SO-AYW-704

THE AMERICAN ALPINE JOURNAL
2006

Josh Wharton on the free crux of the Casarotto Route on Fitz Roy. *Jon Walsh*
Cover: Rolando Garibotti on the last pitch of Cerro Torre's El Arca de los Vientos. *Ermanno Salvaterra*

Stefan Glowacz and Robert Jasper crossing the Patagonia icecap during their approach to Cerro Murallón. (above) *Klaus Fengler*

Sam Johnson on the second ascent of Mt. Hunter's Diamond Arête, Alaska. (right) *Freddie Wilkinson*

"Shipton et al," showing, right to left: The Flame, Shipton Spire, Cat's Ears, Hainabrakk, Uli Biaho, Paiju. (below) *Renan Ozturk*

Evening peaks over the Tawa Glacier, Miyar Valley, India. (lower left) *David Kaszlikwoski*

A very white Russian snowbathing on the Root Canal Glacier before climbing the Tooth Obsession. (left) *Sergei Matusevich*

Sean Jones on Mama, his new 1,000-foot 5.12c in Yosemite. *Shawn Reeder*
Right: Looking down pitch 9 on Grin and Barret, Stewart Valley, Baffin Island. *Pete Dronkers*

Corporate Friends
of the
AMERICAN ALPINE JOURNAL

We thank the following for their generous financial support of the 2006 AMERICAN ALPINE JOURNAL

Guaranteed To Keep You Dry
GORE-TEX® outerwear
GORE Creative Technologies Worldwide

Title Sponsor

Ben Heason redpointing pitch 17 (E7 6b) on Rainbow Jambaia, the first free ascent of Angel Falls, Venezuela. *John Arran*
Right: The Grandes Jorasses rises above gondolas crossing the Vallée Blanche. *John Harlin III*

Friends

OF THE

AMERICAN ALPINE JOURNAL

We thank the following for their generous financial support:

BENEFACTORS:

The H. Adams Carter Endowment Fund for the American Alpine Journal
Yvon Chouinard

PATRONS:

Ann Carter, Neale E. Creamer
John Harlin III, Peter D. McGann M.D.
Joseph E. Murphy Jr., William R. Kilpatrick M.D.
Gregory Miller, Dr. Louis F. Reichardt
Mark Richey, Steven Schwartz
New York Section AAC

SUPPORTERS:

Robert Crawford, Richard E. Hoffman M.D.
Louis W. Kasischke, John G. McCall M.D.
Glenn E. Porzak

SPECIAL THANKS TO:

Robert J. Campbell
Jim Edwards
Z. Wayne Griffin Jr.
Michael John Lewis Jr.
Royal Shannon Robbins
Fredrick J. Wenzel

THE AMERICAN ALPINE JOURNAL
710 Tenth St. Suite 140, Golden, Colorado 80401
Telephone: (303) 384-0110 Fax: (303) 384-0111
E-mail: aaj@americanalpineclub.org

ISBN 1-933056-01-0

THE AMERICAN ALPINE JOURNAL
2006

VOLUME 48 ISSUE 80

CONTENTS

Climbs and Expeditions

Including: On the Ridge Between Life and Death: A Climbing Life Reexamined, *by David Roberts;* I'll Call You in Kathmandu: The Elizabeth Hawley Story, *by Bernadette McDonald;* The Villain: A Portrait of Don Whillans, *by James Perrin;* Possessed by Shadows, *by Donigan Merritt;* Mountain Rescue—Chamonix Mt. Blanc: A Season with the World's Busiest Mountain Rescue Service, *by Anne Sauvy;* Into the Unknown: The Remarkable Life of Hans Kraus, *by Susan E.B. Schwartz;* On Thin Ice: Alpine Climbs in the Americas, Asia and the Himalaya, *by Mick Fowler;* The Forgotten Adventure: Mount Everest, The Reconnaissance, 1935, *by Tony Astill;* Let My People Go Surfing: The Education of a Reluctant Businessman, *by Yvon Chouinard;* Breaking Trail: A Climbing Life, *by Arlene Blum;* Learning to Breathe, *by Andy Cave;* Broad Peak, *by Richard Sale;* Mountain Ranges of Colorado, *by John Fielder;* The Rage: Reflections on Risk, *by Steve De Maio;* The Longest Climb: Back from the Abyss, *by Paul Pritchard;* Bradford Washburn: An Extraordinary Life: The Autobiography of a Mountaineering Icon, *by Bradford Washburn and Lewis Freedman;* Losing the Garden: the Story of a Marriage, *by Laura Waterman.*

Remembering Morgan Harris, Robert F. Kamps, Vera Komarkova, Heather L. Paul, P. Jim Ratz.

The American Alpine Journal

John Harlin III, *Editor*

Advisory Board
James Frush, *Managing Editor*
Rolando Garibotti,
Mark Jenkins, Mark Richey

Senior Editor
Kelly Cordes

Associate Editors
Lindsay Griffin
Dougald MacDonald

Art Director
Lili Henzler

Photo Guru
Dan Gambino

Contributing Editors
Steve Roper, *Features*
Joe Kelsey, *Climbs & Expeditions*
David Stevenson, *Book Reviews*
Frederick O. Johnson, *Club Activities*

Cartographer
Martin Gamache, Alpine Mapping Guild

Translators

Konrad Kirch	Martin Gutmann
Molly Loomis	Adilet Imambekov
Tamotsu Nakamura	Nicholas Mailänder
Henry Pickford	Todd Miller
Bean Bowers	Pam Roberts
Rolando Garibotti	Caroline Ware

Indexers
Ralph Ferrara, Eve Tallman

Regional Contacts
Malcolm Bass, *Scotland*; Danny Kost, *Wrangell-St. Elias;*
Drew Brayshaw & Don Serl, *Coast Mountains, BC*;
Matt Perkins, *Washington Cascades*; Raphael Slawinski,
Canadian Rockies; Antonio Gómez Bohórquez,
Richard Hidalgo and Juanjo Tome *Peru;* Rolando
Garibotti, *Patagonia*; Damien Gildea, *Antarctica*;
Harish Kapadia, *India*; Elizabeth Hawley, *Nepal*;
Tamotsu Nakamura, *Japanese expeditions*;
Lindsay Griffin, *Earth*; Mark Watson, *New Zealand*

With additional thanks to
Mike Anderson, John Arran, Christine Blackmon,
Tommy Caldwell & Beth Rodden, Jeremy Collins,
Damien Gildea, Chad Kellogg, Dieter Klose,
Mike Layton, Roy Leggett, Vladimir Linek,
Bronson MacDonald, Chris McNamara, Ade Miller,
Anna Piunova, Joe Puryear, Corey Rich, Daniel Seeliger,
John Scurlock, Marcelo Scanu, Dr. Brian Wieder

Rolando Garibotti negotiating the final pitch of Cerro Torre's north face during the first ascent of El Arca de los Vientos. *Ermanno Salvaterra*

THE AMERICAN ALPINE CLUB

OFFICIALS FOR THE YEAR 2006
*Directors ex-officio

HONORARY PRESIDENT
Robert H. Bates

President
Jim Donini*

Vice President
Steve Swenson*

Secretary
Greg Miller*

Treasurer
Charles J. Sassara, III*

DIRECTORS

Terms ending
February 2007

Sam Streibert
C. James Frush
Travis Spitzer

Terms ending
February 2008

Steven M. Furman
Steven Schwartz
Charlotte Fox
Nancy Norris
Ralph Tingey

Terms ending
February 2009

Ellen Lapham
Bruce Franks
Michael J. Lewis
Conrad Anker
Jack Tackle
Brent R. Bishop
Monty Mayko

SECTION CHAIRS

Alaska
Harry Hunt

New England
William C. Atkinson
Nancy Savickas

Central Rockies
Greg Sievers

Southeast
David Thoenen

Northern Rockies
Brian Cabe
Tom Kalakay

Blue Ridge
Simon Carr

New York
Philip Erard

Sierra Nevada
Dave Riggs

Cascade
Alfred Schumer

Oregon
Bob McGown

Southwest
David Rosenstein

Midwest
Benjamin A. Kweton

EDITORS

The American Alpine Journal
John Harlin III
Kelly Cordes

Accidents in North American Mountaineering
John E. (Jed) Williamson

The American Alpine News
Staff

STAFF

Executive Director
Phil Powers

Library
Bridget Burke
Maria Borysiewicz
Gary Landeck
Kath Pyke

Controller
Jerome Mack

Membership Manager
Jason Manke

Membership Coordinator
Dana Richardson

Marketing and Development Director
Nigel Gregory

Ranch Manager
Drew Birnbaum

PREFACE

Strung-out deep in the remote mountains of northern Pakistan in early September, Vince Anderson and Steve House heard drumming. They saw fires burning in the valley below, a region reportedly rife with Islamic militants. In the ensuing days, all the way out to the village of Tarshing, locals repeatedly stopped them. They wanted to offer congratulations, for they'd been watching with binoculars and tracking Anderson and House's progress by spotting their headlamps at night as they completed one of the greatest alpine climbs in history, an ascent in pure style on the biggest mountain face in the world, a climb refreshingly done sans pre-event hype, reality TV-show website drama, and senseless publicity stunts. Everything about their climb was real, and worthy of celebration. Some 200 school kids greeted them with flowers in Tarshing, where the mayor and school headmaster gave speeches at a ceremony to commemorate their incredible climb.

The picture easily forms in my own mind, as during my first visit to Pakistan, in 2004, I was greeted with more kindness and warmth than anywhere in my world travels. That trip gave me the strongest memories of my life, ones that still come to me almost daily and extend far beyond just the climbing. Once you've been somewhere and made a personal connection, your ability to relate to the place changes.

Likewise, my disappointment and irritation at ignorance deepens when, predictably, people get a frightened look when I tell them I'm going to Pakistan. Or they say something worse. Before a friend's trip in 2004, another climber called him an idiot for going and predicted he'd get his head cut off. Such a fool's game, blindly succumbing to the political power of fear. As if you can divide the world, based on countries and broad categories of people, into "good" and "bad." Indeed, South Asia and the greater Middle East, including "-stan" countries, tend to make the news a lot these days. As does the United States. Pakistan is the world's second most populated Muslim country, and though hardly anybody will come out and say that all Muslim areas are places to universally avoid, the de facto portrayal of Muslim countries in our culture, media, and propaganda causes people to react in a way that would be considered abject racism or sexism were we talking about black people or women. War-fed nationalism is no excuse for the absolutely stunning ignorance too-often displayed by citizens who, ironically enough sometimes, hold themselves in such high regard. After all, as far as good and bad go, there can

Steve House and Vince Anderson trying to maintain a low-key presence while slipping past Islamic extremists in Tarshing on their way home from Nanga Parbat. *Steve House*

be no denying the fundamental evil of selling and starting a war over bad information, analyzed through the lens of prejudice. We should all be careful about judging an entire nation or group based on the actions of a sinister few, lest we become what we despise.

In light of our seemingly polarized and corrupt world, it's easy to tune out and just go climbing. But we fail as human beings if we use climbing as an excuse to avoid at least a basic level of conscientious behavior, whether in our day-to-day interactions with neighbors or on a more global scale.

On October 8 a horrific earthquake struck northern Pakistan, killing more than *80,000* people and leaving *3.3 million* homeless. Many of those hardest hit faced a Himalayan winter in remote mountain villages that had been completely destroyed. Scores of climbers—and as a group, we're rarely accused of being a selfless lot—pitched in to help.

Going through the piles of clothes, sleeping bags, and tents in my little cabin, the difference in what I had versus the people I saw in the villages of Pakistan, people living *hard* lives with smiles on their faces, overwhelmed me. My local friends, none of whom had been to Pakistan, didn't need the personal connection—helping was the right thing to do. Soon I'd filled my car with warm clothes and tents to bring to the AAC, where boxes upon boxes of donated gear lined the hallways. AAC staff and volunteers set aside their other obligations for the relief efforts. Contributions poured in from companies, both outdoor industry and others, as well as individuals. The AAC shipped 28 tons of materials, and people helped out first-hand, like Renan Ozturk, whose painting of the view from Shipton Camp on the Trango Glacier during his summer 2005 trip graces this *Journal*. He and a crew of North Face athletes traveled to the devastated Kashmir region around Thanksgiving, spending several weeks helping with the relief efforts. Danika Gilbert and Sallie Dean Shatz each spent nearly two months, beginning in mid-January, delivering supplies and helping in the most remote villages. Many people and organizations, including the AAC, continue to help through the ongoing and epic recovery.

Indeed, it becomes exponentially harder to harbor prejudices when, no matter how different our cultures, we see people face-to-face, experience their warmth and kindness, and share their grief. We soon realize that, despite a fair share of nutballs and religious fanatics (yes, including here), the world is full of wonderful people and the boogeyman just might not be who we're led to believe. I've heard it said that if we don't travel, we stagnate. This certainly holds true for us as climbers, if we spend time only in our home crag wiring the same patterns, but even more true for us simply as humans.

Our climbing in distant places fills most of this book's pages. Whether we go there as tourists or something more perhaps depends on how we do things. After all, if we were just looking for a vacation, why not Disneyworld? Hell, it'd be safer and probably cheaper. It's also more than just the climbing. For pure climbing quality, most climbers would never leave Yosemite. (I've got some excellent bouldering right by my house, too.)

Once we form an emotional connection with a place, its people, and its landscape, our travels transcend basic tourism and become unforgettable parts of our lives. And though most of us will never have an entire village celebrate our climb, that matters little relative to the richness of these connections and the power we experience in the world's mountains. When climbing our best, it seems we don't succumb to irrational fears, but remain open and aware, look at risk objectively, and seek good information. I hope you'll do the same and see the world. The *AAJ* gives you just a tease.

KELLY CORDES, *Senior Editor*

DELIGHTFUL EXECRATION

An alpine-style new route up Nanga Parbat's Rupal Face.

VINCE ANDERSON

Vince Anderson at dawn of the third day on the Rupal Face. This 16-hour climbing day would prove crucial to the ascent, as Anderson and Steve House diverged from House and Bruce Miller's 2004 attempted line and pioneered a more direct route up the central pillar of the face. *Steve House*

W ake up!

We were at 7,500 meters on the Rupal Face, and the urge to sleep was overwhelming. It would have been so easy to rest my head on my ice axe and drift off into a more comfortable place, somewhere beyond the present slaughter. Amphetamines would have helped—they worked for Buhl. The bit of caffeine in the GU seemed to help for half an hour, then I would be back to fighting to stay awake. At times we both sensed a third person in our presence, and I am not talking about Jesus. My state of mind was a kind of madness.

Steve House was strong in heart, body, and mind: driven and focused. There was no better person to be with up there. Still, he too is human, and five long, hard days in thin air had taken its toll. We were marching to hell, if ever so slowly.

My experience on the Rupal Face exists now only in abstract memory, vivid, surreal: eight days of my life that have burned a mark deep into my soul. It was my closest glimpse yet toward the essence of purity. The dearest catharsis.

The direct Rupal Face: 4,100 vertical meters from the Bazhin Glacier to the summit. *Arne Hodalic*

Leaving base camp had been easy, though life there was comfortable. Conditions looked good and we were hungry to climb. We had waited patiently for weeks while the weather taunted and teased. With a satellite phone, we called Jim at Mountainweather.com for a forecast. His service was as valuable as the few pieces of equipment we used on our ascent. He nailed the forecast: clear, stable weather for the next six days. Weather during our ascent was a non-issue. Three weeks of light precipitation had, however, left moderate accumulations of snow on the face, and now the sun caused it to release from the slopes above. Large avalanches poured down the face every 20 minutes in the morning sun, so we waited one more day for it to clean before beginning our climb.

On the first day we climbed more than 1,600 vertical meters. Avalanches roared constantly; fortunately, they remained confined to the deep channels they had carved into the slopes throughout the summer. We felt some sense of security when outside the channels. Every time an avalanche ran, these channels became raging torrents. Crossing them between bursts was unnerving.

We climbed on rock as much as possible. The climbing was easy and pleasant, but short-lived. Eventually, a bergschrund at the base of the first real difficulties provided an adequate bivy site with running water, which saved precious fuel, time, and energy. A steep rock wall rose above the bivy, broken by several thin ice and snow ribbons. Only one ribbon appeared mostly unthreatened by falling ice, snow, or rocks. We flittermice ventured out early the next morning under the frozen cover of darkness.

Anderson grapples with the crux pitch on the second day of climbing. This passage consumed most of a day.
Steve House

Convenience is king these days. Recognition has replaced respectability. Ethics are compromised. Aesthetics mean almost nothing. For Steve and me, climbing the Rupal Face was meaningless unless accomplished on our own terms: pure alpine style. In July, a team of Koreans had repeated the Messner route, established 35 years earlier. The Pakistani Ministry of Tourism heralded the Korean ascent as "history making." Yet the Koreans had not bettered the style of 1970. Have we come nowhere in 35 years? They could have done better. The Rupal Face deserves better.

Our decision to climb without high-altitude porters, oxygen, fixed ropes, radios, or pre-trip hype stemmed from our desire to climb in a manner we could feel proud of. Summiting was less important than being able to face ourselves in the mirror and not feel like we had cheated.

The first technically difficult pitches came in the dark. Thin ice ribbons threaded through the steep rock band. The new water ice was junk but easy enough. After three pitches, things got steeper. There appeared to be two options. To the left, a fat-looking ice ramp. To the right, a much thinner but shorter mixed passage. Against Steve's advice, I went left. Though I had the lead pack, which was much lighter than the follower's pack, it was still heavier than what I'd normally carry to lead ice. The ice was atrocious: just a thin veneer over snow, under which lay better ice. The outer ice layer and the underlying snow had to be completely cleared to get purchase. The climbing was time-consuming, exhausting, and virtually unprotected. At wit's end, I downclimbed and started up the thin mixed ground on the right. The ice here was similar, but not as steep.

Losing the protection of darkness, the face warmed rapidly in the sun and rocks began to bombard us with alarming frequency. Most came down the ramp to the left, from which I had just, thankfully, retreated. I was halfway up the right side, moving very slowly and cautiously. The climbing was insecure and poorly protected, though technically not too hard. Eventually, near the end of my rope, I got an A3 anchor in a horribly exposed spot for a belay. I brought Steve up a bit to give me more rope for leading and then continued, now getting a savage pump from spending so much time clearing ice and snow for tool placements and protection, of which there was distressingly little. A couple of times my feet slipped, causing my butt to pucker tight. Whipping was out of the question here. Rocks bombarded us, and the situation became chaotic. A bit further up, I placed a trustworthy cam and regained the confidence to engage the steep dry tooling above. I cautioned myself not to push the boat out too far. I was physically and mentally shattered. After a few futile attempts to work out a sequence and protect it, I downclimbed to the cam and Steve lowered me to the belay. Without a pack, Steve moved quickly to my high point and judiciously got down to business with the mixed section. I asked him how it was. Steve, prone to understatement, replied "Desperate!" Yet, I knew he was loving every bit of it.

At the belay, I understood why he had been eager to take over the lead: The stance was exposed to rocks hurtling down from the left. It was terrifying. All I could do was put my head down and try to keep my pack above me to protect my neck and back. A couple of baseballs hit me on the shoulder; fortunately, the big ones missed. Once Steve had me on belay, I was psyched to get out of there.

This pitch proved to be the technical crux of the route. Though we were still at only 5,300 meters, we sensed we had surpassed a major obstacle. Now, however, we began to really feel the effect of the altitude as we moved much more slowly up 100 meters of easy ice and mixed terrain to a protected ridge crest at 5,400 meters. It was 1 p.m. and we had been climbing for 10 hours, much of it on the crux pitch. We opted to bivy there to rest for a big day ahead.

The Rupal Face is quite complex. Viewed from afar, it appears as a series of rock bands intersected by left-angling ice ramps. It rises abruptly an honest 4,000 meters, so its scale is hard to appreciate. What appeared from below to be smooth, glaciated slopes would sometimes be menacing, active serac bands. The (relatively) safest areas were the rock bands, which provided protection from the continual snow and ice avalanches. Because of the avalanche threat, traversing the ice fields to gain the rocks was often dangerous and always exciting. The avalanche runnels were scoured clean and hard, which required deliberate placement of both ice tools. Doing this while moving as fast as possible was like doing anaerobic interval training. At this altitude, it was painful to exceed our aerobic thresholds, and it put us in an energy deficit from which it would take hours to recover.

The frequency and scope of the avalanches made me realize that climbing this face alpine-style was the safest way to go. The risks were acceptable once, but not for numerous excursions along fixed ropes.

Our third day would prove to be crucial. We crossed a couple of avalanche runnels that had unleashed tons of ice and snow during the night. The blast wave from them had shaken our tent on its tiny platform and pelted it with debris. We continued up seemingly endless 50° snow and ice until we reached the base of another steep rock wall, which offered protection from serac fall. Steve and Bruce Miller had climbed up left of this buttress during their attempt on the face in 2004, but now that route appeared to be threatened by seracs. To avoid exposure, we opted for the rock wall via a potential weakness on its left edge. A few pitches of high-quality mixed climbing led to more ice and eventually a ridge. As day moved into afternoon, I began to suffer from fatigue. Steve suggested that I needed to eat more, and he was right. Somehow, the Organic Food Bars were not as tasty as they were at home. I choked one down and drank some water, but I was cooked. Steve led on into the late afternoon. The ridge did not let up, and bivy spots were scant. I was grinding to a standstill and having serious doubts about my ability to continue.

Day gave way to night, and still we had not found a decent bivy site. There was a hanging glacier to our right, above the seracs, but getting there did not look easy. We stopped, ate, and put on the headlamps. Steve led a pitch in the dark that seemed to take forever. He told me later that he puked at the belay. Following, I could see why. It was steep ice followed by steeper, slabby rock covered in snow, with no pro. We were both exhausted; we had been out over 16 hours without sufficient food or water. A final traverse across the glacier led us into a niche underneath a severely overhanging bergschrund at about 6,000 meters. It took us another three hours to make camp and brew up. We really needed some sleep.

We slept late the following morning. I was not sure if we could continue. I was still tired from the previous day, and I did not get enough sleep. The altitude was debilitating and we were only halfway up the face. Nevertheless, we left camp at about 10 a.m. in the brutal heat

Anderson leading steep mixed ground on Day 3. *Steve House*

of the sunlit face. The ground immediately above was seductively easy, so going up was agreeable. We moved very slowly. The easy ground yielded to moderately steep ice. The wall above was even steeper and more complex. We had gambled by coming this way to avoid the threat of the seracs

The spectacular site of Camp 4 at 6,800 meters, where House nearly fell when the snow collapsed as he tried to gain the ridge. *Steve House*

and were not sure we would find a way through the complex rock wall above. We followed the ice up the path of least resistance and hours later discovered the key passage. Our gamble had paid off. A nice, fat ice flow poured over the shattered rock, providing passage to lower-angled ice above. After three or four pitches, we were back on steep snow. For the first time we felt that we might actually climb the face, if only our strength and will would hold out.

Once again the hunt for a bivy spot was on, and short of an exhausting three-hour ice-chopping fest there was little to be found. The ridge up to our left looked like it might be somewhat level, and it was snow-covered so we could dig in. Steve led as we simul-climbed up easy ice toward the ridge. As Steve neared the crest, he began climbing near-vertical snow on the bottom of a cornice. He tried to mount the ridge, and the snow gave way. TV-sized blocks hurtled down at me. I clung to my tools as the blocks disintegrated and showered me with shrapnel.

It's always a good feeling to look up and see your partner dangling by one axe. Somehow, Steve had kept one of his tools in the snow above the fracture line and avoided a fall that may have pitched us both down the face. He swung back up and made his way along the ridge to where it met a rock wall. We dug in there at around 6,800 meters. The ridge crest started out about 30 to 45 centimeters wide. After an hour of work, we had excavated it to about a meter on one end and less than that on the other. It was barely long enough for the tent, one end of which hung over each side of the ridge. The front end butted up to the rock wall. We stayed tied in for the night and hoped we would not get broadsided by a gust of wind. Another exhausting 12-hour day.

Four breaths, one stick, four breaths, another stick. The altitude was undermining the strength that years of training had given me. After another late start, we rapped from our airy perch to climb the ice field we had been on the previous afternoon. I really had to concentrate on my breathing. If I tried to move quickly, I would go into oxygen deficit and have to rest for several minutes. I had to keep it slow. Simul-climbing with a Ti-bloc clipped to an ice screw for pro, we combined two 50-meter pitches into one of 100 meters. We led in blocks of 300 meters. After a few blocks, the angle eased and we put the rope away. We were getting up there now, over 7,000 meters. The summit seemed close. We carried on as if wading through thick sludge to the top of a snow ramp. It was late in the afternoon and now we could see, for the first time, the Merkl Icefield below us. Our fear lessened somewhat, as now we had an easier escape down the Messner route, if necessary. We were at 7,400 meters and needed one more good day to summit.

Each minor effort brought me to my knees. Digging out the tent platform took hours. Eating, drinking, and melting sufficient water for

Shell-shocked: Anderson (left) and House at high camp. *Vince Anderson*

House drying out at 8,000 meters, just before summiting on the sixth day of the climb. *Vince Anderson*

the following day lasted well into the night. We discussed for some time when we should try to get up. We needed to get some sleep, but we also needed enough time to get to the summit and back. We decided to leave at 3 a.m.

A t 1:30 a.m. on September 6 I heard Steve's alarm. I had suffered a completely sleepless night, but the decision to head for the summit was easy. The weather was perfect. We carried only bare essentials: one pack with three liters of water, one liter of Spiz energy drink, a few energy bars, an ice screw, and our two ropes.

It was pitch black, but far to the south terrific lightning storms raged over the Punjab region. There was not a sound, just a constant strobe of flashes.

After two moderate mixed pitches, we stashed one of the ropes and continued with a single 5mm cord for rappelling. We entered another steep snowfield and found ourselves chest deep in rotten snow. It was the faceted snow I knew oh so well from the continental snowpack of my Colorado home. I've had plenty of experience wallowing through that shit. Hit it with the axes and hands. Knock some more down with the knees, then try to grovel up a bit more. Repeat. 100 meters of climbing took us over an hour. We would never succeed if the snow did not improve. It was almost daylight. I began fighting sleepiness. The days of work and sleep deprivation had taken their toll. I had to keep it together. I would put my head down on my axe to rest and would catch myself drifting to sleep.

We were going nowhere very slowly and feared running out of time and/or energy long before the summit. We took turns at the drudgery, carving a deep trench up the slope. The going was marginally better for the second. Eventually, the surface began to bear our weight. The new day dawned.

I loose inches toward the summit. *Vince Anderson*

Above us was a complex structure of rock headwalls and gendarme-strewn arêtes. We climbed slowly up the snow and ice toward sunny rock. The arête to the left seemed the most appealing. I desperately fought sleep. I had no illusions about the consequences of a lapse in focus here. It was engaging to be in this state. It captured all of my attention. The further I journeyed into this semiconscious state, the fiercer and more delightful my torture became.

Drifting up, following Steve as if in a trance, I scanned the horizon for signs of flatter ground. Somewhere we found it, and I promptly lay down and rested for 20 minutes. In our base layers, we continued climbing over snow and rock in brilliant sunshine, trading the lead. Though Steve and I climbed together, I still felt alone. I continued my battle to stay awake. Being in front helped, as the routefinding gave me something to think about, but soon I'd have to yield to Steve, who moved like a machine: slow and steady.

As I had shed my outer, physical layers, my inner self was revealed. This is what I had come for. I could no longer feel, only think. The physical suffering had ceased. I had the will to keep going. I was spurred on by a personal soundtrack, the measureless blast-beats of black metal music pulsing through my head and coursing through my veins. Introspection was the catalyst I needed.

At 7,900 meters, to our surprise, we noticed faint footprints in the snow. We had reached the intersection with the Messner route, which the Koreans had climbed a month earlier. Mindless drones, we plodded upward.

At 4 p.m. we crested a ridge and reached the foresummit. The true summit was only a hundred meters above. The way was obvious and easy. Nothing left but the crying. For me, that would wait until I took another nap. We knew now that we would summit, and we also knew that darkness would descend upon us shortly thereafter. We needed to be prepared. Steve took off his boots to dry his socks while I slept at our lovely perch at 8,000 meters. When I awoke 10 minutes later, Steve put his boots back on and we lumbered toward deliverance.

The setting sun cast shadows to the east. As we passed into them, we felt the cold creeping in. We staggered on for an hour and a half to cover the final 120 meters to the top. We were both destroyed. After 4,100 vertical meters we ran out of mountain. K2, the Gasherbrums, and Masherbrum were clearly visible far to the east. Their odd symmetry bewildered me. The Hindu Kush mountains of Afghanistan lay closer to the north. Far below was the Rupal valley, where we started five days ago. It seemed so far away.

Steve and I embraced. Few words were needed, and we lacked the energy to say them. In our melancholic bliss, we sat in the pallid light of the setting sun and stared out into the eastern horizon, where Nanga cast her long, lurid shadow.

I looked down the Diamir Face that the Messners had chosen to descend. It did not hold the same allure for us; we found comfort in descending familiar ground.

Shortly after we left the summit, night rose from the valley. "At last," I thought, "the gates have been opened." In the dark, fear and pain seemed more appropriate. In our exhausted state, we gazed into the abyss and it gaped back. We retraced our path through a dark labyrinth of rock and snow. At one point we dropped the rope. Steve thought I had it; I thought he had it. Luckily, we found it not far away.

Eventually, we made it back to the trough we had carved through the faceted snow, which had now hardened into boilerplate ice. Facing in, we frontpointed down to its terminus, where we had cached the other rope. Two rappels, some messing around with a stuck rope, and we reached the bivy we had left 24 hours earlier.

Ours was a delectable suffering.

We woke late the next morning to overcast skies. The stretch of good weather was ending. We were still very tired and had a long, long way to go. We could see the Merkl Icefield below, down which we could escape via the 1970 route. Half a dozen raps took us to the ice field, where the Koreans had abandoned a four-person tent filled with supplies. I recalled seeing posters on the way in heralding their "Clean Mountain" expedition, or something like that. We were now on well-traveled ground littered with fixed anchors and ropes, and in a few places we used the Korean ropes. It seemed pointless to walk down a steep slope without at least grabbing onto them. We found a bag with new gas cartridges, which we carried down for future use. We left nothing on the face of our own but several anchors scavenged from our meager rack.

The air thickened, filling our lungs with the purest of heavenly nectars: oxygen. We could see our base camp, some 3,300 meters below. Strangely, it seemed close. But by the end of the day, we were still far above the valley, and again we needed to bivy. We were on steep ground, it was warm, and we felt pretty good, so we kept descending into the night. Steve's headlamp was burning out, and when I stopped to take off my hat I inadvertently dropped my headlamp. Now, we had to bivy. As my eyes adjusted to the dark, I made out a serac to the side. Steve led over to it and found a perfect bivy spot under the serac, where we pitched our small tent for the last time.

Two thousand meters to go in the morning, and it was not trivial. Most of it was face-in downclimbing on ice. My feet and calves were beat. My crampon points were dull and skittered

Sweet release: Anderson on the summit. *Steve House*

from time to time. Below me, I saw Steve finally dismount from the face and set foot on dry land. What a relief! I was just a hundred meters from salvation when I glanced up to see a huge volley of rocks cut loose and headed right for me. All I could do was put my head down and hang on. It was Nanga's goodbye kiss. The rocks ricocheted around me, but when they stopped I was still standing. I quickly downclimbed to Steve's protected perch. We hauled our weary carcasses down the last few kilometers to the valley floor. Our jubilant liaison officer greeted us and, with the help of a few others, carried our packs to base camp.

We were transformed by our experience on the Rupal Face. Steve realized a lifelong dream and vanquished the pain of last year's rebuff. I discovered my physical, intellectual, and emotional limits, and pushed them much farther than I had imagined possible. Having annihilated our outer skins, perhaps we glimpsed, if only for a moment, our true selves. Neither of us will ever be the same.

Summary:

Area: Pakistan, Nanga Parbat

Ascent: Alpine-style first ascent of a direct route (4,100 vertical meters, ABO) up the Rupal Face of 8,125-meter Nanga Parbat; Vince Anderson and Steve House, six days up and two days down via the Messner Route, September 1-8, 2006.

A Note About the Author:

Vince Anderson, 36, lives in Ridgway, Colorado, home base for his international climbing and skiing guide service, Skyward Mountaineering. Asked for more information on his background, he provided a quote from Friedrich Nietzche's Beyond Good and Evil: *"He who fights with monsters should look to it that he himself does not become a monster."*

CERRO TORRE'S NORTH FACE

Putting to rest the 1959 mystery.

ERMANNO SALVATERRA

Thirteen long years have passed since I first tried to climb Cerro Torre from the north, with Guido Bonvicini and Adriano Cavallaro. We made our first attempt during October, and we managed to reach the base of the so-called English Dihedral, climbed by Phil Burke and Tom Proctor in 1981. We had climbed 550 meters to that point, but were turned back because the face was covered in snow. While we waited for better conditions, we climbed the Franco-Argentinean route on Fitz Roy and the Compressor Route on Cerro Torre. In November we made a second attempt and slept at the base of the dihedral, inside the box portaledge left by Burke and Proctor. The following day the weather was terrible and my partners wanted to descend, but I asked them to give me at least a couple more hours to climb a little higher. I wanted to get to the Col of Conquest, simply because I was curious to see it. There, the storm forced us to retreat.

In 1994 I made another attempt on the same route with the Austrian Tommy Bonapace. He had already tried this line half a dozen times. By afternoon we reached the base of the triangular snowfield, some 300 meters above the glacier. After an awful bivouac Tommy told me, "Finish, Ermanno, never more." I knew then that his relationship with this line had come to a definitive end.

The years passed and every now and then I was seized by the memory of this line. For a long time I had defended Cesare Maestri, who claimed to have climbed the north side of Cerro Torre in 1959 with Toni Egger, who was killed during the descent. I had done so in public debates and bar conversations, and I had argued tooth and nail with Maestri's most determined accuser, Ken Wilson, the editor of the English climbing magazine *Mountain*. But little by little I started changing my mind. I reread and studied everything that had been said and written in defense of Maestri, and I started to have some serious doubts. I had no doubt, however, that I still wanted to climb his supposed "route." This dream of mine never died. In November 2004, I returned home from Patagonia after completing a new route on the east face of Cerro Torre, and two months later celebrated my 50th birthday. For the first time I realized that time was passing. Yet my desire to climb the north face remained strong.

Toward the end of winter, my friend Rolando Garibotti wrote to me proposing a project. He had suggested before that we climb together in Patagonia, but I had always declined, feeling he was much younger and stronger than I was. The idea that he proposed intrigued me, but I responded that first I'd like to try the north face of Cerro Torre, Maestri's supposed route. At first Rolo didn't seem convinced, but finally he accepted enthusiastically. Alessandro Beltrami, with whom I climbed the east face in 2004, also accepted.

Throughout the summer, controversy brewed in the Italian press. During an interview,

Rolando Garibotti starts up the first pitch above the triangular snowfield, racing toward the Col of Conquest. The summit of mighty Torre Egger looms to the right. *Ermanno Salvaterra*

I was asked what I thought about Maestri's supposed ascent, and I responded honestly that I thought it was "pure fantasy." Since I live only about 10 kilometers from Maestri, the local press had a field day with my answer, and the controversy grew. Despite this, I decided to carry on with our project.

While I was excited to look for signs of Maestri's purported ascent, my principal motivation was the climb itself. The idea of climbing a line that reached the summit of Cerro Torre without using the bolts on the Compressor Route that Maestri and partners established in 1970 had haunted me. And not just me. Austrian Toni Ponholzer and his partners had tried the north face more than a dozen times; they were stopped on two occasions just 250 meters from the summit, after climbing a direct line up the right side of the north face. Burke and Proctor, after climbing the big dihedral in the east face, traversed into the heart of the north face and stopped just 30 meters shy of the west ridge. Our original objective was to follow the Austrians' line, but we found it very iced up, so we were forced to look for an alternative. As the great Bruno Detassis once said, "One must look for the easiest solution through that which is difficult."

We arrived at El Chaltén on October 14 at 5 p.m., and 10 minutes later we met up with Rolo, who had just arrived from Bariloche. The weather was good, and by the following afternoon we were standing at the base of Cerro Torre. We were ready to begin the climb, but at dawn the following morning it was snowing, and so we went back to El Chaltén. We returned to the base of Cerro Torre three more times and climbed the first four pitches, fixing our three

Ermanno Salvaterra just above the Col of Conquest, with Cerro Rincon (foreground) and Volcan Lautaro (back) rising from the Continental Icecap. *Rolando Garibotti*

climbing ropes. One morning, carrying our whole kit, we jumared to the top of the fixed lines, but it began to snow again. We couldn't attempt a climb of this magnitude in those conditions. The fourth time we left early, and at 5 p.m. we reached a small pillar just above the Col of Conquest, between Torre Egger and Cerro Torre. From there we made a short rappel that allowed us to access the northwest face, and after a few pitches we found a good place to bivouac. The following day the wall steepened, but Rolo, despite having to clear snow to find the cracks, climbed very quickly.

By late afternoon we had arrived at a small ledge on the very edge of the north ridge. We had a good look at the north face, above and to our left, and it looked feasible. We were encouraged. The summit of Cerro Torre was only about 300 meters above us. Across a gap and only about 50 meters higher, was the impressively beautiful summit of Torre Egger. Toward the north we could see Cerro San Lorenzo, more than 200 kilometers away. We decided to chop out a ledge so we could sit comfortably through the night. Unfortunately the weather started getting worse. Black clouds approached from the west and strong gusts of wind buffeted us. What should we do? Go down or continue? We knew that turning back meant that we wouldn't return. On these peaks it's common to climb 200, 300, even 400 meters, and get turned back by bad weather. But after getting this high it's difficult to find the physical and mental strength to return for another attempt.

At eight in the evening, with a lump in our throats, we decided to descend. It was snowing hard and the wind blew intensely. First we rapped the northwest face, then we did three

Like visitors to another planet, Ermanno Salvaterra and Alessandro Beltrami traverse Cerro Torre's northwest face. *Rolando Garibotti*

Looking down Cerro Torre's north face at the belayer and the top of Torre Egger. *Rolando Garibotti*

Cerro Torre
East face
fot. R. Garibotti

Cerro Torre
North-west face
fot. Beth Wald

Cerro Torre
North face
fot. Jay Smith

(1) Bragg-Donini-Wilson line (1977) to the Col of Conquest. (2) Maestri gear cache below the triangular snowfield. (3) El Arca de los Vientos (Beltrami, Garibotti, Salvaterra, 2005). (a) Bivouac site. (4) Southeast ridge (Compressor Route), 1970. (5) Ragni di Lecco Route (Chiappa, Conti, Ferrari, Negri, 1974). *Left to right, Rolando Garibotti, Beth Wald, Jay Smith.*

rappels along the north ridge to get to the small pillar just above the Col of Conquest. In total darkness we continued descending another 200 meters past the col. At about the same height as the bottom of the English Dihedral, we decided to stop and wait for the dawn. Our headlamps weren't working well, it was 1 a.m., and we were quite tired. We dug out a platform with our axes to make the wait more comfortable and to be able to prepare something to eat. At 5 a.m. we set out again. We were half-asleep, and we descended carefully in order to avoid mistakes. We recovered all the gear we could because we had decided against another attempt. Four hours later we got to the snow cave. The weather wasn't too bad, but we could hear how hard the wind was blowing up high.

We decided to stay until the following day before descending to El Chaltén. In the afternoon, around 3 o'clock, an incredible buzzing startled us. I looked up and yelled. An enormous avalanche was thundering down the wall. Ale grabbed the shovels and fled inside the cave. Rolo, barefoot, began to run down the glacier. I thought he was just going down to get photos, but he had fled fearing the worst. Having seen this type of avalanche on the wall before, I managed to stay calm, found my camera, and took a few pictures. Probably a huge ice mushroom had detached from the uppermost part of the tower, sweeping down the east face and covering it entirely. The resulting spectacle was terrifying, but the strong winds that day began to blow the enormous white cloud horizontally toward the south, and only two small cascades of snow arrived at the base.

At four in the afternoon, after discussing the avalanche, I went to sleep. At midnight, Ale gave me a piece of cheese and some crackers. Then I got up and went outside to smoke a cigarette. The sky was clear and I was overcome with a heavy sadness. I cried, and the clear sky hurt me deeply. We had taken everything off the wall and all that remained was to return home. Around 2 a.m. I fell back asleep. When we woke up, I proposed to my partners that we make another attempt. There was a moment of silence, but soon enthusiasm took hold of them and they agreed.

It was snowing while we hiked back to El Chaltén, and as we descended we planned our next attempt. We would travel as light as possible. We would leave behind absolutely everything that seemed superfluous. We were quite tired, so we knew that we would need a few days of rest.

The following day, the 10th of November, the weather was bad and we enjoyed a well-deserved rest day. In the morning, the sky seemed to be clearing, and although we had wanted to rest a couple more days we decided to go back up. We didn't talk much during our walk, but our legs felt good and in less than six hours we arrived at the cave. We quickly prepared to climb. Rolo and I started up the wall and, as before, climbed the first four pitches and then fixed our three ropes. Ale stayed behind to work on the new snow cave, which, for security's sake, we had moved underneath Torre Egger. In little more than two hours, Rolo and I returned. The weather was turning out to be fantastic, without even the tiniest breeze.

The alarm went off at 3:45 a.m. Breakfast was just a few morsels. The weather was perfect, and there wasn't a second to lose. At 4:45, with headlamps on our helmets, we began to jumar the ropes we had fixed the day before. We climbed another two pitches and soon arrived at the triangular snowfield. The rising sun began to warm us up. We moved fast, reclimbing meter by meter the stretches we had climbed just a few days before. Rolo climbed quickly, short-fixing to gain 10 to 20 meters each pitch while Ale and I ascended the ropes behind him.

The slabs above the triangular snowfield are difficult, but because we knew exactly where to go we were able to move fast. The snow that covered the ramp up to the pillar above the Col of Conquest was in better condition than before, and again we were able to save a lot of time. It was barely noon when we got to the pillar, 50 meters above the col.

On the northwest face the cracks were still clear of snow from our previous attempt, and we reached the small terrace on the edge of the north ridge at around 4:30 in the afternoon. It had taken us two days to get there on our first attempt. We decided that this would be a good place to bivouac, but with a few hours of light left we decided to fix a couple more pitches. After a short pause I set out. The wall was now in shade, and the cold bit our hands. Rolo and

Beltrami trenches through the ice mushrooms of the second to last pitch. *Rolando Garibotti*

Ale then climbed one more pitch, also fairly hard. While we were busy on the north face, the northwest face began to release huge pieces from the frozen mushrooms above, but on the ridge we were safe.

The bivouac spot was phenomenal: in front of us Torre Egger, to the right Fitz Roy, and to the left the immense Continental Icecap and its mountains. The cold was sharp and penetrating, but the sky was filled with stars. The night passed quickly, and we even managed to sleep a bit.

The next morning, November 13, I felt like I was in a movie or a dream. We started getting ready at six in the morning, but weren't ready to begin climbing until eight. Luckily, the sun soon began to warm our frozen bodies. The wall was nearly vertical and quite difficult. From the top of the ropes we had fixed the day before, Rolo climbed another two pitches, zigzagging between ice mushrooms to arrive at the end of the north face. When I got up to Rolo at the last belay, we hugged each other with emotion. We spoke breathlessly. Now below us, the north face was no longer a problem. With another pitch on perfect ice we joined the Ragni di Lecco Route (the west face), climbed in 1974 by Daniele Chiappa, Mariolino Conti, Casimiro Ferrari, and Pino Negri.

It was around one in the afternoon, and above us huge, unconsolidated ice formations promised to make progress difficult. The summit of Torre Egger was now far below us, but we still couldn't see Cerro Torre's summit. We began a series of pitches that took a lot of effort. The ice wasn't solid or consistent, and sometimes we had to dig more than 50 centimeters before we could find ice or snow that was solid enough to climb. We only had two snow pickets, and, since ice screws were useless, protection was nearly nonexistent. But we weren't about to surrender. The sky had clouded over, and it began to snow and blow a bit. We did the last pitch in sections, each of us going up a little. The cold once again became penetrating, but at 11:15 p.m. we all reached the highest point on Cerro Torre. Ale reminded me that exactly one year before we had arrived on this same summit, after climbing a new route on the east face. It was a profoundly emotional moment. After taking a few pictures, we descended the mushroom and sat under a snow overhang to wait for night to pass. The next morning we descended via the Compressor Route on the southeast ridge.

We decided to name our route El Arca de los Vientos (Ark of the Winds). In all, we climbed 37 pitches, 21 of which were new. We dedicated our route to the memory of two dear friends, Spaniard Pepe Chaverri and Argentinean Teo Plaza. Back in 1994, these two amazing youngsters made a great alpine-style ascent of the east face of Cerro Standhardt. Unfortunately, not long afterward, Teo's beautiful life was cut short by an avalanche. A few years later the mountains also claimed Pepe.

EPILOGUE

Above Maestri's gear cache at the top of the initial dihedral, some 300 meters above the glacier and 20 meters below the triangular snowfield, we did not find any trace of the passage of Egger, Maestri, and Fava, their other partner. During the ascents and descents of our first try and successful climb, we covered three-quarters of the north ridge, one of three lines that Maestri described as his line of ascent above the col. (Maestri described three different lines in different accounts: in the newspaper *L'Europeo*, published in April 1959, the magazine *La Montagne*, published in April 1960, and the *Rivista del CAI*, published in 1961.) In this 450-meter section above

Salvaterra traverses during the descent via the Compressor Route. *Rolando Garibotti*

the col, Maestri says he placed 60 bolts, and yet we found nothing. Toni Ponholzer's attempts and our ascent covered three-quarters of the ground on the three different lines described by Maestri as his supposed line of ascent. Neither Toni nor we found any trace of Maestri's passage. Based on these observations and other reasons, we are convinced that the first ascent of Cerro Torre was done by the Italians Chiappa, Conti, Ferrari, and Negri in 1974 via the west face. For anyone interested in this history, I suggest reading "A Mountain Unveiled," by Rolando Garibotti, in the 2004 *American Alpine Journal*.

SUMMARY:

AREA: Cerro Torre, Patagonia

ROUTE: First ascent of El Arca de los Vientos (1,200m, 37 pitches, VI 5.11 A1 90°); the route follows parts of the Bragg-Donini-Wilson (1977) Torre Egger line on the lower east face to the Col of Conquest, then moves onto the northwest face, climbing a few sections in common with the 1994 Giarolli-Orlandi-Ravizza attempt, and then moves onto the north face, which it ascends to the west ridge and then follows the Ragni di Lecco Route for three pitches to the summit; Alessandro Beltrami, Rolando Garibotti, and Ermanno Salvaterra, November 12-13, 2005. Descent via southeast ridge (Compressor Route).

A NOTE ABOUT THE AUTHOR:

Ermanno Salvaterra, 51, lives in Pinzolo, Italy, and works as a mountain guide, ski instructor, and hutkeeper of the Rifugio Dodici Apostoli in the Brenta Group of the Dolomites. He has completed two new routes to the summit of Cerro Torre, a 1,350-meter new route that ended 100 meters below the summit, and the first winter ascent.

CHOMO LONZO

A French national expedition pioneers two 7,000-meter-plus peaks in Tibet.

YANNICK GRAZIANI

Yannick Graziani and Christian Trommsdorff work up the ice slopes on the northwest flank of Chomo Lonzo North at around 6,500 meters. They climbed a weakness in the cliffs above to reach the ridge at 6,800 meters and followed this to the 7,199-meter summit. *Patrick Wagnon*

For the first time in my experience, a high-altitude expedition is entirely sponsored. This makes it so easy to leave—all we have to do is to show up at a set time and board a plane. We owe this to Jean-Claude Marmier, our friend and president of the Fédération Française de la Montagne et de L'Escalade (FFME) Himalayan Committee, and to the FFME itself.

The idea for an expedition to Chomo Lonzo was hatched in 2003, and about 15 climbers were interested in the project, then 10, and the team ends up consisting of eight. We talk a lot before leaving—meetings, dinners, e-mails—and come up with a plan (rather vague and flexible, as the information we have on the mountain is sparse) according to which we will climb with our usual partners: two teams of three and one team of two.

On April 14 we arrive at base camp. The porters have left, the weather is beautiful, and winter snow still sticks to the northern aspects of the mountains. During our meetings in

The beautiful eastern flanks of Chomo Lonzo. The team first attempted the northeast ridge in the foreground of the central summit. During their successful ascent, they followed the west face of the north (right) peak to join the northwest ridge (right skyline) about midway. They followed this to the top. Then they descended to the saddle and spent two days climbing the steep, rocky ridge to the central summit. *Patrick Wagnon*

France, each team member had suggested ideas on how to climb and what routes might be possible. I hold a secret dream of traversing the three summits of Chomo Lonzo, the mountain that represents the goddess of birds for Tibetans, but the idea is still premature.

The next day, with a stable weather forecast, our small team of three decides to go acclimatizing. Our team is based on friendship and trust; we've known each other for five years and have grown closer as each expedition has unfolded.

Christian is 41 and used to work as an engineer all over the world; now he's a mountain guide in Chamonix. He lives with Karine, a ski patroller. He did many expeditions before our paths crossed, and he has been able to share his experience with us. He's a stubborn, adorable person.

Patrick, 35, is a glaciologist who lives in Grenoble with his wife and three children. We tease him by saying he is the fourth kid. He crossed India on a bike at age 20.

As for myself, I live off of guiding and reside in Chamonix; Kelly, a U.S. citizen, has been living with me for the past five years. I find it hard to describe myself. I feel that I live the extremes, even though my ideal is wisdom. I like my opposites.

Our unorthodox team has found a meeting point: high mountains as a passion and adventure at high altitude as an ideal.

We acclimatize in the classic way, never too fast. We explore the northeast arête of the central summit to 6,000 meters, but conditions are not favorable—too much snow. During the next week we move to the other side of the mountain and find that the west face holds considerably less snow than the gigantic and difficult east face. Even if we don't want to admit it, the dice have been rolled, and we will be back on this face. We even leave gear at 5,600 meters.

When you head out on such a mountain, you have to check out the face you want to climb to make sure the itinerary you have picked will work out. This seems obvious, but let me explain. Choosing your line is also determining the style and the ethic. Ours is simple: climbing in alpine style. If the route is well chosen, it will match the technical and psychological level of the climbers. Modesty and ambition thus become a capricious couple, difficult to satisfy, manageable yet dangerous.

In early May we complete the first ascent of the 7,199-meter north summit of Chomo Lonzo by its northwest ridge. Now it is time to regain strength at base camp for our next project. We are aiming for the 7,540-meter central summit. We'll start by repeating our route over the north summit to reach the notch between the two peaks; we have left camps in place to wait for our return. The wind that blows constantly up high forces us to wait. At base camp, springtime is back. Golden marmots, eagles, and spotted does visit us daily.

Doubts set in as we leave the grass for the world of ice and rock. At 6,000 meters we find our VE-25 tent has survived the wind in perfect shape, but our camp 800 meters higher has disappeared according to the youngsters Yann Bonneville and Aymeric Clouet, who returned from their attempt on the route a few days ago. We're going to have to carry gear back up.

We have brought enough food for eight days. We reach Camp 2 at 6,800 meters after eight hours of intense effort on a bare ice slope. Winds gusting to 100 kilometers per hour suddenly pick up in the afternoon, and it takes us two hours to set up two tents. As I lie inside the tent to hold it down with my weight while my friends anchor it solidly, I am scared I might fly off. How about those on the outside? Their faces are all puffy from the wind and their hands are frozen. The wind lasts another two hours and then dies at dusk. Great! We will be able

Trommsdorff leads toward the steep ramp that gained the ridge at 6,800 meters on Chomo Lomo North. *Patrick Wagnon*

to sleep without all the commotion outside.

Six weeks have passed on the expedition, and we have used up much of our strength. Doubts set in again, and we discuss our plans. The weather forecast reassures us. The wind should die, but not tomorrow. So we decide to rest for a day. Going on would be a waste of energy considering what lies ahead. Christian has the lips of a silicon bimbo, and I laugh. But his chapped lips make him suffer enormously. After hearing from the meteorologist, it's time for the doctor to bring him a little comfort over the satellite phone; he recommends a painkiller that we hold in our little pharmacy. Patrick and I head out to anchor our two ropes to the rock headwall at 7,000 meters. The wind and storms again pick up like crazy in the afternoon. Our instinct has been correct, and this rest day gives us strength to spare.

The fourth day is splendid. The north summit of Chomo Lonzo is close by and we quickly reach it. Ahead lies a corniced ridge. The doors to the unknown now lie wide open.

Graziani descends a gendarme en route to the col between the north and central peaks. *Christian Trommsdorff*

What's the value of a virgin summit? Is it even possible to quantify a mountain? For the high-altitude climber, every summit is worthy and gratifying, whether it has already been climbed or whether no one has yet set foot on it. Only the adventure matters, and mountains will never belong to somebody or to something: a country, a man, a religion. They bring extraordinary joy to those who climb them, that's all.

We progress down the ridgeline toward the pass between the two summits. We lose 150 meters of elevation over one kilometer. Pinnacles block the way, but we find a way over or around them. Approaching the pass at 7,050 meters, we grow worried as we realize the route up the central summit starts with a very steep, 100-meter rock ridge. Before settling in for the night at the col, we to try to find an easier way around this granite barrier. We would like to reach the summit tomorrow. It might be possible to rappel 50 meters to reach a hypothetical line of weakness that could lead us higher up on the ridge, where it becomes easier. But it's late and the wind is picking up. It's time to set up our camp.

Tough road ahead: Graziani and Trommsdorff head for the steep buttress above the col. *Patrick Wagnon*

There will be no D-day the next day, only D-minus-one. Despite giving it our greatest effort, reaching the summit seems inconceivable. We leave around 8.30 a.m. in snow flurries and gain barely 100 meters in elevation. Around 3 p.m. we come back down, making sure that our 100 meters of ropes are well-anchored. We have every reason to believe the weather is going to be favorable the next day. As we reach our little tents at the base of the ridge, we have to spend another two hours anchoring them properly because the ropes we had used before are now up on the rock with our jumars.

On the sixth day of our climb, at around 10:30 a.m., we head up our ropes to their high point at 7,150 meters. We are now 400 meters away from the summit. It's scary to hang from the ropes with a 2,000-meter drop down the east face beneath our feet! There is one 40-meter pitch of really hard rock left to complete the steep barrier. It's vertical and completely rotten and unstable. This crux takes us yet another hour and a lot of cold sweat. What would you think of falling at such an elevation? It's unthinkable, and every measure of concentration must be brought to bear.

The next section is more straightforward, or let's just say it's more "classic;" nevertheless it requires some belayed pitches. Now we are moving faster. Christian leads, his intuition and experience helping to find the right way. We rapidly gain altitude, and Chomo Lonzo lets us in on her secret passages and lines of weakness each time we're presented with an obstacle. It would only take a single featureless wall to stop us, but each tower can be bypassed on either its left or right side. Making the right choice on such climbs is often the key to success. We are well into the day when dark clouds start surrounding Everest. We only have one thing in mind: be fast. We are starting to feel tired from all the effort, and we haven't swallowed any food since the morning.

The ridge had looked like a straight line from the col, but in fact it zigzags, which adds to its length. We get over the last difficult section at around 4 p.m., and now we should be able to climb even faster. We drink a little melted water. We're at 7,400 meters and the summit is really close,

Graziani leading at around 7,150 meters on the rock buttress of the central summit. "What would you think of falling at such an elevation? It's unthinkable." *Patrick Wagnon*

but so is our deadline for turning around. The storm kicks in; wind and snow work together with violence; we are forced to wear our goggles and hide our faces. We are roped up 25 meters apart in this raging storm, and we can't even see each other. The commitment is intense and we all feel it. Our goggles freeze up and I can no longer see anything. What to do? Go on or turn around? We stop to talk it over. The summit is too close—we decide to keep going. Christian comes to a halt 20 meters below the top, and these are some 20 meters! When I reach him, I see that he is anchored to a single ice screw only halfway in at the bottom of a large crack. The wind is a little calmer now, but we are overwhelmed by what lies ahead. Yet this is the only way up. I decide to try it. There is no way to protect the pitch. My only chance is to reach the snow on top with my ice axes and pull myself over. I can only hope that my ice axes will hold!

It's 6:45 p.m. when Chris and I reach the summit. Patrick is 100 meters away, saving strength to make it back down. This instant, this stolen moment, belongs to us. An exquisite happiness invades us. It's late, time to head back down fast. It's 7 p.m. when we start. Within 15 minutes, the weather turns nice again; the sun is bright as we rejoin Patrick. We rappel down each tower we had bypassed on the way up. We are eager to lose as much elevation as possible before night sets in. We turn our headlamps on at 7,300 meters. The sky is clear and there is no wind. We know the full moon will soon show up, and we decide to wait for it It's almost 11 when we stop under a big boulder to melt snow. We then head out again on a long series of exhausting rappels that lead to our camp at 4 a.m., after 20 hours of effort. We light all our stoves to melt as much water as possible. It'll take us two hours to melt just two liters! We definitely have to sleep, but we must rehydrate first to recover. It's survival.

On the seventh day, a whole week on this climb, I wake at 8 a.m., get out of the tent, melt snow, and nibble on a few cookies while the others are getting ready inside. To go down, we need to climb up! The exit door lies at 7,200 meters, through the north summit. At 11 a.m. we start our descent, first climbing over the north peak and then rappelling past 6,800 meters.

We gather the extra gear there and head down the last rappels as terribly violent winds pick up again. It takes another 15 rappels on steep ice to reach 6,000 meters, and it's 8 p.m. before we reach a place where we can walk without a rope. We're in hurry to see grass and lose altitude, so we keep going all the way down to 5,300 meters. We're dead tired and collapse on the ground. It's 2 a.m. on the eighth day.

When we reach Kathmandu a few days later, we laze out and take advantage of the Nepali lifestyle before heading to Europe, its luxury, its despair, and its contradictions.

SUMMARY:

AREA: Kangshung Valley, Tibet

ASCENTS: First ascent of Chomo Lonzo North (7,199 meters) via the northwest ridge (1,500m, TD), Yannick Graziani, Christian Trommsdorff, Patrick Wagnon, May 3-7, 2005. First ascent of Chomo Lonzo Central (7,540 meters) via traverse over north peak and north ridge (ED), Graziani, Trommsdorff, Wagnon, May 15-22, 2005.

A NOTE ABOUT THE AUTHOR:

Yannick Graziani, 33, reached the summit of Makalu alone in 2004 and made the first ascent of the southwest face of 7,070-meter Chaukhamba II in India in 2002.

Translated from the French by Caroline Ware.

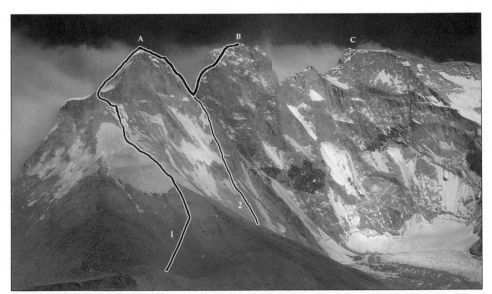

1) Graziani-Trommsdorff-Wagnon line on Chomo Lonzo North and Central. 2) Benoist–Glairon-Rappaz line on Chomo Lonzo North. A) Chomo Lonzo North (7,199m). B) Chomo Lonzo Central (7,540m). C) Chomo Lonzo Main (7,790m). *Patrick Wagnon*

CHOMO LONZO NORTH

Alpine style on a difficult new route to a Tibetan summit.

PATRICE GLAIRON-RAPPAZ

Stéphane Benoist leaves the first bivouac site, with the west face of Chomo Lonzo Main (7,790m) looming behind. *Patrice Glairon-Rappaz*

I am lying in my tent, listening to some sweet music and daydreaming about our climbs on this amazing expedition. Tomorrow, we will start our journey back home after two months in this remote area. I close my eyes and let my mind drift back….

For Stéphane Benoist and myself, the ascent of Chago, a beautiful, 6,893-meter summit between Everest and Makalu, provided the first intense experience of the expedition. We were both frozen by the time we reached the bergschrund. Really strong winds were hammering the summits around us that day.

"Let's try to get over the bergschrund and then decide whether we go on," Stéphane suggested.

A few hours later we were admiring the incredible views from Chago's summit. We had climbed a very logical yet strenuous line up the northeast face and then followed an airy ridge-line to the top. We were surrounded by some of the Himalaya's most prestigious peaks: Makalu, Baruntse, Ama Dablam, Nuptse, Lhotse, and the Kangshung side of Everest—better than anything we'd seen on postcards!

We felt strong and our enthusiasm seemed unbreakable. We had been successful on our first climb in the range, and I could feel the sweet, hard drug that runs in your blood anytime you reach a summit. We had worked hard to stand there, yet that test now made us more confident. A few minutes earlier we had been cursing and suffering from exhaustion, but soon we were feeling ready for an even harder climb. This surely had to be a drug, and a hard one too!

I hear a whistle outside the tent and crawl out to see our sirdar waving for me to come down to the main tent for lunch. We are all gathered at base camp except for "the Renegades"; they are still fighting high on the mountain. The last we've heard, they were on a pass and heading out to the main summit of Chomo Lonzo.

As we sit around and talk, we all agree that if they make the summit their ascent will surely go down as one of the most challenging and exposed routes yet climbed in the Himalaya. We all enjoy being able to share their climb "live" through the radio connection and to give them all the support we can!

Once lunch is over, I decide to return to my tent and open up Shackleton's story where I'd last left off. Reading about his adventures makes my mind drift back to my own recent adventure....

The end of our stay was nearing and only windy and unstable weather was being forecast. Steph and I hadn't even picked our definite line yet, and we were only 10 days from heading home! This was a new experience for us because on other expeditions we had decided on our objectives before leaving home and had been able to closely study the route. This time the approach was different because the mountain would be deciding for us, setting the rules of the game as we climbed. We were going to have to adapt and quickly pick what would seem the best option.

Finally, Steph and I decided on what looked like a really interesting line up the west face of Chomo Lonzo's northern summit. On the night of our departure it snowed heavily and doubts again arose in our heads. They had been there the whole time, yet we had finally managed to quiet them down. And now it was snowing again. The weather forecast was unstable, and we could only imagine how we would be hammered by the spindrift that would now certainly be washing down the face.

Our alarms sounded at 3 a.m., and we were soon on our way, hiking up a boulderfield and then a low-angle slope to the bergschrund. Our packs were heavy and the ice was incredibly hard on the first part of the route. We didn't yet realize it would stay this way throughout the entire climb! By 9 a.m. our calves were already on fire. We reached the gully after a delicate mixed pitch. A rather steep pitch with a vertical section led to the start of a beautiful ice line,

Just like a fun *goulotte* above Chamonix, only it's above 6,500 meters. *Patrice Glairon-Rappaz*

which we followed for 10 pitches up to 6,800 meters. It was 1:30 a.m. when we found a place to set up our bivouac on a shoulder. Ravaged by this long and painful day, we dove into our tent and fell into a deep sleep as soon as our heads touched the ground, forgetting all about food and water.

We woke late the next day and drank, drank, drank, and drank some more. We needed to rehydrate and feed ourselves if we hoped to keep going.

We started moving again around 1 p.m. We were climbing snow slopes now, which enabled our calves to finally rest a little. These slopes led to a series of exciting mixed pitches. It was eight in the evening when we decided to stop for the night. We put up our tent on a comfortable flat boulder that hung over the void. Ambience guaranteed! As strong winds picked up during that night, thoughts of being blown off that rock ran through our heads. But once again, gravity spared us.

I felt drowsy in the morning and knew I would have to gather every bit of energy remaining in my tired body to get out of there. Steph took the lead up to the summit ridge, which appeared much longer and more difficult than we'd hoped. He was in better shape, and I followed the rope he dragged up the snow slopes, around the crevasses, up and over seracs and rocky sections. It seemed like this ridge was never ending. It's hard to move fast when you're at 7,000 meters. We bivouacked for the third time 50 meters below the summit in a sheltered spot.

We slept well but I still felt totally drained. I will never forget what a nightmare the first pitch of that next day was for me. We had to break trail through very deep snow and felt like we were getting nowhere. My body wouldn't respond at all. I screamed from the top of my lungs to shake myself up. I had to reach deeper than I ever had for each step upward. This remains one of the toughest moments I've experienced as an alpinist, and to this day it is still hard for me to analyze. I was full of strength, somewhere inside of me, but I had no access to it.

Soon, though, the snow on the ridge became more solid, and then we were standing on the beautiful northern summit of Chomo Lonzo. This was an indescribable moment of shared joy.

Our descent followed the northwest ridge that the Renegades had climbed a few

Chance meeting, just below the summit of Chomo Lonzo North: From left, Patrice Glairon-Rappaz, Christian Trommsdorff, Stéphane Benoist, and Yannick Graziani. One team headed down, the other headed up. *Patrick Wagnon*

weeks earlier, when they did the first ascent of the north summit. After a few rappels we met the three of them headed back up for their attempt on the central summit. Seeing them there felt both surreal and yet so warm. We spoke only a few words and exchanged friendly embraces. Patrick took pictures of us. They were happy for us, and we cheered them on for their ascent.

After a long series of rappels we reached the 6,000-meter high camp at around 10 p.m. We were on solid ground now.

I open my eyes slowly and see my book at my side. I am lying deep within my sleeping bag. Nothing wrong with a nice siesta, especially when you've had such sweet dreams!

SUMMARY:

AREA: Kangshung Valley, Tibet

ASCENTS: Ascent of Chago (6,893 meters) by the northeast face to the northwest ridge, Stéphane Benoist, Patrice Glairon-Rappaz, April 25, 2005. New route (1,100m, ED M5+ WI4-5) on the west face of Chomo Lonzo North (7,199 meters), Glairon-Rappaz, Benoist, May 13-16, 2005.

A NOTE ABOUT THE AUTHOR:

Patrice Glairon-Rappaz, 35, lives in southern France. His new route on the north face of Thalay Sagar with Stéphane Benoist was featured in the 2004 American Alpine Journal. *He writes: "I would like to take this opportunity to thank Jean-Claude Marmier, president of the FFME Himalayan Committee, for his unlimited support."*

Translated from the French by Caroline Ware.

THE LINE OF LIFE

Chasing dreams on the alpine-style first ascent of Broad Peak's southwest face.

DENIS URUBKO

The southwest face of Broad Peak rises about 2,300 meters above the Faichan icefall. Samoilov and Urubko spent six nights on the face, two more than planned. *Marko Prezelj*

The first ascent of Broad Peak (8,047 meters) was accomplished in 1957 by a small Austrian team from the west side, and this became the normal route. It is a rather easy ridge that leads all the way to the summit. Other routes gain the mountain's northern ridge from the east or west, and then follow this ridge to the top. But by 2005 no one had been able to reach the summit from the southern side.

As far as I know, attempts from the south started in 1984. The great Polish trio of Jerzy Kukuczka, Krzystof Wielicki, and Voytek Kurtyka tried going up the southwestern ridge but turned around at 6,400 meters. Four other attempts by the expeditions of Goran Kropp, Alberto Iñnurrategi, Rick Allen, and Andrew Lock also failed. These well-known and experienced climbers were very determined but had to retreat below 7,000 meters. While the steepest walls of Nanga Parbat, Makalu, and Dhaulagiri were conquered, Broad Peak's southern side remained unclimbed.

Our goal was to climb the 2,500-meter southwest face. The expedition consisted of six Italian climbers—Roberto Piantoni, Marco Astori, Stefano Magri, Matteo Piantoni, Domenico Belingeri, and Mario Merelli—and two Kazakh climbers, Sergey Samoilov and myself. Before meeting in Pakistan, I knew very little about the Italian climbers, but Sergey and I had climbed together for many years as members of the Central Sports Club of the Kazakhstan Army. As the Soviet Union collapsed, Sergey was one of the leading climbers, having done many 7,000-meter peaks in the Pamir and Tien Shan ranges. He had also climbed Peak Communism (7,495 meters) and Khan Tengri (6,995 meters) in winter. In 2000 we climbed Khan Tengri by its 3,000-

Starting up the main face at 5,750 meters. The two climbers shared a single sleeping bag, down jacket, fleece jacket, and windshell. *Sergey Samoilov.*

meter north face and won the Commonwealth of Independent States championship.

"It's good that you are going together," said my wife. "Of course I believe in you, but I'm sure that with such a partner you are much better off."

"Vika, sweetheart," I replied, amused, "sometimes I believe in him more than in myself."

We established base camp on the moraine of the Godwin-Austen Glacier, opposite the southwestern wall. On July 5, with our tents pitched at 4,700 meters, we started the reconnaissance. The wall looked formidable. Seracs and rock bands guarded the way, and icefields rose into the sky. Avalanche debris littered the base of the wall. After spending several days in the cirque of the Faichan Glacier, at 5,200 meters, we had a clear idea of the difficulty and dangers of this route. Our leader, Roberto Piantoni, informed Sergey and me of his new plan: to climb the peak by the normal route.

"But I have already climbed the standard route," I said. It was hard for me to accept this. "What should I do now?" At the base of this tremendous wall, after a year of serious preparation, it was nearly impossible to turn down the challenge. After a week of acclimatizing on the standard route, up to 7,200 meters, I started dreaming about the southwest wall again.

"Let's be logical," Sergey said, smiling. "First, we have enough experience. Second, we should do something new. And third, I like this route…and this is the most important thing! Why should we retreat?" After a good rest and careful preparation the two of us left base camp by ourselves.

Urubko searches for passage through the black belt of rocks at around 6,300 meters. *Sergey Samoilov*

In 1975 Reinhold Messner and Peter Habeler opened the era of alpine style in the Himalaya by climbing Hidden Peak (8,068 meters) via a new route. Since then, very few climbs in the Himalaya have pushed alpine-style climbing to the extremes. By this I mean climbs that reach a main summit of more than 8,000 meters via a difficult new route, in pure alpine style, with a small team of two to four people. In the 100-year history of mountaineering in the Himalaya and Karakoram, only seven or eight ascents fulfill these criteria.

After spending the night at the base of Broad Peak at 5,100 meters, we abandoned all our doubts and fears. We started moving into the Faichan icefall early on July 19, still in the dark. By sunrise we were at the base of the route. The wall had looked big from a distance, but from

Chopping a tent site below the yellow band at 6,500 meters. *Denis Urubko*

here, with kilometers of ice and rock hanging over us, it seemed tremendous.

At our first bivouac on the wall, at 6,100 meters, we felt more confident, and when the next day brought up more difficulties we were ready for them. I led across the first difficult rock band via a diagonal slab stretching several dozen meters under an overhanging section. The black rock was reminiscent of the roofs of old buildings in Europe, very steep and smooth. Holds were almost absent, but a 15- to 20-centimeter-wide line of ice came down from the overhang. I climbed with my Awax axes, my crampons sliding on the smooth slab. I wondered how it looked from the side. Sergey was smiling but didn't say anything.

After some sections of ice above the black rock band, we found ourselves under a band of yellow rock. Rising above us like a medieval castle, it looked intimidating. With no way to the right or to the left, we had to attack it directly, tackling the steep buttress. The freedom of alpine style often implies a return to ancient wild times. Nature brings the climber to the age when survival depended only on the strength of muscles, resourcefulness of mind, and the speed of reaction. A climber becomes like a predator; his perception sharpens. He becomes part of the surroundings. We spent two days at the yellow rock band, dealing with great difficulties. Three 6a pitches and one 6b pitch [5.10a to 5.10d] at nearly 7,000 meters gave me enormous pleasure. All through the spring I had been working really hard on the rocks, honing my technique. And now it was paying off. What makes the mountaineer happy? Maybe it is the feeling that you can reach your dreams. Or perhaps it's the feeling that all that hard work wasn't in vain.

We set up camp on a small rock ledge above the yellow band. Our tent looked like an awkward jellyfish. Its sides hung over the void, and there wasn't enough space to lie down. Nonetheless, we slept like babies, shoulder to shoulder. The night was mystical and full of stars that seemed so close we could just clasp them in our palms, and the wind sang its sad melody of the void. After that hard day I dreamed of my little daughter. Her blue eyes warmed my heart.

So far the weather had been perfect. But after our night at 7,000 meters clouds from the west dumped a fresh layer of snow on the slopes. Early in the morning, just after taking our tent down, we sank in the snow and had to dig a trench to move through it. When we reached 7,400 meters, avalanches poured down as the light snow gave way to a real snowstorm. Fortunately, the steep rock couldn't collect a lot of snow, but tons of it came down neighboring couloirs. We followed our old doctrine of climbing only buttresses and ribs. Though harder than the couloirs, they were safer from rockfall and avalanches.

Urubko surmounts a bulge in the yellow band at around 6,700 meters: 5.10 climbing and no sticky rubber. *Sergey Samoilov*

Dry tooling in a thick fog, when you can see only five or six meters, brings you into a special world, without feelings, without a sensation of space or time. Just a piece of snow-covered rock in front of you. Unable to see anything, I followed my intuition. After spending a night on a small ledge in the middle of the sea of fog, we had nothing to do in the morning but follow our way to nowhere, toward the snowfall and wind, up the snow-covered rock.

The next evening we discovered that we had reached the top of the southwestern wall of Broad Peak. The rock got a little easier and less steep, with more ledges and cracks. We were extremely tired, and only by sheer willpower were we able to continue. We had nothing left to eat, and this was the last day we could melt enough snow to drink. We had planned to reach the summit in five days and based our rations on that. For the backup day, we planned only to drink and use leftovers from the previous days. But the bad weather and the unforeseen difficulties of the route had added an extra day on top of that.

After reaching a tiny, sloping ledge at about 7,800 meters, we pitched the tent with great difficulty and collapsed, with no energy left. One sleeping bag, one down jacket, one windshell, and one fleece jacket for the team—the notorious weight saving. That night we didn't take off our boots, and we barely managed to quench our thirst.

"Sergey, how are you?" I wheezed as the first sign of sunrise arrived. "How cold are you? Do you feel your feet?"

"Please pass me a piece of ice," my friend said stubbornly. "My mouth is completely dry. There is a sea of water near us, but everything is frozen."

The morning was, to put it mildly, horrendous. But the clouds stayed in the valleys, scared off by the west wind. We could see the final sections before the summit ridge, and we started making our way through the snow. It was extremely difficult. Only the idea of moving up kept us going. Our brains couldn't accept the possibility of going down, and we kept kicking steps in the hard névé. Thick clouds covered the mountains below 7,500 meters, and only the pyramids of Masherbrum and Gasherbrum IV were visible.

At the southeastern ridge of Broad Peak, which we joined at 7,950 meters, the wind turned into a hurricane. The mass of air was alive, trying to blow us into the valleys. It was like war—I hurried from one small bit of cover to another. Step by step, roped together, we kept going into the dark blue sky. The summit appeared all of a sudden. Three meters down the slope I had been exhausted, feeling the last sparks of my will burning down in this thin air. But seeing the flags of previous expeditions fluttering in the wind, I felt a new wave of energy, as if the end of the route had become its beginning. Sergey and I had turned our dreams into reality. It was 11:30 a.m. on July 25.

The wind was still trying to rip us off the ridge, searing our clothing and faces. The horizon consisted only of the highest points on earth: K2 to the north and the massive summits of the Gasherbrums on the other side. A free and empty world, with only two tiny climbers in it.

Camp III on the normal route, at 7,200 meters, was calm when Sergey and I arrived as the purple sunlight faded away. No wind, no fuss. No need to hurry or do anything important. Neither a soul nor a tent disturbed the pristine beauty of the snowfields. Digging out some-one's cache, we couldn't restrain ourselves from using one gas canister. Two bodies exhausted by the high altitude desired their reward of several cups of water. Why don't I feel the same sharp taste of the water in the city, in the valleys? Why are the best things I have tasted in my life so simple, and why does it always happen at altitude?

As Omar Khayyam said, "If you want to feel happiness, go to the desert. And after you come back, the first dirty puddle will become the source of divine satisfaction for you."

The gas canister we borrowed belonged to a commercial expedition. When we met them the next day at Camp I, we tried to justify our actions, but they just laughed as they looked at our fatigued faces. They announced that their expedition was over.

"There's lots of gas now. Take as much as you want."

"No, thanks, we've had enough this season. We would rather have more chocolate…. And those cookies, please…. And more tea…. And…."

Robi and Marco met us that evening on the glacier at the base of the mountain. After offering sincere congratulations, they took our backpacks despite our weak protests, and all we had to do was walk down the moraine. The wide summit of Broad Peak faded into alpenglow, as if the mountain were saluting the two dull and extremely tired men, two insects, who had managed to rise above the world and their weaknesses. Soon we found ourselves at base camp, full of friends, warmth, coziness, and the strong feeling of safety.

Every person, at every moment, has the possibility of expanding his horizons. It doesn't have to involve a sporting achievement. The horizons of dreams are endless, and one just needs to stretch a hand to touch them. The ascent of Broad Peak was such a moment for me, the climb during which I found things I had been looking for during many years of mountaineering. The expedition was over, but I won't ever forget those intense days on the slopes of one of the most beautiful mountains on earth.

Summary:

Area: Karakoram, Pakistan

Ascent: Alpine-style first ascent of the southwest face of 8,047-meter Broad Peak (2,500m, 6b A2 M6+ 70°), six and a half days of climbing, with one and a half days on the descent, Sergey Samoilov and Denis Urubko, July 19-26, 2005.

Grants: This expedition was sponsored by Salice, Camp, La Sportiva, The North Face, Electrolux, and the Rescue Service of Almaty.

Exhaustion: Urubko in Skardu and Samoilov flying home. *Sergey Samoilov (left) and Denis Urubko*

A Note About the Author:

Born in Russia in 1973, Denis Urubko lives in Almaty, Kazakhstan. A Snow Leopard of the former Soviet Union, Urubko has climbed nine 8,000-meter peaks without supplementary oxygen and has won numerous speed-climbing competitions on the high peaks of Russia and the CIS.

Translated from the Russian by Adilet Imambekov.

THE KHUMBU EXPRESS

Two Himalayan solos in 12 days, on Cholatse and Tawoche, Nepal

UELI STECK

Base camp for the north face of Cholatse, with less ice and snow on the mountain than Steck had expected. See Climbs and Expeditions for route lines on the face. *Ueli Steck*

I have recently climbed a variety of mountains and routes solo. This type of climbing fascinates me because of the deep and powerful experiences you can get only when forced to live in the present moment. Before leaving for Nepal, I soloed long rock routes, spent time at the crags, ascended frozen waterfalls, and climbed the north face of the Eiger in winter.

Even so, I was unsure if I was ready to handle the pressure of the Himalaya, because it's an entirely different environment from what I was familiar with. Up there, no one could come to my rescue. My goal was to solo three big faces in one short season—the Khumbu Express.

CHOLATSE

Pictures from the fall show lots of snow and ice on Cholatse's north face; in such conditions the face should be climbable in 24 hours. When I arrive, however, I notice that a lot more rock is visible than in my picture, which makes for more interesting climbing!

I decide to take my sleeping bag, but my gear still has to be minimized. Without a partner you end up with twice the weight, and in climbing every kilogram counts. One thing is clear: with the equipment I'm taking, I will be unable to rappel from the upper half of the face. It's a one-way street over the summit and back down the south side. Ten stoppers, the same number of pitons, four ice screws, four quickdraws, five spare carabiners, one meal of spaghetti, and four Powerbars. A nice diet....

At 3 a.m. on April 14, I get out of my warm sleeping bag at base camp. It's slightly unsettling to walk into the dark night. At daybreak I reach my cache at the base of the face. The wall rises steeply above me into the morning sky. I begin to climb and immediately find myself in a meditative state. Focused on climbing in the absolute present, I suppress all thoughts of what could lie ahead.

Trusty roll of duct tape at the ready, Ueli Steck starts up Cholatse. *Ueli Steck*

Pitch after pitch I move upward, belaying frequently in this sketchy and steep terrain. A blend of mixed rock and ice provides a nice variety of climbing, and I feel like I'm flying up the face. It's 11 a.m. when I reach the first couloir, a few hundred meters of pure ice. I drag the rope behind me like a long tail.

Slowly night descends. Exhausted, I stay on the lookout for a suitable bivouac site. At 6,000 meters I find a small cornice with a cave. Small but nice! I fall asleep as I'm cooking, and half the spaghetti ends up in my sleeping bag. The instant coffee tastes terrible.

Now come the hard hours as I try to sleep. The vulnerability won't leave my thoughts in peace. What if I break a hand or ram a crampon into my calf? The briefest lapse of focus could have lethal consequences. The darkness in my snow hole is depressing, yet somehow I manage to sleep.

In the morning the journey continues—450 meters remain to be climbed. My psyche is once again in better shape, but my muscles are not as fresh as they were yesterday. The face shows its ugliest side. Not quite as steep, but my ice tools cut right through the packed snow. That means careful footwork! Protection is nonexistent in this terrain. For the first time I contemplate retreat. But how would I do that? There is no way with this little gear. There's only one direction to go! Hours later I reach the summit ridge. Now you've made it, I think. But then I spot the largest cornices and mushrooms I have ever seen. Over there I see the flat south ridge—I wish I could be there.

The angle of the dangle: Steep ground below, more steep climbing ahead on the first day of climbing on Cholatse, about 300 meters up. *Ueli Steck*

A crevasse in the ridge blocks the way to the summit 50 meters before the top. The crevasse is deep, and the mountain drops 1,500 meters on both sides of the ridge. I dig deep and take a step across. I'm wedged in the crevasse as if it were a big chimney. The lip of the crevasse on the other side is now two meters above me. Somehow my ice tools must find purchase. I try a few different spots. Finally I dare to make the move and pull myself over the lip. My heart is pumping and I'm out of breath. Ten minutes later I'm on the summit. Tension flows from my body as I relax.

The long descent lies ahead. Fog starts to envelop the mountain, and I'm not familiar with the south ridge. But onward! In the fading light I spot the flat glacier below me. That's where I want to bivy. In my mind I feel like I'm already there. There I will be able to unfold my sleeping bag and take off my harness—no need to tie in anywhere. I start to rappel.

It is already pitch black. I look for a crack for my final anchor. Down I go. The rope just makes it down to the glacier. I've used all my gear to get down, but that's practical—less stuff to haul tomorrow.

I feel more at ease at the second bivy. Unfortunately, I have nothing left to eat. I drink some warm water. That's better than nothing.

A 5,000-meter pass stands between me and base camp. My legs are like Jell-O, but slowly and surely I'm getting closer. At Chola Pass I ask the first trekker I see for something to eat. He gives me a Twix. After three days with so little food it tastes revolting, but I eat it. After eight hours of trekking I reach base camp. Content with the first solo ascent of Cholatse, I drink real coffee made from my espresso machine.

TAWOCHE

On April 22 I find myself at the bottom of the rocky east face of Tawoche. I have everything with me—a portaledge, food for nine days, and a bunch of other gear. The morning sun bathes the face from 6 a.m. until 11. It's quite warm, and the wall roars to life. Ice fall, rockfall, and spindrift. Giant blocks tumble down the face. At noon I decide to descend. This route is suicidal. A short while later I reach my friends in base camp.

I scan the face with binoculars for a safer line. On the left side I spot a nice-looking ice line. Not too difficult, but beautiful. I change my plans and pack my bag for this new line. It's been seven years since the last team stood on the summit of Tawoche. I'm motivated to give this peak a try.

The weather is very unstable. I wake up each night at 11 to look outside my tent. Fog, snow....

On April 24 I notice a starry sky with just a few scattered clouds. I have to go for it. I leave my 5,020-meter base camp at 11:30 p.m. I have one 20-meter, 5mm Kevlar rope and three ice screws. I feel the benefits of my "acclimatization climb" on Cholatse. Except for the final part of the route, the terrain is between 50 and 60 degrees. Huge seracs rise above me toward the top. I climb several pitches of vertical ice without any protection. At 4 a.m. I find myself on the summit. Four and a half hours for the first solo ascent of Tawoche, by a possible new route. It's cold, so I immediately begin the descent.

I reach base camp at 8 a.m., just in time for breakfast.

AMA DABLAM

On to Ama Dablam, with my last permit and my liaison officer in tow. The weather stubbornly remains unstable, with constant snow showers. With my time running out I begin the northwest face on May 3. The weather is actually good. But quickly, around noon, the curtain closes again. It begins to snow lightly. I feel good and keep climbing; the ice is hard and the rock quite good.

The steep ramp beyond the glacier plateau is impressive. I place protection for pitch after pitch. The small avalanches and spindrift continue to grow in strength. I turn around just below the crux pitch (according to Tomaz Humar, who pioneered this route). It is too dangerous for me. In the bergschrund at the edge of the glacier plateau, I'm safe from the avalanches. It snows all night. In the morning I use a short break in the weather to return safely to base camp. The wall is covered in snow and the weather is terrible.

After a few more days at the bottom of the face, I decide to depart. It's a difficult decision, but the conditions are simply too dangerous.

Content, I return to Switzerland.

Steck's line on the east-southeast face of Tawoche. He first started up the rock face to the right but retreated as warm weather set loose ice and rockfall. *Ueli Steck*

SUMMARY:

AREA: Khumbu Region, Nepal

ROUTES: North face of Cholatse (6,440 meters) via a direct variant to the French Route (1995) and the 2003 Korean attempt (1,400m, V+ M6 90°), Ueli Steck, solo, April 14-16, 2005. East-southeast face of Tawoche (a.k.a. Taboche, 6,495 meters) via a possible new route (1,500m, M5 50°-60°), Ueli Steck, solo, April 24-25, 2005. Northwest face of Ama Dablam (6,814 meters) via the Furlan-Humar Route (1,650m, V+ A2+ 90°), Ueli Steck, solo attempt to 5,900 meters, May 3-4, 2005.

A NOTE ABOUT THE AUTHOR:

Born in 1976, Ueli Steck is a carpenter turned professional alpinist who lives near Interlaken, Switzerland. He has climbed new routes on Pumori (2001), Mt. Dickey (2002), and the Eiger (2001), and he made two attempts on the north face of Jannu. In 2004, with Stefan Siegrist, he linked the north faces of the Eiger, Mönch, and Jungfrau in 25 hours of climbing.

Translated from the German by Martin R. Gutmann.

THE WALL

Two climbers on the north face of Khan Tengri, Kyrgyzstan.

ILIAS TUKHVATULLIN

PREFACE

The world has gone crazy for records of all kinds. For that reason I want to say right away that we do not make our ascents for the sake of setting records. It's simply the case that when you undertake some pursuit for a long time, you want to accomplish something that hasn't been done and to show that, if a person wants something enough, then surely he'll achieve it. Moreover, we never go into the mountains in order to struggle or die for an idea. We go in order to live another page of our life.

This ascent was distinguished from our others by silence. We enjoyed the silence. Between us there arose such a rapport that we spoke without words and sensed each other without sounds or gestures. Our souls virtually grew together into a single whole. The source from which we drew our energy was the Wall; we had never encountered a more willful and beautiful mountain. We were walking along the road that has no end; we simply dissolved into our surroundings. That is why we were able to push ahead for so long. Every day vouchsafed to us by fate was a gift, and all its manifestations made us happy, even the sudden hurricane—wind of such strength you would think it miraculous, and perhaps it was.

Even when it seemed that we had reached the point of no return, we were certain that this path continued, the path leading back home. And the more we were pulled homeward, the greater the strength with which nature rained down its forces upon us, as though wanting to say, "Where are you hurrying off to, wasting the remnants of your strength? Your home is right here. Relax, you've already arrived at where you wanted to go." Nature, as it were, reminded us that man should have no attachments; they only hinder his ability to live and to make true decisions, free from the past. There is only the present.

In my expeditions with Pasha, time long ago stopped playing any role. Time simply does not exist. We are happy that we are climbing together again. It doesn't matter where we are climbing to, how much we are climbing—there is no end, there is no beginning. This was and will be forever: me, Pasha, and the mountain. When the expedition is over, we come to the surface, and then from the sea onto dry land, but only so as to again be on the sea of salty sensations, which are so good for the soul.

That's the way it was this time too....

August 15. We fly in to the Northern Inyl'chek Glacier as usual, at the beginning of August. The acclimatization proceeds smoothly, and by the 15th we are ready for takeoff. We decide to leave at 2 a.m., but we have hardly gone out when we are plunged into thick mist. Without talking we sprawl in our tents, and at 4 a.m., when it clears up, Pasha asks, "Well, what do you think, shall we start?" I reflect a bit, then say, "We won't have time to cross the lower snowfields; we could end up under an avalanche. Let's wait." It turns out we are right: during the next few days horrid weather rages, and this time we avoid the trap the weather has set for us.

But there is nothing more difficult than waiting. The days drag on and the weather does not improve. The Wall rises above us in a white shroud, and it seems this year an ascent will not shine for us. I accept the caprices of nature with equanimity. If it's impossible to

"Frozen," by Jeremy Collins (www.jercollins.com).

change the situation, then take it for what it is. To be honest, I'm even happy about the poor weather because it is the sole good argument for backing off from the Wall. This is the first time that I hadn't wanted to go into the mountains. We had already been on the Wall, in 2003, and we knew just how hard it was. At the time, I had decided this place would never see me again. During the year I hoped Pasha would not succeed in finding sponsors for this expedition. But in May he called and screamed into the phone, "Everything's first class! We're going!" The mousetrap snapped shut, and so now I wander along the Wall, casting elliptical glances at it. Will it let us up or not?

August 19. The sky clears and in the evening frost sets in, a sign of good weather. Once again we check over our packs. There's some tension over the fact that we're taking only four canisters of gas, but Pasha stresses a quick climb, and I yield to his arguments.

August 20. At 3 a.m. the whole sky is filled with stars but it's not cold. We are dressed just as we were in 2003, in the absolute minimum: long underwear, fleece suits, and windproof outer layers. In our packs we have only light down sweaters, spare gloves, and mittens. With headlamps we cross the zone of crevasses, and when the sunrise begins to glimmer we're already standing below our route. Everything is clear and businesslike: Pashka (I have many nicknames for my friend) is in the lead, and I'm following. This sequence became established between us long ago and does not upset me. I am able to lead, but I'm better at carrying heavy loads and Pasha has no equals when it comes to climbing mixed sections. This wall is no plaything, and for that reason each person does what he does best.

Little by little the mountain wakes up. It clears itself of the snow that has accumulated during the past week and sprays us with dry avalanches. Our ice tools and crampons hold us fast to the ice, and we move quickly up our planned path. The weather is brilliant, and in good spirits we rush upward. Because of our work we don't notice that the day is late until the sun appears to the right of the wall, reminding us that we have only an hour of daylight left. We putz about until darkness without finding a

The north face of Khan Tengri rises about 9,000 vertical feet. Shabalin and Tukhvatullin spent nine nights on the face, including two nights at their penultimate camp. *Chad Kellogg*

suitable site, so we have to swing our tools and cut out a shelf for a sitting bivy. Having finished our business, we sit down, cover ourselves in the tent, and begin to melt ice and prepare dinner, which this day consists of red caviar (no joke) with dry biscuits and tea. First class! Below, like a tiny star, our base camp twinkles. We're at an altitude of 4,800 meters. We are completely satisfied with the amount of work we've done. Only one thing irritates us: we can't remove our boots because they might drop.

August 21. The weather is good; a few clouds are floating in the sky. We breakfast and then head onto the route. Ahead wait complicated rocky sections. And again our tools satisfy: they cling to the rock faces covered in snow, finding invisible catches. Evening comes. Pasha keeps climbing and climbing, and still there is no tent site. I begin to get angry: "How many walls do you need to climb to understand that you have to start looking for a campsite two hours before sunset? You can see that the mountain is not disposed to give us gifts! It's time to stop and carve out a ledge." If you start late on the sleeping arrangements, then you'll start late the next day. The body demands a certain amount of rest. Finally, we find a suitable place, and in an hour of stamping down snow we create a small platform. We cover it with the remnants from our water bottle and our own urine in order to "cement" it, and then we set up the tent.

Inside we remove our boots with delight. We need to let our feet relax completely and restore themselves; otherwise frostbite is inevitable. We prepare dinner and then sink into sleep.

And suddenly, in complete darkness, an avalanche comes down upon us from who knows where. Something hard hits me on my head. This is courting disaster. Thank God, the tent remains standing and there is no visible damage to it. We drink 50 milliliters of vodka to relax and sit back to sleep. But just in case, we spend the rest of the night wearing our helmets.

August 22. In the morning we discover that the avalanche has swept away our shovel, which we left outside the tent. That's too bad: we'd planned to use it as a snow anchor on the upper snowfields. The weather is good and so, not lingering, we set to work. Pasha climbs in the direction of a rocky triangle. It seems the rock face is close, but this is an illusion. To reach it we must plow and plow. Turning a corner, we discover a scrap of old rope frozen in the ice. Hooray! These must be the ropes from Myslovsky's team, we decide. Such finds always warm the heart and bolster one's confidence. Pasha climbs a vertical section with the aid of his ice tools, and I catch myself thinking, "And how is he any worse than the great Mauro Bole, the Italian with the nickname Bubu, who is praised across the globe for his technical prowess?"

"The fixed ropes are ready," Pavlik cries unexpectedly quickly, and I, loaded down with rope, hoist the hated pack and climb upward. After consulting with each other, we decide to stop early to set up camp—we have to conserve our strength. In spite of the wind we quickly set up the tent and reinforce it with help of our ice axes. Gathering a bag of snow for preparing water, we tumble into the tent. The wind gets stronger, but our home is warm and cozy, the stove hums, dinner is cooking. Finally we can pull off our boots. Such bliss cannot be experienced while lying on the couch! Happy, we sink into sleep.

August 23. In the morning, looking out of the tent, I notice narrow feathers of clouds in the sky. In general this means the weather is changing. "Well, okay, time will tell," I think. We set about preparing breakfast. And then, yet another surprise: the stove refuses to work. Now that's a problem! We begin to consider our options and there aren't many. If we don't repair the stove, we'll have to descend. That's the deal. Going for lightness, we did not bring pliers, and without them it's difficult to disassemble the stove. But, as they say, "If you've been eaten, there are at least two ways out." With the aid of a small file we twist the fuel injector of the stove against the latch of a carabiner. Unsealing it, we discover that some kind of dirt has fallen inside. It's not clear how, but facts are facts.

After losing half a day repairing the stove, we set out. Awaiting us is the rocky triangle, the crux of the lower part of the wall. Pasha takes the lead while I belay. After many years I'm now accustomed to the feeling of waiting for a fall. It's wonderful to think the leader has it harder, which is usually true. But I would not hasten to divide our work into hard and easy. Try sitting immobile in the wind and cold for a few hours, visualizing the actions you'll take in case of a leader fall. From this point of view, it is easier to be climbing than to be constantly in a state of nervous tension. Pasha runs out the whole rope without any protection, and my belay station is anchored with one stopper. "That's precious little to hold a fall," I think. The face is snow-covered and devoid of cracks, like much of Khan's northern wall. One has to know how to climb confidently with his ice tools. This my partner clearly demonstrates.

Above, we reach more snowfields, and for Pashka this insecure work in loose snow is the most difficult. On our last climb together he had a failure of nerves and I had to take the lead. It will be interesting to see how he conducts himself this time. I'm prepared to take his place, but it will be better if he masters himself and works through it. Step by step, overcoming the shifting show, we slowly make our way to the next rocky ridge. Although the snow is deep, there is no avalanche danger and we gain ground monotonously, hour after hour, meter after meter. We climb together to traverse some rock and scramble up an inside corner to a small ridge. Ahead of us are the slanting "sheep's brows," covered in snow. As usual, toward evening the wind becomes stronger. We are in luck: we find a suitable tent site, one where we can actually lie down.

August 24. This day is like the previous one, just like two drops of water. The shattered rock faces again give way to deep, loose snow. After floundering in this "cream of wheat," exhausted, we climb onto a huge, two-meter by two-meter platform of thin slate slabs, which the Red Army soldiers laid during their climb in 1988.

August 25. The sky is socked in with clouds; the weather has decidedly worsened. We feel the exhaustion that has slowly accrued during the last few days. Pasha's boots are a cause for concern. Although they are advanced models, they are half a size too small and his toes are squeezed all the time. We climb up a snowy ribbon at the level of the "wine glass" and finally, hooray, reach a belt of reddish rock, our cherished goal. A vertical chimney pulls us into its belly. Steep, very steep. Pavel leads upward for a long time. From above, snow and large chunks of ice fly down onto me. I twist and turn away from them as best I can. When it is already completely dark, I hear, "The fixed ropes are ready." I pull myself up and see that, under a cupola-shaped rock overhang a meter and a half tall, my Pavlik sits and obstinately hacks into a snowdrift. By the light of our headlamps, we set up the tent with difficulty. It's a sitting bivy again, but we're thankful. Everything else is the usual: we have to melt snow, prepare dinner, sit down to sleep in the pose of meditating monks. The wind roars the whole night. What is it bringing us?

August 26. Altitude around 6,350 meters. The wind does not abate. Very cold. After such a night, one's condition is loathsome. Pasha goes out ahead. I belay and mentally prepare to take down our camp. Today will not be easy: there are many horizontal sections and no way of avoiding pendulums. Climbing two pitches, we turn to the right. It seems to me that Pasha is off route. But when he stumbles upon an empty box of sugar, stuck by chance into a fissure, I calm down.

The next pitch is of the category "super," starting in a chimney that leads to a shattered vertical wall. Usually, in places where the probability of a fall is high, Pasha commands, "Watch me!" But he proceeds through this section without hesitation. All that remains is for me not to lag behind. From time to time Pasha rubs his hands together to warm his frozen fingers. It has become perceptibly colder; now that we're above the col to our right, as we expected, the wind is considerably stronger. Wherever you look it's blowing. But we have only one path home: via the summit. We've managed to climb too high to turn back now.

On a small snowy ledge we carve out a platform about half the size of the tent bottom and make this our little home. Inside the tent, I suddenly notice that I'm shaking all over. I really froze today. With melancholy I look at our last gas container; it will last only a day, maybe a day and a half. The only hope is the cache that we left on the summit in 2003. Pavlik is also suffering from the cold; his toes have noticeably whitened. Has he really got frostbite? I want to think positively. After all, we took Trental before we went into the mountains to improve our circulation. I'm becoming more and more worried about some kind of pain in my stomach. There's nothing to be done—I have to bear with it. Outside the wind is gaining strength. Usually, after dark it subsides a bit, but today it seems to have forgotten this and blows at full force.

August 27. Outside storm-force winds are blowing. At such moments we take longer than usual to prepare to leave, as if considering whether to stay or wait it out. It's already around midday (to the extent that we can tell by feel, because we have no watch and there is no sun) before we reluctantly crawl outside. The storm is raging around us. It's a good thing that yesterday we fixed about 20 meters above our bivouac site. Pasha begins to climb slowly up the fixed rope, while I pack up camp. The wind is howling like we're in a wind tunnel, a horrible shriek all around us. Through the wind a sound reaches me: "The fixed ropes are rea…." I understand that it's my turn. In a second my glasses are pasted over with snow and I'm blind. There's no possibility—and no sense—of cleaning my glasses, and so I proceed blindly up the rope. I begin to gasp for breath. There is no oxygen: the wind is carrying it away, leaving a vacuum. My heart is working like a machine gun just at the point of overheating and jamming up. Bad thoughts creep into my mind: "Probably, this is how Salavat died on Makalu—his heart wore out." Dismissing these stupid thoughts, I force myself to crawl to Pavlik. He is thoroughly frozen. Through the shriek of the wind I hear, "Set up the tent, we have to wait it out." We still harbor the faint glimmer of hope that the storm will not last forever.

We nestle together like tiny fledglings on a narrow ledge, sitting on our packs and hiding under the tent. How long we sit there I don't know. It seems an eternity to us. We've long since lost the feeling in our feet, like they are made of wood, and the wind does not decrease for one second. One of us, I don't remember which, comes up with a great idea: descend to our platform below. With unbelievable effort we descend and set up the tent. Crawling into it, we pray for one thing: "Just don't let it be torn to pieces!" Somehow we melt snow and assuage our thirst and hunger. A spark from the stove starts to melt a hole in the wall of the tent, the size of a fist, but it doesn't burn completely through. Again we're lucky! We pass the night without closing our eyes.

August 28. We listen closely to the howling wind in the hope of catching the least indication of a change for the better. Sometimes it seems that the wind is abating and then we look at each other: "Well, what do you think, shall we work today?" We can't lie about very long—our gas has almost run out. We have to go! Most of the chimney has been climbed; just a little remains. All around the snowstorm still rages, but at times we can see blue sky through a break in the clouds. Slowly, step by step, Pavlik gains tempo, and at last we finish the endless chimney. A steep, rocky ridge juts into the sky, and it still seems a long way to the top. We proceed simultaneously on some sections, by turns at others. The ascent seems endless, but ahead we can see the white summit capped by huge plumes of snow. Finally we stumble across a light-blue auxiliary rope. "Hooray! We're on the upper part of Kuzmin's route. We've climbed the Wall!"

To descend from the summit of Khan Tengri (6,995 meters), the two men first downclimbed to the saddle at 5,900 meters and then climbed over 6,150-meter Peak Chapaev and down the ridge in the right foreground. *Chad Kellogg*

In our tent we try to burn the residual gas from our last canister, but it's in vain. We chew a little snow. Although we're tired, for some reason we can't sleep. We lie and talk. According to our schedule, today is the day we were supposed to evacuate our base camp. If the last helicopter leaves, we'll have a very hard time. Imperceptibly, the conversation moves to the topic of our coming expedition to K2. I confess that I haven't yet decided whether to take part in this project. Pasha, as if not hearing me, continues to talk of the beauty of the face, about equipment and clothing. We sink into sleep, ignorant of the tribulations waiting for us. The wind continues to roar, but we don't care because the Wall has been climbed.

August 29. For breakfast we gnaw at some dry biscuits, which give us heartburn. But we have to eat something. Today we have to climb to the summit and descend at least as far as the col. We have to find our cache with the gas canisters—then everything will be fine. Outside: hurricane force winds, although the sun is shining. Getting ourselves together, we move out slowly, very slowly. Where has our strength gone? After an hour we crawl out of the deep snow onto a firm crust of ice. Next to a line of footprints lies a lemon. Unbounded joy! We break apart this frozen fruit from overseas and divide it fraternally. In our souls everything is transfigured.

Ahead of us looms the tripod, long awaited and familiar to the point of pain. The summit! This is where our cache should be. We walk around and look under every stone. Alas, it's nowhere. If only we could find this cheapskate climber! We clip into the fixed rope on the normal route and descend. At 6,400 meters we find some abandoned sugar, crackers, nuts, two frozen apples, and two cucumbers. Okay, that's something. But to our great regret, we find no gas canisters. We drag ourselves downward. Our strength continually ebbs. We go 100 meters and collapse into the snow, then move the next 100 meters. "If only somebody has waited," goes round and round in my mind. "Just one more day and we'll arrive."

We reach the col around 3 p.m. The sun is shining brilliantly and the wind is roaring. Tossing down our packs, we start to rummage in the garbage bags that someone has left at the col. Four canisters! They appear to be empty, but perhaps we can squeeze something out of them. We start to set up the tent, but, just as we've always feared, a burst of wind tears the tent out of our hands and carries it away toward the Northern Inyl'chek. I stand as if paralyzed, imagining how we will spend the night in a shallow snow cave. With unbelievable speed, considering his condition, Pavlik runs through deep snow after the tent and just as it appears above the cornices he catches one end of it and falls into the snow. "Cornices!" is all I manage to cry. Pasha remains lying in the snow a long time, regaining consciousness. But the tent is securely clutched in his hand. We're going to survive!

The canisters we found turn out to be empty. Have you ever eaten fluffy snow? There's no nourishment in that. For an hour and a half we swing a frying pan with snow, mixing the snow with some kind of powder from overseas we'd found in the garbage. And, O miracle! After shaking it about, the snow becomes moist and we enjoy some rather nice ice cream. Only after eating three bowls of this delicacy is our thirst somewhat assuaged. Pavlik's fingers are black and blistered. I prepare an injection of prednisolone. We can't feel our feet. We don't know what's wrong with them because we don't remove our boots—we stay ready to leave at a moment's notice, even at night, if only the wind will abate. My stomach doesn't give me any peace; apparently an ulcer has developed. I'm forced to go on ketorol, which relieves the pain in my feet and stomach.

August 30. Morning does not bring any improvement in the weather. There's a strong wind and visibility is only 50 meters. I give another injection of prednisolone to Pashka. At close to noon it clears up and we set off. Slowly we ascend Peak Chapaev, seemingly without end. The mountain does not want to release us. The visibility deteriorates to the point that we can't even see the flags marking the route. We stay roped up in case of crevasses. Up to our belts in snow, battling gusts of hurricane-force winds, we creep up to 6,150 meters on the shoulder of Chapaev. It's all downhill now. We toss our tattered rope and I go ahead, pulling the fixed ropes out of deep snow.

Slowly we descend into Camp 2 at 5,600 meters. Surely no one is there. By the standard of the Tien Shan Range, it is already the beginning of winter. And suddenly: "Pasha! Look! A tent, or am I wrong?" I call hoarsely, "Hey, below, water, water!"

We have not had anything to drink in three days. No one responds to my cry. "Probably there's no one there," I think. And then a head sticks out of the tent.

AFTERWORD

Everything that happened to us has already happened to many others. Although you don't refuse journalists the right to use enthusiastic epithets like "super-extreme," "first-ever," "high-speed," and so on, I'm certain their efforts are futile. We didn't climb for such reasons, even if only because no achievements can justify frostbitten fingers and undermined health. If someone tells you something different, he's simply not being sincere with you; indeed, he's not being sincere with himself.

People often ask me, "How much are you paid for your ascents?" They have forgotten that there are things one can't pay for, even for lots of money. How much does goodness cost? How much does friendship cost? How much does love cost? Answer me, people! How much does the feeling of happiness cost, when you're standing on a summit? You can't buy happiness—you arrive at happiness through the losses and experiences that life and mountains give. People: be happy!

SUMMARY:

AREA: Tien Shan Range, Kyrgyzstan

ASCENT: First two-person ascent of the north face of Khan Tengri (6,995 meters) in alpine style, via a linkup of the Studenin Route, the Myslovsky Route, and the upper chimney of the Zacharov Route, Pavel Shabalin and Ilias Tukhvatullin, August 20–29, 2005, followed by a day and a half of descent.

A NOTE ABOUT THE AUTHOR:

Ilias Tukhvatullin from Tashkent, Uzbekistan, has climbed new routes on the north faces of Ak-Su North and Mt. Everest, as well as the first winter ascent of Ak-Su North's north face, all with Pavel Shabalin and various partners.

Translated from the Russian by Henry Pickford.

KAJAQIAO

"Technical wading" to an unclimbed summit in Eastern Tibet.

MICK FOWLER

Chris Watts pauses during the third day on Kajaqiao's west face, unclimbed peaks rising behind. *Mick Fowler*

Chris Watts and I peered out the window of our hotel in the town of Nagchu, Tibet. The temperature hovered stubbornly below freezing, and a dusting of snow blew around the courtyard. It was October 17, still a few months to go before winter. At 6,447 meters, the summit of Kajaqiao, the mountain we had come to climb, was 2,000 meters higher than this. What would the conditions be like up there, we wondered?

Kajaqiao is situated in the Nyainqentanglha East Range, about two days' drive east of Lhasa. This is officially a closed part of Tibet, and numerous permits are required to secure access. Permits tend not to be issued until the last minute, with the result that visits entail a fair bit of pre-trip anxiety. In 2004, it was not until 17 hours before our flight was due to leave London that we finally had to acknowledge that we had failed on the bureaucratic challenge.

But we persevered and now, armed with nine separate permits, we kept our fingers crossed that no bureaucrat would stand in our way.

A photograph taken by the Japanese explorer Tamotsu (Tom) Nakamura first gave Chris and me the irrepressible urge to visit this part of the world. Not only did the mountains look fantastic, but Tibet had long been on my list of places to visit. Adam Thomas and Phil Amos were among the select group of westerners who had traveled to Eastern Tibet, and their enthusiasm for a return visit was such that we readily decided to team up. And so, after a year and a half of bureaucratic challenges, the four of us, together with Jimi, our liaison officer, and Tenzing, from the China Tibet Mountaineering Association (CTMA), were on our way. In the meantime, Tom, in his characteristically helpful manner, had forwarded detailed maps and photographs from earlier Japanese expeditions.

The 250 kilometers of dirt track from Nagchu to the regional center of Lhari was notable for wild scenery, yaks, and building my respect for four-wheel-drive vehicles. We had reason to believe that Lhari could be the bureaucratic crux, so we kept our fingers crossed as a stern-looking policeman peered closely at our paperwork. He appeared mystified, but to our relief I left clutching a letter asking the headman of Tatse, the last village, to arrange for our equipment to be carried to our base camp.

Some 35 kilometers from Lhari, the village of Tatse sits on meadows above the beautiful Yigong Tsangpo River. Young villagers were friendly and very interested in what we were planning to do. They told us that Kajaqiao is pronounced Chachacho and that the mountain was named after its likeness to hands drawn together in prayer. An elderly woman expressed concern that it would snow forever if anyone ever stood on the summit.

"I think 10 porters will be enough," announced Tenzing.

We looked around at the enormous amount of gear that Tenzing and Jimi had brought. There were huge gas cylinders, a marquee-style tent, several large yak steaks, crates of beer… and on it went. Ten porters seemed ridiculously inadequate.

Tenzing clearly recognized the look of concern on our faces. "We will have base camp here," he reassured us, pointing to the meadows next to the river. This was all very curious. With security in mind, we had specifically made clear that Tenzing and Jimi would be staying at our base camp. Something had clearly been lost in the translation, but there wasn't much we could do about it now. CTMA policy, it seemed, was to establish base camp at the roadside wherever possible.

The porters arrived on motorbikes, a first in my experience. They roared away on their bikes with us trailing far behind. After six hours or so, we arrived at the site of the base camp used by the Japanese. The only evidence of their expedition was rudimentary tent platforms, which we gratefully occupied.

We awoke to perhaps 25 centimeters of snow. It was considerably colder that we expected, to the extent that the eggs the porters had caringly carried had frozen solid and were to stay that way for the duration.

Our acclimatization explorations revealed that the head of the valley was dominated by two mountains, Kajaqiao at 6,447 meters and Menamcho at 6,264 meters. Both looked inspirational but seriously snow plastered. The amount of snow was a real concern. By the time we were ready to attempt an ascent, a meter of new snow had fallen. This wouldn't have been so bad with plenty of freeze and thaw, but with the temperature continually below freezing the snow simply accumulated as deep powder. With no snowshoes, traveling around was absolutely knackering.

Bad weather and deep snow slowed us to the extent that it took two days of heavy panting to get from base camp to the foot of our chosen line at about 5,300 meters on Kajaqiao. Clouds had prevented us from getting a good view when we were acclimatizing, but now we could see that the west face sported a series of shallow, left-trending couloirs leading up to the crest of the northwest ridge.

Perched on the crest of a projecting rib of rounded slabs, we managed to cut a comfortable tent-sized platform for our first bivouac. The day had been exhausting, largely because of the vast amounts of soft snow. Technical wading, the best way to describe it, is not my favorite style of climbing. But at least we were making progress. As the evening sun bathed us we relaxed and soaked up the view. The skyline to the west was opening up with a myriad of unclimbed, toothlike peaks.

Above, it was steeper, good in that the deep snow that had plagued us so far would not stick. The problem, though, was that sections that looked easy were in fact granite slabs covered with a thick dusting of powder. We proceeded cautiously. Nothing was particularly difficult, but it all felt horribly precarious and insecure. At one point I was reduced to a gibbering "watch me" call on ground where we would have moved together if the snow had been nicely frozen. By dint of judicious routefinding we progressed safely, if slowly, ending with an open bivouac on the left-bounding rib of the main couloir line.

"This is a crap bivouac ledge," announced Chris emphatically.

Chris' comment was disturbingly apt. There was nothing for it but to fashion a narrow,

The west face of Kajaqiao, with about 1,100 meters of relief. *Chris Watts*

nose-to-tail ledge out of a thin snow band. Fortunately, the clouds that had swirled around for much of the day had lifted, and a glorious evening had developed.

Some hours later I awoke with a start. I had been wrapped cozily in the tent fabric, but now it was billowing around me like a huge sail and spindrift was blowing into my sleeping bag. Moving too hastily to rewrap myself resulted in my end of the ledge collapsing and me spending the rest of the night perched uncomfortably on the remains. Chris woke briefly to curse the spindrift runnel pouring onto his head

The paperwork: Nine different permits were required to enter this remote region of Tibet. *Mick Fowler*

before settling down and snoring loudly. By daybreak I had given him a good kicking on several occasions with no positive response.

Experience and determination are probably the key factors that dictate success or failure in the greater ranges. At the bleak and windy break of dawn, both were tested to the full, and we made a hesitant and weary team as we scrabbled and dithered over the best line. This sort of climbing is so difficult to grade and describe. Above we could see that the angle increased slightly, which could make things much more difficult. But mountains are nothing if not surprising, for the steeper ground was closer to the windswept ridge and the conditions actually improved. Able to move faster, by afternoon we were enduring a character-building crosswind on the ridge. On the windward side the wind was fierce and the ground technical, whereas on the lee side excitingly steep powder snow presented its fair share of problems. We alternated uncomfortably, reaching an easing of the angle an hour before nightfall.

"Time for a snow hole," Chris shouted above the sound of the roaring wind.

Snow holes have always distressed me. Perhaps it's because I have never had the time to dig out a nice, spacious one. Or perhaps I have latent claustrophobic tendencies that surface only when I am surrounded by snow. Chris, though, had such enthusiasm that I found myself reluctantly digging into the slope. Inevitably, snow ended up inside my clothing and I became damp. The calm atmosphere in the hole was encouraging, though. After an hour Chris pronounced it big enough, produced his sleeping gear, and settled down. I peered in. Length and width looked okay, but the height of our little room was only about 40 centimeters. Hesitantly, I decided to test my feelings before committing myself. It felt awful. A quick bit of experimenting revealed that even the weedy Fowler shoulders were broad enough to dislodge copious quantities of snow when I turned over. The snow fell in my face and down my neck. I was beginning to feel really cold.

"No way. Sorry, Chris. Can't do it."

For me, the last hour had been a complete waste of energy. I now felt an immediate need to arrange something safe; otherwise matters might go horribly wrong. Chris, who appeared very comfortable with the snow hole, was understanding. In the dark we struggled against the wind to erect the tent. After 15 minutes we sat in the flapping fabric together. The hastily stamped-out snow platform was ludicrously uneven, and the outer edge overhung the slope.

"Sorry, Mick. Can't sleep here."

Laughably, Chris ended up in the snow hole with me outside in the tent. Fortunately, the wind seemed to have dropped slightly, and my initial concerns about being blown away without Chris' weight lessened.

One section of the tent ledge was shaped like a small volcano, and I curled myself around this in as comfortable a manner as possible. For a few hours all was well. Then, when I must have been half asleep, I had the awful sensation of my small volcano erupting. All hell let loose and then my face was planted firmly into something hard and cold. Fortunately I had a small torch around my neck, the light from which revealed that the tent was now upside down and the cold hard things against my face were the crossed poles that are normally at the top. My immediate urge was to escape, but a few things had priority. Jumping out only to watch the whole show blow away would not be clever. While I was putting my boots on I came across Chris' inner boots. This was worrisome. He must have put only his outer boots on to return to the snow hole. But where was he now? Clearly the tent had been hit by a snow slide, but what had happened to the snow hole? If it was damaged he would certainly need his inner boots. Having located the entrance zip, I stood on the tent fabric, cursed the situation that had ended up with us sleeping apart, and scoured the slope for signs of the hole. The narrow beam picked out nothing but windswept snow. Securing things as best I could, I started to search for the entrance. I had taken only a few steps when a surprisingly loud and urgent shout stopped me in my tracks.

"Fowler! Fowler! I'm stuck! Fucking well get me out of here!"

A section of the cave had collapsed, leaving Chris disoriented and partially smothered. It was easy to grab his extended hand and pull him to safety, but it turned my stomach just to look in at the partially collapsed low roof. In the confusion Chris had been unable to find his head torch. I could only imagine how terrifying it must have been milling around in the dark in such constricted circumstances, aware that further collapses were possible.

Together we retrieved items from the remains of the cave, dug out the tent, put it the right way up, and squeezed inside. It was good to be back together again. Remarkably, nothing appeared to be lost or damaged. It was light by now, and I was uncomfortably aware that the hours had slipped past quickly. The wind seemed stronger than ever, we were in a cloud, and it was one of those situations where a negative decision could come all too easily. We decided to contemplate our fate over a hot drink and half a chocolate bar. In the end we recognized that nothing was really wrong apart from frayed nerves and the weather. Onward it would be.

The north (lee) side of the ridge was composed of frighteningly steep, bottomless powder that appeared to defy gravity. This meant that we were forced onto the rocky crest, which was technically challenging and outrageously windy. Nevertheless, clearings in the cloud cover showed that we were making progress. By midafternoon nearby Menamcho was below us, and we knew we were close. At about 6,300 meters my camera ran out of film. The wind and spindrift were such that changing the roll was out of the question. Fortunately, for the first time ever I had packed a cheap, lightweight spare camera.

It was with some relief that I completed the final section of wind-blasted technical mixed climbing and hung from a small but secure nut belay. Above me, overhanging snow protected the summit snow/ice slope. We were nearly there.

Our altimeter read 6,500 meters as the slope started to ease off. The highest point was still about six meters above us, but huge cornices were visible on the other side, and we had that uncomfortable feeling that we were close to the breaking point. It was past six in the evening. The skies had cleared a little on the final section, and I had been looking forward to a glorious panoramic view.

In fact, the views were obscured by the cornices and clouds. And the wind still howled incessantly. My hopes for indulging in photographic frenzy were dashed as I fought to hold the camera still while taking shots that I instinctively knew were destined to be blurred and unremarkable. After not very long at all we retreated to our last ice screw and abseiled into the gathering gloom.

An exciting bivouac was followed by three days of abseiling, avalanche dodging, and serious wading to rejoin Adam and Phil at base camp. They had reached about 5,800 meters on Menamcho but had been stopped by the wild weather and low temperatures. But they were still smiling. Exciting mountains have that affect on people.

Chris and I also felt great. Excess blubber had been used up, and Kajaqiao, our objective of two years, was climbed. And with the cornice tip untouched we slept comfortably, knowing that the old lady in Tatse would be happy to know that it wouldn't snow forever.

Night six: "An exciting bivouac followed by three days of abseiling, avalanche dodging, and serious wading." *Mick Fowler*

SUMMARY:

AREA: Nyainqentanglha East Range, Eastern Tibet

ASCENT: First ascent of 6,447-meter Kajaqiao (a.k.a. Chachacho), via the west face and northwest ridge (1,110m, TD), Mick Fowler and Chris Watts, October 2005. See Climbs and Expeditions in this journal for an account of the Amos-Thomas attempt on Menamcho.

EDITOR'S NOTE: The photo in *AAJ 2003*, p. 134, which also appeared on the front cover of the *Japanese Alpine News Vol. 2 (2002)*, shows Menamcho (a.k.a. Chakucho), not Kajaqiao as captioned.

A NOTE ABOUT THE AUTHOR:

Mick Fowler's urge for first ascents has led him from crumbling Devon sea cliffs to unclimbed 6,000- and 7,000-meter peaks in Asia. He lives in South Derbyshire, England.

UP AND DOWN GREAT TRANGO TOWER

Going light on a stormy new route and harrowing descent in Pakistan.

GABO ČMÁRIK AND DODO KOPOLD

Gabo Čmárik enjoys good weather and a light load (for a 2,000-meter route) on the first day of climbing.
Dodo Kopold

Dodo Kopold: An ascent of Great Trango Tower meant more to me than all the routes I had done before. It was a big dream, and, not wanting to leave anything to chance, I spent a lot of time training and choosing the line, equipment, and tactics. But the hardest job was to find the ideal partner. We needed to form a good team, to be capable of all kinds of climbing, and to be very strong physically and mentally. To survive all possible situations, we needed the perfect partnership.

Gabo Čmárik: Dodo and I share the same ideal, which is to go alpine style on the biggest faces. We focused our training on long routes; for example, we did the Colton-McIntyre route on the Grandes Jorasses in winter with one bivy. There, we tested our minds and ability to survive in cold conditions. But I knew that Trango would be much more difficult.

Dodo: Neither Gabo nor I could be sure what would be involved with the actual climb, how many days of climbing it would require, how difficult the headwall would be, if there would be no way down except over the top. We thought a long time about such possibilities, about snowfall, a slow descent, or an injury to one of us. Great Trango

The southwest and south faces of Great Trango Tower: Azeem Ridge (2004, Cordes-Wharton) on left; Assalam Alaikum (2005, Čmárik-Kopold) on right. *Courtesy of Vladimir Linek*

is almost 6,300 meters high, and the altitude difference between base camp and the summit is more than 2,000 meters. Crack lines in excellent rock start just above the talus and finish very high. We chose the south-southwest face, one well suited for alpine style, but dangerous in case of bad weather. Climbing such a big face is not only about experience, but also about luck. We knew that if we were to be successful everything had to be okay, from a good spell of weather to excellent acclimatization. We wanted to do a new line on our first try, and our plan was to climb it in four days. That meant to go as fast as possible, as light as possible, and to climb even into the night.

Gabo: We thoroughly examined the face before the climb and chose our starting point. In the evening we packed our equipment. Everything had pluses and minuses. To climb quickly means to be light, and so we decided not to take our sleeping bags. We started at 4:30 a.m. The first pitches were up to me. Our tactic was not to lose time with changing equipment, so I was to lead all day. There were a lot of hard offwidth cracks, and I had only one big Camalot that I moved many times with me. Sometimes this Camalot was not big enough. The difficulty was between 7 and 8 [5.10–5.11]. It was very hot, and we had only three liters of water, which we drank very soon. Later, we had no water for cooking, so we were both thirsty and hungry.

Dodo: I don't know who was more dead after the first bivy, but neither of us spoke about going down. I started leading in the morning. After five pitches we found water. We were so happy that even falling rocks and a coming storm could not spoil our enjoyment. But our picnic finished soon—we had to climb smooth slabs with poor protection, and the rain was coming. Finding a good place for a bivy was a big problem. We climbed many hours in the rain and finally found a small cave not even big enough for us to extend our legs. We sat on our packs, listening to our MP3 players and writing in our diary. It rained all night.

Gabo: It was not possible to descend because of falling rocks and because of the nature of the terrain. We realized that our only chance was to climb to the summit ridge. With this idea in mind, I nestled next to Dodo and tried to sleep. I was praying for good weather.

Dodo: In the morning the rock was completely icy. I climbed toward a crack and chimney system with big problems. Later, we had to make many pendulums to get to another climbable crack line. At the end of the day we did mixed terrain to a big ledge for a comfortable night.

Gabo: The fourth day began once again with icy pitches, followed by long runouts on slabs. Cirrus clouds appeared, a sign of more bad weather. I climbed as fast as possible, despite not feeling my toes in my climbing shoes. At 3 p.m. I reached the headwall in a heavy snowstorm.

Dodo: We had not been sure how we would climb the headwall. The bad thing was that we had minimal gear to tackle this 400-meter-high face. We had only seven pitons, so we had to climb mostly free. At the beginning, the face was vertical and overhanging. We climbed a crack system to a wide chimney and then slabs into the unknown. The climbing would have been good, but it was snowing. I fought until dark but did not find a good place for a bivy. So we rappelled 80 meters to a col and found a small ledge. The wind was strong, the temperature –15°C, and it was snowing hard. The night was terrible. We nestled together to gain warmth.

Gabo: It continued to snow on the morning of the fifth day, and it was terribly cold. I was climbing with aid and cutting ice from cracks to make places for protection. I did two pitches to a snowy ledge, where we bivied. We ate our last food. It snowed again all night.

Dodo: I didn't sleep at all. In the morning I had to force myself to climb. The rock and our equipment were all icy, and hard climbing lay above us. For the next four hours I fought to complete one pitch. I was dreaming about serious sleep in a warm room far away from Trango. I knew that with no food we would not survive for long if we didn't keep climbing. In spite of the cold and the snowfall, I headed up smooth slabs. It was not possible to climb them with aid, only to do them free. My fingers and toes were stiff and frozen. Gabo was shaking at the belay. In the evening we had to rappel 60 meters to find a bivy. We left one rope fixed and used the second as a pad.

Gabo: We spent the night in a snow cave on a small ledge. By now we were accustomed to nonstop snowfall. During this day I had problems with my vision, probably from high-altitude illness, and from time to time I was unable to see anything. We were tired, without food, battered in body and mind. We crawled into our bivy sack and lit our stove in desperate need of warmth. This worked, but immediately we fell asleep and I dropped the stove. Miraculously, Dodo woke up and caught it.

Dodo: In the morning, conditions were even worse. I tried to ignore this and focus on climbing. We were only a few meters below the summit ridge. Unluckily, I fell eight meters and bashed my hip. But my fear and powerlessness were transformed into unbelievable energy. I climbed to my high point and in a rage did the icy crack free. I crawled the last meters in the snow. We were on the summit ridge. One ordeal was finished but the second was just beginning. There was lot of snow on the ridge, so we were not able to climb to the summit

Day 4: Čmárik leads icy rock toward the 400-meter headwall atop Great Trango's south face. The two spent that afternoon and the next two and a half days surmounting this steep wall in severe weather. *Dodo Kopold*

Circles mark the Slovaks' positions partway through their rappel descent of the enormous northwest face of Great Trango Tower. See Climbs and Expeditions for the descent line. *Courtesy of Vladimir Linek*

and descend via the normal route. Our only choice was to rappel the northwest face, yet we had only our rack of nuts and cams, eight bolts, and four pitons. We were not sure if this was enough for such a big wall. Brilliant idea.

Gabo: We decided to rappel via the Russian route in hopes of finding their anchors. The top half of the face is vertical and overhanging and plunges 1,000 meters. We found only two old anchors. We rappelled either from one bolt or from nuts, pitons, or cams, using up our gear frighteningly fast. The face overhung so much in places that we had to place gear during the rappels so we wouldn't lose contact with the rock.

Dodo: By 7 p.m. of the seventh day, we had descended half the face. I slipped 10 meters during one rappel and almost died. Then I fell 150 meters in an avalanche and was only stopped by a miracle. I lost one of our 60-meter ropes in the slide, so this meant that we could make only 30-meter rappels. It was dark, and we could see lights in the Trango base camp, but nobody came to meet us. We were lost and tired. Gabo fell down an icy slab and disappeared but stopped after 30 meters. We found our other rope, but we were moving so slowly now. Only several hundred meters to go, but I felt I could not do it. When we reached the talus, I moved only a short distance before collapsing. Gabo went ahead, hoping to wake someone at base camp. I started down on my own, and when I reached camp it was 5 a.m. Gabo was asleep on the ground. I fell next to him. Then somebody grabbed my hand. It was over.

SUMMARY:

AREA: Trango Valley, Baltoro Region, Pakistan

ROUTE: Alpine-style first ascent of Assalam Alaikum (ca 90 pitches, ABO VIII A2) via the southwest and south faces, finishing on the summit ridge of Great Trango Tower's southwest summit (ca 6,250m), Gabo Čmárik and Dodo Kopold, August 4-11. The two descended the northwest face from right to left (looking in) to reach a gully on the left side, making about 60 rappels. Other members of this Czech-Slovak expedition climbed new routes on Hainabrakk East and Shipton Spire. See the full report in Climbs and Expeditions.

A NOTE ABOUT THE AUTHORS:

Gabo Čmárik was born in 1982, lives in Trencin, Slovakia, and works in the building trade. Dodo Kopold, born in 1980, lives in Bratislava, Slovakia, and designs outdoor clothing. The two began climbing together in 2005.

Happy to be alive: Kopold (left) and Čmárik collapsed at base camp just before dawn after their 16-hour descent.

SPICE FACTORY

An Alaskan debut ends with a major new route on Mt. Bradley.

MAXIME TURGEON

Maxime Turgeon stretches for a placement on the Jalapeño Headwall during the first attempt on Spice Factory. Turgeon used a bit of aid this time but returned to free the pitch at 5.10R M7 during the successful climb. *Louis-Philippe Ménard*

Everyone spices differently. Some carefully measure quantities, make sure aromas will match, and never make a mistake, while others just pour it on and see what happens. With the latter approach, sometimes you blow your brains out and think you're going to die, but sometimes you come up with something really memorable. —*Brian Baxter*

Scrickk! The dull tip of my blade rips from its catch, my hammer hits me right on the lip, and I'm off. That's it! This is the end! The psychological belay won't hold this fall. We'll both end up down in the bergschrund.

Suddenly I wake up, the fabric of the bivy sack crushed onto my face. My toes are frozen and I cannot feel my right arm. Leaving the sleeping bags behind was probably not the best idea. In the last 18 hours we've climbed 600 meters up the highest face either of us have ever attempted. Flashbacks from the committing climbing and my four-meter fall onto a marginal belay—my closest call ever—are running through my mind like an overbroadcast song. Uncertainty about what's above makes my uncomfortable position even more torturous. We're not even at the one-third mark on the face, and the business is far from over. The angle won't ease until the summit. Our two-man bivy kit worked well in the comfort of our

Maxime Turgeon rations his three screws for the WI5+ ice of On the Frozen Roads of Our Incertitudes, London Tower. *Louis-Philippe Ménard*

living room, but now the clock is running pretty slowly and I'm wondering, "What am I doing here?" A couple of minutes later we decide to keep moving.

Mt. Bradley sits proudly between Mt. Wake and the massive Mt. Dickey on the Ruth Glacier. Its north face is around 1,400 meters of steep, gray granite supporting summit seracs. This imposing, compact face first caught my eye as I scrolled through past expeditions' pictures on the Internet. All my senses awoke simultaneously when I fell on that stunning white line splitting the face, like a thin filigree of icing dripping from the summit. The steep face marinated in my mind—the thought of climbing this line made any other project seem insipid.

On April 30 my friend Louis-Philippe Ménard and I are dropped on the Ruth Glacier, our home for the next 25 days. Having met three years ago at engineering school, we are on our first trip to the bigger ranges and we're seeking some spicy thrills. We've already climbed a couple of big routes in Québec together, and we share the same interest in the mystical aspect of the unknown—in which we are fully immersed right now. The steepness and massiveness of the surrounding faces is breathtaking.

Shirtless shoveling of our camp quickly puts us in the mood for the unseasonably warm month to come. Despite our expectations, the frozen lines are really few and we can hear the background sound of rocks coming down the east- and south-facing gullies. In front of our camp, Bradley's north face has a grayish, intimidating aspect, with few white ornaments. Our dream line doesn't even exist!

With almost a month in front of us and with all the granite faces surrounding our camp, the situation is far from desperate. Worst case: we'll have to use our "just in case" rock shoes. Attracted by the few ice stripes in the gorge, we cut our teeth on the east face of Mt. Johnson:

the second ascent of The Escalator. We take 13 hours on the route and another 13 on the spicy descent. After two rest days, our legs are back to life and we take a ride up On The Frozen Roads of Our Incertitudes, on London Bridge. In less than a week, two second ascents have given us just enough confidence and courage to return—binoculars in hand—to the base of Bradley's north face. Scrutinizing the whole face in sections, we imagine a linkup of snow and ice ramps, broken by some blank and mysterious sections, making a big "S" path across the compact face.

The line of Spice Factory on Mt. Bradley's north face. The east ridge (left skyline) was climbed in 1987, and the mixed slopes and steep rock buttress of the northeast spur, to the left of Spice Factory, were ascended in 2002, using some fixed ropes. *Joe Puryear*

Drawn by the mystery of that line, we decide to have a peek at the first few pitches, carrying only a small rack. We could not ask for a better intro: the mixed climbing—a thin runnel of ice in a saffron-orange dihedral—is cinnamon sweet! The second pitch's tricky traverse quickly cuts the pleasant candied taste, foreboding what might lie ahead. Nonetheless, a huge, slanting, snow-filled chimney presents itself and suggests a way forward, so we decide to wrap it up and save our energy for an alpine-style ascent the next day.

Turgeon follows a sketchy traverse on Spice Factory's second pitch. *Louis-Philippe Ménard*

At 2 a.m., after a few hours of light sleeping, perturbed by all those first-ascent demons, we are trying to get into a rhythm as we enter the narrow gap between Bradley and Dickey. The shadow of the two walls closing the sky overhead makes us feel like intruders. As the light grows in the Ruth Gorge, we make good progress through our previous high point and meet up with the sun at the base of the first mysterious section: the headwall. From the ground, this steep and almost blank wall had seemed to be the most problematic section of the line. Swapping leads the whole way (chance or bad luck?) gives me the sharp end of the rope for the improbable-looking wall.

My heart is going crazy as I sort the small alpine rack on my harness. As I'm working my way up a shallow seam I let go of one tool, thinking it is still leashed to my wrist, but it's not. It flies into the air and falls on the snow right beside LP. It's too far to downclimb, so I decide to keep going with the remaining ice tool; soon I clip it to my harness and then strip the gloves and go bare-handed. Attracted to a crack as if by a magnet, I hit a dead end and have to pendulum back left. Soon I find myself on delaminated ice. "I'm at the end of the rope!" I yell to LP. Shivering and sweating like I just threw up, I finally figure out how to make a decent belay among all the loose blocks. I've really pushed my limits this time. As I belay LP up, I don't want to think about what is lying above.

What we had dubbed the "ramp" is pretty intimidating from this point of view: a slightly overhanging dihedral clogged by big, hanging snow mushrooms. Dejected by the superexposed ground, but determined to keep up the momentum, LP unballasts from the heavy pack and takes the lead. At this moment a pattern is set up between us. After seconding a hard pitch we feel it is our turn to commit, in tribute to our partner's boldness. Three more pitches, a four-meter fall onto the belay, and a couple of hours of avoiding falling projectiles, and the "Hot and Spicy Ramp" is born.

We are still under the halfway point on the face and the climbing isn't looking any easier. If we want to be able to continue, we have to find a decent bivy site to brew and try to sleep a bit. To our surprise we find a semiclosed cave made by accumulated spindrift at the edge of the névé that will give us access to the next ramp system. After digging a bit, we end up with a pretty comfortable two-man bivy. Without a sleeping bag, we wrap ourselves in our single bivy

Louis-Phillipe Ménard tiptoes across the fifth-pitch traverse used to bypass the insecure "quarry" pitch during the second attempt on Spice Factory. *Maxime Turgeon*

sack. An hour later, our feet are numb and we start moving again.

In semidarkness, we quickly get into the bath. The first pitch takes an hour and a half to lead, and I have to resort to aid to pull through the roof of a big cave. Then LP has to sling a huge loose flake to a tiny knob before it plunges onto me. While I'm seconding, the block falls right onto my belay stance and makes that deathlike burning smell. I've got goose bumps for several minutes afterward, as if we had just missed getting swiped by a 10-wheeler on the highway.

Through the rest of the day we cover four more pitches of new ground. We exit another hard-won pitch, a rock groove that forces us to pull on gear, and continue onto more forgiving, lower-angled terrain to the base of a nasty-looking chimney. Hidden under our hoods at the belay, we are trying to figure out which way to go from the pictures we'd taken earlier on our digital camera. The pixels are convincing me that the snow-filled chimney on our right is the best way to go, giving us rapid access to the summit seracs. LP is more convinced that the way the spindrift is coming down from the left is the correct way. Finally he decides to let me have a look at the right option.

The steep, snow-filled groove doesn't allow me to get all the way inside, so I start working my way up the rounded outer edge. The climbing quickly turns awkward, forcing me to clip the pack to a piece of gear. Soon, I resort to aid. I'm transferring my weight onto a hook placement when I get knocked off balance. My foot sticks in my aider and I flip upside down. I look down to see the block on which I was hooking fall right onto the pack. The sling holding it to the piece breaks, and the pack bounces into the air.

It takes us some time to figure out what has happened. LP is completely dumbfounded. We've lost a pack, but we're both unharmed and the ropes are undamaged. We're both shaky, so we decide not to push our luck. Wondering if our small rack is enough to rappel the face, we hesitantly start our descent.

Forty-eight hours after leaving, we savor the pleasures of our camp, the bitterness easing away in the sweet-clove warmth of food and shelter.

It dumps for almost five consecutive days. In between storms, we spot our high point on the face with binoculars and realize we'd gotten completely off route. We find the fallen pack two days after our retreat, its contents all there. When the weather improves we need something to bring back our good spirits—perhaps the Moose's Tooth; we both agree we can't go home without having climbed it.

We leave camp at 4:30 p.m. with the intention of doing Ham and Eggs at night to get the best conditions. We simulclimb the entire route, clipping belay stations as we see them. What a great couloir—just what we needed to restore our psyches.

Since our retreat from Bradley it has been impossible to take our eyes off the peak. It's always there, like a good-smelling meal passing under your nose when your stomach groans with hunger. With all the technical ground still to cover above our high point, plus the complexity of the summit seracs, the prospect is very intimidating. We spend a lot of time scanning and reviewing each section of the wall with binoculars to convince ourselves that the recent snowfall and the melt and freeze cycle may have improved conditions on the second half of the route. Climbing this face was the reason for our trip to Alaska, and we agree we have to give it another try.

At 2 a.m. on May 20, with five days to go before our plane will arrive, we are once again gliding through the Ruth Glacier for a last-chance attempt. Our positive vibrations are dampened fast, as the first pitch has deteriorated a lot. The climbing is much scarier, with unstable sugar snow and delaminated ice. We are very worried about how the ramp will look in these conditions. However, LP says, "We didn't wake up this early to turn back right away!" The sun rapidly touches the face and starts to heat everything. As the elements come alive, we manage to get to the base of the headwall. Rockfall on the south face of Dickey creates a terrifying atmosphere.

Ménard chimneys out of the bivy site before dawn on the second day of climbing. *Maxime Turgeon*

Turgeon waits to escape the precarious second bivy, below a cornice near the top of the wall. *Louis-Phillipe Ménard*

I wanted to lead the headwall again, and now it's time to fulfill my wish. Back in the comfort of our camp, climbing it free sounded good, but at this moment I don't really care. I slump my tool into a small seam and trade the security of the névé ledge for the first small edges. "Allez, Max, focus!" LP shouts. Hold by hold, I link the crimp sequence, flashbacks from the first attempt searing my mind. Soon I'm at the pendulum section, hesitating. "Come on Max! There's plenty of rope out! I'm with you!" Tool in hand, I fully stretch my body and swing for a shallow dimple. As soon as my tool hooks, my feet rip. I can't downclimb now. Every muscle tightens and I throw for the good crack. I'm above the crux....

To our surprise, the ramp is in quite the same condition as the first time. We stretch the rope, making fewer pitches, and pass the bivy site sooner than expected. Still, we stop at the chimney just above, as it's our last opportunity to rest at a decent stance. Since we brought a sleeping bag and extra instant oatmeal this time, our bivy proves restorative.

Just before sunrise, LP stands at the cave entrance below the roof. Hood on, his headlamp moving in circles, his tools leashed to his wrists and bouncing back and forth, he looks like an alien coming out of my dream. We have agreed to switch leads so he can tackle the harder pitches this time. I silently hope he will be able to free the aid sections, and the first one is served for breakfast! As we scratch our way up with crampons flat on the rock, palming our hands next to our feet and leaning back against the opposite wall, I can't imagine we're supposed to be ice climbing! But higher up we find better-looking ice and LP manages the improbable, freeing the roof and the next remaining aid section.

Totally absorbed by our progress, we don't notice the big clouds building around us. An instant later, we find ourselves in a total whiteout, amid a world of seracs. Four hundred meters higher, out of breath, we chop a ledge that allows us to sit and cover our legs with the now totally wet sleeping bag.

Our words are few, giving way to sporadic spasms as hypothermia starts to take over. An hour later, the fog clears just enough to see the mountaintops and our proximity to the ridge. I give LP a shake: "Let's get out of here!"

For two pitches we head toward what seems to be the only breach in the corniced crest. Passing through it first, I search for the next obstacle and for a possible view of the summit, but there's nothing else—we are on the summit!

The euphoria lasts for a few minutes as we contemplate the half-light that lends a supernatural pink glow to the glacial amphitheater below. The remaining low clouds emphasize the steepness of the surroundings faces. It's 11 p.m. and the unstable weather pushes us to start our descent to the Bradley/Wake col before total darkness. Eight hours later we crumple in camp, not fully realizing that we have just done the biggest route of our lives.

The fog breaks and light emerges from behind Dickey. The only remaining cloud over Bradley's summit glows incandescent red, as if the mountain is catching fire, angry at having been violated. Down on our snow couch, we savor the outstanding moments of this 55-hour spice fest, a satisfying result from our "pour it on and see what happens" approach.

Summary:

Area: Ruth Gorge, Alaska Range

Ascents: Second ascent of The Escalator (1,220m, Alaska Grade 3 50°, Shaw-Wagner, 2000) on Mt. Johnson (2,579m). Second ascent of On the Frozen Roads of Our Incertitudes (950m, V M6 WI5+, Constant-Mercader, 2003) on London Bridge (2,250m). Ham and Eggs (850m, V 5.8 AI4, Davies-Krakauer-Zinsser, 1975), Moose's Tooth (3,171m). First ascent: Spice Factory (1,310m, Alaska Grade V 5.10R M7 WI5) on the north face of Mt. Bradley (2,775m), May 20-22, 2005.

All climbs by Louis-Philippe Ménard and Maxime Turgeon.

A Note About the Author:

Maxime Turgeon lives in suburban Montréal, Québec, and has recently completed a degree in mechanical engineering. The experience in Alaska, he writes, "definitely opened my mind to an infinity of new possibilities and the call from the bigger ranges."

Ménard (left) and Turgeon, wet but happy, atop Mt. Bradley. *Maxime Turgeon*

THE GREAT GORGE
OF THE RUTH GLACIER

An overview of Alaska's legendary alpine valley.

JOSEPH PURYEAR

Set in the heart of the central Alaska Range, the Great Gorge of the Ruth Glacier is a massive geographic rift that has shaped a climbing area like no other. More than 20 peaks border the sides of the north-south-trending valley, with walls up to 5,000 feet rising directly off the smooth and gentle glacier that lines the floor. Although not often compared to Yosemite, up north this is the Valley, Alaska-style. With easy approaches and huge walls just a short distance from a fly-in base camp, the Ruth Gorge may be North America's ultimate alpine climbing destination. However, climbers won't always find endless splitters, perfect granite, plastic ice, and ideal weather. Instead, they will find some of the most intimidating mountains in the world. Written into the history of these walls are stories of struggle, survival, and death, but also of triumph, camaraderie, and, above all, respect for an immensity found in few places in the world.

The Ruth Glacier, nearly 35 miles long, feeds off the slopes of Denali and Mt. Silverthrone. Numerous forks of the glacier merge into the huge icefield known as the Ruth Amphitheater. This vast snow arena encompasses some 25 square miles. Then, with nowhere else to go, the great mass of ice is pushed down a mile-wide constriction rimmed by walls up to 5,000 feet high. With so much ice being squeezed through such a narrow slot, it's no wonder that the glacier has been measured to be more than 3,800 feet deep and moving at a rate of over three feet per day. Without the ice, this canyon would have a sheer 8,700-foot rise to the top of Mt. Dickey.

The western side of the Gorge holds most of the great stalwarts—huge granite monoliths rising abruptly out of the glacier. Any one of these peaks would be a major destination. The east side, although generally less impressive, still holds several 2,000- to 3,000-foot walls. One of these is perhaps the area's most remarkable peak: the complex façade of the Moose's Tooth. This, along with several other "Tooth" peaks, creates a seemingly impenetrable alpine bastion that oversees the entire Ruth Glacier.

In the minds of most climbers, the Gorge historically has had two strikes against it that have kept it from becoming popular. The legendary Alaskan weather has been responsible for numerous epics and has left many climbers empty-handed. However, although major storms do occur often, the snow tends to quickly slough off the steep routes, and the rock dries rapidly after even torrential rainstorms. The area also has gotten a bad rap over the years for poor and occasionally treacherous rock. This is definitely true for much of the Gorge, and climbers looking to do first ascents should be ready to attack the infamous "Cracker Jack" granite that can literally require one to chop steps. Also, atop many of the western-side peaks is a layer of black schist that has been likened to ascending stacked china dishes. That said, there are long stretches of exceptional and highly textured granite on several formations, including the south face of Bradley, the Eye Tooth, the Stump, and Hut Tower, to name a few.

Skiing across the Ruth Amphitheater toward the Gateway to the Great Gorge, with the Moose's Tooth (left), the Incisor in the right center, and the pointed Bear Tooth behind. *Joe Puryear*

A BRIEF HISTORY

The first humans to venture into the Ruth Gorge were the infamous Frederick Cook and a guide in 1906. Cook claimed to make the first ascent of Denali via this approach, but this was soon discredited as a hoax. They succeeded only in climbing 5,350-foot "Fake Peak," a small bump on a side glacier. Cook named the Ruth after his stepdaughter, Ruth Hunt.

In 1910 Belmore Browne and Hershel Parker wandered up the gorge on a quest to debunk Cook's claim. Naming peaks as they went, they weren't overly creative, designating some with individuals' names like Johnson, Wake, and Dickey. They named the most fantastic peak they saw Mt. Hubbard after the president of the Perry Arctic Club. This name fortunately was changed to the Moose's Tooth, a translation of the indigenous Athabascan name. With

Chris McNamara leads the eighth pitch of Dream in the Spirit of Mugs, on the west pillar of the Eye Tooth. *Joe Puryear*

Mark Westman climbs the final bit of the west ridge of the Moose's Tooth, with the middle and west summits behind him. *Joe Puryear*

names like the Gargoyle, Werewolf Tower, and the Bear Tooth, the rest of the peaks on the eastern side also fared much better.

A group of four from Oregon's Mazamas was first to surmount a peak in the gorge with their climb of Mt. Barrill by its northwest slopes in 1910. Bradford Washburn surveyed much of the area in 1955 and climbed Mt. Dickey by its western slope. It was Washburn who perhaps first realized the extensive potential of the area. In his 1956 article in this journal, he wrote, "It would be hard to find a spot more easy of access where glorious glacier walks, easy lower climbs, and magnificent major ascents can all be accomplished out of the same air-supplied base camp, set amid North America's finest scenery and hardly a day's travel from New York!"

The first technical climb in the gorge was on the Moose's Tooth in 1964, when its long west ridge was climbed by a German party. Defining the bold style that came to dominate climbing in the Ruth Gorge, they ascended the entire spine of the Moose's Tooth in a single push from a camp low on the route.

In the mid-1970s the first big-wall routes started going up. The southeast face of Mt. Dickey (climbed in 1974 by David Roberts, Galen Rowell, and Ed Ward) was the first of seven major ascents on this monolith's 5,000-foot south and east walls. Although fixed lines were employed on the lower 900 feet, this groundbreaking big-wall ascent set the standard for committing routes. The same year, in similar style, Gary Bocarde, Michael Clark, Charles Porter, and John Svenson climbed the sheer southwest face of the Moose's Tooth—the second route to be climbed on this multifaceted mountain. On their "Moose Antler" ascent, the climbers carried an actual moose antler that proved easier to haul than the bags. Bocarde was a big mover in the early stages of climbing in the Gorge, accomplishing the first ascents of many of the peaks on its west side.

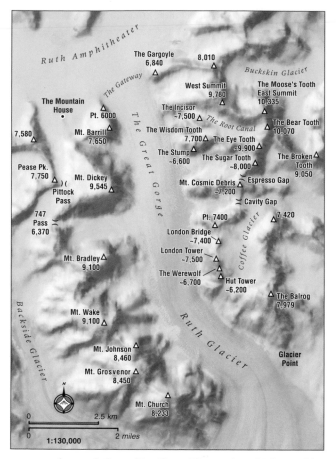

Ruth Amphitheater

The Gargoyle
6,840

8,010

The Gateway

Buckskin Glacier

West Summit
9,780

The Moose's Tooth
East Summit
10,335

The Mountain
House

Pt. 6000

The Incisor
~7,500

The Root Canal

The Bear Tooth
10,070

7,580

Mt. Barrill
7,650

The Wisdom Tooth
7,700

The Eye Tooth
~9,900

The Great Gorge

The Stump
~6,600

The Sugar Tooth
~8,000

The Broken
Tooth
9,050

Pease Pk.
7,750

Mt. Dickey
9,545

Mt. Cosmic Debris
~7,200

Espresso Gap

Pittock
Pass

Cavity Gap

747
Pass
6,370

Pt. 7400

7,420

London Bridge
~7,400

Coffee Glacier

Mt. Bradley
9,100

London Tower
~7,500

The Werewolf
~6,700

Hut Tower
~6,200

The Balrog
7,979

Backside Glacier

Mt. Wake
9,100

Ruth Glacier

Mt. Johnson
8,460

Mt. Grosvenor
8,450

Glacier
Point

N

0   2.5 km

Mt. Church
8,233

0   2 miles

1:130,000

After a lull in the early 1980s, the Ruth Gorge saw a climbing boom when Austrian Andi Orgler came onto the scene. During the late 1980s and early 1990s, Orgler and a few key partners were responsible for a surge in new-route activity, including major ascents on Mt. Bradley, Mt. Dickey, Mt. Barrill, the Eye Tooth, and several of the smaller east-side peaks. On his first trip to the Gorge in 1987, Orgler, along with Sepp Jöchler, raced up the nearly 5,000-foot east buttress of Bradley in a mere 14 hours. In 1988 he and Tommi Bonapace completed the 51-pitch Wine Bottle Route on Dickey. This was one of the finest alpine-style ascents accomplished in Alaska, climbed at a high technical standard without drilling a single hole. Orgler and partners went on to climb a huge route on the south face of Bradley—The Pearl—which, in addition to other Ruth Gorge achievements, gained them world recognition with the Piolet d'Or award in 1995.

The past decade has seen its share of equally impressive ascents. Hard, technical, early-season mixed climbs have been the biggest focus. The Elevator Shaft on Mt. Johnson was an extraordinary achievement on a dangerous ice climb that saw no fewer than four attempts and some major epics before it was finally climbed by Doug Chabot and Jack Tackle in 1995. The Gift (That Keeps on Giving) on Bradley (climbed in 1998 by Jonny Blitz, Steve House, and Mark Twight) was a bold and cold undertaking that brought mixed climbing in the Gorge to a new level. In 2002 Scan Easton and Ueli Steck undertook an audacious early-season climb with their ascent of Blood From the Stone on Mt. Dickey. Linking incipient ice ribbons, they pieced together a line directly up the mountain's massive east wall—a line that doesn't often form and had never seen a prior attempt.

There is still some great new-route potential for climbers up to the task. The 2005 season can attest to that, as major first ascents were accomplished on Mt. Bradley, the Moose's Tooth, and Mt. Grosvenor. One of the Alaska Range's last great problems is located on the east buttress of Mt. Johnson, which has thwarted attempts for over 20 years by some of the world's finest alpinists, including Yvon Chouinard, Mugs Stump, and a noteworthy attempt by Renny

Jackson and Doug Chabot, who climbed 38 pitches to a prominent tower on the ridge. After difficult free and aid climbing low on the route, the duo was horrified up higher when entire pitches required steps to be chopped with ice tools in 5.10 gravel. With many more appalling pitches ahead, they decided retreat was in order. Other major unsolved problems include the north face of Mt. Church—a 4,000-foot straight-shot ice and mixed route directly up the center of the face—and the direct north face of Johnson.

LOGISTICS

Climbing in the Ruth Gorge is best done from March through July. Although there are rumors of dry rock and late-season ice in the fall, the first winter storms have perplexed more than a few parties. Early season is best for technical ice and mixed routes, as they generally fall out of shape by mid-May. The best rock climbing season starts in June and tends to get better as more snow melts off the cliffs. Easier snow climbs can be done throughout the season, although crevasse and icefall difficulties can make late-season ascents interesting. The low elevation (between 4,500 and 10,300 feet) precludes much need for acclimatization.

A fly-in approach is necessary from the town of Talkeetna. Most parties start from the Mountain House airstrip above the Ruth Amphitheater. For climbing the south-face routes on the Moose's Tooth, the Root Canal airstrip can be used. Landing in the Ruth Gorge itself can sometimes be preferable, although it is often necessary for climbers to haul their gear back up to the Mountain House for pickup. The Ruth Gorge is located within Denali National Park. Climbers are required to pay a small entrance fee and are encouraged to register with the ranger station in Talkeetna. Check the NPS website (www.nps.gov/dena/home/mountaineering/index.htm) for more details.

Although it is home to many of the most difficult routes in North America, the Ruth Gorge also hosts a variety of novice and intermediate routes that climbers have enjoyed for years. Nearly 80 routes have been opened, but the route lines shown in the photos in this article reveal as much of what hasn't been climbed as what has been.

For nearly a century, Ruth Gorge climbers have shown exceptional respect for the great forces of the natural environment and for a spirit and history that has helped define the essence of alpinism. While the entire sweeping, 500-mile arc of the Alaska Range is an alpine mecca, the Ruth Gorge and its solid core of outstanding alpine achievements have created a valley of legends.

A NOTE ABOUT THE AUTHOR:

Joseph Puryear has been climbing and suffering in the Alaska Range for more than a decade. He is the author of the new book Alaska Climbing, *a comprehensive guide to 30 of the best routes in the central Alaska Range; visit Puryear's website, www.cascadeimages.com, or www.supertopo.com for more information. (Several Ruth Gorge routes can be found in this book.) When not enjoying their small cabin in Talkeetna, Joe and his wife, Michelle, make their home in Leavenworth, Washington.*

All photos by Joseph Puryear.

PHOTO 1: **(C)** Mt. Johnson (8,460'). (1) Bocarde-Head-Lee-Thomas Route (4,400'). G. Bocarde, C. Head, J. Lee, J. Thomas, May 1979. (2) The Escalator (4,000', 50+°), S. Shaw, T. Wagner, May 2000. (3) East Buttress (attempt) (5.10 A3), D. Chabot, R. Jackson, July 1999. **(D)** Mt. Wake (9,100'). **(E)** Mt. Bradley (9,100'). See Photo 5. **(F)** Mt. Dickey (9,545'). See Photo 6. **(G)** Mt. Barrill (7,650'). See Photo 7. **(AA)** Denali (20,320'). **(BB)** Mt. Silverthrone (13,220'). **(I)** The Gargoyle (6,840'). **(N)** The Wisdom Tooth (7,770'). See Photo 12.

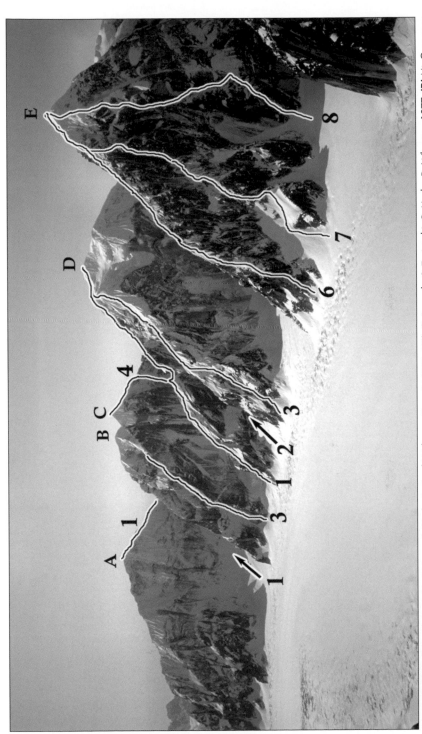

PHOTO 2: **(A)** Mt. Church (8,233'). (1) Bocarde-Henke-Taniguchi-Wheaton Route (4,200', 60°). **(B)** Mt. Grosvenor (8,450'). See Photo 3. **(C)** Mt. Johnson (8,460'). See Photo 3. **(D)** Mt. Wake (9,100'). (1) Pilie' de la Tolerance (1,500m, 5c A1, 90°), M. Desprat, M. Lestienne, F. Salles, May 1996. (2) East Face/Lowney-Teale Route (1,500m, VI M4 WI5), P. Lowney, B. Teale, April 2002. (3) Northeast Buttress/Screaming Blue Messiah (1,500m, VI 5.7 A2 70°), C. Atkinson, B. Kay, May 1990. **(E)** Mt. Bradley (9,100'). (6) East Buttress (1,400m, 5.10 70°), S. Jöchler, A. Orgler, July 1987. (7) Welcome to Alaska (1,400m, VI 6b A3+ M6-), V. Charon, A. Faure, C. Moulin, J. Ponson, May 2002. 8. Spice Factory (4,30C', VI 5.10R M7 WI5), L. Ménard, M. Turgeon, May 2005.

PHOTO 4: **(D)** Mt. Wake (9,100'). 1. Pilier de la Tolerance (1,500m, 5c A1, 90°), M. Desprat, M. Lestienne, F. Salles, May 1996. 2. East Face/Lowney-Teale Route (1,500m, VI M4 WI5), P. Lowney, B. Teale, April 2002. 3. Northeast Buttress/Screaming Blue Messiah (1,500m, VI 5.7 A2 70°), C. Atkinson, B. Kay, May 1990. 4. Wake Up (900m, IV WI5), M. Desprat, M. Lestienne, F. Salles, April 1996. 5. Bocarde-Dendewalter-Parker Route (3,600', 60°). G. Bocarde, P. Dendewalter, N. Parker, February 1979.

PHOTO 3: **(B)** Mt. Grosvenor (8,450'). 1. (not shown) South Face (4,400', III 55°), A. Walsh, M. Westman, April 2005. 2. Once Were Warriors (4,400', V M6 WI6), A. Walsh, M. Westman, April 2005. 3. Bocarde-Head-Lee-Thomas Route (4,400', 70°), G. Bocarde, C. Head, J. Lee, J. Thomas, May 1979. **(C)** Mt. Johnson (8,460'). 1. Bocarde-Head-Lee-Thomas Route (4,400'), G. Bocarde, C. Head, J. Lee, J. Thomas, May 1979. 2. The Escalator (4,000', 50+°), S. Shaw, T. Wagner, May 2000. 3. East Buttress (attempt) (5.10 A3), D. Chabot, R. Jackson, July 1999. 4. The Elevator Shaft (3,000', 5.7 A3 AI5), D. Chabot, J. Tackle, May-June, 1995.

PHOTO 5: **(E)** Mt. Bradley (9,100'). 1. (not shown) Adamson-Stover Route (5.8X), S. Adamson, J. Stover, March 2005. 2. The Gift (That Keeps on Giving) (3,200', 5.9 A3 WI6 XX), J. Blitz, S. House, M. Twight, March 1998. 3. South Face/ Williams-Schaefer Route (4,000', VI 5.10 A3), M. Schaefer, B. Williams, July 2000. 4. The Pearl (4,000', 5.11 A3), H. Neswadba, A. Orgler, A. Wutscher, 1995. 5. Bourbon Bottle Route (4,000', 5.8+ A1+, presumably harder), G. Crouch, J. Donini, June 1996. 6. East Buttress (1,400m, 5.10 70°), S. Jöchler, A. Orgler, July 1987.

PHOTO 6: **(F)** Mt. Dickey (9,545'). 1. (not shown) West Face (3,800', II 40°), D. Fisher, B. Washburn, April 1955. 2. Crime of the Century (1,550m, VI 6c A4), G. Avrisani, Y. Bonneville, C. Cruaud, P. Robach, R. Wagner, May 2002. 3. South Face/Italian Route (5,000', VI 5.11 A4), G. Bagatolli, P. Borgonovo, B. de Dona, F. Defrancesco, F. Leoni, M. Manica, D. Zampiccoli, June 1991. 4. Southeast Face/Roberts-Rowell-Ward Route (5,000', VI 5.9 A3), D. Roberts, G. Rowell, E. Ward, July 1974. 5. Snowpatrol (5,000', WI5+), S. Chinnery, A. Sharpe, April 2004. 6. Gross-Kormarkova Route (5,000', VI 5.8 A3), T. Gross, V. Kormarkova, May-June 1977. 7. Blood from the Stone (5,000', VI M7+ AI6+X), S. Easton, U. Steck, March 2002. 8. The Wine Bottle (1,600m, 5.11 A3+), T. Bonapace, A. Orgler, July 1988. **(DD)** 747 Pass (8,370').

PHOTO 7: **(G)** Mt. Barrill (7,650'). 1. Japanese Couloir (2,700', III 70°), T. Segawa, M. Suemasa, K. Suga, E. Tsai, July 1975. 2. Southeast Buttress/Feeling Randy (2,700', VI 5.10R/X A2+), C. Amelunxen, S. Easton, D. Marra, April-May 2001. 3. The Cobra Pillar (2,700', 5.11 C1+ or 5.11), J. Donini, J. Tackle, June 1991. 4. Happy End (2,700', 5.10+ A3), T. Bonapace, A. Orgler, July 1988. 5. Forever More (2,700', ED+ VI 5.10 A3, V. Babanov, June 1999. 6. (not shown) Baked Alaska (10 pitches, no summit, IV+ 5.10 A1), B. Teale, S. Thelen, July 2001. 7. (not shown) Northeast Face/Donini Route (ca 1,500', 5.10), J. Donini and partner, June 1990. 8. (not shown) North Ridge (2,000', 60°), unknown, 1977. 9. (not shown) Northwest Face (2,000', 50°, Mazamas, July 1910. **(H)** Peak 6,000'. *See Photo 8.* **(AA)** Denali (20,320').

PHOTO 8: **(G)** Mt. Barrill (7,650'). *See Photo 7.* **(H)** Peak 6,000' (ca 6,000'). 1. Hebert-Spaulding-Medara Route (900', 5.10+ A1), C. Hebert, D. Medara, D. Spaulding, July 1996. 2. Phanerotime (900', 5.11b A1), J. Kalland, L. Mjaavatn, July 2004. 3. DeClerk-Brueger Route (900', III 5.10c), J. Brueger, A. DeClerk, June 1992.

Photo 9: **(I)** The Gargoyle (6,840'). *See Photo 10.* **(J)** Peak 8,010'. 1. South Route (500'), H. Allemann and N. Lötscher, July 1968. **(K)** The Incisor (ca 7,500') 1. Northwest Face (700m, 70°), E. Helmuth, et al, 1996. 2. (not shown), East Route (300', easy snow), D. Lunn, D. O'Neil, M. Young, 1973. **(O–P)** The Moose's Tooth (West Summit, 9,780'; East Summit, 10,335'). 1. West Ridge (5,200', V 80°), K. Bierl, A. Hasenkopf, A. Reichenegger, W. Welsch, June 1964. 2. The Moose Antler (800m, VI 5.8 WI4), G. Bocarde, M. Clark, C. Porter, J. Svenson, June 1974. 3. Shaken, Not Stirred (2,600', V AI5), G. Crouch, J. Donini, May 1997. **(Q)** The Bear Tooth (10,070'). See Photo 11. **(R)** The Eye Tooth (ca 9,000'). *See Photo 12.* **(N)** The Wisdom Tooth (7,770'). *See Photo 12.* **(H)** Peak 6,000' (ca 6,000'). *See Photo 8.*

PHOTO 10: **(I)** The Gargoyle (6,840').
1. New Mother Nature (1,650', V 5.10+
A1), D. Medara, D. Spaulding, July 1996.
2. Electric View (1,650', 5.11a A2+), S.
Holden, J. Kalland, M. Lund, L. Mjaavatn,
July 2004.

PHOTO 11: **(K)** The Incisor (ca 7,500') *See Photo 9.* **(M)** The Stump (ca 6,600'). *See Photo 12.* **(N)** The Wisdom Tooth (7,770'). *See Photo 12.* **(O–P)** The Moose's Tooth (West Summit, 9,780'; East Summit, 10,335'). 1. West Ridge (5,200', V 80°), K. Bierl, A. Hasenkopf, A. Reichenegger, W. Welsch, June 1964. 2. The Moose Antler (800m, VI 5.8 WI4), G. Bocarde, M. Clark, C. Porter, J. Svenson, June 1974. 3. Shaken, Not Stirred (2,600', V AI5), G. Crouch, J. Donini, May 1997. 4. The Tooth Obsession (2,900', V 5.10+ A0 WI4), S. Matusevych, D. Shirokov, A. Shuruyev, K. Vorotnikova, April 2005. 5. Ham and Eggs (2,900', V 5.9 WI4), T. Davies, J. Krakauer, N. Zinsser, July 1975. 6. Levitation and Hail Marys (2,900', V M7), S. Adamson, J. Stover , May 2004. **(Q)** The Bear Tooth (10,070'). 1. Original Route (2,600', 60°), D. Lunn, D. O'Neil, M. Young, 1973. 2. White Russian (2,600', 70°, S. Matusevych, T. Mytropan, A. Shuruyev, April 2004. 3. The Unforgiven (350m, M5 WI6), G. James, I. Ramirez, May 2004. **(R)** The Eye Tooth (ca 9,000'). *See Photo 12.* **(S)** The Sugar Tooth (ca 8,000'). 1. West Face (650m, V 5.10+ A2), T. Bonapace, R. Hass, A. Orgler, July 1994. **(T)** Mt. Cosmic Debris (ca 7,200'). 1. (not shown) North Route (1,200'), T. Davies, J. Krakauer, N. Zinsser, July 1975. **(U)** Peak 6,400' (ca 6,400'). 1. (not shown) North Route (1,700', Alaska 1), J. Forrester, D. Hoven, J. Irby, June 2005. **(CC)** The Broken Tooth (9,050'). 1. West Ridge (600m, IV 5.9), T. Bauman, J. Lewis, 1987. 2. Stump-Quinlan (600m, 5.10+ A3), S. Quinlan, M. Stump, 1987. 3. (not shown) Southeast Ridge (600m, VI 5.8 A3), C. Haire, B. Plumb, May 1982. **(EE)** Espresso Gap (ca 6,500').

PHOTO 12: **(L)** Wisdom Tooth Cragging Area (1–2 pitches, 5.6–5.11), Various. **(M)** The Stump (ca 6,600').
1. (not shown), Stump-Quinlan attempt (5.10), S. Quinlan, M. Stump, June 1991. 2. Goldfinger (1,800', IV 5.11a),
C. McNamara, J. Puryear, June 2004. 3. Stump-Quinlan (1,800', 5.10 A2), S. Quinlan, M. Stump, June 1991.
4. Game Boy (1,800', 5.11-), H. Neswadba, A. Orgler, A. Wutscher, July 1995. **(N)** The Wisdom Tooth (7,770').
1. Novocaine (2,600', 5.10 A2), K. Daniels, M. Davis, B. Gamble, G. Frontella, May 1997. 2. (not shown) North
Route (700', 50°), D. Lunn, D. O'Neil, M. Young, 1973. **(O–P)** The Moose's Tooth (West Summit, 9,780'; East
Summit, 10,335'). See Photo 11. **(Q)** The Bear Tooth (10,070'). *See Photo 11.* **(R)** The Eye Tooth (ca 9,000').
1. West Pillar/Dream in the Spirit of Mugs (3,300', V 5.10c), T. Bonapace, R. Hass, A. Orgler, July 1994.
2. The Talkeetna Standard (3,300', 5.9 WI5), J. Hollenbaugh, S. House, September 2003. **(S)** The Sugar Tooth
(ca 8,000'). *See Photo 11.*

PHOTO 13: **(V)** Peak 7,400'. 1. Southwest Face (3,000', 5.10-), T. Bibler, D. Klewin, 1989. **(W)** London Bridge
(ca 7,400'). 1. Miss Keli (1,000m, 5.9 WI4 M6+), B. Hasler, U. Stöcker, I. Wolf, May 2003. 2. On the Frozen
Roads of Our Incertitudes (sur les chemins gelés de nos incertitudes) (3,110', V WI5 M6), S. Constant, J. Mercader,
May 2003. 3. Northwest Couloir (3,200'), unknown. 4. Cornhole Couloir (3,200', 60°+), B. Gilmore, O. Samuel,
F. Wilkinson, 2004. **(X)** London Tower (ca 7,500'). *See Photo 14.* **(Y)** The Werewolf (ca 6,700'). *See Photo 14.*
(Z) Hut Tower (ca 6,200'). 1. West Face/Men's World (600m, 5.11+), H. Neswadba, A. Orgler, A. Wutscher, July
1995. 2. Southwest Face (600m, IV 5.10c), S. Jöchler, A. Orgler, July 1987. 3. (not shown) South Ridge (600m,
5.9), P. Mayfield, G. Meyers, J. Otteson, 1988. 4. (not shown) Southeast Face/Boy's World (600m, 5.9), B. Sem-
borski, S. Wayker, June 1999. **(DD)** The Balrog (7,979'). 1. (not shown) Southwest Face (1,300m, 5.7), H. Arch,
H. Neswadba, July 1990.

PHOTO 14: **(X)** London Tower (ca 7,500'). 1. The Trailer Park (3,200', VI WI6 M6+), K. Cordes, S. DeCapio, May 2000. 2. Big Time (1,000m, VI 5.11d A2), H. Arch, H. Neswadba , July 1990. **(Y)** The Werewolf (ca 6,700'). 1. Freezy Nuts (800m, TD+ 95°), M. Guy, M. Pelissier, May 1996. 2. West Pillar (800m, 5.10+ A1), A. Orgler, M. Rutter, July 1990. 3. Anemone Pillar (800m, 5.10), K. Geisswinkler, A. Orgler, July 1991. **(Z)** Hut Tower (ca 6,200'). 1. West Face/Men's World (600m, 5.11+), H. Neswadba, A. Orgler, A. Wutscher, July 1995. 2. Southwest Face (600m, IV 5.10c), S. Jöchler, A. Orgler, July 1987.

SOME KIND OF MONSTER

Could this Yukon route be the longest ice climb in North America?

JOE JOSEPHSON

Joe Josephson starts the first ice pitch of Flowers for Blaise on the northeast face of Catenary Peak. *David Dornian*

Adjacent to Mt. Logan in the Yukon's remote St. Elias Range, Mt. McArthur is to Logan as Mt. Hunter is to Denali: a beauty of a mountain dwarfed by the heaping mass of a neighbor and often overlooked as a result. McArthur sees what might, at best, be called "random attempts."

1) Some Kind of Monster (6,000' vertical), north face of Mt. McArthur. 2) Flowers for Blaise (4,500' vertical), northeast face of Catenary Peak. Mt. Logan (19,550 feet) rises to the right of this picture (out of view). *Joe Josephson*

In 1991, three of Canada's top alpinists, Don Serl, Michael Down, and Jim Haberl, flew in to climb a sweep of ice rising directly to McArthur's main summit. The trio decided to start with the seemingly easy, and also unclimbed, west ridge to prepare for the north face. Reading Serl's concise yet dramatic report of the epic they suffered in the 1992 *Canadian Alpine Journal* was when I recognized the First Golden Rule of the St. Elias Range: there is no such thing as a warm-up.

I first "discovered" McArthur's north face while flying by in 1998. Steve House and I were on our way to try the 7,500-foot southwest face of King Peak in single-push style. We made the sixth overall ascent of the continent's ninth-highest peak, encountering serious WI6 ice at 15,000 feet and tackling the entire route with only 30 pounds of collective gear in a 36-hour push. Our route, Call of the Wild, may be my personal high-water mark in the world of alpinism. We also learned the Second Golden Rule of the St. Elias Range: everything is bigger and farther away than you imagine.

In 2002, Rich Searle, Jesse Thompson, and I took the single-push strategy to McArthur. Our goal was the north face, but we decided to warm up on the sunnier south face. Ignoring the First Golden Rule was my first mistake. Despite a malfunctioning stove, I didn't worry when clouds seemed to be developing into something more because I thought we could always bail down the east ridge. And then we learned the Third Golden Rule of the St. Elias Range: there is no such thing as an easy ridge. Having never been to the range so early in May, I didn't realize how dark it gets, particularly in a whiteout. Hours of stressful routefinding, downclimbing seracs, and dodging gaping yawns and inexplicable cornices forced me to throw down my tools and declare "no more!" at the first flat spot. The open bivi in −25°C cold, with a fading stove, left an indelible impression on all three of us. We stumbled back to camp 35 hours after leaving.

Such were the lessons I brought with me in 2005, when David Dornian and I arrived at Kluane Lake. By now I had been burned enough to create my Fourth Golden Rule of the St. Elias Range: always, and I do mean always, carry a photo of your planned descent along for the climb. I also had a brand new stove.

We landed on the upper Logan Glacier with two main objectives, the 6,000-foot north face of McArthur and the 4,500-foot northeast face of Catenary Peak (Dak Tower). Some two weeks later, when we flew out, we had seen no more than 20 hours in a row of good weather, but it was perhaps the best climbing trip of my life, and certainly the most successful.

At 6 feet, 5 inches, thin as a rail, and deeply involved in sport climbing, David would not appear to be the archetypal single-push alpinist. But 35 years of mountaineering in western Canada is résumé enough for me, not to mention our friendship, earned during my tenure in Calgary. Holding a graduate degree in philosophy, David remembers everything he reads, and I seriously doubt it's possible for any form of normal communication to keep up with his creative brain. His sometimes annoying tendency to stutter along, waving his hands frantically, while trying to make a literary connection or articulate some pithy anecdote, appeals to my own version of intensity.

Unlike our solitary line on McArthur's north side, Dak Tower coughs up numerous options across its broad flank. There is no shortage of moderate new routes to do, and we focused on what we thought to be the best, a fine chute of steep water ice leading to ice slopes, with more mixed gullies connecting directly to the upper ice slope at the highest point of the face. It's a beautiful thing.

Fighting bad weather on two quick attempts, and sitting out a healthy storm, we headed up for a third time on the afternoon of May 29, after the sun had left the face. Classic climbing with a spooky bergschrund, water ice, firm snow, and a little rock on fractured but good granite kept us going until close to midnight. Heeding my earlier lessons, I told David, "We could go around this big rock buttress to maybe a better spot, but we need to brew up now." I was bonking and it could be hours before we got around the buttress. After at least two sucker punches in the range, I had given up on any chance of lying down on one of these rigs. I was learning. Or so I thought.

David Dornian surmounts the bergschrund to begin Some Kind of Monster on Mt. McArthur. *Joe Josephson*

Hunkered on a rock the size of a volleyball but not at all as smooth, I managed to balance the stove between us in a little alcove. Despite a melting-out perch that dumped the first full pot of water onto David's leg, my new stove was functioning wonderfully. I even mentioned to David how nice it was, for once, to not be having a stove epic. Less than 15 minutes later, just as we were about to drain the next pot, David stood up to pee. To avoid jabbing my friend with my frontpoints, I straightened my cramped leg. At the sound of this motion, David lunged back toward the sit-down. We both watched in horror as I kicked two liters of lukewarm water over our rope and rack. The pot strode down the mountain.

The next two hours were spent melting eight liters, two tablespoons at a time, on the only part of the pot we still had: the lid. After this diligent and none-too-restful stop, we unraveled from our stance and were moving once again near sunrise. As we topped out on the rock buttress, I could finally see to the north, only to discover the ubiquitous stormy weather was moving in again. Needing to make a fast decision, I changed course and abandoned the wicked-looking mixed gully above us for the easier and shorter snow gully to the right. Wandering down the northeast ridge in swirling snow and making 11 long rappels, we returned to the tent 27 hours after leaving.

We called the route Flowers for Blaise, in tribute to the flowers growing from a crack just above the bergschrund and for David's wonderful dog, who had died earlier in the spring.

It took a few days after we arrived in base camp to realize that the constant background noise we heard was the spindrift pouring down our intended line on the north face of McArthur. It was obvious we would have to wait for clear weather to even get close. I stated unequivocally to David, "We were not stopping on that face until we are on the summit." Although this sounds definitive, experienced, and filled with exactly the gusto required for stripped-down alpinism, it is the sort of statement that has gotten me into trouble.

Recovering from Dak Peak and waiting for the skies to clear, I soon remembered another Golden Rule of the St. Elias Range: the nearby Gulf of Alaska is a perpetual source of low pressure, and therefore the barometer may or may not go up in good weather. Relying on the prevailing patterns instead, we began swimming over the bergschrund at 8:30 in the morning of June 2 with clearing skies. Armed with 17 ice screws and a few stoppers and pins, we began simul-climbing the glass-hard, spindrift-tempered ice, placing screws every 60 to 100 feet. We'd carry on until the leader ran out of screws or otherwise just couldn't take it any more.

While scoping the line, we had clearly seen that the lower section was bereft of snow, as indicated by the black, pitted appearance. It appeared that we would encounter a number of snow runnels and easier ground beginning a third of the way up the face. Yet in my desire to climb the route, I had forgotten the Second Golden Rule (everything is bigger and farther away). By the time each of us had done a full block of pitches, we had turned the corner onto the main face but were still in the middle of a relentless sweep of clean ice with no easy runnels in sight. The rolling, spindrift-formed bubbly at the start had given way to a prehistoric shield of 60- to 70-degree iron plate. After six hours of steady climbing, about half the time I thought we'd be on the face, we were not even a third of the way up.

I was finally playing my trump card. All my mistakes, everything I'd learned on six other trips to the Yukon, even the dropped pot on Dak Peak—all those lessons were rolled up into the singular event of this climb. The ice remained unrelenting and even required a few places where

Dornian approximately 30 pitches up Some Kind of Monster. Black circle marks base camp. *Joe Josephson*

we had to lever our modern screws in with our axes as in the old days of ice climbing. But this time, unlike all my other single-push climbs, we stopped to rehydrate at just the right time and stood in front of the stove, guarding it; we put on all our extra clothes just as the sun started to dip; we stayed organized and consistent.

Around midnight, we finally reached the attractive summit cone. David had been openly wondering about the way through the complex-looking terrain. I was distracted and blew off thinking about it until we arrived at the base of a mixed gully. Thankfully, it was David's turn to lead. I needed a rest.

Spindrift started slithering down the green ice tongue David had entered. I was convinced the spindrift was from David knocking snow off holds as he scratched up some mixed variation. Had we been six hours earlier I'd have thought, "Go for it." But as the temperature plummeted, I just wanted to arrive at the glorious final pyramid, where we'd follow our long-lost cruiser névé and bask in the rising sun on the top of my favorite mountain. Some time later it occurred to me David was not causing the spindrift—it was the ferocious wind blowing over the summit. After what seemed like hours of expecting to see David rappelling out of the nightmare, the rope came tight. If David ever yelled down, I never heard it. As I moved into the maelstrom, it was evident by the slow crawl of the rope that we were simul-climbing again.

Although my view of the pitch was almost entirely looking down, the climbing was clearly brilliant. Not too hard but interesting, with thin runnels winding around rocks and changing directions. It is one of the best pitches I've ever climbed in the mountains. Too bad I couldn't enjoy it. In a desperate attempt to escape the gully, we made an awkward traverse left and up some broken cliffs to seek shelter next to a large rock tower.

By now the storm was mostly wind; some blue sky was poking through the streamers of snow swirling off the summit like so many prayer flags. After I led up another rope length I insisted that David head left for the skyline, where it looked like we might get some sun. Few people would consider –30°C in a steady 50 mph wind with only intermittent sun as basking, but it might as well have been Hawaii. It was 9 a.m. We had spent more than 25 hours on the face.

The true summit was only a pitch or two away. We were on low-angle ground and we could see snow all the way. Deep beautiful snow. But the clouds were still there and the wind was still howling. Was the storm clearing or was it a sucker hole? Herein lies the moment that defines single-push alpine climbing. We headed down.

When I got home and described the climbing, everyone commented on what a burn it must have been on the calves. Maybe it was because I've never been able to wear tube socks, but my calves didn't even notice it. Instead, it was my feet that suffered. After an estimated 50 pitches of pure ice climbing, no one could escape the pain of the pediatric gripping required between one's feet and crampons. The magical runnels of névé that every alpinist dreams of just didn't materialize. Even when snow appeared, it often would be little more than crust over two inches of air over black ice. The real demoralizer was the short stretches of ankle-deep powder that left us scratching into bulletproof ice without the added security of any visual cues. For a month after I got home, the first 30 minutes out of bed were spent wobbling on my heels, followed by extended showers just because my toes liked it.

Most of the ascents I've done in the Yukon are not "hard" when measured by the numbers. Not even close. But regardless of any single grade one wants to attach to it, our McArthur route, Some Kind of Monster, is the "hardest" climb I've ever done. More importantly, this was the only time in the greater ranges where I've put together all my experience in a way it was truly meant to be used. It is my most meaningful climb.

Mark Twight writes about a conversation he had with Scott Backes prior to climbing Deprivation on Mt. Hunter in 1994: "Look, let's do the thing we're good at. Let's carry the light packs. I'd rather climb something easier in three days than struggle day after day with a few hard pitches at a time and sit out the storms and ration our food and all that rule-book bullshit." As this was Mark writing, all most readers may remember is the rant. What climbers really need to understand is the wisdom and significance of doing something they are good at.

SUMMARY:

AREA: St. Elias Range, Yukon Territory

ROUTES: First ascent of Flowers for Blaise (4,500', Alaska Grade III) on the northeast face of Catenary Peak (a.k.a. Dak Tower), ca 12,790 feet. First ascent of Some Kind of Monster (6,000', Alaska Grade V) on the north face of Mt. McArthur (14,248 feet). David Dornian and Joe Josephson, May-June, 2005.

A NOTE ABOUT THE AUTHOR:

Joe Josephson was born in June 1967 and has spent 13 percent of his birthdays on the slopes of Mt. Logan. He is working on a historical guidebook to the Logan massif that will be published by First Ascent Press (www.firstascentpress.com) in early 2007.

COMING OF AGE

Solo first ascents in Queen Maud Land, Antarctica.

MIKE LIBECKI

Mike Libecki stands beneath Windmill Spire, his 1,500-foot consolation prize in Queen Maud Land, climbed after near-fatal rockfall drove him off his first objective. *Mike Libecki*

As the gales of November whipped and thrashed my fragile nylon tether, I felt like a lone sailor out at sea. But the sea I explored consisted of solid blue ice, and I sailed with a kite connected to my harness, skis, and sled. I had come to reconnoiter and climb remote granite islands that are both threatening and magnificent. They are like giant granite bouquets blooming out of vases of ice—by far the most uniquely shaped formations I have ever seen.

To go alone to Queen Maud Land had been on my list of dreams for many years. All the solo expeditions I had done had been part of a staircase of training to prepare for this journey. Then, after a year of meticulous planning, there was a sudden shift in logistics: the Russian company making it possible for me to get there switched the date of departure from December to October. It was either go early and gamble on risky weather, or don't go at all.

Greetings! Disembarking from the "Millennium Falcon" aircraft at the Russian base Novolazarevskaya. *Mike Libecki*

For the last 15 years, I have looked through my eye-windows into the world with the feeling of being 17 years old, an adolescent boy. I am 32 now, and I can see and feel myself changing. For the first time in my life, when I look into a mirror I can see my dad looking back. Goodbye adolescent boy, hello adult man.

All the homilies that I heard growing up pertained to other people, to older people, to adults. I remember hearing adults share their wisdom: "Curiosity killed the cat," "Don't judge a book by its cover," "One day at a time," and the ever-so-popular "Don't bite the hand that feeds you." Such age-old sayings had always made a bit of sense to me, but now they have come to define my life, not only in the trials of relationships and building a career but also on intense expeditions around the world.

My initial reaction to the new feeling of adulthood was like a rebirth, with renewed optimism and the courage to take life to greater heights. I felt something like a professional kid, with newfound strength to continue my lifestyle of climbing in the remotest areas of the planet, and to do so while being a father, having a comfortable home for my family, and giving back to the community. Now I even listen to the news channel in my truck instead of rocking out to bootleg Grateful Dead jams circa 1977. What happened to me? As surely as a compass needle points north, I was becoming an adult.

Random events during my Antarctic trip in 2005 confirmed this metamorphosis. For the first time, I indulged in what I had always considered the classic adult vices: coffee and tobacco. My entire life, I had made fun of my parents for indulging in this combo. How could a cancer stick followed by jitter juice be a delight? Just before leaving Cape Town on my way to Antarctica, as I bought a few back-up salamis at a market, a pouch of tobacco caught my eye. I left with a pouch of Old Toby and 50 rolling papers. Unfortunately, with changing into an adult also comes hypocrisy.

I flew from Cape Town to the Russian base Novolazarevskaya. When we touched down on the ice runway it was October 31, Halloween. The sun was below the horizon and the temperature was −15°F without factoring in 60 mph winds. Before my sixth step onto the frozen continent my face was numb and my nostril hairs had turned to ice. I was welcomed by hot borscht and long skinny wieners for breakfast. A celebration among the crew was under way for the start of another Antarctic season, as they unloaded boxes of Stolichnaya from the plane.

According to my map, a few hundred square miles of Queen Maud Land are home to countless spires, towers, and ship-prows of granite. I had made friends with the Russian pilots and had the opportunity of a lifetime to spend almost three hours flying over the area for a stunning aerial reconnaissance. It seemed impossible that so many unclimbed world-class formations could exist in such a relatively small area.

At one point, perhaps in the time of Gondwanaland and Laurasia, these geographic works of art must have been home to dragons and wizards and are part of the reason fairytales exist. I felt like an ancient warrior right out of a book, coming to save a sweet, beautiful maiden imprisoned at the top of the unclimbed spear-tip summits, guarded by subzero temperatures and fierce numbing winds, like ferocious, frost-breathing dragons.

I pointed to a group of granite swords to signal where I wanted to land. The toylike, bi-wing airplane landed on the glassy ice and slid back and forth like a fish swiveling around a boat deck. The Russians laughed and gunned the single-propeller engine like kids in a go-cart. The pilots seemed perplexed that I would attempt to climb one of these strange towers of stone by myself. When I stepped out into the numbing breeze, I felt the same way.

The sound of the propeller faded to silence, and I stood alone on the clear icecap; perfect sculptures of shiny ice flames surrounded me. It was 0°F when the last light of the sun winked away. The tall, ominous granite and I regarded each other with suspicion. I shuttled loads to set up my camp. When the rustling of gear and skis gliding on ice subsided, there was only the breeze, my heartbeat, and my breath. Utter solitude. Living alone in temperatures as cold as my home freezer for the next five weeks would prove another adulthood slogan: "Be careful what you wish for, because you might just get it."

The unnamed "ship's prow" formation Libecki first tried to climb. His high point on the prow is marked. Later in the expedition, he followed the Dragon Back Ridge to reach the summit from the left. *Mike Libecki*

Mike Libecki poses amid the kitty-litter rock of the eighth pitch of Frozen Tears, Windmill Spire. *Mike Libecki*

There were two real concerns: the katabatic winds and the rotten granite. I had learned to fear both during the Antarctic summer of 2003–04 when I climbed a big wall about 40 miles away. The lurking wind had turned balmy, sunny, 20°F days into dangerous negatives in minutes. I also would never forget my previous experience on the worst rock of my life. Since I left Salt Lake City on this journey, I had been possessed with worry about the rock quality. But I wore a halo of hope that I would find solid stone, and the steep-sharp granite formations disguised their danger in gorgeous grandeur. The towers are so fantastic that one's fear is replaced with a feeling of eroticism.

My first objective was to attempt a stunning shield of rock that reminded me of the Ship's Prow off the coast of Baffin Island. In 1999, on my first solo expedition to the Arctic, I was able to climb that ominous formation in temperatures that never rose above 25°F. I was now back in a similar situation on the opposite side of the planet, and though the temperatures here would be colder, at least I would not have to worry about polar bears raiding my camp.

Before long I had three pitches fixed, with the high winds and freezing temperatures forming the crux. As I traversed a small ledge under a hollow spider web of cracks, two haul-bag-sized flakes stood in my way. They were balanced so perfectly it seemed that a gust of wind could set them loose. They had to go.

On a good stance, with bomber gear, I gently touched one of the flakes, and they both went crashing toward the ground. I was expecting the simple thrill of a wall trundle, but then a chain reaction started and pool-table-size flakes in a dihedral about 10 feet to the right of me exploded and roared with fury. Before my adrenaline had a chance to kick in, a truck load of granite let loose, continuing the thunder and destruction. I tucked into a fetal position. The earth shook and screamed like King Kong. It sounded like the entire wall was

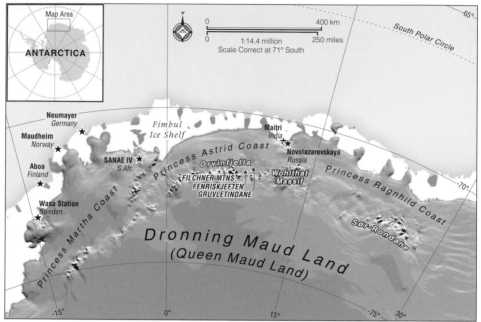

Many peaks in this area likely were climbed first by scientists and surveyors, starting in the late 1940s. The expeditions listed below completed technical climbs. *Map by Martin Gamache, Alpine Mapping Guild*

(1) Ulvetanna (2,931m, 1994)
   Fenriskjeften Massif
   Caspersen-Nesheim-Tollefsen (Nor.)
In all, the 13-member expedition climbed 36 peaks, including Gessnertind (3,021m), Holtanna North (2,630m), Jøkulkyrkia (3,148m), and Kinntanna (2,724m).

(2) Rondespiret (2,427m, 1996-97)
   Sør-Rondane
   Aastorp-Caspersen-Staver-Tollefsen (Nor.)

(3) Rakekniven (2,365m, 1996-97)
   Filchner Mountains
   Anker-Graber-Krakauer-Lowe-Ridgeway-
      Wiltsie (U.S.)
Four other peaks in the area also were climbed.

(4) Kubbestolen (2,080m, 1999-2000)
   Holtedahlfjella
   Lukes-Oehninger (Switz.)
The duo first climbed a new route on Mundlauga in the Fenriskjeften, then skied three days to reach the Holtedahlfjella, where they climbed six peaks.

(5) Holtanna (2,640m, 2001)
   Fenriskjeften Massif
   Dujmovits-Georges-Hubert-Mercier-Robert-Zangrilli
   (international expedition)
The expedition climbed nine other new routes in the massif. A Spanish expedition climbed in the same area during this time, doing at least one new route.

(6) Peak Valery Chkalov (2,510m, 2003)
   Svarthorna Peaks, Wohlthat Massif
   Khvostenko-Kuznetsov-Sokolov-Zaharov (Rus.)
The expedition climbed five peaks in all.

(7) Fenris, west face (2,680m, 2004)
   Orvinfjella
   Helling-Libecki (U.S.)

8. Windmill Spire (2006)
   Gruvletindane Group, Orvinfjella
   Libecki (U.S.)

A Kazakh expedition may have climbed in Queen Maud Land during December 2005, but no further details were available.

crumbling: doomsday. All of the stone to the right of me that would have been part of my route erupted in the most intense movement of earth I have experienced. I smelled fire, heat, raw organic energy.

After the end-of-the-world explosions bellowed across the icecap and boomed off the nearby walls, I heard only ringing and a deep hum in my head, then the crackling of stones bouncing down the wall toward me. I hid behind my eyelids, curled into a ball, and took the stoning like an accused witch tied to a post. Then there was silence, a chilly wind, bright blue sky, and a happy sun gleaming. It was as if I was in a straight jacket. I suddenly gasped for breath as if I had been under water for three minutes. I was hot and wet despite the freezing wind—then I realized I had peed my pants.

I rappelled the route, shivering. Fortunately, my route had been veering right, and my ropes below were unscathed. As my tears slowly seeped, I thought of my daughter. I thought of my adult duties, and not only how much my daughter needed me but also just how much I needed to be with my daughter. Tears froze on my face. I crawled into my bag, drank the rest of the warm liquid in my thermos, bit off a few chunks of hard salami, and tried to sleep. My iPod fed me therapy in the form of Johnny Cash songs: "One," "Nobody," "Solitary Man," and "I See A Darkness." In my mind I could still hear the crashing roar of the earth. I could still smell it.

When I awoke I felt a new energy. I took the day to digest the experience and consider my options. It was the first time I had backed off a solo route, and it humbled me to the bone; I had to come to terms with the fact that this experience had been near ultimate danger, and I had had no choice but to go down. But my psych-addiction-obsession for solo climbing is energy I cannot control; it guides me like iron to a magnet. I had put every bit of my heart and soul on the line to get here. I thought of another bit of adult wisdom that my mom had always told me: "Be true to yourself, and be thankful for what you've got." I still had plenty of time to find another objective.

I put on my skis to look at a beautiful, tall, skinny spire nearby, a route I had scoped earlier that led to a café-table-sized summit. Despite the lingering terror from the first route I had attempted, I still yearned to stand on the top of this spire.

I found some solid stone but also, of course, pitches of kitty litter. There were times I would try to place a No. 1 Camalot and, after finally whittling down the pebbles, I'd end up placing a No. 3; a knifeblade placement would turn into a 3/4-inch angle hole. The wind chill controlled my schedule, and I often had to rappel back to camp due to dangerously numb feet and toes. I tiptoed with each move and wore free climbing shoes the entire time for precision, despite the frozen toes I obviously would have to endure. I fixed ropes and used only one wall camp. I could barely sleep while thinking of the next day's work in the steeps, shadowed by fear from that first monumental rockfall experience.

I made the summit after 16 days. Standing on top was glorious, but most of my enjoyment while getting there had been consumed by fear of the rotten rock. Nonetheless, I found myself screaming with joy as I put on my Year of the Cock mask atop the needlelike Windmill Spire.

Safely back at camp, I was hypnotized by a magnificent horizontal sunset of Barbie pink and sherbet orange rolling across the horizon. The ship's prow I had attempted mocked me in glorious sunlight. I still wanted to stand on top of its amazing summit. Three days before the Russians picked me up, I skied to the back of the formation, and after several hours on a beautiful dragon-back ridgeline I found myself on top. I thought of my daughter again, but this time I was laughing instead of crying.

Back home I had to take pain pills for the after-effects of frozen toes. Before long I was pulling off dead flesh that looked like strings of dried squid. I felt deeply honored to have witnessed such raw power on this journey.

I am back to my usual green tea and coffee a couple of times a week. The tobacco didn't make it home, and I mock myself for the brief nicotine fix. Transformation into adulthood is an interesting journey. The single most important thing I have realized, as I evolve from boy to adult and to father, is that I need to teach my daughter that she must believe in her dreams, regardless of what they may be, and to go after them. Old age and death are inevitable. The time is now.

SUMMARY:

AREA: Orvinfjella, Queen Maud Land, Antarctica

ASCENTS: Solo first ascent of Frozen Tears (1,500 feet, 9 pitches, VI 5.10 A3) on Windmill Spire. Solo first ascent of Dragon Back Ridge (2,500 vertical feet, 5.5) on unnamed "ship's prow" formation. Oct. 31–Dec. 8, 2005.

A NOTE ABOUT THE AUTHOR:

Mike Libecki's life revolves around raising his three-year-old daughter, Lilliana, and seeking out remote, unclimbed walls and mountains of the world. He lives near the mouth of Little Cottonwood Canyon in Utah with his daughter, dogs, cats, birds, rabbits, and his newest family addition, a potbelly pig.

GRANTS: This expedition was sponsored by the Banff Centre, Black Diamond, Clif Bar, Mountain Hardwear, and the W. L. Gore Shipton/ Tilman Grant.

Summit view: a successful finale to Libecki's Year of the Cock expeditions. *Mike Libecki*

Gone with the Wind

A three-year struggle to climb the north pillar of Cerro Murallón, Patagonia.

Stefan Glowacz

No trail to the peak: Stefan Glowacz (left) and Robert Jasper ford an icy river en route to Cerro Murallón.
Klaus Fengler

Silence. Not the slightest trace of noise. Even Robert's breath made no sound. Small clouds of mist escaped from his mouth at regular intervals and vanished instantly in the icy air. I kept staring at the same point on the ceiling, as if my gaze could drill a hole into the crushing hopelessness. The halogen bulbs of my headlamp filled the ice cave with a harsh glow. A velvety layer of frost covered our sleeping bags, ropes, pitons, and dry rations. –3°C. I couldn't help but think of the refrigerator room of a slaughterhouse. For days a hurricane-force storm had been raging outside. The snow and ice walls—over a meter thick—absorbed all sound and every ray of light. We were buried alive. Nevertheless, we were here of our own free will. And for the third consecutive year we were possessed by a 1,000-meter-high north face at the end of the world on the Patagonia ice cap. This wall was as precious as a jewel to us, and we courted it like we would a beautiful woman. Always at the same time of the year, in the months of November and December of 2003, 2004, and 2005, we struggled to the foot of the wall. Twice we had been harshly turned back. Diva Murallón enchanted us and—with total disregard for logic and common sense—we would have returned even a fourth or a fifth time in case we failed again. Until she would give in to our desire.

Years ago a picture of Cerro Murallón, an almost unknown mountain even among expedition climbers, captivated Robert Jasper and me. Murallón rises into the sky south of Fitz Roy like a huge fortress. At 2,831 meters, its elevation is negligible. However, the technical difficulties and remoteness make it quite a challenge. In this photograph we could see a huge, mostly overhanging pillar soaring some 600 meters, followed by a ridge leading to a 400-meter-high wall that reared up like a gigantic breaking wave. The line was of unsurpassable simplicity and beauty. Our appetites were additionally whetted by the words of the great climber Casimiro Ferrari, who wrote of Cerro Murallón, "If Cerro Torre is the mountain that left its deepest mark on me and if Fitz Roy was technically the hardest, then Murallón was the peak that put my mental and physical powers to the toughest test." What kind of mountain must it be to make the great Ferrari pay such obeisance? It took him four expeditions between 1979 and 1984 to reconnoiter an approach to Murallón and subsequently to climb the colossal northeast pillar.

     Prior to Ferrari, only one expedition had been successful. It was the untiring Briton Eric Shipton who, together with three others, reached the summit plateau in 1961. Their route from the northwest is perhaps the easiest line. However, the weather conditions were so terrible that it remains uncertain if the team really climbed the highest ice mushroom. This detail is unim-

Crossing the ice cap toward Cerro Murallón. The north pillar rises above the long snow and ice tongue below the left side of the face. The Ferrari Route (1984) climbs the light-gray pillars left of this. The Lost World (2003) is out of view to the right. *Klaus Fengler*

portant on a one-kilometer-long plateau with small, technically easy protuberances, and Robert and I consider Shipton and his team to be the first ascensionists of Cerro Murallón.

2003

The shortest distance from the last outpost of civilization—the Estancia Christina—to Murallón is 40 kilometers as the crow flies. It took me, Robert, our cameraman, Sebastian, and our photographer, Klaus, almost three weeks to carry our equipment and provisions

The right tool for the job. *Robert Jasper*

through pathless terrain and dangerous glaciers to the foot of our wall. Filled with awe, we stood under our pillar, realizing that our equipment and—most of all—the remaining time, would never suffice to reach the summit via our planned route. We vowed to return. In spite of everything we managed to pluck a very nice first ascent at the right edge of the north face. We called this route The Lost World and deposited most of our gear at the foot of our original goal for another attempt the following year.

2004

This time we planned to reach our mountain from the north via the ice cap. The approach was double the distance of last year's, but we had to do equipment carries only from Piedra del Fraile up to the Passo Marconi. From there we could pull our belongings over the ice cap on sleds.

It took us not quite a week to get our gear up to Passo Marconi. After a few days of bad weather we set out across the ice on November 2. Our friends Sebastian, Tobias, and Pater were to accompany us to base camp and return to civilization via Estancia Christina. With their help we could drag our equipment to base camp without further depots and portages.

Four days without a breath of wind, a crystal-clear sky, and hard snow turned the approach into an exhausting but nonetheless pleasurable experience. It was the typical Patagonian lull before the storm. On the morning of day four, Pater, Sebastian, and Tobias set out for Estancia Christina while Robert, Klaus, and I headed for Murallón's north face.

For the next five weeks we had to fend entirely for ourselves. We did not see a human soul, nor another creature, nor a flower. When we reached the foot of the wall, we realized it was impossible to build a safe ice cave as a base camp as we had the year before, for there was not nearly enough snow. The next day we constructed huge snow walls around our tents so we would not be entirely without shelter in the devastating storms we knew would come.

By evening the good weather had already turned into a nightmare. The wind carried snowflakes horizontally over our wall and in no time buried the tents. At 2 a.m. I awoke from a restless slumber. Snow, hard as concrete, pressed against the side of my head. I pounded my fist against the roof of the tent. Panic began to well up; Klaus and I had to get out of there as fast as possible. Robert, lying near us in an even smaller tent, had surely been completely covered. The back of our tent had already caved in. Like two maniacs we carved out an upward-leading tunnel, using our cooking pots. Outside, all hell had broken loose, but Robert at least was okay. Gusts of wind repeatedly blew us off our feet. We battled the elements with our pots and shovels until eight in the morning.

How vulnerable we were! If one of us got injured, our fancy sat phone would be of little use. By the second night we were stumbling like punch-drunk boxers. However, this is exactly why the mountains in Patagonia count among the biggest challenges alpinism has to offer. On Cerro Torre or Fitz Roy you at least can weather the storms in base camp, but on Murallón every storm could mean the end. The mountain was playing cat-and-mouse with the tiny, two-legged intruders. Two days after showing its claws, the kitty started to purr. Up went the air pressure, the storm died down, and one morning the sun shone from a cloudless sky. While Klaus started to put the camp in order, Robert and I finally laid hands on our dream pillar.

It was an incredible feeling to climb the first meters in these hostile but grandiose surroundings. For almost two years we had prepared ourselves mentally and physically for this moment. In this instant we were rewarded for all our deprivations and trials.

Pitch by pitch, the climbing got harder. Robert and I had decided from the beginning to do without bolts entirely, even at belays. We were climbing in wonderful cracks and corners, and as we gained height, the wall got steeper and steeper. We had brought 850 meters of line to fix; the rest of the route would have to be done alpine style. Late at night, we rappelled to base camp.

Although the air pressure had increased by only a few millibars and seemed to predict unstable conditions, the spell of good weather lasted over a week. On the following days we climbed until we could barely lift our arms. Every morning we started out at first light, hiked for two hours to the start of the climb, and jumared to the previous high point. Robert or I would lead most of the day while Klaus documented the climbing. At the belays we put in pitons; in most cases nuts worked well as protection. Most of the climbing was at a level of 5.11 to 5.12. We were trying for a pure free ascent, but 400 meters up we reached a compact over-hanging section split by a fine crack. To speed up our ascent we aided two pitches, planning to free them later. We estimated the difficulties to be hard 5.13—or even a digit more. After five days of climbing, 600 meters of elevation, and 17 pitches, we finally stood on the top of the lower pillar. Halftime.

Climbing simultaneously along the easy ridge, we reached the second section of the north face. As we set up the belay on a narrow ledge, the sight above almost took our breath away: the wall curved outward like a huge petrified wave. The first two pitches were extremely overhanging, with technically hard cracks of every width. I was able to free the first pitch at 5.13. On the second I had to succumb to aid, but it should also go free. Late in the evening Robert aided another overhanging pitch. For the first time we began to believe that we might reach the summit. From our high point it was about 300 meters to the summit plateau. It would take one day in alpine style, or two at the most, to reach the top. Robert and I were euphoric while rappelling to the base in the dark.

Murallón had been merciful, but during the night the mountain started to display its ugly side. During the next day the storm tore the flysheet of Robert's tent to pieces. With needle and thread in numb fingers, we tried to repair the damage while the storm pelted us with slush. We felt like demonstrators attacked by police water cannons. In the evening we had to take down Robert's tent. Now the three of us had to lie in a small two-person tent. Each of us spent the night clinging to a tent pole; in the morning our flysheet also tore to shreds. It was apocalyptic.

We moved to a high plateau in hopes of being better protected. The following days were hell. We deposited the sleds, a bag of climbing gear, skis, and most of our Powerbars at the foot of a talus gully leading up to the plateau. The storm continued to rage for several days. As it began to get warmer, the fresh snow started to melt, and in the night torrents poured from the rocks and turned our campsite into a lake. Everything got drenched. It continued to storm, the rain turning again to snow. While pitching the tents on a new campsite, I saw my sleeping mat blow away; for the remainder of the expedition I had to lie on the aluminum bags from our dry rations.

Gone with the Wind, completed in 2005. *Klaus Fengler*

Every day the tents became more and more damaged, until they were hardly recognizable. As the storm continued to strengthen, we decided to make our way to the distant Pascale Hut to wait out the weather. We knew this decision drastically reduced our chance of reaching the summit, but it was out of our hands. With snow pelting our faces, we broke camp and tried to arrange an orderly retreat. But when we reached our cache at the foot of the gully, we found that it had been buried by a landslide; with luck we managed to salvage our bag of climbing gear and the skis. The rest was gone.

For two days we struggled over the Upsala Glacier to the Pascale Hut. The miserable weather imprisoned us for a week, but then the barometer started to rise, the storm let off, and after more than three weeks Murallón re-emerged from the clouds. With our questionably repaired tent, dried sleeping bags, and fully recuperated bodies, we covered the two-day hike back to base camp on the plateau in one push. On the following day the sky was cloudless, but hurricane-force winds raged around the summit. In the evening the pressure was declining. Despite this, we stuck to our attempt, knowing it would be our last. Belaying each other, we jumared up the alarmingly frayed ropes for 400 meters before our ascent was brought to an abrupt stop. Above, the ropes were completely tattered, hanging from shredded strands. We had lost the Patagonian poker game. We cleaned the first 400 meters of fixed rope and deposited it on the plateau with the rest of our equipment. Then we returned to the Pascale Hut in another forced march and reached Estancia Christina the next day.

Jasper leading the eighth pitch of Gone with the Wind in 2004. *Klaus Fengler*

We had lost and won simultaneously. We had climbed most of a route on one of the hardest mountains of the world. To us it was a magic line worth a good struggle. We were possessed by a dream and knew that only if we realized this dream would we be free again. This time the dream had "gone with the wind"—and with this the route had its name.

2005

In the ice cave we were safe. We could sleep and cook or even go on a fantasy trip with a good book. Nonetheless, we were under great pressure. At the beginning it was only two of us on the mountain; Hans Martin Götz and Klaus the photographer were planning to follow three weeks later. So Robert and I lay in our sleeping bags, continuously pondering our possibilities, the strategy, and, of course, the dangers. With just two of us, the approach to our climb through a maze of seracs and crevasses brought a fair amount of danger. We didn't dare contemplate the possibility of an accident up on the wall. The line we drew was definitely on the side of safety.

Now on our third attempt, we had learned from our previous mistakes. This time we had chosen the southern approach route via Estancia Christina. As we knew the way perfectly, we could reach base camp even in unfavorable weather. As we didn't want to waste our valuable strength, time, and gaps of good weather on hauling equipment, five Argentinean friends helped us with the transport.

Excluding the last 300 meters, we knew exactly what was awaiting us. Our biggest fear was failing once more and having to suffer through the void that would follow. In our ice cave we were condemned to idleness, which is always difficult to bear. We ruminated and talked about our worries and fears, but in the end each of us had to sort things out for himself.

We already had prepared ourselves for the horrific scenario of spending another two or three weeks in the ice cave. Then, suddenly, the pressure stabilized. Although it had risen no more than five millibars, the storm suddenly lost its force and the sky cleared entirely during the night. It was three in the morning when we climbed out of the ice cave. For the first time in more than a week, we took more than 10 steps, and the effort almost caused a breakdown. We felt like patients forced to run a marathon after spending a week in an intensive-care ward. Each of our packs weighed more than 30 kilograms. At the base of the climb we sank into powder up to our hips and burrowed our way to the rock inch by inch. The cards had been remixed, and a brand new game was about to start.

Again, we had to climb all the pitches, put in protection, and fix new lines. But now just two of us had to do the work. That meant we had to shoulder more weight and jumar with heavier loads. On the other hand we experienced every moment more intensely. Although Robert and I had gotten along extremely well the year before, now we seemed to synchronize even better. We were doing the climb in a style both of us considered ideal. Number one, we were adamant about ascending the wall without putting in a single bolt, even if the technical difficulties were extremely demanding. Second, we did not want to share leads with other members of a big team. We were getting frighteningly close to our ideal of modern expedition climbing.

The first three pitches were entirely covered by verglas. So, the following morning, Robert, the great mixed climber, was able to let off steam to his heart's delight with his ice tools and crampons. It was much harder than the year before, but, contrary to our expectations, we made good progress. On the second day we climbed halfway up the lower pillar. That evening, back in the ice cave, we developed a plan that could get us either to the top or into deep trouble. In the next window of good weather we wanted to reach the ledge under the headwall, bivouac there, and climb the following day until we reached the summit—with headlamps, if need be.

Three days later, after a short stormy interlude, we shot up the face like cannonballs. To save time we jumared for two pitches up the tattered shreds of our fixed ropes from the year before, belaying each other for these antics. I was leading one of these pitches, hanging by my ascenders from an old fixed rope, five meters out from my last shaky nut, when I started to race downward, as if somebody had cut the cables of an elevator. When I came to a halt, I was hanging 10 meters lower, frantically clasping the ascenders that were still fixed to the old rope. The sheath had peeled off, and I had whizzed down the core until the compressed sheath jammed in my jumars.

On the northern horizon Cerro Torre and Fitz Roy were holding an impressive glowing contest when we reached the bivouac ledge under the headwall. We had been on our feet for 17 hours. We had traded down jackets and sleeping bags in our packs for more ropes, so we huddled in bivy sacks wearing just rain shells above our clothes, slurping our soup with an angle piton. Suddenly, we noticed two black dots on the glacier below. It was our friends arriving, but unfortunately too late. We exchanged greetings with our flashlights before Robert and I started our extended shivering session.

During the night, clouds started to move in. I began to box against the inside of my bivy bag in the vain hope of warming up. Shortly after 5 a.m. Robert took the vertical stage for the final act. Only three pitches had to be climbed to reach last year's highpoint. This section was so overhanging that we were forced to install fixed ropes, as we wouldn't have had a chance of rappelling it otherwise. Laboriously, Robert aided his way up; it was much too cold for free climbing. More and more clouds arrived, hiding the rising sun.

It took us until 11 to reach untrodden

Glowacz leads the 5.12 sixth pitch in 2004. *Klaus Fengler*

ground. There it was again, this feeling of
discovery, coupled with the hope that this
time we might reach the summit.

I took over the lead, and with every
pitch the wall became a little less steep.
We reached a huge system of cracks and
chimneys, completely frozen in the back.
Almost every nut and Friend placement
had to be painstakingly chopped out of the
ice as a deep black cloud raced toward us.
Immersed in a surrealistic glow, Fitz Roy
and Cerro Torre were swallowed by the
cloudbank. Again, Robert took the sharp
end of the rope, as my free-climbing abili-

Glowacz tucks in for the night midway up Gone with the
Wind, 2005. *Robert Jasper*

ties were powerless against the ice-covered cracks. In our single-mindedness we had lost all
sense of time. We saw the summit plateau almost at touching distance, but we also saw the
threatening storm at our backs. It was growing colder and darker. Snowflakes drifted down as
harbingers of the approaching storm. It was a race against the forces of nature.

At nine in the evening Robert reached the summit plateau. Shreds of clouds whirled
around its edge. We embraced. That was it. In my dreams I had tried to imagine what this
moment would feel like. Every time tears had welled up. But reality was different. For three
years we had been obsessed by this magic line. Perhaps in this moment of success we were
nothing but relieved.

SUMMARY:

AREA: Hielo Continental, Patagonia

ROUTE: First ascent of Gone with the Wind (1,200 meters, 27 pitches, 7c+ A2 M4), north
pillar of Cerro Murallón (2,831 meters), Stefan Glowacz and Robert Jasper, summit
plateau reached November 13, 2005. Glowacz notes: "During our descent in the night we
cleaned the fixed ropes from the upper part. In the lower part it was impossible to clean
the ropes because of the storm. We waited another week to return to the wall to clean the
last 500 meters of fixed ropes, but the weather was horrible for another month. Before
leaving for Estancia Christina, we cached two haul bags of gear and dry food, and our
Argentinean friends will return to Murallón in the fall of 2006 to recover them."

A NOTE ABOUT THE AUTHOR:

*Born in 1965, Stefan Glowacz lives in Garmisch-Partenkirchen in southern Germany. During
the late 1980s and early 1990s he was one of the world's top sport and competition climbers, but
since then he has focused on climbing remote big walls by "fair means," approaching by sea kayak,
sailboat, or by foot.*

Translated from the German by Nico Mailänder.

A LETTER HOME

The first free ascent of Linea di Eleganza, Fitz Roy.

TOPHER DONAHUE

Topher Donahue zigzags on the first day. *Tommy Caldwell*

February 23, 2006

Dear Daddy,

A few days ago, when I scattered a few of your ashes at the base of Fitz Roy, I had no idea we'd be going up for another try. Now we're standing on top after the most outrageous climb of my life. Had I known, I would have scattered you from here. But I guess the way the winds are in Patagonia, you probably beat us here.

It's about 4 p.m. and we've been going almost nonstop for 36 hours. Clouds are rolling over Cerro Torre, and the winds are growing stronger every minute. It's time to get out of here, but I want to linger a moment and share some thoughts with you about the climb we just completed.

I wish you and I had tried to climb Fitz Roy a couple of years earlier. Then I might have stood here with you, rather than with your memory and a few of your ashes on the breeze. Since I couldn't try it with you, I chose to come here with the only climber in the world who knows our family and is also capable of doing the climbs on the east face of this amazing peak: Tommy Caldwell. Earlier on this trip, we had a couple of great adventures trying a famous climb right up the center of the face that a team of Germans decorated with a couple hundred bolts. It is called the Royal Flush, but with its soaking-wet corners the Toilet Flush would have been an equally fitting name. It's ironic that the first-ascent team bolted it for the masses, like a crag in the Alps, but then the Torre gods pour water or ice across the bolts some 364 days a year.

We got tired of the flush factor, so when the last storm broke we decided to check out a drier and slightly longer climb on the same face called Linea di Eleganza. Until today, it had been climbed only once, by an Italian/Argentinean team. They fixed many ropes and spent multiple seasons to reach the summit. Their vision for the line was fantastic, but their housekeeping skills were not. They had a once in a lifetime climbing experience, but then left fixed ropes and equipment strewn across the lower portion of the climb and a couple of haul bags full of trash at their high camp.

For some reason we thought it would be fun to leave all our bivouac gear behind and just climb nonstop for as long as we could go. We invited Erik Roed to join us. At the bottom of the face we were able to step right off the flat glacier onto quality rock. The sun was shining, and we were all having a great time. To go as fast as possible but still experience the peak as a free climb, the leader climbed free and the two seconds quickly ascended the rope.

The rock was excellent, and the pitches went quickly. Awesome cracks and corners appeared, with some exhilarating face climbing in between. To begin with, Tommy and I took the leads and Erik carried the lion's share of the weight. Erik is a good climber, but Tommy and I have much more experience with routefinding during first ascents. For a while, the two climbers at the belay would giggle and make jokes while the leader solved the problems of onsight free climbing. Eventually the sun sank low, the climbing got a lot harder, and everything changed. It was my lead, and I started up an overhanging thin crack on an exposed arête. I began by chimneying behind a 40-foot dagger of rock until I could stand on the very point. From there I jammed a slightly wet crack and cranked on sloping face holds until my strength gave out and I blew a sequence, taking an exciting fall about 1,500 feet above the glacier.

While lowering to the belay, I thought about my chances of quickly dispatching this fierce lead, and then decided to let Tommy have a go. After pulling the rope, Tommy sent it first try. Watching the best granite climber I've ever seen contrive rests with double heel hooks and strain through powerful laybacks while slamming in gear from strenuous positions confirmed my choice to give up the lead.

A few hours later it was dark, no one was having much fun, and I was leading again in the middle of the most demanding five hours I have spent tied into a rope. Lack of gear forced me to traverse out of the original aid line and link up a series of flakes that offered minimal protection and slow climbing. Alone in my little world in the glow of my headlamp, I slowly moved up the wall. Enduring a cold belay, my partners managed to yell happy words of encouragement when I finally clipped into a complicated anchor of five small nuts.

From the belay I peered into the darkness as far as my light would shine. Ice dripped menacingly from the steep corner above. I hoped to stem around this, but after climbing a few body lengths it became apparent I would need to climb the ice as well. I pulled up an ice tool and began to get creative. Chalking with one hand and gastoning a series of flakes, I swung my tool into the thinly iced corner. Without years of experience of old-fashioned mixed climbing on granite, I never could have climbed the pitch. If I hadn't grown up guided by your view of the climbing world, Daddy, and how you saw bad conditions as a new season and new challenge, I simply would have declared the pitch out of condition. Instead, I stemmed around paper-thin smears of ice, switching the tool from hand to hand. Sometimes I would use it to clear rotten ice from the crack to make room for a jam or a cam. I kept free climbing, but the exertion became nauseating. I thought about retreating for boots and crampons, but the rock was too smooth; I often holstered the tool or left it behind for a few moves of insecure granite smearing.

While I was warm and gripped, Erik and Tommy were cold and gripped. I was bombing them with small pieces of ice, and I could hear their boots beating rhythmically against the rock to warm their toes. Nausea from exertion and the massive pump were forcing me to dangle frequently in the wrist leash of my single tool to regain strength, but since I was still free climbing I knew my partners would want me to take whatever time I needed. Finally I reached dry rock at a strenuous, thin hand and finger crack. Sixty feet later, with no gear, no energy, and no hangs, I fixed the ropes and collapsed onto the belay.

One pitch later, Tommy took over the lead, jamming efficiently up a steep crack into the blackness. Erik belayed while I passed out in my harness. Daddy, I have to wonder, did you have any idea all those years ago, when your 5-year-old son would take your climbing equipment and lead circles around your cabin floor, that one day he would be half a mile off a glacier, delirious from fatigue, without bivy gear, at the southern tip of the Americas? Was it more terrifying or exhilarating to watch me gain enough climbing experience to get into such a spectacular and ridiculous position? I wish I could ask you.

Erik and I slowly ascended the ropes to Tommy's anchor. Erik fell asleep, hanging in his harness with his head jammed in an offwidth, his headlamp shining strangely around his still figure. Our only information about the climb was a photo with a line drawing that I had pulled off the Web. We somehow lost that before even touching the rock, so now we were going by feel and the fixed anchors from the first ascent. Tommy ran into blankness 20 feet above the belay. A series of holds ran right, and Tommy tension traversed below us around the corner to see if the next system held promise. It didn't. As he tried to make his way back to our belay, his feet skittered and he came soaring past Erik and me, the rope slapping us, back and forth, until his momentum ceased.

Retreat, or at least some recovery, was mandatory. We rapped to a rounded ledge to rest for the last hour until dawn. For a few minutes we all fell asleep in our harnesses, leaning against each other like three drunks on the back of a motorcycle. Minutes later, we awoke shivering and fired up our stove to melt snow and greet the sunrise with a hot drink. When the sun hit the face and we turned to pull our ropes from our rappel, we all laughed. The ropes hung across the steepest part of the face. In daylight we never would have gone off-route the way we did.

Linea di Eleganza is the first free route up Fitz Roy's east face. The free ascent involved two 5.12 pitches, one pitch rated 5.12 M8, and numerous 5.10 and 5.11 pitches. *Rolando Garibotti*

We headed right on much easier terrain and began a dash for the summit. Clouds rolled across the ice cap, and the wind was increasing. We were a long way from the summit and the descent of the Franco-Argentinean Route on the other side of the mountain. We measured our progress against the massive north pillar; it was slower than we wanted, but we toiled onward. Ice appeared in all the cracks just as the angle of the wall broke. I led a wacky double offwidth choked with beautiful blue ice before handing the lead to Erik for the anchor leg. A few pitches later, Erik tied off a huge boulder on the summit and Tommy and I jugged happily.

Now, standing on top, I wonder what you would have thought of climbing Fitz Roy. I know you would have loved the uncertainty of the weather and the psychology of trying against all odds. You always wished the world had a mountain so big and so difficult that no one could reach its summit. Climbers would merely try hard and go as far as possible with no hope of actually making it to the top. Climbing in Patagonia is a little like that. To succeed on the first free ascent of this face, we had to forget the summit and immerse ourselves in the process. We had to leave behind anything that did not directly fuel our ascent. We forgot about success, and by doing so we succeeded.

Our climb is far from over. We will watch our third sunrise before we reach our tents and the other comforts of base camp. I wish I could have shared this lofty peak with you, but I guess in some ways I did. I am thankful for all the peaks we did share, and certainly without you I never would have been here.

Your son,
Topher

SUMMARY:

AREA: Fitz Roy, Patagonia

ASCENT: Alpine-style first free ascent of the east face of Fitz Roy, via the second ascent of Linea di Eleganza (1,250m, 33 pitches, VI 5.12+ M8, Codo-Fava-Orlandi, 2004); Tommy Caldwell, Topher Donahue, and Erik Roed, February 22-24, 2006. Free attempts on Royal Flush (ED+ 5.12b A1, Albert-Arnold-Gerschel-Richter, 1995) to 23rd pitch, Tommy Caldwell and Topher Donahue; Caldwell led crux pitch 19 free at "probably around 5.12c if dry, but since there was not an inch of dry rock on the pitch it felt more like 5.13 to me."

A NOTE ABOUT THE AUTHOR:

Topher Donahue, 34, lives in Nederland, Colorado, and works as a writer and photographer. He learned to climb as a child in nearby Rocky Mountain National Park, which he considers the best training ground in North America for high-standard rock climbing in alpine regions. His father, Mike Donahue, was the longtime owner of Colorado Mountain School, the guide service in the park. Mike died on November 16, 2005, at the age of 59.

Caldwell (top) and Donahue greet the day. *Topher Donahue*

Twice as Nice

The all-free ascent of two El Capitan routes in a single day.

Tommy Caldwell

Sunday, October 30, 2005

I'm strolling nervously to the base of the Nose with Beth and her dad, who will carry my shoes and empty water bottle back to the car. The night is calm and the stars are out. El Cap shimmers in the moonlight, massive and intimidating. I was in my sleeping bag for only about four hours and slept less than two; logistics and doubts kept playing in my head like a skipping DVD with no stop button. By the time I got out of bed I was frustrated and wondering if I was crazy for thinking I might be able to free climb two El Cap routes in a day. The egg sandwich I fixed for breakfast sits like a lump in my stomach.

1:00 a.m. (pitch 1)

"C'mon, you need to relax!" I feel tense and uneasy, and at this rate I'll run out of energy before sunrise. At the top of the first pitch, I fix the rope and close my eyes.

"Only 64 pitches to go," I laugh to myself. "This is totally ludicrous."

1:15 a.m. (pitch 2)

I'm feeling a little more relaxed. Beth's excitement and encouragement are contagious. At times, just her presence can melt all my worries away and replace them with focused concentration. Two weeks ago, we free climbed the Nose together. It was one of the most amazing experiences of my life, and we probably should have gone straight into retirement. How could we top that? But some flaw in my genes always pushes me forward, creating curiosity and a need to discover what I am capable of. Beth somehow puts up with it; her company has become an addiction, an essential fuel for my existence. Two and a half days after finishing our free ascent, I went back to the Nose and led it all free in around 12 hours. Five days later, I led Free Rider in a day. Now, after another eight days, I'm back again.

2:00 a.m. (pitch 4)

I short-fix on Sickle Ledge and keep going, getting into a rhythm. Climbing is starting to feel effortless, and my confidence is building. I plan to climb pitch by pitch 90 percent of the day, with very little short-fixing or simul-climbing. My tendency is to get caught up in the climbing and not think enough about the dangers. In the past this has led to some long falls and near misses. I want to be with Beth for at least 100 more years, so dangerous tactics don't seem worth it. Besides, the rest at the top of each pitch is a good way to pace myself and keep my heart rate low.

2:30 a.m. (pitch 8)

The Stovelegs have the potential to consume a lot of energy, with wide cracks and continuous climbing. But I'm feeling great. The pitches are flying by, and the calm, quiet night is relaxing. My arms feel no fatigue and my feet no pain. At each belay I close my eyes for a few minutes and take deep breaths. I want this so bad. Doubts have disappeared. My world lies within the small beam of my headlamp, and I am unaware of anything else. In the shadows cast by my lamp, the footholds seem to look a little bigger.

4:00 a.m. (pitch 11)

At Dolt Tower I wake a party of five out of a deep sleep. Their first reaction is to offer me water. I discover that it is Thomas Huber, Ivo Ninov, Ammon McNeely, and a couple of their friends. Thomas hopes to free a variation on the Nose, and the others are there for support and for the ride. I tell them my plan, and they look a little shocked and bewildered. I had told almost no one, not even some of my closest friends, what I was planning to attempt today.

5:30 a.m. (pitch 19)

Pitches continue to fly by. My arms are feeling a little tired but surprisingly good after 2,000 feet of climbing. Even though I'm not thirsty I keep drinking electrolyte mix. Dehydration is the last thing I want. Just a few pitches from the Great Roof, it's still completely dark. I climb slower, hoping to take off my headlamp at the Great Roof. It feels strange to slow down when I still have 4,000 feet of climbing to do by the end of the day.

6:45 a.m. (pitch 21)

Looking up at the Great Roof I feel intimidated. An early-morning breeze chills me to the bone and I'm shivering. I've brought very little clothing, trying to minimize weight. We've got some energy bars and gels, plus a bit of beef jerky and salty nuts; we carry only three liters of water, having cached additional water during our recent ascents. I've got two pairs of shoes: one for the cruxes and a more comfortable pair for everything up to 5.12a. I've brought a single rope, a set and a half of Camalots up to a No. 4, a few stoppers, six draws, six runners, and a few extra biners. Before each pitch I hand any extra gear to Beth, carrying only what is essential to protect the pitch. When we freed the Nose together, Beth led the Great Roof; she has the gear list wired and now she helps me rack the necessary pieces in order.

I methodically slide my fingertips into the crack and tiptoe up ripples in the rock. I feel jittery but try to stay relaxed. Most hard pitches on El Cap are all about precision and foot-work. One sloppy foot placement and you slip. It makes for nerve-wracking climbing. Exertion warms my body and gives me a boost of confidence. I begin shoving my fingertips in the crack as hard as I can. Nearing the end of the roof, I start getting pumped, my body quivers, and I watch my feet slowly creep off the edges. I reach for a sinker fingerlock and pull myself to the end of the pitch, fixing the rope with a big sigh of relief.

9:35 a.m. (pitch 24)

I start up the Glowering Spot pitch feeling more confident. Beth yells encouraging words. I reach for a one-finger pin scar just as both feet slip. I dangle for a moment from a single finger and manage to grab a lower lock with my other hand. "That was close!" I say out loud. My finger goes numb. I scramble to the top of the pitch and compose myself. Beth is there in a few minutes. We sprint up the next pitch to Camp Six.

10:15 a.m. (pitch 26)

Just before the crux moves of the day on the Changing Corners, I wedge my hip in the crack and close my eyes. I can feel my heart racing as I take deep breaths. This pitch takes such precision, such focus, and I'm nervous. My first attempt ends quickly with a foot slip. I lower, pull the rope, and start again from the belay stance. On my next attempt I make it a little higher and slip again. "I better not keep this up," I mutter. Extra time and energy are not in abundance.

12:20 a.m.
Top of
Free Rider

Noon
Top of
the Nose

10:15 p.m.
Two falls
and a flicker
of doubt

10:15 a.m.
Changing
Corners
Pitch

7:30 p.m.
Free Rider
Crux Pitch

6:45 a.m.
Great
Roof

5:30 p.m
Monster
Offwidth

4 a.m.
Dolt
Tower

3:30 p.m.
Heart Ledge

2 a.m.
Sickle
Ledge

1:30 p.m.
Start of
Free Rider

1 a.m.
Start of
The Nose

Chris McNamara

On my next attempt I feel more focused, placing my feet and hands with precision and applying just the right pressure to hold on. Halfway up, I switch from scissoring my feet and legs to hip scumming, then back to scissoring. With calves and forearms burning, I try to place a small nut, but my body tension starts to give out. I throw the sling around my neck, aggressively palm the wall behind me, and smear my foot high on a small edge. The bolt is 10 feet below, around the corner, and I try not to think about the fall. With a high knee-scum, I palm my hand hard and reach for a jug. My fingers latch it securely and I let out a yell.

Noon (top of the Nose)

I scramble to the summit tree, fix the rope, drop the rack, and down a turkey and cheese sandwich that's waiting with a friend. Before Beth is even up to the top, I've pulled on my descent shoes and started running toward the fixed rappels down the East Ledges. I won't see her until I've climbed El Cap again.

1:30 p.m. (start of Free Rider)

Beth's dad picks me up at the Manure Pile parking lot and drives me to El Cap Meadow, where I meet Chris McNamara, my new belayer. I down a bunch of water and another sandwich, and then Chris and I head straight toward the base of Free Rider. I'm feeling a little tired but surprisingly good. Although we had never climbed together, I knew Chris would be great

Tommy Caldwell pauses to warm his hands and psyche up for the Great Roof on the Nose. *Corey Rich*

as a partner. He has climbed El Cap 67 times, and he knows the Big Stone better than anyone. Our systems click immediately. Belay transfers take less than a minute. He jumars so fast I dub him Rocket McNamara, and I have to ask him to slow down occasionally so I can rest a bit more at the belays.

3:30 p.m. (pitch 42)

Already on Heart Ledge. The hottest part of the day starts to wear on me. My feet have swollen and my skin hurts. I curse myself for forgetting Advil. With the pain comes doubt. I start taking off my shoes at each belay and rubbing my toes. Chris distracts me by chatting about home remodeling.

5:30 p.m. (pitch 47)

I start up the 180-foot offwidth called the Monster, probably the most tiring pitch of the climb. I'm not worried about falling—just about puking. I climb as efficiently as possible, but it's hard to finesse arm bars and knee jams.

6:30 p.m. (pitch 51)

A 10-minute breather on El Cap Spire and a Red Bull help me regain a little energy. The sun goes down and my feet

Two views of the famed Changing Corners pitch, the 5.14a crux of the free Nose. Caldwell starts the crux sequence about 20 feet below the protection bolt and eyes the finishing jug about 10 feet past the bolt. *Corey Rich*

instantly feel better. My arms, though, are beginning to feel like lead weights. As I start the next pitch I get pumped shockingly fast. It's a good thing Chris is jumaring so quickly because I'm slowing down and I need all the time I have.

7:30 p.m. (pitch 53)

The crux of Free Rider is only a short, 5.12d boulder problem, but it definitely takes some power. I take some deep breaths and start pulling hard. My stomach is queasy and I struggle for a clear mind. Climbing into the darkness always gives me an uneasy feeling. "What am I doing here?" I think. I compose myself and try to ignore all conscious feelings and just pull hard. My fingertips are now numb and bleeding, along with my right big toe. I inch my way onto a small crimper and tediously reach for a large side-pull; my foot slips and I swing hard into a corner but somehow manage to hold onto the side-pull.

10:15 p.m. (pitch 58)

My eyes jolt open as Chris arrives at the belay. I cannot believe I've fallen asleep hanging in my harness. The night is getting cold, or at least I feel like it is. Goose bumps cover my body, and a chill scampers up my spine. My body may be shutting down from overexertion. I click

Late-afternoon sunlight illuminates Caldwell as he grunts up the Monster Offwidth (5.11) on Free Rider, "the most tiring pitch of the climb." *Corey Rich*

my headlamp on high, slip my shoes over my swollen, red, tender feet, and began stemming up the steep, smooth granite corner. The stars provide just enough light that I can see the base of El Cap 2,500 feet below. I switch to a lieback and continue grunting up the rounded corner. My arms are quivering with pain and fatigue, and as my hand starts to cramp I desperately switch back to stemming. I know that if I fall here it will seriously affect my chances. My feet start to slide and I pull a little harder, but then I'm off.

"Whose idea was it to try and free climb two El Cap routes in a day?" I whimper to Chris.

He lowers me, we pull the rope, and I start up again. The new moon gives little help with finding footholds. I climb as methodically as I can, but keeping a clear mind is a struggle at this point.

Five feet higher, my fingers peel open and I fall again.

"Damn it!" I slap the wall with the pitiful amount of strength I have left. This pitch is 5.12b, much easier than the other cruxes I've faced today, but I'm exhausted. Even though I only have four pitches to go, it seems like miles.

The radio clipped to Chris' harness squawks to life.

"How are you doing down there, Tommy?" Beth says. She's only 300 feet above me at the summit, and just the sound of her voice fills me with adrenaline. "I'm coming for you, baby," I reply.

The truth is, even though I saw her less than 12 hours earlier, I miss her. We started this project together seven weeks ago, and her energy keeps pushing me beyond what I think is possible.

I pull the rope again, tie back in, and start climbing. My mind and body are malfunctioning. I can't figure out which foot to move up, and I'm moving clumsily. I feel like I'm going to puke. But I am so close to completing my goal. I close my eyes, breathe deeply, and summon every ounce of power I can find. I tell my feet to stick like glue. As I reach my high point, determination takes over. I place my hands carefully and stem my feet with precision. I reach the anchor with a nauseous stomach, swollen feet, and yet another big sigh of relief.

12:20 a.m. (top of Free Rider)

I grovel up the last bit of offwidth and stumble to the top, where I collapse on the ground. A small group of friends and my wife are waiting for me. Beth gives me a big hug and fixes the rope for Chris. I feel euphoric but also completely floored. My arms and fingers have fallen asleep. I take some Advil, and within minutes I can feel the blood flowing through my arms once again. I crawl into a sleeping bag and pass out, not able to fully appreciate and understand what I have just accomplished.

After a month I still had not completely recovered. The ends of my toes remained numb, and climbing just hurt. Maybe for the first time in my life I felt a little burnt out, but I also felt a deep sense of contentment. I knew the urge to climb would soon return. I have lived my entire life with it and don't know any other way.

Free climbing two El Cap routes in a day was an idea a friend had mentioned four years earlier, after I freed the Salathé Wall in a day. My first reaction was to laugh at him, and I continued to shrug off the idea for the next two years. But, as my wife and friends know, once the seed is planted I have a hard time letting it go.

SUMMARY:

AREA: El Capitan, Yosemite Valley

ASCENTS: Free ascent of the Nose (VI 5.14a), Tommy Caldwell and Beth Rodden, sharing leads, October 12-14, 2005. One-day free ascents of the Nose, October 17, and Free Rider (VI 5.12d), October 22, Tommy Caldwell. Sub-24-hour free ascent of the Nose and Free Rider, Tommy Caldwell, belayed by Beth Rodden on the Nose and Chris McNamara on Free Rider, October 30-31.

NOTE: In this article, Caldwell numbers the pitches according to guidebook descriptions (31 pitches for the Nose, 34 pitches for Free Rider); during his one-day linkup, he climbed the Nose in 25 pitches and Free Rider in 26 pitches.

A NOTE ABOUT THE AUTHOR:

Tommy Caldwell, 28, lives in Estes Park, Colorado, with his wife, Beth Rodden. He has free climbed eight different routes on El Capitan.

RAINBOW JAMBAIA

The first free ascent of the main Angel Falls wall, Venezuela.

IVAN CALDERÓN

Bedroom with a view: Ben Heason, Miles Gibson, and Anne Arran hang out at camp, about 450 meters up the Angel Falls wall on Auyan Tepui. *John Arran*

In December 2004, after receiving a letter from John Arran inviting me to climb the concave wall of Angel Falls, I grabbed the telephone and began making the contacts necessary to organize a complicated expedition. I had attempted this wall twice before with John and his wife, Anne, but without success, due to logistical errors. This time it would be different, as we were perfectly aware of what lay ahead of us.

In Venezuela, big-wall climbing is not popular. No more than five climbers here are dedicated to the big-wall discipline. However, Angel Falls has become a national symbol for Venezuelans. In school we learned how important the world's highest waterfall was to our country;

our largest denomination bills are stamped with the image. For years I had dreamed of completing the climb.

Angel Falls lies in a region without any services, and even the most minute logistics of an expedition must be carefully thought out. All the necessary gear and supplies must be obtained before leaving Bolivar City, the last place where shopping can be done. Culturally, Venezuelans aren't so punctual, and the famous saying about arriving a half hour late for appointments is true. This complicates expedition logistics, but with patience all will be resolved.

John and Anne arrived March 10 and began finalizing logistics. The following day, the rest of the team—Miles Gibson, Ben Heason, and Alex Klenov—met at my

Black route line: Ruta Directa (1,150m, VI 6b A4, Gálvez-Medinabeitía, 1990). White route line: Rainbow Jambaia (31 pitches, E7 6b, 2005). *John Arran*

small apartment on Caracas' east side. With five climbers and nine haul bags packed with ropes and gear inside, it literally was difficult to walk through the small space. At the market we left people in shock with the huge quantity of food we bought—almost $2,000 worth. This is a fortune for the majority of people in Venezuela.

After the 10-hour bus journey to Bolivar City, we met our final team member, Alfredo Rangel, who lives in the Gran Sabana region. Alfredo is an expert on the tepuis, the flat-topped mountains of the region, and furthermore is an excellent expedition chef. We had to charter flights into the Kamarata region, where Angel Falls is located. The logistics of traveling in small planes (the only option) is a crucial step in the planning process—the weight and size of the luggage is critical. We used three airplanes to transport the entire team and all our gear.

The route from Bolivar City to Kamarata flies over Angel Falls, and this was the first time the majority of the team had observed our objective from the air. The magnitude of the place left a lasting impression. Fifteen minutes later we landed in the Kamarata Valley, home to an indigenous community of approximately 5,000 people belonging to the Kamaracoto ethnic group. Pemon is their language, but the majority of them also speak Spanish. These people played an important role in this expedition because they knew every centimeter of the region.

We contacted Santos, one of the community leaders, to help organize our approach, which would begin with a three-day journey downriver in a *curiara*, a boat the locals carve from a huge tree only found deep in the jungle. It was the end of summer and the river was low, so we would need the local knowledge and manpower to make it through. This route is incredibly beautiful, running along jungles and green savannahs and through dark red water that gives the place a mysterious feeling.

We took advantage of the journey to begin organizing all the logistics of the climb. Our first mishap happened while pushing the canoe through a shallow section of the river. A small crocodile appeared, and Ben, the only one of us with a phobia of these animals, almost stepped on its head in his bare feet. He was back in the boat in less than a second, yelling, "Crocodile! Crocodile!" It was a surprise, as one normally doesn't see crocodiles in this region.

After two nights of camping on the river's shore, we reached Isla Raton (Rat Island), the last point where the *curiara* can travel. That same day we began carrying loads toward base

John Arran launches up pitch 14, which he onsighted at E6 6b. *www.thefreeclimber.com*

camp, two hours away. La Cueva de Los Españoles (Spanish Cave) is a huge, leaning block that provides refuge for three tents. It's not very comfortable, but from there it is just 20 minutes to the base of the wall. The following days were filled with work. Since we were not using porters, we carried all the gear ourselves.

Boatmen from Kamarata. *Anne Arran*

The intensity of the climb became clear right away. Several days of heavy rain had swollen the waterfall, making the outlook bleak for the first two pitches, now wet and extremely slippery. Ben and Miles encountered many difficulties climbing the first 200 meters. Meanwhile, the rest of the team carried all the food and gear to the base of the climb. Ironically, considering the wet early pitches and the enormous waterfall nearby, one of the most complicated aspects of this climb is that not a single drop of water is available on the upper wall. We decided to carry 300 liters. Once all the gear was at the base, we immediately began hauling. Every night, John, as expedition leader, would organize logistics for the following day, and the work was shared evenly. For every two days of climbing, we each did three days of carries.

It took five days to fix the first 300 meters of the route. Alfredo kept us well supplied with food, of which his morning bread was the most appreciated. Once the entire team was on the wall, we organized on three distinct levels, 100 meters apart, and communicated by radio.

Climbing consistently overhanging and poor rock creates a subtle yet ever-present tension. The English climbers were very comfortable with poorly protected and run-out pitches. The ethic was strict: our goal was an all-free ascent and to place no bolts for protection. (We used only two pitons on the route.) We would onsight whatever we could and redpoint what we couldn't, sometimes leaving protection in place.

After three days on the wall, we found a huge ledge above the 11th pitch, where for the first time the entire team could reunite with all the gear. This was a very special night. We had a little party, with a great dinner and Peter Tosh and Bob Marley entertaining us. We were getting close to the most overhanging section of the route, baptized by the Spanish as the Derribos Arias (Demolition Zone) because of the awful rock quality. Alex, Ben, John, and Miles were in charge of figuring out this section, which had numerous pitches of E6 and E7. At least the totally overhanging wall facilitated hauling the bags to Camp 4, located at the beginning of a big roof exiting the wall, where the view was spectacular and the roof provided a respite from the wind and rain.

After 10 days on the wall, the team was working tightly together, each one doing his job solidly and professionally. Confidence reigned and we had totally bonded. All modesty had disappeared, and going to the bathroom had turned into a comedy. Whoever was taking care of his personal business would participate in conversations as if the bad smell was the only issue. Still, there was a lot of uncertainty because the route was so overhanging. Each night when those who had been working on the route returned, our first question was if they could see the top. The answer: two more pitches. This was how the next four days passed. The last section of the route was extremely technical; the rock was broken and the climbing was insecure, and on

Miles Gibson redpoints pitch 27 (E7 6b). *John Arran*

top of this we wanted to climb the route as cleanly as possible. We placed only five bolts on the route, used to anchor the bivouacs.

On the 11th day on the wall we arrived at Camp 5, our last bivy and the most comfortable: a ledge one meter wide and fifteen meters long, big enough to hold the entire team. Alfredo created a celestial sound with his flute, entertaining us as we were relaxing. The energy that exists in this place is indescribable, and in these moments it filled all of us. Still, after 12 nights of bivying without a sleeping bag, I was ready to get to the top. All that was left for food was Ramen, sardines, and water whose quality had degraded considerably. Physically, we all were eroding from the constant work. On the 13th day of living on the wall and the 18th day of climbing, Miles topped out at approximately 2 p.m. When he yelled, "I am at the top!" there were shouts of celebration and laughter from everyone. That night we had another small party, eating huge amounts of food and hydrating as best we could.

The 19th day was a general workday, cleaning the bivouac site and hauling all the loads toward the summit. By 5 p.m. we were all at the top with our gear. After so many years of training and thinking about this wall, this was a very special day for me, and part of my spirit could finally rest. We had a good fire that night, a cave for our bivouac, and even a visit from a coati.

The following morning we linked together all the ropes, totaling approximately 1,100 meters. We tied two huge haul bags to the end, lowered them, and then threw everything off the steep wall to the ground. The haul bags landed 100 meters out from the base of the route, demonstrating its angle.

The summit pose, from left to right: Ben Heason, Miles Gibson, Alex Klenov, Ivan Calderón, Alfredo Rangel, Anne Arran, John Arran. *John Arran*

We descended via an existing route a half hour's walk away: 29 rappels on steep rock and 300 meters in vertical jungle. We then walked another hour back to base camp, where lots of food and two bottles of vodka awaited our celebration. The route is named Rainbow Jambaia in honor of the rainbows that formed every day in the waterfall's mist and the initials of each expedition member's name.

SUMMARY:

Area: Auyan Tepui, Gran Sabana, Venezuela

Route: Rainbow Jambaia (31 pitches, E7 6b): All-free ascent of the Angel Falls wall, following the general line of Ruta Directa (1,150m, VI 6b A4, Gálvez-Medinabeitía, 1990), with many variations and an independent finish for the final eight pitches; Anne and John Arran (U.K.), Ivan Calderón (Ven.), Miles Gibson (U.K.), Ben Heason (U.K.), Alex Klenov (Rus.), and Alfredo Rangel (Ven.), March 18-April 5, 2005.

A NOTE ABOUT THE AUTHOR:

Ivan Javier Calderón Andrade was born in 1972 and started to climb at 16 at La Guarita, near his hometown of Caracas. He learned to climb big walls in Yosemite Valley and has since climbed many Venezuelan tepuis, including half a dozen first ascents, as well as other routes throughout the Andes. He works as guide and hopes to move soon to Monagas with his wife and four-year-old daughter to open a climbing school.

Translated from the Spanish by Molly Loomis.

EAST OF LAKE BAIKAL

Introducing the big granite walls of Transbaikalia, Siberia.

KONSTANTIN BEKETOV

The mountains of the Stanovoi Range are located to the east of Lake Baikal in southeastern Russia. This vast territory, referred to as Transbaikalia, is crossed by the central part of the Baikal-Amur Railroad (BAM). The mountains have an alpine appearance with occasional 1,000-meter walls, the majority of which still remain virgin. Despite their relatively low altitude (reaching a little more than 3,000 meters), the mountains rise as much as 2,000 meters from the valley floors to the summits.

In this article, the Transbaikalia Mountains refer to the southwestern and highest part of the Stanovoi Range. This mountain system stretches for approximately 1,000 kilometers from southwest to northeast; its western part drains to the Lake Baikal basin, while the eastern part drains to the Vitim River.

The continental climate of the region is characterized by sizable seasonal and daily temperature fluctuations. The coldest month is February, with mean daily temperatures below −30°C. The warmest month is July, when the air temperature in the intermountain basins occasionally rises to 30°C to 35°C. The amount of precipitation decreases as you move eastward; the mountains near Lake Baikal are known for their high humidity, and especially intensive precipitation occurs in the Barguzin and Upper Angara ranges. In the mountain basins common in this region, the climate is much drier. The Chara Basin, known as Chara Sands, is the northernmost sandy desert in the world. In winter, the rivers are covered with thick ice, simplifying access to the mountains along river valleys. Waterfalls also freeze, especially in the eastern part of the region, where the climate is more severe.

Transbaikalia is a region of high seismic activity. As a consequence, rockfall is common and spontaneous avalanches are possible in winter. Due to all the tectonic activity, there are many hot springs in the region. The mountain ridges are experiencing uplift, "growing" a few centimeters every year. This is a possible explanation for deviations in altitude estimates on maps of different years.

Another important characteristic of the region is the abundance of bloodsucking insects. Their quantity varies from year to year; in certain years one can observe very few insects. Mainly, this misfortune is concentrated in intermountain basins and in river valleys. High in the mountains, there usually are no mosquitoes or midges.

The mountains described here do not reach the permanent snow line, but the central part of the Kodar Range has several dozen glaciers totaling approximately 20 square kilometers.

The highest point of the Transbaikalia Mountains is considered to be Peak BAM (3,071 meters) in the Kodar Range, followed by Muiski Giant (3,067 meters), located in the South Muiski Range. Ascents to Peak BAM along the easiest route (2B) are made every year, generally in summer; however, only four ascents to Muiski Giant are credibly known, all in summer.

The unclimbed White Wall, South Muiski Range, Stanovoi Mountains. *Konstantin Beketov*

TRANSPORTATION

The main means of transportation is the Baikal-Amur Railroad (BAM). The railway goes along large intermountain basins, crossing the Baikalski, North Muiski, and Kalar ranges. Distances from the railway stations to the mountains average between 10 and 60 kilometers. The largest towns are Severobaikalsk, Novyi Uoyan, Taksimo, and Chara (sta-

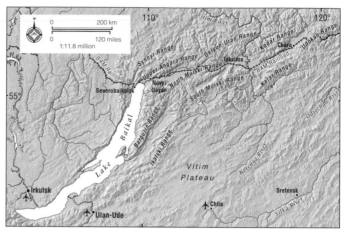

Transbaikalia map by Martin Gamache, Alpine Mapping Guild

tion Novaya Chara). Nijne-Angarsk is connected by air transportation with Irkutsk, and Taksimo and Chara have flights to Chita. In summer there is a motorboat that goes back and forth across Lake Baikal from Irkutsk to Nijne-Angarsk.

In order to get farther into the mountains, one can use various off-road vehicles and helicopters. In winter, heavy loads can be transported deep into the mountains by sledge along frozen rivers. Access to particular mountain areas will be described in more detail below.

UPPER ANGARA RANGE

This range forms one side of the Upper Angara Valley, towering abruptly over a marshy intermountain hollow. The highest peak (2,641 meters) is located in the eastern part of the range. The central part of the range, at the rise of the Asikta River and its tributaries, is the

The seldom-visited peaks of the Upper Angara Range, guarded by numerous canyons and loose rock walls. *Konstantin Beketov*

most interesting; the mountains here are in the form of rock towers with broad walls. The rocks are highly deteriorated, and rockfall caused by seismic movements is not rare. The distinctive feature of these mountains is numerous canyons, the crossing of which demands much time and effort.

The mountains can be reached from a small, unmanned BAM railroad station between Kitchera and Novyi Uoyan stations. The distance does not exceed 20 to 30 kilometers, but the absence of trails makes it difficult. This is possibly the reason for the rarity of visits to these mountains.

To the northwest of the Upper Angara Range lies an isolated massif: Inyaptuk (2,514 meters), the highest point of which apparently has not been reached. (A few attempts are known, including one in winter; all failed to climb the final summit ridge.) The remoteness of this massif—approximately 100 kilometers from the railroad—contributes to a scarcity of information and low popularity.

BARGUZIN RANGE

This range stretches along the eastern shore of Lake Baikal. The area is visited relatively often in summer for hiking and rafting trips; it is considerably less popular in winter. The southern part of the range belongs to the Barguzin reservation, with rather strict visiting rules. The highest point (2,841 meters) is located in the southeastern part; it rises more than 2,300 meters over the Barguzin Basin.

Alpine walls are found in all parts of the range, especially at the headwaters of the Talinga, Alla, and Kabanjya rivers. About 10 climbing routes of high difficulty have been done here.

Access to the mountains is by hiking from the north from the BAM railway or from the south from the villages of Urumkan, Alla, and Ulyukhan, which are connected by a road with Ulan-Ude.

IKATSKI RANGE

These mountains lie to the east of the Barguzin Range, between the Barguzin and Upper Tsypa valleys. At its north end, the Ikatski Range meets the North and South Muiski ranges. The highest point, a nameless summit of 2,574 meters, is located at the origin of the Barguzin River. Nearby is also the highest alpine cluster of the range. The mountains here are composed of skeletal towers, ridges, and rock fingers several hundred meters high. This little-known area has many possibilities for rock climbing routes.

The mountains can be reached from the Barguzin Valley in winter by the Ulyukhan-Kumora road. The closest towns are Ulan-Ude in the south and Novyi Uoyan on the BAM railway in the north. Unfortunately, the road can be used only in winter; in summer, the marshy road and river bed can only be used by hiking or a special off-road vehicle (which can possibly be rented).

In winter, the Ikatski Range is characterized by a more stable climate than the other mountains described above. There is less snow here, and the rivers freeze more often. The best time for winter trips is February and March; for summer trips July through September.

Big peaks of the South Muiski Range, seen from the northeast. *Konstantin Beketov*

Peak Zorro from the upper Bambukoi River. The line marked is the last section of the 1994 route (4A) from Kuanda Pass, led by V. Ryzhii. *Konstantin Beketov*

SOUTH MUISKI RANGE

This range stretches more than 300 kilometers between the Muya Valley on the north and the Tsypa Valley on the south. In the western part of the range, Dorong Peak (2,661 meters), at the origin of the Inamakit River, and the surrounding mountains have some interest. But the main attraction of the South Muiski Range is its highest part in the east, at its junction with the small Mudirikan Range. Here is the second-highest summit of the whole region: 3,067-meter Muiski Giant. (On older maps one might find another name—Spartak Peak—and for a long time its altitude was considered to be approximately 2,700 meters, but later it was discovered to be 350 meters higher.) In the "fork" of the two Bambukoi rivers' sources, Muiski Giant rises for 1,400 meters. There is no easy way to the top; the easiest one (4A-4B) is the route from the north. Muiski Giant has the appearance of a monumental cathedral. Numerous routes are possible.

Base camp can be easily organized at the junction of the Bambukoi's sources, where extensive flat ground is available. From this point, the foot of the mountain can be reached in 1 to 2.5 hours, depending on the route. Heavy rains may flood this camp, however, so base camp can also be organized higher, directly under the flanks of Muiski Giant, on the lower or upper lake in the valley of the Bambukoi's left (northwesterly) source. Here the climate is more severe; there are fewer mosquitoes but no wood for a fire, and even in summer it might snow. From the lower lake, it is convenient to start the interesting routes to the summits of Dvurogaya (meaning "Double Horns") and Imeninik. The upper lake is close at hand to the routes on Peak Zorro. For the routes in the valley of the southwestern Bambukoi source, base camp can be set along Kholodnoe Lake (meaning "cold"), which justifies its name.

The south face of Imeninik ("the person whose birthday it is") on the right, with the 1994 route (2A) led by V. Ryzhii marked. Dvurogaya ("Double Horns") is on the left. *Victor Ryzhii*

Besides the above-mentioned summits, Solovyev Pyramid has intriguing steep sides formed by extensive rock slabs. Also interesting are the northern flanks of Dvurogaya and Imeninik, with 900-meter walls.

Despite its remoteness and difficult access, the South Muiski Range might become a popular area for expeditionary alpinism in the near feature; one will not find such a diverse collection of interesting and new routes anywhere else in Transbaikalia.

The base for access to the Muiski Giant area is the village and BAM railroad station of Taksimo. Here is located the local airport, from which helicopter flights can be organized. Muiski Giant is 50 kilometers from Taksimo. Hiking to the area along the old, often disappearing trail will take three to five days with a load. Especially difficult is the hike along Mudiriskamskit River to the saddle in the dividing range, due to the fact that the altitude difference is almost two kilometers.

The new route Ciao Victor (900m, 33 pitches, TD 5c obl., A. Studnev, M. Studnev, August 2005), on the north face of Muiski Giant. *A. Studnev*

In winter, there is a route passable for off-road vehicles along the Muya Valley, which allows closer access to the mountains. But it should be taken into account that not all rivers of the South Muiski Range are suitable for traveling on ice; one can face several kilometers of loose rocks covered by deep, dry snow. Movement on such surfaces is very tiring and time consuming.

NORTH MUISKI RANGE

This range stretches from its junction with the Ikatski Range in the southwest until the Vitim Valley in the northeast. In its southern part, the North Muiski Range is crossed by the BAM railroad via a 15-kilometer-long mountain tunnel. In general, the area is characterized by little relief; alpine relief can be found at the origins of the Upper Angara and Amnunda rivers, where the highest point of the range (Peak 2,493 meters) also can be found. The mountains can be reached from the railway stations at Angarakan, Tonnelnyi, and Severomuisk. The North Muiski Range is still waiting for explorers; in the 1980s and '90s several ski expeditions were made in the area, and so far these have provided the only available information.

KODAR RANGE

These mountains are among the best known in Transbaikalia because of easy access and a high concentration of interesting objectives. The first difficult ascents here were made as far back as the 1980s.

The range stretches from the southwest to the northeast for about 200 kilometers, to the north of the Chara Basin. Three main parts are distinguished: Western, Central, and Eastern Kodar. The most interesting are the central section and the eastern part of Western Kodar. Here, the mountains have highly broken alpine relief with recent glaciers.

The highest point is BAM Peak (3,071 meters), and several other summits rise above 3,000 meters. Central Kodar is characterized by very complicated orography. The dividing range makes incredible twists and turns, and spurs are often higher than the main ridge. (BAM Peak, in particular, is located on a spur.) Kodar also has very narrow valleys, and the mountains are tightly compressed.

BAM Peak, high point of the Kodar Range, from the north. First climbed in 1963 via its eastern flank, the peak sees several ascents each year. *Konstantin Beketov*

Besides the routes on BAM, climbs have been done on Pioneer Peak (Obrez), Tron Peak (Tzar Tron), Moskva Peak (Polivanova), and Tchitinets Peak. Almost untried are the interesting summits above the Sygykta River Valley, and also the northern spurs of the main range.

Due to the presence of glaciers and high altitude, one can find mixed routes and ice couloirs. The rock is very deteriorated, causing a high danger of unpredictable rockfall due to seismic activity.

Access to the Kodar Mountains is relatively easy. The route starts in Chara (Novaya Chara train station), which can be reached by railway or by airplane from Chita. For access to the mountains, three valleys are used (listed from west to east): Upper Sakukan, Middle Sakukan, and Upsat River. The most popular is the way along the Middle Sakukan, with a forest road passable for off-road vehicles for seven kilometers up the gorge. The winter road along the Upsat River to Lake Nichatka has not been operating for the last 15 years and has become partly overgrown. The way along the Upper Sakukan requires a long hike, but this is the only way to get to BAM Peak without crossing additional mountain passes.

LOGISTICS

Rus' Peak in the Western Kodar Range. First climbed in July 1993 along the ridge from Rus' Pass (2B-3A) by Viktor Ryzhii and Viktor Solov'yev. *Victor Ryzhii*

All climbing in the region is expeditionary. The area is very sparsely inhabited, and for many days you won't see a person or even traces of human life. Such autonomy requires additional attention to safety. Rescue teams are only present in Severobaikalsk and Chara, and their capabilities are rather limited. From the mountains, they can be reached only by satellite telephone or by a very powerful base radio set. As a consequence, rescue help can not be received immediately.

In this context, such factors as experience, sober estimates of one's strength and capabilities, and the necessary equipment for technical climbing as well as surviving in a severe climate are all essential. Compared to other mountains, you might need more reliable camping equipment, additional food reserves, and skills in such things as making Tyrolean traverses, canyoneering, orienteering in the taiga, and so forth. In the Transbaikalia, only the high-altitude factor is absent. In everything else, these are not toylike mountains, and they impose high demands on mountaineers.

A NOTE ABOUT THE AUTHOR:

Born in 1971, Konstantin Beketov lives in St. Petersburg. A former Russian ski-mountaineering champion, he has led exploratory skiing expeditions in remote mountainous areas across Russia.

Henry Pickford provided translation assistance for this story.

CLIMBS AND EXPEDITIONS

2006

Accounts from the various climbs and expeditions of the world are listed geographically. We generally bias from north to south and from west to east within the noted countries, but the priority is on a logical flow from one mountain range to the next. We begin our coverage with the Contiguous United States and move to Alaska in order for the climbs in Alaska's Wrangell Mountains to segue into the St. Elias climbs in Canada.

We encourage all climbers to submit accounts of notable activity, especially long new routes (generally defined as U.S. commitment Grade IV—full-day climbs—or longer). Please submit reports as early as possible (see Submissions Guidelines at www.AmericanAlpineClub.org/AAJ).

For conversions of meters to feet, multiply by 3.28; for feet to meters, multiply by 0.30.

Unless otherwise noted, all reports are from the 2005 calendar year.

NORTH AMERICA
CONTIGUOUS UNITED STATES

Washington

CASCADE RANGE

Summary of activity. [Note: this summary supplements individual reports, mostly of bigger routes, below—Ed.] Mountaineering activity appears to be in slight decline in Washington. In recent years the Park Service has been reporting fewer climbers registering for permits at Mt. Rainier and some of the popular mountaineering destinations in the North Cascades, and climbing clubs are also reporting fewer new members. Meanwhile, growing traffic on Internet discussion boards is facilitating the exchange of information on routes and route conditions, along with pictures, stories, and detailed beta, thus more than ever funneling climbers to specific routes in specific seasons and, in some cases, stimulating new route activity. Also, the Internet publication of John Scurlock's outstanding collection of winter aerial photographs is giving climbers a tantalizing view of possibilities they never would have noticed without being able to peruse prospective new routes from home. This is playing a particularly important part in the selection of "worthy" winter projects in the north and north-central Cascades.

A prominent example of an active bulletin board is found at www.cascadeclimbers.com, and the Scurlock photos are available at www.pbase.com/nolock/root

Sod On Me on Castle Peak. *Mike Layton*

The winter season of 2004-05 had one of the lowest snowfall totals on record, and the resulting relatively easy road and trail access facilitated a lot of climbing activity. In addition to those climbs reported in the 2005 *AAJ*, Peter Hirst and Rolf Larson climbed a new route (III AI3+) left of the north face routes on Mount Buckner in the Cascade Pass area on February 20. They had spotted this line in one of the Scurlock aerial photos.

After near-record moisture in May, the 2005 summer season was fairly normal. However, as happened in 2004, September brought a lot of rain to the Cascades, despite this normally being a reliable month for good weather. In addition to climbs reported individually below, local climbers established many excellent rock routes. Darin Berdinka and Allen Carbert climbed the 2,000' Green Creek Arête (III 5.7) in the Green Creek cirque on the east side of the Twin Sisters Range, south of Mount Baker, on July 1. Berdinka returned with Mike Layton to climb a steep wall to the right on July 21 (Mythic Wall, III 5.10). These routes featured exciting climbing in a gorgeous setting on unique peridotite rock; their Internet reports led subsequent parties into the cirque for further exploration.

Near Lake Chelan, east of the main North Cascades crest, Blake Herrington and Tim Halder climbed the East Ridge (III+ 5.7) of Tupshin Peak on August 9. The ridge is over a mile long, with scrambling and climbing. On September 29 Darin Berdinka and Mike Layton climbed a new route up the northwest buttress of Castle Peak, on the northeast edge of the North Cascades, just a mile-and-a-half south of the Canadian border: Sod On Me (III 5.10+ A2 M4 [M for moss]).

In the Enchantments, near Leavenworth, on July 10 Rolf Larson and Mike Layton established a new route (Thank You Baby Jesus, 5.10) up the 1,500' Boola Boola Buttress. Then, on July 31 on the south face of Enchantment Peak, Dan Cappelini, Larson, and Layton climbed a possible new route (Acid Baby, IV 5.10+), though they found an old nut on pitch two. Their line ascends steep cracks to a slender ridge on a 1,000' tower, found along the approach to Asguard Pass, that blends into the skyline until one is directly beneath it.

On August 23 Peter Hirst and Eric Wehrly climbed a new line (20-Sided Dihedral, IV 5.11 A1) between the Dragonfly route and the Cauthorn-Stoddard variation of the northeast buttress on Dragontail Peak in the Stuart Range.

Closer to Seattle, Mark Hanna and Eric Gamage completed a new route on the first tower of the Tower Route on Big Four Mountain, near Granite Falls, on July 30. Hanna, with Stephen Packard and James Lescantz, had previously completed the largely bolt-protected climbing on the first five pitches, comprising what makes an interesting crag climb on pebble conglomerate

(5.10a). The full climb of the tower was grade III+ 5.10a and distinctly subalpine, perhaps even arboreal in a way that only a Cascades mountain climber can appreciate.

A rare blessing came with the formation of a deep high-pressure cell on President's Day weekend, 2006, and, bolstered by the previous weekend's report of good ice even at low elevations, along with relatively easy travel below timberline, everybody seemed to go climbing. Climbers around the state enjoyed great conditions on a variety of peaks. On the east face of Whitehorse Mountain, near the town of Darrington, on February 19 Peter Hirst and Rolf Larson climbed a line (III/IV AI4) unseen from the road but prominent from the air, which they had targeted after viewing a Scurlock aerial photo. This face had reportedly seen no prior ascents, though rumor of an unreported ascent subsequently appeared on the Internet (presumably a summer ascent).

Internet discussion and Scurlock's aerial photography continue to stimulate not only mountaineering, but a number of exciting ski descents, including formerly unskied lines on Hurry-up Peak, Jack Mountain, Mount Goode, Sinister Peak, Mount Maude, Robinson Mountain, Bonanza Peak, Spider Mountain, Argonaut Peak, Three Fingers, Big Four Mountain, Guye Peak, and Mount Formidable. Nearly all of these descents were directly stimulated by the Scurlock collection. An active bulletin board at www.turns-all-year.com hosts frequent discussion of Northwest ski mountaineering.

For further information about these and other climbs, see the *Northwest Mountaineering Journal* at www.nwmj.org

MATT PERKINS, *Northwest Mountaineering Journal, AAC*

Southeast Mox Peak, Devil's Club to top of east face. The east face of Southeast Mox Peak (a.k.a. Southeast Twin Spire) is something I never expected to climb. The 2,400'-vertical face rises out of mist and clouds deep in the heart of the North Cascades and had an almost legendary status for being unclimbable. Its reputation came from Cascade legends like John Roper, who called it "the greatest face in the North Cascades." North Cascades historian Harry Majors wrote, "The intimidating 2,500'-high east face of Southeast Mox is one of the 'Last Great Problems' of the North Cascades, and should probably remain so. The rock on the Southeast Spire is notoriously unstable and treacherous. … There are routes of great difficulty, which should be climbed only once, and there are routes of such great danger and unfeasibility that they should never be climbed. The central 800' of the east face of the Southeast Twin Spire probably falls into this latter category. The Northwest Spire has already proven to be deadly. The Southeast Spire has an even greater potential." I stumbled upon a description of an earlier attempt on the face: "Each hold required testing—most pulled out like drawers. Pitons could not be solidly placed, and firm projections for runners did not exist—all ledges were piled high with loose rock. It seemed that one had only to locate and pull out the keystone, and the entire mountain would collapse into a heap of smoking rubble. What, we wondered, was holding this precipitous pile of junk together? Every crack you find—and they're pretty scarce—means that something's ready to peel off the mountain." Fred Beckey had made an attempt on the face years earlier, and the experience left him shaken enough to never ever want to go back. Fred told me that it was "a good place for a funeral." Pilot John Scurlock told me that he had flown over just about every peak in the Cascades and admitted that the east face of Southeast Mox was the biggest, most awe-inspiring face he has seen. Scurlock took me on a reconnaissance flight, and when we flew over the gut-churning east face, I knew I had to climb it.

The climb did indeed live up to its reputation, once we got to it. With a 14-hour approach, spread over two brutal days in the rain, and enough bushwhacking to beat the life and every ounce of will to climb out of you, Southeast Mox must be one of the most heavily guarded mountains in the range. We will need years of therapy to deal with the dehumanizing, savage, brutal beating we received. Our path took us in and out of the ice-cold river and the carwash of sopping wet slide alder, devil's club, and blueberry bushes. Things went from shitty to wretched in the forest. It just went on and on and on in an endless valley of tangled vegetation. The forest seemed to mock forward progress and took delight at screwing us over almost every slow and horrid step of the way. I uttered the most violent string of expletives to ever pass my lips, cursing every rock, tree, bush, tree, river, mountain, and valley in this godforsaken hole. Finally, Erik Wolfe and I arrived at the Mox basin, exhausted and unable to see anything in the mist.

Unwilling to accept defeat, the next morning, August 31, we began to climb, and the clouds parted long enough for us to spend two days forcing a line up a face that did not want to be climbed. The leader could not see where the next piece of protection would be on the upper 1,500' overhanging headwall, so every move required total commitment. The climbing spiraled out of control as the run-outs grew longer

The Devil's Club on Southeast Mox, shot on a fly-by during the climbers' (circled) second day on-route. Lifelong Cascade climber John Roper said to Layton afterward: "You tamed the beast!" Layton's reply: "No, the beast tamed us." *John Scurlock*

Mike Layton on the crux pitch of The Devil's Club. *Erik Wolfe*

and the rock became steeper, coming to a climax at a 5.11- X pitch to surmount the final over-hangs. The pressure of forcing a way up, constantly trying to dig for gear, and getting very little, worrying about poor belay anchors, not knowing if I'd totally blank out, and just the whole enormity of the situation almost got to me. I tried to seize control of my mind and calm down before Erik got to the anchors, so he wouldn't see how fucked up I was.

We both pushed and pushed until we were spread to the limit of our physical and mental capacity. It was full-on until the very last pitch. Our route stuck to the right edge of the east face, and I could see the summit up ahead. The rock above was devoid of cracks and solid rock, so we traversed over to the northeast ridge to get a look at our planned descent (over the sum-mit and down the back), then traversed back to the face. It looked like a short scramble to the summit of what's been called "Hardest Mox" [the unclimbed sub-summit atop the east face but before the true summit of Southeast Mox—Ed.] would lead to a heartbreaking full day's climb over ridges and gendarmes to the true summit of Southeast Mox, then an unknown number of rappels into the extremely broken glacier on the backside. One more easy pitch to the Hardest Mox summit, but on sandy blocks of stacked garbage where we wouldn't be able to get a rappel anchor, would have committed us to another full day of trying to get off the peak. John Scurlock told me later that he saw this on his flight and hoped to God that we wouldn't try going that way to get down.

We had to regain control of the situation and get off this mountain. We had completed the east face and were so close to topping out, but we felt that if we summited we would have climbed past the point of no return. So we put a Joker playing card in a plastic bag to mark our ascent (The Devil's Club, 2,400', V+ 5.11-), shook hands, and decided to rappel the entire face, in places staying closer to the northeast ridge than our ascent line did, especially down the lower half. We placed no bolts. I can barely describe how relieved we were when we heard the whump of rope on the talus below. A few hours later, at 3:30 a.m., after wading chest-deep in the river to avoid more punishment from the alder and devil's club, we finally found our camp. We had to retrace the entire approach later that day in order to make the next morning's ferry ride back to our car; we didn't want to be reported late and deal with a rescue cluster. By the time we returned from our adventure, the rains returned and Mox Peak went back into hiding.

MIKE LAYTON, *AAC*

Silver Star Mountain, Central Couloir to near West Summit. Anne Keller and I had both noticed a classic-looking alpine couloir splitting the west face of Silver Star (8,800'), and I couldn't wait for spring. The 1,900-foot-long ribbon of steep snow and gully ice shoots the whole relief of the face and seemed to cut deep into the face at uniform width.

On March 15 we began our day at 6:15 a.m., and the morning started off with demor-alizing post-holing until we gained the bare trail. We finally got to the base at 8:30 a.m. and noticed a flow of water ice marking the couloir entrance. The ice was not climbable, though, so we scrambled around on easy rock and began to simul-climb perfect névé and smears of gully ice. The walls became high around us and the couloirs slightly steeper as we progressed. We came to the first of two mixed cruxes: a large chockstone with steep ice smears pouring off both sides of the rock's interface with the couloir walls. The left side offered rotten ice, but the right side went at fun M4 for a short pitch. The couloir again narrowed and became slightly steeper, and conditions and climbing continued to improve with every step. We looked out to the Cascades, the walls perfectly framing the Liberty Bell group. Before we reached the summit ridge, we met a second chockstone. This crux is shorter, at M3; we climbed it on the left up a small column of ice. Above, Anne stepped off the snow and up the final 125 feet of the line on easy rock, finishing the couloir on the flat slopes a few hundred feet north of the West Peak. We continued south up the ridge and stopped approximately 20 feet below the West Peak summit, where we took a break to grub on a flat bench. Then we descended down the glacier to Burgundy Col and back to the Methow Valley.

MARK ALLEN, *AAC*

The Central Couloir on the west face of Silver Star, showing conditions like those from the March 15 ascent. Only isolated snow patches remained in August during The Washington Pass Traverse, which roughly follows the skyline ridge for its middle third (through the crux climbing of the Wine Spires, the line deviated some to the NE and briefly to the SW). The Vasiliki Ridge is farther left, not shown. *John Scurlock*

The Washington Pass Traverse. At the end of day two, August 25, Mark Allen and I had just completed three-fourths of a traverse that we'd talked about for three years, and we were about to bail and go home. Mark said he had to guide in Mazama the next day, and, regardless, we were out of water. The trip was a series of heartbreaking near-failures anyhow.

The traverse was supposed to be a complete circuit of over 20 high points of the famous Silver Star massif of Washington Pass: the spine-backed ridge of Silver Star, the monoliths of the Wine Spires, and the final continuation of the long, towered Vasiliki Ridge. Although each part of the traverse is on a different mountain, the entire ridge is a continuous four-mile-long knife-edge.

The trip almost ended the first night, when I set my sleeping bag on fire during our below-freezing bivouac. Later that night we ran out of fuel, forcing us to load our camelbacks full of snow to melt against our backs. It almost ended again the next morning, when our morale plummeted after staring down the long rappel off Silver Star that led to the start of the Wine Spires traverse: 1,500 concentrated feet of climbing on four separate towers, with summits only 50-100' apart.

But after beating the odds and getting through what we thought was the worst of two days of solid climbing, carrying minimal packs that looked loaded for a day of cragging rather than a grade VI traverse, we had to go home.

"Yeah, I gotta work Saturday morning, tomorrow. Bummer," Mark said. "Mark, today is Thursday, not Friday," I exclaimed.

Instantly gaining a day, we could yet make the traverse happen. We were still out of water, though, and a tiny trickle draining from the glacier below wouldn't accommodate our bottles. But the whiskey bottle we polished off the night before fit perfectly!

The final day of climbing looked like it would go fairly quickly, but it was just as challenging as the first two days. Constant ridge climbing, tricky routefinding, and a bit of garden-ing on the Vasiliki Ridge led us to the final summit and the end of a long traverse: 26 summits, 28 rappels, 4 miles and 34 hours of climbing, up to 5.9+. We stuck to the ridgeline the whole way, in the process establishing new lines on several of the peaks, including the Direct East Ridge of Silver Star and new routes on Pernod, Chianti, Burgundy, and the Vasiliki Spires.

We called it the Washington Pass Traverse because the ridge is one of the most promi-nent lines you see in the Washington Pass area as you come up over the crest of the North Cascade Highway. This long and uninviting ridge screamed at us to climb it every time we descended to the Methow Valley. Now we can look up and rest, knowing that we finally did it. Vote for Pedro.

Note: the original trip report with photos can be found at www.cascadeclimbers.com

MIKE LAYTON, *AAC*

Northern Pickets Traverse. No matter how content with success a climber gets atop the heights, the compulsion to gaze from one summit to the next goal is irresistible. In 2003 we had just completed my dream traverse over all 14 summits of the indescribable southern Picket Range. Even before the high fives met atop the final summit, my eyes were working out the intricate ridge of incredible summits to the north.

Cascadeclimbers.com introduced me to a character named Josh Kaplan. I could see he had the spirit for the project, based upon his discourse on the site. We planned it over the phone, eventually meeting the day of departure for our first go in 2004. But a whiteout, fog, and rain forced our retreat from the Phantom-Ghost col. I didn't think I would be back for another attempt.

The next July we made our way up Access Creek to our second bivy, at the start of the ridge itself. The view from Luna Col is one the most incredible I have seen. But the weather totally sucked again, and we had only one small fuel canister left for the traverse.

After the east summit of Fury in a whiteout, the commitment zone lay ahead. From here on, climbing would be difficult and treacherous, the descents scarce. After climbing the Furies we started a staggering series of rappels. Severe, difficult leads took us across the ridge, until we rapped into a glacier col after West Fury. We camped on the snow in a wind hollow.

On day four we rejoiced at the clear skies and raced over the remaining small peaks and ridge mazes, reaching the Spectre Plateau and finding the easy way up Swiss Peak. Phantom Peak provided some off-route fun as we went over the "Cub Scout Salute" and back. As high clouds crept in, I said, "All we need for tomorrow is six good hours to finish the climb." We were to get four.

Across Ghost Peak we zoomed together on day five, in a smooth simul. The amazing knife-edge arête of Challenger turned desperately steep and slippery, as rain began to fall. The winds picked up, and the rain briefly turned to ice pellets. Handholds were the only things keeping us up there. With all we had put into it, we simply weren't going to bail. It was as if the great range was making sure we were worthy. We came over the end with not a bang, but a whimper. I could not talk or think. I saw the same look in my partner; we had survived this time. We had pushed our lives into a zone we may deserve to be criticized for. There would be no time for celebrating; we were two days from being dry or warm. Tough-guy Josh had no rain gear, relying on a down jacket. A miserable and long night was in store, but as we reached the valley below, the warmer air brought relief. We began celebrating the biggest thing we could have imagined.

We enjoyed our caches and early departure after six life-changing days. It was truly the greatest of times. We had gone 60+ miles, 10 of them on an alpine crest. We had crossed nine of the most remote peaks out there (VI 5.7 (old school): Luna, East Fury, West Fury, Swiss, Spectre, Phantom, Crooked Thumb, Ghost, and Challenger (and Whatcom on our previous attempt)). The mighty Pickets had been crossed.

With a heavy heart we share this jewel of a wilderness with the masses. May it be our supreme wish that all the wild lands be kept as pure as they can be.

WAYNE WALLACE

Johannesburg Mountain, The CK Route. On August 27, we climbed a new direct line on the 4,600' north face. In 2002 we had retreated after underestimating steep, unprotectable rock sections. The route begins in a vertical cleft with a waterfall, midway between the 1985 Desvoigne-Kloke and the northeast buttress routes. We climbed six pitches of rock, from 4th class to 5.9, to a steep, over-hanging, blank wall. After an hour of scouting we skirted under this to the left to gain a ramp from which Jens led a long, overhang-ing, stemming pitch (5.10b) in

The CK Route on Johannesburg Mountain's north face, shot from across-valley in upper Boston Basin. More than 10 other routes ascend this face. *Loren Campbell*

a chimney next to a prominent eyebrow over-hang, to gain easy slabs below two large ice cliffs. Above the slabs, we soloed three pitches of exposed, unprotectable rock, to 5.7, between two cascading waterfalls, to gain the amphithe-ater rim below the right-hand ice cliff. Shortly after we were out of the way, a large portion of the right-hand ice cliff calved and scoured the pitches we'd just soloed. After 4th class scram-bling along the rim of the amphitheater, we belayed one final rock pitch along a horizontal seam and then downclimbed, to gain the glacier above a seemingly impassable crevasse. Ascend-ing to the head of the unclimbed glacier was technical, requiring many hours of complex navigation while weaving back and forth and

Loren Campbell climbing glacier ice on The CK Route. *Jens Klubberud*

descending into and climbing out of many crevasses. Loren led a pitch of AI3 to pass the final obstacle. A rock ramp gave access to the base of the northeast buttress snow arête. Three simul-climbed pitches of AI2 led to its crest, where we joined the 1951 and 1957 Northeast Rib routes. We reached the summit at dusk and made our descent under headlamp, via the East Ridge route. Just below the Cascade-Johannesburg col, after 22 hours of continuous climbing, we made an open bivouac. Forecast rain held off for 18 hours, and we enjoyed a cold but dry bivy and descent via Doug's Direct. We rate the route V 5.10b AI3. Pictures and a trip report are available at www.cascadeclimber.com/theckroute.htm

LOREN CAMPBELL AND JENS KLUBBERUD

Mt. Index's North Peak (A), Middle Peak (B), and Main Summit (C). From left to right: North Face (Chute-Kaartinen, 1929; first winter ascent, Callis-Davis 1963), Murphy's Law (Miller-Taylor, 2006), EDM/Supercouloir (Nelson-Bebie, 1988). *John Scurlock*

Mt. Index, Murphy's Law. Stuart Taylor and I went in to check out the west face of the North Peak of Mount Index (5,353') on Friday, February 17, 2006. We planned to attempt the unrepeated Eve Dearborn Memorial (EDM)/Supercouloir route. The approach wasn't that bad although the bushwhacking up the lower part of the face was tedious. We soloed the lower gully and bypassed the second ice step by mixed terrain to the far left. From there we simul-climbed the left fork of the couloir, to above where it is split by a small rock spur.

We climbed higher but moved left too early, thinking we were higher on the face than we were, essentially mistaking a lower snow patch for the upper one described in Jim Nelson's guidebook. Call it ineptitude or an inexplicable enthusiasm for steeper terrain.

The route we took leaves the EDM approach couloir and climbs an ice step, before heading up an ice runnel on the left side of the couloir. This leads to a snowfield level with the EDM bivy site (as marked in Nelson). We bivied at the top of the snowfield, below a rock buttress.

It wasn't possible to continue up the runnels, the next pitch being discontinuous sn'ice. Failing upwards, we traversed left about half a ropelength across the snowfield and climbed another ice system on the left side of the buttress. From there the route stays to the right and climbs steep snowfields and ice smears for four pitches. It finishes immediately to the left of the North Peak; another ropelength leads to the summit.

After a brief trip to the summit, to make sure we were descending the right way, we traversed the ridge to the false summit of the North Peak. This required a short but awkward rappel to get across a notch in the ridge. We made it about 200' below the false summit before nightfall, and bivied. The following morning we descended the North Face route, rapping off trees almost the whole way. We used some existing fixed anchors lower on the face. Murphy's Law (V, snow and ice to 80°, steep mixed ground).

ADE MILLER, *Redmond, WA*

Oregon

Oregon, various activity. On Mt. Hood's Illumination Rock, on April 24 Mike Layton and Marcus Donaldson climbed a route that starts to the left of the south chamber on the south face of the southwest ridge. It follows a series of chimneys and crack systems for 800 feet of sustained dry-tooling on andesite rock and rime gargoyles to a point west of the main summit. They believe the line to be new (Bitchin' Camero, M6 AI4), and say it's one of the best mixed lines in the Cascades.

Bitchin' Camero on Illumination Rock. *Mike Layton*

The winter of 2005-06 produced rare cold snaps in December and February, allowing several significant ascents of ice in the Columbia River Gorge outside of Portland. Though the *Journal* rarely reports on ice routes this short, we note these routes for their rare nature and the world-class potential of the Columbia River Gorge as an ice-climbing destination. Granted, the ice hardly ever forms, but we read that climate change might actually make some areas colder, so who knows?

Many routes in the Gorge saw repeats, and in addition to several new single-pitch lines being established, the oft-tried, north-facing Ainsworth Falls (600', WI5) received its first complete ascent on December 16, by Hal Burton and Marcus Donaldson. The next day, Lane Brown and Wayne Wallace established Black Dagger (600', M4 WI5+), located two miles east of Multnomah Falls. The impressive line (some had dubbed it "Black Diamond") has reportedly never connected, and the pair started from the rock on the right.

California

Yosemite Valley, El Capitan, free ascent of the Nose and monster linkup. On October 30-31, in a 23-hour and 23-minute continuous push, Tommy Caldwell freed both the Nose (5.14a) and Free Rider (5.12d). Earlier in October, Caldwell and Beth Rodden swung leads on a free ascent of the Nose. Caldwell then returned and freed the route himself (leading every pitch, becoming the only person to repeat Lynn Hill's much-heralded 1994 feat) in 12 hours. He also hucked a lap on Free Rider before his linkup. For a first-hand account of Caldwell's 6,000-vertical-foot day freeing two El Cap routes, see his story earlier in this *Journal*.

Yosemite Valley, Mama, Flying in the Mountains, Homeworld. On January 9 I experienced the most crushing and empowering day of my life, sitting by my mother's side as she took her last breaths. One of the last things she said to me as we held each other was, "Don't worry, my son, I'll always be with you, flying in the mountains, flying in the mountains, yeah (with a big smile) flying." She was so into my climbing. So much of my love for nature comes directly from her. I always wished she could be with me on so many of my adventures, but the laws of nature didn't allow for that. But these days, with every move I make, and her words echoing in my head, all I have to do is think of her and it's like she's riding on my back. She's everywhere I go.

Anyway, we did a few routes in Yosemite with her in mind. In the Bridalveil Falls area, 150' right of Rattlesnake Buttress and 300' left of Yellow Corner, Jake Jones and I established a new free route called Mama (IV 5.12c), seven pitches and 1,000' high. Wild, steep climbing, like a Thailand route, but trad. Pro from #0 TCU to #6 Friend. Rappel the route.

At Parkline Slab, 300' right of the Cockshead, Robbie Bouchard and I put up a seven-pitch route, 1,000' long, called Flying in the Mountains (IV 5.11a). One hundred feet right of that we established Homeworld (IV 5.10c), nine pitches, also 1,000' long. Both Parkline routes require a set of stoppers and one each from #0 TCU to #3 Camalot; they meet at the last anchor. At Parkline, I led all of both routes, but Robbie freed all the moves on second and worked his butt off. The recommended rap route is Homeworld, which can be descended with a single 60m rope.

Detailed topos should be in Don Reid's new, 2006 book, *Yosemite Free Climbs*. See you in the mountains!

SEAN JONES

SIERRA NEVADA

Balloon Dome, Into the Pit and Netherworld; "Cat Wall," Heaven and Hell. For the longest time I've wanted to do a route on this dome, which lies a few miles upcanyon from the Fuller Buttes. It sits in the San Joaquin River's canyon, dead center of the Sierra, and rises nearly 3,000' from the bottom of the canyon. The canyon is filled with unclimbed walls. The stone is just like Yosemite, nearly as much of it, and nearly as big. The difference is long, steep, trail-

The upper portion of Balloon Dome, with Netherworld taking the left skyline to the summit. *Blair Dixson*

less, bushy approaches. No people and no noise, except the simple things like water, wind, birds, and on occasion a mountain lion. In the fall I decided to finally get in there. I needed a partner who could take a serious beating and keep coming back for more. That would be none other than my friend Jake Jones.

We started from the Squaw Dome trailhead and headed south, cross-country, for three miles downhill (including 1,400' of rappelling) to the canyon bottom. The north face of Balloon Dome, across the canyon, faced us as we dropped into the canyon.

On our first trip in October, we planned to just scope a line up Balloon Dome, deposit huge bags of gear, then return home to stock up for the real push. But it took so much longer to reach the bottom than we expected, with all the bushwhacking and rappels, that we were committed to climbing back out by a new route. We scoped an obvious line up what looked to be a not-so-big wall and started climbing at 4:30 p.m., knowing darkness would be upon us by 7:30. The line goes directly up the center of the largest south-facing wall opposite Balloon Dome, but slightly upstream, thus taking us back toward our approach descent. We named this wall the "Cat Wall." But cracks that looked open from the ground pinched down in places and didn't all connect. Our sweet 5.9 simul-climb and jog to the beer store turned into a thin-at-times, run-out, 1,400' 5.11c. We had no bivy gear, extra food, or other way out, so we had to focus and keep pushing. We managed everything onsight and topped out at 10 p.m. on a moonless night. Wearing shorts and T shirts, with fading headlamps and no extra batteries, we ditched our gear and bushwhacked uphill for four hours, worshipping the car like a god, when we finally found it, and drove home, arriving just before sunrise. We named the route Heaven and Hell. The route name fits the entire canyon.

During the rest of October and November we humped several loads to our base camp and pushed what I believe is the first line from the bottom of the canyon to the summit of Balloon Dome. A forested section splits the upper dome from the wall below, and a few routes exist on the upper dome. (You can approach the upper dome by a 12-mile hike from the Cassidy trailhead in the Oakhurst area, without having to descend to the river.) Fred Beckey, of course, was the first to climb the upper dome. What we did was more like two separate routes, linked during our final push.

Our line on the 2,000' lower wall, Into the Pit (V 5.11d), ascends an obvious line of cracks leading to an obvious, left-angling dike. The dike leads straight to the most amazing, splitter, right-facing corner on the whole lower wall. More straight-up cracks, then some 4th class, lead to the upper dome. Our line on the upper wall, Netherworld (1,100', 5.11c), could be accessed by the 12-mile hike (i.e., without starting from the valley bottom). It ascends our left skyline view as we approached from the opposite side of the canyon.

Whether climbing our line or any future line from the river to the summit, one should plan on a grade VI wall. As for the logistics of getting the gear and yourselves to and from the wall, plan on that being more work than the wall.

SEAN JONES

Angel Wings, Right Wing. Chris LaBounty and I made the first ascent of the Right Wing (IV 5.10d) on Angel Wings on July 15. This route ascends the striking arête to the right (east) of the South Arête. We approached from the start of the South Arête, by making a 35m rappel from bolts into the gully below. In 100m 3rd and 4th class becomes easy 5th. Three 5.10 pitches and four easier pitches lead to the top of the arête. After reaching the stacked rocks atop the arête, make a 60m easy 5th class traverse west, toward the South Arête. Make a 30m rappel into the gully from a chickenhead and head north for 100m of 4th class to a notch. Continue north for 60m on a 4th class orange band into another notch. Make a 30m rappel off two fixed nuts onto the backside of Angel Wings. From here hike east, almost toward the summit of Cherubim Dome, descend the summit ridge, and follow the gully toward Upper Hamilton Lake; you will meet the High Sierra Trail.

BRANDON THAU

Palisade Traverse in a day. Gravity takes hold of my legs, and I stumble. My lungs still bursting, I see a flash and suddenly my father, dead seven years, turns into Norman Clyde on a bergschrund slide and screams, "Here I go to Hell!" Piss runs down my leg.

Squirming between reality and dreams, I pull myself from the nightmare and open my eyes to a full moon shining in my face. A rumble to the north brings my attention to a storm over Mammoth.

Rough trade, this mountaineering gig, I mutter to myself. Only seven hours in and the adventure has taken its toll on my body and mind....

California is unique in that one can ski and surf in the same afternoon, the weather almost always perfect in both climes. For me, it is the perfect place to raise a family while exorcising the demon shakes. When friends took me to these mountains, I rediscovered my childhood joy of wandering for days without the intrusion of another, while, as a climber, I understood that going up is the easy part of the battle. The mountaineers, the true climbers, of which I am not one, would recount tales of horrific approaches and descents, while the deaths reported occurred during the complacent periods. It is a Zen-like realm where awareness of one's surroundings dictates life and death. For me, it is nirvana. The mountains of California, Mecca. And in this Mecca lies a grand jewel: the Palisade Traverse, eight miles long, 26 peaks, six over 14,000'.

In July 1979 John Fischer and Jerry Adams made the first traverse of the Palisades, in seven days after spending a week caching supplies. In June 2004, after a week of caching supplies, Scott McCook and Adam Penney made the second ascent, in 12 days. The rock varies from perfect granite to jigsaw death to sandy scree. One can climb in a T-shirt and jeans while straddling blue ice, only to become embroiled in a storm worthy of Everest minutes later if caught unprepared. It is the stuff of nightmares and dreams. And during one glorious day last August I laughed, cried, and dry-heaved my way into a level of climbing that awaits those willing to sacrifice everything for the ultimate beauty of life. It was truly a grand adventure.

Strictly the facts: Palisade Traverse (VI 5.9), third ascent, in 22 hours. No supplies cached along the way. I started on August 18, 7:00 p.m., at Southfork Pass (12,560'), traversed the ridgeline, and finished on August 19, 5:00 p.m., at Bishop Pass (11,960'). By 10:00 p.m. I was back to Glacier Notch below Mt. Sill.

MICHAEL REARDON

Sierra and Yosemite, various activity. Climbing.com reported that Dave Turner soloed a new route, Block Party (VI 5.9 A4), on the southeast face of El Capitan. He fixed ropes for three days and spent 18 days on the wall, finishing June 21. The route shares parts of Tempest and

Mt. Marcus Baker (13,176') from the northwest, showing Sanctuary Ridge (Smith-Turner, 2005). The Knik Glacier route (Hoeman-Tschaffert, 1966) reaches the pre-summit plateau (solid line) from the southwest, then finishes left of SR up the summit pyramid. The Matanuska Glacier route (Bright-Dyhrenfurth-Gabriel-Washburn, 1938) approaches from the northeast, climbs over the ca 12,800' point on left, and roughly finishes along the left skyline. *Gordon Smith*

for a gentle line to the summit, but found the gentle ice slope broken by steps of up to 70°. One could probably ascend left and climb névé or ice no steeper than 40°.

We descended the route, reaching camp after a 17-hour round-trip. Our total time from Talkeetna, including a reconnaissance day on the northwest ridge, was less than four days, making this a quick, moderate route to the summit. In addition the climbing was enjoyable and safe from objective hazards.

GORDON SMITH AND ALASDAIR TURNER, *Seattle Mountain Rescue*

Pt. 6,000' of Mt. Yukla, The History of Things to Come, and The Positive Side of Negative Thinking. After many failed attempts, with several partners, I finally got up two new routes this winter, 2006, on the northwest face of Mount Yukla (7,535'). I approached both routes from Icicle Creek, and both top out on the 6,000' subpeak that's approximately 0.75 mile northeast of Yukla's summit.

From the toe of the Icicle Glacier there are three obvious ice/mixed lines on the far left side of the face that feed from a hanging glacier. In the last week of January, Josh Varney and I climbed a steep, narrow chimney that starts right above the toe of the glacier. We third-classed about 700' of steep snow and ice, to WI3, to where the three lines separate. From here a ramp system heads out left, a snow and ice couloir goes right, and a narrow chimney goes straight up. We climbed six pitches up the thin ice/mixed chimney, making one bivy. Once above the chimney we crossed the hanging glacier and traversed left to the summit of the 6,000' subpeak. We descended the Northeast Ridge route and headed down the glacier back to our high camp. We named the route The History of Things to Come (2,800', V M7 WI5 A1). The warmest it got on the route was -20°F.

In the third week of February I hiked back in alone (Josh had broken his arm snow machining). After a night at the boulder bivy, I hiked up the left side of the valley and crossed the glacier between the two major icefalls heading for the base of a large ice-filled couloir. The couloir consisted of 1,200' of excellent waterfall ice before reaching the base of the hanging glacier. I climbed up the left side of the hanging glacier and finished with a short, easy mixed pitch that topped out on the subpeak. I descended the Northeast Ridge route. It's one of the best routes I've done. I called it The Positive Side of Negative Thinking (1,800', IV WI4+).

In last year's *Journal* I reported the route that Dan Petrus and I did as being the northeast couloir and the second ascent. In fact, it faces northwest and was probably the third or fourth ascent. I also called Little Cub "Little Bear" by mistake.

JOHN KELLEY

Mt. Yukla's northwest face. (1) The History of Things to Come (Kelley-Varney, 2006) on Pt. 6,000'. (2) Northwest Couloir. Note that this angle seriously distorts the relative distances between the glacier, Pt. 6,000', and the main summit of Yukla (upper right, 7,535'). *Josh Varney*

ALASKA WRANGELL MOUNTAINS

Peaks 10,320' and 9,110', possible first ascents. On May 14 Cory Hinds, James Dietzmann, and I drove from Anchorage to Chitina to meet Kelly Bay of Wrangell Mountain Air. After being flown in, we hiked west along the Chitina Glacier to reach a camp at 2,600' near the Ram Glacier's terminal moraine. Two hard days later, we reached base camp at 5,650', near a western fork of the main glacier.

At 5:00 a.m. on May 19 we headed off for reconnaissance. We turned our attention to a 10,320' peak, on the north side of the

Peak 10,320'. The route takes the skyline ridge, from right to left, to the summit. *Danny Kost*

glacier, with two nice lines on the south face. A thin couloir broke right of the summit and a broader snow ramp farther right led to a saddle about a mile east of the summit. We opted to try the snow ramp, since it might offer safer avalanche conditions because of rock outcrops.

The bottom of the 30-35° snow ramp was littered with avalanche debris, and we postholed through the debris on snowshoes. A few hundred feet below the crest we donned crampons. The ridge was exposed, with a mixture of broken rock and knife-edge snow and the occasional cornice. There was a 30' tower of loose and broken rock midway along the ridge. Once over the tower, we traversed a corniced ridge to the base of the summit pyramid and belayed a couple of pitches. We crossed a narrow notch, broke through a small cornice, and continued up a short mixed section to a rock outcropthat afforded a belay. We unroped for the final slopes. Exposed traversing and another short mixed section led to the final icy traverse and, finally, we reached the summit and enjoyed awesome views. Mountains everywhere.

Before long we were back in camp looking back up at the summit—our recon turned out to be 15½ hours and over 5,000' of elevation gain.

The weather then turned and kept us in camp for a couple of days, and on May 22 we started down. We struggled back down the rock-covered glacier onto solid ground, and the next day finished the hike to Hubert's Landing and set up camp on the huge gravel plain near the airstrip.

From this camp, on May 24, Cory and James got a 3:00 a.m. start to try Pk. 9,110'. James turned around at 7,950', but Cory kept going and summited via the south-southwest ridge and face. Hubert's sits at around 2,150', so it was a 7,000' elevation gain from camp. On their descent, they surprised a large boar grizzly that had sprawled out across a tiny knoll to sleep the afternoon away. They said he looked up a couple times, but paid them no attention. They said he looked like a big dog stretched out snoozing the day away.

On May 25 Kelly was right on time to pick us up. He got us all on one flight, and we enjoyed sightseeing on our flight back to civilization. It is possible that our climbs of Peaks 10,320' and 9,110' were both first ascents of the peaks.

DANNY KOST, *AAC*

ALASKA SAINT ELIAS MOUNTAINS

Note: Climbs of Mts. Alverstone and Cook, border peaks between Alaska and the Yukon (Canada), are covered in the Canada section of this Journal.

ALASKA COAST MOUNTAINS

Mt. Boullard, Foster-Ricci. Mt. Boullard, a relatively benign-looking peak bordering both the Juneau Ice Field and the terminus of the Mendenhall Glacier to the east, rises abruptly from just above sea level to its 4,200' summit. Unusually good ice conditions in January proved just adequate enough for Nick Foster and me to get up a rarely formed line I have been looking at for several years. We started up the left of two promising ice formations on Boullard's southwest face. We began by simul-climbing for several hundred feet, with ice up to 80°. The steep ice eventually gave way to lower-angle snow, before steepening again. The middle of the route was characterized by brittle, rolling, and ever-thinning 60-80° ice covering compact and poor-quality rock. For lack of a belay, we were forced to simul-climb through the crux section, which, being generally off-vertical save the odd move here and there, was not particularly strenuous, yet insecure and hard to protect. The final 1,000' to the ridge consisted of perfect 50-70° styrofoam, with gear every so often among the rocks, which we quickly shot up in the setting sun. We climbed the face in five long pitches, taking nine hours, and walked off, taking 15 hours car-to-car. 3,000', IV+ 5.7R/X 85°.

On March 19 Nick Foster, Will Wacker, and I completed the second winter ascent of the Main Tower of the Mendenhall Towers (possibly the second winter ascent of any of the seven towers) by the standard route (IV AI4). The first winter ascent, by John Svenson and company, took place more than 25 years ago. Our ascent took 13 hours round-trip from the south branch of the Mendenhall Glacier.

STEFAN RICCI

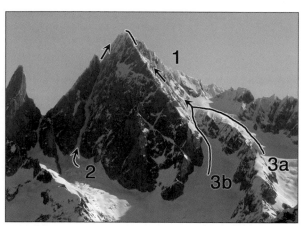

Mt. Burkett (9,730') from the southwest. (1) Southeast Ridge (Bryan-Harthill-Liddle-Thompson, 1965). (2) Golden Gully (Bearzi-Klose, 1980). (3a) South Face (Cauthorn-Collum, 1994). (3b) South Face (Hoyt, 2005). The prominent spire on the left is Burkett Needle. *Zac Hoyt*

Mt. Burkett, South Face, solo. After waiting in town for three weeks of unsettled spring weather, Leo Smith (Paines Ford, New Zealand) and I (Petersburg, Alaska) flew via helicopter on April 23 to the Baird Glacier below the southwest face of Mt. Burkett (9,730'). The moon was full, the weather unseasonably warm with little to no wind, and the forecast for extended good weather. After much scrutiny from both the helicopter and spotting scope, we determined that only the south face was in condition. The three-plus weeks of unsettled weather had left the upper reaches of the mountain heavily rimed, and with warming conditions the southwest face and Golden Gully (Bearzi-Klose, 1980) had great objective hazards. I left camp at 22:30 with a bivy sac, 40m of rope, and two days' worth of food and fuel. The snow was soft and the going slow for the first 400m. Near 00:00 on April 24 the temperature dropped, conditions improved, and climbing was superb, with the full moon lighting the south face until sunrise. The climbing remained moderate until the final 200m, where the face grew steeper. Gaining access to the southeast ridge was challenging, and finally I left my pack and dug a small tunnel through the rime. The rime allowed for fast travel over the exposed ridge, below the south summit to the middle summit (which was believed to be the highest; however, the south summit may be higher). Using the 40m rope, I fixed the exposed and rimed summit pitch for the descent and reached the summit at 6:30 a.m. Once off the ridge and reunited with the pack, I called Leo at base camp via VHF and enjoyed views of the northwest face of the Devil's Thumb and Cat's Ears, along with a breakfast of smoked salmon and Snicker bars, before making a rapid descent by the ascent route. I made six 20m rappels along the summit ridge and upper headwall. I down-climbed the remainder of the route, except for two raps over 'schrunds on the mountain's lower reaches. I returned to camp extremely exhausted at 12:00 p.m., before the mountain shed its skin that afternoon. Difficulty AI3, Alaska Grade 4.

On the afternoon of the 26th Leo and I put up five new routes on Burkett's Boulder (15m), a large erratic on the lateral moraine closest to Mt. Burkett, from grade 14-22. The next two days consisted of skiing south-facing slopes, eating, and sun bathing, before we were whisked back to Petersburg on April 27.

ZAC HOYT

Editor's note: Upon entering the concave south face (sometimes called southeast), Hoyt's line generally follows the 1994 Cauthorn-Collum route. Hoyt's climb was the first solo of Burkett, and the peak's fifth ascent overall.

Devil's Thumb, first winter ascent and epic, solo. On March 11 Zac Hoyt had an early breakfast at his home in Petersburg and helicoptered to base camp below the southeast face of the Devil's Thumb (9,077'). Immediately he soloed the Krakauer route, calling me on his sat phone from the summit before lunch. Afterward he started on the three-day ski to tidewater, and his luck changed. While negotiating an icefall, he fell 100 feet into a crevasse, deeply injuring a shoulder and bloodying a hand.

The climb had gone quickly in calm, sunny skies, at 0°F, but the crevasse incident happened during a vicious, unpredicted storm, with 70 mph winds and temps of minus 24°F.

Zac spent the night in the 2½' wide crevasse on a false floor, alternately shoveling out the tent and warming himself. The amount of spindrift pouring in was suffocating at times. His fingers became frostbitten. In the morning he climbed out of the crevasse with just one axe and crampons; he says it was the hardest climbing he's ever done. Standing there in the raging tempest, he called me again.

"Hey Dieter, it's Zac!" "Zac, where are you?" "In the middle of the icefall." "How's it going?" "Not so good." Then the phone went dead. I initiated a rescue.

Zac rappelled back into the crevasse and packed only the very essential items. After a grueling ascent of the free hanging rope with a Tibloc and a prussik, he had an exhausting episode hauling the pack up and over the lip of the crevasse. He managed to set-up the tent. Using snow that had remained in the tent, he brewed tepid water mixed with blood, hair, and detritus. "It was really gross, but it went down just fine," he said.

He soon heard our helicopter (they invited me on board), a Coast Guard Jayhawk, and called in on his VHF radio. He couldn't see us, nor could we see him. He said he couldn't get his frozen boots on with frozen fingers. I hung out the open door, since the windows were too frosted to see thru. Finally, after 20 minutes of harrowing flying I spotted his half-buried tent. It took two tries to get to him, with the chopper operating fully at its margins. The flight crew displayed extraordinary heroism, saying, "We pushed ourselves to our maximum limits." The pilot radioed Zac: "This is a one shot deal. If you can't get your boots on, forget them." They lowered the basket, and he got in with socks on. Immediately after the basket became airborne, a gust of wind blew the helicopter sideways. The basket slammed into the side of a serac, almost ejecting Zac. A minute later he was on board, saying, "Hey! What's up?"

He is expected to make a full recovery from his injuries. Zac left about $4,800 worth of gear on and in the glacier. I am accepting bids for the Booty Trip. Winner gets the GPS coordinates.

DIETER KLOSE, *Stikine Icecap Manager*

Canada

ST. ELIAS RANGE

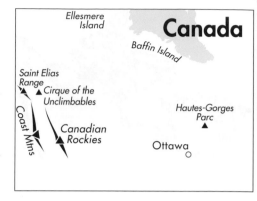

Kluane National Park Reserve, mountaineering summary and statistics. During the 2005 climbing season 86 persons participated in 29 mountaineering expeditions, accounting for 1,535 person-days in the icefields of Kluane National Park.

As usual most expeditions were concentrated in the Mt. Logan area, with 17 parties attempting various routes on the mountain. Twelve expeditions attempted the King Trench route, while five attempted the East Ridge route. The mountain allowed only four expeditions to successfully reach either the main or east summit, with weather and time being the main obstacles. A huge storm, with over a meter of snow, and then extreme winds stranded climbing groups on the summit plateau during the latter part of May. A number of people came back with a new respect for the forces of nature in the St. Elias Ranges.

Other mountains that witnessed climbing this year were Mt. Vancouver (twice), Mt. Kennedy, Mt. Hubbard, Mt. Alverstone, Mt. Wood, Mt. McArthur, Mt. Badham, Mt. Queen Mary, Mt. Saskatchewan, and the Donjek Ranges. There were four ski-touring-specific expeditions into the icefields. Ski-touring is a wonderful lower-risk option for experiencing the Icefield Ranges of Kluane National Park.

Of note this year was the first ascent of the west face of Mt. Alverstone, by a pair of British climbers (one from the now-famous *Touching the Void* book and movie). Also, an American crew scaled a new route on the north face of Mt. McArthur. A couple of Czech climbers scaled Mt. Logan by the East Ridge route to the main peak, traversed the summit plateau, and descended the King Trench route, all in 11 days. A crew of skiers did a north-south traverse of the icefields from Kluane Lake to Yakutat, AK, and another couple of Swiss mountaineers/kayakers did a 41-day unsupported west-east traverse of the icefields from Cordova, AK, to the Alsek River and Dry Bay, AK. The latter crew failed to register for their trip and were dealt with accordingly by park officials. (Registration is mandatory for all overnight activity in Kluane National Park.)

One major search-and-rescue operation occurred during the climbing season. A group of climbers on Mt. Logan's summit plateau lost much of their camp gear in a fierce storm. They were forced to huddle in a small snow hole and were saved from certain death when other members of their party were able to reach them and render assistance. Satellite phones carried by both groups allowed this to take place. The three men were evacuated from their location near Prospector Col (5,500m) by an international rescue operation consisting of personnel of the U.S. National Guard and Wrangell-St. Elias, Denali, and Kluane national parks. A high-altitude helicopter brought from Denali National Park facilitated the highly technical heli-sling operation. The three men suffered severe frostbite and have subsequently spent much time in hospitals.

On a sad note, a young Canadian woman was killed in an avalanche/fall on the East Ridge of Mt. Logan. The young woman had five years earlier been the youngest person to successfully climb Mt. Logan and was climbing it for her third time when the accident occurred.

Mountaineering in the Icefield Ranges of Kluane National Park is an inherently danger-ous activity but with proper preparation and planning, most groups have positive experiences and return with memories that last a lifetime.

Anyone interested in mountaineering in Kluane National Park should contact:

Mountaineering Warden, Kluane National Park, Box 5495, Haines Jct. Yukon, Y0B 1L0, CANADA. Phone 867 634 7279; Fax 867 634 7277; e-mail Kluane_info@pch.gc.ca and ask for the "mountaineering package"; or visit the Parks Canada web site: http: www.pc.gc.ca/kluane

RICK STALEY, *Mountaineering Warden, Kluane National Park*

South Walsh, attempt. Our flight in was delayed for five days due to poor weather, and we left three days early due to the high probability of further poor flying conditions. Paul Geddes, Willa Haraysm, Dave McCormick, Ted Rosen, and I were on the Donjek Glacier from June 16-26. Iso-thermic snow provided many opportunities for post-holing, and very warm afternoons resulted in rock and serac falls and running water, which persisted through the night. We made a route on the northwest side of the lower icefall in order to reach the main hidden cirque. The cirque appeared to provide access to the col lying below Pt. 4,050m. However, at the 3,400-3,600m ele-vation there is a complex crevasse system traversing the entire cirque, immediately below the shelf leading to the col. This was as far as we reached. On June 21 Geddes and Haraysm climbed Pt. 3,450m (GR544590) in order to view the upper part of the proposed route. South Walsh (4,223m), if considered an independent summit, is the highest unclimbed peak in North Ameri-ca—see *CAJ* vol. 75, 1992, p.8, for more information. [Just as we went to press, we received word that Paul Knott and Graham Rowbotham climbed South Walsh, summiting on May 28, 2006, via the southwest ridge and upper south face. Details will appear in the 2007 *AAJ*—Ed.]

ROGER WALLIS, *Toronto Section, Alpine Club of Canada, AAC*

Skiing on the Donjek Glacier, with South Walsh in upper left. The line shows the upper portions of the peak's May 28, 2006, first ascent, which will be reported in the 2007 AAJ. *Roger Wallis*

Donjek Glacier, first ascents. On June 1 Jonathon Wakefield and I flew into the Donjek Glacier, where we made first ascents of eight peaks around the East Donjek Glacier, a spur off the head of the main Donjek. Geoff Hornby and I had researched the area for our 2002 expedition, but circumstances beyond our control prevented our accessing the correct area. We had researched American, Canadian, and British alpine journals and believe the peaks still unclimbed prior to our 2005 visit. Named peaks included Donjek 3, 4, and 5. Others peaks were identified by spot heights.

On June 2 we climbed Peak 3,390m via the south face, finding generally uniform 45° steepness, with snow on hard glacier ice. Our route took a rightward-rising line to a small col between the main and lesser summit. At the col we turned west along the easy ridge to the summit. The round-trip took five hours.

After several days of heavy snow, on June 6 we climbed the north face and glacier to the col between Donjek 3 (3,650m) and Donjek 4 (3,700m), and climbed both peaks. We arrived back in camp after 11 hours' climbing.

On June 8, via the southwest ridge that falls from the summit, we climbed Peak 3,480m, taking 8 hours 40 minutes round-trip.

The next day we climbed Peak 3,330m via the southeast ridge, weaving between outcrops and finding climbing up to 55° and 60°. Eight hours after leaving, we returned to camp.

We then moved camp closer to Donjek 5 (3,610m) and on June 12 climbed it via the west face and north ridge. A small couloir, breaking through the lower rock bands, linked the lower and upper faces and offered climbing to 55° to gain the foot of the widening main upper face. Six and a half pitches, most at 50° but rising to over 60° near the top, took us to the main ridge, a knife-edge rising to the summit, which we climbed in five short pitches. Steep faces dropped off on three sides from the pinnacle-like summit of what was the crown jewel of our trip. Ten hours round-trip.

Heavy snow dumped the next day, but in a four-hour trip from camp on June 14, we ascended Peak 3,390m via the east face and south ridge, with easy climbing, never steeper than 40°.

The following day we climbed Peak 3,560m. The lower east face led to a higher ridge, which led directly to the summit. From the foot of the face, we made a diagonal ascent up 50° slopes to the foot of a rock buttress. We followed the base of the rock diagonally left for two pitches, turned the buttress, and climbed diagonally right to the buttress top (and the base of the steepening ridge) in another two pitches. Two more pitches along a sharp 55° ridge took us to the summit, and we returned to camp after a five-hour round-trip.

All our climbing was on snow and/or ice. What little rock we encountered was poor, broken, and generally worth avoiding. We used snowshoes on all glacier work and the approach to each route. We were able to snowshoe all the way to a high point on the col between Donjeks 3 and 4 before changing to crampons. On all other routes we changed to crampons on the glacier at the foot of the route. We descended our lines of ascent.

We thank the Mount Everest Foundation and The British Mountaineering Council for their great help and support of this expedition.

GLENN WILKS, *U.K.*

South Donjek Peaks, various ascents. Although thwarted in our attempts on Pt. 4,223m, Paul Geddes, Willa Haraysm, Dave McCormick, Ted Rosen, and I did climb some of the South Donjek Peaks (1:50,000 topo sheets 115C/16, 115B/13):

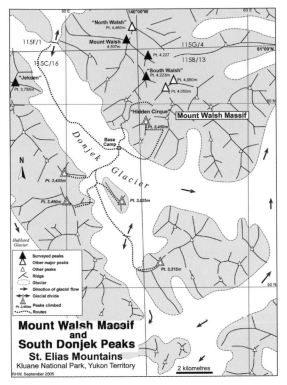

**Mount Walsh Massif
and
South Donjek Peaks
St. Elias Mountains**
Kluane National Park, Yukon Territory
RHW, September 2005
2 kilometres

Pt. 3,433m (GR499562) via east ridge, June 18, 1st ascent, PG, WH, DM, TR

Pt. 3,450m (GR 501547) via east ridge, June 23, 1st ascent, PG, WH, DM, TR, RW

Pt. 3,315m (GR552513), via west-southwest ridge, June 25, 1st ascent, PG, WH, TR, RW

Pt. 3,025m (GR531546) via northwest ridge, June 19, 2nd ascent, PG, WH, DM, TR; and June 23, 3rd ascent, PG, TR, RW. First ascent was by Helmut Microys (solo) in July, 1967, when he and his two companions skied out from Mt. Steele to the Slims River bridge on the Alaska Highway (*CAJ 1968*).

ROGER WALLIS, *Toronto Section,
Alpine Club of Canada, AAC*

Kaskawulsh/Hubbard divide area, various ascents. After waiting five days for suitable weather to fly, Andy Williams put Jean Boyd, Cathryn and Nigel Wallis, and I down on July 1 at a superb "photo opportunity" location 10½ km north of Mt. Queen Mary: the Kaskawulsh/Hubbard divide area, north of Mt. Queen Mary (1:50,000 topo sheet 115B/12). Excellent weather allowed fabulous views of virtually the entire St. Elias Mountains. Yakutat's helpful weather-forecasting service let us know that the next deep low was fast approaching from the Gulf of Alaska, so we climbed and flew out while we could. We climbed the following peaks:

Pts. 2,915m (GR 692313) and 2,890m (GR 679315), July 3, by traversing the ridge crest. We located no previous cairns, so we presumed ours were first ascents.

Pt. 3,000m (GR713347) "Family Peak," July 4, via a steep snow/ice line up the northwest ridge from the col between our peak and a subpeak lying to the northwest. Then traverse the kilometer-long summit ridge over numerous subsummits. Finding no cairn, we presume ours to be a first ascent.

We ascended Pt. 2,941m (surveyed height; GR670332) on July 5, via the east-northeast ridge. We found a cairn on the summit, but no written record.

ROGER WALLIS, *Toronto Section, Alpine Club of Canada, AAC*

Dak Tower, Flowers for Blaise, and Mt. McArthur, Some Kind of Monster. Between spells of consistently bad weather, Joe Josephson (Bozeman, MT) and David Dornian (Calgary, AB) climbed two new routes in the Mt. Logan area between May 29 and June 3. On Dak Tower, they established Flowers for Blaise (4,500') in a 27-hour round-trip from camp. After two days' rest, they took 38 hours from camp to climb the 6,000'-vertical north face of Mt. McArthur, their *Some Kind of Monster* offering sustained calves-of-steel ice the entire way. See Josephson's feature article in this *Journal*.

Various first descents and possible first ascents. Inspired by our friend Nevada Christianson and her quest to solo Mt. Logan's East Ridge, Trevor Hunt and I found ourselves wandering the giant glaciers of Kluane Reserve like ski safari nomads. On May 6 the three of us flew in with Andy Williams to the Hubbard Glacier. After skiing a steep warm-up run on the lower east ridge of Hubsew Peak, we left Nevada to her bold task and headed south down the Hubbard toward Mt. Vancouver, the most striking ski-objective visible from our plane ride.

Neither Trevor nor I had been to the St. Elias before, so except for the topo map this was an on-sight mission. As we reached the confluence of Mt. Vancouver's north glacier with the flats of the Hubbard Glacier, we gained a view and the realization that there was a skiable route up the base of Vancouver's north ridge and into the upper northwest face of the North Summit's formidable pyramid. As the sun began to drop and the temperatures cool, we crossed the low-angled terrain, exposed to the seracasaurus, and started up the ridge into the pseudo-darkness of the Yukon night.

We were feeling the dramatic altitude gain, and the summit kept looming far above this never-ending 40° face. Finally, around 4:20 p.m., we reached the North Summit (4,812m; 15,783'), in awe of our 360-degree view. Just as we began to ski, sharp winds from the south tubed us with the chalky spray of our turns, and it felt as if we were being hustled off the mountain. The windswept upper face was real "mountain skiing" conditions. On the mid-level ice tongue the snow had warmed up nicely, and we dropped in on the steeper, undulating north

The line of ascent and descent on the 10,000'-vertical north ridge of Mt. Vancouver. *Ptor Spricenieks*

aspects of the lower ridge and slashed backlit afternoon turns in preserved powder. Back on the flats of the Hubbard Glacier at 1,680m (5,510'), we had completed an uninterrupted 3,132m (10,273') run. Another couple of hours in the sunset touring back to the camp made it a 30-hour round trip. I watched the northern lights, took off stinky boots, and fell asleep.

Trevor Hunt on the lower third of the Mt. Vancouver descent. *Ptor Spricenieks*

After four restful days, tent-bound while it snowed, we moved base camp to an unnamed peak (which we called "Nice Peak") on the ridgeline between the Hubbard and Seward Glaciers, just south of the pass between the two. Its 400m north face had good snow and enticing steepness.

For the remainder of our time, we focused on the north ridge of McArthur Peak. With time running out we broke camp at the first sign of clearing and wound our way up through the McArthur-Lombard col onto the Logan Glacier, inspired by the fresh snow. The full moon was a day away and was accompanied by cooler temperatures and high pressure. For the evening session we hustled up a nice 2,500' northwest-facing couloir on a close-by unnamed peak (located on the next ridge northwest of Lombard Peak's north summit) to scope out McArthur and ski some sunset steeps.

After a three-mile approach paralleling the daunting northern flank of McArthur, our rapid progress skinning up its lower ridge and boot-packing the steeper sections was finally slowed by a 100' ice and rock gully (WI3 M3). I led the pitch and set an anchor for a rappel, gaining us access to the upper glacial plateau, covered in sweet, boot-deep powder. Above, McArthur's main summit loomed impressively but was unskiable, while the east summit was rather inviting. The sun was already on the horizon by the time we topped out at 14,130'. We watched as cold blue shadows mixed with the last splashes of pink and orange on the summits of Logan and St. Elias, and then pushed off in the chilly arctic powder making big, long turns into the pale night.

Back at camp on the Logan Glacier, 6,600 vertical feet later, our nap was interrupted by a thundering avalanche from McArthur that crossed our approach track. A raven appeared for the first time as well. It was time to go. That evening Nevada appeared from the misty clouds and hanging ice madness, and we were overjoyed to be reunited safely. She had made it to the top of the East Ridge, at the first ice plateau high on Mt. Logan, where she placed a special peace vase.

After six months of research, I think that all of our descents were premieres. Our ascent route on Vancouver may have been a new variation to the North Ridge (in the upper portion, where we went direct up the northwest face), and the ascents of "Nice Peak" and the peak near Lombard may have been firsts as well.

By lunchtime on the 25th we were flying high above the Kluane Reserve, riding the winds from the approaching storm. Kluane Lake had melted, and the trees were now green. A lone moose waded through the river, as Andy banked the plane around for final approach to the dirt runway in Silver City. We walked around stunned for the first bit, trying to assimilate the transformations we had experienced by exposing ourselves to Kluane for 20 days. While getting water at the adjacent Arctic Institute, I met university geology students who were inquisitive about my "vacation," which only reminded me of why I was in these mountains in the first place.

PTOR SPRICENIEKS, *Canada*

Mt. Cook, first ski descent and probable third ascent. On May 5 Paul Swanstrom of Haines (Alaska Mountain Flying and Travel) flew Peter Linn, Andrew McGarry, Kiajsa Krieger, Scott Morely, and I from Yakutat to a landing zone on the upper Seward Glacier. We were dropped at about 7,000', near the Canadian border, under the southeast arm of Mt. Vancouver, with the aim of skiing Mt. Cook. Although the pilot reported that the previous week had been unseasonably warm, and huge runnels prevented us from landing closer to Mt. Cook, a short tour on the first day unveiled soft conditions on the northern aspects. Better yet the view from camp showed a near perfect and likely continuous run down Mt. Cook.

Incredulous that we were indeed in the St. Elias Range, and that indeed we were not yet "digging for our lives," we packed up and launched on the second day. We threw our stuff together planning on several nights at the base of the route, and maybe a couple of nights on the mountain.

"Tobey, you threw that gallon of gas on your sled right?" "I thought you had it?" "Shit! I hope the weather holds."

So we started up the next morning with barely enough fuel for two nights on the mountain, and one back at the base—*if* we ate mostly dry food and didn't boil our water. No storming allowed!

After dashing under a couple of seracs, we ducked into the scant shelter of our chosen rib and started booting up the route, over ever-steepening undulations, to beneath a severely overhung serac. We detoured left and over two short ice bulges. One long ascending traverse brought us to the pass at the head of the North Fork of the Turner Glacier. The following day we skinned and booted, weaving around gaping cracks, and traversed all the way around the north side of the mountain, finally gaining access to the summit pyramid via the northwest aspect. After slamming a couple of golf balls off the summit, we clicked in and schussed back to camp.

With our egos inflated from the ease of skiing on the top half of the mountain, we underestimated the severity of the lower half. With us carrying our bivy, the initial slope from the pass proved to be absolutely puckering and twice as steep as we remembered. However, perfect wind-buffed soft snow saved us from certain death as we sketched across the traverse. Two 20' rappels got us around the ice bulges and another 2,000' of severely steep skiing got us around the 'shrund and back to our lower camp.

Our route of appears to be the descent route of the second ascent party (*AAJ 2000*, pp. 219-220).

TOBEY CARMAN

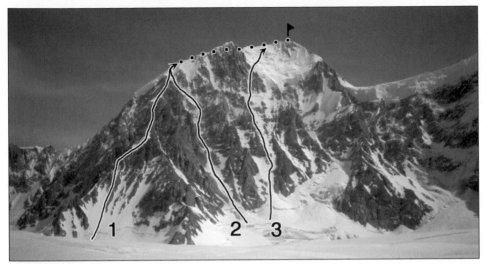

Mt. Alverstone's 6,000' west face: (1) Diedrich-Pilling (1995). (2) Blanchard-Wilford (1998, to summit ridge). (3) Schweizer-Yates (2005). *Paul Schweizer*

Mt. Alverstone, west face. In early May Simon Yates and I climbed a new route on the 6,000' west face of Mt. Alverstone (14,565'/4,439m). We knew very little about the mountain, except that the west face was huge, and apparently only two routes had been done on it. A couple of inspiring aerial photographs kindly supplied by Mick Fowler tipped the scales. Alverstone is a border peak, and the west face [At least its lower portion—Ed.] technically belongs to Alaska. However, we flew in from Kluane Lake, on the Yukon side. After being dropped off on a high lobe of the Alverstone Glacier by ski plane on May 5, we set up base camp, then made an initial reconnaissance of the approach and studied the massive wall for plausible new lines. The prominent west buttress to the left side of the face had been climbed in 1995 (Diedrich-Pilling), and the main gully system to its right in 1998 (Blanchard-Wilford, to summit ridge). Both these routes intersect the final ridge/glacier fairly far from the actual summit. On the right-hand boundary of the main west face we spied a classic unclimbed couloir that lead almost directly to the top of the massif—definitely the route to do.

On the evening of May 7 we left base camp with four days' food and fuel and bivied below the face. We started climbing early the next morning in perfect weather, soloing up good névé and trying to gain as much height as possible before the sun hit the upper rock towers, and projectiles began to launch. At one point, about 2,500' up, the couloir narrowed, and Simon was walloped on the forearm and shoulder by several falling stones. This resulted in a swollen, badly bruised arm, but thankfully nothing more serious. The sun was now out, the plush névé was turning into bare ice, and a well-fatal drop yawned below, so we decided to pull out the ropes and start pitching. An alarming number of rocks continued to whiz past in the hot sunshine. Late in the day we excavated a tent platform in a snow bank atop a mini-icefall, about 4,000' up the route. From our bivy site we could look out over the blue Pacific and watch the sunset.

Due to general sloth and the need to rehydrate, we got less than an alpine start on the second day of climbing. But seven pitches of good 55-60° ice eventually led to a col in the summit ridge. We dumped our sacks at the col and reached the summit on the evening of May 9, again in perfect weather. After descending back to the col and bivying, we took another two days to return to base camp on the Alverstone Glacier. Our route, while not particularly technically difficult, was long, serious, and committing, with a complex descent [their descent included downclimbing north to "The Great Shelf" and onto the Dusty Glacier, then west to a fork of the Hubbard Glacier and a miserable climb up a long ridge to regain the Alverstone Glacier and their camp]. We reckon it warrants an overall alpine grade of TD+.

PAUL SCHWEIZER, *Alpine Club*

Paul Schweizer about 4,000' up Mt. Alverstone, at the start of day two, with Mts. Vancouver (L) and Logan (R) in the distance. *Simon Yates*

LOGAN MOUNTAINS

Terrace Tower, Brent's Hammer. On Terrace Tower in the Cirque of the Unclimbables in July, A. Mawson, D. Lavigne, and J. Lavigne established a steep route on the southeast face. Their route, Brent's Hammer (200m, 5.11+), climbs mostly hand cracks and is approached by scrambling left up the ledges toward the loose gully below the face. The first pitch begins after you head up and right 5m into the gully, climbing an arching, right-facing corner. The initial four pitches range from 5.10- to 5.10+, with the final two being 5.11+. The line receives plenty of sun and reportedly remains dry when other climbs in the area are wet. Descend via fixed rappels. Bring triples of hands- and small hands-sized cams. A 4" or 5" piece can be helpful on the final pitch.

COMPILED WITH INFORMATION FROM GEORGE BELL'S EXCELLENT
CIRQUE CIRQUE WEBSITE: HTTP://WWW.GEOCITIES.COM/GIBELL.GEO/CIRQUE/

COAST MOUNTAINS

Coast Mountains, remote areas summary. Craig McGee, Sean Easton, and Eamonn Walsh spent time on the south side of Waddington late in July. Their major accomplishment was an outstanding new ice route (Uber Groove, 600m, ED1 ice to 90°) well left of the Haberl-Reid. The line is under the Epaulet Glacier, but the seracs, while vertical, looked stable, and there was no debris below, so the climbers were "somewhat at ease." They climbed nine 60m pitches of water ice, the first being the crux at WI5X, then consistent WI5 and WI4, easing to WI3, and a 5.9+ pitch to the serac bands (they skirted right under the seracs). Craig reports that Eamonn and Sean (ice gods, for sure) called it their best pure water ice climb ever.

The crew then got about 80% of the way up the rock headwall on the prominent south buttress of the Northwest Summit, but some looseness, lack of compelling climbing features, cold, and finally a developing snowstorm put an end to the attempt.

The threesome then flipped over to the Tiedemann, where they made the coveted (and oft attempted) first ascent of the Grand Cappuccino, via the southwest buttress (Morgenlatte, 450m, ED1 5.11). The first four pitches were 5.8, then the buttress steepened, and the next six pitches finished with a 5.11 crux on the final pitch. Craig says "Great line, awesome position and climbing."

Jia Condon and Jon Walsh got scooped on the Cappuccino, but did a 200m direct variation on the South Ridge of Serra 2, climbing directly up the crest from the Phantom Tower col. This gave six or seven pitches to 5.10. The upper section of the crest had been rappelled, then reclimbed, on an abortive Grand Cap attempt by Janez Ales and Graham Rowbotham in 2003.

Condon and Walsh then went onto the South Buttress of Tiedemann with no bivy gear, starting at 2 a.m., intent on a speed ascent. They had a "sit" above the second tower the next night for four hours, having freed all the climbing to that point (FFA? 5.10+/11-). They then finished via a major new variation, up the snow/ice/mixed gully left of the upper Direct South Buttress. They topped out about 30 hours after starting and got the majority of the long complicated descent done, down through the Chaos Glacier cirque, then up and over Combatant to the Waddington-Combatant col, before getting stymied by isothermal snow and impassable crevasses on the final slope down into the Tiedemann Glacier. Late in the day, with the weather breaking down a day earlier than forecast, they plugged back up to the col and over to the west shoulder of Hickson, from which Mike King was able to chopper them out. The boys were lucky: the following two and a half days saw six *feet* of snow dumped on an American Alpine Institute party high on Waddington! Woulda been mighty unpleasant to bivy.

Simon Richardson returned from Aberdeen for another Coast Mountains adventure, this year with Mark Robson, and they climbed a new route on Mt. Zeus in the Pantheon Range (25km north of Waddington). See report below.

Steve Harng, Jordan Peters, and Ben Stanton spent a week climbing among the peaks at the head of Sunrise Glacier in the northeastern Waddington Range. They made several smallish ascents, but their "class" outing was the eight-pitch South Buttress on Isolation Peak #2 (250m D 5.9). This was reported as "beautiful and obvious… a fantastic climb."

Sergio Aragon, David Rangel, Peter Renz, and Mickey Schurr spent a week doing Waddington Range "light classics" out of a camp at Cataract Col. Of note, they climbed a prominent tower on the eastern rim of the Mt. Shand horseshoe, above and northwest of the Four Horsemen. This they named "Knudson Knob" to commemorate David Knudson, the prolific and long-time Coast Range mountaineer, who died in Seattle on July 22. Dave's first trip into these mountains was organized by the legendary Joe and Joan Firey, into Combatant Col in 1972. Until failing health curtailed his activity in the last few years, many other outings followed, often into little-explored far-flung corners where intriguing discoveries and first ascents lurked; there are 25 attributions including Mr. Knudson out of 444 numbered routes in *The Waddington Guide*, for instance. The high-quality photographs that he brought back, and enthusiastically shared with all who asked, will remain an important legacy.

Chris Barner, Paul Rydeen, and friends returned to the steep peaks near Doran Creek, climbing numerous summits, around 2,600m high, surrounding the head of the first major south-side feeder drainage. A few summits sported ancient John Clarke registers; some were likely virgin. Later the crew moved north to the Reliance area, again making numerous ascents. The best of these was the Southeast Ridge (550m, D 5.9 A1 or 5.10+) on Determination. This fine route required a few aid points on a 5.9 pitch low down, climbed with mandatory boots and full alpine gear in the packs, as there is snow on the upper sections.

Bruce Fairley and Harold Redekop knocked off the big, steep, imposing, and long-ignored East Face (750m, D+ 5.8) on the superb Mt. Queen Bess. Snow and ice for 350m led to 10 pitches of rock, mostly mid-5th to 5.6, with three pitches of 5.8. They climbed the face in a day, bivouacking during the rappels, which they did via the route of ascent.

Andrew Rennie and I flew to Bifrost Pass on the northern fringe of the Waddington Range and climbed new routes on all three of the surrounding 2,800m+ peaks. The West Ridge (400m, AD 5.10) of Delusion mostly consisted of scrambling on nice, featured, solid rock, with three belayed pitches on the obvious steps, at 5.8 and 5.9, with a finishing 10m steep right-facing 5.9 corner leading to a short, harder bulge. The prominent southeast buttress on the east tower of Frontier proved to be an attractive line (Miles from Ordinary, 300m, D 5.10+). About 150m of scrambling was followed by seven or eight roped pitches, with a fair amount of 5.8, a few 20m stretches of easy ground, a couple of 5.9 sections, and one full-on, pull-like-hell, left-leaning crux crack past a bulge. The looming headwall went surprisingly easily, despite appearances, with good 5.9 face-climbing low down, then a left-angling crack system through solid rock to the flats beneath the previously unclimbed 2,800m+ subsummit. A severe two-and-a-half-day storm interrupted proceedings, after which we attempted one of the fine 250m pillars on the west side of Cornelia. Various difficulties quickly brought the attempt to an end, but we reached the summit by a west-facing snow/ice gully and the upper north ridge (250m, AD+ mid-5th). We passed over the northern subsidiary summit (ca. 2,900m; also previously unclimbed) en route.

DON SERL, *Alpine Club of Canada, AAC*

Southwest British Columbia (southern Coast Mountains and Canadian Cascades) summary. The most notable event of 2005 was not a single ascent but rather an unusual winter. Bitter cold in early January was followed by a short rainy season and then two months of unseasonably warm, sunny weather in February and March. While dealing a crushing blow to local skiers, the thin January snowpack, once it consolidated, provided near-perfect conditions for winter alpine ascents, enabling an unprecedented tally of routes in the local mountains, including the following first ascents and/or first winter ascents.

In the Coquihalla alpine zone in March, Wayne Wallace and Lane Brown of Oregon made the first winter ascent of the popular Yak Check link-up on Yak Peak, a summer line that checks in at 12 pitches and 5.9. The first portion of the route follows the diagonal groove of Yak Crack (D III 5.9), while the upper half moves left to climb the finish of Reality Check (D III 5.10c) above that route's crux. Several years ago Yak Crack saw a winter ascent, featuring thin ice, powder snow, and runout dry-tooling on somewhat crumbly granite slabs. What was unusual about Wallace and Brown's ascent of Yak Check was the summery conditions encountered. They had only intermittent verglas, snow patches, and wet rock to deal with, far different from the true winter conditions of the earlier ascent, despite both climbs having been done during calendar winter.

In the Mt. Rexford area Andrew Rennie made the first winter ascent, solo, of the North Ridge route (summer AD+ III 5.8) of North Nesakwatch Spire. Most of the route consisted of rock climbing, with snowy ledges, but the crux chimney pitch was iced and required dry-tooling.

As knowledge of the excellent alpine conditions spread over the Internet, more disgruntled ice climbers and skiers ventured out into the hills. Attention turned to the Cheam Range, a popular winter climbing area with a couple of well-known unclimbed objectives. Don Serl and Andrew Rennie made the first ascent of the north face (III/IV D+) of Welch Peak, via a system of interconnected snow ramps and mixed steps with WI3 ice, with serious runouts and sparse belays. On the same day, Jesse Mason and Toby Froschauer climbed the northeast ridge (III D 5.8 WI3) of Foley Peak, featuring a mix of snow, ice, and mixed ground as well.

In early March, I found firm névé and a 40m water ice pitch while making the first ascent of the east face of Mt. Outram, via a 400m gully line (III AD+ WI3 60°) that tops out between Outram's two summits. There are numerous other potential gully lines on this broad face; the approach via Ghost Pass trail from Highway 3 takes about five hours.

Once the unusual winter conditions normalized with the return of spring rains, a lull ensued that lasted until May and the next period of good weather. On Needle Peak, above the Coquihalla Highway, Merran Fahlman and I set out to repeat the 1972 Douglas-Starr route on the southeast buttress, a route with an obscure history (Fred Douglas, credited in the guidebook as a member of the first ascent party, does not believe he ever climbed the route) and sandbag grade (the guidebook mentions a bit of 5.6-5.7, but recent ascents found sustained 5.9). However, we never actually climbed the Douglas-Starr route, instead following a parallel line of corners and cracks about 70m right of the buttress crest on the northeast face. Wet cracks, extensive vegetation, loose rock, and even a small hanging snowpatch avalanche combined to make our route somewhat less than classic (III 5.9 A0). Don Serl and Andrew Rennie found better conditions on the north ridge of Mt. Roach, near the Stein River, where they found much scrambling, to about 5.7, on the lower ridge, leading to three 30m-40m pitches to 5.9 at the top (D- III 5.9). They were accompanied to the base of the route through the forest by a dog from the local Native reserve, who was rewarded with half the sausage supply for chasing off bears three times.

In the Slesse area, Shaun Neufeld and I climbed a new route on the east face of Labour Day Summit in midsummer. The climb begins at the base of the northeast face and climbs slab and snowpatches to the notch behind the obvious gendarme. From there it crosses the existing (2003) route and climbs steep cracks on the upper pillar to the summit (D III 5.10d).

Big news from the Powell River area over the summer was the completion of Call of the Granite, in the Eldred Valley, by Aaron Black and Sean Easton [see report below]. A DVD called "No Permanent Address" is now available which documents the climb and Aaron's seven-month road trip in preparation for it.

On Mt. Ossa in the Tantalus Range, Don Serl and Andrew Rennie climbed a direct route up the north face that they dubbed Reaction Time (D+ IV 5.10-). The route begins off the north glacier with a difficult 'schrund crossing and climbs up the shadowed face above on generally good rock. They completed the route in 15 hours round-trip from camp, with a day to approach and a third day to walk out.

Few new routes were reported in the fall, owing to an infestation of wasps in the forest. Some climbers were stung up to 36 times while bushwhacking to the base of a route near

Chilliwack Lake. One much talked about face that did finally get climbed was the north face of Grant Peak, which gave Tyler Linn and Nick Elson a long 5.7 (AD+/D- III) on good rock. Climbers had been eyeing the face for years, but it took a local—Linn from the nearby town of Hope—to work out the best approach to the relatively remote face, which is guarded by massive thickets of slide alder in the valley below.

DREW BRAYSHAW, *Canada, AAC*

Athena Tower (A) and the main (Z) and west (W) summits of Mt. Zeus: (1) Northwest Face (de Saussure-Firey-Knudson-Renz-Rose-Schurr, 1980) of Zeus. (2) East Buttress of Athena (Collum-Pilling, 1983). (3) 2005 attempt on Athena. (4) Northwest Ridge of Zeus (Richardson-Robson, 2005). *Simon Richardson*

Mt. Zeus, Northwest Ridge. The many rock towers and pinnacles in the Pantheon Range often get overlooked in favor of the better-known peaks around Mt. Waddington, just south. The Pantheons have seen only a handful of visits from technical climbers. Mt. Zeus (2,959m) is the second highest peak in the group. It comprises solid granite and dominates the central part of the range.

Mark Robson and I visited Zeus to attempt the striking 500m-high northwest pillar of Athena Tower on the north side of the mountain. Athena Tower was first climbed by Bill Pilling and Greg Collum via the East Buttress in 1983, but had seen no further ascents. Unfortunately, our attempt ground to a halt at one-third height, when we encountered an almost featureless 50m-high wall. With no cracks for aid or protection, we were forced to retreat.

Instead, we turned our attention to the 2km-long northwest ridge of Zeus. We left base camp on the Zeus-Pegasus col early on the morning of August 7, crossed the glacier, and front-pointed up a short snow slope to the foot of the ridge. The route followed corners and chimneys, interspersed by smoother slabs (5.7 to 5.8), and although the climbing was technically not too testing, the rock was loose in places and covered in black lichen. Once we reached the narrow ridge leading up to the West Summit, the quality of the rock improved, and the climbing became increasingly exposed. The crest was clear of snow, and we were able to continue in our rock shoes, even though steep, mixed icy faces fell away just below. When we reached the unclimbed West Summit, we saw the Waddington group for the first time, gleaming white with fresh snow.

The character of the ridge changed abruptly at this point, as it widened to a 1m-wide gangway of perfectly flat rock, which led over a series of subsummits toward a snowy col. The continuation ridge above the col was deceptively difficult, narrowing to a series of steep towers. Fortunately they were bathed in the setting sun, and we climbed a series of absorbing pitches, some up to 5.9, to reach the summit slopes just as night fell. We bivouacked in a hollow of boulders approximately where the Northwest Face route (de Saussure-Firey-Knudson-Renz-Rose-Schurr, 1980) reaches the summit slopes.

We talked, dozed, joked and shivered our way through the night, and were away at first light up boulder fields and snow. We arrived on the summit at 6 a.m. on August 8. It was a magical morning with the surrounding peaks tinged by the red of dawn. We plunged down the southern slopes that narrowed into a hanging glacial valley, below Kali Peak, that led down to the glacier leading up to the Zeus-Manitou col, and made a long abseil down a cliff onto the Zeus Glacier. What we saw descending from the col was evidence of rapid glacial recession in the area. The first party to climb Zeus in 1966 commented on snow slopes reaching to the col but made no mention of the rock wall below.

From the Zeus Glacier it was a long slog back up moraines to our base camp. We arrived tired but happy late in the afternoon, having completed a satisfying alpine route (550m, TD 5.9) and traverse of the peak. The weather stayed settled, so a few days later we crossed the Ragnarok Glacier and made the second ascent of the superb Northwest Ridge of Mt. Fenris (450m, AD, de Saussure-Schurr, 1981).

SIMON RICHARDSON, *Scotland, AAC*

Eldred Valley, West Main Wall, Call of the Granite. Due west from Squamish, the Eldred Valley is the backyard of the small coastal mill town of Powell River. Large mountains, deep valleys, and inlets prevent direct road access to the peninsula, but government ferries shuttle cars for easy access. The Eldred Valley is home to five granite walls, the biggest of which is the West Main, whose east face rises 3,000' above the valley floor.

In 1993 two Powell River locals, Colin Dionne and Rob Richards, claimed the first ascent of the West Main Wall. They worked on their route for a couple of summers before committing and climbing the 18-pitch Mainline (VI 5.11 A4) capsule-style in seven days, using only 18 bolts. Mainline was likely the biggest and proudest route to go up in Canada that year, but it saw little press; Colin and Rob wanted to keep the Eldred Valley a secret.

It wasn't until 1999, when Matt Maddaloni and the late John Millar made the short two-ferry journey, that other climbers began to take notice. Matt and John spent three weeks in the Eldred and established a hard aid line on Carag Dur, the valley's second biggest wall. Upon his return to Squamish, Matt beguiled me with wild tales of untapped big walls easily accessed by a two-wheel-drive vehicle.

In October 1999 I was fortunate enough to climb with Colin during the first ascent of Amon Rudh. Although not as big as the valley's other walls, Amon Rudh was the last unclimbed wall in the Eldred. It was on this trip that Colin opened my eyes to the process of large-scale new routing. I watched Colin, shod in blown-out Boreal Ballets, take off on lead, climbing at least 20' before swinging a power drill from his hip to place a bolt, then climbing another 20' or 30' and repeating the process. In three days Colin and I, along with Chris Wild and Victor Ting, established ten new pitches.

The Eldred Valley's 3,000-foot West Main Wall (left to right): Mainline (Dionne-Richards, 1993), Call of the Granite (Black-Easton, 2005). *Aaron Black*

In 2002, with the success of Amon Rudh still in the back of my mind, I teamed up with Ben Culhane and Ope (Dave Gemmel) to try and climb the Eldred's biggest and most imposing face: the West Main. But after 16 days of hard work, our time was up, and we had established just a handful of pitches.

Ope and I returned to the valley the next two summers and fumbled for efficient ways to equip and clean the route. During our third trip we made it to within three pitches of the top, before running out of drill-battery power, food, and motivation.

By the fourth season Ope was done with the Eldred Valley, and life had pulled him in other directions. Looking for a partner, I left messages on answering machines scattered across the continent. Sean Easton was the first to call me back, and he was psyched to come in for what would hopefully be the glory round. Back when I was starting to climb, I read articles that Sean had written about his first ascents in far-off places like Patagonia. I was excited to climb with him.

Sean and I decided that the easiest way to equip and free the upper pitches would be to rap in. For a week we worked long days on the route from the top down, before we felt it was ready for the ground-up ascent. The route follows a line of shallow corners and face holds up the middle of the bottom slab. Upon meeting the headwall, the route stays right of the amphitheater-like feature known as the "Scoop" in the middle of the wall, and continues on a direct path through the largest part of the headwall.

Rain kept us off the route for the following week. Then, in late August, a questionable forecast changed for the better overnight, and six hours after I phoned Sean he arrived back in Powell River from visiting his girlfriend in Squamish. The next day started at 4 a.m., and by 8 a.m. we were at the base. The route was mostly dry, and on the first day we climbed 15 pitches of mostly 5.11-ish rock to a pre-placed bivy.

Day two launched us onto the headwall's steeper terrain. On pitch 18, I wound up for a long move and sprang for a hold past the limit of my static reach. As I caught the hold, my entire weight sagged onto a finger with a "pop!" that vibrated down my arm, the sharp pain forcing me to let go and fly off. Only five pitches from the top, good finger or bad finger, going up would be the fastest way off the wall. Except for a 20' bolt ladder and one other move, I had freed every move on the route at some point. Our goal was always to free climb as much as possible, but I had to change into survival mode to get off the wall. I taped my tendon to the bone and continued wrapping the finger until it was splinted half-bent. Sean was now on rope-gun duty.

Aaron Black on pitch 19 (5.12b) of Call of the Granite. *Dave Humphreys, www.dh-photos.com*

The last pitches went as smoothly as could be expected, and at around noon Sean pulled me over the West Main's summit lip to complete the first ascent of Call of the Granite (23 pitches, V 5.12 C1).

AARON BLACK, *Canada*

SELKIRK MOUNTAINS

Mt. MacDonald, North Pillar. At 7 a.m. on August 19, after a heinous two-hour approach, Bruce Kay (Squamish, B.C.) and I racked up at the toe of the steep pillar on the right side of Mt. MacDonald's 1,000m-high north face, for our first adventure together. We were surprised to see a bolt at the first belay, although we knew the pillar had been attempted a few times before. On the second pitch (5.7), two unnecessary and appalling protection bolts appeared, both within a few feet of bomber Camalot placements. The nut on the first one was tight, but Bruce managed to get the second one loose, remove the hanger, and unleash the fury of his hammer on the stud. It was the first time he had chopped a bolt in some 30 years of climbing. The pillar now steepened, and Bruce led a nice pitch of 5.10-. One final bolt appeared at the belay above the third pitch. The fourth pitch and the technical crux of the route involved moving right onto the arête. I welded two knifeblades for protection, before pumping out and having to hang on a short section of 5.11 face climbing. At the top of the sixth pitch we passed the last signs of other attempts. Pitch after pitch of sustained 5.10 climbing followed, with one more section of 5.11 on the eighth pitch. Finally, after 11 pitches, eight of which were sustained 5.10 and 5.11, we topped out on the pillar. Ahead, the angle eased a little, as the wall split into a series of gullies and buttresses.

It was 4 p.m., and we knew it was going to be a long night. We moved left into the gully, the line of least resistance, and simul-climbed for three long pitches to the final headwall. A more direct buttress line had been our original goal, but time was of the essence. In the fading light Bruce led a pitch of 5.10, to a small ledge below a dripping squeeze chimney. By headlamp I found a way to avoid spending the night there, by climbing a knifeblade-protected 5.10 face to the right, followed by a desperate 5.10+ bulge above a ledge. Climbing by headlamp

Mt. MacDonald: (1) North Pillar (Kay-Walsh, 2005). Little Face: (2) Prime Rib (Moorhead-Walsh, 2004). (3) North Face (Waterman-Waterman, 1974). *Jon Walsh*

seemed better than shivering away the seven hours of darkness. More pitches of 5.10, 5.9, and 5.8 followed. Finally, at 1:30 a.m., we hit the ridge just below the summit, after 18 hours of continuous climbing. The full moon lit the Southwest Ridge descent route, allowing us to descend without headlamps. Near the base of the ridge we made five rappels: two to the col and three down a chossy couloir into a bowl. The bowl descends to the highway, where talus, creeks, and bear tunnels led us through the jungle and back to the car, 30 hours after leaving it.

Summary: 1,000m, 19 pitches, 5.11- A0 (for a couple of hangs—would go free at about 5.11b). Nice corners, cracks, and featured face climbing up excellent quartzite, with excellent protection the entire way. Rack: a double set of cams (one #4 Camalot), one set of nuts, and a couple of KBs and LAs. We placed about six or seven pitons and left three fixed.

JON WALSH, *Canada*

PURCELL MOUNTAINS

BUGABOOS

Snafflehound Spire, Snaffleophagus. The northern part of the Bugaboos has a collection of less-impressive spires called the Vowells. The rock tends to have less-perfect lines and less-climbable features than the Bugaboos proper. Overall we were a bit disappointed in the many lines that turned out to be unclimbable seams, but in late August Vera Schulte-Pelkum and I did find an eight-pitch new line up the previously unclimbed east face of Snafflehound Spire. We climbed it after two attempts, following a corner system up the middle of the face. It was mostly good crack climbing in the 5.10-5.12 range, with one heinously thin 5.13- pitch that is probably the first 5.13 in the Bugaboos. It follows a nearly blank, overhanging corner that is unfortunately positioned above a teetering pillar the size of a truck, which would make a painful landing if too many of the thin pieces pulled out. I redpointed the dicey pitch with pre-placed gear, which included thin pins and a beak. The beak did hold a fall when a handhold broke, but I have no ethical insecurities if someone wants to add bolts to the pitch to make it more fun. Vera skipped the crux redpoint but had her own thrilling moments on other pitches. We rapped from the top of the face rather than join the East Ridge route, which follows a broken but beautiful ridge to the summit. Snaffleophagus (IV 5.13- R).

TOPHER DONAHUE, *AAC*

Pigeon Spire, first winter ascent. On March 12, 2006, Marc Piché and I made the first winter ascent of Pigeon Spire, via its North Face. During summer Pigeon sees constant traffic up its classic West Ridge, a 5.4 ridge scramble, but in winter this ridge has thwarted all attempts. Double cornices, unsupportable rime, and sketchy snow slabs hovering over smooth rock slabs turn this benign romp into an alpine nightmare. Marc, assistant manager of the CMH Bugaboo Lodge and co-author of the Bugaboo guidebook, had tried this many years ago and got shut down. Our plan was to try the North Face route, originally done by Fred Beckey in 1948 at 5.7 A2. This forgotten route was most likely unrepeated, as in summer it climbs an unappealing wet, mossy gully that offered perfect alpine mixed climbing in the cold of winter.

Marc and I flew via helicopter from the CMH Bugaboo Lodge to the west side of the Howsers and landed just outside of the park boundary. We skied over the Pigeon-Howser Col and down the Vowell Glacier to the base of our proposed objective. Just below the bergschrund, we dug a luxury snow condo and crawled in for the night. The sky was clear, and the temperature dipped to -30° C. Getting up in the morning was difficult, to say the least, but we managed to be climbing by 8 a.m. We both struggled with frozen toes and fingers, making upward progress slow. A short snow slope gained the gully, where Marc stretched our 60m ropes with some simul-climbing up the first pitch. The next lead had me tapping up a vein of water ice 2' wide by 2"-4" thick. When the ice ran out, steep rock with good dry-tooling and turf shots deposited me into a snow gully. Two pitches worth of steep snow went fast, but the pace screeched to a crawl as Marc did battle with a tight squeeze chimney. A blank section had him stumped, but he finally overcame it by lassoing a boulder from 10m away. More snow groveling, and we gained the West Ridge one ropelength below the top. We reached the summit at 5 p.m., as the last helicopter of skiers buzzed by, then rappelled the route back to our snow cave. The route offered eight pitches of classic mixed climbing, going at M6 A0 (A0 for one hang to warm hands on pitch 2 and the lasso on pitch 5).

The next day we packed up and skied back up to the Pigeon-Howser Col in a whiteout, then survival skied down 1,500 vertical meters of the Bugaboo Glacier to the valley bottom.

SEAN ISAAC, *Canada*

North Howser Tower, Hey Kool-Aid!; South Howser Tower, Lost in the Talus; Pigeon Feathers, Peek-A-Boo and ICU. I never thought that here in the Bugaboos I would hold my breath for a crappy forecast. Bruce Miller and I had completed four new routes in eight days, from a camp in the East Creek Basin, and our weary bodies needed rest. Our hands were swollen, sore, and dinged, and our thumb pads were split and oozing blood. But with warm sunshine, high pressure, and a colossal amount of solid rock greeting us every morning, how were we supposed to relax?

Bruce and I had each climbed in the Bugaboos twice previously without setting foot on the area's showpiece. So, for our first climb together in the range we focused on one of North America's greatest alpine walls: the 3,000' west face of North Howser Tower. Our spotting scope revealed an intriguing series of untouched cracks and corners, which appeared climbable, on the right margin of the face.

By 3:15 the following morning (July 30) we were underway, carrying just enough gear to survive a bivy, which we hoped to avoid. The first crux came at the base of the face, with a sketchy transition from snow to rock, without crampons or a solid anchor. The first few pitches

Chris Weidner on the crux of Hey Kool-Aid! during the first ascent. *Bruce Miller*

Hey Kool-Aid! on the 3,000' west face of North Howser Tower. For other lines on this face, see *The Bugaboos Guide: Rock and Alpine Climbs in the Bugaboo Spires and Vowells. Chris Atkinson*

ran with water in places from a large snowpatch at half-height, but in a drier year or later in the season the rock may be dry. By day's end we had climbed over 2,000', of which at least 1,500 were new terrain. The crux involved the only aid on the route: a 10' near-featureless traverse on which I used tension to lead, but which Bruce followed clean. By 8:45 p.m. it was nearly dark. We had been moving for more than 17 hours and had climbed two-thirds of North Howser Tower. These factors made our decision to bivy an easy one, although our bed of sloping granite blocks perched next to a 2,000' drop-off was unalluring. Deep reds in the west segued into a long, torturous night of shivering and moaning, huddled together in just our clothing and paper-thin bivy sacks.

By 2:00 p.m. the following day we stood atop the highest summit in the Bugaboos, and by 5:30 p.m. we were back at camp. The top half of our climb coincides with pitches of a previously established route, Young Men On Fire, but many pitches deviate to its right or left. The quality of rock on the entire route surpassed our expectations, and unlike some parties who have climbed the face, we experienced no rockfall.

Two sunny rest days provided motivation for another new route. A short approach just above camp brought us to a highly featured wall in between the classic Beckey-Chouinard and the Catalonia Route on South Howser Tower. Eight hundred feet of new climbing in five long pitches led to a point between the fifth and sixth pitches of the Beckey-Chouinard, which

Bruce Miller climbing through the cold on pitch 15, day two of the first ascent of Hey Kool-Aid! *Chris Weidner*

we then followed to the summit. Lost in the Talus (V 5.11-) offers a steep and sustained variation to the low-angled start of the Beckey-Chouinard route.

With clear skies prevailing, we climbed for two more days, establishing new routes on a previously unclimbed 300' face in the Pigeon Feathers. The south face of Peek-A-Boo Pinnacle hides behind Fingerberry Tower, and now contains two excellent routes of vastly different character: Peek-A-Boo (III 5.11+) climbs an overhanging finger crack on the right side of the face, while ICU (III 5.11+) attacks a steep offwidth and roof on the left side.

In the back of our minds lurked unfinished business that we began 12 days earlier on North Howser Tower. Would our new route go completely free? And if so, could we do it in a day? On August 11 we carried lightweight crampons, two mini-ice tools, a pared-down rack, a lead line, an 8mm haul line, two belay jackets, two liters of water, and some food. We carried no bivy gear. Before the sun reached us, and despite numb fingers and toes, Bruce led the crux tension traverse free on his first attempt. Inspired by his success, I

Bruce Miller leading the 5.10+ fourth pitch of Lost in the Talus on South Howser Tower. *Chris Weidner*

also climbed this delicate section free, relieved to have the most difficult moves behind us. But with 2,300' to go, and with the clock of daylight ticking away, we focused on climbing quickly and without mistakes. Fifteen hours after starting we once again stood atop North Howser Tower, having made its first one-day free ascent (21 hours round-trip from camp). With loads of 5.10 crack climbing and a short crux, Hey Kool-Aid! (24 pitches, VI 5.11+) is the second free route on the west face.

CHRIS WEIDNER, AAC

CANADIAN ROCKIES

Summary. After the incredibly dry summer of 2004, which turned faces like that of North Twin into rockfall-strafed nightmares and peaks like Mt. Alberta into overgrown scrambles, the summer of 2005 turned out to be one of the wettest on record. The big peaks never cleaned up, curtailing serious alpine activity. The wet calendar summer was followed by a beautiful Indian summer in October and into November. Unfortunately the fall dried off much of the summer moisture, resulting in an above average, but not exceptional, 2005-06 ice season. Nonetheless, climbers took advantage of fine early-season ice and alpine conditions. Classic "hard" routes like the Andromeda Strain (700m, V M6) in the Columbia Icefields and The Drip at the Centre of the Universe (400m, WI5+) in Kananaskis Country were both climbed during this time. In a solo effort, J. Mills contributed The Brink (450m, IV WI3 5.8): the route follows a couloir on the northeast face of an unnamed summit in the front ranges southwest of Nordegg. Two interesting mini-alpine routes went up on the north face of the unassuming-looking Wedge in Kananaskis Country. Klatu Verata N... (200m, M6), by Robert Rogoz and Raphael Slawinski, was a warm-up for The Maul (300m, M7), by Will Gadd and Slawinski. The second route especially offered high-quality naturally protected thin ice and mixed climbing up a compelling line.

The east face of the East End of Rundle, affectionately known as EEOR, is visible from every bar in Canmore. For this reason the obvious line which most seasons tries to form between the rock routes Balzac and Dropout had been sieged, aided, rappelled into, just about everything but actually climbed. Last November Dana Ruddy and Eamonn Walsh finally remedied this state of affairs by climbing Balzout Direct (500m, M6 A0 WI5) from bottom to top in a long day. They did, however, French-free their way up the bolt ladder leading to a hanging dagger. In January Slawinski and Ian Welsted repeated the route, freeing the bolt ladder onsight, at give-or-take hard M8. For those with eyes to see, another dribble of ice lurked a few hundred meters to the left, in the huge corner left of the Guides' Route. In February Ben Firth, Slawinski, and Walsh climbed some ten pitches of moderate snowed-up rock, followed by five increasingly difficult ice and mixed pitches to put up The Great White Fright (500m, M6), so named for the massive cornice overhanging the route. Although technically easier than Balzout Direct, the route proved quite adventurous, the crux pitch featuring climbing up to a hanging dagger, with shaky pins for protection.

On the pure-ice front, in early December Rich Marshall and Jon Walsh were rewarded for their patience when a line they had been eying for several years finally formed to the ground (well, almost). Situated up the Blaeberry River drainage west of Golden, Blaeberry Express (220m, M6 WI6) was one of the most aesthetic new routes of the season and quickly received several repeat ascents. The Elk Lakes area, just across the Divide into British Columbia from the Kananaskis Lakes, likely saw more activity this past season than in all other seasons combined. While this might be an exaggeration, the area did prove popular, with most attention centering on EMF (140m, WI4). Originally climbed with a short section of aid to an unformed dagger, the route this past season formed as a beautiful pure ice route. Two new routes also went up, the ephemeral Nightmare Before Christmas (150m, WI6), by Slawinski and Walsh, and Elk Horn (70m, WI5-), by Janes Ales and Donald Otten.

Between trips abroad to Patagonia and such, Jon Walsh had an excellent winter season. In January, with Chris Brazeau and Jon Simms, he finished off Drama Queen (140m, WI6 M7) on the famous Stanley Headwall, a route he and Simms had started the previous season. Two pitches of scrappy, traditionally protected mixed climbing led to an amazing pitch of ice up splattered mushrooms, topped off by bolt-protected dry-tooling to a dagger overhanging the base of the route. Sean Isaac also had a good season on the Headwall, completing two new multi-pitch routes. Dawn of the Dead (M8+) is a two-pitch direct start to the upper ice (WI5+) of The Day After les Vacances de Mr. Hulot. Isaac and Dave Thomson, the father (or is it grandfather?) of new-wave mixed climbing in the Canadian Rockies, had started the route some years ago, but never did finish it until this past winter. Taking advantage of good ice conditions on the Headwall, Thomson came out of quasi-retirement to complete the project in December. Toward the end of the winter Isaac teamed with Shawn Huisman to contribute Rhamnusia, a completely independent line left of the classic Nemesis. The route featured both traditionally and bolt-protected mixed climbing to a steep ice finish.

Things were relatively quiet on the winter alpine front proper. In January, in a fine effort, visiting Quebecois climbers Yan Mongrain and Maxime Turgeon climbed the Andromeda Strain. Winter climbing in the Canadian Rockies is rarely a walk in the park, and this was no exception. Between deep snow in the lower couloir and a wrong turn on the descent, the roundtrip took over 30 hours. Farther south, in Kananaskis Country, on the east face of Mt. Sarrail, Slawinski and Eamonn Walsh added an extension to the ice route Riders on the Storm (500m, WI4), climbed the previous winter by Valeriy Babanov and Slawinski. Slawinski and Walsh continued up for another 300m on challenging snow to the summit ridge and creatively named the line Riders on the Storm Integrale.

One of the finest creations of the winter season came in early April. Jon Walsh and Caro-lyn Ware capped off a remarkable tour of Canadian Rockies ice, which saw them link up many classic lines in single-day efforts, by climbing The Shadow (220m, M6 WI6+R), a thin and narrow line of ice up the prominent corner to the left of the hard classic Riptide. On the first attempt, carrying but a meager rock rack, they stopped a pitch short of the top of the climb. Returning with a beefed-up rack and a bolt kit to back up one of the belays, they pushed the route to the top of the cliff.

RAPHAEL SLAWINSKI, *Canada, AAC*

CANADIAN ARCTIC

Axel Heiberg Island, ski traverse and first ascents. Over six weeks, from April 19 to May 31, our team made an unsupported north-to-south traverse of the island. The team consisted of Louise Jarry (Canada), Vicky Lytle (USA/Australia), Sarah Boyle (Australia), and I (Canada). A three-hour charter ski-plane flight from Resolute Bay dropped us off on the south side of Rens Fiord. Each skier pulled a pulk 1.75m long and weighing 80 to 100kg, with all their equipment, food,

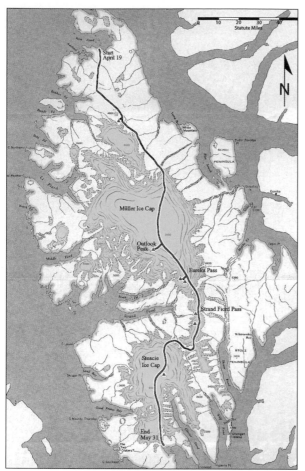

Route of the Axel Heiberg Island ski traverse, with triangles indicating major peaks climbed. *Greg Horne*

and fuel for 47 days. We used no resupplies or caches. The rate of travel ranged from 2 to 24km per day, depending upon snow conditions, terrain steepness, and obstacles present. Including side trips, we skied about 475km.

Our principle route went from Rens Fiord into the headwaters draining to Aurland Fiord, across a watershed divide to the lower Bukken River, then up the Bukken through its spectacular canyons to its headwaters. Next, we crossed the length of the Müller Ice Cap to Eureka Pass. We made a side day trip to ascend Outlook Peak. The web site of The Atlas of Canada by Natural Resources Canada lists Outlook, at 2,210m, as the highest mountain of the island. The 1:250,000 topo map likewise corroborates this height by positioning the summit above the 7,000' (2,134m) contour line. However, at the summit two Garmin GPS units indicated a much lower height, 1,963 to 2,012m. Something is amiss. A nearby peak, White Crown Mountain, was previously thought to be the island's highest. On the same topo map its spot elevation is indicated to be 6,720' (2,048m). Due to the distance away and time constraints, it wasn't possible to cross-check the elevation of White Crown by GPS. Undoubtedly, Outlook had been ascended previously, but we don't know details.

South of Eureka Pass we climbed two more peaks above 1,700m. Then we continued south across another icefield to Strand Fiord Pass and over two more icefields to the pass separating Wolf and Strand fiords. We then traversed the Glacier Fiord/Steacie Ice Cap and finished at the head of Surprise Fiord. In total, we ascended seven mountains and three minor viewpoints en route [see table below], using ice axe and crampons, with all but Outlook probably first ascents. Mammals seen included fox, wolf, hare, caribou, and musk ox.

The Royal Canadian Geographical Society, Mountain Equipment Co-op, Integral Designs, and The North Face Canada supported this expedition.

GREG HORNE, *Alpine Club of Canada*

The Eureka Pass area on Axel Heiberg Island. *Greg Horne*

Axel Heiberg 2005 Peak Ascent List

DATE	PEAK	ELEVATION	ROUTE	UTM GRID REF[1]
Apr 29	"Cone Mountain"	898m	NE slopes	E 0508099 N 8942832
May 9	Outlook Peak	1963 to 2012m[2]	ENE ridge	E 0531789 N 8852723
May 13	"Reconnaissance Ridge"			
	(north peak)	1244m	N slopes	E 0443492 N 8836914
	(central peak)	1233m	N slopes	E 0443050 N 8836604
May 15	"Piper Mountain"	1795m	NE ridge	E 0443259 N 8828842
May 16	"Ikulliaq (Calm) Mtn."	1760m	W slopes	E 0446681 N 8826906
May 20	"Junction Mountain"	1342m	S slopes	E 0458846 N 8798268
May 21	"Diversion Peak"	1580m	E slopes	E 0459687 N 8793311
May 26	"Grand Vista Point"	1470m	W ridge	E 0553112 N 8745646
May 30	"Bumble Bee Hill"	305m	NE ridge	E 0548781 N 8695595

1 - Summits of April 29, May 9, 26, and 30 are in UTM grid zone designation 15 X, NAD 27.
   Summits of May 13 to May 21 are in UTM grid zone designation 16 X, NAD 27.
2 – Elevation differences from Garmin 12 and Etrex models.
All elevations and grid references are by a Garmin 12 GPS unit using the position averaging function.

Baffin Island, Wilson Wall, Grin and Barret, and tragedy. On April 24 Drew Wilson (24), Kyle Dempster (22), Grover Shipman (32), Ross Cowan (41), and I (25) left Ottawa for the Stewart Valley. I knew of only four routes there, two of which were professionally organized expeditions to Great Sail Peak. We left Clyde River in subzero temperatures and sledged across Sam Ford Fjord to Stewart Valley, establishing camp beneath Great Sail Peak. We knew of no other climbers in northeastern Baffin.

We chose a 2,200' unnamed, unclimbed, overhanging spire 2½ miles southwest of Great Sail Peak, on the same side of the valley, and moved camp to the spire. Dempster and Wilson began fixing up snow and rock slabs, while Cowan, Shipman, and I brought loads up the 2,000' approach. Wilson and Dempster continued fixing over loose rock above a hanging snowfield, and Shipman and I narrowly avoided being hit. Wilson completed the free crux, a 5.11 traverse on loose flakes.

Wilson Wall, showing Grin and Barret. *Pete Dronkers*

Shipman would remain in base camp, while the rest of us climbed in teams of two in shifts around the clock. While sorting food at base camp, though, Cowan decided not to participate, so we climbed as three.

After the final hauls, we drilled our camp below a dihedral. We had pulled up 1,100' of rope, and were suspended 400' up overhanging rock. Lacking spotting scopes, we had to route-find as we progressed. We climbed 60m and 70m pitches, generally continuous and thin, in extreme cold, over many days. Dempster and Wilson—cousins and long-time partners—did most of the leading, as Cowan had been my intended partner. Wilson accomplished the aid crux, an A4- hook traverse, and Dempster led an 80m pitch by tying ropes together.

With 1,000' of rope fixed above, it appeared that our high point was within 600' of the summit, so we didn't move camp higher. By our 10th day on the wall we could fix no more and packed for a summit push, not knowing if it was day or night. We left camp in poor visibility and light snow. Dempster excavated snow and ice from wide cracks above the high point. The angle finally eased, and Wilson quickly drilled up a blank slab to gain a corner. Then we saw the first blue skies in a week. The clouds sank, revealing the most impressive view imaginable.

I aided to a pendulum point, then Wilson began free climbing in rock shoes, using bare fingertips in snow-filled 5.10 cracks. He continued up an overhanging bowl and arrived at a ledge 10 feet from the summit. It had been 25 hours, and we rested and talked in the warm sun, gazing over distant summits protruding from the massive ice caps beyond the Stewart Valley.

Wilson and Dempster displayed their summit costumes: Dempster's hoola skirt and Wilson's inflatable monkey. We had succeeded on the most significant climb of our lives. We began rappelling and collecting hardware and ropes. We slept well that day.

Fourteen hours later we had a casual breakfast and packed our haulbags. I jumared to retrieve two remaining ropes, while Dempster and Wilson arranged the lowering system.

Wilson had fixed a 300' static line to the anchors with a figure eight on a bight, leaving a 15' tail to safeguard himself while maneuvering around the anchors. He was clipped to the tail end with a Grigri. We would need another rope to reach the snowfield, so he clipped a spare cord to his harness. He didn't tie knots in either end of the 300' line.

Wilson would rappel first, then Dempster would lower the bags. I would descend last with the remaining ropes. Wilson must have forgotten that he was still on the short end and weighted the Grigri. He was speaking to Dempster as he began rappelling. It was the last time he was seen alive.

From above I heard Wilson's scream. I looked down to see him falling, impacting hundreds of feet below, and coming to rest 700' below. I descended to Dempster. There was enough rope to reach Wilson, so he rappelled, to be sure there was no pulse. He wanted to lower all the bags immediately, so he returned

Jumaring high on the Wilson Wall soon after a storm clears the Stewart Valley. *Pete Dronkers*

to the anchors to set up a lowering system. I descended to the snowfield to dock the bags, dodging the rocks they dislodged. Fifteen hours after waking, everything was near Wilson's body.

I drilled an anchor where Wilson rested, retrieved my personal haulbag, and continued rappelling. Dempster found a way to walk down and met Cowan and Shipman, explaining what had happened. Temperatures on the lake had turned styrofoam snow to wet slush. We post-holed to our knees in ice water, and the three-mile walk took five hours. At camp Shipman notified the police using our satellite phone, and we rested before retrieving Wilson.

After we got Wilson's body down, an outfitter snowmobiled to our camp and retrieved it. We carried camp to Sam Ford, and the police took Dempster and Wilson's body to Clyde River. Cowan, Shipman, and I waited for three more days for our outfitters, who told us that an unusually rainy spring had come early in the arctic. We were the last people in the region; a month had passed.

The Inuit gave us permission to name the mountain in Wilson's memory, and we named the route Grin and Barret (VI 5.11 A4-). Barret is the middle name Kyle and Drew shared. I will remember Drew for his simple approach to life, sense of humor, amazing climbing skills, and sharp intellect. I remember, once while discussing plans before the climb, I referred to it as a "project." Drew said, "I don't see this as a project. I'm just here in this beautiful place, under a beautiful wall, having fun climbing every day." For Drew Wilson, life on the wall was the life he loved most.

PETE DRONKERS, *AAC*

Greenland

Greenland ▲ North Peary Land

Upernavik ▲

Staunings Alps ▲▲
Liverpool Land ▲
Knud ▲
Rasmussen Land

▲ Trillergerne
Mountains

Nuuk ○ ▲ Thor's Land

▲ Tasermiut Fjord &
Maujit Qoqarsassia

EAST COAST

*Watkins Bjerge and Gunnbjorns Fjeld areas, first ascent
claims.* As a frequent visitor to Greenland (10 expeditions)
perhaps I can offer some corrections and additional information that might clarify claims of ascents in the region of
Gunnbjorns Fjeld.

In 1999 I was a member of Scott Umpleby's expedition
to the Watkins Bjerge (*AAJ 2000*, pp. 241-243). Among our
first ascents was Pk. 3,249m or Midnight Peak. Subsequent
groups seem to have mistakenly identified the position of
this peak, and as a consequence some later claims are erro-
neous. This is borne out by checks I made with original
reports available here in the U.K. In 2000 the Watkins Mountains International Female Expedition, led by Christine Watkins, visited the area. This group made the first ascent of Ladies'
Peak (2,992m), which lies midway between Terra Nova (3,020m) and Midnight Peak, both first
climbed by the 1999 Umpleby expedition. The women then appear to have misidentified Midnight Peak, climbing it but wrongly claiming a first ascent and naming it Pyramid Peak. They
then climbed its neighbor, Pk. 3,256m, in the belief that they were repeating Midnight Peak. In
fact their ascent of Pt 3,256m was a first ascent. (A photograph of it appears in the 2000 *Alpine
Journal*, where 3,256m is visible on the left as "One O'clock Peak." We did not climb it. On the
right can be seen the snowy top of Sphinx, a first ascent that the women did make, overtopped by
the rocky summit of Big Top, first climbed by Jim Lowther's group in 1988.)

In 2004 the Rucksack Club expedition led by Jim Hall (*AAJ 2005*, p. 235) also seems to
have mistaken the identity of some peaks in the area. Their "Afternoon Peak" (3,020m) seems
to me to be Terra Nova, and Pk. 3,249m to be Midnight Peak. Perhaps the 2004 expedition
repeated Ladies' Peak? The map accompanying Hall's report suggests this. In addition, Minaret
lies southeast of Wyvis and not southwest.

In 1999 I corresponded with Todd Burleson and Hans Christian Florian about their
groups' ascents in the Watkins Bjerge. Florian and his Austrian group (Reinthaler) made the
first ascent of Pk. 3,535m (close to Gunnbjorns) in 1998. Therefore the ascent reported by
Nigel Vardy (*AAJ 2005*, p. 234) was not the first. The "other" peak (3,265m), also claimed by
Vardy, *is* marked on the map; it just doesn't have a spot height. In 1998 Florian and the Austrians also made the first ascent of Pk. Oestereich, the fourth "top" along the ridge east of Pk.
3,535m. It is an obvious pointed summit, well-seen on p. 106 of the fine Florian-Reinthaler
book, *The Unknown Mountains of East Greenland*. In 1998 Todd Burleson's guided American
groups made first ascents of U-Turn (Pk. 3,307m), northeast of Gunnbjorns, plus another peak
across the glacier just northwest of Pk. 2,919m and Pk. 3,175m. The latter peak and its neighbor to the south, together with Pic Cappuccino (Pk. 3,266m), were also climbed by Florian's
group in 1998.

JIM GREGSON, *The Alpine Club*

Kangerdlugssuaq Mountains, first ascents. A British expedition comprising Carole Feldman, Peter Hawksworth, Cath Walton, and I made 11 first ascents in the region south of the Hutchinson Glacier. The landing site, logistically about as far as a Twin Otter can fly from Isfijordur, Iceland without refuelling, was at N 68° 04' W 33° 20' and an altitude of 1,395m. The area was previously unvisited, although a 2003 British expedition camped just to the south during a ski tour from their base camp to explore other peaks.

We climbed the following peaks (names provisional): Pk. 1,487m ("Crowley Peak," N 68° 03' 76.2" W 33° 10' 66.1", via east ridge, July 26); Pk. 1,481m ("Diana's Peak," N 68°05'88" W 33°15' 67.2", snow/rock at Scottish II/III, July 28); Pk. 1,679m ("Jess's Peak," N 68° 05' 88.9" W 33° 15' 67.2", steep snow/ice at Scottish II, August 2); Pk. 1,526m (N 68° 04, 57.7" W 33° 05' 70.5", August 3); Pk. 1,905m (N 68° 07' 88.1" W 33° 17' 47.8", via the long, snowy southeast ridge at Scottish II, August 7); Pk. 1,733m (N 68° 05' 89.6" W 33° 16' 51.4", Scottish I/II on August 8); Pk. 1,708m (N 68° 07' 48.2" W 33° 20' 55/6", Scottish II and a rocky scramble, August 9); Pt 1,583m ("Laura's Peak," N 68° 01' 93.6" W 33° 16' 90.7", Scottish I/II to fine snow summit, August 11); Pk. 1,364m (N 68° 06' 18.7" W 33° 15' 94.6", a rounded snow dome, August 11); Pk. 1,554m (N 68° 06' 28" W 33° 20' 13.3", small easy snow peak, August 11); Pk. 1,648m ("James Whyley Peak," N 68° 06' 24.1" W 33° 19' 53.9", a fine peak via four roped pitches and heavily corniced summit, August 14). We climbed all peaks at night, leaving camp between 10 p.m. and 11:30 p.m. to profit from best snow conditions. All readings are GPS.

PETER WHYLEY, *United Kingdom*

Kangerdlugssuaq Mountains, first ascents. To celebrate the centenary of the Cambridge University Mountaineering Club, eight members planned an expedition to East Greenland during July. As our departure time from the U.K. approached, it became obvious that bad weather in Greenland was going to force a change in plans. Our intentions had been to fly directly to an unexplored region of the Kangerdlugssuaq Mountains, landing at N 67° 57' W 33° 15', close to the head of the North Parallel Gletscher. However, our arrival in Iceland coincided with 1.5m of fresh snow in Greenland, forcing our landing site to be switched 60km inland, to where another group, awaiting evacuation, was able to prepare a runway.

On June 30 the first plane carried Alex Cowan, Matt Harding, Tom Stedall, and I to the new landing site, at N 68° 11' W 34° 05'. We pitched our tents in the gathering gloom and spent the next three days in a total

On the first ascent of Mt. Jaeggi, east of the Nordre Parallel Gletscher, Kangerdlugssuaq: Tresurer's Ridge gave 20 pitches of wonderful and intricate climbing mostly on immaculate rock (500m, D IV, Harding-Sample). *James Sample*

Pear Buttress on the northwest face of Peak 11, Kangerdlugssuaq. This was the highest face on the biggest mountain in the area visited by the Cambridge University expedition. The upper headwall provided the most difficult climbing (850m, TD V, Harding-Sample). *James Sample*

On the lower section of the north ridge of Peak 4 (PD+) looking west to Base Camp Peak. The latter is the furthest right of the three high summits on the ridge. It was climbed via the right skyline (northeast ridge) by Cowan, Moss, and Stedall at AD+ (IV+). During an attempt at a repeat ascent Jenny Marshall snapped a foothold while climbing into the little notch before the final steep rise to the summit. The resulting fall injured her leg, resulting in a rappel descent of the thin couloir below the notch and a subsequent tow back to base camp in a pulk courtesy of her climbing partner, Leah Jackson-Blake. *James Sample*

whiteout, digging out tents from under a further meter of fresh snow. When the weather finally cleared, a second plane brought in the rest of the team: Alison Ingleby, Leah Jackson-Blake, Jenny Marshall, and Mike Moss.

We climbed a number of small peaks in this area, most of which had been climbed for the first time by the group that had prepared our runway. However, a beautiful triple-headed mountain towering above our base camp, undoubtedly the jewel of the area, remained unclimbed. Toward the end of the first week Mike and Tom made its first ascent, by a long mixed ridge with immaculate rock. The 500m route was PD.

We had now consumed enough food to contemplate moving toward our original area. With overloaded pulks and bulging rucksacks we set off on a ski-tour that would take four magical days. We traveled by night, skimming across crisp snow with the midnight sun on our backs, weaving a path between unclimbed peaks, spindrift whirling round our ankles. In the growing warmth of the sun we pitched our tents, using ski poles and axes, and settled down for a day of feasting and sleep, moving on again when the sun dipped low, and the snow began to harden. On the fourth day we reached the head of the North Parallel Gletscher and carefully negotiated a region of crevasses, to arrive at our original landing site.

For the first time in the trip the weather became settled and, with less than 14 days before our return flights, we felt desperate to do more climbing. Mike, Tom, and Alex got us started by making the first ascent of one of the most striking mountains in the region, by a 600m route at F+/PD-. After five hours of hard up-hill skinning, they were rewarded by 45 minutes of off-piste ecstasy as they skied down.

Matt and I made the first ascent of "Mt. Jaeggi" (named after our friend and treasurer back in Cambridge), by a long ridge involving approximately 20 pitches, up to IV, on immaculate granite (500m, D-). Meanwhile Ali, Leah, and Jenny climbed a short rock ridge to a fine snow summit (300m, PD-, short sections of IV).

The 250m Thumb, Kangerdlugssuaq, showing the first ascent route via the south face (PD, IV+, Harding-Ingleby-Sample). Short, steep and technical, this has some of the best granite in the region visited by the Cambridge University expedition. *James Sample*

The Three Angels lie close to the original landing area of the Cambridge University Kangerdlugssuaq expedition. The first ascent was made via the long north ridge (left skyline) and gave super climbing on solid granite (PD, short steps of II, Moss-Stedall). *James Sample*

During the last few days Mike, Tom, and Alex made their way along a spectacular, complex granite ridge just behind our base camp, spending 10 hours linking ledge systems and crack lines to reach an exposed summit (500m, AD, pitches of IV+). Ali, Matt, and James spent a morning climbing "The Thumb," a steep 250m granite tower with some of the best rock in the area (PD, IV+).

Next day Matt and I attempted a direct route on the northeast face of the biggest mountain in the region. This gave a long, complex, and committing route, generally on good rock and always in spectacular positions. We climbed the route in a continuous push of 28 hours bergschrund-to-bergschrund (850m, TD, pitches of V).

But after so much fantastic climbing the trip was to end on a low note. While attempting to repeat the ridge behind base camp with Leah, Jenny slipped and fell, sustaining a serious wound to her left shin. Unable to return along the ridge, the pair began multiple rappels down the flank to reach snow slopes. Leah bravely returned solo to her skis, then skied back to Jenny and towed her in the sledge to base camp. We used our satellite phone to arrange an evacuation, and 36 hours later Jenny had an operation in Isafjordur, Iceland. The operation was successful, and there has been no lasting damage. We are extremely grateful to Fridrik Adolfsson and Paul Walker for their help in co-ordinating our rescue.

In many ways the trip didn't go according to plan, but in others it exceeded all expectations. We made 12 first ascents ranging in standard from PD to TD and had the unexpected bonus of traveling a new route from the ice cap almost to the sea. With the exception of Jenny's accident, I wouldn't change a thing.

Further information can be found at www.greenland2005.co.uk

JAMES SAMPLE, *United Kingdom*

CAPE FAREWELL

Tasermiut Fjord, Sermitsiaq region, Hermelnbjerg northwest pillar; Ketil region, Ulamertorssuaq, Moby Dick, ascent; and Nalumasortoq, Non C`è Senza Tre, ascent. Between mid-June and mid-July eight Norwegians visited the Tasermiut Fjord in the yacht *Sumithra*. The two sailors, Reidar Gregersen and Audun Hetland, were making their last stop in a round-the-world voyage, which ended in late August back in Norway. The climbers, Bjarte Bø, Rune Halkjelsvik, Lars Hetland, Anders Mordal, Torkel Røysli, and I used the opportunity to explore the fjord.

Bø and Røysli left the boat in the Ketil region and climbed Non C`è Due Senza Tre on Nalumasortoq and Moby Dick on Ulamertorssuaq. They thought that Non C`è Senza Tre

The Hermelnbjerg (1,912m) near the head of the Tasermiut Fjord. Marked is the new route Alle vil til himmelen, men ingen vil dø (1,300m of climbing, Norwegian 6+ and A2, Halkjelsvik-Hetland-Mordal-Nessa) on the northwest pillar. The party descended by rappelling left to gain the top of the concave snow slope, then descending this to easy ground. *Lars Nessa*

was a magnificent route but had doubts that the "first ascensionists" had really climbed as far as the actual summit. Their disbelief was based on the original topo, which is inconsistent with the rock at the top of the route.

The rest of us wanted to explore the unnamed valley south of the Sermitsiaq that leads to the eastern flanks of the Tininnertuup Qaqqat Group, where we made our main goal the northwest pillar of Hermelnbjerg. We had studied the pillar on the map and seen Erik Massih's pictures of it taken from the valley [Massih visited this valley in 2002, making the first ascent of the northeast pillar of 1,725m Tininnertuup—Ed.], which gave us an indication of what to expect.

The approach to the start of the climb took us four hours. It was easy to avoid the worst dwarf birch jungle, a problem that can prove a big challenge in neighboring valleys. The worst

Silhouetted above a cloud sea during the first ascent of the northwest pillar of Hermelnbjerg. *Lars Nessa*

obstacles were large boulder scree and some river crossings. However, the approach overall was a beautiful trek.

The first four pitches of the climb ascended good rock on the right flank of the pillar, following big features on a clean slab. The next three pitches lay in a wet, dark, scary gully. Hauling sacks was hard work and dangerous, as the bags knocked off plenty of rocks. Once we left the gully the rock became much better. In general the granite is coarse and granular, which means it can be a little porous, but it is comparable with the granite on Ulamertorssuaq.

The remainder of the route followed dihedrals and chimneys, interspersed with slabby sections. We wanted to free-climb as much as possible, but wet conditions

Three of the five summits that comprise the Tininnertuup group (1,725m), as seen from the northeast pillar of Hermelnbjerg. All five summits were first climbed by the 1971 Irish expedition via routes that were, in the main, straightforward. The highest summit on the left, which the Irish, unaware of any local name, christened Aurora Borealis, was revisited in 2002 by Martin Blixt, Erik Massih and Bjorn Andreas Krane, who climbed the fine prow facing the camera to give Qivtooq (1,000m, 7a+ A2). Two years later Martin Jacobsson and Ola Knutsson climbed the two consecutive pillars to the left, finally reaching the summit from behind to create Rapakivi Road (1,000m but 1,300m of climbing, 5.11 A2+). *Lars Nessa*

and bad weather forced us to use aid in some sections. These were relatively easy, and I think the route will go free easily in good conditions.

Above the seventh pitch the flank of the pillar got increasingly steeper, until we reached the crest at the top of pitch 20. We followed the crest for another five or six pitches, until we got to the top of the pillar but we did not continue to the 1,912m summit of the Hermelnbjerg. [The main summit was first climbed in 1971, via the northeast ridge by two members of an Irish expedition. It is not clear that it has been reached again.]

Five rappels got us down to the snow slopes on the north side of the mountain. From here we slanted down to the plateau between Hermelnbjerg and spot height 1,339m on the map. Then we walked south, crossing a glacier, to regain our valley

We called the route "Alle vil til himmelen, men ingen vil dø." It is 26 pitches long and offers 1,300m of varied climbing at a grade of Norwegian 6+ and A2.

It took seven days to climb the route (with portaledges) and one day to descend. A normal free rack is fine, as long as it includes big cams. Although the weather was excellent for most of the climb, with sunshine and temperatures between 10-15°C, on the last two days we got first snow and a strong breeze, then heavy rain.

After a week resting and fishing, Hetland, Mordal, and I spent three days climbing Moby Dick on Ulamertorssuaq. We also made two free ascents of Mosquito Attack (seven pitches, 6b A0, Körner and Redder, 2000) on the west face of Little Ulamertorssuaq (a.k.a. The Pyramid). The grading of the route by the first ascensionists was very inconsistent, both on the climb and compared with other grades in the area. It was also bolted in a way that is not normal in our climbing ethic, with several bolts placed right next to perfect cracks.

LARS NESSA, *Norway*

(A) Titan I (1,811m) and (B) Titan II (1,736m) with the route of the first ascent of the southeast pillar of Titan I (Wounded Knee, 900m, 6b+, Bekendam-Fickweiler), and bivouac site on the shoulder. *Roland Bekendam*

Titan I, southeast pillar. Dutch climbers Martin Fickweiler and I visited the Tasermiut Fjord in July. We camped in the Klosterdalen Valley close to the fjord and below the famous tower, Ketil. We spotted interesting rock spires at the end of the valley, on its northern flank, and decided to have a look. Later we found that these peaks are known as Titan I (Pk. 1,811m) and Titan II (Pk. 1,736m). We chose the prominent southeast pillar of Titan I as our goal. On July 6, after several rainy days, we walked to the base of the mountain and camped. Just before reaching the campsite Martin fell and got a nasty

Martin Fickweiler during the first ascent of Titan I in the Klosterdalen, Tasermiut Fjord. *Roland Bekendam*

cut to the knee. In order to continue climbing, he had to stitch it. However, we now knew that if we got up the route, there was at least a name for it: Wounded Knee.

After a day's rest we fixed the first two rope lengths. On July 9 we climbed 15 long pitches to a perfect bivouac spot to the right of the foresummit. We could melt nearby snow for drinks. Next day we climbed the lichen covered connecting ridge, which steepened into a near-vertical summit wall. The wall looked intimidating, but we found a way through. Finally, a 15-minute scramble took us to the summit, where we left a piton. The view was superb, encompassing hundreds of peaks and the nearby icecap. On our descent we bivouacked at the same spot and reached the base of the mountain during the afternoon of the 11th. Here we were attacked once again by the ubiquitous mosquitoes (head nets are indispensable).

Wounded Knee is 900m high, with 21 pitches of mainly 5+ to 6b. There is one beautiful but somewhat run-out pitch of 6b+. The climbing is mainly in cracks and corners just on the right flank of the pillar. The rock is sound, with the exception of one pitch through a brown-colored band. Each belay is equipped with one hand-drilled 8mm bolt (with a red sling). Apart from the belays, we did not use bolts, only Friends and wires. We are almost certain that the mountain had not been climbed previously from this side but cannot rule out an ascent in the 1950s or 60s from the glaciated north side.

On the July 18 we tried another probably new line: the northwest pillar of Pk. 1,727m at the bifurcation of the valley. We climbed the pillar for about 800m, negotiating difficulties from 3 to 6b on rock that was not always solid. However, when the pillar steepened, the rock became increasingly compact and, more seriously, covered with thick black lichen. We decided not to continue up the remaining 200m, made three rappels, then down-climbed the rest, in order not to lose gear for another route (we took no bolts on this climb). However, the weather became more unstable, forcing us to abandon a plan to climb the fabulous west face of Ketil. On the 24th we left base camp.

ROLAND BEKENDAM, *The Netherlands*

Attempt to reach Apostelens Tommelfinger; Ulamertorssuaq, Moby Dick ascent. Jens Richter and friends returned to South Greenland for another attempt on Apostelens Tommelfinger, which lies above the Lindenows Fjord and of which they had almost reached the top via a new route on the south face in 2003 (*AAJ 2005*, pp. 238-239). They sent 14 boxes by air freight from Germany, thinking that they would be handled by a courier company. In fact they were sent by normal air freight four weeks in advance. When the team arrived in Greenland, they discovered that three boxes were missing, including all snow and ice equipment. In 2003 they travelled by boat from Nanortalik around to the east coast and then up the Lindenows. This was very expensive, and last year they decided to add to the adventure by travelling over the ice cap from the head of the Tasermiut Fjord, repeating a journey that was probably first made by an Irish expedition in 1971.

In Nanortalik they met the two Dutch climbers, Bekendam and Fickweiler, retuning home after their climbs reported above, and the Dutch kindly lent them some gear. Optimistic that the boxes might catch up with them, and despite Richter not having plastic boots, the German team sailed to the head of the Tasermiut, from where they decided to reach the glacier from the left (Itivdlerssuaq), in order to maximize the time spent load carrying over grass and scrub before reaching the ice.

After two days walk in bad weather they got their first look at the glacier falling from the ice cap; it was steep and crevassed. Deciding that the terrain ahead would prove too difficult for ferrying loads and getting no positive information on their boxes, they decided that 2005 was not the year of the Tommelfinger and called for a boat.

They returned to the relatively popular Ketil area farther down the fjord, where the rest of their group from Dresden was trying to climb a new route on Nalumasortoq.

An Austrian team was just down from an ascent of Moby Dick on Ulamertorssuaq, climbing free as far as the Black Man but using aid above. They'd had four days of more or less good weather. Normally, base camps in South Greenland are characterized by millions of mosquitoes but this year there were almost none. Endless days of rain had seen to that.

During short weather windows Richter's group attempted Moby Dick as far as the Black Man, fixing five pitches. Three days before they were due to leave, their friends having already abandoned the new route, the weather cleared. They swiftly climbed the face again to the Black Man and slept in hammocks under a cloudless sky, with the temperature around -20° C. Next day they climbed in full Goretex. Conditions were quite icy, so they were unable to enjoy a free ascent, though they did free-climb all pitches graded VIII and below. As darkness fell they arrived at the little bivouac ledge three pitches from the top. Here, they had another cold night but for the only time in their four-week expedition, saw the northern lights. Next day they reached the summit in excellent weather and had a perfect view of the distant Tommelfinger. They rappelled to the base of the route, to be greeted by the next big weather front.

Postscript: The missing boxes eventually made their way back to Germany, arriving two months after the climbers got home. Apparently the contents were considered too dangerous for the Danish post. However, with all the bad weather it was a good decision to abandon the Tommelfinger, and the climbers left equipment in Greenland for a return match.

LINDSAY GRIFFIN, *Mountain INFO, CLIMB Magazine*

Ulamertorssuaq, Moby Dick, previously unreported ascents. In 2004 Marco Kuppianen and I came close to onsighting Moby Dick. I fell on the 28th pitch and had to make a couple of aid moves on the 30th (7c+) pitch. We led in two blocks. Marco led the first 15 pitches, and I led the remaining 17. We completed the route from our base camp in a roundtrip of 36 hours. We found the route to be very nice but tainted by all the bolts, at times next to perfect crack placements.

Annicka Bergquist and Sofia Sandgren from Sweden also climbed Moby Dick. I believe this was the first all-female ascent.

ERIK MASSIH, *Sweden*

Tornarssuk Island, various ascents. On July 19 Dan O'Brien, Marylise Dufaux, Carl Pulley, Dave Whittingham, and I left the U.K. on a multi-stage journey to Tornarssuk Island, near Cape Farewell. Having previously visited Pamiagdluk Island (*AAJ 2005*, pp. 244-247), we had the idea to try somewhere new. Tornarssuk is the next island west.

We could find little evidence of exploration and therefore little more than aerial photographs to help us plan. However, on these images we noted a number of interesting-looking shadows. Tornarssuk is linked to the island of Quvernit, which a Swiss-German team visited in 2004 (*AAJ 2005*, pp. 240-242), and contact with them encouraged us to press ahead. After establishing a base in the Kukasit valley on the western coast, we set out to explore and establish new routes north of Pk. 1,120m. The western and northwestern flanks of Pks. 1,250m, 1,388m, and 1,230m, at the head of the valley, and other smaller faces above a series of lakes appeared to offer potential.

After a rushed journey, the Tourist Office boat landed the team at mid-day on July 21 amidst boulders on the north side of Kukasit Bay. The valley above was fairly barren, with much rock and little greenery. The latter looked very dry after a prolonged spell of wonder-

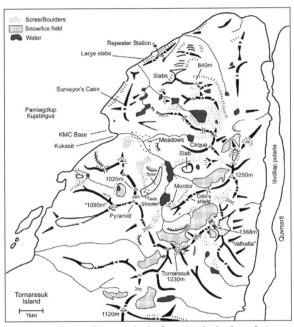

Sketch map of the northern two-thirds of Tornarssuk Island, South Greenland, showing the area visited by the KMC expedition. *Dave Bone*

Tornarssuk (1,230m) seen from Pyramid Peak to the northwest. The route of the first ascent climbed out of the top left side of the glacier via the light-colored ramp/spur to gain the skyline ridge. This was then followed to the right, first along and then more steeply up to the highest point. The slightly lower Tornarssuk summit to the right, and separated from the main peak by the deep, partially snow-filled gully, was not attempted. *Dave Bone*

Valhalla (1,388m) from the west-northwest. The first ascent of this peak was made from the southeast via an easy scramble up a couloir. Notable, just right of center and with its top almost in the cloud base, is the unclimbed, squat, Odin's Tooth (ca. 1,100m), its various faces seamed with fine lines of excellent granite. *Dave Bone*

fully dry weather; this was soon to change.

An investigation of the valley to the watershed col north of 1,388m revealed that the approach to most peaks would be generally arduous, with considerable amounts of scree, boulders, and crevassed ice fields. However, we did discover striking objectives such as "Odin's Tooth," a massive, steep-sided rock tower southwest of 1,388m ("Valhalla"). The weather then became unsettled, with many days of low cloud. Two major depressions passed through, and strong winds from the second wrecked the base tent. As a result most of our efforts were directed towards mountaineering-style routes and exploring access to various areas.

We made a likely first ascent (Alpine PD) of Tornarssuk (1,230m), by the north ridge and couloir on the east flank; there are some big walls below this summit. Arete B Route was a five- or six-pitch HVS/E1 attempt on the central rib of the north face of 1,020m "Twin Shooter Ridge," on the southern Kukasit skyline. Having failed by small margins to reach

The "hidden" northwest-facing Black Walls, which lie below the summit of the second peak north of Pt. 1,250m, just west of Itivdliap Pularia, the inlet separating Tornarssuk from Quvnerit to the west. Unfortunately, black rock at this altitude in South Greenland generally means variable amounts of lichen. Smooth rock walls in the far distance lie on Quvnerit. *Dave Bone*

the top of a peak that we called the Pyramid via complicated ground to the west or southeast, we discovered a route around the coast that gained the summit of Pt 1,090m, and from there continued east-northeast to gain the boulder problem top of Pyramid by its southwest spur (PD+). We made two attempts on 1,388m by the northwest spur, with the second terminating on the "Blind Pew" pinnacle after 10 pitches up to VS/HVS; the mountain turned out to be even more complex than it appeared from below. We eventually gained the big domed top of 1,388m from the "back" (F+), by scrambling up its southeast couloir.

Sustained damp conditions, until we left the island on August 11, frustrated further attempts on key projects, so there's still much to do

DAVID BONE, *Karabiner Mountaineering Club, U.K.*

Mexico

Candameña Canyon, Macuchi, Raramurí Lenguaje. To further the evolution of climbing, our team of six Mexican guys (Diego Delmar Garza, Pablo Fortes González, Marcos Madrazo Rodríguez, Daniel Castillo Migues, Julio Tabares Fernández, and I) opened a new long sport route on the southeast face of the Basaseachic Waterfall wall in Candameña Canyon, Chihuahua. We opened the route ground-up, free-climbing the moves and hanging from hooks to drill the bolts, over eight days between March 19 and April 8.

We studied the wall and decided on a line to the left of the waterfall. The route starts with two pitches of mixed face and crack climbing by a dihedral. The third pitch crosses the left side of a roof via face climbing; this is the longest pitch, 57m. Pitches four and five climb beautiful face features, and pitch six finishes the climb. Macuchi, Raramurí Lenguaje [route name] is 300m long, V 5.12+ in difficulty, and well protected. Although we didn't send it free, we think it's probably 5.12+. Necessary equipment: helmet, one 60m rope, 23 long quickdraws. It awaits an all-free ascent. For more information: simuchi@yahoo.com

LUIS CARLOS GARCÍA AYALA, *México*

Pico Candela, Northwest Ridge. In January 2006 Ralph Vega and I established the first technical route on this obvious 1,000' granite spire off Highway 1, north of Monterey. After a four-hour hike to the base, we started up the northwest ridge for two long pitches, then traversed right into a crack system, which we followed for 400' to a ledge. One long pitch off the left end of the ledge took us to the summit. Eight pitches, 5.10+, summit elevation 6,200'. Rappel the route to the ledge, then five 50m rappels straight down the west face, using a lucky combination of oak trees. Full rack to three inches.

ALEX CATLIN

Peru

CORDILLERA BLANCA

La Esfinge, Salida desde la Oscuridad, and Waiting for Jurek. The Polish team of Arkadiusz Grządziel, Bogusław Kowalski, and Jerzy Stefański climbed a new route on the south face of La Esfinge. Their painful acclimatization included climbing up the normal rappel route that descends from the col/saddle. Three steep pitches were presumably new; they named their variation Waiting for Jurek (270m, 6 pitches, UIAA V+). They climbed directly toward the ledge midway up, although they didn't use the ledge while climbing; this ledge is where descending climbers traverse off to easy ground. Grządziel and Kowalski made this ascent on June 22. The three also onsighted the Original Route on the east face (700m, 7a). During these climbs, they saw no place for a logical new route on the famous east face, so they attacked the shaded, rotten, and icy south face.

After fixing 170m of rope on June 29, 30, and July 1, they started climbing on July 3 at 7 a.m., climbed until 10 p.m., and had a cold bivy without sleeping bags. They completed the route the next day, reaching the top at 5 p.m. The route tackles a logical line on the left side of the

The south face of La Esfinge: (1) Salida desde la Oscuridad (Grzadziel-Kowalski-Stefanski , 2005). (2) appx line of The Furious Gods (Beaulieu-Légaré, 2003). *Boguslaw Kowalski*

wall, 100m left of The Furious Gods (Beaulieu-Légaré, 2003), and offers free-climbing with difficulties around French 6b+ and A2+. The route is 680m long (16 pitches); they did no drilling but left fixed pitons. The rock is rarely good. Actually it is mostly very rotten; cracks are sometimes full of earth and big, loose stones are waiting to sweep climbers off the wall or at least cut the rope. "You have to be very committed to start such a wall," the team declared, but they don't regret it. The route's name is Salida desde la Oscuridad, because the most important moment was when they made their Exit from the Shadow [the route name in English] into the sun again.

JAKUB RADZIEJOWSKI, *Warsaw, Poland*

Nevado Ulta, Toy's Band. After our climb in the Huayhuash [see below], we returned to Huaraz to learn about conditions. The guide Alfredo, of the agency Mountclimb, helped us considerably. We needed two or three days of rest to recover from a night spent in the El Tambo discotheque, but do not regret it. Benoît Montfort and I then took the bus to Chacas, in the Cordillera Blanca, crossing a 4,900m pass before coming down to Chacas. We got off around 4,200m and made our first bivouac at the foot of the glacier below the east face of Nevado Ulta (5,875m). The following day we crossed the glacier and bivied on the northeast shoulder. We suggest leaving early because of threatening séracs. Ice fell almost everywhere and didn't have the politeness to avoid our tracks. We left early and ascended the first part by slopes of easy ice. A rocky projection above, where it's helpful to have cams, contained the route's most technical part (V+ max [French rock grade]). There were beautiful icy passages before we arrived at the summit. We rappelled the route and found two old pitons in a block in a mound of ice (attempt or unknown success?).

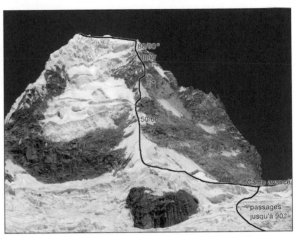

The east face of Nevado Ulta, showing Toy's Band. Given the scarcity of old route line photos and dramatically different conditions, it is difficult to know whether this route climbs substantial new ground. The summit ridge has been climbed at least twice prior, and the remaining line may share portions of the 1961 NE Face/Rib (Bogner-Hechtel-Kämpfe-Liska). *Benoît Montfort*

PIERRE LABBRE, *France*

Nevado Chugllaraju, British Route to summit ridge. On June 24 John Pearson and I climbed a new route on the west face of Nevado Chugllaraju (5,575m), southwest of Nevado Ulta and between it and Nevado Cancaraca. A complex approach led to the route, which started with an icy runnel on the right side of the face, followed by several steeper sections of ice (up to Scottish IV/V) before we reached a mixed upper section. This section proved to be the crux, a couple of pitches going at Scottish V. The rest of the route was mostly 55-60° and, although short (350m, 8 pitches), we thought the route warranted a grade of TD-. We stopped on reaching the ridge and rappelled the route.

ANTHONY BARTON, *U. K.*

Nevado Chugllaraju, west face. American Thai Verzone and Australian David Clinton climbed a new route on Nevado Chugllaraju's west face. Their route angles up and right, atop a prominent hanging glacier from the lower left side of the face on 45-60° snow and ice, then climbs a 60-75° runnel for five pitches to the ridge at the left-side base of the summit pyramid. It follows the ridge for 30m to the summit.

Churup, Northwest Ridge, direct variation. On May 24 Ben Ditto and I climbed a direct line up the northwest ridge of Nevado Churup (5,493m), beginning on the west side of a squat rock buttress separated from the main peak by a narrow col. We dubbed this formation the "Entrance Stool" and climbed it in six short pitches, with a downclimb and rappel into the snow gully that drops from the north side of the col.

From this notch we climbed a low-angle mixed pitch, followed by several pitches of steep and, in places, rotten rock. I crept up the first (and worst) of these pitches using tools and crampons, then happily relinquished the rack to Ben in our single pair of rock shoes. Seeking solid rock, he traversed left to the very arête of the ridge in a wandering pitch, which I scratched and sparked my way up wishing for sticky rubber of my own. The next lead angled up and sharply right to reach the snowfields on the upper ridge, near their highest point. With darkness settling in, we climbed four long pitches up the snow ramp to the summit slopes.

For the real adventure, we descended the '76 American Route, which follows a wide, mixed gully on the right side of the southwest face. We renovated a number of old anchors and built new ones, as we rappelled through the night over a jumble of loose rock and rotten snow. We returned to our camp at the lower lake 30 hours after leaving it, having encountered difficulties of 5.9 M4 R/X 65°. The descent was more frightening than the climbing. From the research I've done, both in Peru and through the AAC library, the pitches on the rocky lower half of the northwest ridge appear to be a new variation.

Given the great Andean thaw, over the last few seasons this once-classic mixed objective has dried considerably, exposing lots of exfoliating rock. While the climbing on the lower Northwest Ridge is less than superb, the climb's position and awesome views, including that of a lone condor buzzing us at the col, made for a fine outing easily accessible from Huaraz.

ADAM FRENCH, *AAC*

Cayesh, Slo-Am Route, and other activity. In May, Marko Prezelj and I visited Peru, where neither of us had been. We started our acclimatization with cragging on La Esfinge (5,325m). We first climbed the first three pitches of Cruz del Sur, originally graded 7c+ (5.13a), 7a (5.11d) obligatory, 800m, to ascertain the rock quality and the protection.

The next day we climbed the Original Route, originally graded 5.11c, free, onsight, in five-and-a-half hours, with the rarely done direct finish, which provided some of the best climbing on the route. After two days of rest, on June 1 we climbed Cruz del Sur free (onsight except the first three pitches) in seven hours.

All the pitches we climbed on this cliff seemed overgraded. At sea level I would say that the Original Route is probably 5.10b and Cruz del Sur is 5.11b. That said, Marko and I probably acclimate better than some parties that don't have altitude backgrounds. Also we had fine sunny and cool temperatures during these climbs.

Our next destination was the west face of Cayesh (5,721m), a peak that I had long felt epitomized hard climbing in the Blanca. We spent June 6 packing in to the head of the valley, and the next day we made a bivy just below the edge of the glacier. On June 8 we left the tent just before first light and in 16½ hours (round-trip from the base) opened a new line between the German and Charlie Fowler routes.

The climbing was uncertain from the start to the summit, which is just the kind of thing we like. After the initial 150m of

The west face of Nevado Cayesh, showing the Slo-Am Route. Several other routes and variations exist on this face. *Marko Prezelj*

an ice/snow couloir and 11 steep pitches with real mixed climbing, one pitch of pure rock and a final pitch of super-funky ice/snow led to the corniced summit. The difficulties were up to M7+ (M8?) on the mixed sections and 5.10c on rock. Dry conditions and unreliable protection made the route hard to grade, but we both managed to free it all onsight.

We rested for two days in Huaraz, then hiked up to the north face of Huascaran Norte. We planned to spend a day observing the face, and between 7:00 a.m. and 7:43 a.m. I counted 17 significant rockfall events down the center of the face, in the vicinity of the Casarotto Route. Instead of scoping the face, we retreated to Huaraz.

For our last week we chose Taulliraju (5,830m) and the Italian Route (900m, ED1 VI 5.9 A1), a beautiful and logical line to the summit. On the first third of the route we found good conditions, with dry/mixed sections that we climbed free (up to M6+). On the middle third,

Steve House well past the "end of the difficulties" (as the common refrain goes), high on the summit ridge of Taulliraju's Italian Route. *Marko Prezelj*

Steve House scratching his way toward the first icicle, low on Cayesh. *Marko Prezelj*

conditions were not so good: deep sugar snow on steep slabs and dry parts. Overall the terrain left the impression that we had to use every trick in the book to route-find (and climb) this rig. Super-fun.

The first night we bivied in a strange flat-floored ice-box, which required minimal chopping. The multiple chambers were hidden inside the cornice that forms on the crest of the spur. During the second day, we reached the long summit ridge, which was very cor-niced with poor-quality snow and ice. It took a lot of energy and some dangerous snow-climbing/crawling to get to the summit mushroom, where we made our second bivy just 15m below the top. We crossed the summit the next morning and descended the other side of the mountain, having freed the entire route.

STEVE HOUSE, *Bend, Oregon, AAC*

Andavite/Chopiraju Central, Fight Club. In the summer we, both 21, spent several weeks in the Cordillera Blanca. During our first stay in the Cayesh Val-ley (climbing Maparaju, San Juan, and Andavite's South Ridge) we got a good view of the south face of Andavite (a.k.a. Chopiraju Central), which looked really nice. We then left, but a few days later returned to Cayesh base camp. After a day of bad weather, on July 27 we started at 2:30 a.m. from base camp, and two hours later roped up and started climbing. The face was quite dry, and we followed an intermittent line of frozen waterfalls leading to the big snowfield halfway up. (Here an

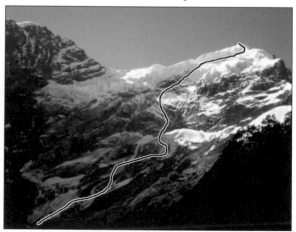

Fight Club, on the south face of Andavite (a.k.a. Chopiraju Central). *Moritz Wälde*

escape to the south ridge would be possible.) Then the crux followed: steep, bad rock covered with thin ice, difficult to climb either with or without tools, poor protection. Pitch after pitch of steep snow brought us close to the final serac barrier. It looked frighteningly big and unstable, but we found a narrow couloir and, three pitches of steep, hard ice later, we reached the snow slopes leading to the summit. It was noon; the 800m face had taken seven hours. What a climb! We called the route Fight Club and, based on the information we got in Huaraz, it was the first

ascent of Andavite's south face. We think
that conditions were extraordinarily dry,
and under different conditions the seracs
might be even more dangerous. The difficulties were varied, and we climbed most of
the route simultaneously. We descended the
southwest ridge, with one rappel from snow
anchors.

TOBI LOCHBÜHLER AND MORITZ
WÄLDE, *Germany*

*Editor's note: Antonio Gómez Bohórquez
reports that Peruvian guide José A. Castañeda
and his Swiss client Catherine Bertui climbed a
route on Andavite/Chopiraju Central in 2000
that may be similar to the above route. Further
details could not be verified.*

Tobi Lochbühler near the top of the final serac barrier on Fight Club. *Moritz Wälde*

Itsoc Huanca, Dominguerismo Vertical. The
wall is situated in the Quebrada Rurec. To
get there obtain transport to Olleros. Here you can get burros to carry gear to base camp, four
hours' walk from town. Three hours into the hike the walls become visible, and Itsoc Huanca
[a.k.a. Risco Ayudin—see note below] (4,700m) is located to the right as you ascend the Quebrada, the third of three small peaks (the second is Punta Numa).

The rock quality is exceptional, though perhaps a little dirty at the beginning where it is
hard to get in pins or camming units. We (Jordi Barrachina, Daniel Gutierrez, Jorge Ferrero,
Maria Lopez, and I, all from Spain) put in 13 days in July to climb 700m up the west face,
10½ days spent actually climbing, using five bivy sites. We placed bolts, and from the top we
descended the route, using the same anchors as on our ascent, apart from pitches 17, 12, 5, and
4. Gear: two sets Camalots, 1½ sets Aliens, 10-15 pitons, a variety of small hooks. We named
the route Dominguerismo Vertical (ED- 6b A2).

RAMON PEREZ DE AYALA, *Spain (translated by Bean Bowers)*

*Note on naming: Antonio Gómez Bohórquez reports that Itsoc Huanca is the native (Quechua) name of
the crag reported above and below. The reporting climbers, presumably unaware of the original name,
called the formation Risco Ayudin.*

Quebrada Rurec, Pietrorrrago: Vaffanculo; and Itsoc Huanca, Libertad es Partecipacion. On
August 12, after some preparation, Italians Enzo Arciuoli, Giulio Canti, and Roberto Iannilli
put up Pietrorrrago: Vaffanculo! (420m of climbing: 6a/6a+) up the middle of the northwest-
facing compact slabs that lie at the start of the Rurec Valley (on the right side, upon entering,
under Cerro Pumhauagangan). The route is sustained and on perfect granite, but with little
in the way of protection (13 bolts were placed; take quickdraws and small wires and RPs).

Beginning on August 15 Canti and Iannilli put up Libertad es Partecipacion on Itsoc Huanca's northwest aspect. The route ascends the wall immediately left of the corner system that sepa-

rates Itsoc Huanca from Punta Numa to its right. It is 1,600m long (6c+ A2), but only 600m (13 pitches) involve difficult rock, the rest being easy ground. The pair started up a slanting dihedral, followed by a crack system with two prominent roofs, then continued on more compact slabs. Higher they crossed a huge amphitheater of rock and vegetation to reach a short headwall, which they climbed in one long pitch to the top of Itsoc Huanca. A full rack is required (RURPs to #5 Camalot). The climbers placed five protection bolts, plus a bolt on every stance. The route took four days, with one bivouac on the wall.

LINDSAY GRIFFIN, *Mountain INFO Editor, CLIMB magazine,* AND ROBERTO IANNILLI, *Italy*

Itsoc Huanca's 2005 routes, thought to be the only lines on the face. *Roberto Iannilli*

Rurec, Caravaca Jubilar. After installing base camp in mid-July 2003 below Rurec (5,080m) and fixing the initial pitches, we began our first capsule-style attempt carrying food, water, and gear for three weeks. The team: Alfonso Cerdan Sandoval, my brother Juan Carlos Garcia Gallego, and I. After climbing 250m Alfonso came down with gastroenteritis and Carlos suffered from a respiratory infection, so we descended to base camp to recover and get medical attention.

By early August we were on our second attempt. Alfonso remained sick and abandoned the climb. Carlos and I continued, and on August 23 we reached the top. The new route (1,000m, 21 pitches, VI 5.11 A4) climbs the central part of the wall. The first half is abundant with blind seams, while in the upper half we encountered numerous expanding flakes.

JOSÉ LUIS GARCIA *Gallego, Spain (translated by Bean Bowers)*

Shaqsha Sur, southeast face. In June Peruvian guides Elias Flores and Miguel Martinez, with Cesar Rosales and Italian Tizianoi Orio, made the first ascent of the southeast face of the slightly lower South Summit (ca. 5,697m) of Shaqsha. The elegant, narrow, triangular snow-and-ice face rises 350m above the bergschrund and gave climbing up to 70-75°. Shaqsha (occasionally referred to as Huantsan Chico) lies southwest of Cashan and could be climbed in a long day from Huaraz via the Rurec Valley and South Ridge (350m, PD+ 45-50°, Maardalen-Martens, 1988).

In mid-May, 2004, Martinez, with Michell Araya and aspirant guides Quique Apolinario, Maximum Efraim, and Elias Flores, from the Don Bosco School, are thought to have climbed a new route to the main summit of Shaqsha (5,703m), above Laguna Azulajacocha. After weaving through 250m of serac, they found the final 150m snow-and-ice face to involve climbing up to 60°.

LINDSAY GRIFFIN, *Mountain INFO Editor, CLIMB magazine*

Huaketsa Punta, Eder Sabino Cacha. On June 11, 2004, Mauro Floret, Massimo Sacchi, and Marco Sterni, from Trieste, reached the summit of Huaketsa Punta (a.k.a. Amahuagaychu, 5,134m) after completing the first ascent of the west face. Huaketsa Punta is a steep rock forma- tion set amongst pleasant, grassy meadows east of the well-known Olleros-to-Chavin trail. From Olleros, close to the Rio Santa Valley south of Huaraz, it is possible to take a 4WD for 15-16km to the village of Sacracancha, from where a three-hour walk south leads to the foot of the rock wall, at 4,740m (S 09° 39.49'; W 77°). The rock is porphyry and therefore not always perfect, but allows natural protection throughout. The route follows a prominent dihedral in the center of the face. The climbing was largely free up to 6c, with a 60m section of A2 in a right-facing dihedral close to the summit. Every belay was equipped with one 10mm bolt. The 500m climb, Eder Sabino Cacha, was named after a young Peruvian guide who was killed in an avalanche the previous day while skiing Tocllaraju. The climbers recommend the area as being easy to reach, generally dry, and having little vegetation compared to, say, the Paron Valley.

LINDSAY GRIFFIN, *Mountain INFO Editor, CLIMB magazine*

Cordillera Blanca, other activity. The following information supplements the new routes individually reported above.

In addition to their climbs on La Esfinge (above), Polish climbers Arkadiusz Grzązdziel, Bogusław Kowalski, and Jerzy Stefański added a 300m variation, to the right of the Normal Route, on the upper portion of Artesonraju (6,025m).

In the Ishinca Valley in early May, Jamie Laidlaw made two extremely steep ski descents, likely firsts. He climbed and skied (same line) the West Face (750m, D+) of Tocllaraju (6,032m), and two days later climbed and skied the 800m North Face (D+) of Ranrapalca. For Ranrapalca he climbed a ridge on the east side of the hanging face to minimize rockfall exposure. He climbed to the 6,162m summit but skied down from just below a short band of 5.5 rock that guards the summit plateau, and skied farther to climber's right than his ascent.

Also in the Ishinca, on June 18 Americans Wayne Crill and Kevin Gallagher returned to their 2004 route on Hatun Ulloc, Karma de los Condores, to make its first free ascent at 5.11d. One week later Americans Andy Wellman and James Woods repeated the route, free, and con- tinued up Ulloc's previously unclimbed upper tiers on rock up to 5.9R. About 60m from the summit they retreated due to dirty and vegetated cracks.

On August 15 Wellman and Tyler Anderson climbed the south face of Mururaju (a.k.a. Nevado Pongos Sur, 5,688m), likely making the second ascent of the 1999 Argentine-Israeli route, the South Face Direct (600m, TD WI3). They made some minor variations while climbing the face in 10 hours (16 hours roundtrip from base camp).

Wellman made many impressive repeats during the summer, including a 6:32 trailhead- to-summit solo of Artesonraju (6,025m) via the Normal Route.

The prolific Spanish climber Jordi Corominas made several speed solos, including the Ecuadorian Route on Santa Cruz (6,259m) in six hours, and the 1979 route on Sarapo (6,127m, in the Cordillera Huayhuash) in just three hours. Corominas also soloed a new variation to the Northeast Face of Huascaran Norte (6,654m) in a 12-hour roundtrip from camp, starting right of the other routes on the face, joining the 1973 French Route, and going left for an M5 pitch just below the ridge, which he then followed to the summit.

Basque climbers Kepa Escribano and Fernando Ferreras opened a nine-pitch rock route, Matxinsalto (ED-), on the northwest face of Huamashraju (5,434m). The granite route report-edly climbs runout slabs and vertical cracks, has difficulties to 6b, and finishes via the north ridge to the top.

On La Esfinge, Escribano and Ferreras repeated the 2004 route Killa Quillay, climbing it mostly free at 7a+/7b. Also on Esfinge, Americans Brian McMahon and Josh Wharton made a free variation to the 2000 route, Riddle of the Cordillera Blanca. Their free version, which they called King of Thebes (V+ 5.12b/c), took them seven-and-a-half hours onsight; they used no pins or bolts. The pair also onsighted Cruz del Sur in seven hours, reporting it, as other parties have, to be severely overgraded (originally 5.13a) but of high quality. They'd climbed the 1985 Original Route in four-and-a-half hours onsight, and on Wharton's last day in Peru he made likely the first free solo, and certainly the fastest ascent, in 1:28.

Climate change continues to dramatically alter conditions in the Cordillera Blanca, as noted by many teams visiting the region. Josh Wharton writes of the north face of Huascaran Norte, from which he and Brian McMahon retreated (as did Steve House and Marko Prezelj a few days later) without setting foot on the face because of rockfall: "Someone will climb the north face again, but it will likely be a much different experience than Casarotto's. Most of the ice on the lower face is gone, only measly snow patches remain, and the ice routes that once existed on the wall's left flank seem to have entirely disappeared."

Compiled with help from ANTONIO GÓMEZ BOHÓRQUEZ, LINDSAY GRIFFIN, *and* RICHARD HIDALGO

CORDILLERA HUAYHUASH

Yerupaja Sur, Furieux Mais Romantiques. The participants on our expedition were Benoît Mont-fort, François Nadal, Julien Laurent, and I. Intending to open a route on the west face of Siula Chico, we left on foot from Llamac, arriving at base camp on the banks of Laguna Sarapococha in three days. It took another day to reach advanced camp beneath the southern arête of Yeru-paja Sur (6,515m). Regrettably, the face on Siula Chico was dry, and the glacier very cracked. We thus took refuge on the south face of Yerupaja Sur, where we saw a way to be opened. A short, technical gully marked the start of the route, which then continues up a hanging glacier, at the top of which we bivouacked (5,600m). The next day we climbed endless slopes of ice leading onto the west arête. To reach the summit we followed ice arêtes in the middle of the ice-flutings. We descended by rappel by another line to our bivy, then followed our route the rest of the way down. We left some pitons in place, but it would be useful to take pitons for a repeat.

PIERRE LABBRE, *France*

Trapecio, Southeast Face Direct. On July 10 Branko Ivanek, Miha Lampreht, and I (all from Slovenia), and Aritza Monasterio (Spanish-Basque, living in Huaraz) completed the central route (800m, ED+ AI6 M5 A2) on the southeast face of Trapecio (5,644 m). We climbed the route in

Furieux Mais Romantiques on Yerupaja Sur. Although conflicting information exists regarding the exact locations of the 1965 and 1981 routes, the 2005 route likely shares some terrain with these lines. In 1977, Carrington and Rouse climbed the obvious ice face to the right. *Benoît Montfort*

single-push lightweight style, taking 12 hours to the summit and nine hours to descend the north face. The hardest part of the route was climbed by Jeff Lowe in 1985, but he retreated 250m below the top. He graded his 700m climb ED+ and considered it one of his hardest solo climbs.

After acclimatizing on Chopicalqui, we took the fastest approach to Trapecio, starting from the village of Queropalca. In two days we reached base camp at a small lake just below the face. Weather and conditions were good, although there was much less ice on the face than usual (from past photos). On July 10 we started from base camp at 3 a.m.,

The southeast face of Trapecio: (1) South Spur (Dionisi-Ferraro-Malvassora, 1974). (2) SE Face (Donini-Tackle, 1986, to ridge). (3) SE Face Direct (Ivanek-Kozjek-Lampreht-Monasterio, 2005). (L) Marks the appx highpoint of Jeff Lowe's 1985 solo. This face, shown here in July 2005, has melted so dramatically that the previous routelines barely resemble their original conditions. *Pavle Kozjek*

and at about 5 a.m. entered the steep ice gully where the route begins. Overhanging rock soon stopped our rapid progress. We climbed it (M5 A2) before dawn. The rest of the lower part was

Pavle Kozjek leading an overhanging chimney to gain the upper icefields, high on Trapecio. *Miha Lampreht*

easier, although there were further mixed parts before we reached the wide icefield halfway up the face.

The steeper upper part began with an excellent narrow gully (AI5) and continued with mixed climbing (M4-5), until we reached the hanging icefall that opens to the upper icefields. We noticed an old piton (probably Jeff's) at the base of it. Since the ice looked unstable, we looked around the edge on the right and found a steep overhanging chimney (UIAA 6-), which we climbed in two pitches. From the upper icefields another two steep pitches reached the east ridge, which leads to the top, where we stood at 5 p.m.

We descended the north face, in the night, for nine hours. The main problem was orientation. We found old slings and made four rappels before we got off of rock and ice and reached the grass on the northern slopes.

PAVLE KOZJEK, *Slovenia*

Puscanturpa Sur, El Guardian de Pachamama, to top of rock wall. Oriol Anglada (Catalunya) and I wanted to make our own contribution to the mountains. When we arrived in Lima, a mountain

El Guardian de Pachamama, the only route on the wall. *Oriol Anglada*

guide mentioned the walls of Puscanturpa, describing their beauty and how little it got visited. After seeing a photo and speaking with a friend who had been there, we decided to direct our efforts there.

An exhausting three-day hike brought us to base camp (4,700m), a special place in a meadow directly below Puscanturpa Norte and the impressive north wall of Puscanturpa Sur (5,550m) [see note below]. Once we saw this wall, knowing there were no routes on it, we told ourselves it was here that we wanted to climb. With a lot of psyche and a hand drill, we opened the route in four days, from July 17 to 20. The route is 7c (6c+/A2 mandatory) with 16 pitches (670m), combining face and crack climbing on high-quality granodiorite that provided perfect dihedrals and some weaving between loose blocks, but mostly enjoyable climbing on good rock. [Of the two rock buttresses on Puscanturpa Sur, this route takes the more continuous, right-hand buttress.] Although two seracs threaten the peace of the valley, our route is free of serac danger. The base of the wall is at 4,800m, so acclimatization is important. We used 38 bolts, for belays and for protection. The rappel route reverses the climb. Our route ends before crossing a snow-field of penitentes (we only had rock shoes), about 200m from the summit.

MARISOL MONTERRUBIO, *Mexico*
(translated by Bean Bowers)

Note on naming: As with many peaks in the region, some confusion surrounds this peak's name and location. The name "Cuyoc" has been used synonymously with Puscanturpa Sur by some climbers (including Monterrubio), locals, and even maps. The true Nevado Cuyoc, or Cuyocraju, however, is just southwest of the Puscanturpa group, on the other side of Cuyocpunta (Cuyoc Pass). Puscanturpa Sur sits between the well-known Puscanturpa Norte and Cuyoc Pass, and likely picked up the incorrect name of Cuyoc due to this proximity to Cuyoc Pass.

Oriol Anglada having no trouble routefinding on pitch 5 of El Guardian de Pachamama. *Marisol Monterrubio*

CORDILLERA CENTRAL

Pariakaka, Peru 6 Mil. Pariakaka is located in the Yauyos area between the borders of Lima and Junin, where such other snowy peaks as Collquepurco, Vicunita, Tunshu,

Puscanturpa Norte (A) and Puscanturpa Sur (B), with route line roughly indicated, from the Quebrada Huanacpatay. *Oriol Anglada*

Tatajaico, and Paca are found. From the main highway between Lima and Huancayo, go through Oroya and Pachacallo, finally arriving in Tanta, where there are telephones, hotel, and food, and one can arrange for an arriero and burros to get to base camp. It's 17 km from Tanta to Pariakaka and took Guillermo Mejia and I a bit more than half the day. The moraine at the end being too difficult for the Burros to pass, we had to ferry loads.

The next day we went on a recon to the base of our proposed route, to mark our approach and get oriented. The weather was bad, cloudy and snowing lightly by 3 p.m. The following morning the weather continued poor, so we waited in base camp. On day three, September 1, we left base camp at 3:30 a.m., taking two hours to get to the base of the climb and our gear deposit. We

Pariakaka's southwest face, showing Peru 6 Mil, the only route on the face. The triangle near the top marks their bivy, and the arrows their descent. *Diego Fernandez*

Guillermo Mejia near the top on Peru 6 Mil. *Diego Fernandez*

started up the southwest face, by a 75° ice slope with a small rock step, gaining a little more than 100m. We then arrived at a verglased wall, where Guillermo put in an anchor and, after bringing me up, set off on a 50m pitch. We continued, simul-climbing for 500m on an 80° ice slope, with vertical steps and easy mixed ground.

At 4 p.m. we gained another mixed section, the crux, vertical and technical, probably due to never getting sun. The exit was crowned with seracs that guard the summit. At 6:30 p.m. we placed an anchor and chipped at the ice to make a small bivy ledge.

The next morning we ate some chocolate and quickly got under way to reach the warmth of the sun and the top. Two mixed pitches with some aid, the second going through a roof formed by the serac looming overhead, followed by 20m of rock, deposited us on top about mid-day.

We descended the Normal Route, starting with a wall of rock, then going through a field of penitentes and crossing a couple of bergschrunds. The entire descent is riddled with crevasses and requires roping together. We arrived at base camp at 7 p.m., 40 hours after leaving our tent.

Peru 6 Mil, 650m, VI AI7 (75°-95°) M8 A2

DIEGO FERNANDEZ, *Peru (translated by Bean Bowers)*

Tunshu, Direct Northeast Face. To reach Tunshu (5,730m), take the main highway from Lima to Huancayo through Oroya and Pachacallo. From there take the road to Hauylacancha Lake (60km, 3 hrs), and then to Siuracoha Lake and base camp, in the moraine. Water can be found in the glacial drainage nearby, and from the moraine it is 20 minutes to the glacier. The northeast face of Tunshu is visible from camp, and in three hours (follow the right side of the lake) you can reach the base of the wall.

Axel Loayza, Guillermo Mejia, and I began to climb the northeast face at 4 a.m., starting on the right side of the wall, then traversing on the glacier to a 50° slope and a bergschrund. From there we did our first pitch, over a snow/ice bridge; the pitches tended up and left. Pitch five involved loose snow on rock with patches of verglas. By the ninth pitch the terrain got more vertical, with sections of hard, brittle ice. Near the summit rock cap we did a diagonal traverse to where we could get in a piton and make our last anchor (11th). We were 40m from the summit. This was the most vertical section of the route. At 3 p.m. on November 1 we got to the summit and appreciated the view of the surrounding peaks: Pariakaka, Tatajaico, Collquepurco, and Vicunita.

We got to the summit in good weather but took so much time taking pictures that we didn't notice a building thunderstorm. The rappel from the summit was complicated, and a bit hair-raising due to the lightning. After getting off-route, and a cold, open bivouac (at least the snow and lightning had ceased!), and a long walk to the tent, we arrived at camp at 11 a.m. the day after summiting.

Direct Northeast Face, 660m, V AI3 (50°-80°)

JENNY POSTILLOS, *Peru (translated by Bean Bowers)*

CORDILLERA ORIENTAL

Various ascents. On an expedition I led to the Cordillera Oriental with Tim Riley, we did several climbs. Our first climb, on August 9, was of a nameless ca. 5,200m peak that extends from the long ridge west-southwest of Nevado Huaguruncho. We climbed the northeast ridge, grading it AD, and descended the southwest ridge/western slopes in a round trip from base camp of 12½ hours. I could find no evidence of this peak having been climbed, although the French gave it a go in 1968.

Our next climb was on the southwest face of Nevado Nausacocha and was just awesome, 16 pitches of perfect climbing. Snow, ice, and perfect granite led to the summit. I thought this peak may also have been unclimbed but found a bolt anchor and fixed ropes on the summit; the ropes headed down the southeast ridge. I could find no details of this ascent, although I found a krab with "Made in Japan" stamped on it. [Subsequent research revealed a Japanese ascent unpublished in western journals: Southeast Ridge, Kumagai-Kubo-Nishikawa-Moriya-

The ca. 5,200m peak climbed by Barton and Riley, showing their NE ridge ascent and SW ridge/W slopes descent. *Anthony Barton*

Sawamura-Tomomura, 1978.] We rappelled our ascent route and were back in high camp after 18 hours of climbing. We rated this route D+.

Our final climb was on August 23, of a minor rock peak, near Cerro Barraco, which we climbed by its east ridge, with one short pitch of severe (British grade), to gain the moderate east ridge.

ANTHONY BARTON, *U.K.*

CORDILLERA VILCABAMBA

Cordillera Vilcabamba, various ascents. In 2004 Canadians Conny Amelunxen and Neil Maedel visited the eastern end of the Pumasillo group, climbing the small peaks, north of Totora, that form the end of the long curving ridge running generally east from Lasunayoc (5,960m). The weather was particularly bad, and the pair was only able to climb on two days. On the first they

Nevado Nausacocha from the east, showing the Barton-Riley route. *Anthony Barton*

made an 18-hour traverse over the three most easterly peaks, which were separated by two minor subpeaks; this involved one-to-two pitch ascents. They climbed the most easterly peak by the north face and west ridge, with pitches of 5.8 and 5.9 to reach the summit. They traversed the next main peak from east to west via three pitches of 50-60° snow and a 30m summit section of 5.6. The third, highest peak gave a convoluted glacier ascent, after which the two descended south to camp.

On the second day, in a 22-hour push, they climbed two more peaks, including a traverse of the highest in this area, a large granite summit. Reaching the notch west of the previous day's third peak, they moved onto the north flank and climbed two pitches of 65° ice to a gap between two tops. A pitch of 5.9 led to the west top. They climbed the more easterly top in four rock pitches up to 5.10. From here a knife-blade ridge led south to a col in front of a second, possibly higher peak. This gave two pitches (5.8 and 5.9), followed by scrambling to the top. A convoluted descent, first north, then back east to cross the south ridge, led to a glacier, down which they headed south and eventually walked out to Totura. The five summits ranged from ca. 5,000 to 5,300m, and gave intricate climbing up to 5.10 and WI4. Although no trace of previous ascents was found, it is not known how many of these peaks were new. It is believed the two westernmost were likely climbed by a 1969 Australian expedition.

In June, after visiting a valley called Pumasillo (the only glaciated peak in this area, west of the Mandor group, is confusingly marked on the map as 5,189m Cerro Pumasillo, but it should not be confused with the main Pumasillo Massif farther east) but not reaching any summits, Germans Christoph Nick, Frank Toma, Katja Angerhofer, Christian Klant, Ingo Mittas, and Katja Weil, and Peruvian brothers Alejandro and Hermenegildo Huaman Olarte, trekked south across the Mandor and eventually reached the village of Yanama, known to Nick and Toma from previous visits. Leaving the Yanama Valley they headed north to place a camp at 5,200m, close to the Lasunayoc Col. From there Angerhofer, Klant, Nick, and Toma ascended Lasunayoc via the huge eastern glacier and a final steep ice face of 60°. This 5,936m peak was first climbed by Americans in 1956 and had been reconnoitered by Nick and Toma in 2002. Good conditions allowed them to complete the ascent in a roundtrip of nine hours from camp. Like all peaks in this region, Lasunayoc is rarely climbed. The next day Angerhofer, Klant, Mittas, and Nick climbed Pk. 5,447m on the east side of the col, dubbing it the "Mirador de Lasunayoc." In 2002 Nick and Toma had failed to climb the 30m summit tower, but this time the four Germans were successful, after a pitch of UIAA VI on less than perfect rock. They rappelled from an in-situ snow stake hammered into a crack on the summit. Pk. 5,447m has both a rocky and a snowy top. The snowy summit was climbed by New Zealanders in 1962 and Australians in 1969, but the rocky top was not ascended until 2003, when Conny Amelunxen and Sean Easton climbed it, at 5.9. Today it is undoubtedly the highest point of the mountain but may not have been so 40 years ago.

The team then split, with Klant and Nick trekking to the Palcay Valley for an attempt on Salcantay (6,271m), while the rest returned via the village of Mollepata (2,800m) to Cuzco. Part of this trek is being promoted by agencies as an alternative to the very popular Inca Trail, and Toma notes the once pristine environment has now become a huge garbage dump.

On the June 21 Klant and Nick established a camp below the Normal Route (Northeast Ridge) of Salcantay, which rises from a col at 4,500m and is generally considered ca. alpine AD in standard. Klant was ill, so on the 23rd Nick left for a solo attempt. When he hadn't returned by the 25th Klant descended for help. The subsequent helicopter search by two rescue teams, one from a private organization and the second from the Policia di Alta Montagne, found a high bivouac and steps leading to the base of a rock wall, above which they vanished. The search was called off after a week, and Nick's body has not been found. His previous new routes, during the last few years, in the Vilcabamba (Pumasillo and Panta groups) and Urubamba (Terijuay Group) with Toma were reported in Mountain INFO.

LINDSAY GRIFFIN, *Mountain INFO Editor, CLIMB magazine*

CORDILLERA VILCANOTA

Auzangate Massif, mapping and new approach route. In early May, Brad Johnson and I, accompanied by three American clients and supported by five Peruvians, spent 10 days in the Cordillera Vilcanota collecting field data for an upcoming map of the range. We entered the region through Tinqui, Upis, and Arapa Pass and traveled counterclockwise around Auzangate, using the regular trekking route to Jampa. From there we crossed Huayruru Punta to Sibinacocha Lake and made a high traverse through Laguna Huarurumicocha and down to Laguna Mullucocha, between Señal Nevado Tres Pico and Nevado Chumpa. A Czech team in 2004 explored this pass and did several, as reported in the 2005 *AAJ*. Although the approach we took from the south is possible on foot, the trail and terrain are still too difficult for pack animals; this may change as more people travel the route. This southern approach may provide quicker access to this part of the range, from a trailhead at Sibinicocha, which is accessible by road from Cuzco. A significant number of unclimbed lines exist in this region, which is becoming easier to access. We plan to complete our fieldwork and publish a map of the range in 2006.

MARTIN GAMACHE, *Alpine Mapping Guild*

CORDILLERA CARABAYA

Cordillera Carabaya, various ascents. I led an expedition to the Peruvian Cordillera Carabaya in June, and we believe we made a few first ascents and new routes. This is a very remote part of Peru, and in two weeks traveling in the mountains we saw no other westerners. One local alpaca herder said that in over 20 years no other climbers had been to the first valley we visited. The weather was unbelievably good, with only one partly cloudy day in our three weeks. It was also a dry year in the mountains, and the glaciers were quite icy, with little snow on the rock routes that we climbed. Glacier recession over the last few decades has

Chichicapac from the northwest. At least one route has been climbed from this side, but details are sparse. The route climbed by Biggar et al ascends the other side, beyond the right skyline. *John Biggar, www.andes.org.uk*

clearly been dramatic in this range, but there remain some substantial glaciers, particularly on the north and east sides of the highest peak, Allincapac. The Carabaya is exceptionally scenic and the rock solid granite, reminiscent in places of the granite in my home climbing area in the Galloway Hills, Scotland, but with more dramatic scenery and fewer bogs and midges.

We spent the first week camped southeast of the second highest summit in the range, Chichicapac. From a base camp just above beautiful Laguna Chungara, the whole team (guides Pere Vilarasau and I, clients John Bell, John Cadger, Bob Cole, Alan McLeod, Sarah Maliphant, and Jill Robertson) climbed Chich-

Enjoyable travel on the northeast ridge of Chichicapac. *John Biggar, www.andes.org.uk*

icapac (5,614m) by the east glacier and northeast ridge on June 14. This route was only alpine F, but we have found no record of a previous ascent of the mountain from this side, perhaps explained by the route being well hidden. The next day Vilarasau, Cole, and I made what we believe to be the first ascent of the minor peak of Chichicapac Southeast (ca. 5,285m), by an easy glacier climb from the south, followed by scrambling and climbing on rock to about British VS (5.6 or 5.7) on the northwest ridge.

After a brief rest in Macusani we walked to a base camp at Laguna Chambine, located in the unnamed valley between Chichicapac and the highest peak in the Cordillera Carabaya, Allincapac (5,780m). On June 19 Vilarasau, Cole, Maliphant, and I climbed an unnamed ca. 5,267m rock tower by two different rock routes, on the north ridge and west face. Although the tower may have been climbed by an expedition in the 1950s, it is pretty certain that the routes we climbed have only recently emerged from the glacier. John and Bob then crossed the glacier to climb another peak of 5,411m, believed to be the one referred to as White Sail in previous expedition reports. A view from there of the north side of Allincapac revealed that there is currently no easy or safe route to the relatively flat summit of Allincapac, which has become isolated on all sides by a continuous 360° serac. On June 20 Sarah, Bob, and I climbed another possibly previously unclimbed line, on a ca. 5,192m peak, which is possibly the peak marked Red Peak by previous expeditions. This was a straightforward scramble by the south ridge from the camp by Laguna Chambine.

As good weather continued, the next day Sarah, Bob, and I, now starting to tire, climbed another unnamed peak, ca. 5,044m, by the north buttress. The climb gave 300m of easy, enjoyable V.Diff (5.2) on good granite. This summit had clearly been reached before.

Various members of the team climbed three other 5,000m peaks: 5,294m Quenamari, which lies south of the main range; 5,270m Iteriluma, just south of Chichicapac; and an unnamed ca. 5,057m peak near Laguna Chambine.

With Bob Cole and I making nine 5,000m+ summits in two weeks, this was a very successful expedition, demonstrating that there is still plenty of exploratory mountaineering at easy grades to be found in the more forgotten corners of the world.

JOHN BIGGAR, *U.K.*

Venezuela

Pico Ruiz Teran, Idos en Guate, and Pico Humboldt, Five Pitches of Good Weather. During January 2002 Carlos Pineda and I climbed a direct route up the north face of Pico Ruiz Teran (4,924m). We christened the route Idos en Guate (IV 5.9 C1 AI3). I attempted to climb the face a year earlier with Mario "La Palida" Dos Reis, but we turned back after the first pitch due to very loose rock and bad conditions.

It took Carlos and me two days to do the approach. The first day we took a small bus from the city of Merida to the town of Tabay. From there we took a jeep to the entrance of the Sierra Nevada de Merida National Park in La Mucuy. After registering with the rangers we started the uphill hike up to Laguna La Coromoto (3,100m), where we camped. The next day we hiked up to Laguna Verde (4,100m) where we set up base camp. The day after, we got an early start, approaching the route by the northern side of the base of Torre Condor, until we reached the north slopes of the glacier between Pico Ruiz Teran and Pico Humboldt. We began with 80m on 30-45° snow, which we soloed to the base of the wall. I noticed that the glacier was a meter or so lower than the year before. Carlos started the route, and we switched leads to the top. We encountered enough loose rock that the going was slower than expected. Once on top of Pico Ruiz Teran we realized that the hardest was yet to come. We had to make a delicate traverse to the summit of Pico Humboldt (GPS 4,917m, map 4,968m; the second highest mountain in the Venezuelan Andes) that involved a few raps and more loose rock. Alter reaching the summit of Pico Humboldt we started the descent and reached the comfort of camp after 16 hours. After speaking to some of the locals, we presumed this to be a new route.

In mid-September 2005 Carlos and I climbed the north ridge of Pico Humboldt. Although we do not know if the north ridge had been climbed, we believe this to be the first ascent from this side. We called the route Five Pitches of Good Weather (700', III 5.8 C1). The route could go free at 5.9 in dry conditions, but we had to use points of aid in places due to dirty cracks and wet rock. We approached by a loose gully, with exposed 4th to low-5th class,

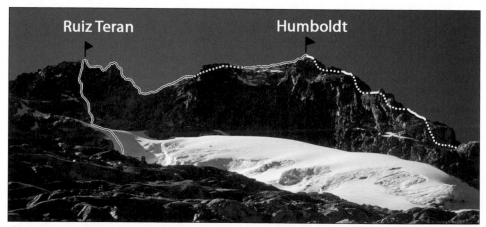

Idos en Guate on Pico Ruiz Teran, with the traverse to Pico Humboldt, by Lopera and Pineda in 2002 (stroked line). The pair's 2005 route, Five Pitches of Good Weather, ascends the right skyline of Humboldt (white line). *Maikey Lopera*

between the base of the west face of Torre Condor and La Corona Glacier. This gully put us in the col between Torre Condor and Pico Humboldt, where the route starts (GPS 4,736m N08°33.067' W070°59.833'). After much debating about continuing in uncooperative weather, Carlos had the honors of doing the first pitch. Switching leads, we went through four more pitches, under changeable conditions of fun: sun, rain, hail. Three of the pitches are moderate (5.6-5.9) and two are 4th class, with interspaced sections of 5th class. There is plenty of loose rock. As usual we topped out just before sunset and had a fun descent in the dark (right!).

MAIKEY LOPERA

Auyan Tepuye, Gran Sabana, Rainbow Jambaia. In March and April, Anne and John Arran, Ivan Calderón, Miles Gibson, Ben Heason, Alex Klenov, and Alfredo Rangel made a free ascent of the Angel Falls wall. Their line (Rainbow Jambaia, 31 pitches, E7 6b) roughly follows Ruta Directa (1,150m, VI 6b A4, Gálvez-Medinabeitía, 1990), with many variations and an independent finish for the final eight pitches. See Calderón's feature article earlier in this *Journal*.

Suriname

Duivelsei, first ascent. Intending to ascend an unclimbed mountain in the southern Suriname jungle, Gerke Hoekstra, Ronald Naar, and I traveled to Paramaribo in September. We chartered a small plane that flew us to an isolated airstrip south of the Wilhelmina Mountains. From the Kaysergebergte airstrip we headed for adventure the next day. Smaller, lower-angle rocks abound in the area, but from the plane we saw Duivelsei, a steep mountain with a big rock face. The native aviators, who have flown people in this area for years and years, told us that they never met people so crazy that they wanted to climb Duivelsei.

With a reporter from a Dutch newspaper and four strong Surinamese, we started the journey in long wooden boats. For the first day we went down the Zuidrivier, and for the next five days we headed up the Lucierivier.

It seemed so unreal to push the boats through difficult passages of the river, standing up to our waist in the fast running water, while seeing cayman every hour and catching 40cm-long piranhas while fishing. The most dangerous fish, however, are the anjumaras. People have left with fewer toes than they started their trip with. Luckily these monsters are easy to catch and provide a good meal at the start and at the end of a hard day's work. More than once, one of the boats turned over, and our belongings floated away. This is how we lost a map, a lot of rice, and all our coffee just three hours away from the airstrip. For six days we fought with the water, until finally the river became too narrow, and we traveled by foot. The life we were getting used to changed dramatically the next day. Instead of sunshine, water, and dangerous fish, we faced shadows, tough vegetation, spiders, snakes, and monkeys who tried to scare us by throwing branches. Our diet changed with the surroundings and we ate pig for dinner, nothing for lunch, and smoked, salted pig for breakfast. After six days our stomachs were messed up for real.

After six days walking east-northeast, we saw our objective for the first time. While the others slept in camp 3, Gerke, Ronald, and I headed toward the mountain and started the climb. With only one package of dried food and too little water, we hoped to be back down in two days. The first part of the climb goes through steep and sometimes vertical vegeta-

The first and only route on Duivelsei. *Martin Fickweiler*

tion on the west (left) side of the south face, and we spent the night on a narrow shoulder, an obvious spot nearly around to the north side of the mountain. Here we ate the only food we had. The lack of breakfast gave us a very early start the next day. More vertical jungle took us to the base of a steep, smooth rock face on the north side. There was no way around it, and I started leading, drilling batholes and bolts. After 20m I free-climbed a scary, unprotected section into the next vegetation and belayed from a tree. Another rock wall stood above, but after traversing and creative routefinding I got around it. Then I climbed another short vertical, vegetated section and stood on top of the mountain that the natives call "het Duivelsei" (Egg of the Devil, because the lower summit has a big egg-shaped rock on top). With Ronald and Gerke I enjoyed the view from the summit, already dreaming of climbing the 600-800m high south face. But then we were so tired, hungry, and thirsty that all we wanted was to go back to civilization. It took us another five days to get there.

Our route was 600m, 5.9 jungle, A2 rock. This expedition was supported by Gore-Tex and Haglöfs.

MARTIN FICKWEILER, *Vlaardingen, Netherlands*

Bolivia

Bolivia, various ascents. Although more may come to light, Bolivian contacts and regular visitors know of little pioneering activity in 2005. However, they do report that the mountains are in bad shape, crumbling and with marked glacial retreat. The general view is that climbing conditions are really tenuous.

In July a young British team of Tom Bide, Carl Reilly,

Graeme Schofield, and Sam Walmsley visited the southernmost group of mountains in the Apolobamba. These peaks (sometimes referred to as the Pupuya Group), which run south from the Ulla Ulla-Hilo Hilo road to Acamani (ca 5,400m) and culminate in Huelancalloc (5,836m/5,847m), appear to have seen little traffic compared to the rest of the Apolobamba, and their history is unclear. Available reports suggested the steep southern aspect of these peaks were unclimbed. The team set up base camp at 4,730m, after a short approach from the road-head at Mankha Canuma to the west. On July 21 they climbed Canisaya (GPS 5,652m) by two different routes. Bide and Walmsley followed the southwest ridge (500m, D- 60°), while Reilly and Schofield climbed the southwest face to the left (500m, D 60° sustained snow and ice). Both parties descended by the southwest face. The following day all four climbed the west face of Casalaya (GPS 5,423m, 600m, D 60° with a convoluted serac section in the middle). From the summit they traversed the southeast ridge all the way to the exit of their route on the southwest face of Canisaya, down which they again descended. They estimated the grades of their routes relative to grades in the Condorini Massif, in which the group acclimatized, but believe their routes easier than those of the same grade in the Alps. Route lengths given here indicate the amount of climbing, not the vertical interval of the face.

On July 24 Bide and Schofield climbed the southeast face of Huelancalloc, by a serious ice/mixed line that took a narrow gully below the overhanging seracs of the summit ridge. They encountered difficulties of Scottish 4/5 and UIAA IV+, but moved together on much of the climb, often due to the lack of protection or belays. The 600m route was TD-/TD to the summit ridge, well left of the highest point. From here they descended the southwest ridge and regained camp after a 14-hour day. On the same day Reilly and Walmsley climbed the objectively safer southeast buttress (800m, D+). They followed a pronounced spur on the right side of the face, which, apart from a rock buttress, was mainly snow and ice (70° max). Below the crux chimney they found an ancient peg and assume the previous climbers completed the line to the summit. From the top Reilly and Walmsley descended the southwest ridge. Two days later Reilly and Schofield climbed the southwest gully on the left side of the face (500m, D-/D, generally Scottish 2 but with rock sections, the hardest IV+/V on good granite).

The group then moved north to the Cololo area, where they established base camp in the Kotani Valley east of Cololo (5,916m). The highlight was a new, though incomplete, line on the south face of Kotani North (ca 5,350m), the central summit on the valley rim northwest of Kotani Lake. This group of peaks forms the eastern extension of Cololo's northeast ridge, which is characterized by steep rock walls capped by a broad serac barrier. On August 1 Reilly and Schofield climbed a thin, right-slanting icefall for 480m, to below the serac cap. There were at least four pitches of sustained Scottish 4 and 5, plus short sections of 2/3 and rock to IV+. The approach to the route is seriously threatened by collapsing seracs down a more major gully system to the left. On reaching the seracs they could see no easy way through and, as the day was getting late, decided to rappel the line of ascent using Abalakovs. They thought the climb to their high point (more than 200m below the summit) to be TD (90°).

LINDSAY GRIFFIN, *Mountain INFO, CLIMB magazine*

Argentina and Chile

NORTHERN ANDES, CHILE

Sierra Nevada de las Lagunas Bravas, exploration and various ascents. During the four campaigns that we undertook in 1998, 2000, 2002, and 2005, several members of our Iberia Mountain Group visited the Sierra Nevada de las Lagunas Bravas, located northeast of the town of Copiapó. To access the area, we drove through the valley of the Juncalito thermal springs, or Río Negro, and up a road (in bad condition on our fourth trip) that left us near the Laguna del Bayo (lake). In those four campaigns we ascended numerous peaks, most of them first ascents. North of the Laguna del Bayo, our main ascents were of Cerro Tridente (5,417m), "Vértice Zurich" (4,852m, second ascent), and two unnamed heights we christened "Cerro Cobrizo" (4,718m) and "Cerro Entre Dos Aguas" (5,015m). South of the area in which Lakes Jilguero and Bayo lie, we also reached a number of untrodden summits: Cerro Plomizo (5,392m), as well as several heights situated west of the Sierra Nevada (Cerros 5,273m, 5,355m, 5,519m, 5,530m, 5,497m, and 5,529m) and the peaks of the main massif of the Sierra Nevada itself (5,928m, 6,013m, and 6,127m). The first two were first ascents and the highest one a second, as without our knowing it, an American group had been active in the district and had made the first ascent.

In the Cordón de la Azufrera we also reached several mountain tops. This massif had felt the impact of human visitors previously, since we found traces of mining activity at a high altitude, even on the summit of the main peak (Cerro Azufrera de los Cuyanos, 5,921m). Southeast of this imposing chain we made two more ascents: of Cerro 5,732m, which we deemed a first, and of Cerro 5,710m, which members of the Club Alemán Andino of Santiago, Chile ascended in 1976. From the thermal baths area, to acclimatize, we climbed Cerro Juncalito Oeste (5,266m), on whose summit we found no traces of human occupancy. Participating in these campaigns were Rodrigo Bernardo, Carlos Bravo, Maribel Fernández, Luis Bernardo, Francisco Gómez, Fernando Laguna, Carlos Gómez, Alfonso de la Iglesia, Pedro Gómez, Jorge Pérez, Eduardo Ruiz, Alfonso de la Iglesia, and José Martinez. And always in our thoughts was Evelio Echevarría, who had indicated to us the climbing possibilities of these fantastic places.

JOSÉ MARTÍNEZ HERNÁNDEZ, *Madrid, Spain*

NORTHERN ANDES, ARGENTINA

Pissis-Bonete region, various activity. In March, Andrés Fabeiro and I were transported to the slopes of Cerro Pilar (erroneously stated on the official map as Cerro Azul). We erected camp on a barren desert not far from Laguna Brava. My friend had problems acclimatizing, so on the 21st I tried the mountain, but could only reach a lower summit, at 3 p.m., which I called "Cerro Pilar Pequeño" (ca. 4,820m, S28°23'48.8" W68°50'12.4"). It had no previous ascents. Later, I learned that an archeologist had ascended three peaks around Laguna Brava: Cerro Pilar (5,075m), Cerro Fandango (5,612m), and a secondary summit of Cerro Morado o Tambero (5,230m). He found Inca remains on the top of these, but no modern evidence. The major peaks around the lake have now been ascended.

After our February expedition to the same area, we met a Swede, Janne Corax, and his girlfriend Nadine on bikes. They went to Laguna Brava. Corax ascended, solo, Bonete (6,759m) by its southwest face (first solo of the route and possibly its second ascent). They continued north to the little-visited slopes of Pissis, which, at 6,882m, is the second highest summit in the hemisphere and the highest volcano on earth. They found a lot of snow but managed to reach a summit 2 km south of the higher summit. They named it Pissis II or Pissis East (6,811m, S27°46,137 W68° 46,800) and found no traces of other ascents. This summit can be found on the official map. They then went north and ascended main Pissis and other summits in Catamarca.

Another first ascent in the Pissis region was made by Rafael Solana Plaza on April 10, 2004 (www.andeshandbook.cl). He ascended a virgin peak that he christened "Cerro Peña Vieja del Pissis" (S27°47'16" W68°44'00"). On the new Argentine maps, these coordinates roughly match those of Pk. 6,195m.

MARCELO SCANU, *Buenos Aires, Argentina*

Cordon Cachi-Palermo, first complete traverse. Cachi-Palermo is an isolated range located in the Argentine province of Salta. Its two main summits, Cachi-Libertador (6,380m) and Palermo (6,184m), are linked by a long and previously unexplored ridge, and surrounded by a number of 6,000m peaks.

In October, we (both Argentine) made the first complete traverse of the entire range in a 10-day, self-sustained effort. After four days of acclimatization, which included the approach to the range from Liquín de las Pailas (3,050m) and the ascent of Pelicelli Peak, we reached the main ridge at La Hoyada Peak (6,012m). Then we traveled north for about 26 km, never dropping under 5,470m, climbing the 6,000ers Hoygaard, Cachi-Libertador, Palermo, Quemado, Guanaco, and Ciénaga Grande peaks (the three last just by Vitry). We descended the beautiful and partially unexplored gorge of the Salado River.

Beyond mountaineering, we had two other two goals. First, as no good local cartography is available (the only map is IGM's 1:250,000, which shows no details), we did a preliminary geographical exploration, measuring all the passes and summits with GPS and clinometer. We found that Cachi-Libertador and Palermo are the only peaks in the range with more than 400m of prominence, that the highest point of the flat Ciénaga Grande Peak is its western summit, and that Pelicelli Peak, traditionally considered to be higher than 6,000m, measured just 5,831m. The complete set of gathered info is available via email: chvitry@yahoo.com, dariobracali@yahoo.com.ar

Our other purpose was a brief archeological study of these mountains, as Vitry is an archeologist. The Incas climbed La Hoyada, Cachi-Libertador, and three minor summits between 1480 and 1532 AD; on top of the first are little ceremonial centers. At La Hoyada's feet are two more archeological sites, and clear traces of an Inca trail still can be seen heading up it. We also found two historical mines and a forgotten arriero pass across the ridge.

DARIO BRACALI, *Argentina, AAC, and* CHRISTIAN VITRY, *Argentina*

CENTRAL ANDES, CHILE

Cerro Marmolejo, Senda Real and The Nook. Austrians Harald Berger and Albert Leichtfried established a wild ice route on the south face of Cerro Marmolejo (6,100m, about 20 km from Baños Morales) in the Cajón del Maipo in January 2006. Their line, Senda Real, climbs six difficult pitches of glacial ice with enormous roofs and pillars (WI5, 6-, 7-, 7+, 5, 6-), at over 4,500m, before continuing up lower-angle slopes to the summit. After onsighting the first three pitches, they used redpoint tactics on the crux pitch, including preplaced screws and hook placements in the ice of a 20' roof. For photos and information, see www.escalando.cl/marmolejo.htm

In February 2002 Canadians Ben Firth and Eamonn Walsh established what was probably the first steep ice line on Marmolejo. Their route, The Nook, climbs five pitches on the southwest face, starting with climbing up to WI4 to reach a prominent scree ledge. From the ledge they took the rightmost of three independent lines. A 60m WI6/6+ pillar, reminiscent of the famous Canadian route French Maid, followed by a 30m WI5 pitch, led to a plateau, which they crossed, then continued to the summit. Although warm temperatures limited their options, they saw many promising-looking lines for colder months.

Cerro Marmolejo's West Ridge apparently sees some traffic as a mountaineering objective. Firth and Walsh note seeing several bivy sites and cairns as they descended that route, and also encountered another party coming up the ridge.

Cordon Granito, overview and various ascents. Cordon Granito is part of the Río Cipreses National Reserve, located in Chile's VI Region, about 100km south of Santiago and just north of the better-known Torres del Brujo Range. Before we visited the area I spoke with a few people, some of whom described remote and unexplored granite walls supposedly up to 900m.

The area was first explored in 1883, when German pioneer Paul Gussfeldt climbed several 3,000m peaks and even photographed the Agujas del Palomo. In 1959 Eduardo García, Pedro Durand, and Francisco Vivanco made the first ascent of one of the range's most challenging peaks, Dr. Hernán Cruz (4,565m). Since then only a handful of teams have climbed in the area, the last to put up new routes visiting in 1993.

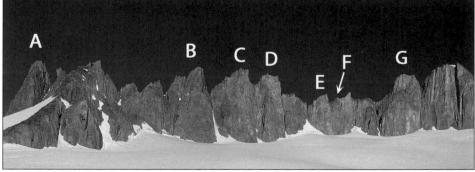

The Agujas del Palomo granite spires: (A) El Velero. (B) La Maestra. Las Mellizas (C) Grande and (D) Chica. (E) El Penitente. (F) La del Lado. (G) El Búho. *Jose Ignacio Morales*

We left Santiago in January 2005, a team consisting of Basques Mikel Martiarena and David Segurado, German David Bruder, and Chileans Waldo Farías (from the 1993 expedition), Jose Edwards, and I. Given the remoteness of the range, we hauled gear and food to last for 30 days.

We knew it wouldn't be easy to get to the walls. It took five long days to finally reach them. As we got closer, the walls got smaller, and we could not help but feel disappointed after such a long approach. Instead of 900m walls, we found mostly 200-300m walls, although longer routes exist in the Dr. Hernán Cruz area.

Punta María Ángeles: (1) Directa (600m, D+ 5.9, Martiarena-Segurado, 2005). (2) Normal (350m, 50°, Bruder, 2005). (3) Arista Este (400m, 5.6/7, Bruder-Farías, 2005). *Jose Ignacio Morales*

Our disappointment, however, didn't keep us from putting up several new routes, including a 700m alpine line on Dr. Hernán Cruz's west face, two on Sandra's west face of about 300m, three new routes, up to 500m, on an apparently unclimbed peak we dubbed "Punta María Ángeles" (ca. 4,300m) and several shorter routes on a nearby crag. All the action took place above 4,000m.

Cerro Dr. Hernán Cruz: (1) Normal (Durand-García-Vivanco, 1959). (2) Las Mulas del Apocalipsis (770m, D+ IV 5.9 45-50°, Edwards-Morales, 2005). (3) Sur Directa (700m, 5.10a WI4 80°, Besser-Farías, 1993). (4) UC-DAV (700m, 65°, García-Huidobro-Flowree, 1993). *Jose Ignacio Morales*

After two weeks, part of the team left. David Segurado and I stayed, moving camp to the Agujas del Palomo, a magnificent chain of a dozen granite spires, up to 200m high, with steep west faces. There wasn't a single climb reported from this area.

Our plan was to climb a spire a day for as long as our supplies lasted. In five days we climbed five spires. Overall, we put up more than 20 new routes in 21 days. All the routes were climbed ground-up in alpine style, without the use of a hammer and only leaving slings and jammed knots for rappels.

Cordon Granito is still a wild and remote range, and to date there is not a single piece of fixed pro. It is our responsibility to keep it like this, as a wild adventure-climbing destination for future generations to enjoy.

JOSE IGNACIO MORALES, *Chile*

CENTRAL ANDES, ARGENTINA

Aconcagua, 2005-2006 season overview. From November 15, 2005, to March 15, 2006, the Parque Provincial Aconcagua had 7,285 visitors who trekked or climbed. This is 12.5% more than the preceding year. There are now 40 rangers (34 in the early season). Even after the season finished, rangers and climbers still were active in the park. There were 4,271 individuals who attempted the summit, 65 more than during the 2004-2005 season. An estimated 35% reached the 6,959m summit. Eighty-five percent of the visitors were non-Argentineans, who can now get permits by Internet or with help from their consulates. Three people died (two Spanish and a Swiss).

There is now a GPS and weather station on Aconcagua's summit, and the information is sent by automatic radio command. The park has improved waste and garbage disposal. Even the 780 mules in the park suffered fewer injuries, thanks to a special project to assist them. There is now an ambulance in the lower park, and the Mendoza police rescue team is active, even using a helicopter. The Horcones hut, which burned last year, has been improved and now has bathrooms.

The Club Andinista Mendoza made its third consecutive winter ascent, reaching the summit on July 24. The team consisted of Popi Spagnoli, Gonzalo Dell Agnola, and Horacio Cunietti. Spagnoli is the first female to ascend Aconcagua in winter.

Sometimes Aconcagua is a circus. A Peruvian named Holmes Pantoja Bayona made a record by ascending Aconcagua from Horcones in 13 hours (4,112m of altitude gain). He summited on February 3, 2006, in sneakers, and returned to his starting point after 20:35. Another Peruvian, Jaime Ramirez Quiroz, made a new record on February 24. He went from Horcones to the summit in 9:30, 14:59 round-trip. The first sea level-to-summit ascent was made by a 17-member Argentina Navy team. Each member ran a sector of the 1,600km between Mar del Plata (on the Atlantic Coast) and the summit, which the anchor man reached on January 17, 2006.

Italian Angelo D'Arrigo set a world record by flying a non-motorized delta wing to 9,100m while flying over Aconcagua's summit.

MARCELO SCANU, *Buenos Aires, Argentina*

Pico Polaco, An Offer You Can't Refuse. On January 12, 2006, Scott Vanderplaats and I completed a new route on Pico Polaco (6,001m), in the central Argentine Andes. The route follows an obvious couloir up the northwest face, then summits via the north ridge. This face was previously unclimbed. The route begins at the lower snowfield and traverses up and left over loose

An Offer You Can't Refuse on the north face of Pico Polaco. *Jarrett Tishmack*

mixed rock, followed by an excellent traverse into the main couloir. The couloir contains headwalls of excellent moderate ice and mixed pitches. We accessed the ridge by a chimney system in the upper headwall, passing through gigantic towers with beautiful icefalls on all sides. The ridge offers scary and exposed rock, with excellent views of the Argentine foothills to the east and the Chilean highlands and the Pacific Ocean to the west. We reached the north summit by a steep face of alpine ice for the last 50m, while the main summit was a 15-minute traverse to the south. We descended the normal south face route. We had believed our route would link up with the Austrian north ridge route of 2002. However, we found that there are two distinct ridges, separated by a large snowfield, on the north side of the mountain. Our route climbs the ridge visible from base camp, and thus climbs new terrain all the way to the summit. We named the route An Otter You Can't Refuse, due to its aesthetic quality on a beautiful mountain. It took 43 hours to traverse the mountain (including an open bivy), bergschrund-to-bergschrund, with 1,000m of technical climbing (5.7 R/X M4- 70°).

Scott Vanderplaats taking caution not to send down any watermelon-sized rocks on the first pitch of technical climbing, Pico Polaco. *Jarrett Tishmack*

JARRETT TISHMACK, *Ft. Collins, Colorado, AAC*

NORTHERN PATAGONIA, CHILE

COCHAMÓ

Valle Cochamó, overview and various ascents. At pitch 13 on the white granite of the 1,000m Trinidad wall, Argentine Esequiel Manoni and I were interrupted by a condor's 2m wing span slicing the air, as the curious bird swept by our position. Below was the Cochamó River valley, a.k.a. the Yosemite of South America. The sun shone on the thick rainforests, waterfalls, and 1,000m walls dominating our views. The typically dry, stable February [2006] weather was here. Our predetermined line began on the west face of the north Trinidad Tower but worked its way over to the north face halfway up. The route began on flaring 5.10 butt cracks, later taking us to classic 5.10 face and dihedral-crack pitches. After we exchanged prolonged stares with the condor, we continued up. The following seven pitches ascended a mixture of cracks, including an easily protected 5.9 offwidth, an excellent 50m 5.10a fingertip splitter, and finishing with a perfect 5.9 hand crack. After a 14-hour push from the base, we inaugurated the longest fully free line in the valley: Bienvenidos a Mi Insomnio, 5.10d, 920m, 20 pitches, nine being 5.10. We walked the last 300m to the peak and took in the incredible views before the sun set. Volcan Tronador's immense-ness, capped by glaciers, stood out among other snow-capped summits: Volcan Orsono, Calbuco,

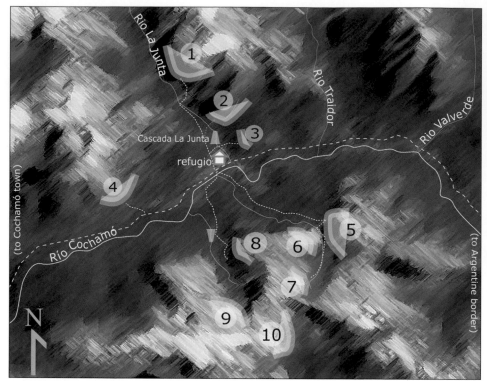

The walls of Valle Cochamó:

1. Cerro Capicua (a.k.a. Roca Grande de la Junta; 1,000m, two routes)
2. Cerro La Junta (1,000m, four routes)
3. Paredes Secas (cragging area)
4. Pared Arco Iris (approximately 1,000m, one unfinished project)
5. Cerro Trinidad (just less than 1,000m at the wall's highest part, more than 15 routes)

6. Piedra de Gorila (500m, five routes)
7. Cerro La Laguna (400m, two routes)
8. Pared lindi (600m, one unfinished project)
9. Cerro Walwalun (900m, one route)
10. El Monstruo (more than 1,000m, Cochamó's biggest wall, one route)

Map and caption info from Daniel Seeliger

Puntiagudo, and even far away Aguja Principal outside Bariloche, Argentina.

Other new and recommended routes include the German route Viaje a la Luna Creciente (5.12d A0, Jens Richter-Sabine Tittel, December 2004), which ascends 1,070m in 24 pitches, following a prominent crescent-moon dihedral on the south face of Cerro La Junta. All 24 pitches go free, except for one rappel/pendulum. The American route Camp Farm (5.11c, Andy Hoyt-Daniel Seeliger, December 2004) makes its way for 300m up less-than-vertical faces and dihedrals on the lower west face of La Junta. In February 2005, after getting shell-fish poisoning and visiting the local hospital in Puerto Montt, an Italian team established Nunca Mas Mariscos (5.12d, Simona Pedefenni-Giovanni Ongaro-Cristian Gianatti-Ismaele Fosti-Lorenzo Lamfranchi), which ascends 17 pitches up the center of Trinidad's central tower. Another impressive Italian line, Vista del Condor (5.12b A2, Helmut Gargitter-Much Thaler-Bernhard Mock-Pauli Trenkwqloler, February 2003) climbs 15 pitches up the left side of Piedra de Gorila's north face. The Brazilian route Vida de Ogro (5.10a A2+, Rian Mueller-Daniel Fernandes, February 2005) climbs nine pitches of a prominent left-facing dihedral on the north face of Trinidad's south tower. Two climbers who have left their mark on Cochamó are Brazilian "Chiquinho" Jose Luis Hartmann and Sergio Tartari. While camped for months in the valley, they established new lines on or near Trinidad almost every year since the valley's first route in 1997. One of their classic lines, Alandalaca (5.12b, February 2000) ascends nine long pitches up the left-side arête of Trinidad's southern tower. Chiquinho's newest line, Pegadito a la Pared (5.11c A0, Jose Luis Hartmann-Valentin Reimay, February 2006) climbs seven pitches up the right-side arête. Other Chiquinho-Sergio routes include the 340m Velho Alerce

Routes established on Trinidad in 2005-06: (1) Bienvenidos a Mi Insomnio. (2) Nunca Mas Mariscos. (3) Vida de Ogro. (4) Pegadito a la Pared. *Daniel Seeliger*

(5.11b A2+, February 2000) on Cerro La Laguna, the 800m Mucho Mucho Granito Arriba (5.10d A4, February 1999) on Trinidad's overhanging north tower and the 750m Tabanos na Cara (5.10+ A3+, March 2003) on Trinidad's central tower.

This Patagonian valley lies in the Chilean Andes 100km east of Puerto Montt and 18km northeast of the town of Cochamó. The approach to the refugio by foot or horse takes four hours along a muddy, eroded trail. The Refugio is run by climbers, has topos and info for almost every route, and is strategically centered near the biggest and more developed walls. On rest days you can fill up on their homemade bread and beer. Cochamó is notorious for wet weather; the driest time of year is from mid-January to mid-March, February being the most stable. December 2005 and February 2006 saw almost no rain. For more information, go to www.Cochamo.com and www.StoneDance.com.

DANIEL SEELIGER, *Bariloche, Argentina*

Cerro La Junta, Trinidad, and Roca Grande de la Junta, new routes. I made my first Cochamó expedition, from the DAV and supported by the Section Bayerland, with Stephan Schanderl (30, mountain guide, also from Munich). We spent six weeks between mid-December 2003 and the end of January 2004 there.

After a complicated journey, starting in Argentina, we wanted to find good, high, untouched walls. We found the 800m south-southwest face of the first mountain behind the La Junta junction, and called the peak Puta Bayerland. [Cochamo locals and most climbers know this peak as Cerro La Junta, which is the name we use elsewhere in this *Journal*—Ed.] The weather was bad: rain and snow for days. After three days of jungle-cutting and transporting equipment to the face, we started on wet rock. We finished in fine weather on December 29, 2003. It was mostly green, sometimes dirty and easy climbing: 23 pitches to the top jungle, without bolts. Alter Gartenweg (IV 5.10a A0).

At the very end of 2003 summer weather arrived. We turned to our second project, the

Roca Grande de la Junta (a.k.a. Capicua): (1) Pluja, Fam i Feina (Barrios-Barrios-Esquirol-Farreres-Solís-Teixidó, 2001). (2) Adios Michi Olzowy (Frieder-Schanderl-Tivadar, 2005). *Thomas Tivadar*

face's steeper left side. We began climbing with fixed ropes. However, on January 1, 2004 we found that our money (nearly $1,000 U.S.) had been stolen from base camp. We lost three days of dream weather while reporting this to the police at Cochamó village. The following days we climbed and fixed up to the 11th pitch. Then in four days we climbed to the top jungle and rappelled our new 18-pitch route, which we called 1000 Dollar Gedächtnisweg (VI 5.11b A4c). We did the aid without drilled protection (clean, new wave) on good hardware: 20 beaks, cams, heads, pins, hooks, etc.

At the end of our trip, on January 23, we climbed a new alpine route on the north face of the north tower of Trinidad. Dick and Doof (15 pitches, IV 5.10b plus one point of A0) has good slab and crack climbing on excellent granite, with a few runouts and no bolts.

On our second visit to the Cochamó Valley, in 2005, there were of us: Schanderl, Felix Frieder (29), and I (44). Our aim was a first ascent on the biggest wall in Cochamó, the 1,000m west face of Roca Grande de la Junta [a.k.a. Capicua]. After cutting a new trail we transported equipment to the base. We found a possible line, without too much drilling, on the right side of the face. On the left side is the 2001 Spanish route Pluja, Fam i Feina. Nice weather and rain had been alternating every few days, so we started with fixed ropes. Our portaledge would not have a chance in the rainstorms, so we commuted daily between base camp and the wall. Later we put up a small tent on a ledge to save time.

The lower half of the climb had hard slabs (5.11) and easy vegetated cracks. In the middle of the wall we climbed steeper rock, mixed aid and free. The cracks were mostly dirty or green, limiting

Felix Frieder (L) and Stephan Schanderl (R) atop pitch 15 on Adios Michi Olzowy. *Thomas Tivadar*

our free-climbing possibilities. We used hardware ranging from 23 beaks to a #4 Bigbro. After 19 pitches (up to 65m) we reached easy terrain and climbed about 300m (5.0-5.3) up and down to the main summit. We rappelled the wall, mostly down our route. We named the route with our dead Bavarian friend and climber in mind: Adios Michi Olzowy (VI 5.11b/c A4b/c).

THOMAS TIVADAR, *Munich, Germany*

Cerro La Junta, Viaje a la Luna Creciente. In the grassy meadows of a high plateau, after six hours of horse packing along a muddy trail with several delicate river crossings, Jens Richter and I were surrounded by snowcapped mountains that towered over a valley that holds stunning granite walls of more than 1,000m. Yosemite Valley must lose in any comparison. The Valle Cochamó offers both more and higher walls, and you do not share the breathtaking views with anybody else.

Up the valley lies the Refugio Cochamó, a tiny old wooden cabin with nearby camping (and a loo with lots of view). Some days, the neighbor who lives 3km up the river comes riding by, stops for a cup of maté and a quick chat about what's new in the valley. It's never much, just a couple of cows and horses and the everlasting sound of waterfalls. Condors circle majestically around the granite walls.

Cerro La Junta: (1) Alter Gartenweg (Schanderl-Tivadar, 2003). (2) 1000 Dollar Gedächtnisweg (Schanderl-Tivadar, 2004). (3) Viaje a la Luna Creciente (Richter-Tittel, 2004). Not shown: Camp Farm (Hoyt-Seeliger, 2004; ascends only the lower part of the wall, starting as (3) for 3.5 pitches, then same as (2) for pitches 5 and 6, before an independent finish). *Jens Richter*

Some climbers have left their traces on a few of these walls, but free-climbing remains in its infancy. A dominant and beautiful line on Cerro La Junta captured our attention. Shaped like a delicate crescent moon, a system of crack lines and dihedrals shoots up the 1,000m-high wall.

During our four weeks in the Refugio Cochamó, the unpredictable Patagonian weather and other bad circumstances gave us only seven days of climbing. We used the first days to clear the very old trail that leads through the dense, wet rainforest to the base of the wall. But after we fixed ropes and stored food and water high on the wall, an accident stopped our ambitions and reminded us of our vulnerability. Tired after a long, happy day of climbing, Jens slipped as we stumbled along the muddy path, and a bamboo stick ripped his cornea. Not a nice thing, when the clinic is a six-hour hike and one-and-a-half-day bus ride away.

Days of sunshine came and went while Jens sat in the cabin, blind and inpatient. Ten days later he seemed well enough to try again, but the weather changed, a north wind bringing five days of ridiculously strong, incessant rain. Eventually, the first day of sunshine found us back on the wall. It seems, though, that the Patagonian St. Peter is not a climber: the sky broke open and untamed rains poured down again. The wall became a massive waterfall. We were on pitch 10, diving desperately for cracks in which to place bad gear to abseil from, as the water rose to our hips.

After another drenching week in the cabin, we got two days of reasonably good weather. This allowed us, after 39 hours of climbing, to finish our free route [except for one rappel point], climbing beautiful and beautifully exposed granite slabs, hard vertical faces, and steep, perfect cracks and dihedrals all the way to the summit. There we stood with the day fading, soaking up the breathtaking view and drinking home-brewed German schnapps.

We can recommend Valle Cochamó to anyone who wants to experience the unique nature of Patagonia (rain included), who wants to hike on old gaucho trails through a mossy rainforest, who wants to find himself in a remote and overwhelming paradise. It is a peaceful, precious place.

Andy Hoyt on pitch four of Viaje a la Luna Creciente, Cerro La Junta. *Jens Richter*

Viaje a la Luna Creciente (1,070m, 24 pitches, 7c (7a obl.) A0, Jens Richter-Sabine Tittel, December 2004). Belay stations are established, and important bolts and pitons remain in place. Climbers need 60m twin ropes and two complete sets of cams and nuts.

SABINE TITTEL, *Germany*

El Monstruo, La Gran Raja. Jerzy Stefanski and I (both Polish) created a new line on the previously unclimbed east wall of El Monstruo. After transporting our equipment to Barranca Pass (sort of our advanced base camp), we descended the next morning to the Barranca Valley, through a vertical forest. At 2 p.m. on February 18, 2006, we started our climb, leading a few pitches up to 7a. After a cold, uncomfortable bivouac with no sleeping bags or other bivy equipment, we climbed the rest of the wall the next day, up to a snowy headwall ridge, encountering difficulties up to 6c. We reached the top exactly when the sun set, then followed the ridge down north to our bivouac on the pass.

The east wall of El Monstruo (the name given by climbers in Cochamó) is 1,000m high and has one weak point: a series of dihedrals that, after about 10 pitches, becomes a crack and then a chimney. That is why we called our line La Gran Raja (*Big Crack* in English, *Wielkie Pekniecie* in Polish). The route has 22 pitches, difficulties up to 7a (we climbed it onsight), climbing distance of 1,100m plus 200m of snowy ridge to the top.

Before El Monstruo, we tried to repeat the Alandalaca on Trinidad Sur but didn't succeed (bad weather and lack of energy).

We also tried a new line on Piedra de Gorila. After two days of cleaning dirty and grassy cracks, an uncomfortable bivouac, and a few falls, we gave up.

Cochamó Valley is located in northern Patagonia, close to Puerto Montt. Summer weather makes this area similar to Yosemite Valley. There are five 1,000m big walls and a few smaller

La Gran Raja, the first and only route on El Monstruo. *Boguslaw Kowalski*

walls, mostly unclimbed. Thanks to Daniel Seeliger, an American living in Bariloche, for the friendly atmosphere in Cochamó. Nice place, nice people.

BOGUSLAW KOWALSKI, *Poland*

CENTRAL PATAGONIA, CHILE

Allevano Tower: (1) Conquistador Ridge (Anderson-Grez-Herlighy-Selda, 2004). (2) Avellano pal Verano (Grez-Morales, 2006). (2a) Costumes Rehearsal (O'Neill-Roseberry, 2006). Dots indicate hidden portions. *Jose Ignacio Morales*

Allevano Tower, Avellano pal Verano, and Costumes Rehearsal. While working for a month by massive San Lorenzo Peak as a mountain instructor, I thought about a third attempt to climb a direttissima up the northeast pillar of Avellano Tower in the XI Región de Aysén.

My first time in the valley as a climber ended with the first ascent of the spire by a snow, rock, and ice route (Conquistador Ridge, IV 5.10 80°, *AAJ 2004*, pp. 307-308). Bad weather persisted for 26 out of 28 days, allowing us to climb only one route but leaving us with a taste of the potential of the valley, in particular for the direttisssima, which my partners Dave Anderson and Jamie Selda attempted on that trip.

In 2005, with less time than the previous summer, Marcelo Mascareño and I made a second attempt to the direct route. Conditions were a bit better, but poor weather and a lack of time kicked us out off the wall and back to Coyhaique to enjoy New Year's eve. That same season, a Basque team (Azier Izaguirre and Xavier Amonárriz) also attempted the direct route, but failed due to bad weather.

Jose Ignacio "Nacho" Morales, editor of *Escalando* (a recently launched Chilean climbing magazine) and my climbing partner this time, had asked me, "What about Avellano for the summer?" I thought about the poor weather, the time spent in the tent staring at the wall getting fat and swearing at the weather. And I said, "I'll do it."

I finished work in the San Lorenzo area on February 12, 2006, and returned to the Avellano Towers on the 14th. Along with Nacho and me came Wyoming climbers Becca Roseberry and Brendan O'Neill, and my girlfriend Julie, from France. We settled into base camp, with the conditions quite dry. Most of the snow was gone, and the cracks looked clean of ice. On February 16 Nacho and the Americans scouted the best approach from our base camp. There were some significant avalanches tumbling down from the hanging glacier at the foot of the wall, which made the approach not casual. Plus, routefinding was required on the upper glacier to reach the upper snowfield.

Overcast skies the next two days had us eating under the tarp, but on the evening of February 18 Nacho asked me to set up the alarm for 3 a.m., so we could check the weather.

In the morning clouds partially covered the skies, but the anxiety to get climbing was strong, and we left camp at 5 a.m. Before it was clear we were scrambling up the 4th- to easy 5th-class slabs at the beginning of the approach. At dawn we began the glacier travel and quickly crossed the snowfield. At 7 a.m. we switched from mountain boots to climbing shoes.

The first four pitches follow a straightforward crack/corner system, with a potpourri of cracks up to 5.10-. Then several splitters, a couple of roofs, and face climbing on great granite led to the summit in five more pitches, with consistent 5.10 moves. At 5:15 p.m. a scream from Nacho, who had reached the summit, put a smile on my face.

The descent was not casual. Stuck ropes delayed our return. The glacier seemed longer on the way down. After 22 hours we arrived at camp, at 3 a.m. At 4 a.m. Becca and Brendan left to attempt a variation of the direct route set by Nacho and I, and made the second ascent of the northeast face, by Costumes Rehearsal, which went at about the same grade as our route.

We named our route Avellano pal Verano (360m, TD- IV 5.10).

IGNACIO GREZ, *Coyhaique, Chile*

CENTRAL PATAGONIA, ARGENTINA

San Lorenzo, Café Cortado. The Up Project is a series of expeditions I conceived, in order to bring some strong climbers to remote locations around the globe. Our first trip was to Pakistan (see report elsewhere in this *Journal*). Our second trip, which had two parts, took us to Patagonia.

In the first part Italians Hervé Barmasse, Elia Andreola, Kurt Astner, Yuri Parimbelli, and I attempted to complete an unfinished line on the west face of Cerro Piergiorgio, which I climbed to within 200m of the ridge with Maurizio Giordani in 1995. After several attempts

The north face of San Lorenzo: Café Cortado (L) and the Hauf-Rawson-Walter route (R). *Giovanni Ongaro*

that involved placing a number of fixed ropes, we completed the first 11 pitches, but I was hit by rockfall and we retreated.

The second part of the Up Project Patagonia adventure took Italians Giovanni Ongaro and Matteo Bernasconi and Swiss Lorenzo Lanfranchi to Cerro San Lorenzo. It early March they met Barmasse, who was waiting in the town of Perito Moreno. They had intended to approach the mountain via the Rio Oro Valley, but since Mario Sar, the owner of a piece of land one needs to cross to reach it, demanded $1,200 per person, they changed plans and approached from the Chilean side instead [but climbed on the Argentine side; San Lorenzo is a border peak—Ed.]. They crossed the border and traveled to Cochrane.

It took two days hiking to reach base camp, which they established next to a small glacial lake at the base of the mountain's northernmost flank. Barmasse, Bernasconi, Lanfranchi, and Ongaro originally intended to attempt the northeast face, but due to continuous precipitation its gullies and snow ramps were not in condition. They changed their objective to the massive couloir in the north face, which leads straight to the summit. Two weeks of continuous bad weather kept them in base camp, allowing only one outing, during which they dug a snow cave near the foot of the face.

On March 26, in spite of the bad weather, the foursome moved up to the snow cave, breaking trail through more than three feet of new snow, only to find no trace of the cave or the equipment they had left. Unable to find their shovel, they dug a new cave using their cook pot. On the morning of the 28th, although the sky was covered, the barometric pressure was high, so they made an attempt. They left the snow cave in the early hours and climbed two pitches of 80° ice to reach the gully itself, following the line climbed by Americans John Hauf, Timothy Rawson, and Tom Walter (see *AAJ 1988*, pp. 173-174). After 1,000m, where the Americans veered right toward the north ridge (from where they retreated along the De Agostini route without reaching the summit), Barmasse, Bernasconi, Lanfranchi, and Ongaro continued straight up toward the summit headwall. Here lies the crux of the climb: a short but difficult S-shaped gully that brought them to the summit mushroom. After 10 hours of climbing they reached the summit, having completed a line that they christened Café Cortado.

LUCA MASPES, *Sondrio, Italy*

SOUTHERN PATAGONIA, ARGENTINA

CHALTEN MASSIF

Patagonia summary. [Note: this summary supplements the individual route reports below—Ed.] Unlike the past few years, this season did not offer an extended good weather period in late January and February, which climbers had come to expect and rely upon. There have been no major changes in the National Parks Service policy regarding climbing permits, which are still free. A definitive review of the measure enacted in late 2004, which established permit fees, is still pending. This season was characterized by several important repeat ascents, particularly on Cerro Fitz Roy, where during February five of its longest climbs were repeated. These included the second complete ascent of Ensueño on the west face, climbed in two days by Slovenes Rok Blagus, Tomaz Jakofcic, and Miha Valic; the fourth ascent of the Slovak Route on the southwest face, climbed by Slovenes Boris Lorencic and Urban Azman; the second ascent of the French route on the northwest pillar, climbed over two days by Argentine Gabriel Otero and Brazilians Edemilson Padilha and Valdesir Machado; the first free ascent and first one-day ascent of the Casarotto route (Kearney-Knight variation), by Americans Bean Bowers and Josh Wharton in 15 hours bergschrund-to-summit (24 hours roundtrip from Paso Superior), at about 5.11+; and the first female ascent of the same route, by 23 year-old American Crystal Davis-Robbins, with Canadian Jon Walsh in a 27-hour push, bergschrund-to-summit. Davis-Robbins' ascent is particularly significant because, unlike some "first female ascents," she shared equally the leading duties. Just three days later American Helen Motter, also swinging leads, climbed the Franco-Argentine route with Bowers (his second Fitz Roy ascent in 72 hours), completing the third or fourth female ascent of the route. Elsewhere on Fitz Roy, veteran American Jim Donini, who first visited the Chalten massif in 1974, attempted a new route on the west flank of the Goretta (north) Pillar with Tom Englebock. They climbed 14 pitches before retreating in deteriorating weather. They intend to return next year to complete it. Elsewhere in the massif, Americans Sean Leary and Bean Bowers did a nine-hour, no-falls ascent of the Red Pillar (550m, 5.12b) route on Mermoz, with both climbers climbing all pitches.

Cerro Torre continues to be climbed almost exclusively by the Compressor Route, but ironically this year the long-disputed first ascent route was both disproved and climbed, and the true first ascent route, the Ragni di Lecco west face route, was repeated. In early December a Franco-Argentine team led by Bruno Sourzac and including Ramiro Calvo, Walter Rossini, Max O'Dell, and Gabriel and Luciano Fiorenza completed the fifth ascent to the summit of this route (previous ascents to the summit: Chiappa-Conti-Ferrari-Negri, 1974, now known to be the true first ascent of Cerro Torre; Bragg-Carman-Wilson, 1977; Bearzi-Winkelmann, 1986; Elias-Merino, 1997).

ROLANDO GARIBOTTI, *Club Andino Bariloche, AAC*

Cerro Torre, El Arca de los Vientos. On November 12 and 13, Alessandro Beltrami, Rolando Garibotti, and Ermanno Salvaterra became the first to climb Cerro Torre from the north. Their route, El Arca de los Vientos (1,200m, 37 pitches, VI 5.11 A1 90°), starts with the Bragg-Donini-Wilson (1977) Torre Egger line on the lower east face to the Col of Conquest, then moves onto the northwest face, and then the north face to the west ridge to the summit. See Salvaterra's feature article on their historic climb, earlier in this *Journal*.

Cerro Torre, The Long Run; and Cerro Standhardt, Extreme Emotions. On Janurary 3, 2006, Stephen Koch and I went to Chalten and the next day to the Agostini/Bridwell Base Camp at Laguna Torre. The weather was unstable, as described in many Patagonian reports. Our first idea was the Marsigny-Parkin to the Ferrari route to the summit of Cerro Torre. At the Noruegos camp we met Dean Potter, who was waiting for weather to improve. He wanted to BASE jump from Cerro Torre. After we returned to BC together, I suggested that Dean join us on the climb. He was happy to.

After several days of bad weather we returned to Noruegos, but on the way up the glacier we noticed that conditions on the Marsigny-Parkin were not good for safe and fast climbing, so we decided on a route we'd previously considered as a second option.

On January 17 we started to climb from the glacier up the 250m El Mochito via new

Stephen Koch on pitch 9 of Extreme Emotions. *Marko Prezelj*

ground (F6a), and then joined the Piola-Anker route on El Mocho to reach its top. We used a single rope, the leader climbed without a pack, and the seconds carried small packs. We were climbing fast and started to rappel down the north side of El Mocho around midday, when the weather turned bad. After 150m of rappels we climbed snow and ice slopes toward the Col of Patience and luckily missed a big wind-slab avalanche. The crux of this section was a steep mixed pitch 150m below the col. It took me almost an hour to free-climb it, though I took a fall on the exit slab: my first leader fall in the mountains in ten years. Very interesting and challenging pitch with wet snow and rotten ice.

We reached the Col of Patience in unmotivating weather and spent an uncomfortable, wet, cold night in a crevasse, before descending in the wind and rain the morning of the 18th. At Noruegos the next day, the weather improved.

On January 20 we started again with the same idea and same tactics. Before dawn we climbed El Mochito and at 1 p.m. reached the Col of Patience, where we rested and prepared water before continuing up the Compressor Route. The climbing there is nice, and we found plenty of mixed sections before complete darkness set in, two pitches below the ice towers. The weather had been perfect—no wind and no clouds. After midnight we cut a small ledge in an ice bridge [a short snow/ice feature linking the tower and the headwall] under the headwall, where we sat and prepared water. At first light we started climbing the headwall and the infamous bolting monument, reaching the windy summit around 1 p.m. We spent more than an hour taking pictures and looking for a good BASE jump spot, but Dean decided that Cerro Torre isn't steep enough for a safe jump and joined us for 10 hours of a more "classic" descent of the Compressor Route.

On January 29 Stephen and I went up to study some possibilities on Torre Standhardt, finding an interesting new line on the bottom half of the east face. At first light the next morning we started up the rock buttress just left of Tomahawk, following steep cracks and logical passages. Atop pitch eight we rappelled 15m into a deep chimney, which we climbed in "interesting" mixed conditions. It was late in the afternoon, and a small waterfall ran over the steepest section, where the ice was thin and rotten. At the top of the chimney, luckily we caught the last half hour of sun. We waited there until 3 a.m. for cold temperatures before continuing. In the dark, windy morning with fog, we missed the start of the Exocet chimney, but soon found the right way and climbed Exocet to the summit ridge, where we noticed that the weather had gone (wind, clouds, rain). However, the cold temperatures kept the ice in place. We continued up one short rock pitch to the summit snow and ice. It took two more ropelengths to reach the bottom of the summit mushroom. The 30m mushroom was quite challenging, due to poor snow conditions on the upper half. It took me almost an hour to reach the top, at 3 p.m. February 1.

The descent was a story in itself; we were under time pressure because we had a bus to catch early on the morning of February 3, and a flight that same day. We rappelled, and after about eight rappels our rope stuck, and the sheath was destroyed. We had to climb back 150m to the ramp on Exocet, by which we descended. We reached the couloir at midnight and continued the descent with 30m rappels. We made it to our tent at Noruegos around 4 a.m., slept for four hours, and descended to BC.

It was interesting trip, with most of the elements an expedition needs to stay in my memory. We were motivated and ready to climb most of the possible climbing days, which were rich and intense with new experience.

MARKO PREZELJ, *Slovenia*

Fitz Roy, Linea di Eleganza, second ascent and first free ascent. In a single push from February 22 to 24, 2006, Tommy Caldwell, Topher Donahue, and Erik Roed made the first free and first alpine-style ascent (second overall) of Linea di Eleganza (1,250m, 33 pitches, VI 5.12+ M8, Codo-Fava-Orlandi, 2004) on the east face of Fitz Roy. For the story of their incredible ascent, see Donahue's feature earlier in this *Journal*.

Aguja Rafael Juarez, Blood on the Tracks; and Desmochada, The Sound and the Fury. In December, Taki Miyamoto (Japan), Freddie Wilkinson (New Hampshire), Paul Tureki (Alaska), and I (Maine) established a new route on Cerro Innominata (also known as Aguja Rafael Juarez). We climbed the steep, 2,000' north face, following a continuous crack system up its western side near the skyline. Our first attempt was thwarted by strong winds, but, during an unusually stable period of weather around Christmas, the four of us returned and finished the route,

Freddie Wilkinson on pitch five of The Sound and the Fury.
Dave Sharratt

using some aid. I then returned with Taki and Fred and free-climbed the aid pitches, creating Blood on the Tracks: 11 long pitches, 5.12. The route is characterized by steep, clean crack climbing and is quite sustained until pitch nine, which is the free-climbing crux, then eases into 5.10 terrain. [For the route line, refer to Jon Walsh's Aguja Rafael Juarez photo on p. 297, *AAJ 2005*. Where the line for Comono begins to angle slightly left, Blood on the Tracks continues up, traverses slightly right to the left side of the shaded, triangular roof, and then continues straight up to the summit.—Ed.]

Upon descending to El Chalten, Taki departed for his final semester of law school, Paul turned his attention to new routing in El Chalten, and Fred and I waited out poor weather for most of January, until the following scenario played out:

It is 4 a.m., January 23, 2006, the wind is ripping and rain drips into our bivy cave at high camp. When a big gust comes, or the wind suddenly changes direction, it snaps loudly, like the crack of a whip. Freddie groans, and I roll over and try to sleep a bit more.

By 8 a.m. the wind still blows strongly, but the rain has stopped. We sip instant coffee and recommence strategizing. A large portion of our mental energy over the past five weeks has been spent strategizing, plotting, and scheming, to be ready to strike out when the elusive weather window arrives. Having learned the hard way that attempting a summit on a marginal day can waste time and energy, this past week—the last week in our trip—we blew it on one of the best sunny streaks of the season. Now, bivied at high camp, we are riddled with angst and hungry.

At 10 a.m. the wind suddenly quiets. It's late, but rather than something we know we can do quickly, we set out for a new route we have been eyeing on Desmochada. We will scramble up 3,000' of 4th- and 5th-class terrain to reach a 2,600' vertical wall, split with continuous crack systems. We have 44 hours before we have to be 15 miles from here, in El Chalten to catch our flight home.

At 1 a.m., January 24, we sit on the summit in strong and increasing wind. We have climbed a new route (The Sound and the Fury) up the 2,600' south face, on a steep, continuous crack system between El Facón and El Condor, mostly free (5.11+, with short sections of A0). We have made the fourth ascent of Desmochada, and now have 29 hours to get from the summit to El Chalten. As we descend our line, winds whip into cracking gusts by our fourth rappel, sending one of our ropes sailing sideways, snagging too far away to pendulum out to. We are forced to leave the rope and make 20m rappels. Halfway down, a whiteout engulfs us. We make it back to town after a slow, cold, harrowing descent: a 38-hour push from high camp to summit to town.

After a celebratory steak and liter of beer we pass out in a field and sleep through our 6 a.m. alarm clock. Magically, Fred wakes up as the bus is leaving. I chase it down in my skivvies, successfully convincing the driver to wait for us.

DAVE SHARRATT

Desmochada, Golden Eagle. On January 29 German Alexander Huber and I went from Bridwell Camp to Campo de los Polacos, directly below the west face of Aguja Desmochada. The next morning at 6 a.m. we started up the lower slab to the beginning of the actual climbing, at the base of the prominent southwest buttress of Desmochada.

At 9 a.m. we started climbing and reached the end of the vertical, central part. We fixed our two climbing ropes and rappelled back to the "Eagle's Nest," a perfect bivy platform. After a beautiful and exposed bivy, we started again at first light and, despite the chill and wind, made the summit at 11 a.m. We descended via the fully equipped The Sound and the Fury [see above] and made it back to Campo de los Polacos at 6 p.m. The next morning saw us, with all our equipment, walking back to Campo Bridwell.

Our new route, Golden Eagle, more or less follows the line of the prominent southwest buttress. We climbed the lower, less-than-vertical part just left of the buttress, while the dead-vertical central part of the route follows the obvious continuous crack system just right of the

Aguja Desmochada: (1) El Condor (Bridwell-Dunmire-Smith, 1988). (2) El Facón (Bowers-Bransby-Tresch, 2004). (3) The Sound and the Fury (Sharratt-Wilkinson, 2006). (4) Golden Eagle (Huber-Siegrist, 2006). Not show: Dieta del Lagarto (variation to El Facón; Cortes-Walsh-Zegers, 2005). *Alexander Huber*

buttress. Above the "Eagle's Nest" the route joins The Sound and the Fury. The rest of the route follows the low-angle line of the buttress.

We made the first ascent of Golden Eagle without any prior exploring or preparation: fully alpine style from Campo Bridwell to Campo Bridwell. Because of snowfall in the days just before our ascent, the cracks of the first three pitches of the vertical, central part of the wall were iced up and made the climbing difficult. Thus, we had to aid two short sections of the first of these pitches, but under better conditions this pitch should go free at 5.11. The rest of the route went free, even though, due to the cold, we had to rest several times on several pitches (French free, difficulties up to 5.11).

The central part of the route offers mostly steep climbing in hand and fist cracks. The granite is typically very rough, and tape might be helpful. The rest of the 25-pitch route is moderate and not-too-steep face climbing.

We recommend bringing Camalots 0-4, with doubles in the midrange sizes, plus a full set of stoppers. Though not necessary, a small set of pitons might be sensible. Except for one piton in pitch nine and one stopper at the belay after that pitch, there is no gear in place.

STEPHAN SIEGRIST, *Switzerland*

Various ski descents. In the fall Bean Bowers, Ben Ditto, and I completed a ski mountaineering circumnavigation of the Fitz Roy massif. Christened the "Southern Patagonia Ice Cap Expedition"—SPICE Tour for short—we traveled 65 miles, completed several ski descents, used traction kites for high-speed glacier travel, and endured some of the most notoriously bad weather on earth.

Starting from El Chalten we walked and horse-packed up the Rio Electrico valley, then shuttled heavy loads up talus slopes and crevasse fields to the edge of ice cap. After establishing a camp on a rocky ledge, we endured a four-day wind, rain, and snow storm, with steady winds of 40-50 mph and gusts of over 70 mph.

After a break in the weather, we ascended the nearby Gorra Blanca Peak and made a ski descent from the mushroom-capped summit down the southwest face to the west ridge.

Ben Ditto leading some high-speed glacier travel, with Cerro Torre in the background. *Andrew McLean*

During this descent Bowers made an airborne variation near the summit and survived a serious fall that took him over a 50' cliff, before he miraculously stopped, unhurt, on a steep ribbon of powder. After regrouping, we used traction kites to fly downwind to the Circo de los Altares, where we established Camp 2.

Basing out of a camp located in the middle of the cirque, we spent the next week making day trips to nearby couloirs. We warmed up with a descent of what we called Effecto Venturi, a short, south-facing corner/couloir on the western flank of Cerro Rincon, then moved on to ski the steeper and more committing Col de Bloque Empotrado Couloir on Torre Egger. After enduring another storm, we skied two more couloirs, which we called The Shark's Fin and Sacrificial Virgin. The former was a prominent south-facing arête on the western flank of Cerro Rincon, the latter a north-northwest-facing couloir on the ridgeline leading west from Cerro Adela Norte. The final and most spectacular descent in this area was from the Col de la Esperanza on Cerro Torre, which was first reached by Bonatti and Mauri during their 1958 attempt on the peak.

We then kited over to the Mariano Mereno mountain range at speeds up to 30 mph, while towing our heavy sleds. This area had less skiing potential and more bad weather, but we accomplished two more ski descents of remote peaks (shorter, likely unnamed subpeaks near Dos Cumbres), before running out of time.

ANDREW MCLEAN

HIELO CONTINENTAL

Cerro Murallón, Gone with the Wind. On the north pillar of Cerro Murallón (2,831m), Stefan Glowacz and Robert Jasper made the first ascent of Gone with the Wind (1,200m to summit plateau, 27 pitches, 7c+ A2 M4), in November. See Glowacz's feature article earlier in this *Journal*.

Cerro Lliboutry, first ascent, winter ascent. On July 20 Abdo Fernández and I, both Chilean, flew to Punta Arenas and from there traveled overland to Chalten. We intended to accomplish the first ascent of Cerro Lliboutry (1,980m), located 10km northwest of Paso Marconi in the Cordon Gaea. We had attempted the mountain during the 2004 winter, with four other partners, but were driven back by bad rock and lack of adequate protection, a mere 60m from the summit. After carrying our gear to the vicinity of Paso Marconi, we moved into the Eduardo García Soto hut, located north of the pass, on the Chilean side of the border. Bad weather pinned us down for five days, with 5°F temperatures inside the hut. Finally the weather improved and, using sleds and skis, we crossed Glaciar Chico to reach the base of the mountain, where another storm pinned us down for a further five days. On our last available day before we had to start our journey back, the weather improved. We woke at 5 a.m. and started up, climbing the southwest face while it was still dark. Deep snow slowed our progress, and we did not reach the technical part of the climb until well past midday. The upper portion consisted of several pitches of ice and mixed terrain, with difficulties up to WI3 (70°) and M3. We reached the summit at 4 p.m. on August 6. Ours was the first ascent of the mountain and the first winter ascent.

CRISTIÁN VÁSQUEZ ORTIZ, *Club Andino Universitario, Santiago, Chile*

SOUTHERN PATAGONIA, CHILE

TORRES DEL PAINE NATIONAL PARK

General information. Riders on the Storm (1,200m, 5.12d A3), first climbed by Germans Norbert Bätz, Peter Dittrich, Bernd Arnold, Wolfgang Güllich, and Kurt Albert on the east face of Torre Central in 1991, received its fourth ascent, from a Belgian team composed of Olivier and Nicolas Favresse, Seán Villanueva, and Mike Lecomte. After fixing the first six pitches they committed themselves to the wall, spending 11 days up and down to complete the ascent in capsule style, using portaledges. They summited on February 8. Time and weather kept them from freeing everything. They free-climbed all but three pitches, plus two that they didn't redpoint. They describe finding a three-pitch variation to the right of the original line that might go free, but would be quite hard, perhaps 5.13. The other two ascents of this route took place in 2002, by Czechs David Stastny and Jan Kreisinger, and by French Arnaud Boudet, Martial Dumas, Jean Yves Fredericksen, and Yann Mimet.

Other Paine news involves CONAF's (the national park management's) growing concern about rescues and insurance. After the death of a U.S. climber during the 2004-05 season, CONAF now requires that climbers present proof of rescue insurance, including an insured number, and a letter from a helicopter operator confirming that they will come in case of need.

To help those who might visit Paine, below are the basic guidelines, which will help avoid problems when securing the climbing permit, which is free. We thank Hernan Jofre, of Antares Patagonia in Puerto Natales, for this information.

1) Because Paine is located close to the border with Argentina, all foreign visitors must first secure DIFROL (border patrol) clearance. This needs to be done at least 20 days before the start of the expedition. Go to www.difrol.cl, click on the "Autorizacion de Expediciones" link, then go to the bottom of the page and click on the "Si lo desea, puede completar el formulario Aquí" link and fill in the application. This clearance is free.

2) Bring proof of travel insurance or rescue insurance. Note that though AAC membership includes rescue insurance, because the AAC does not issue specific rescue insurance cards and print individual member or policy numbers on membership cards, presenting your AAC membership card probably won't suffice. You will be asked for your own personal rescue insurance number and card. Make sure that information about how to contact the company is included in the proof of insurance. The AAC is working on this issue, so check the website for further updates.

3) Visit www.dap.cl, and contact them at ventas@aeroviasdap.cl and ask for a quote for a possible rescue in Torres de Paine Park. Indicate that it will involve approximately five hours of helicopter time. Present this quote to CONAF, along with your rescue insurance info and your DIFROL clearance to secure the climbing permit, which, as mentioned earlier, is free.

Compiled by ROLANDO GARIBOTTI, *with information from*
HERNAN JOFRE *and* STEVE SCHNEIDER

Cuerno Este, first ascent, Lauchon Este. In early March 2006 Milena Gomez and I, both Argentine, completed the first ascent of Cuerno Este. We approached the peak from the Bader Valley.

Our new route, which we christened Lauchon Este, climbs a line on the east face. We found some traces of passage in the lower part. The first 120m involve easy slabs (5.8), but after the third pitch difficulties increase, with three pitches following perfect cracks (5.10+). We reached the upper basalt formation at the base of an obvious dihedral, which we climbed in one pitch and which is the only feature on the east and north faces that gives access to the upper ridge. We followed the ridge for 120m (easy), climbed a 30m step, then more easy ground, to reach the final summit tower, which required a 45m pitch. At the summit we did not find any traces of passage, and this, combined with Buscaini and Metzeltin's conclusion from their research that all routes stop at the base of the upper basalt formation, lead us to believe that ours is likely the first ascent to the summit. We climbed 500m in nine pitches, with difficulties to 5.10+. The basalt section involves difficulties to 5.9, with little protection. We left belays equipped with threads, pins, or bolts. Because Cuerno Este is lower than some of the neighboring formations, and because our route faces east and is therefore protected from the wind, it is a good objective for a bad weather day. The climb took us 12 hours.

RAMIRO CALVO, *Club Andino Bariloche, Argentina*

Peineta, Capicúa Pastor. In October, Darío Arancibia and I summited Peineta, the fourth Paine Tower, by a new route (Capicúa Pastor, 12 pitches, 500m, 5.9 A1+), making what seems to be the seventh climb of the spire. Our route ascends the west face, facing the Valle del Silencio (opposite the east faces of the Fortress and Shield).

We were a three-climber team, Francisco Rojas being the other member, with the idea of opening, in winter, a new route on the Shield, but we had problems with it from the very beginning. We entered the Paine Towers on August 1, in winter conditions, with loads totaling 1,000kg. After 15 days we were established in the Japanese Camp; then we took two weeks to put a cache in Valle del Silencio and, finally, five days to sculpt a snow cave in the glacier between the east faces of the Fortress and Shield.

The weater, although harsh, was more than acceptable.

Peineta tower, showing Capicúa Pastor. Other routes exist to the right of this line. *Rodrigo Fica*

But after we had climbed the first 50m of the Di Donna Couloir, the avalanches began. After additional incidents in the following days, we retreated and changed our focus to Peineta.

On September 11 a severe storm arrived and stayed for 17 days, and Francisco Rojas had to leave because of his job. In the first week of October, Arancibia and I fixed nine pitches, and, after another week of bad weather, on October 14 we summited. Two weeks later, on November 1, we left for civilization after retrieving our ropes and garbage.

According to information we received (though we don't know if it is 100% correct), the first climb of Peineta was made in 1986 by Cristophe Delachat and Pierre-Jean Pradalier (MD+ 6b A2). The second was made in 1990, from the east side, by Yvan Boullen, Pierre Faivre, Lionel Pernollet, David Ravanel, and Jerome Ruby (28 pitches, ED 6c A3). Thereafter, several new routes and repeats have been made.

Our expedition was the only mountaineering activity in Paine Towers this winter. Ours was the third winter expedition ever, after Mario Manica and Luca Leonardi in 1987, and Rodrigo Traub, André Labarca and Claudio Retamal's attempt on Paine Grande in the late 90s.

Peineta should be considered the fourth Paine Tower. If it isn't, it's because most people see the towers from east, where Peineta seems to be more a granite wall than a spire-like mountain. A lot of space for new routes remains on Peineta.

RODRIGO FICA, *Chile*

WEST OF PAINE

Meseta de los Franceses, various first ascents. In July, Pablo Besser, Ismael Mena, Nicolás von Graevenitz, and I made the first winter ascent of Cerro Balmaceda, at southern end of Continental Icecap [see below]. From the summit the Tyndall Glacier and surrounding mountains attracted our attention. Nicolás and I started planning an expedition to the seldom-visited Meseta de los Franceses, the glacier just west of Tyndall. The only recorded ascent in the area (by Gino Buscaini) was of Cerro Manzano, a 1,500m peak west of Tyndall. After difficulties fulfilling CONAF's permit requirements, we camped near Cerro Manzano on our fifth day. Three days later, having given up the idea of visiting the northern part of the Meseta, due to a highly crevassed glacier, we camped at the base of the east ridge of an imposing peak, which like most peaks in the area is unnamed. The next day we made a reconnaissance of a tributary glacier that runs east-west, to the north of our camp. We were pleased to find that several beautiful peaks surrounded it. Finally we had something to climb! The weather kept us in the tent for two days, but on the third day we decided to climb, despite bad conditions, and ascended three small peaks: Piojo (1,601m, S51°07'696" W73°31'692", PD, 600m) and Ciego (1,595m, S51°07'640" W73°32'453", PD, 500m) and Cerro Dormido (1,717m, S51°07'766" W73°32'781", AD, 700m). The next day we climbed Cerro Desconsuelo (2,011m, S51°11'594" W73°29'057", PD+, 1,000m), which is at the southern end of the Meseta. The weather finally improved, and we attempted the prettiest peak in the entire area, the one whose ridge protected us from the wind. We started up at 8 a.m., climbing a long ice couloir leading to the icy north face. The first pitch was 50°, followed by another with steps to 85°, and a third that involved a traverse (70°) to avoid vertical ground above. The fourth was 80° and deposited us on the east ridge. The weather was perfect, no clouds or wind. To reach the corniced summit we climbed two more easy pitches. We named the peak Cerro Travesia (1,913m, S51°09'470" W73°31'342", MD, 700m

85°). The next day, though we were tired, we climbed one more peak, Cerro Kaweskar (1,580m, S51°08'221" W73°33'730", PD 500m), at the end of the Travesia Glacier (the glacier north of our camp), just above the fjords. After resting in bad weather for a few days we headed back. Having climbed six previously unclimbed summits, we were pleased with our adventure.

FRANCISCO URZÚA, *Santiago, Chile*

SOUTH OF PAINE

Cerro Balmaceda, first winter ascent. Cerro Balmaceda (2,260m) is located at the southern end of the Continental Icecap, some 40km south of the Paine Massif. Being surrounded by lakes and major rivers, it is difficult to reach. Since its first ascent in 1957, it has had only three other ascents. On July 11 Ismael Mena, Francisco Urzúa, Nicolás von Graevenitz, and I, all Chilean, traveled by Zodiac boat for three hours from Puerto Natales and were dropped off at the Laguna Azul beach, south of the mountain. We spent the following two weeks contouring the mountain and Lago Balmaceda (frozen in winter) to the west, finally reaching Gallina Pass, located high on the mountain along the first ascent route, on the 24th. The next day, after six hours of nontechnical but somewhat treacherous glacier travel, we reached the main summit. It took us only three days to return to Puerto Natales. Faster and shorter access to the mountain would be from the east, via Puerto Toro, but we strongly recommend the western approach. Due to its remoteness, it is one of the most pristine areas in Patagonia.

DR. PABLO BESSER JIRKAL, *Club Aleman Andino, Santiago, Chile*

Antarctica

ELLSWORTH MOUNTAINS

Union Glacier, "Mt. Hervé," possible first ascent; Horseshoe Glacier, "High Nunatak," possible first ascent. Previously unreported from the 2004-05 season, the Heritage 2004 Expedition comprised three alpinists/geologists of the Universidad de Chile, Rodrigo Fernández, Christian Vásquez, and I. We traveled 350km studying part of the Ellsworth Mountains, using two skidoos and four sledges. We had food and fuel for two months and one satellite phone. We had no external support, and you might describe our journey as an Alpine-style snowmobile traverse.

We began by heading south from Patriot Hills and climbed the south summit of the Three Sails. We next moved back north on the west side of the Patriot Hills, at every stop exploring and collecting rock samples. Unlike most expeditions, ours increased its load with time. We continued to the north end of the Horseshoe Valley, crossed the Eureka Pass, and stopped on the southern section of the Union Glacier, installing "Unexpected Camp" in the middle of a field of crevasses at S 79° 54' 20.871", W 83° 30' 52.483", 1224.22m (GPS reading).

Twenty-five days into the expedition we decided to continue on ski, due to the high risk of crossing crevasse fields in Skidoos with heavily loaded sledges. The route north took several days of exploration and planning in order to find the best route across the Union Glacier. Six days later we were celebrating Christmas by pulling sledges across the middle of the Union Glacier at midnight in full sunshine. Finally we reached the northernmost point of our journey, which we named "Christmas Camp" (S 79° 45' 12.406", W 83° 28' 01.352", 815.11m).

From this camp we reached the summit of a nunatak peak we later referred to as "Mt. Disappointment" (S 79° 44' 47.6", W 83° 28' 8.5", 1,049m), because we discovered a

Against a backdrop of unclimbed peaks, Chileans Rodrigo Fernández and Christian Vásquez, move north along the Union Glacier during the 2004-2005 exploration of part of the Heritage Range. Mauricio Duran

bamboo wand on the summit. The following day we climbed a similar peak we called "Mt. Hervé" (S 79° 43' 51.3", W 83° 11' 56.8", 1,112m). This was six kilometers from our camp and gave a four-hour climb to the top, with a fine view of the great Union ice stream to the east. Both peaks were technically straightforward.

Three days later we returned to Unexpected Camp and in a marathon 28- hour skidoo journey established "High Nunatak Camp" in the middle of the Horseshoe Valley at S 80° 04' 07.623", W 82º 53' 04.507", 1,055.94m. Next day we climbed the "High Nunatak" (S 80° 03' 24.2", W 82° 38' 02", 1,149m) in two hours. The climbing was easy but rather exposed, and the final 50m, which we climbed unroped, gave a pitch of 5.6. This summit provided a fine panoramic view of the entire Horseshoe Valley. Finally, after 45 days, we returned safe and sound to Patriot Hills with 500kg of rocks and two broken sledges.

MAURICIO DURÁN, *Chile*

ELLSWORTH MOUNTAINS - SENTINEL RANGE

Vinson Massif, summary. Around 140 climbers summited Vinson during the 2005-2006 season, with only four climbers unsuccessful. There were no new routes reported on the mountain, though at least one team climbed Mount Shinn (4,661m) by the normal route, and one pair climbed Pico Jaca. The weather was slightly worse than usual, with one particularly bad storm on and just after December 10. However in the case of some Vinson climbers the effect was exacerbated by their inexperience and poor judgment, an increasing problem on the mountain as the number of visitors rises. On a more positive note, Antarctic Logistics & Expeditions (ALE) has been proactive in dealing with potential waste problems arising from the greater number of climbers. In recent years all teams have carried out their human waste, but now they are given special bags to deal with fecal waste in a better manner. They are also encouraged to put urine only in specific areas and to use a pee bottle (rather than the ground), if possible, when between camp sites. However, enforcement of these measures on the mountain is necessarily largely up to the guides, and the standard of guiding on the mountain varies considerably.

DAMIEN GILDEA, *Australia, AAC*

Craddock from the southwest, showing the line of the new route up the west face climbed by the Omega Foundation expedition in December 2005. (A) The Pinnacle, (B) Craddock Central (4,402m), (C) Craddock (4,368m). Bugueno and Rada made the first ascent of Craddock Central during their descent from the summit of Craddock. The Pinnacle is unclimbed, as is another, possibly higher, summit, Craddock North, off picture to the left. *Damien Gildea*

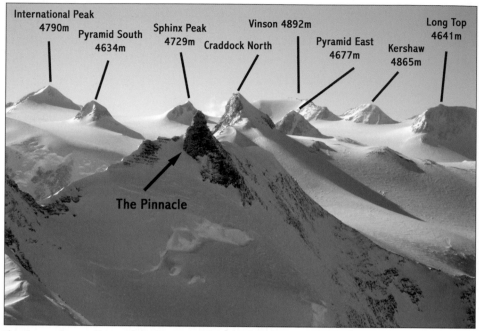

The view north toward Vinson from the summit of Craddock (4,368m). *Damien Gildea*

Stephen Chaplin descending the north ridge of Gardner with the northern Sentinel Range beyond. (A) Shear (4,050m), (B) Ostenso (4,085m), (C) Giovinetto (4,089m), and (D) Anderson (4,157m). *Damien Gildea*

New altitude survey; Mt. Craddock, west face; Mt. Gardner, ascent; Mt. Tyree, attempt. As a continuation of previous GPS work on Mt. Shinn (2002), Livingston Island (2003), and the Vinson Massif (2004), another expedition from the Omega Foundation planned to climb and measure Mts. Tyree, Craddock, and Gardner during 2005-06. These mountains were believed to be the second, fourth and fifth highest, respectively, in Antarctica.

On November 23 we landed on a previously unvisited glacier west of Mt. Craddock and set up base camp, lower than expected, at 1,455m. During the following days we climbed a small virgin 1,978m peak to the west (via the east face and north ridge on the 24th; 500m; PD), sledged loads farther up the glacier, and made an advanced base at 2,041m, close beneath the west face of Craddock. All the team climbed the lower slopes of the face and dug a site out of a rock ridge for Camp 1 (3,258m). Steve Chaplin (U.K.) and I spent four nights there in poor weather.

December 7 was a brilliant day, and we quickly climbed the 45° snow and ice slopes of the 1,000m upper west face to reach the summit in the evening. The climbing was never difficult but sustained and sometimes on ice, so a fall would have been serious. The 2,300m route was AD. There are no flat places to put a tent, hence our excavation of the ridge.

The huge and unattempted east face of Gardner (4,573m) from the Patton Glacier. The summit is the high point on the extreme left. *Damien Gildea*

This was the second ascent of Craddock, first climbed by Conrad Anker and Jay Smith in 1992 by a different route from the west, accessed from the glacial basin to the north of ours. Mt. Craddock has a number of high tops at its southern end but we placed the GPS on the highest rock summit, at the eastern extremity of the summit plateau, then walked back west over to a slightly higher snow dome before descending. Our Chilean teammates, Manuel Bugueno and Camilo Rada, repeated our route next day to retrieve the GPS. Processing the data at base camp via the Australian government AUSPOS website, accessed via laptop computer and Iridium satellite phone, we determined that Craddock is in fact only 4,368m: 282m lower than the previously published official height of 4,650m.

After descending to base camp we sat out extremely bad weather,

Tyree (4,852m) from the Patton Glacier. (A) The unclimbed east ridge, (B) northeast face: Grand Couloir, climbed in 1997 by Antoine Cayrol and Antoine de Choudens, and repeated a month later by Conrad Anker and Alex Lowe, (C) the unclimbed northeast ridge. In December 2005 Steve Chaplin and Damien Gildea climbed the crest to around one-third height, planning to move left into the couloir. However, bad conditions and incoming weather forced a retreat. (D) Northwest ridge, climbed by Barry Corbet and John Evans in 1967 to make the first ascent of the mountain. *Damien Gildea*

but were finally picked up by ALE on December 17 and flown north to a new base camp, on the flat ice 5km west of Mt. Gardner. The next day we carried loads to a site for advanced base beneath Gardner's west face, then occupied it the day after. Wanting to take advantage of the now-excellent weather, Steve and I departed the following day and climbed 2,100m to the summit in a single nine-hour push. We climbed the original 1966-67 route up a 1,200m, 45° couloir on the northwest face, followed by the long north ridge. This was the fifth ascent of this route (AD+) and the sixth overall of the mountain. The discarded food cache from the 1966 American expedition is still visible and intact near the bottom of the face, and in the couloir itself we found short lengths of old fixed rope from the same expedition. The final section of the summit ridge was severely corniced, requiring a short bout of exposed and delicate climbing. We placed the GPS right on top. Manuel and Camilo repeated the route the following day, retrieving the GPS. This later showed that Gardner is 4,573m, 14m lower than its old official height.

In continuing good weather, we flew to the east side of the range and landed in soft, deep snow on the beautiful Patton Glacier. There, we established a base camp with marvelous views of Tyree, Gardner, Ostenso, and Evans Peak. We spent Christmas and New Year's Eve in bad weather—cloud, fog, wind, and light snow—but managed to place a cache at the foot of the east face of Tyree. Our intended route was the Grand Couloir, first climbed in November 1997 by French alpinists Antoine Cayrol and Antoine de Choudens, from the GMHM expedition that also made the first ascents of Mt. Shear (4,050m) and Evans Peak (3,950m). One month after the French ascent, Conrad Anker and Alex Lowe summited via a slight variant on the same route, with Dave Hahn turning back up high. Tyree has not been climbed since.

We climbed a variant of the lower route, not using the couloir but going directly up the northeast ridge from its base, moving unroped with heavy packs. We placed a small tent at 3,247m in a small exposed col, where Steve Chaplin and I spent two nights. However, the condition of the couloir above was not good, with very hard ice lying under just a few centimeters of soft, sugary snow. Higher, large patches of slick blue ice were visible. These conditions, combined with incoming bad weather, led me to decide against climbing the route at this time. Two days later we descended in a whiteout to our base camp on the Patton and several days after that flew out of Antarctica.

The height order of Antarctica's highest mountains now looks like this:

1. Vinson Massif 4,892m

2. Mt. Tyree 4,852m *

3. Mt. Shinn 4,661m

4. Mt. Gardner 4,573m

5. Mt. Kirkpatrick 4,528m *

6. Mt. Elizabeth 4,480m *

7. Mt. Craddock 4,368m

Note: * denotes *not* measured by the Omega Foundation. These peaks are probably lower than the figures indicate.

The resulting data from this survey will be included on a new topographical map of the Sentinel Range, to be published later in 2006 and distributed worldwide, free of charge, in the interests of furthering knowledge of Antarctica and contributing to Antarctic science.

DAMIEN GILDEA, *Australia, AAC, Omega Foundation*

Vinson Massif, west face, Purple Haze Couloir. It was January 15, 2005 and we had been stuck in Vinson base camp for several days, waiting for clear weather so we could fly to Patriot Hills and then home. The weather was cloudy enough to prevent a safe landing but not bad enough to keep us from climbing. Around midnight we put together a small amount of gear and prepared for our climb. Neither of us had brought technical gear; we were there to guide people up the Normal Route on Vinson, not to climb steep snow and mixed ground. So, with borrowed technical tools, 30m of rope and a few screws, we set out.

On our ski to the base of the west face we discussed which of the gullies to try. We both had thoughts of the unclimbed gully just left of Banana Friendship Gully but shared doubts of

The central section of the west face of Vinson Massif seen across the Branscomb Glacier. (A) Branscomb Point (4,520m), (B) Main Summit (4,892m). (1) Branscomb Ridge (probably first crossed in descent by Mike Hood and Roger Mear in 1994: ascended in 2004 by Miguel Angel Vidal). (2) Linear Accelerator (ca. 1,700m, WI3 5.9: Jay Smith, solo, January 6, 1994). (3) Purple Haze Gully (1,700m, 70° and Mixed: Dave Morton-Todd Passey, January 15, 2005). (4) Friendship Banana Gully (ca. 1,700m, 50-55° and rock/mixed at UIAA IV: Miguel Angel Vidal, solo, December 31, 2004:). (5) Central Ice Stream – Rudi's Runway (ca. 1,700m: Rudi Lang, solo, January 1991). (6) Just off picture is the Central Ice Stream – Right Side (ca. 1,700m: Conrad Anker, twice in 1999, the second time to the summit: repeated by Spanish on December 23, 2003). *Damien Gildea*

its feasibility, given our meager rack. We decided to give it a try, but were willing to back off if it became too difficult to climb safely without proper gear.

At 2 a.m. we began climbing. From the Branscomb Glacier the route starts with a bergschrund, followed by a 40-50° snow slope through broken rock bands. The climbing was on perfect névé that gradually got steeper. The angle approached 70° as we entered the gully, which, higher, narrowed until it ended in a 10m chimney barring access to a low-angle slab. Once above the chimney we discussed turning back, but it seemed more dangerous to retreat than to keep going, so we carried on.

From the low-angle slab we traversed left to a sloping ledge, which led to a snowy ridge. The crest looked like it might offer a direct shot to the top of the face, but instead it led to another 500m of 50-60° mixed climbing. It was a spectacular night with colorful skies and an ever-present "purple haze" above. We topped out in the late morning and, knowing planes were now likely to be flying, opted to forgo the last few hundred meters of straightforward climbing to the summit.

The route, which we named Purple Haze Couloir, gave 1,750m of climbing on snow and short sections of mixed terrain up to IV 70° (we started from the Branscomb Glacier at 2,800m and reached the ridge atop the face at 4,600m). We went from base camp to base camp in 13 hours, descending by the normal route. As we suspected and as Murphy's Law would have it, not long after we started our climb the weather improved sufficiently to get our clients on planes to Patriot Hills. However, the gracious ALE staff were kind enough to wait until they saw us coming, before calling the last plane of the season to Vinson base camp.

DAVE MORTON AND TODD PASSEY, *AAC*

Epperly (4,359m, left) and Shinn (4,661m), seen from Pico Jaca to the west-southwest. The line of the Lewis-Nonis route to the Epperly-Shinn col (ca. 4,100m) is marked, with X the site of the accident during the descent. The obvious, narrowing couloir in the middle of the southwest face of Epperly was climbed in December 1994 by Erhard Loretan to make the first ascent of the mountain. He returned in December 1995 to solo it again for a film. The Standard Route on Shinn finishes up the gently angled snow slopes on the right. The ridges leading from the Epperly-Shin col to either summit remain unclimbed. *Damien Gildea*

Epperly-Shinn col, west face, attempt and accident. Tom Nonis and I were dropped off in the cirque to the west of Mt. Epperly on November 23. We planned to climb the west face of the Epperly-Shinn col, with the idea that after having reached the col we might be able to attempt the first ascent of Mt. Epperly's south ridge and/or the first ascent of Mt. Shinn's northwest ridge. Leaving camp at 6 p.m. on the 25th, we skied to below the west face of the col and started climbing at around 7:30 p.m.

Our route went up a 55° gully to the right of the icefall and, where the snow quality deteriorated, moved onto mixed ground. The buttress consisted of good quality quartzite, which was easy to protect and allowed us to move together for the majority of the route. The temperature was most of the time around -25°C, with no wind. However, at around 2 a.m. on the 26th we lost the sun and donned more clothes, to cope with dropping temperature and increasing wind.

Toward the top of the gully we moved leftward onto a terrace, where the angle dropped to a more manageable 45°. Here we spent three hours searching for a

Tom Nonis in the west-facing couloir leading to the Epperly-Shinn col, November 2005. *Nick Lewis*

bivouac site, as we were unable to find any ledges big enough or flat enough for our tiny tent. The wind speed increased, and both of us suffered minor frostbite.

Finally, at 8 a.m., we discovered a split in a stable serac at 4,100m, which allowed us to set up the tent. We had climbed 1,500m.

On account of the high wind and extremely cold temperature we stayed put for 28 hours, trying to rest and rehydrate. The estimated temperature was below -45°C, a figure recorded in the sun at around the same time by a guided party on the Vinson-Shinn col, which is 300m lower.

At midday on the 27th we decided to downclimb the route and wait in base camp for warmer weather. The sky was blue, and there was no wind, but it was still extremely cold. Five hours later we were traversing the lower slopes near the bottom of the route, when a snow slab, lying on hard ice, sheared from beneath my feet. I fell 10m, cart-wheeling, and breaking my tibia and fibula. I eventually managed to ice-axe arrest, but in the process of coming to a halt, ripped the pectoral muscle off my arm.

Nonis established a secure belay and made a satellite phone call to the ALE base camp at Patriot Hills. He then lowered me the remaining 150m to the glacier, where an ALE Twin Otter picked us up on the morning of the 28th. We arrived in Patriot Hills on the 29th, having been forced to sit at Vinson Base Camp for 24 hours due to bad weather. At Patriot Hills I was put in plaster and finally evacuated to Punta Arenas on December 4. I subsequently had operations on both the leg and the shoulder in Santiago.

Although we both had a lot of experience of cold conditions in New England, Alaska, the Yukon, Poland, Greenland, the Patagonian winter, and Antarctica, we had never been on a technical route before in such a low temperature, and it required a significant amount of our experience just to get through the bivouac. In addition, neither of us had previously taken so long to find a bivouac site where we felt we could survive the conditions.

NICK LEWIS

QUEEN MAUD LAND

Orvin Fjella Mountains: "Windmill Spire," first ascent, by Frozen Tears; Unnamed Peak, first ascent, by Dragon Back Ridge. In November and December, Mike Libecki spent five weeks alone in a region of granite spires that forms part of the Orvin Fjella Mountains. He first attempted a buttress on an unnamed peak but backed off after four pitches because of serious rockfall. Libecki then spent 12 days climbing a fine tower he named "Windmill Spire." He graded his 450m, nine-pitch route, Frozen Tears, VI 5.10 A3. He then returned to the peak he originally attempted and climbed a long ridge, Dragon Back Ridge (5.5), with 750m of elevation gain to the summit. A full account of this committing expedition appears earlier in the *Journal.*

Mike Libecki camped below Windmill Spire, Queen Maud Land, with the line of his first ascent marked (Frozen Tears, 450m, VI 5.10 A3). *Mike Libecki*

ANTARCTIC PENINSULA

Peninsula summary. As usual, there were numerous yacht journeys down the Peninsula, some of them for climbing. The season was somewhat busier and more successful than the previous few. The highlight of the climbing season was the first ascent of Wandel Peak (980m), the highest point of Booth Island, by a strong Spanish team (see below). Carl Wandel was a Danish hydrographer on de Gerlache's 1897-99 Belgica expedition, which overwintered in Antarctica. (The expedition was an international affair; the doctor was Frederick Cook and a young volunteer was a certain Roald Amundsen.)

Booth Island forms the western side of the narrow Lemaire Channel, the entrance to which is known in the Antarctic cruise industry as "Kodak Gap." The Channel, with Booth Island on one side and Cape Renard Towers ("Una's Tits") on the other, is probably the most photographed area of the Antarctic Peninsula, which is now receiving around 20,000 shipborne tourists a year. Wandel had been attempted numerous times with no success, including two attempts from the north. It was probably the most coveted first ascent on the Peninsula.

Australian yacht *Spirit of Sydney* carried both a sea-kayaking expedition and a group of climbers. The climbers were Jytte Christensen of Denmark and Darrel Day, Grant Dixon, Peter Itaak, and Megan Noble from Australia. Day, Dixon, Christensen, and Itaak made what is probably the third ascent of Mt. Hoegh (890m), by the west face. The latter three, with Noble, then climbed the popular Mt. Scott (880m) by the normal route up the east ridge. The only overnight trip undertaken by the climbers resulted in Christensen and Dixon summiting Mt. Shackleton (1465m) via the east ridge. This route, accessed from the Wiggins Glacier, has been climbed numerous times, but the team was almost certainly only the third private (i.e., non-government) group to do so. The first such group was an international team of three in March 2001, and the second the Spanish team this season, as reported below.

Dixon and Christensen climbed the south ridge of a southern summit of the Miller Heights, a feature above Prospect Point that runs eastward from Sharp Peak. Dixon also joined Rob Clifton and two others from another yacht, *Australis*, to make an ascent of the aesthetic little Mt. Demaria (635m), in Waddington Bay. The group aboard *Australis* was led by the experienced Peninsula guide, Kieran Lawton, who took clients up both Mt. Scott and Mt. Demaria. Dixon, who in 1999 was one of the team that made the first north-south traverse of South Georgia, finished his busy southern sojourn with a solo ascent of Jabet Peak (545m) above Port Lockroy, probably the most popular climb on the Peninsula.

While their friends were climbing, the kayak team of Laurie Geoghegan, Andrew McAuley and Stuart Trueman achieved their objective of paddling over 800km from Hope Bay to Darbel Bay, where they crossed the Antarctic Circle.

A commercially guided expedition of New Zealand-based Adventure Consultants was also active on the Peninsula during February. It was led by Kiwis Guy Cotter and Mark Sedon, with the American guide Luis Benitez, all aboard Steve Kafka's *Evohe*. Cotter kicked off with an ascent of Jabet Peak, while Sedon and Benitez took the group up Doumer Hill (515m), the high point of Doumer Island, a snowy dome near Port Lockroy and situated between Anvers and Wiencke islands. Most of the group descended on skis.

Four days later the whole group made an ascent of the highest point of Edwards Island in Leroux Bay. On February 15 the whole group climbed on Chavez Island, also near Leroux Bay, but were turned back on three different attempts by dangerous avalanche conditions. However, a fourth attempt resulted in the ascent of a peak that they measured at 630m and called "Will's Peak," in memory of a guiding colleague killed in the mountains at home. Two days later the group visited the popular Prospect Point area and, after an unsuccessful attempt on Sharp Peak (475m), climbed an unnamed peak to its west, which they called "Kiwiana Peak." Benitez, with some of the clients, all on skis, also climbed another peak yet farther west. Nearby, Cotter made ski ascents of two small peaks close to the sea, while Benitez and Sedon made a ski ascent of a larger peak slightly farther inland. They named this peak "Chloe's Gift" after one of the crew on *Evohe*.

On February 24 Benitez, Cotter, and Sedon made a possible first ascent of a larger mountain, of around 1,300m, on the Peninsula mainland above the waters of Errera Channel. The map stated the presence of "100' ice cliffs at sea level," a common problem along the Peninsula when trying to get ashore to climb, but these particular ones seem to have disappeared, and the climbers had no difficulty accessing the ground above. The climbing initially required snowshoes but then involved steeper slopes and finally seven roped pitches on variable snow and ice to gain a ridge. Benitez, Cotter, and Sedon traversed moderate ground along the ridge, then climbed a short, steep slope to arrive on a rounded summit dome six hours after starting. They proposed the name "Hiddleston Peak" in memory of fellow guide Dave "Hip" Hiddleston, who died with several other climbers in an accident on Mt. Tasman recently. Hiddleston was a well-known and respected UIAGM Guide who had taken clients up Everest and other Himalayan peaks, as well as working extensively in New Zealand.

A group of New Zealand climbers aboard the perennial visitor *Northanger* is said to have climbed Savoia Peak (1,415m, often erroneously called "Mt. Luigi" or "Mt. Luigi de Savoia") on Wiencke Island and attempted a route on one of the impressive peaks in the Cape Renard area.

DAMIEN GILDEA, *Australia, AAC*, WITH INPUT FROM GRANT DIXON, KIERAN LAWTON, ANDREW MCAULEY AND MARK SEDON

Mt. Shackleton, south face-west ridge; Wandel Peak, north ridge to summit mushroom. At the end of January 2006 we headed for the Antarctic Peninsula on board the yacht *Le Sourire*. Our Spanish TVE expedition comprised Sebastian Alvaro, Ester Sabadell, Alex Txikón, and I. On the 28th we put ashore at Pleneau Island and the next day climbed the normal route on Mt. Scott (882m). The following day, January 30, we all climbed Mt. Mill (734m).

On February 1 we set out for Mt. Shackleton (1,465m). After crossing the Wiggins Glacier we set

Shackleton (1,465m) on the Antarctic Peninsula, as seen from the southwest. Marked is the route followed on the first ascent of the south face in January 2006 by the Spanish team of Sabadell, Tamayo, and Txikón. The "normal route" is the east ridge (right skyline), climbed on the first ascent of the mountain in August 1965 by MacNee, Murton, and Thoday from the UK. *José Carlos Tamayo*

Wandel Peak (980m), reflected in the waters off Booth Island. The route taken on the first ascent by Alvaro, Sabadell, Tamayo, and Txikón in February 2006 follows the north ridge (left skyline) from the shore to the point marked 1. From there the Spanish team rappelled to the glacier on the far (east) side and continued to the summit. See also the photo in AAJ 2001 p. 312. *José Carlos Tamayo*

up camp on the big plateau under the south face of the mountain. The following day Alex, Ester, and I made the first ascent of this 600m snow/ice face (55-60°), to reach the corniced west ridge, and then followed the crest for 200m to the summit. We tried descending the normal route (east ridge) but after 300m were stopped by thick mist. Unable to see a thing, we waited until dawn, but February 3 wasn't any better. The mist was still too thick for a safe descent. We returned to the summit and reversed our ascent route, rappelling the steepest parts.

Back on *Le Sourire*, rain and strong winds stopped us for a week. Later, we moved to Charcot Port on Booth Island, and on February 15 all four of us made the first ascent of Wandel Peak (980m). The huge summit mushroom was deemed just too risky, so we stopped 10-15m below.

We first climbed the rocky north ridge, which after the first 30m of IV is generally easy but loose. This gave access to a snow ridge, from which we rappelled to the glacier on the east flank, between the continuation of the north ridge and the shorter, steeper northeast ridge, which overlooks the Lemaire Channel. Once on the glacier, we found the route to be easy, although one crevasse nearly stopped us. We descended the same way.

The north ridge had been tried several times previously, with the best effort coming from Ed Birnbacher and Greg Landreth in March 2003. They reached a height of 650m but were thwarted by the long corniced ridge above (see *AAJ 2003*, p.335). We felt a little guilty about our ascent as we later met Landreth, skipper of the yacht *Northanger*, at Port Lockroy. He'd planned to climb the route with his New Zealand passengers. In fact, he later attempted to repeat our route but couldn't cross the bergschrund on the final section. After leaving Booth Island, we traveled north, enjoying views and walks before sailing back to the Drake Passage.

JOSÉ CARLOS TAMAYO, *Spain*

Oman

Western Hajar, various first ascents.
In December 2004 and January 2005, Geoff Hornby (U.K.) and I climbed on the mountain limestone of the Western Hajar. We based ourselves around Wadi Al Ain west of Al Hamra, three hours drive from the capital, Muscat. Thanks to Geoff's extensive knowledge of the area, we were able to climb seven new routes.

The majestic Jabel Misht (2,090m), perhaps Oman's finest "high mountain" rock climbing venue, seen from Hibshe. Facing the camera, the ca. 900m south (a.k.a. French) pillar divides the extensive south face to the left from the steeper southeast face to the right. *Paul Knott*

Attracted by the huge southern aspect of Jabel Misht (2,090m), we climbed Palestine (800m, TD-), taking the full length of the southeast pillar, via a black band at the bottom and a groove and amphitheater on the upper face. We also climbed Mishts of Time (540m, D) to the right of existing routes on the southwest face. Opposite, on the north face of the isolated Jabel M'Saw, a pyramidal summit between Asala and Misfah, we climbed the first route on the formation, White Magic (570m, TD-), which follows a clean white slab to a surprising

Jabal M'Saw from the northwest. Marked is the January 2005 British route on the north face: White Magic (570m, TD- F5+). This is the first rock climb on the formation. *Paul Knott*

traverse through the overhangs. On the east face of Jabel Asait we climbed Buzzy Bee on the loose lower tier and the more satisfying Arch Wall (385m, TD-), which leads to a rock arch on the narrow summit ridge. We finished by climbing the first route on the north face of Jabel M'Seeb opposite the southern pillars of Jabel Kawr. This was the enjoyable Juggernaut (435m, D-), a steep groove festooned with holds.

Paul Knott leading pitch 5 (F4) during the first ascent of White Magic, Jabal M'Saw, Western Hajar. *Paul Knott*

We climbed from the road each day, carrying just a light wind top, a pair of trainers for the descent, a few liters of water, and energy bars. The rock was hard and smooth in water-worn grooves, but elsewhere it was sharply pitted. We descended by long boulder and

The southwest face—Coxcomb—of Jabel Misht. Routes marked here in the central section of the face are typically in the 5.7 - 5.9 category and around 500m maximum. (1) Tindetinix (Cicogna-Manica, 2003), (2) Watergate (Brachmayer-Precht, 2001), (3) Misht as a Newt (Barlow-Nonis, 1999), (4) Sorely Misht (Hornby-Sammut-Turnbull, 2003), (5) Gorillas in the Misht (Hornby-Ramsden, 1999), (6) Red Misht (Chaudry-Hornby, 2000), (7) Mishts of Time (Hornby-Knott, 2004). *Paul Knott*

scree slopes, which added to the challenge. During our visit heavy rain flooded the roads, and afterwards the temperature was surprisingly cold for several days. Traveling through the country was a pleasure, and we received great hospitality from the people living in the mountains.

PAUL KNOTT, *New Zealand*

Jordan

WADI RUM

Autumn 2005-Spring 2006, summary. In 2005 climbing slowly began to pick up again in Wadi Rum, and just before Easter 2006 many climbers and trekkers were active. Visitors are advised to have travel and sports activity insurance, even if climbing with Bedouin guides, who are unable to obtain rescue insurance. Long-time activist Wilf Colonna, a French guide who runs a Jordanian travel agency, notes that local guides have formed the Wadi Rum Volunteer Rescue Society. They are looking for contributions, so they can purchase much-needed rescue equipment. Donations should be made to Sabbah Eid al Zalabieh, who is looking after the Rum Rescue Fund in the Arab Bank. Guides have identified accident "hot spots" and are training aspirants about hot spots on popular routes, before issuing a guiding permit that will be recognized by the Aqaba Special Economic Zone Authority (ASEZA). The Guides also hope that the French Mountaineering Federation (FFME) will assist, by providing a technical guiding course. Visitors are also advised to leave notification of their intended treks or climbs at the Tourist Police Office in the Rest House and not at the new Visitors Center, as originally proposed, a sensible precaution in this area of unusual complexity.

Now to the climbing. Autumn 2005's first developments were several new single-pitch routes, at F4 and 5, on Seifan Kebir in the eastern sector of Rum, put up during October by Harry and Lose Adshead. November saw more serious stuff appear, on the south face of Jebel Kharazi opposite the Rest House. Although still incomplete, the eight-pitch Ish Hazak (Strong Man) was climbed by Joel Etinger and Gili Tenne at 6a maximum. It takes a direct line up the obvious water-polished cracks that begin left of Vanishing Pillar. Descent is by five rappels.

Even nearer the Rest House, the rock Mecca of the east face of Jebel Rum's East Dome received yet another top-quality route. Named Rock Empire and put up by Ondra Benes, Michal Rosecky,

Top Bedouin guide, Mohammed Hammad, bouldering out the start of an unclimbed line in the Barrah Canyon, Wadi Rum. Hammad has climbed new routes up to 7b. *Di Taylor*

and Tomas Sobotka, this 15-pitch route is bolt-protected and at least 6b to 7a for most of its length, with a crux of around 8a. [See report below—Ed.] Their verdict? "A great sport climb on perfect rock. Take 10 quick draws, slings, two 60m ropes, and Friends for the final pitches of Raid Mit the Camel."

Jebel um Ishrin was climbed by a route that is technically easy but long and complex. Bedouin guide Talal Awad, with Robert Mandi and Rum regular Gilles Rappeneau, made the ascent in November and named it Bedu Majnun (Crazy Bedouin). Wilf Colonna, who spends half of each year in Rum, made the second ascent in April 2006 with aspirant Bedouin guide Mohammad Hammad. Supposedly a long-lost Bedouin route up the east face, it was graded 4 by Awad, Mandi, and Rappeneau, who found it necessary to place protection on the exposed crux pitch. While finding evidence that ibex had almost certainly used this route (scuff marks are visible on the sandstone), Wilf and Mohammad believe it unlikely that Bedouin hunters would have climbed up and down this pitch. They were not convinced that this is an old Bedouin way, and Mohammad should know. Not only is he the youngest and best of today's Bedouin climbers, creating new routes up to 7b, but both his father, Hammad Hamdan, and his grandfather, Sheikh Hamdan Amad, were well-known guides, hunters, and two of the most illustrious pioneers in the region. Sheikh Hamdan led the first guided route in Rum, with clients Charmian Longstaff (wife of British Himalayan explorer Tom Longstaff) and her daughter Sylvia. The three climbed the Great Siq on the west face in 1952, "Hamdam climbing with bare feet as surely as a mountain goat." They reached the summit in around three hours, a time that is still rarely bettered.

There is talk of continuing the search for a Bedouin way on Jebel Um Ishrin and also on North Nassrani. Climbers have discovered ibex droppings (carried down and confirmed) on the latter, a difficult summit to reach. However, a new route on North Nassrani's southeast face is definitely not a Bedouin way. Sandy Silence, climbed by M. Dorfleitner and F. Freider on January 3, 2006, lies on one of Rum's most impressive walls, between Guerre Sainte and Muezzin. It is a nine-pitch route on good rock, described as "long, sparsely bolted, and more demanding than Guerre Sainte to the left." All you require are 13 quick draws, slings, two 60m ropes and "a good head."

Only Austrians Albert Precht and Sigi Brochmeyer seem able to climb Rum's big faces in traditional style. They were out in Rum again this spring, climbing on the west side of Jebel Rum, but there is no news yet of their activity. Although the number of big-wall bolt routes is increasing, bolts on smaller cliffs are frowned upon, even by the Bedouin guides. Some guides, without being aware of British ethics, have suggested that sport climbs with fixed gear should be limited to selected cliffs. In fact, the leaflet provided for climbers at the Visitor Center states that "the use of power drills is not permitted in the Protected Area."

So it is a great shame that a bolt-protected line has been added between Perverse Frog and The Beauty, both traditionally protected routes, climbed in 1985 by Alan Baker and Wilf Colonna. The new route, Priez pour Nous (Pray for Us: were they expecting condemnation?) is six pitches of mostly 6b and 6c, with a 7b crux. Twenty-five bolts were placed, shiny ones. They are even visible from the Rest House over a kilometer away, glinting in the sun. It may be an enjoyable climb, but in my opinion and also Wilf Colonna's, the use of bolts here is out of order, unsightly, and detracts from the ambience of the nearby traditional classics. The cliffs of Rum were developed as an adventure playground with few signs of man. Let's keep it that way.

In early 2006 the weather was most unusual. During late February a torrential rainstorm during the night flooded the whole Rum valley, from the new Visitor Center south to Khazali and on into Khor al Ajram south of Wadi um Ishrin. A river rushed down that valley, carving a new wadi in the heart of the old one. Bedouin had to be rescued from the floods. As the water evaporated, vast mud flats, then dust bowls, appeared, producing dust storms throughout the spring. The rains continued, albeit at rare intervals, until mid-April. This is unusually late for Jordan; north Jordan hills still had snow in March. And Mr. Bush says climate change is still in doubt!

Elsewhere in Jordan new three-day treks are being organized between Dana Reserve and Petra. Canyon exploration is also continuing, and some canyons now have fixed gear placed by guides. Wilf Colonna and Mohammed Hammad have been exploring the cliffs below Shaubak Castle, north of Petra. Between 20-30m in height, these cliffs are steep, with good quality limestone, similar to those around Ajlun Castle in north Jordan, where Tony Howard and Di Taylor have located a dozen cliffs. These cliffs have easy access, and the surrounding landscape is particularly beautiful in spring. The cliffs look over rolling green hills with flower-filled meadows and forests of oak, pistachio, and pine. There are also a few caves in this area, the best of which, Zubia, was recently trashed by well-meaning locals. Having discovered that it was being visited, they removed the obligatory roped descent and entry crawl, and people can now walk in. However, they thereby opened the venue to non-cavers, and most of the features have been destroyed. Such is life!

Despite the political problems, Jordan is still reasonably busy with tourists. Why not give it a try this autumn or next spring? The climbing is unique, the people are wonderful, and the Red Sea, with its superb snorkeling and diving, is just an hour away. For general information on, and links to, climbing in Rum visit www.nomadstravel.co.uk

Tony Howard, *U.K.*

Jebel Rum, east face, Rock Empire. In November Michal Rosecky, Tomas Sobotka, and I visited Wadi Rum. We were interested in this area because we come from the Czech Republic, where most rock climbing is on sandstone. We've put up many new routes in our country and wanted to make a first ascent in Jordan using the ground-up ethic we employ at home. Although we were away from home for a month, we only spent two weeks in Wadi Rum, the rest of the time traveling and climbing elsewhere in Jordan and Israel. November may not be the best time to climb in Wadi Rum. Nighttime temperatures were 8-10°C, and climbing in the shade could be chilly. However, we put up a new route on the 500m east face of 1,560m Jebel Rum.

Rock Empire is a 15-pitch line with the hardest climbing on pitches three to five. We redpointed the crux fourth pitch at UIAA IX+/X- or an Elbe Valley sandstone grade of Xb. It was a vertical wall with small finger holes and a very technical finish. Pitches three and

Ondra Benes making thin moves on the new Rum super-route, Rock Empire (500m, 8a), east face of Jebel Rum. *Ondra Benes Collection*

five were IX-. We completed the route from November 8-11 and believe it could be the longest hard climb in Wadi Rum. This is the Arabic world with its own rules and food, but we enjoyed the experience

Ondra Benes, *Czech Republic*

The east face of Demirkazik (3,757m) in Turkey's Ala Dag Mountains. The line of the new Larcher-Paissan-Oviglia route, Uc Muz (650m, 8a (7b obl)), is marked. *Maurizio Oviglia*

The slender limestone spire of Parmakkaya (2,800m) in Turkey's Ala Dag Mountains. The line of the new Italian route, Mezza Luna Nascente (7c (7a+ obl)), on the 270m east face is marked. *Maurizio Oviglia*

Turkey

SOUTHERN ANATOLIA

Ala Dag Mountains, Demirkazik, east face, Uc Muz. Parmakkaya, east face, Mezza Luna Nascente. Occasionally in jazz three people from different backgrounds join forces to form a trio, with the aim of playing just one type of music. In 2003 Rolando Larcher, Michele Paissan, and I found ourselves in the Atlas Mountains with the fine prospect of spending 25 days together on the great walls of Taghia. The new route we created is, according to Arnaud Petit, the best he has ever climbed. Two years passed, during which time each of us was involved with our own projects.

When it was time to play the music again, the trio regrouped. We searched for new ground in which to express ourselves. We are interested in creating modern hard routes in unknown areas, where we have to locate an objective, possibly without knowing what the rock will be like, or whether there will be rock at all. Improvization is the name of the game.

After a slideshow in Turin, Renzo Barbiè, a passionate ski-mountaineer. approached me. He confided, "I know a place in Turkey like Taghia. I've been skiing there. I'll e-mail you photos, and when we meet up again you can show me photos of the new routes you climb."

You can imagine the rest. At the beginning of July the trio landed at Ankara. We spent the first days exploring the length of the mountain range, until we suddenly discovered the wall of our dreams. We established base camp at 2,900m and walked up to the foot of the wall. Damn it! There were no holds, and we couldn't climb the line. However, there was another wall, 700m high, on a formation directly above base camp. We decided to go for it.

At times rocks whistled down, and the environment felt more high-mountain than craglike. However, the weather was splendid, often without a cloud in sight. It was hot in the sun and cold in the shade, T-shirt to down jacket in less than 15 minutes. In 10 days we finished and freed an outstanding route, reaching the 3,756m summit of Demirkazik at 5 p.m. on a clear, colorful day. It seemed as though the world was truly at our feet. We named our 650m east face route Uc Muz; it had 13 pitches, with difficulties of 8a (7b obl).

With two Turkish climbers, Recep and Zeynep Ince, we attempted the much-feared French route on the 270m obelisk of Parmakkaya (2,800m), which had only received three ascents in the 10 years since it was first

Rolando Larcher leading the fourth pitch of Mezza Luna Nascente (270m, 7c (7a+ obl)) on the east face of Parmakkaya, Ala Dag Mountains. *Maurizio Oviglia*

climbed. The maximum difficulties are 7b, but we had to climb the entire route with the potential for 20m falls. We managed an onsight ascent on another memorable day. On the way down Rolly stopped too often to look at Parmakkaya. As if in a trance, blown over by the beauty of the obelisk, he couldn't go away without another line.

Two 14-hour, hailstorm-ridden days brought us again to the slender summit of Parmakkaya, climbing in turns and freeing the pitches the same day. Some pockets were still filled with hail, but our new line on the east face, Mezza Luna Nascente, had difficulties of 7c (7a+ obl). Is this improvisation, or simply desire to play the music, and to continue even when the concert is over and the audience has gone home?

Note: Climbers interested in putting up new bolt-protected routes in the Ala Dag should know that bolting is currently the subject of vigorous debate. Contact local climbers first, to clarify the current situation. Prospective visitors are encouraged to write to Recep Ince at ince-recep@yahoo.com

MAURIZIO OVIGLIA, *Sardinia, Italy*

Africa

MOROCCO

Taghia, Tagouimmt N'Tsouiannt, Fanta-sia. On entering the Taghia Valley you are immediately captivated by two walls. The first is the tooth of Oujdad, 700m high; the second is 800m Tagouimmt N'Tsouiannt, one of the largest walls of the Atlas. In May, Eliza Kubarska and I opened the 700m Fantasia on Tagouimmt N'Tsouiannt. Maximum difficulties were 7b+/7c, with many pitches of 7a or more, making it one of the longest free climbs in the High Atlas.

Hidden deep in the mountains, 85km from the nearest city, Taghia has recently become a climbing Mecca for Europeans. However, this region has been quietly explored since the 1970s, mainly by Spanish. Massive limestone walls and deep canyons form a fabulous labyrinth of crags. These attract like a magnet, drawing pioneers intent on climbing the great walls.

After climbing on Oujdad, where in 2004 our Polish team of Kubarska, Szybiński, and I opened Barracuda (590m, 7c+, 7a obl), we dreamed about coming back to one of the most spectacular projects in Taghia. The established routes on Tagouimmt N'Tsouiannt are mainly aid climbs, and the bravest lines had been left untouched. Our project was to climb the smoothest part of the wall, which resembled the Verdon Gorge in France.

On April 21 Eliza and I started work on the new route. Halfway through the trip we were joined by Przemek Klimek, who helped to open the upper part of the route. We climbed the line from the ground up, using a combination of free and aid, always assuming that we would eventually free climb it. Protection, typical for Taghia, requires drilling while hanging on sky hooks.

Eliza Kubarska on pitch eight (7a) of Fantasia, during the first ascent in May 2005. *David Kaszlikowski*

Most of the wall is compact, without possibility of protection other than bolts. We didn't use a portaledge, only ca. 400m of fixed rope. At the end of each day we rappelled and spent the night in the village, living for a month in a friendly *gite* owned by Said Mesaouidi.

Eliza and I made the redpoint on May 23 and 24, with a bivouac on the face. A few days before, I had been sick. My inner ear was inflamed, and I had trouble walking and keeping my balance. However, on the fourth day of sickness I felt well enough to try the ascent. Not long into the climb, though, I realized I was still having trouble with my balance. On the first few pitches I was fighting to overcome the feeling of dizziness and was still uncertain if I would be able to lead the more difficult rope-lengths. However, after a couple of hours the malady passed, and the 6th pitch, the first difficult one, went smoothly.

Although we had a comfortable bivouac on a 120cm-wide ledge, we began to get dehydrated and were out of water by the following morning. A dry wind and the effort we put into the climb tired us completely. By evening we were seriously exhausted, tasting thick saliva, and seeing black spots before our eyes.

Fantasia is one of the most diverse routes in Taghia, with chimneys and dihedrals mixed with slabs. The backdrop of magnificent canyons just made things sweeter.

The line of the 700m Fantasia (7b+/7c) on Tagouimmt N'Tsouiannt, Taghia, one of the longest free climbs in the High Atlas. *David Kaszlikowski*

But climbing is changing in Taghia. In 2004 we met only 15 climbers during our month in the area; in 2005 there were around 60. More and more people are coming, not only to create new routes but also to repeat existing lines. While there is an increasing number of both sport and trad routes, the scope is still vast, and many sizeable walls remain more or less untouched. The impressive Bou Iourlanene has only one route, which is 25 years old. See more photos on www. StudioWspin.com.pl.

DAVID KASZLIKOWSKI, *Poland*

Editor's note: Two of the numerous climbers there at the time were the well known South Tyrolean, Christoph Hainz, and Roger Schali. This pair concentrated on a 300m-high exposed arête on the right side of Oujad, climbing the 13-pitch La Mano del Maroc (7b+, 6c obl, bolts and pitons) in four consecutive days. Such is the pace of development in Taghia that it didn't wait long for a second ascent, an impressive onsight by Martin Moser. In October Jack Geldard, Dave Pickford (both U.K.) and Juha Saatsi (Finland) repeated Fantasia. These three almost made an onsight ascent, redpointing only one pitch.

Mali

Hombori region; Hand of Fatima, Hombori Tondo and Naama Tondo various new routes. In January our team from the Groupe Militaire de Haute Montagne traveled to the Hombori region of Mali, our goal being to put up new routes on the Hand of Fatima. We chose the steepest and blankest walls in the group and, with the help of a power drill, managed to open seven new lines.

On January 6, 7, and 8 Thomas Faucheur, Arnaud Petit, and I put up Black Mamba (320m, 7a+, 6c obl) on the north face of Suri Tondo, the most northerly of the main formations that comprise the Hand of Fatima. This is a superb, sustained, and strenuous climb, right of Grains of Time, that is partially protected by 10mm bolts but needs some Friends for the cracks. We equipped the belays with chains for a rappel descent. On the 18th, 19th, and 20th Guillaume Baillargé, Francois Savary, and I climbed Le Cri (320m, 7a+, 6b obl) a little to the right of the previous route. It is less sustained and less equipped than Black Mamba but on exceptional rock.

On the east face of Wanderdu, south of Suri Tondo, Baillargé, Thierry Pellirrat, and Savary put up Panique à Gotham City (250m, 6c, 6b obl), a super seven-pitch route, with an exposed last pitch through the capping roofs. On Hendu Tongo, on the north side of Suri Tondo, Lionel Albrieux, Baillargé, Pellirrat, and Savary established Vol au Vent (280m, 9 pitches, 7a+, 6b obl).

Our main objective was the virgin north face of nearby Hombori Tondo, a wall 400m high. Arnaud Petit, who had joined us, knew the mountain from a previous visit. At first sight we were all impressed by the steepness of the wall, which looked devoid of holds. However, after our success on Suri Tondo we decided to give it a shot. The first pitch was what we expected: tricky 7a+ on small holds. Then everything went well until the middle ledge, where large vultures witnessed our efforts from their nest. A blank section of 50m curtailed our enthusiasm. The rock got worse, and Arnaud and I spent the whole day on the first 20m, cleaning, equipping, and finally sending the crux of the route: 7c+ on very small edges. The rest of the route went more easily, and after five days of climbing by five different people (Albrieux, Faucheur, Pellirrat, Petit, and me), Futuroscope was born. The route is totally equipped; five of the 12 pitches are 7a or above. Later, Albrieux, Faucheur, and Pellirrat returned and, at the far left side of the wall. put up L'Echappée Savatrice (230m, 6c, 6b obl), a fine seven-pitch route with two strenuous final pitches.

Finally, on Naama Tondo in the Naama Massif, Baillargé and Pellirrat climbed the northwest spur of the northwest tower of Torre Escondida. This gave a 250m route (seven pitches) with obligatory difficulties of 6b. Traditional protection is mandatory, but there are 10 bolts on the route.

All our days spent going up and down fixed ropes had cost a lot in time and energy. However, the game was to open everything from the ground up, hauling or carrying the drill, and free-climbing as much as we could, We used bolts only where necessary and when it made the climbing nicer. These rules forced us to spend sometimes more than four hours on a single pitch and achieve no more than two or three ropelengths a day.

The last week of the trip was spent climbing the classic routes on the Hand of Fatima, such as the North Ridge and Abert, but we also enjoyed some bouldering and sport climbing close to the campsite, using the last of our bolts to create some difficult lines.

One of the best days involved a football match, organized by the school kids of Hombori. The great French climbers lost a little dignity but won a lot of friendship.

MANU PELLISSIER FOR THE GROUPE MILITAIRE DE HAUTE MONTAGNE, *Chamonix, France*

Ethiopia

The Sandstone Towers of Tigray. The province of Tigray, in northern Ethiopia, is a region of sandstone mountains and high desert; it has been compared to Arizona. It may seem an unlikely place to go climbing. Apart from being close to the troubled border with Eritrea, the region is always one of the worst hit in times of famine. However, if you like Africa, Africans, and climbing adventurous routes on spectacular sandstone towers, it is a wonderful destination.

As one of the oldest Christian cultures, Ethiopia has an amazing

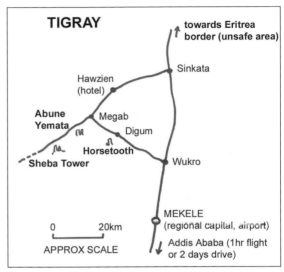

Sketch map of the recently explored sandstone towers of Tigray, Northern Ethiopia. *Pat Littlejohn*

Tigray's Nevelet Towers, seen from the southwest. The left and most impressive tower is Sheba and 500' high. The route of the first ascent, the south face, starts up the right side of the smooth wall more or less facing the camera and continues right of the big bulges. All other towers in this picture are unclimbed. *Pat Littlejohn*

Pat Littlejohn bridging up the final (sixth) pitch (5.10) of Sheba Tower in the chimney between the two summits. *Stephen Sustad*

heritage of rock-carved churches reminiscent of Petra. The story of its ruling dynasties begins with the legendary liaison of King Solomon and the Queen of Sheba, their son Menelik being the ruler who brought the Ark of the Covenant to Ethiopia, where it has supposedly remained for the past 3,000 years. Ethiopians are knowledgeable and proud of their culture, which remains strong, partly because they are the only Africans never to have been colonized. The Tigray province is famous for its rock-hewn churches concealed high in the cliffs. Some of these require 5.4 climbing to reach (uniquely challenging for both priests and parishioners!).

Stephen Sustad and I flew to Tigray's regional capital, Mekele, and based ourselves at Hawzien, a village three hours drive to the north near the Mountains of Gheralta. All the climbing that we discovered could be easily accessed from here. Other teams may wish to explore somewhere completely different; there is plenty of rock. Climbing at Tigray was like being pitched back into the early days of exploring the desert towers in the U.S., a golden age if ever there was one. We investigated a fairly limited area, climbing three big towers during an eight-day stay. Our style of climbing? Start at the bottom with a rack of nuts and cams, and do your best. Adventure guaranteed.

One of the most remarkable rock-hewn churches in Tigray is carved into the base of a great castle of rock, which appears impregnable on every side. Beside it is a slender tower called Abune Yemata, which we climbed via a line of chimneys on the west face to a saddle, then up a crack line on the south face till about 80' from the top, where it became a repulsive overhanging off-width. We then squirmed *through* the tower to the corresponding crack on the north face, which gave some very exposed climbing to our first virgin Tigray summit. The grade was about 5.11.

The queen of all towers we discovered was Sheba Tower, a 500' monolith of beautifully sculpted sandstone in the Nevelet group, just 15 minutes drive along the track from Abune Yemata. The fissures on the north side looked smooth and scary, so we chose the south face, where a more featured chimney, leading to a massive bulge, looked like it might be a bit of a problem. Four pitches of enjoyable and atmospheric climbing led to a great chamber in the heart of the tower. We belayed on a huge jammed block at the level of the bulge, and Steve led upward and outward through a bottomless slot that cut through the giant overhang. From here a relatively normal pitch, featuring a 5.10 bulge at the end, led to the summit. This was a fantastic spot, with the whole of Tigray province spread below us, and very inter-esting-looking rock peaks shim-mering in the distance.

The extensive sandstone escarpment of Gheralta, Tigray province. To date no rock routes have been climbed on this massif. In fact no routes, and they could potentially reach 400m in height, have been climbed on any of the massifs, just the free-standing towers. *Pat Littlejohn*

Horsetooth Tower was the first we'd investigated, and it hadn't excited us as much as the others, being a bit smaller (400') and less striking. We left it till the end, for an easier day. What a joke! With the usual group of children in tow, we slogged up to the base and chose our line, again, unfortunately, on the sunny side. Steve took the first pitch, which looked straightforward but had a mean bulge. I took over and got some great 5.10 climbing up grooves in the crest of the tower. An intermittent crack took Steve to a hanging belay. It then got steep and required 5.11 climbing to pass a bulge and reach a long, narrow shelf. I thought we'd cracked it, till I looked at the face ahead, which was lower-angle but essentially devoid of cracks. Traversing back and forth revealed neither easier ground nor protection. This was one of those situations where you have to commit yourself into unknown hostile territory, risking a huge fall if it doesn't pay off. "Why always on my pitch?" I thought, till I remembered Steve's lead on Sheba Tower. Delicate climbing, which I would have hated to reverse, brought a thin bendy flake within reach. The RP placed behind it was purely psycho-logical but still important, helping me press on across a precarious traverse, the odd foothold snapping for that extra buzz. Finally, I sank hands and runners into a decent crack. This was British HXS territory, and the toughest climbing of the trip.

Ethiopia was a bit of a revelation. The poorest country to which I've been but rich in so many ways, including its climbing potential. A very special climbing area that we'll be revisiting.

Getting there: There is a direct flight from London to Addis Ababa with Ethiopian Air-lines, and EA passengers get half-price on internal flights (e.g., to Mekele). You can hire 4WD (with compulsory driver) and get all the supplies you need in Mekele.

Accommodation is cheap, if you don't mind it basic. Rooms from $10/night in Addis to $3/night at the "hotel with no name" in Hawzien.

Maps and guidebooks. We used Lonely Planet, which was fine, and bought maps from www.stanfords.co.uk

Gear and ethics. Take nuts and cams, mostly medium and large, cams to at least a 4 Camalot. All climbing done so far has followed a "clean climbing" ethic: no drills, hammers, or pegs. Many cliffs are important archaeological sites containing rock-carved churches, shrines, and burial chambers. Try to leave as little trace as possible.

PAT LITTLEJOHN, *U.K.*

Kenya

Mt. Kenya, Diamond Couloir, ascent. The Diamond Couloir is an African classic, an elegant ice couloir on the south face of 5,199m Mt. Kenya that was first climbed in October 1973 by Thumbi Mathenge and Peter Snyder. At that time the steep headwall leading to the Diamond Glacier was not well-formed, and the climbers logically cut out left below it to reach the hanging glacier. A direct line up the headwall was climbed in January 1975 by Yvon Chouinard and Michael Covington, and most parties repeating the route have followed this line. The recent and generally increasing desiccation of Africa's high mountains has led visitors to believe the climb now impossible because the steep entry pitch has failed to form.

In August Kitty Calhoun and Jay Smith climbed the full Diamond Couloir, starting with 10m of difficult M7 dry-tooling on overhanging volcanic rock, followed by 50m of thin WI5 ice [not long before their ascent an Italian party had retreated after the first 15m of scary mixed climbing—Ed.]. This long pitch gained the easier-angled and undulating middle section of the couloir, where several pitches of moderate ice led to the base of the headwall. Two pitches of WI 4+ led them onto to the hanging glacier. The following day, Jim Donini and Brad McMillon repeated the route.

DOUGALD MACDONALD, *AAC*

Fred Salamin on the now rarely formed entry pitch of the Diamond Couloir, Mt. Kenya, in October 2005. *Fred Salamin Collection*

Mt. Kenya, Diamond Couloir, complete ascent. On October 26 my girlfriend Séverine Bornet, who is aspirant guide, and I climbed the Diamond Couloir. It was not in fat condition. The ice was fairly thin, aerated and a little soft, due to warm temperatures. The entry pitch was completely iced and comparable to a French 4+, though the ice was not attached to the rock in some places. The headwall was of similar difficulty to the Modica-Noury on Mt. Blanc du Tacul, which is graded 5+. We easily used ice screws.

On the day before the ascent, as we were approaching the route, there was a considerable amount of rain. Next morning there were 5cm of new snow covering the base of the couloir, which near the top increased to 10cm. We took six hours from the start to the summit of Nelion. The weather was perfect that day and the next three, in which we climbed the north face of Batian before going home.

FRED SALAMIN, *Switzerland*

Editor's note: In August, Asa Firestone and Ken Ford climbed the Ice Window Route (Laulan, LeDain, and Snyder, August 1973), immediately right of the Dia-

Fred Salamin on the headwall pitch of the Diamond Couloir, Mt. Kenya, October 2005. He likened this section to the Modica-Noury Route on Mt. Blanc du Tacul, France, which is 5+. *Fred Salamin Collection*

mond Couloir, *negotiating steep and often thin ice in a 3m-wide runnel. They noted the "Window" had long since disappeared. They continued to the Gate of the Mists and over the summit of Nelion, for what local porters report was the first ascent in six years.*

Back in the winter of 1997-1998 three local climbers, with a total of more than 50 years experience on the mountain, were surprised to find the Diamond Glacier reduced to almost half its size and no ice to be seen anywhere in the couloir. The following Christmas (1998) the Diamond Glacier had all but disappeared, and not even running water could be seen in the couloir. However, during the previous October the couloir was climbed direct at hard Scottish V Mixed. Anecdotal evidence suggests that glacial decline has been taking place on the mountain at an increasing rate since the 1980s. However, during this time there have been periods when the classic ice routes have been climbable, if not in their original fat state.

Uganda

Rwenzori Range, traverse, various ascents, and new peaks. From January 31 to February 12, Cam Burns, Charlie French, 12 porters, one ranger, and I traversed the central portion of the Rwenzori range, from Roccati Pass south to Kilembe. The traverse included ascents of Mounts Speke (16,042'), Stanley (16,763'), and Baker (15,889'), as well as an ascent of Keki (13,760') in the Nyamugasani Valley and two previously unclimbed peaks (13,400' and 13,440') in the Kamusongi Valley.

Leaving Nyakalengija on January 31, we hiked four days up the Bujuku and Mugusu rivers to the northeast side of Mount Speke, making camps at Bigo Hut, Skull Cave (named for human contents), and on Speke's "upper eastside." On February 4 Cam, Charlie, Josiah Makwano, Peter Babughagle, and I traversed Speke from the northeast to the southwest, by way of the Vittorio Emanuele summit. We intended to ascend the Vittorio Emanuele Glacier; to our surprise the glacier was gone. The slope that once held the glacier was bare rock. We hiked this slope toward the ridge connecting the Ensonga and Vittorio summits. We needed crampons and ice tools just beneath the ridge. On the crest we scrambled south through dense mist to the Vittorio summit, encountering some technical climbing. We descended Speke's southwest ridge.

On February 6 and 8, respectively, we made ascents of the Margherita and Edward summits of Stanley and Baker.

On February 9 we bushwhacked south around the east side of Kitandara Lake. East of the Butawu River the vegetation opened up in a large burn area (the result of a Ugandan Army skirmish with rebels). Skirting Weismann Peak's west ridge, we climbed a steep slope into the Kachope Valley, camping at Kachope rock shelter. The porters enjoyed reading the graffiti in this shelter, as the signatures were those of "very old men" they knew back in the village.

From Kachope we crossed Bamwanjara Pass (14,600') to the Batoda Valley. After descending halfway to Lake Batoda, we headed east over a low pass to the Nyamugasani valley. Here we surveyed our approach to the Kamusongi River valley and identified a peak called Keki (*cake* in English), which was named by Humphreys (1933) because of the impression the peak left on his hungry expedition. Osmaston and Pasteur described Keki as "steep sided and maybe difficult to climb. No ascent has been recorded." While the porters went to set up camp at Bigata rock shelter, Cam, Charlie, Fred Bosco, Peter, and I headed to the mountain. Keki's northwest face is an uninviting cliff, its west side steep vegetation. After dumping our packs north of the summit, our team broke ranks, with each person aiming for what he thought was the best route to the top. After 30 minutes of climbing we coalesced just beneath the summit,

There's still some ice left in the Rwenzori. Climbing Mt. Stanley in February 2005. *Cam Burns*

One of the local guides working for Rwenzori Mountain Services being introduced to rock climbing on the lower slopes of Mt. Baker, overlooking Lake Kitandara. The RMS is the local cooperative with more or less exclusive rights to operate visitor services on the central circuit and south of the range. Guides developed from headmen in charge of local porters and have recently begun to have proper training. *Cam Burns*

sweaty and scratched. We noted Keki's elevation and coordinates, and found a cairn beneath some moss. Keki had obviously been climbed in the past, probably from the east, which is the side we descended. After traversing the peak we circled back to our packs to find our porters. They had been unable to locate Bigata rock shelter. Following a short discussion we descended the Kamusongi Valley to Mutinda rock shelter and camp.

On February 11, Cam, Charlie, Peter, Fred, and I cut through steep jungle to a col between two rocky spires south of Mutinda. From here we climbed a three-pitch lower-fifth-class route to the summit, sometimes via vegetation and sometimes beautiful rock. We marked the summit with a cairn, noting elevation and location: 13,400'; N 0° 16' 37.2", E 29° 55' 3.6". Later that day Cam, Charlie, and Fred soloed another slightly higher peak farther southeast. As it was one of Cam's daughters' birthday, we dubbed the peaks Zoe's Needle (the lower summit) and Mollie's Tower (higher).

BENNY BACH

Editor's note: Guide to the Rwenzori - Mountains of the Moon; 336 pages including 48 color plates, 25 grayscale, and 30 maps and drawings; ISBN 0-9518039-6-4. Publication date June 2006. £16.00.

The 1972 Osmaston and Pasteur "Guide to the Rwenzori," long out of print, has been expanded and completely revised. It describes changes in the status of the range as a National Park and World Heritage Site, and records the great retreat of the glaciers. As before, it contains a detailed history of exploration, climbing, research, and management in the range and has been funded by the Rwenzori Trust, to which all proceeds will accrue. The objectives of this trust are to support scientific research, environmental conservation, and mountaineering education in Uganda or for Ugandans.

Henry Osmaston notes that naming of features in "other people's" mountain ranges is something that has to be both appropriate and modest. The following has been abstracted from the guidebook and could be pertinent to other mountain ranges.

Onomatology (the study of name origins). Places, like people, must have names to identify them. The Bakonzo have lived and hunted in the Rwenzori for millennia. Naturally they gave names to features important to them: rivers, lakes, rock-shelters, etc. These are often either descriptive or historical but have been awarded in a limited and uncertain fashion to features such as mountains, which have only become important in the last century to explorers with other interests. The first explorer of all, Stanley, did his best for local names with *Ruwenzori*, though he was not entirely successful and recently *Rwenzori* has been adopted as nearer the vernacular. Later explorers, such as Johnston, tried to identify local names, such as *Duwoni* and *Kyanja*, with particular mountains, but did not know enough about them: these names later had to be discarded.

"New places" must have new names. Humphreys was diligent in manufacturing (not always correctly) and applying apparently local names to the minor peaks he climbed. These continue to be used, e.g., *Keki* for one shaped like a cake. In 2006 we celebrate the centenary of explorations that resulted in Abruzzi applying the names of European royalties (*Margherita*), German professors (*Kraepelin*), and earlier explorers (*Scott Elliot*) to most of the major peaks, passes, and other features. These were in accord with the political climate then, and had the official approval of the Royal Geographical Society (which had to urge on him the application of his own name, albeit modestly, to the smallest of the five main mountains). This tradition was continued by the Belgian de Grunne (*Albert*) and by Busk, with *Philip* and *Elizabeth* (but Busk was a Queen's Ambassador, so he had some justification).

Whatever we may feel about such names now in our different political climate, name changes cause great confusion and the Ugandan authorities have shown praiseworthy restraint in retaining the plethora of foreign names, which do represent an interesting historical record.

As the exploration of the Rwenzori becomes more detailed, there will be a justified need for the naming of more and more features so that they may be conveniently identified. Each fresh expedition, flushed with its achievements and impelled to write about them, is liable to produce a rash of new names of its own invention. Some of these names fail to become commonplace, either because they are unsuitable or incorrect, or because they appear in a publication of limited circulation. This causes much trouble to those who later wish to study accounts in which these names are used.

In future, appropriate descriptive or personal Lukonzo (or other Ugandan) names would be preferable for naming new features, such as *Kitasamba* and *Nyabubuya*, recommended by the MCU and officially approved in 1953. All those who wish to propose new names should get in touch with the Uganda Wildlife Authority, responsible for this national park, which can guide and approve the choice of suitable names, then record them for permanent use in future editions of this guide and on Survey Dept. maps. The only recent examples of foreign personal names, *Guy Yeoman Hut* and *Kurt Schafer Bridge*, are perhaps justified, as each played an important role in the conservation and development of the Park: both names were locally proposed and both features are possibly no more than ephemeral structures.

DR HENRY OSMASTON, *United Kingdom*

Madagascar

Tsaranoro Atsimo, new route in 2004. The Tsaranoro Massif is now well known and attracts climbers from all over the world, because of its beautiful summits and walls of excellent compact granite. An hour on a jeep from the last village of Ambalavao will take you to Camp Catta, a permanent camp facility below the walls. We visited the region from September 23 to October 20, 2004 and over four days climbed a new route, Avana (Rainbow) on the east face of Tsaranoro Atsimo. We used fixed rope and found it impossible to place natural protection. We placed 10mm stainless steel bolts: 84 for protection and 20 at belays. All you need is two 60m ropes and quickdraws. The height of the route is 530m,

On the lower slabs of the 2004 Italian route, Avana (530m, 7a+ (7a obl)), on the east face of Tsaranoro Atsimo, Madagascar. *Alberto Zucchetti*

with difficulties of 7a+ (7a obl). Pitch grades are as follows: (1) 6a, (2) 6a, (3) 6c, (4) 6c, (5) 6b, (6) 7a+, (7) 6c+, (8) 7a+, (9) 7a+, and (10) 6b+.

ALBERTO ZUCCHETTI, *Italy*

Scotland

Scottish winter season summary. It is early April as I write this. Despite the birdsong and spring flowers, here in Northern England, 90 miles south of the Scottish border, it's snowing. Up in the Scottish Highlands the cliffs are buried beneath blankets of unconsolidated snow, the avalanche risk is high, and snow continues to fall. Winter is still in ascendancy. The best winter conditions came late this year, as they did in 2004-2005; again it was mid-February before there was a major snowfall. Until the mid-1980s, late February, March, and early April were the prime times for winter climbing. Then the big snow and ice routes on Ben Nevis and elsewhere were most likely to have completed their complex evolution and be at their best. Many well-known classics had their first ascents in March and April: Astronomy (VI, 5) in March 1971, Hadrian's Wall Direct (V, 5) in April 1971, Galactic Hitchhiker (VI, 5) in mid-April 1978, Gemini (VI, 6) in March 1979. This tardy tendency hasn't been restricted to pure snow and ice routes. The classics Red Guard and Mitre Ridge, from the 1950s Aberdonian mixed school, saw their first winter ascents in March and April, respectively.

But since the resurgence of mixed and snowed-up rock climbing during the 1980s, the season's usual focus has shifted to earlier in the winter, when the sun is lower and the steep ground less prone to being stripped of its snow and rime. Activists expect to get going in

Tim Emmett leading the crux pitch during the first ascent of Pick n' Mix (IX, 9) in Coire an Lochain. This route is typical of the increasingly technical routes being climbed in winter in the Northern Corries of the Cairngorms. The crux involves hooking through moves of summer 5.11 with the potential for 40' falls. Spice is added by the fact the climber usually has to dig through a foot or so of hoar ice to find the holds. *Ian Parnell*

November and to have a decent tally of routes under their belts by February. This year's dry early winter, with its scant, ephemeral snowfalls, resulted in frustration being expressed on internet forums as early as December. These "when will winter start?" threads can be seen as examples of what Will Gadd refers to in his blog as "pushing the seasons": the desire for the onset of winter and spring to fit with our impatience rather than climatic reality.

Scottish winter traditionalists will have enjoyed the shape of the last two seasons. Scottish winter climbing in spring is a joy; less governed by the tyranny of onrushing darkness, and ending in a leisurely descent from winter hill to budding birch woods. (Scottish *winter* climbing in *spring* may sound like a contradiction but the winter status of a Scottish ascent is defined by the condition of the cliff rather than by the calendar.)

Climbing in November is anything but leisurely. Try something hard, and you may well find yourself warming up for the season by battling up a rime-encrusted wall, with plenty of air beneath your feet, in pitch darkness. This was Rich Cross's almost enviable fate as he led the technical 7 exit groove on Hydroponicum's first winter ascent last November. Jon Bracey and Martin Moran were his ropemates on this frozen, snowy, rimed-up E1. Moran had spotted the sensational undercut ramp line on the savagely steep Far East Wall of Beinn Eighe, but on his first attempt, in winter 1993, had been thwarted by a sudden thaw. Two years later the route received a summer ascent, by John Allott and Andy Nisbet, who found it a rather dirty rock climb. This, of course, added to its winter allure. Ten years later Bracey's impressive onsight lead of the bold and technical crux pitch, and Cross's efforts above a hanging belay in the dark, brought the threesome to the top of a fine VIII, 8: a grade that is still rarely climbed onsight.

Hydroponicum adds yet another fierce test piece to Beinn Eighe, a fantastic mixed-climbing venue in the North West Highlands about 60 miles north of Ben Nevis. The mountain's main coire, Mhic Fhearchair, is dominated by the Triple Buttresses. The first winter ascent of the 300m Central Buttress took two days (Spence, Rowayne, and Urquhart, 1971, VI, 7). The first one-day winter ascent was made by those doomed heroes of British Alpinism, Alex MacIntryre and Al Rouse, in 1978. Even they were forced to use a couple of points of aid, as they fought their way up the final tier in swirling snow and obligatory darkness. Since then, many superb mixed routes have been added to the buttresses and its steep flanking walls, such as the compellingly named and savagely steep Blood, Sweat, and Frozen Tears (VII, maybe VIII, 8), the lengthy West Buttress Direttissima (VII, 8), and the brilliant chimney lines of Kami-Kaze (VI, 7) and Shang-High (VII, 7). The special attraction of Beinn Eighe is that its rock is particularly helpful for mixed climbing, giving solid hooks and positive edges, allowing improbably steep ground to be climbed. This was exemplified later in November by Andy Nisbet and Jonathon Preston's ascent of Bombs Away, a steep and exciting wall at a pretty reasonable grade of V, 7. If you add to this helpfulness the corrie's weeping walls, general dirty dampness (there are some notable evil-looking thin weeps still unclimbed), it is clear why some people see Beinn Eighe as the future of Scottish mixed climbing.

December and January were difficult months. Although it was often cold, there was a distinct lack of snow. Success went to those who knew the Highlands intimately and could predict where conditions might be good, or to those committed to going the extra mile. Camping on Ben Nevis on New Year's Eve (Hogmonay) and climbing on New Year's Day counts as going the extra mile, so Olly Metherell and Ian Parnell richly deserved their reward of the first winter ascent of Sioux Wall, a Hard Very Severe rock climb high on Number Three Gully Buttress. This imposing climb up a clean cracked wall proved to be a sustained and pumpy winter proposition meriting VIII, 8. Metherell fell at one point, leaving his axes embedded in the belay ledge he'd so nearly reached (the pair were climbing leashless, which is still relatively unusual in Scotland), and the first nightfall of 2006 overtook Parnell on the top pitch. However, it was only a couple of weeks before the climb was repeated by Duncan Hodgson and Andy Turner, and it seems likely to become one of the modern mixed classics of Ben Nevis.

Mid-February finally brought a huge snowfall across the Highlands, and conditions stayed largely wintry through to April. A lot of pent-up new-routing energy was released by this improvement in conditions, and activity was hectic. As I mentioned last year, a great many new routes get climbed each winter in Scotland. The majority are up totally new ground, rather than first winter ascents of summer lines. Many are on cliffs that most climbers, even Scottish climbers, won't have heard of, let alone visited. These new climbs spread across almost the entire grade range. Many are fickle, and their suitors have waited years for the correct conditions. Taken together, they represent a huge amount of exploration, commitment, energy, enjoyment, and opportunism. How can I capture all that in one brief report? Trying to choose the most significant routes doesn't seem to get us far—significant in what sense? Technicality? Purity of line? Alpine stature? Ephemerality? Speed of ascent? In a faint echo of the Piolet d'Or debate, I deliberated how to select some climbs over others for this report.

I have tried to work by a couple of principles that I find more in common with the ethos of this *Journal*. I try to select climbs of a more alpine nature, either longer or more remote. I also try to showcase the variety of winter climbing in Scotland by selecting routes of different types from across the Highlands and trying to draw the attention of potential visitors to great cliffs beyond Ben Nevis. Whilst holding these principles in mind, I do find myself defaulting to harder new climbs, perhaps because I find it hard to judge the qualities of climbs on cliffs I don't know. Of course, my favorite selection principle would be simply to choose my own climbs.

Foinaven is about as far north as it's possible to go on the Scottish mainland. From its flanks you can see the north coast. It's also a confusing and slightly mysterious hill, with seven named cliffs and a history of poor documentation and unfathomable route descriptions. Many of the cliffs, including the steep and unpredictable Lord Reay's Seat, are remote. The unpredictability of this crag comes from the fact that a lot of snow is needed to produce adequate winter conditions. When it does snow sufficiently, the snow may be of the wrong type (as Simon Yearsley and I discovered in 2004, when we found mounds of graupel beneath a totally black crag), or the roads may be blocked many miles south. This combination of remoteness and unpredictability verges on the annoying. The last winter addition to the crag was Fishmonger (VI 6), which required three treks along Strath Dionard for Roger Webb and Neil Wilson before they were successful in 1998. Fishmonger takes a line of chimneys on the right of the crag's steep central nose. To the left of the nose is another line of chimneys taken by the summer route Pobble (160m, Very Severe). The chimneys are steep and often wet in summer, providing a compelling winter proposition that until last winter had attracted several unsuccessful suitors.

The northerly winds of late February and early March deposited a lot of snow on the hills of the far north. They also dropped a lot of snow on the Chamonix Aiguilles, so Simon Yearsley and I abandoned an alpine trip in favor of Foinaven, where fresh snow would be an asset rather than a hazard.

We set off at 5 a.m. on mountain bikes, along the snow-covered track (mountain bikes are commonly used to ease long approaches), We switched to snowshoes for the walk up to the

The steep and remote Lord Reay's Seat in Foinaven is about as far north as it is possible to go on the Scottish mainland. *Simon Yearsley*

crag and began climbing at 10 a.m. Eleven hours later we were on top of Lord Reay's Seat in darkness and a snowstorm, after climbing a superbly varied VII 7. The chimneys had been as steep as expected but helpfully supplied with hooks and torques. It was the slabby sections that proved most technical, their slight features hidden deep beneath the powder. Snow had been falling for most of the day, and so it was another six hours, most of them spent pushing the bikes, before we were back in the tent toasting the far north with frigid vodka.

The Southern Highlands is the generic term for the hills south of Glencoe. Climbing here feels different from the rest of the Highlands. The hills are more rounded, the corries and cliffs less blatantly rugged. With a couple of exceptions the corries are often quiet, and the area has the feel of a backwater compared to Glencoe, Ben Nevis, and the Cairngorms. Many of the cliffs are very vegetated, so summer rock-climbing opportunities are more limited than the amount of rock would suggest. Water-ice routes are the main draw here, as they form quickly. The mixed routes, of which there are many fine examples, tend to be approached with more caution. The rock has a reputation for being compact and hard to protect, and the vital turf blobs are often invisible from below, requiring a confident approach. The steep mixed lines often go through or around friezes of free-hanging icicles, so the routes have an appearance akin to Continental or North American mixed lines. In March, Beinn Dorain saw Dave MacLeod and Fiona Murray pushing the standard of onsight winter climbing in Scotland with their ascent of Defenders of the Faith (IX 9). This is an archetypal Southern Highland mixed line: hard to protect, icy, and reliant on thank God blobs of turf ("tufts") appearing just when you need them. Where this route differs is in its relentless steepness; the huge 60m crux pitch is gently overhanging. MacLeod, who has considerable M-climbing experience, rated the crux, which he led, as technically M8+, but he could place traditional protection onsight. Defenders of the Faith is well named: a winter line only, the ideal route for many activists, as the leader climbs with no prior knowledge of the terrain ahead (in contrast to following the known features of a summer line under snow, ice, or rime). The style of ascent was impeccable, and, despite its cutting-edge technical standard, the route still used that characteristic Scottish medium: frozen vegetation.

The speed of an alpine ascent seems to be an increasingly important dimension in the international reporting of climbs, and there seems to be a slowly emerging interest in the speed of Scottish ascents. Although the short days provoke a feeling of rush, high-standard Scottish mixed climbing is notoriously slow (or maybe it just feels that way when you're belaying in the wind and spindrift, as your leader scratches around in the gloom above). The need to find tool placements beneath a uniform cloak of snow, to chop ice from cracks to place protection, and to wear or carry sufficient clothing to survive long belays, all count against speed. Three-hour leads of crux pitches aren't uncommon. When darkness falls, time begins to balloon away.

All this makes Pete Benson and Guy Robertson's 12-hour second ascent of The Steeple (IX 9) on the Shelter Stone crag in the Cairngorms a superb achievement. The climb is 240m, with nine pitches, six of which are technical 7 or harder. The first winter ascent by Alan Mullin and Steve Paget in November 1999 took a planned 24 hours and involved a lot of climbing in the dark. Benson and Robertson finished in the weak evening light of a mid-March day.

Sometimes it's good to wait.

MALCOLM BASS, *The Alpine Club*

Norway

TROMSØ REGION

Kvaloya Island, Blamann, north face, Arctandria, first free ascent. After meeting a Swedish guy in Squamish, Canada, who told me about a north-facing wall somewhere in Norway where the sun shines through the night, I was totally psyched. Looking at Marten Blixt's website, I was almost sure there would be good crazy stuff to free-climb. It would be fun to visit somewhere few people go, trying to do something no one has tried. It's bad to be a sheep.

Two months later I was in Tromsø airport with fellow Swiss Giovanni Quirici and Laurent de Senarclens, the latter accompanying us as photographer. We spent three weeks at Blamann, mostly hiding from the rain in our little tent.

Norway

Lofoten Islands/
Vagakallen

Sweden

Troll Wall

Oslo

Stockholm

We first climbed Atlantis on the left side of the wall. We climbed it in a single push of 10 hours, falling on pitches one, three, six, and eight (wet) but following free. At the top we

Didier Berthod making the first free ascent of Arctandria, Blamann, North Norway. *Laurent de Senarclens*

had the best sunset of our lives (and the longest as well). Wet crack climbing no longer held any secrets. [The 400m Atlantis was first climbed in June 1980 by Frode Guldal and Harvard and Sjur Nesheim, at A1/A2. It was climbed free in July 1990 by Per Hustad and Johan Nilsson at Norwegian 8-/8 or F7b+. It has now been freed several times. While the north face of Blamann is generally overhanging and composed of compact, solid granite, giving mainly well-protected aid routes of 10-12 pitches, Atlantis has a few loose sections—Ed.]

For the rest of the trip we focused on the best-looking line on the wall, Arctandria. [Arctandria was first climbed in May 1981 by Finn Daehli and Harvard and Sjur Nesheim, at A2+ with copperheads, hooks, and knife-blades. During subsequent ascents drilled protection was added—Ed.] We climbed the first five pitches on aid in two days, fixing ropes and returning to our base camp to sleep. We spend six separate days climbing on the wall, and working the route, with both Quirici and I leading every pitch.

The second pitch, a beautiful corner, finally went free at 8a+, on the third day of attempting it and the last day's climbing, and then we only pinkpointed it. There were good Friend placements, reasonable nuts and copperheads. The third pitch was a perfect finger crack, and the roof on the fourth pitch provided a wet lay-back. Unforgettable!

Every pitch was of high quality, and we had much fun climbing them. It was also interesting to climb the route free without changing its character by adding bolts. This ethic definitively makes the free-climbing side of our activity much richer.

Three weeks is a short time. Rain often made the pitches wet and harder, so we never got the opportunity to try a single-push ascent. The challenge is still there.

DIDIER BERTHOD, *Switzerland*

The north face of Blamann, North Norway, showing the two lines mentioned in the report: Atlantis (400m, 7b+, left) and Arctandria (450m, 8a+). There are at least six other routes on this face, all but one being to the left of Arctandria. *Laurent de Senarclens*

Laurent de Senarclens adds: Arctandria is one of the most beautiful and perhaps one of the hardest big trad routes in Europe. The quality of the rock and the quality of the pitches left a good impression. In addition, the surrounding area is stunning, and the local climbers, of which there are few, welcome foreigners with open arms. The weather on our visit could have been better; during one spell we spent seven days in the tent because of wind and rain. Nevertheless, Didier and Giovanni at least pinkpointed every pitch and propose the following pitch grades: 7c, 8a+, 7c, 8a, 7b, 7c+, 7b+, 7a+, 6b, 6c, and 6b, with three more easy pitches to the top. The first, second, fifth, and sixth pitches were only led with preplaced gear. The crux of pitch two is only protected by two copperheads, making it a serious lead. There are six protection bolts in the entire route.

The island of Kvaloya, where Blamann (861m) is located, also has a few crags and bouldering. More info on www.blixt.no.

Another view of Didier Berthod making the first free ascent of Arctandria, Blamann. *Laurent de Senarclens*

LOFOTEN

Austvagoy Island, Vagakallen, second ascent of Freya. Dusan Janak and I arrived on the island of Austvagoy hoping to climb on the big north face of Vagakallen (942m). We were welcomed by six days of perfect weather and made the second ascent of Freya, the 800m, 30-pitch route climbed by Daniela and Robert Jasper in July 1998. Freya climbs the front face of the mountain's most prominent feature, the Storpillaren (*Great Pillar*), which was once dubbed the "Bonatti Pillar of Lofoten," and was graded IX or 7c and new wave A3+.

We climbed Freya from late afternoon on June 12 to early morning on the 16th. Our first bivouac was on a grass ledge at the top of pitch eight, the second at the top of pitch 13, below the big corner with the hardest climbing. The corner gave three pitches: IX, which we climbed AF [AF means that all the moves were climbed free but with rest points—Ed.]; IX-, also AF; and VIII+/IX-, which we climbed onsight. We climbed the next three pitches on aid, at A3+, A3, and A2+. We then rested for a few hours on a small ledge, before finishing the route and descending to the valley.

Apart from the belays, there is only one bolt, on pitch three. Although we hauled a portaledge, one is probably unnecessary, as there are good ledges on the wall

JAN KREISINGER, *Czech Republic*

Austvagoy Island, Vagakallen, second ascent of Storm Pillar. From June 16 to 18 Vasek Satava and I made the second ascent of Storm Pillar on the Storpillaren of Vagakallen. The route was first climbed in September 2003 by Louise Thomas and Mike "Twid" Turner (U.K.). This pair spent two days fixing the lower section, then made three portaledge camps on the wall, climbing for three days and waiting out two days of stormy weather, to complete the 19-pitch route at British E5 6a and A3.

We had a small amount of information from Twid and felt it might be possible for us to make a free ascent. We got a detailed topo from the climbing pub in Hemingsvaer. On the first day we onsighted the lower slabby part of the wall and slept at a grassy spot above the big terrace (top of pitch eight). Next day we continued, planning to make a free ascent of pitch 12, the first aid pitch. However, we met three ugly pitches, including the very steep "water-

1. Storm Pillar E5 6a A3
2. Freya 7c A3+

The north face of Vagakallen, Lofoten, looking steeply up the Storpillaren (Great Pillar) and showing (1) Storm Pillar (800m, E5 6a A3, Thomas-Turner, 2003) and (2) Freya (800m, 7c A3+, Jasper-Jasper, 1998). *Pavel Jonak*

fall" 11th pitch, which had been given the grade E4 5c. We managed to onsight this hard pitch; the grade was a joke. Above, we discovered that we would be unable to bivouac, as we were not carrying a portaledge. It took us over three hours, using all the gear we had, to overcome the A3 pitch. Without resting for part of the day, we couldn't even attempt to free this pitch. We also felt that we would probably need to replace much of the gear or drill a few bolts. Although there was gear every half a meter in the crack, it was generally poor.

On the top of the Storpillaren, Vagakallen, after a successful repeat of the 800m Storm Pillar. Behind is part of the coastline and off-shore islands of Austvagoy, the main island of Lofoten. *Pavel Jonak*

We continued up, looking for a place to rest, but there wasn't a ledge big enough even to sit on, so we continued through the night, which was still quite light at this time of year. At the top of pitch 16, which we reached at 9 a.m., we found a big square block that we could sit on and sleep for three hours in the morning sun. After this rest we climbed the A2+ pitch, which again might be possible to free-climb except for problems with protection. Above, easier pitches led to the top of the pillar. After taking photos we rappeled the route. Due to overhangs and poor belays, rappeling was almost as adventurous as the climb, but we made it down in a few hours.

During my visit to Wales in 2004 I tried to understand the British grading system. Here in Norway I stopped worrying about it, accepting that just about anything could fit any grade.

PAVEL JONAK, *Czech Republic*

Flakstadoy Island, Stortinden, Slovakiaruta. Miro Mrava and Brano Turcek, two climbers from the Slovak Mountaineering Union, JAMES, spent two weeks in northern Norway from August 2 to 17. On the 10th they made a new route on Stortinden, an 866m peak on the island of Flakstadoy. This, the first recorded rock route on the mountain, climbed the west face (the summit is easy to reach from south or north). They completed the 1,200m route (climbing length), which they named Slovakiaruta, Alpine style in 12 hours, beginning at 6 a.m. It has two distinct parts, separated by a large terrace. The lower half is generally

The west face of Stortinden (866m) on the island of Flakstadoy, Lofoten. Marked is the line of the Slovakiaruta (1,200m of climbing, VIII-, Mrava-Turcek), the first recorded rock route on the mountain. *Miro Mrava-Brano Turek collection*

slabby, with lots of vegetation, leading to an easy gully. The upper section is clean, quasi-vertical, and significantly more difficult. The route has 24 pitches, with difficulties up to VIII-.

The rock proved to be of good quality, solid granite (even in the grassy sections), and there are plenty of places to use nuts and Friends, though pitons and birdbeaks were also useful.

VLADO LINEK, *Slovak Mountaineering Union, Slovakia*

Moskenesøy Island, Helvetestind, west face, The Next Best Thing and Norwegian Sheep Ranch. On July 3 Adam Stack and I climbed a six-and-a-half pitch line on what is locally known as Den Franske Pillaren (*the French Pillar*) on the west face *(Hell's Wall)* of Helvetestind (606m). The route, which we named The Next Best Thing, was 5.10+ and probably shares some common ground with the original line on the French Pillar, which was put up over six days in 1983 by Anne and Eric Lapied and party, though no one here quite knows where the Lapied line goes. From the top of the pillar we continued with 150m of easy simulclimbing/scrambling to the summit ridge, making our route 450m long. It was great climbing in a beautiful setting. We descended by the normal route on the south ridge (4th Class).

The west face of Helvetestind, on the island of Moskenesøy, Lofoten. Two routes on the French Pillar, which almost certainly share some common ground with the original 1983 line, are marked: (1) The Next Best Thing (ca. seven pitches, 5.10+, Stack-Wiik, 2005), (2) Norwegian Sheep Ranch (six pitches, 5.11, Caldwell-Rodden, 2005). In the middle of the face to the left is an incomplete route that stopped two pitches short of the top (11 pitches, 5.8 A1, Jensen-Meyer, 1984). *Odd-Roar Wiik*

Tommy Caldwell and Beth Rodden climbed a route on the French Pillar that was a bit harder than ours. They climbed six pitches of mostly excellent rock that was relatively sustained, with the first, third, and fourth pitches each 60m and 5.11. They called it "Norwegian Sheep Ranch."

To the left, somewhere in the middle of the face, is an incomplete 5.8 A1 route climbed in 1984 by Finn Jensen and Arild Meyer. They climbed 11 pitches but retreated two pitches from the top of the wall. I recently saw a description of a line done way over on the left side of the face, but details are lacking.

ODD-ROAR WIIK, *Norway*

The 250m east face of Ølkontind, Moskenesøy Island, Lofoten. The only two lines to date are marked: (1) It's all About the Numbers (six pitches, 5.10+, Stack-Wiik, 2005), (2) Looks Can be Deceiving (four pitches, 5.10, Caldwell-Rodden, 2005). *Odd-Roar Wiik*

Moskenesøy Island, Ølkontind, east face, It's all About the Numbers and Looks Can be Deceiving. On July 7 Tommy Caldwell, Beth Rodden, Adam Stack, and I climbed two lines on the previously unclimbed east face of 735m Ølkontind. This peak lies just east of the village of Hamnoy, close to Reine. The 250m wall has two obvious lines. Adam and I climbed the wide central line in six pitches to give It's all About the Numbers (5.10+), the name a bit of a joke reflecting the "adventurous" nature of the route, with its grassy chimneys and offwidths. Tommy and Beth climbed a line well to the right. It followed a large ramp/dihedral system and was quite adventurous, with vertical grass climbing and bad rock in the wrong places. Not destined to be a classic. The route had four pitches, with the two hardest at 5.10. A further 500m of 4th

Adam Stack dealing with the vegetation at the start of It's all About the Numbers (250m, 5.10+), east face of Ølkontind, Moskenesøy Island. *Odd-Roar Wiik*

Class terrain would lead to the top of the peak. Descent follows the south ridge down to the valley to the east.

This general area has loads of potential. Some of the most obvious lines are quite vegetated, but there are dozens of interesting walls with few or no lines to date.

Lofoten has been popular by Norwegian standards since the mid-1990s, but there is now also a steady flow of foreign climbers, and a number of them are putting up new routes. The biggest change over the last few years is that more people are climbing the longer/harder routes. This summer there were many occasions when more than 10 parties could be seen on Presten. This would have been unheard of 10 years ago.

ODD-ROAR WIIK, *Norway*

New guide to Lofoten climbing. Ed Webster's classic guide *Climbing in the Magic Islands* was reprinted last year. However, the Nord Norsk Klatre Skole and RockFax are collaborating to produce a new rock-climbing guide to the Lofoten Islands, including all new routes put up in the 10 years since the last guide. There is also a plan to produce a small guide to the superb granite peaks around Narvik, which are virtually unknown outside Norway. Publication dates have not been fixed but are not likely to be before 2007.

CHRIS CRAGGS, *U.K.*

SOUTHERN NORWAY

STAVANGER REGION

Lysenfjord, Kierag, La Vida es Bella. Spaniards Edu Marin and Toti Vales, the former reputed to be one of the strongest rock climbers in Spain, climbed a new route on the 1,000m-high south-west face of Kierag. After climbing the first 12 pitches of the existing route Hoka Hey, the two Catalans forced an independent line to the top of the wall, with a crux of 8a+. They completed the route, which they named La Vida es Bella, in 22 hours. They used only traditional protection, and it is reported that Marin led the hard pitches onsight.

LINDSAY GRIFFIN, *Mountain INFO, CLIMB Magazine*

Russia

SIBERIA

SAYAN MOUNTAINS

Kupol-Stol region, Peak ca.
3,000m, Pofigo. In June, Heidi Wirtz and I made a first ascent at a climbing area known as Kupol-Stol, in the remote Barun Valley of the Sayan Mountains, just west of the southern end of Lake Baikal. We were the first Americans to grace the Siberian taiga, as well as the first women and first to put up a traditionally protected route in the region. In 1999 local Irkutsk climbers made a helicopter reconnaissance of this area, then attacked it, rappelling from the tops of the peaks with a stack of bolts, to create 10 sport routes up to 20 pitches long. The climbers who frequent this area do not even own traditional gear, and splitter cracks are accessorized by a line of closely spaced bolts (excluding off-width sections, where they are farther spaced).

We arrived in Irkutsk, the capital of Siberia, with five loaded haulbags and a fat extra-baggage dent in our pocketbooks. After only one day we were itching to get to the mountains, and when our guide asked why we had brought so many bags, then asked us to wait in "the city" for two weeks while he finished another job, we hired an 18-year-old we met in the hotel lobby.

Our proposed helicopter ride fell through, so we trekked ca. 30km into the Sayan Mountains, carrying a minimal amount of gear and food. At base camp, with a double rack and a hand drill, we were told by local climber and area aficionado Pavel Trofimov that it

The Kupol-Stol region of the Sayan Mountains, close to Lake Baikal in Russian Siberia. Existing routes are marked, though details are unknown except for the route on the far left up the obvious prow to an unnamed ca. 3,000m summit, climbed in June 2005 by Roxanna Brock and Heidi Wirtz (350m, 5.11). *Roxanna Brock*

would take "a million years" to drill a bolt in this area. "Cool, we didn't want to drill any bolts!" exclaimed Wirtz.

While in the States, we had seen photos of the area's one large peak without an ascent. After tossing the drill and weathering three days of intense thundershowers, we grabbed the rack and tromped to the base. Benighted on our first attempt, we ended up huddled in a wet cave big enough for two large packs.

Two days later we returned for a first ascent on one of only three days without rain. After completing pitch seven, Wirtz climbed a jigsaw puzzle of balanced rock to our right. I then traversed back left using one point of aid to reach the crack that rose directly from the top of pitch seven. I continued up the crack to a belay below a roof. When Wirtz reached this point she lowered me 60m to the top of pitch seven, and I top-roped a finger crack at 12a. I found it would require a lot of gear we weren't carrying. Wirtz then also top-roped the crack and confirmed the grade. The ninth and final pitch of this 350m route, above the roof, was also loose, and we arrived on the summit late in the day, estimating its elevation to be between 2,900 and 3,050m.

We named the route Pofigo, which means *whatever* or *it does not matter* in Russian. The grade was about 5.11. We chose this name to reflect the numerous changes in plan that took place before and during the trip, and because it is unlikely to be climbed again (unless someone bolts it), since climbers in the region lack traditional gear.

Supporting the expedition, The North Face, in conjunction with Global Giving, provided financial support to the City Bridge Foundation, which gives treatment to children who suffer from a rare auto-immune disease called Plastic Anemia. Many of these children are from the nearby shores of Lake Baikal.

Trofimov, who was initially cold, subsequently declared, "We don't have any women like you here."

ROXANNA BROCK

Afghanistan

Koh-e-Maghrebi (6,040m), probable first ascent. Spanish mountaineers David Cejudo Fernandez and Luis Miguel Lopez made a rare visit to Afghanistan's Wakhan Corridor, where they made the probable first ascent of a 6,040m peak, subsequently named Koh-e-Maghrebi. This is one of the few first ascents made in Afghanistan's mountains since the Soviet invasion during 1979.

The two left Kabul by vehicle on July 29, entered the Corridor via Faizabad and Iskashim, and drove up it to the confluence of the rivers at Qala-e-Panja. It was then five days on foot to a base camp at 4,200m in the West Ali Su valley. They reached there on August 10, having taken time out to make a three-day side trip farther east to Elghunak. On the 12th they established Camp 1 at 5,050m on the West Ali Su glacier, south of Koh-e-Maghrebi. Next day they climbed a 700m couloir (40-55° névé) through the rocky slopes of the south face to reach the easier 300m summit snowfield. This led to the upper section of the west ridge, where the pair had to overcome a 60° section before reaching the summit (N 37° 6' 28"; E 73° 10' 23"). They returned to camp 10 hours after leaving and regained their vehicle on the 18th.

The Spanish note that this area of the Pamir has a dozen or so peaks above 6,000m, the highest being Koh-e-Pamir (6,320m) above the North Issik Glacier, a little northeast of their own peak. Some of these mountains were climbed during the 1970s. They also found the inhabitants of this region, mainly Wakhis, but in the extreme east Kyrghyz, very hospitable.

JOSEP PAYTUBI, *Servei General d'Informacio de Muntanya, Sabadell, Spain*

Kyrgyzstan

PAMIR ALAI

KARAVSHIN

Wall of Dikes, Central Pyramid, various first ascents. In July a team of two Irish climbers (Donie O'Sullivan and I) and four British (Ian Parnell, Mark Pretty, Dave Pickford, and Sam Whittaker) visited the Ak-Su Valley in the Karavashin region. There have been few trips to this area since the incident involving Tommy Caldwell's party in 2000, when the members were kidnapped at gunpoint and fled to safety after a daring escape. Indeed, our thoughts that the situation had improved in the interim were cast in doubt close to our departure. There were reports of the deaths of 200 refugees at a nearby border and political upheavals because of an approaching election. However, as we had already paid our £300 air fares, we rationalized that our lives were unlikely to be worth more than that, so at the beginning of July we flew to Kyrgyzstan.

Donie O'Sullivan on the steep compact slabs of the Pamir Pyramid (3,700m), Ak-Su Valley, Kyrgyzstan. *Niall Grimes*

After a protracted week's traveling, involving missed flights, broken gear boxes, mad drivers, road blocks, five-hour short-cuts, huge spiders, recalcitrant donkeys, and a Polaroid camera, we arrived at our base camp in the Ak-Su. This was a stunning setting, nestled between two parades of the most impressive granite mountains that I have ever seen (and I have seen over a dozen!). Instead of the dusty locale that I had expected, it was an alpine pasture, complete with a huge herd of cows (whose game of Shit In The Humans' Campsite amused us no end and eventually led to us building a tiny corral).

Our first objective was a line on the Pamir Pyramid, to the left of the 1999 Parnell-Pretty route, The Reluctant Chief (530m, British E3 5c). Having climbed three pitches to a ledge (which was littered, as the valley was, with armor-piercing shells, ominous reminders of whatever trouble had occurred over the years—and could happen again), we began the upper section, heading toward a groove high on the wall. However, after a bold slab pitch, we began to find, to our disappointment, bolt belays. From there we followed a line, which we presumed to be roughly that of the existing route, until the climbing eased off. We rappelled the line. The existing bolts illustrate the problem of lack of information. We had gathered all the information we could from the Mountain INFO section of High Magazine, but such surprises still seem inevitable.

Because of bad weather, Pickford and Whittaker spent several days climbing on a one-pitch crag behind the campsite, adding a clutch of surprisingly fine, bold slab climbs ranging from E3 to E6/7. They also climbed a four-pitch route on a small peak to the right of the Central Pyramid, based around the most obvious of a series of left-facing grooves (250m, E5 6a). They found a bolt on the crux, indicating prior ascent, though possibly an aid line.

Donie O'Sullivan holds characteristic remnants of previous activity in the Ak-Su Valley, Kyrgyzstan. *Niall Grimes*

Donie and I then turned our attention to a line ascending the right arête of the huge Wall of Dikes, a formation first climbed by Dave Green and Paul Pritchard in 1997 (The Great Game, 900m, E5 6b) and in 1999 by Anne and John Arran (The Philosopher's Stone, 900m, E6 6b). An obvious ramp led to the base. We gained the diagonal line with three interesting pitches up to E3, but again found a bolt. Carrying on with our plan, hoping that when we reached the main arête we would be on virgin ground, we grazed up the ramp with little difficulty. Actually, this grazing took three days, due to two days of downpour that forced us to retreat. The heavy rain turned the ramp to a drainage channel, giving some idea of what it would be like to be trapped in the U-bend when a toilet was flushed. The ramp ended at a shoulder below the arête, a point from which we could easily escape back to base camp for fried potatoes. We returned to climb the upper section, about 13 rope lengths up to E3, in a day, returning to bivouac on the shoulder long after nightfall. We found no more bolts or other evidence of previous ascents. The route, Amazing Graze, was on superb rock, with good protection, and went more easily than we had expected from below. Presuming it to be a first ascent, it shows the quality of virgin lines to be found in this area, at attainable standards. We later returned and climbed a new direct start up slabby rock directly to the shoulder, at E3/4.

Meanwhile Parnell and Pretty had been at work on the huge area of unclimbed rock right of the Wall of Dikes, to the right of the huge waterfall that comes down the large bowl. Using fixed ropes they climbed an arduous and difficult route, sustained, with pitches up to E4, based around a massive, sweeping, left-facing corner. The route ended at a ledge system about halfway up the peak proper, allowing the pair to descend into the bowl and return to camp. Parnell, who had come on the trip straight from a successful Everest expedition, had the look of an 8,000m veteran as he staggered into camp after this behemoth. The Beast (550m, 10 pitches, E4 6a).

Finally, Pickford and Whittaker added the hardest route of the trip, with an ascent of a pillar, on the very right edge of the Central Pyramid, rising out of the large depression between the Pyramid and the Russian Tower. This 400m, eight-pitch climb had a fourth-pitch crux of E7 6b, led by Whittaker, and reckoned to be one of the hardest on-sight leads he had ever made. The climb was named From Russia with Love.

Towards the end of the trip, while O'Sullivan and I were returning to base camp, having just done our direct start, we heard the unmistakable sound of an AK-47 rifle spitting its hot leaden death. We peeked round a corner to see Whittaker trying to eliminate a small bottle of water set on a rock. We approached to discover we had been joined by an army group, their camo gear and sniper rifles made more sinister by their shades, Coca-Cola T-shirts, bandanas, and Adidas trainers. The long and the short of it was that they were going to have a lot of money from us, and we were to leave the valley. From then on we were seen by anyone with a gun as an ever-diminishing pot of money. The final bizarre episode occurred on the Aeroflot plane, where armed men demanded, "Were you the Alpinists?" "No", replied Pretty, "I collect flowers." We were allowed to fly home with our final few dollars.

This area still has lots of potential for development, although, as stated, what has or has not been done is not always clear, especially if climbers leave no drilled protection. The weather was fairly showery with, on average, afternoon rain every other day, though the rain was often light and would not necessarily mean coming off a route. Flies and other wildlife, cows except- ed, were not a problem, and day and night temperatures were pleasant. The base camp area has excellent bouldering (our team added problems up to V9), and an expedition might bring a pad or two. Apart from boys with guns, the locals were warm, friendly, and generous.

NIALL GRIMES, *United Kingdom*

WESTERN KOKSHAAL-TOO

Kyzyl Asker, southeast face attempt. On August 3 Scott Adamson, Tom Adamson, and I stepped off the plane in Bishkek, courtesy of an AAC Lyman Spitzer Grant. We immediately realized the extent of the communication barrier and were glad to see our contact, Misha Sohorukov (mis48@rambler.ru), waiting at the terminal. He loaded our mountain of gear onto his tiny car and away we went, flying through the early morning darkness, excited and exhausted from so much travel.

Misha is an outfitter who came highly recommended. Our agreement was simple: one flat fee and we were his complete responsibility for a month-and-a-half. He took charge of our meals, lodging, and travel expenses. He also had enormous expertise as a ski mountaineering guide and porter, and was familiar with the areas in which we were interested. Although he speaks limited English, communication was not a problem. We found his services exceptional throughout our stay.

We hashed out details the following day over dinner with his wife (who speaks very good English). We would spend a week or so in the Ala Archa, getting used to our new surroundings and acclimatizing on the 4,500+m peaks around the Ak-Sai Glacier. We'd then head back to town long enough to gather supplies, and then head off again to spend a month in one of the most remote and unexplored mountain ranges in the world. A day later, in an amazing down- pour, we hiked up the grueling 1,500m vertical interval to the Ratsek Hut at the mouth of the

Ak Sai. We then sat in the hut through eight days of rain. The weather cleared long enough to see us through one of the classic 5.9 rock pillars on the south face of Pik Bachichiki and a failed attempt on a new route up the north face of Korona. After eight days we had had enough and steeled ourselves for a muddy descent.

Two days later we headed to Naryn, past ancient relics of the Soviet era and into the Western Kokshaal-Too on the border with China. The final day's drive was one of the most gripping on the trip, as we threaded our way through washed-out roads and bridges for 100km in Misha's tiny car.

Driving along the western approaches to the Kokshaal-Too is extreme, and we slowly rose onto a 3,600m bench that provides a surreal view. Finally, the Kyzyl Asker group came into view, the main summit a huge mountain dominating the southern horizon.

The next few weeks of fall saw our initial five days of sunny weather deteriorate into an early winter. In addition, a nasty stomach bug led to me suffering pulmonary edema, and an attempt on Kyzyl's southeast face by the other two almost ended their lives. Only nine days into our stay on the Komorova Glacier, plagued by sickness and unable to hydrate, I was beset by some alarmingly high respirations while completely at rest. These forced me back to Bishkek and a Kyrgyz hospital. Forging on, Scott and Tom pushed the remaining five kilometers to an advanced base close to Kyzyl Asker, where they waited out weather system after weather system, before finally committing themselves to the face. The weather quickly deteriorated into a tempest, and constant spindrift finally forced a retreat at mid-height. The ensuing storm dumped a full three meters of snow over the following five days, crushing all hopes of another attempt and providing challenges during the 20km hike out. The extreme weather caused Tom to suffer frostbite.

Back in Bishkek on September 9 after a bit of rejuvenation on the soothing shores of Lake Issyk-Kul, we wished we had done things differently. Hopefully our short memories will be an asset in getting us motivated for some more abuse next season.

JAMES STOVER

Fersmana Glacier, Pik Neizvestniy, first ascent, and various attempts. In July and August I traveled with Grant Piper and Graham Rowbotham to the central part of the Western Kokshaal-Too. We climbed in the previously unexplored Fersmana Glacier basin, where we were delighted to find granite columns and steep walls, rather than the friable limestone prevailing immediately to the east. However, the walls of the highest peak, Byeliy (a.k.a. Grand Poohbah, 5,697m), were mostly overhung by seracs, and we saw no suitable routes on the

The north face of Granitsa (5,370m) at the head of the Fersmana glacier, Western Kokshaal-Too. The Anglo-New Zealand party attempted this peak via the west ridge (right skyline), but the peak remains unclimbed. *Paul Knott*

The Byeliy cirque of the Fersmana glacier basin, Western Kokshaal-Too, from the northeast. From left to right: Pik 5,481m, Pik Byeliy (a.k.a. Grand Poohbah, 5,697m), and Pik 5,611m. *Paul Knott*

Grant Piper on the west spur of Pogranichnik's north ridge during an unsuccessful attempt. *Paul Knott*

Looking south across the frontier towards unexplored Chinese peaks in the Western Kokshaal-Too. Paul Knott

northeast, east, or south sides. The route substantially climbed by Mike Libecki's party in 2000 appears to have been the southwest ridge (not southeast as captioned in AAJ 2001, p. 401). Contrary to maps, spot height 5,481m in the same massif turned out to be a quite separate and equally precipitous summit.

We focused our climbing efforts on the smaller but still challenging peaks at the head of the glacier. We made the first ascent of Pik Neizvestniy (*Unknown* in English, 5,240m) via the northeast arête. A sharp corniced ridge high on the route required delicate à cheval technique and in places vibrated as we climbed. We graded this route Alpine D or New Zealand 4. Our descent via the west ridge was straightforward.

Next we attempted Pik 5,370m, a symmetrical peak at the head of the glacier. We named this Granitsa (*Border* in English); it sports several impressive granite walls on the Chinese side. We retreated low on the west ridge when confronted by monolithic gendarmes that we could not bypass. Our next attempt was on the peak in the southeast corner of the glacial cirque. We named this Pogranichnik (*Border Guard,* 5,220m). Climbing the north ridge, we reached the granite "head" at 5,180m but could not see a way around the steep rock above. The next day deep hanging powder on the north-facing slopes of a small peak we named Zastava (*Border Post,* 5,010m), prevented us from summiting on its otherwise straightforward west ridge. This summit lay between Neizvestniy and Granitsa. Our peak names reflect the close border control in the area.

We experienced squalls on almost every day of our visit and were unable to climb during an eight-day period of very unsettled conditions. In early August we waded through melt streams and slush on the upper glacier. Two weeks later the streams were frozen and powder snow covered the surface. On our return truck journey there was snow on the already marginal 4,000m passes.

Our approach to base camp up the Uzengegush valley was affected by a little-known change to the border between Kyrgyzstan and China (see below). As a result we had to complete the last 60-65km on foot, with our luggage on horseback. Previously it had been possible to drive off-road trucks up the braided river as far as our base camp at Pt. 3,392m and on to Pt 3,425m (though definitely not beyond). We also lost time because our vehicle experienced a blown radiator and because we had our border zone permit rejected at Kara-Sai. The colonel who authorized the permit had been ousted following the March coup. We had the permit revalidated in Karakol. During our exit from the mountains, a misunderstanding with our agents left us stranded for three days at the Uzengegush border post. We avoided missing our flights only by persuading the border guards to relay an emergency message via their military telephone system.

PAUL KNOTT, *New Zealand*

Kyrgyzstan-China border changes. During our journey to the Western Kokshaal-Too reported above, we were surprised to find that sections of the border have been realigned. All current printed maps (*Kyrghyzstan, a Climber's Map and Guide,* produced for the AAC in 2005) show the de-facto boundary that has stood since the time of the Soviet Union. The legal border had been ill defined since the 1860s-1880s agreements between Russia and China.

A new agreement, which remains highly contentious in Kyrgyzstan, cedes significant parts of the disputed territory to China. One such area starts west of the Bedel Pass, with the new border following the Uzengegush River from the point where the road meets it from the north to the confluence of the Chon-Tyuekuyruk River (grid ref. 436630 on 2005 AAC map). The border then follows the Chon-Tyuekuyruk east of Pik Koroleva (5,816m). Along the Uzengegush section we saw border posts dated 2001. The originally disputed territory encompasses the whole alpine area of the Western Kokshaal-Too, as well as much of the Borkoldoy range. Only a small part of the affected area appears on the AAC map. The recent agreement also cedes an area of the Kokshaal that lies west of the main massif.

The road up the Uzengegush now crosses into China for some of its length, and we were told only military vehicles are authorized to use it. The road was also blocked by landslides, although these were later cleared. Future parties may find it more convenient to access the

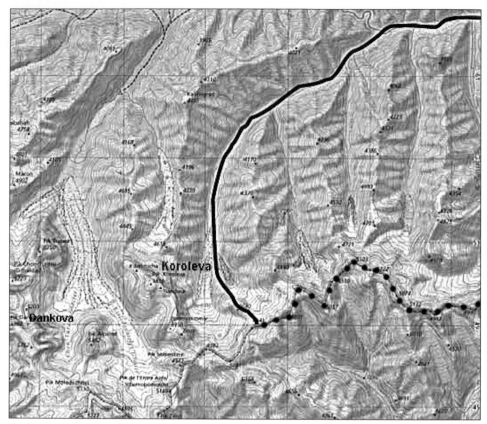

The far eastern section of the map of the Western Kokshaal-Too produced for the AAC in 2005 (*Kyrgyzstan, a Climber's Map and Guide*). The dotted line shows the de-facto boundary between Kyrgyzstan and China that has stood since the time of the Soviet Union. The solid line shows the new boundary, which has been in existence for several years and caused access problems for one expedition last summer.

Fersmana Glacier by approaching via Naryn to the west, driving as far as base camp in the Kotur Valley and then walking the remaining 9km to the Sarychat River. It is not possible to connect east and west sides of the West Kokshaal-Too by vehicle. There is a steep gorge in the middle, and my guess is that the road marked on maps was once planned but never built.

Much farther east it appears that at the eastern end of the Inylchek Glacier the new border turns north at Pobeda East, follows the ridge through Pik Shipilov, and crosses the glacier to Khan Tengri

PAUL KNOTT, *New Zealand*

Editor's note: Kyrgyzstan, a Climber's Map and Guide, which was produced for the AAC by cartographer Martin Gamache, was awarded an honorable mention in the American Congress on Surveying and Mapping (ACSM) CaGIS 33rd annual Map Design Competition, the most prestigious map competition in the U.S. Initial details were posted on http://www.acsm.net/cagis/05mapwinners.html

BORKOLDOY RANGE

Looking west-southwest from Peak Fox (4,446m) in the Northern Borkoldoy: (1) Part of the west ridge of Peak Harvard (4,817m), (2) The north ridge of Peak Omingmak (4,746m), (3) Peak Adventure (4,636m), (4), (5), and (6) are unnamed, unclimbed peaks, (7) Peak of Theoretical Physics (4,856m and the highest summit in Harvard Circus, climbed by the long east ridge facing the camera), (8) An unnamed and unattempted peak. The Harvard Mountaineering Club's Advanced Base Camp was situated just off the bottom of the photograph, at the foot of the long east ridge of (7). *Bjarne Holmes*

Northern Borkoldoy, first ascents. The Borkoldoy Range in southeastern Kyrgyzstan has been explored by a handful of recent expeditions, which reported promising unclimbed alpine peaks: British (1995) in the northeast of the range, British (2002) in the southwest, Russian (2003) in the south, and the International School of Mountaineering to various regions (2003, 2004, and 2005).

In August the Harvard Mountaineering Club, celebrating its 80th anniversary, sent a team of eight climbers to the northwestern region of the Borkoldoy,

Looking south-southwest from the summit of Peak of Theoretical Physics (4,856m). In the foreground (to the right) is the top of what has loosely been dubbed Laursen Cirque. Beyond lie a host of unclimbed peaks in the Central Borkoldoy. The skyline is the Western Kokshaal-Too with Pik Byeliy (a.k.a. Grand Poohbah, 5,697m) in the center and Kyzyl Asker (5,842m) the big peak toward the right. *Adilet Imambekov*

immediately to the west of the second area visited by ISM in 2003 (*AAJ 2004*, pp.347-348). The team included George Brewster, Kelly Faughnan, Laura Fox, Bjarne Holmes, Adilet Imambekov, David Krause, Corey Rennell, and I. Record keeping of first ascents in the Kyrgyz Republic is scattered, but requests for information from the Kyrgyz Alpine Club and the International School of Mountaineering gave us some idea of where unclimbed objectives were located.

On the northwest face of Peak Adventure (4,636m) during the first ascent of Meta-documentation. Behind Corey Rennell, who is "resting" in the foreground, unnamed and unattempted peaks continue to the west. *Bjarne Holmes*

During 15 days of exploratory climbing the team ascended nine peaks along the Ayutor and Koldmor rivers, south of the Chakyrkorum River.

We consider that on each of these we made at least the first recorded ascent. Peaks ranged from 4,400 to 4,850m in height, and routes ran the gamut from scree slogs to a full day of alpine climbing with cruxes of 5.6 and AI 3. We climbed all routes free in one-day alpine-style pushes, except for one, on which a single pitch was fixed above a bivouac site. The more southerly of the peaks we climbed looked into the central valley of the Borkoldoy and offered tantalizing glimpses of months of potential alpine climbing.

We found conditions in August ideal for accessing the area from the north, though minor concerns with avalanche danger on some of the most exposed northern aspects prevented us ascending one peak. Loose rock meant that most of the climbing took place on comparatively reliable ice, covered in about 30cm of snow. The weather was sunny, with afternoon clouds occasionally dropping light snow or rain at base camp (3,500m). We placed advanced base at the snout of the Ayutor Glacier. We hired a driver and cook from ITMC Tien Shan, a company that appears to maintain a good relationship with the military outpost at Karasai. A few cigarettes, beers, and a watermelon got us through, in spite of a problem with our permits. (Watermelon seems to be the key; see Crossland, *AAJ 2005*, p. 341.)

The nine peaks climbed are as follows: Peak Fox (4,446m), northeast ridge (Brewster, Faughnan, Fox, Holmes, and Imambekov, August 10) and north face, Treadmill Gully (Krause, Laursen, and Rennell, August 10); Mt. Powell (4,555m), southwest face, 17-year Gully (Brewster, Faughnan, Imambekov, Krause, and Rennell, August 14); Peak Harvard (4,817m), south face, 80 Years of Harvard Mountaineering (Holmes and Rennell, August 18); Peak of Theoretical Physics (4,856m, the highest summit in Harvard Circus, our name for the three cirques we explored above advanced base), east ridge (Brewster and Imambekov, August 20); Peak Adventure (4,636m), west ridge, Meta-documentation (Faughnan, Holmes, Laursen, and Rennell, August 21); Peak Omingmak (4,746m), northwest face (Brewster and Fox, August 21); Peak Schullinger-Krause (4,727m), south face, Sneakin' Sallie Through the Alley (Krause, August 21); Mount John Bowlby (4,846m), north ridge, Kazakh-Swedish Route (Holmes and Imambekov, August 24). This last ascent crossed the subsidiary summit of Peak Mary Ainsworth (4,612m, via northeast ridge).

We recorded all but one summit height using GPS. Our proposed names have been submitted to the Kyrgyz Alpine Club. Full GPS coordinates, route descriptions, a map, etc. are available to the climbing community at www.borkoldoy.harvardmountaineering.org.

LUCAS LAURSEN, *President, Harvard Mountaineering Club, AAC*

Climbing the west ridge of Pik Alpinistka (4,959m, D) in the Central Borkoldoy during the first ascent. Pat Littlejohn

Central Borkoldoy, Pik Tansovsitsa, north ridge; Alpinistka, west ridge; Pik Koldunia, south ridge; "Pik Borkoldoy," south ridge. The central area of the Borkoldoy Range in southeast Kyrgyzstan is a collection of superb alpine peaks, which are well defended on every side by chains of slightly lower mountains. While it has been visited by a few trekking groups in recent years, the only known mountaineering expeditions have been a Russian attempt on the highest peak (5,171m) in 2003 and our party from the International School of Mountaineering (ISM) in 2004.

ISM returned in September 2005, the team comprising Ben Box, James Bruton, Peter Kemble, Mark Samuels, Bill Thompson, and Dr. Jane Whitmore, with guides Vladimir Komissarov, Adrian Nelhams, and I. In 2004 we had to work hard to re-open an old geologists' track in order to access the area by 6WD vehicle. This year we were pleased to find our work intact and were able to reach the broad river delta quickly, then drive easily for another 20km to base camp at 3,570m. From there glaciers radiate like spokes of a wheel, approximately eight being within easy walking distance. As each is surrounded by great peaks, this is an exceptional expedition venue.

We established advanced base at 4,240m on Ilbirs Glacier West, from where Nelhams, Samuels, and Thompson climbed the north ridge of the big peak on the left (east) side of the glacier, Pik Tansovsitsa (4,911m, Alpine AD). Higher up the same glacier Box, Bruton, Whitmore and I made several attempts and then finally succeeded on the west ridge of Alpinistka (4,959m; D).

After a spell of rock climbing on the 150m limestone crag above base camp, Nelhams, Kemble, Komissarov, Samuels, and Thompson turned their attention to the previously untouched "Hid-

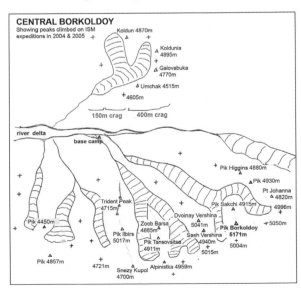

CENTRAL BORKOLDOY
Showing peaks climbed on ISM
expeditions in 2004 & 2005

Koldun 4870m

Koldunia 4895m

Galovabuka 4770m

Umchak 4515m

4605m

150m crag   400m crag

river delta

base camp

Pik Higgins 4880m

Pik 4930m

Pt Johanna 4820m

4996m

Trident Peak 4715m

Pik Sakchi 4915m

5050m

Dvoinay Vershina

Pik 4450m

Zoob Barsa 4885m

Pik Borkoldoy 5171m

5004m

Pik Ilbirs 5017m

Pik Tansovsitsa 4911m

Sash Vershina 4940m

5015m

Pik 4857m

4721m

Snezy Kupol 4700m

Alpinistka 4959m

den Glacier" north of base camp. Over the following days they climbed four fine peaks, the highest and most difficult being Pik Koldunia (4,895m), by the south ridge, at AD+.

The main objective for my team was Pik 5,171m, on which Box, Bruton, and I had been turned back the previous year at 5,000m on the north ridge (*AAJ 2005* p. 339-340). This year, in better snow conditions, we were able to try the snowy northeast flank, picking the safest line through big seracs. We reached the south ridge at 5,000m and followed it on perfect névé to the summit. Though very arduous, the route was technically straightforward at PD+. We gave the peak the name "Pik Borkoldoy," as it is the highest in the range. Clear weather on the summit gave stunning views of the Western Kokshaal-Too and unexplored peaks in the eastern sector of the Borkoldoy, some of which look very inviting.

The trip was rounded off with a brief stay at Lake Issyk-Kul, where the swimming was still pleasant in late September, and our stone-walled hotel gave good training for the keen rock climbers in the team.

PAT LITTLEJOHN, *United Kingdom*

TIEN SHAN

Pik Pobeda, first solo traverse. From August 16-23 Gleb Solokov made the first solo traverse of Pik Pobeda (7,439m) from the Chon-Toren Pass in the east to the Dikiy Pass in the west. [This traverse was first completed in 1970 by Riabukhin's expedition—Ed.] Solokov had previously attempted this traverse on several occasions. In addition, in 1993 he made a high-speed solo ascent of the mountain, via the Standard Route from the Zvezdochka (Little Star) Glacier to the summit and back again, in a record roundtrip of 20 hours, a feat that has not been attempted since. In 2003, as leader of a large team, he made a difficult (6B) new 2,000m route towards the left side of the north face, reaching the east ridge close to Pik Armenia (7,100m) before traversing the main summit.

In the summer of 2005 the weather was generally bad, with frequent heavy snowfall. It was only in mid-August, when conditions started to improve, that teams began major ascents. Sokolov first acclimatized with an ascent (his 20th) of Khan Tengri, spending three

The massive north flank of Pik Pobeda seen from Khan Tengri. (A) Chon-Toren Pass, (B) Pobeda East (ca. 7,050m), (D) Pik Armenia (7,100m), (E) Pobeda Main Summit (7,439m), (F) Pik Pavel Pshavel (Pobeda West, 6,918m), (G) Dikiy Pass (5,800m), (H) Pik Nehru (6,742m: first climbed by Ivanov's expedition in 1970). (1) East Ridge (5B/6A, Erokhin, 1958), (2) Pobeda East, north face (6A/6B, Khrischaty, 1984), (3) Pik Amenia, north face (6B, Sokolov, 2003), (4) Pobeda, northeast face (5B, Zuravliov, 1990), (5) Original Route (5B, Abalakov, 1956), (6) North face (5B, Smirnov, 1986), (7) Standard Route (north spur to west ridge, 5B, Medzmariashvilli, 1961). Gleb Sokolov made the first solo east-to-west traverse of the mountain in 2005 via routes 1 and 7. The skyline ridge is the border between Kyrgyzstan and China; C3, C4, C5 and C6 mark Sokolov's third to sixth bivouac sites on the mountain. *Anna Piunova and www.mountain.ru*

nights camped at 6,400m. At 4:30 a.m. on the 16th he left Ak-Sai camp on the moraines of the Zvezdochka Glacier for Pobeda. The weather was excellent, but at 1:30 p.m. he was forced to stop by sloppy snow when a little short of the Chon-Toren Pass. Next morning he reached the pass at 11:00 a.m. and discovered the initial steep section of the east ridge above to be an unpleasant surprise: deep, unconsolidated snow, and the steeper the slope, the deeper it became. On one 20m section he waded and shoveled through snow up to his neck. Above, he realized that he had passed the point of no return and continued upward in worsening weather. At 5:00 p.m. he erected his small tent at 6,300m.

Snowfall kept Sokolov tent-bound on the 18th, but on the 19th he used snowshoes to progress farther up the crest, following the the 1958 Erokhin Route in reasonable weather. He reached the East Summit (ca. 7,050m) at 11:00 a.m. on the 20th in cold conditions. Just short of this top he found a cache of gear left from 2000. This provided two gas cylinders, concentrated milk, a bottle of juice and some tea bags.

As he moved west, conditions improved as he took to the sunny Chinese flank of the crest, where the snow was only knee-deep. Here he met climbers coming toward him and used their tracks to continue to a prepared campsite. The weather was again excellent, and August 21 would be the main summit day.

The slope up to Pik Armenia was heavily loaded, and toward the top Sokolov was dramatically avalanched. He stopped 100m lower, against outcrops on the northern flank. His left leg was by his ear and his elbow hurt, but there was no major damage, and his equipment was intact. Twenty minutes later he reached the top of Armenia.

Even with snowshoes Sokolov sank to his knees while progressing towards the main summit, and camped for the night just before the final rise to the top. At 11:50 a.m. on the 22nd he reached the highest point of Pobeda, and now simply had to follow the normal route down (the 1961 Medzmariashvilli Route, 5B). Again deep snow made progress tiring and dangerous. The night of the 22nd-23rd was particularly miserable, as tent poles had blown away and zippers were broken. He spent much of the night trying to keep blowing snow out of his bag. On the 23rd he reached Pik Pavel Pshavel (a.k.a. Pobeda West, 6,918m) and later the tents of Georgian friends at 6,600m. In improving snow conditions he regained base camp at 6:30 p.m. that evening.

Born in 1953, Sokolov's most notable high-altitude achievements include the first ascent of Lhotse Middle and the Russian Route, Central North Face, on Everest. His Pobeda traverse was voted the best accomplishment by any former Soviet climber during 2005, but in good conditions Sokolov thinks it is possible in a day.

ADAPTED FROM ANNA PIUNOVA'S REPORT ON WWW.MOUNTAIN.RU

Khan Tengri, north face, ascent. From August 20 to 29 Pavel Shabalin and Ilyas Tukhvatullin made the first two-man ascent of the prestigious north face of Khan Tengri (6,995m) above the northern Inylchek Glacier. The pair climbed the central section of the face, starting up the Studenin Route, climbing the middle part via the Myslovsky Route, and finishing up the chimney of the Zacharov Route. They were forced to spend half a day on the face mending a stove and another full day sitting out bad weather. This is the first time a two-man team has climbed the formidable 2,000m face, previous ascents having involved large teams climbing in expedition style. There are thought to have been six previous attempts by duos to climb the face, the last in 2004 when the well-known Polish climber Grzegorz Skorek was killed while retreating from an attempt on a possible new route (*AAJ 2005*, p. 341). To date no parties outside the CIS have climbed the face. An article on the Shabalin-Tukhvatullin ascent appears earlier in this *Journal*.

TADJIKISTAN

CENTRAL PAMIR

Upper Fedchenko Glacier, possible first ascents and tragedy. Our expedition comprised eight current and former members of the University of Bristol Mountaineering Club. Four of us had climbed in Bolivia in 2003; for the others this was their first expedition to the Greater Ranges. The idea was to go somewhere different and adventurous with scope for first ascents and new routes. The Central Pamir fit these criteria, being both remote and relatively undeveloped, so we headed for the Fedchenko Glacier.

This region is situated in the Gorno-Badakhshan Autonomous Oblast (GBAO) of southeast Tajikistan and requires an entry permit. Recent Western visits have been few, the most recent we could learn of being the 1992 Imperial College London expedition. One of its members, Dr. Phil Wickens, gave us some help.

Getting to Dushanbe, the capital of Tajikistan, was straightforward. We had organized accommodation, onward transport, and porters from the U.K. through a local guiding company. We planned to travel by truck to the Vanch Valley and continue with porters as far as the Abdukagor Pass. From there we would access the head of the great Fedchenko Glacier. From the pass we would need to be self-sufficient until we met our pre-arranged return transport.

Our drive to the mountains took us over roads of varying quality along part of the Pamir Highway. On the latter part of the journey, the road followed the Amu Darya, the river that marks the border between Afghanistan and Tajikistan. The occasional sight of a vehicle lying upturned in the river highlighted the precariousness of this major route. Wrecked military hardware also littered the landscape, remnants of the recent civil war.

After two hair-raising but strangely therapeutic days of travel, the truck was just too large and cumbersome for the road ahead. We soon flagged a jeep, and the driver, unperturbed about removing the back seat and the kids sitting thereon, took our gear a little farther. However, the road was soon blocked by the last remaining snow, and after ferrying our kit across on foot, the porters found a look-alike VW combi. We couldn't all fit into the van, so we took turns walking, which wasn't much slower. The final kilometer was little more than a boulder field, which we had to clear in several places. We reached the end of the road that evening and set up camp.

We spent the following days ferrying kit to the Abdukagor Pass, via two interim camps. We averaged about 300m height gain per day, which was perfect for our acclimatization. By day nine we had reached our first base camp, at the 5,000m pass. We spent a week climbing here before moving up the glacier to a second base camp at 5,200m.

While at the first base camp we managed a number of possible first ascents: Pik Valodiya (5,847m), on July 4 via snow slopes at Alpine PD; Pik Bronwen (ca. 5,500m), on July 5 by the east face from Glacier 9, via a snow slope and ridge traverse at PD (Ed Bailey and Steve Nicholls); Tanymas (5,900m), on July 5 by the west face, 45°-50° snow slopes to a ridge followed to the summit, at D (Amy Marshall and Simon Spencer-Jones); Pik Bronwen, on July 7 by the northeast couloir at D/TD (Bailey, Robert Lavin, and Spencer-Jones); traverse of Pt. 5,390m, on July 10 by a series of couloirs and poor rock at TD (James Byrne and Lavin). In addition we climbed three routes on British Cosmonauts (5,400m?): Zero Gully, on July 6 by 45° snow and ice (Scottish II; Bailey and Nicholls); Fourth Gully, on July 8 by a long easy snow slope and two pitches of WI 2, followed by two final pitches of Scottish 4/5 (Scottish IV; Byrne and Spencer-Jones); Fifth Gully, on July 8 (Scottish III; Ian Hatcher and Sam Smith).

From the second base camp, below the north side of Pik 26 Bakinskish Kommissarov, members attempted Peak Grena (6,500m) but were thwarted at the north col by two days of stormy weather.

Finally, Hatcher and Spencer-Jones set off at 2:00 a.m. on the 13th for a traverse of Pik 26 Bakinskish Kommissarov (6,834m) and Pik Revolution (6,940m). They'd planned to take five days, but bad weather set in a day or so after their departure, and the pair was never seen again.

The loss of Ian and Spen notwithstanding, the expedition was a success. We visited a relatively unexplored mountain area and saw a part of the world of which many of us knew little. The people we met were welcoming and remarkably untouched by the influence of the West. Since the collapse of the USSR, Tajikistan has needed money; mountain tourism is seen as a way of attracting money. Hopefully the Pamir won't be ruined by the transition to a post-Soviet future. The expedition thanks the Mount Everest Foundation and the British Mountaineering Council for grant awards.

ROBERT LAVIN, United Kingdom

SOUTHWESTERN PAMIR

Pik Engels, west face to foresummit, Russian Roulette II. In August the Alpine Fund of Tajikistan organized an expedition to Piks Karl Marx (6,723m) and Engels (6,510m) in the Gorno-Bada-khshan region of Tajikistan. The expedition comprised Murod Akimov and Akai Muzafar from Tajikistan, Anna Crecenti and Mateo Gatti from Italy, Mojca Vajger and Irena Mrak from Slovenia, Johannes Chudoba from Austria, Daniel Passon from Germany, and I from the U.S. Several Soviet expeditions had climbed in this region from the 1960s to 1980s and put up super-hard routes on the north faces. However, since then there had been little or no reported activity. On Soviet topos it appeared that the col between Karl Marx and Engels could be reached from the north, giving access to both summits: Karl Marx via the 1951 Savvonov route (1,200m, 5A) and Engels via the 1963 Snegirev route (1,000m, 5A).

In early August the team gathered in Dushanbe and after an amazing drive along the Afghan border, hired donkeys for final transport. We established base camp at 3,800m on the terminal moraine of the Shaboy Glacier. We set an advance base camp three hours' hike up the glacier, then Camp 1 at 4,900m. From close up we saw that glacier conditions had deteriorated in the last few decades, and the approach to the crucial Zugvand Col was threatened by fragile, immense, and scary-looking seracs.

Members of the expedition warmed up by ascending a sub-5,000m peak above advanced base (mainly a snow walk, with slopes of 30-50°), a sub-5,000m peak up a side valley (unroped scramble up rocks), and unsuccessfully attempting Prudnlkov and the Zugvand Col.

The north face of Pik Engels (6,510m) in the southwest Pamir, Tajikistan: (1) North Ridge (6A, Budanov, 1964), (2) North Face Direct (6A, Khatskevich, 1976), (3) North Face Original (6A, Gass, 1974), (4) Russian Roulette II (stopped at 6,450m, 70-80°, Mrak-Willis, 2005), (5) West Ridge (5A, Snegirev, 1963), (6) East Ridge of Pik Karl Marx (5A, Savvonov, 1951). The Zugvand Col between Engels and Karl Marx is ca. 5,500m. *Garth Willis*

A sub-5,000m peak above an advanced base on the Shaboy Glacier used by members of an Austrian-American-German-Italian-Tajik-Slovenian expedition in 2005. The route followed by members of this expedition is marked (30-50°). *Garth Willis*

On August 15 Mrak and I climbed from Camp 1 toward the Zugvand Col, still planning to reach the col and climb Karl Marx by the Savvonov route. As we approached, though, it looked more and more scary, so before reaching the col we went left on a pure whim and continued up Pik Engels instead. The first section of the climb was a 450m glacier slope with sections of 70°. We then entered a world of crevasses and continued up the broad swath of snow and ice on the west face, at times coming to the edge of the vertical drop over the seracs to our left. That night we dug a snow hole at 5,800m. The next day we continued toward the top. However, clouds that had held back all day rolled over the summit, obscuring the long awaited views of Afghanistan's Wakhan Corridor. We terminated the route on a 6,450m foresummit of Engels, where we joined the Snegirev Route. We started to descend immediately, as our tracks in the snow—our life-link down—were disappearing in a whiteout. We ended with a late night rappel back to Camp 1. Due to the similarities of this route with our 2002 Russian Roulette in the Pamir Alai, which because of objective danger was not the safest climb, we named our new line Russian Roulette II (1,400m, IV 70-80°).

GARTH WILLIS

American Garth Willis during the first ascent of Russian Roulette II, northwest face of Pik Engels. Tajikistan. *Irena Mrak/Garth Willis Collection*

Pakistan

HINDU KUSH

Saraghrar Southeast, first ascent. In July a Neuchatel Swiss Alpine Club expedition, which comprised nine members led by Jean-Michel Zweiacker, made the first ascent of Saraghrar Southeast (7,208m) in the High Hindu Kush. On June 22 the expedition, with assistance from 120 porters from Zondangram village, established base camp at 3,930m (GPS; N 36° 29.32' E 72° 07.43') in the Rosh Gol Valley. Our initial plan was to attempt a direct route to the Southeast summit but this was rapidly abandoned, when we saw how threatened it would be from ice fall. Our decision was confirmed on July 1 when a huge ice avalanche, initiated by an earthquake, swept the approach up the Warsin Glacier. Instead the team chose a safer route to

Looking up the Warsin Glacier from a base camp below the south face of Saraghrar. Saraghrar Southeast (7,208m) is the summit in the center of the picture above the avalanche cloud, initiated by an earthquake on July 1. Saraghrar South (7,307m) is the summit to the left, and the route of ascent to Saraghrar SE is a face/ridge off-picture to the left and around the back of Saraghrar South. *Yves-Alain Peter*

the west on the south face of Saraghrar, passing close to Saraghrar South (7,307m). This summit was climbed by a Japanese expedition in 1967 [Saraghrar South had been climbed only once before 2005. Hara and Satoh reached the top via the south face from the glacier immediately west of the Warsin. It appears that the Swiss team followed a very similar route—Ed.].

On June 27 Camp 1 was set up at 5,076m (N 36° 30.66' E 72° 06.70') on a secondary ridge running west off the main south spur of Saraghrar South. The route above lay over glacier with rocky sections. On the 8th Camp 2 was established at 6,147m (N 36° 31.58' E 72° 06.96'). Above, steep ice gullies (50°) led to more gentle slopes and Camp 3 at 7,007m (July 19; N 36° 32.09' E 72° 06.95'), which was placed to the south of Saraghrar South.

On the south face of Saraghrar South (7,307m) during its second ascent and the first of Saraghrar Southeast (7,208m). The view west into the high peaks of the Hindu Kush includes (A) Istor-o-Nal Northeast (7,276m), (B) Istor-o-Nal North (7,373m), (C) Nobaism Zom (7,070m), (D) Shingeik Zom (7,294m), (E) Noshaq (7,492m), (F) Darban Zom (7,219m) and (G) Gumbaz-I-Safed (6,800m). Below the climber the dry Nohbaiznon Glacier rises to (H) the Udren col at 5,300m. *Yves-Alain Peter*

On July 24, Mazal Chevallier, Sébastien Grosjean and myself reached the summit of Saraghrar Southeast (N 36° 32.26' E72° 07.69'), opening a route through a pass at 7,224m (N 36° 32.33' E 72° 06.85') west of Saraghrar South. This pass led to the Saraghrar plateau from where another pass at 7,210m (N 36° 32.43' E 72° 07.23') north of the South peak allowed us to reach the base of the Southeast peak. The final section was composed of steep rock and ice slopes with a narrow ridge leading to the highest point. From the top there were excellent views of base camp 3,300m below. The same day Fred Morthier, climbing alone, reached the South summit for the second overall ascent, following a rocky ridge directly from the pass to the west. He then snowboarded down very steep slopes from camp 3 to the top of the rocky section above camp 1.

On July 27, Corinne Lerch, Martin Liberek and Jean-Michel Zweiacker repeated the route to the South summit. Finally, on the 29th, Marc Bélanger and Jean-Michel Zweiacker reached the Southeast peak and South peak on the same day.

During the expedition we made the first ascent of a much lower unnamed peak. With a height of 4,950m and situation south of the Saraghrar massif, it offered a perfect observation point for Saraghrar route identification. Bélanger and Morthier reached the top on June 25, and over a month later, on July 29, it was climbed again by Grosjean. Morthier made a snowboard descent via the north gullies.

Yves-Alain Peter, *Switzerland*

Himalaya

Nanga Parbat Range

Nanga Parbat, southeast (Rupal) face. From September 1 to 6 Vince Anderson and Steve House made an alpine-style ascent of Nanga Parbat's Rupal Face, via a new line up the central pillar between the south-southeast spur (a.k.a. Messner Route, 1970) and the southeast pillar (climbed to the top of the face and foresummit in 1982 by Ueli Buhler, completed to the main summit by the 1985 Polish expedition). Over 4,000m high, this face is often described as the biggest wall in the world.

Following the line of House's 2004 attempt, the pair moved steadily up the lower section, passing the route's crux, a pitch of poorly protected dry-tooling up loose 5.9 granite. On the third day they moved right from known ground and climbed the more elegant central pillar to the huge hanging glacier in the middle of the face. An icy ramp through the lower headwall led up left to their final bivouac at 7,400m, near the 2004 high point and directly above the Merkl Icefield. They joined the Messner Route at 7,900m and continued to the 8,125m summit. They rated the difficulty VII 5.9 M5 WI4. The pair used the Messner Route for their descent. Anderson's account of the climb, which was awarded this year's Piolet d'Or, appears earlier in this *Journal*.

Nanga Parbat, Rupal Face, second ascent of Messner Route and traverse of mountain. The Korean Nanga Parbat Rupal Expedition arrived in base camp on April 20, shortly after a storm had deposited a meter of snow, making access difficult. In the next 12 days members established

Camp 1 at 5,280m and Camp 2 at 6,090m, on a line close to the 1970 Messner Route.

However, at the start of May the weather began to deteriorate, with snow every day. On June 14, 43 days after the team began climbing, they sited Camp 3 at 6,850m. By this time seven tents had been destroyed, no more than three were left at Camp 1, and all at Camp 2 had disappeared under fresh snow.

Toward the end of the month the team was set for a summit bid. Four members started their attempt on the 26th, but at 7,550m, while climbing the Merkl Icefield, Kim Mi-gon was hit on the leg by a rock. The injury was bad enough to prevent further climbing, and the next four days were spent evacuating the casualty to base camp. From there Kim was able to ride out on a horse to the nearest hospital.

Kim Chang-ho and Lee Hyun-jo made a second summit bid on July 13. They left Camp 4 (7,125m) at 10:30 p.m. and climbed to the base of an objectively hazardous ice

Gu Hyeong-jun climbing to Camp 1 (5,280m) on the lower section of the Messner Route, Rupal Face of Nanga Parbat. *Lee Young-jun collection*

gully in the Merkl Icefield, using ropes previously fixed to 7,550m. They continued with a single 6mm rope, 50m long. At 9:00 a.m. on the 14th they narrowly missed being hit by a big fall of rock and ice but by 5:00 p.m. reached the summit snowfield at 7,850m. They had originally planned to bivouac but, as night approached, discussed their options and decided to continue.

At 9:00 p.m. they reached the ridge connecting the south and central peaks, and at 10:41 p.m. the first of the two reached the summit. They had been climbing for 24 hours.

Because it was dark the two were unable to take any convincing summit photographs and were a little concerned that their success might subsequently be doubted. They left their rope and sponsor's flag but also discovered a small container holding a note left by Reinhold Messner after his successful ascent (it is not completely clear whether this is from his 1970 Rupal ascent or the 1978 solo of the Diamir face). They decided to take this container as proof of their climb.

At 11:10 p.m. Kim Chang-ho and Lee Hyun-jo began descending the Diamir Face unroped, following the standard Kinshofer Route. Somewhere in the middle section of the face they set off a windslab avalanche. Lee was buried and Kim, who was on a boulder, was swept 50m downhill, scratching his face and losing his head torch. Extracting themselves, the two continued down, reaching the tents of another expedition at 7,100m. However, tempting though it was to stop, they believed that if they went to sleep, they might never get up, so decided to continue the descent. Both were hallucinating that another climber was ahead of them.

Eventually, 68 hours after starting out from Camp IV on the Rupal Face, they walked into the Diamir base camp [climbers in the Diamir base camp at the time report that they were

Climbing the sharp snow arête to Camp 2 (6,090m) on the Messner Route, Rupal Face of Nanga Parbat. *Lee Young-jun collection*

impressed by the Korean's speed of descent and that Lee Hyun-jo, who arrived first, looked remarkably fresh after his ordeal—Ed.]. They radioed their fellow team members on the other side of the mountain and eventually met up with them nine days later. All together, the expedition lasted 109 days.

Messner was able to confirm that the container was his and was later invited to Korea to have it formally returned to him. It is now safely housed in his alpine museum in the Tyrol.

LEE YOUNG-JUN, *Korea*
(translated by Peter Jensen-Choi)

KARAKORAM

Government avalanche warning. After the 2004-05 winter, following the heaviest snowfall in Pakistan for over 40 years, Pakistan's Meteorological Department issued a warning to climbers and trekkers planning to visit the Karakoram and Hindu Kush during the summer. The authorities warned parties of serious avalanche danger on the high peaks in early season. During winter and spring more than 800 military personnel and civilians in higher villages were reported killed in avalanches, though the true death toll was probably more than twice that. Greg Mortenson of the Central Asia Institute, who has made nearly 30 visits to the region since 1993, reported more snow than he had ever seen.

BATURA MUZTAGH

Batura II (7,762m), south face, attempt; probable second ascent of Ya Chish, probable fourth ascent of Batokshi. Batura II is one of the highest unclimbed points in the Karakoram, though its south face was attempted by a German team in 2002. They followed the same route as the 1976 German expedition that made the first ascent of neighbouring Batura I (7,786m), moved left on the upper slopes, and eventually abandoned their attempt in bad snow conditions at 7,100m. Simone Moro (Italy) and Joby Ogwyn (U.S.) made an attempt in July last year. Ogwyn was delayed by visa problems and Moro went ahead, setting up base camp at ca. 4,100m on the Baltar Glacier (higher than the German base camp). He climbed to a foresummit of Ya Chish (5,130m; the cornerstone between the North and Eastern Baltar Glacier) to view the route and decided to follow the 2002 German line up the right side of the glacier that flows down from the summit of Batokshi Peak on the right flank of its west ridge. Ogwyn arrived, and the pair made the probable second ascent of Ya Chish (first climbed by the 1976 German team). On July 8 the pair climbed the glacier on Baktoshi, reached its west ridge, and placed a camp at 5,900m, not far below the summit. The following day they reached the 6,050m top, for the probable fourth ascent. The first ascent was also made in 1976 by the Germans. During the descent to base they took a different line. There was a lot of downclimbing on front points and sections of high avalanche danger. Moro, who was faster, went ahead and was relaxing in base camp when he got a call from Ogwyn over the radio. Ogwyn had been hit by an avalanche and thought his ankle was broken. Moro, his cook, and the cook's assistant went to the rescue and helped Ogwyn down the moraine to base camp, from where he and Moro were evacuated the following day by helicopter.

LINDSAY GRIFFIN, *Mountain INFO, CLIMB Magazine*

Ultar (7,388m), southeast pillar, attempt. Christian Trommsdorff and I met at the beginning of October in Karimabad, Hunza. The earthquake did not appear to have done much damage, but enormous avalanches were sweeping the surrounding mountains. Our project was the unclimbed southeast pillar of Ultar, which I had tried to climb in 2000. On that occasion our expedition didn't even reach the base of the pillar. One good thing about Ultar is its short approach, which would allow easy escape to the valley and prevent us getting trapped by autumn storms. However, we first needed to return to Islamabad for a permit. Once there, though, we found everyone preoccupied with the earthquake and headed back without the necessary signatures. My memories of the 2000 expedition were a bit hazy, and our "two-day" approach took four. We established base camp at 4,200m, just in time for a big storm to deposit 60cm of fresh snow and force us back to the valley.

The crux of the ca. 3,000m-high pillar is probably a difficult rock buttress at 7,000m. After a long discussion we decided to try the climb in two stages: first we would try to reach a small col at 6,000m in order to thoroughly acclimatize; then, if conditions allowed, we would attempt a four-day ascent to the summit. On October 21 we left base camp with seven days food and fuel, hoping to reach the base of the pillar and climb the long couloir on the left flank while conditions were still cold. To reach the pillar we had to cross a serac-threatened glacier plateau, only one hour but a race against fear. Then up the long 45-50° couloir, hemmed on both sides by granite walls. By the time we reached 5,300m, where the gully became increasingly narrow, the warmth of the day, which exhausted us, was also releasing a bombardment of ice chunks. After two hours I felt threatened by a gigantic stalactite hanging 150m above, so we decided to climb rocky ground to the left. On belay after two pitches, ca. 15m to the side of the couloir, I suddenly heard a rumble. At first I thought it came from the seracs just left of the 6,000m col but in fact it was a slope above us (that we had allowed to settle for several days before starting the route). The avalanche channeled into the terrible funnel that, on a hunch, we had escaped from just one hour previously. It was obviously time to bivouac and continue tomorrow, when it would be colder.

Next morning we headed towards the crux of the couloir, a vertical water-ice pitch. It proved rotten, so we had to force our way up a rocky pillar on the left, pitching our bivouac tent only 100m higher than the day before. Next day we hoped to continue to the col and back before nightfall.

The weather was perfect, but we were unable to find the diagonal line we'd seen with binoculars from below and instead decided to climb to the top of the avalanche slope, which was now safe in the colder temperatures, and then traverse the arête to the col: a much longer alternative. Nightfall caught us climbing corniced terrain, and in this realm of vertical snow we felt it best to backtrack to a place where we could at least sit down. We hadn't reached our goal and were already less ambitious.

Next day, October 24—my birthday—a radio message from base camp announced the return of bad weather. We began a series of rappels that eventually got us back to base before nightfall. But each one was torture: should we come back up or not? We had to decide whether to leave our gear at the second bivouac. In the end we didn't and continued down. The expedition was finished. The first time I failed to set foot on the pillar. The second time I got half way. This story is unfolding in a mathematical manner: perhaps there will be a third time?

YANNICK GRAZIANI, *France*

Editor's Note: In May 2000 Jerome Blanc Gras, Graziani, Erwin le Lann, and Hervé Qualizza climbed several good rock routes on the small peaks around base camp, but unsettled weather prevented them setting foot on the pillar. The only other known attempt was made by Toshio Narita and two Japanese friends in August 1992. Bad weather forced them down from a height of 5,400m.

GHUJERAB MUZTAGH

"Boe Sar" (ca. 5,700m) and "Shah Izat Peak" (ca. 5,700m), first ascents. These two easy summits are located in the Ghujerab Muztagh, the range between the Shimshal and Ghujerab rivers [referred to as the Karun Koh group on the Miyamori Japanese maps—Ed.]. They lie close to the Boesam pass on the main route from Shimshal to the Ghujerab Valley and on toward the Khunjerab Pass, where the Karakoram Highway crosses the Chinese border.

With my friend Abdullah Bai, a Shimshal resident, teacher, and trekking guide, I reached the Boesam after a walk of two days from Shimshal village. We had help from a young porter, Abdul Mohamed, and also from the village. We established a comfortable camp near the lake situated just behind the ca. 4,800m pass.

Our initial goal was the first sum-

Shar Izat Peak (ca. 5,700m) rises above the lake just north of the Boesam Pass. On the first known ascent of this peak Abdullah Bai and Francois Carrel followed the skyline (southeast) ridge in its entirety at PD. *Francois Carrel*

mit northeast of the pass. We climbed it in five hours on August 23. It was an easy, pleasant ascent on snow, with just three crevasses to cross (Alpine F, 900m of vertical gain on slopes of 35° maximum). Abdul Mohamed roped up with us and managed the climb without crampons. We descended our route and named the peak "Boe Sar" (in local dialect *sar* is *summit*, while *sam* is *pass*).

On the 24th Abdullah and I climbed the first summit northwest of the pass. We found an easy route horizontally across the glacier to the west of the pass, then walked up the little glacier falling from the summit. After crossing the bergschrund and climbing a 45° snow

Abdullah Bai at around 5,600m during the first ascent of the southeast ridge of Shar Izat Peak (ca. 5,700m) in the unfrequented Ghujerab Muztagh. In the background are some of the big faces that comprise the north side of the Hispar Muztagh. From left to right: Disteghil Sar (7,885m), Malunguti Sar (7,026m), Trivor (7,720m), the Lupghar Massif (ca. 7,200m), and on the extreme right Rakaposhi (7,788m). *Francois Carrel*

slope for 200m, we reached the upper section of the summit ridge, followed it north, then northwest, and gained the highest point after five-and-a-half hours of climbing. The final section of ridge was easy but offered a gorgeous view of most of the Karakoram, from Rakaposhi in the east to K2 far away in the west. The altitude was ca. 5,700m, similar to Boe Sar, and the route PD. Abdullah said it was "the most beautiful day of my life." We called this easy peak "Shah Izat Peak," after Ghulam Ali Shah and Izat Mohamad, two Shimshal porters who in 2001 crossed the Boesam with us, before being killed in an avalanche a few days later near the Chapchingol Pass. No one in Shimshal had heard of these peaks being climbed before, though according to some porters Sar had been attempted.

We believe these two summits could become classic trekking peaks. The campsite near the lake is perfect and the views from the peaks fascinating. Shimshal village can now be reached by jeep, only three hours and some rupees with the daily collective taxi from Passu on the Karakaram Highway. It is not necessary to buy a permit, and the three-stage walk from Shimshal to the Boesam is easy and beautiful (this pass is an easy deviation from the classic trek to the Shimshal Pass).

FRANÇOIS CARREL (FCARREL@CLUB.FR), *France*.

HISPAR MUZTAGH

Shimshal White Horn (ca. 6,400m), attempt. Shimshal White Horn (a.k.a. Ishpardin) is an elegant snow pyramid located to the northeast of Distaghil Sar. In July-August a French team comprising Jacques Autino, Brimbelle Grandcolas, Luc Jarry-Lacombe, Ludovic Lagoutte, and David Marchaland attempted it. The climbers approached via Shimshal village (this formerly remote settlement has had road access since 2003) and established a base camp on the left bank of the Yazghil Glacier, to the northeast of the mountain. They set up Camp 1 at 5,200m, but a reconnaissance above revealed that access to the northeast ridge would be very complex and was covered with fresh powder. Discouraged, the climbers abandoned their plans and returned to Shimshal.

There they talked with one of Pakistan's most famous high-altitude guides and 8,000m climbers, Rajab Shar. Although Shar had failed twice before on the mountain, he persuaded them to continue with the expedition. Two of the team therefore walked up the Goz Valley directly south of Shimshal, from where they could get a view of the northern side of the White Horn. From 4,400m they could see the north face dangerously endowed with seracs, but also saw a possible line well to the right, leading to the northwest ridge.

On August 1 they set off again, with only seven porters and seven days of mountain food. That afternoon they established base camp on the left bank of the Goz Glacier at 4,400m. On the 3rd all the team except Lagoutte, who had a cold, went up toward the foot of the north face and camped at 4,750m. Because of the heat, they elected to climb at night, and set the alarm for 8:30 p.m. A little before midnight the four French crossed the bergschrund at 5,000m on the right side of the face, then climbed an 800m couloir (Alpine D; 50°) to the crest of the northwest ridge, which they reached at sunrise. Conditions rapidly deteriorated, and they biv- ouacked for the day, suffering in the heat before departing again at around 9:00 p.m. At 6,000m they gave up after sinking more than a meter in 50-60° snow. The west flank of the ridge looked better, so on the 5th they descended blind towards the Malangutti Glacier. Thirteen hours of descent, with bad snow and complex route-finding through the seriously crevassed glacier, brought them to a comfortable bivouac site on the moraine. Next day they reached Shimshal.

While Rajab Shar and the French team were under the impression that Shimshal White Horn was a virgin peak, in fact it was climbed in 1999. In early July of that year a small inter- national team entered the Yazghil Glacier and established a base camp at the point known as Parigoz, farther up the glacier than the first French base camp. On an early reconnaissance the group reached the top of a 6,300m shoulder immediately to the east of the White Horn. On their summit attempt they climbed back toward the shoulder, traversing its north face at ca. 6,000m to reach a snow basin below the east face of the White Horn. From there they climbed this flank to the upper northeast ridge, but due to poor snow on the crest made a rising left- ward ascent on the east face. One member of the team reached the summit on July 19. The overall grade was Alpine AD with snow/ice to 50°.

LINDSAY GRIFFIN, *Mountain INFO, CLIMB Magazine*

PANMAH MUZTAGH

Baintha Brakk (a.k.a. the Ogre, 7,285m), attempts to repeat the original British Route and the South Pillar. Basque climbers Juan Mari Iraola, Chus Lizzaraga, Eduard Martinez, and Juan Vallejo attempted the second ascent of the South Pillar, only completed once to the summit, by Huber, Stöcker and Wolf in 2001. They fixed rope to 6,000m on the pillar, free climbing to VII, but were prevented from going higher by bad weather. A second Basque team, Jon Beloki, Alberto Iñurrategi and Jose Carlos Tamayo, operating at much the same time, also failed on both the original British Route (southwest face and west ridge, 1977) and the South Pillar.

LINDSAY GRIFFIN, *Mountain INFO, CLIMB Magazine*

Latok I, north ridge, attempt; various new routes on surrounding peaks; repeat of Indian Face Arête. Last summer my brother Willie and I returned to the Choktoi Glacier with fellow Argentinean,

Matias Erroz. Our goal was another attempt on the huge north ridge of Latok I. Although one of our bags, the one containing much of our technical climbing equipment, was lost during the flight to Islamabad, we continued to our base camp on the Choktoi to acclimatize. On June 26, while still waiting for our gear, we attempted a ca. 6,000m peak on the northern rim of the Choktoi Glacier, a little to the right of Biacherahi Towers. The striking line on the south face, which overlooks the glacier, is a 1,000m névé couloir a little to the right of the summit fall line. It is about 30m wide with an average angle of 55°. We named it the Supercouloir. We left base camp around 2:00 a.m. and climbing unroped were on the summit ridge by 6:00 a.m. Here things got trickier, and the rope came out. Willie spent a long time above me before returning to the belay. He'd been thwarted 60m short of the summit by a slabby headwall. Having no rock shoes and a minimal rack, he decided to back off. We descended and were back in camp at 11:30 a.m.

The following day Willie and Matias did a 10-pitch rock route on a tower just behind base camp: Medocinos Route (5.10). On the 30th the three of us tried a two-day ascent of Indian Face Arête, a prominent rock spur on a minor ca. 5,200m peak below the north spur of Latok III. [The ca. 800m route was first climbed in 1990 by Sandy Allan and Doug Scott at British 5c and A2, but they stopped at least six pitches below the summit and made a rappel descent. In 1999 four Italians climbed to about the same high point. Later that year British climbers Sam Chinnery, Ali Coull, and Muir Morton reached the summit via the upper half of the arête, which they gained after climbing a 400m dihedral (A3) on the quasi-vertical west flank—Ed.] We took a sleeping bag, a stove, and food but at the base of the route left most of it and went for a continuous-push ascent. This decision was influenced by the fact the weather had been perfect for 10 days. When we were half way up it snowed, but we kept going and by dark were 120m below the summit. We spent a miserable night in a sort of cave, continued to the top next morning in 30cm of new snow, and rappelled steeply into the west couloir, down which we bum-slid to the base of the route. This seems to be the only time the original line has been followed throughout to the summit. We climbed 16 pitches, up to 5.10a and A1.

On July 10, after a long spell of bad weather, Willie and Mathias climbed Biacherahi North (5,850m) via the northeast ridge, which although technically easy was a nightmare on a dangerously corniced crest leading to the summit. We then went onto the north ridge of Latok I (7,145m) with a portaledge and haul bag, hoping to make a continuous ascent, but it was not to be. There was too much deep snow and too many dangerous mushrooms. We abandoned the climb on July 20 at 5,400m, noting that the north face, to the left, looked well formed, with good ice runnels and little in the way of avalanche danger. We climbed one more new rock route close to base camp at 5.10+ before returning to Skardu.

DAMIAN BENEGAS, *Argentina*

BALTORO MUZTAGH

TRANGO GROUP

Trango II (6,327m), southwest ridge (Severance Ridge), not to summit. Trango II is the major snow-capped peak immediately north of Trango Tower and Trango Monk. Between August 15 and 19 Jonathon Clearwater (New Zealand), Samuel Johnson (U.S.), and I (Canada) made the

Trango II (6,327m) showing the line on the southwest (Severance) ridge climbed by Clearwater, Frimer, and Johnson. To the right are Trango Monk (ca. 5,900m) and Trango Tower (6,251m). *Sam Johnson*

Superb crack climbing on "the Shield," Severance Ridge, Trango II. Higher, the crack all but disappeared and thin aid plus a pendulum were needed to exit this golden granite headwall. *Jeremy Frimer*

first ascent of a 1,600m-high ridge on its southwest side, naming it Severance Ridge. Despite taking only enough food for three days, we spent five on the climb, being battered by stormy weather much of the time. The route offers quality climbing on orange granite with splitter cracks, all in a fine place. It was the hardest, most spectacular climb in any of our alpine careers.

The route began on a steep, smooth rock face just half an hour's walk north of Trango base camp. On the first day we worked our way up this 900m face, encountering over a dozen sustained 5.9 to 5.11 pitches. The crux two pitches involved run-out stemming in a tight corner, then underclinging beneath a steep arch before surmounting a roof. We finished the day by traversing a long knife-edge atop the smooth rock face.

On the second morning we soloed an ice/mixed gully and, as a storm moved in, climbed simultaneously up moderate rock on a steeply ascending ridge. By noon we had reached the base of a steep headwall, where we found a sheltered bivouac. The headwall, dubbed "the Shield," is a particularly blank feature, save for a perfect hand crack up its center. However, the crack narrows, then disappears, at half-height, requiring thin aid and an aggressive pendulum. With only blankness above, we aided left, exiting the face of the Shield to arrive at an exposed hanging belay, just as a raging storm began. After nearly opting for retreat, we painstakingly aided a 40m pitch, best described as a "flaring off-width garden," using an ice tool for excavation. At its top the crack became a parallel, clean offwidth, requiring a single tipped-out cam as a nerve-wracking mov-

Atmospheric weather on the narrow "Roadway" of Severance Ridge, Trango II. The northeast face of Uli Biaho Tower (6,109m) is visible through the clouds on the far side of the Trango Glacier. *Jeremy Frimer*

ing point of aid. Climbing into the night, we finished the Shield with a pitch of burly and sustained fist cracks.

We'd anticipated that the final ridge would go smoothly but instead found the terrain to be complex and challenging. After a storm on the third night, we began climbing along the narrow ridge above. Yet another storm moved in. We soon came to a series of gendarmes that forced us onto the left side of the crest. Every pitch involved traversing flaring, thin crack systems at sustained 5.10. Overtaken yet again by nightfall, Sam attempted to lead a difficult pitch with poor protection, almost taking a huge pendulum before wisely retreating. We rappelled 60m into an adjacent gully and bivouacked. Having not eaten all day, we had trouble staying warm that night.

On our fifth and final morning we climbed several ice and mixed pitches up the gully to reach the end of the knife-edge, where it met the summit snow slopes. Exhausted but elated, we traversed these slopes and started our descent immediately, without visiting the summit. [The team traversed 150m below the summit to reach the south ridge—Ed.] We downclimbed the ridge, then made six rappels below Trango Monk to reach the Trango Tower approach gully, descending this to the valley floor. We rate Severance Ridge VI 5.11 A2 AI 3 M5; it had 63 pitches.

This trip was funded in part by grants from the American Alpine Club (Lyman Spitzer Award), The Mount Everest Foundation, and the New Zealand Alpine Club.

JEREMY FRIMER, *Vancouver, Canada*

Editor's Note: Trango II appears to be the same peak as that climbed in 1995 by Antonio Aquerreta, Fermin Izco and Mikel Zabalza after their ascent of a new route on Trango Tower. Confusion arises as they reputedly referred to it as Trango Ri (a.k.a Trango I), which according to the new Polish map is the next peak to the northwest.

Jeon Yang-jun jumaring during the first ascent of The Crux Zone (A4), Below him is the snow-covered Shoulder, while above his head can be seen the approach gully from the Trango Glacier. *Lee Young-jun collection*

Kim Hyung-il leading one of the lower pitches of The Crux Zone above the Shoulder. *Lee Young-jun collection*

Trango Tower, southeast face, The Crux Zone. A Korean expedition comprising leader Kim Hyung-Il and members Jang Ki-heon, Jeon Yang-jun, Kim Pal-bong, Wang Dae-shik, and I established base camp on July 12 at 4,150m alongside the Trango Glacier. Nine days later we had sited our high camp on the Shoulder at 5,600m.

Jang Ki-heon (left) and Jeon Yang-jun on the summit of Trango Tower, having completed the first ascent of The Crux Zone (A4). *Lee Young-jun collection*

Our goal was a new route above the Shoulder, up the face between the Slovenian route and Run for Cover. By August 7 we had completed 11 new pitches to a junction with the Slovenian route. After climbing several more pitches up the latter, we reached the summit—one group on August 11, another on the 13th. The hardest pitch was the seventh, which we graded A4. We named our route The Crux Zone after our main sponsor, the climbing gym in Anyang City near Seoul.

WON DAE-SHIK, *Korea*

Trango Tower (6,251m), south pillar, Eternal Flame—Pou Brothers Variant. After arriving in base camp on July 11, mountain journalist Jabi Baraiazarra, my brother Iker, and I spent the next few weeks climbing Eternal Flame. In generally bad weather we spent the first week ferrying loads up to Camp 1 and the next few days fixing lines up to Camp 2 on the Shoulder, at 5,400m. The heavyweight approach was dictated by our desire to free-climb the entire route. After several days rest at base camp we returned to Camp 2 on the 26th, and the following day, after waking up to snow and low temperatures, then checking weather reports via the radio, we fixed ropes up the pillar above. On the way down to camp we checked out the 10th pitch, initially seeing little hope of climbing it free. [This pitch has a 15m bolt ladder in compact granite—Ed.] On the 28th we ascended our ropes and continued to a bivouac at 6,000m on a 50° snow patch. The same day we fixed three more pitches above the site.

Next day, in a weakened state, all three of us reached the true summit of Trango Tower, quite late, and rappelled to our bivouac in the dark. Later that night a severe storm struck, and at 4:30 a.m. high avalanche danger forced us to leave much of our equipment and rappel the ice-covered wall.

After several days rest at base camp, we returned to retrieve our equipment and try to establish a free variation to the 10th pitch. In four more days Iker managed to climb what we have dubbed the Pou Brothers Variant. This 50m pitch at 5,950m required a single bolt to link two crack systems. The hard climbing is in the first part, which Iker redpointed. However, the finishing crack, which is probably no more than 6c, was running with water, and in the prevailing cold he could only climb it with rest points. We estimated the pitch to be 8a, but it could be 7c+, 8a+, or even harder. We hope this effort brings climbers a step closer to the prized first free ascent of Eternal Flame. [The Pous were unable to redpoint pitches 15 and 16, free-climbed at 7c/7c+ and 7c, respectively, by Denis Burdet in 2003. They didn't have enough time to work on these pitches but are full of praise for Burdet's effort, as the pitches looked extremely hard. They did free-climb all other pitches, and their effort on the 10th pitch makes it clear that a strong climber, in good conditions, can climb Eternal Flame free—Ed.] There were several other teams on Trango, and we enjoyed the camaraderie both at base camp and on the wall.

We are also happy that this route takes us another step toward completing our project Seven Walls, Seven Continents. [Their aim is to free climb a big wall on each continent. Starting in 2003 they climbed El Niño on El Capitan, Zunbeltz on the Naranjo de Bulnes (Spain), Bravo les Filles on Tsaranoro Kely (Madagascar), and the Totem Pole (Tasmania)—Ed.]

ENEKO POU, *Spain, translated by Adam French*

View from low in the Trango approach gully: Trango Tower (T; often erroneously called Nameless Tower), Little Trango (LT), and the Southwest Summit of Great Trango (GT). The line shows Čmárik and Kopold's harrowing descent of the northwest face, with (a) marking the gully that avalanched and swept Kopold 150m. The NW face is home to the 1999 American, Russian, and German routes, while the 2003 Ukrainian attempt climbs the prominent detached pillar just left of the NW face, continuing high up the left skyline of GT's summit tower. The Azeem Ridge (2004) roughly follows the right-hand skyline, and the Čmárik- Kopold route (Assalam Alaikum) ascends farther right, out-of-view. *Vlado Linek*

Great Trango, southwest face to south face (Assalam Alaikum), not to summit; Hainabrakk East Tower, south southeast face (Mystical Denmo); Shipton Spire, east face to northeast ridge, to with-in 80m of summit (Prisoners of the Shipton); and Ship of Fools, attempt. A joint Czech-Slovak expedition visited the Baltoro from July 26 to August 31. The team comprised eight climbers from Slovakia: Gabo Čmárik, Andrej Kolárik, Igor Koller, Jozef Kopold, Pavol Pekarčík, Juraj Poděbraský, Erik Rabatin, and I. There were four climbers from the Czech Republic: Milan Benian, Martin Klonfar, Petr Piechowicz, and Miroslav Turek. Čmárik, Kopold, Koller, and I had climbed in this region during 2004 and had unfinished projects. In particular Čmárik and Kopold wanted to climb a new line in alpine-style on the south side of Great Trango (6,286m), right of the 2004 American route, Azeem Ridge.

The two started on August 4 in good weather, taking only two small rucksacks and food for four days, no sleeping bags, no mats, no ropes for fixing, and no radios. They planned to move together up the first 1,000m but found the terrain more difficult than expected and were forced to belay. Their progress was slow and not helped by rain and snow throughout the second day. On the fourth day they reached the headwall. That night was very cold, with the temperature down to -15°C, a strong wind, and heavy snowfall. The pair endured a difficult bivouac without sleeping bags. After that, icy or snow-covered rock slowed them down even more. On fifth day they ate their last food and didn't reach the summit ridge until day seven [this was the summit ridge of the ca. 6,250m Southwest summit and not the main summit—

Hainabrakk East Tower (ca. 5,650m) from the east. The face is a little over 1,000m in height. To the right is the Cat's Ears Spire (ca. 5,550m). (1) Mystical Denmo on the south-southeast face (34 pitches, VII+ A2; Kolárik-Rabalin, 2005) (2) Tague it to the Top (VI 5.11 C2, Copp-Pennings, 2000). (3) For Better or for Worse (VII 5.12a WI3; Baer-Brock-McCray-Schneider, 2000). *Vlado Linek*

Ed.]. The overall length of their climb was more than 3,000m and involved many pendulums, wet slabs with poor protection, and loose chimneys.

Čmárik and Kopold intended to traverse the Southwest summit and descend via the normal route [it is not necessary to cross to the main summit in order to gain the normal route—see *AAJ 2005* pp. 14-23 on the ascent of the Azeem Ridge—Ed.) but, due to large

An unusual view of Shipton Spire (5,885m), showing the northeast face. Marked is the new Slovak line, Prisoners of the Shipton, which has 21 pitches (VIII A3) up the right side of the southeast face, until it joins Ship of Fools (Ogden-Synnott, 1997) at the notch (A) on the northeast ridge. Above, the Slovaks climbed 14 pitches up the ridge (VIII- WI 5+), following the original line of Ship of Fools over two pinnacles (B) and past a second col (C) to the final ridge, where they retreated 80m below the summit. A photodiagram of all the routes on the southeast face appears in AAJ 2005, p. 347. *Vlado Linek collection*

amounts of snow on the ridge, decided instead to rappel the huge northwest face. They descended through the afternoon and all the next night. At one point Kopold was avalanched 150m. At another point Čmárik fell 30m down icy slabs. At 5:00 a.m. on the 11th, after 16 hours rappelling, they reached Trango Base Camp.

Their route, named Assalam Alaikum, had ca. 90 pitches, with difficulties up to VIII and A2. They left three pitons and two bolts (for pendulums). On the descent they had only their rack, five pitons, and eight remaining bolts for making ca. 60 rappels. They rappelled the face from right to left, crossing the Russian and American routes (and using their rappel anchors), to reach the gully on the left of the face.

Andrej Kolárik and Erik Rabatin climbed on Hainabrakk East (ca. 5,650m), with the goal of completing a logical direct line up the central pillar in the middle of the face. They started on August 6 but due to bad weather had to return to base camp on three occasions. They fixed and climbed the first half of the route big-wall style. They completed the second half in alpine-style, reaching the summit on the 23rd. Mystical Denmo gives 1,400m of climbing, with 34 pitches up to VII+ and A2, mainly following cracks. [This new route starts up the 2000 Copp-Pennings line, Tague it to the Top, then moves left to climb directly to the central pillar on the south-southeast face. In the upper half it climbs very close to the Copp-Pennings line, cutting through its leftward horizontal traverse—Ed.]

Koller, Poděbradský, cameraman Pekarčík, and I worked on Shipton Spire (5,885m). In 2004 Koller and I, with the help of Čmárik until he became ill, climbed 17 pitches of a new line up the right edge of the southeast face. Bad weather stopped us just 100 meters below the notch on the northeast ridge where Ship of Fools comes in from the left (*AAJ 2005*, p. 347, photo). Last year we returned to complete it.

We four started up the route on August 1. Through generally unsettled weather we climbed and fixed 10 pitches to a roof shaped like the letter W and dubbed Cassiopeia. In

2004 we had cached rope there. On the 7th we returned to base camp, worried that we might have to organize a rescue for Čmárik and Kopold, who were long overdue on Great Trango. After the latter two returned safely, Koller, Poděbradský, and I began a second attempt. On the 13th we jumared to a ledge at two-thirds height on the face, where we bivouacked. Over the next two days we completed the wall, reaching the notch where we joined Ship of Fools. Although we had climbed the new ground, we wanted to reach the summit. However, on the 16th the weather deteriorated, and as we had no bivouac equipment, we retreated.

We regained the notch on the 19th, this time with a tent, but during the night there was heavy snow, which prevented us from climbing till the afternoon of the 20th, and then only the first two rocky pitches up the ridge. On the 21st we managed three difficult pitches of ice covered with fresh snow and the following day went for the summit. However, Koller took a fall, and the team retreated to our camp at the notch. The 23rd

Igor Koller leading the 10th pitch above the first notch on the northeast ridge of Shipton Spire. This was the first pitch (M5 WI5+ 90°) of the icy headwall that gives access to the summit ridge. Koller led four more pitches to what should have been easy ground below the summit but dangerous snow above and the onset of more bad weather forced the Slovak team down. *Vlado Linek*

was a rest day, and on the 24th we decided that only Koller and I would go for the summit. By 5:00 a.m. we two were at the end of the fixed ropes, in clear, cold weather. With Koller in the lead, we climbed for 10 hours up the sharp ridge, overcoming two towers and a four-pitch ice headwall plastered with snow. At 4:00 p.m. we were hit by a vigorous 30-minute snow storm. At 5:30 p.m., only 80m from the summit, we decided to retreat. We had reached the point where the American topo indicates easy terrain to the top, but we were faced with much snow, dangerous cornices, and hard climbing. As the next storm blew in, we started rappeling and regained our tent in the notch at 2:00 a.m. We named the new route as far as the notch Prisoners of the Shipton (900m), which gave 21 pitches up to VIII and A3. Above, the 14 pitches coinciding with Ship of Fools to the summit ridge gave difficulties of VIII- and WI5+.

After fixing the first two pitches of Ship of Fools, Martin Klonfar and Miroslav Turek made a four-day alpine-style ascent as far as the notch. They waited there for two days in bad weather and on August 9 retreated. From the 14th to the 16th they climbed the first 15 pitches of Prisoners of the Shipton but again were forced by bad weather to descend.

VLADO LINEK, *Slovak Mountaineering Union, Slovakia*
A full article on the Čmárik-Kopold ascent of Assalam Alaikum
will be found earlier in the Journal.

Trango Pulpit, northeast face, Azazel. The spirit of Xaver Bongard is still alive. Grand Voyage remains the ultimate, unrepeated route on Great Trango (6,286m). The steepest flank of the Trango group is the side overlooking the Dunge glacier and our goal was to be a repeat of Grand Voyage. Martial (Cochonette) Dumas, Jean-Yves (Blutch) Fredriksen, and Yann (Mimouse) Mimet, all French, made me an offer I couldn't refuse: to fly from the top of Great Trango while they lowered the sacks and stripped the route.

When we arrived at base camp on the Dunge glacier, the reality we were face-to-face with was different from our dream. Heavy snowfalls in late spring had resulted in bad conditions, even at only 6,000m. Ali Baba, the couloir you climb to reach the base of Grand Voyage was continuously swept by avalanches, even at night. The risk seemed far too great. We changed our objective to Trango Pulpit (6,050m), a prominent shoulder on the long southeast ridge of Great Trango. There was

The northeast face of Trango Pulpit (6,050m). The left skyline (southeast) ridge is more or less the line taken by More Czech, Less Slovak (ca. 1,400m, VII- A2, Dutka-Rinn-Weisser, 1999). (1) Azazel (ca. 1,500m, VII A3+ M6 WI 4 6a, Beaugey-Dumas-Fredriksen-Mimet, 2005). (2) Norwegian Direct (1,500m, VII A4 5.11, Casperson-Karlsen-Skjerven-Wold, 1999). *Sam Beaugey*

an obvious unclimbed 1,500m line left of the Norwegian route. The first section would ascend a yellow wall that we could approach from the left, the second ascend the prow above.

Our "lightweight" expedition suddenly had more than 400kg to take on the wall: food for 15 days; two portaledges, nine "pigs," and a water drum. We also had 500m of rope and 27 bolts. Except for bolts, we left nothing on the mountain.

It took four days to bring all the loads to Camp 1, via a snow couloir and a mixed-terrain ridge. After a few days' rest we began our slow ascent in capsule style. The lower wall turned out to be much harder than expected, with first-class aid climbing on mostly beaks, hooks, and expanding flakes. The sky was a perfect blue for seven days, but the heat of the sun kept

At the bottom of the picture, Sam Beaugey, wearing a black wing suit, just clears the headwall of Trango Pulpit en-route to a safe landing on the Dunge Glacier over 1,000m below. *Sam Beaugey collection*

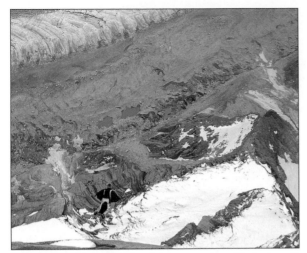

Camp 2 suspended below the massif roof ("the Bunker") on the lower wall of the northeast face of Trango Pulpit during the first ascent of Azazel. *Sam Beaugey*

us from relaxing. Melting snow mushrooms near the top would fall and smash into the upper wall. We suspended Camp 2 below a massive roof—"the Bunker." Above, we were forced to climb at night to avoid the "blitz" and safely reach the left edge of the big inclined hanging-glacier/snow-ice shelf at two-thirds height above the glacier. We established Camp 3 on the shelf at 2:00 a.m. after two nights' work.

Starting the upper wall involved two pitches in the fall-line of "Moby Dick," the name we gave to a huge cornice overhanging our route. On my first attempt, in daylight, there was a loud explosion: Moby Dick's fins had broken off. Down they came, with pieces smashing into the camp and me. I got off lightly with a big fright, but it became obvious we had to move our camp lower down the shelf, where we could dig into the snow. We would also have to continue up the next few pitches at night.

The weather turned bad, and we had to sit out four days in the portaledges. Eventually, in far from perfect conditions, we pushed on. Jumaring icy ropes and hauling the bags through stormy weather was a real pain, but after a mixed pitch and some loose rock, we were able to hang Camp 4. With Moby Dick now some meters to our left, Martial spent five hours climbing the dihedral above camp, mostly through a sweet snow storm. I fixed another pitch to a black roof full of stalactites. Next day was our 16th on the face, and the weather was not bad, just misty. Mimouse radioed from the pitch above, "Sam, I think I've found a possible jump site."

The weather improved, and there were only three pitches left to the top of the wall. However, for the BASE jump it was probably now or never. I checked the fall line and decided to use my winged suit. I'd spent the last 10 days thinking about whether I would clear the big snow shelf at 5,300m while still flying or have to open the canopy beforehand. I knew my flying profile would be seriously reduced at this altitude, and I'd resemble a tiny bird. I cleaned a small ledge for my feet, unclipped from the last Camalot, and, "three, two, one," jumped into the misty air.

I passed close to the first big ledge 40m below and then worked slightly right in an attempt to target the steepest icy gully descending from the snow shelf, just in case. Finally my wings began to work, and I could move left toward Ali Baba. Seracs passed close by for 45 seconds, till I opened the canopy and landed on Ali Baba's avalanche cone. I was there, with thanks to the team above.

The following day, July 8, feeling a bit sad and without food, my three friends set off for the summit. It was still misty, and at the top of the wall, in a whiteout, they decided to forego the narrow corniced ridge leading to the summit. The descent took two full days, with a night at Camp 2 below "the Bunker." The three had spent 19 days on the wall by the time they returned to base camp.

Our new route, Azazel (1,500m, 300m approach, snow/ice/mixed and moves of 5/5+ to gain Camp 1, then 26 pitches at VII A3+ M6 WI4 6a), lies between the southeast ridge (More Czech, less Slovak; Dutka-Rinn-Weisser, 1999) and the northeast face (Norwegian Direct; Casperson-Karlsen-Skjerven-Wold, 1999).

SAM BEAUGEY, *France*

The Muztagh Tower (7,284m), Baltoro Muztagh, showing perhaps its most spectacular aspect, the southeast. The route climbed by the French in 1956 (second ascent of the mountain) is marked. The French gained the crest of the southeast ridge via slopes that are largely hidden in this picture but lie behind the Black Tooth (6,719m), the top of which is situated more or less at the point where the upper solid black line turns to dots. Contamine, Keller, Magnone, and Paragot reached the summit less than a week after Brown, Hartog, McNaught-Davis, and Patey had successfully climbed the northwest ridge. While the British route has now been repeated twice, the French awaits a second ascent. *Bruce Normand*

BALTORO MUZTAGH - OTHER

Muztagh Tower, southeast ridge (French Route), attempt; possible first ascents of surrounding peaks. Our expedition began when I developed an obsession with the unclimbed and rarely seen northeast side of 7,284m Muztagh Tower. The team comprised I (a Scot working in Switzerland) as leader, deputy leader Steve Brown (American), climbers Nicolas Bernard (France) and Philippe Oberson (Switzerland), and high-mountain trekkers Patrycja Paruch (Poland, medic), Markus Schneider (German), and Markus Stratmann (German). The team was rounded out by Akhbar, our cook, assistant cook Javed, and liaison officer Lt. Haseeb Ullah.

A streamlined Islamabad-Skardu-Baltoro approach put the squad in base camp on June 9, our sixth day out from Askole and 12th in Pakistan. The camp was located at the confluence of the Younghusband and Biange glaciers, at the foot of the southeast ridge of Muztagh Tower. The heavy Karakoram winter and cold spring was turning into an unstable summer, and while the team's weather forecasts contained detailed information relayed by satellite telephone from a free U.S. web page, they turned out to be hopelessly inaccurate for all but the most general trends.

Oberson and I found a route up the Younghusband icefall and reconnoitred the flat upper basin to within 2km of Moni Pass. There we found a location for an advanced base camp below the northeast face. Bernard and Brown performed a vertical reconnaissance of the first rock peak on the long southeast ridge, electing not to complete the last 15m of their route up a pinnacle, which fell off less than a week later. We established advanced base just before the arrival of a week of good weather, which saw Brown, Oberson, Paruch, Schneider, and Stratmann climb a foresummit of Pt. 5,850m, directly above camp, and then Schneider, Stratmann, and I climb Pt. 6,001m (Tsetse on the Swiss map) by its south ridge. This ascent, completed on July 18, involved snow climbing at 45°, followed by a descent to the west. From the top we obtained a perspective view of Muztagh Tower's north face. Monstrous cornices on the southeast ridge and seracs threatening the true north face and north ridge (which rises from the Moni Pass) left two available options: a snow/ice line with two rock steps way over to the left, which ascended to the col on the southeast ridge between the Black Tooth (6,719m) and Muztagh Tower; or the poorly defined northeast spur falling directly from the summit with a steep rock barrier between 6,600m and 6,900m. For either route to be feasible, the face would need time to dry.

Schneider, Stratmann, and I continued acclimatizing by tackling a peak on the ridge separating the Biange and Godwin-Austen glaciers, climbing a long slope of hardened avalanche debris to steeper exit gullies. Stratmann was forced to turn back due to inadequate crampons, but Schneider and I reached the summit of Pt. 6,345m on July 21, finding it to be a fine vantage point. There was a unique view of Muztagh Tower, with its southwest and northeast ridges in profile, plus a full Baltoro panorama. Meanwhile Bernard, Brown, and Oberson turned their attention to the Biange Glacier icefall above base camp, in an attempt to make the second ascent of the 1956 French route on the southeast ridge. Two night-time outings resulted in a passage through convoluted terrain to gain snow slopes, at 5,500m, below the Black Tooth.

With the return of unstable weather the trekkers departed, and Oberson and I retrieved much of the technical gear from advanced base. As there were no large accumulations of snow on the mountain, the four other climbers made an attempt at the French route, turning back on the snow face below the Black Tooth, due to illness and exhaustion. A second bid, which reached the same point, was stymied by the arrival of the heaviest snow in two weeks, despite an optimistic forecast.

With time running out, Oberson and I made a final attempt on August 4. We climbed the icefall by night and continued over snow and ice faces to a shoulder, at 6,000m, on the southwest ridge of the Black Tooth. We then climbed, through a snowstorm, up a broad snow slope to the right of the giant serac barrier on the south face. At ca. 6,300m, on the inclined snow terrace above the edge of the serac, avalanche conditions forced a retreat.

On the descent I led down a long snow slope directly to the upper Biange. While crossing a low-angle ice slab, Oberson slipped, pulled me off, and we went for a 100m skid. Although Oberson was unhurt, I sustained impressive facial scratches and a back injury, which was later diagnosed as two compressed vertebrae. Fortunately, I was able to descend unaided, which was convenient, as were too high for helicopter evacuation. I was later assisted through the icefall by Brown, Bernard, Akhbar, and assistant sirdar Mustafa, the last two also high-altitude porters.

The expedition concluded with an immediate walk-out, a bus to Islamabad, adminstrative wrap-up, and medical attention in Europe. The team members thank Wil and Alta Brown, Dima Geshkenbein, Monika Hronska, and Colin Monteath for their generous assistance.

BRUCE NORMAND, *Switzerland*

Savoia Kangri, southeast face, attempt. A seven member Japanese expedition led by Koichi Ezaki attempted unclimbed Savoia Kangri (a.k.a. Summa Ri, 7,263m), just west of K2. The peak had only been attempted twice. In 1982 a team of Czechoslovakians living in Switzerland reached 6,550m on the 1,800m southeast face above the Savoia Glacier, and in 1998 a British team climbed a bow-shaped couloir through the triangular rock buttress left of the Czech Route, then followed the right edge of the big south-facing ice slope above to gain the upper southeast ridge. They climbed the ridge to 7,000m, before retreating in deep unstable snow. The Japanese opted to attempt the British line.

They established base camp on the Baltoro below Angel Peak, at 5,100m, and an advanced base on the Savoia glacier, at 5,300m. On July 25 the team placed a temporary camp at the start of the bow-shaped snow couloir, and on August 7 situated Camp 1 high in the gully, at 6,100m. The same day members climbed another six pitches to 6,300m, close to the top of the couloir, but thereafter were unable to regain this high point.

TAMOTSU NAKAMURA AND THE JAPANESE ALPINE NEWS

K2 - correction. Iván Vallejo was part of the Spanish film crew from the "Al Filo de lo Imposible" TV series, as reported in *AAJ 2005*, p. 352. However, Vallejo is not Basque but Ecuadorian.

MARCELO SCANU, *Argentina*

Broad Peak, southwest face. At 11:30 a.m. on July 25 Sergey Samoilov and Denis Urubko from Kazakhstan stepped onto the summit of Broad Peak (8,047m) after a remarkable ascent of the previously unclimbed southwest face. The two climbed the 2,500m route alpine-style, in six days. On the lower part of the face they had to overcome two steep rock bands, the first at ca.

6,300m and the second above 6,550m. These gave difficulties up to F6b and A2, with an M5 finish. They avoided freshly laden snow slopes higher up by climbing rock ribs, which involved a section of M6+ at over 7,400m. Reaching the southeast ridge at 7,950m also involved tricky mixed terrain (M4+), and the pair then had to battle strong winds before traversing the summit and descending the Normal Route. The full story of this ascent, which was nominated for the Piolet d'Or, appears earlier in this *Journal*.

Central Kharut Peak, attempt. I led a commercially organized expedition for Adventure Peaks to attempt the unclimbed Central Kharut Peak (6,824m on the new Polish map). The mountain is believed to have been attempted only once before. A Japanese party climbed to the col between Central Kharut and the virgin Kharut Pyramid (6,402m on the Polish map), then reached a high point on the rocky shoulder of the ridge above. [The Kharut peaks lie immediately northeast of K2's Abruzzi Ridge. In 1974 Tatsuro Arioka's expedition, which was trying to climb Broad Peak North, reached the Sella Pass, from where two members, Hidenori Iwamot and Isumi Kita, climbed a peak immediately to the northwest, the height of which they gave as 6,394m. This is most likely Central Kharut South, the rocky shoulder on the southwest ridge of Central Kharut, now assigned the height of 6,455m on the new Polish map—Ed.]

Our expedition planned to camp on the Sella Pass and first climb Kharut Pyramid, to aid our acclimatization, but conditions were not good. There was a considerable amount of snow left from the winter (no one summited neighboring K2), and unstable weather did not improve the situation. From base camp we could see that the snow slope leading to the col was covered with avalanche debris, while the glacier approach [up the West Kharut Glacier—Ed.] was seriously crevassed. A client and one of our high-altitude porters had to be extracted from slots. However, our main problem was time, or lack of it. We had experienced long delays in both Islamabad and Skardu due to administrative work at the Ministry, a holiday period when the Ministry was shut, and unexpected military briefings in Skardu. When we eventually arrived at the mountain, there was not enough time to make a serious attempt, and our high point was on the approach glacier. We had reliable weather reports at base camp, and when a good window was finally forecast, we made our escape over the Gondokoro La, rather than take the long trek out via the Baltoro. Adventure Peaks hopes to return in July-August 2006.

NICK CARTER, *United Kingdom*

MASHERBRUM RANGE

CHARAKUSA VALLEY

Chogolisa Glacier: Pk. 5,500m, north face; Raven's Peak, south face; Capucin, south face; Pk. 6,000m, northwest face. Charakusa Glacier: Iqbal's Wall, attempt. As in 2004, when we climbed above the Chogolisa Glacier, north of the Charakusa, completing four new routes *(AAJ 2005, p. 354)* our plan was to visit the Kondus and Saltoro valleys. However, the Pakistan government denied us a permit just two weeks before we were due to leave Italy for the mountains, so we returned to the Chogolisa and established base camp on the north side of the entrance to the Beusten Glacier below Raven's Peak.

On June 18 Hervé Barmasse, Ezio Marlier, and Fabio Salini climbed the north face of virgin Pk. 5,500m, via a line they named Fast and Furious. They climbed the 700m mixed route in a day; it had a difficult upper section of V/4. The second freed a short section of A1 at M6. The trio reached the summit ridge but didn't continue to the highest point, a little spire 10m above. They rappelled the route. [This summit appears to lie a short distance east along the ridge from Pointed and Crested peaks on the south side of the Beusten—Ed.]

On June 22 Marlier and Salini put up a new line on the left side of the south face of Raven's Peak (ca. 5,300m). Green Tea is eight pitches long and 6b, with a short section of A1 (one bolt). In 2004 we had climbed Luna Caprese (1,000m, 22 pitches, 6c+), a similar line to the original 1987 British Route, toward the right side of the main face.

From June 16 to 26 Barmasse, Cristian Brenna, Francesca Chenal, and I climbed a big line up the left and steepest part of Raven's south

Peak 5,500m, on the south side of the Beusten Glacier, showing Fast and Furious. *Luca Maspes collection*

face. We placed fixed ropes on the first 250 difficult meters and used bolts on the first pillar, with a view to a possible all-free, one-day ascent later. We completed Up and Down after six days and 800m of climbing. It has 16 pitches, up to 6c/6c+ and A1, and terminates on the left-hand ridge some distance below the summit. On July 10 Brenna, belayed by Giovanni Ongaro, climbed the route free in one day. They rated the crux (sixth) pitch 7c, but there were many pitches at 7a and 7b. I think this is one of the best and most difficult free climbs in the Karakoram.

From June 24 to 26 Gianluca Bellin and Ongaro climbed the 5,500m Capucin. [This fine spire lies on the south flank of Sheep Peak, up and right from Raven Peak, and was dubbed the Dru by the 1987 British party—Ed.] Duri e Puri is a relatively short (400m, 12 pitches) but difficult "big wall," with difficulties up to 6b and new wave A2. Bellin and Ongaro climbed the route, which ascends the south face and finishes on the southeast ridge below the summit, capsule style, with two nights spent in portaledges.

On June 28 Barmasse and Giovanni Pagnoncelli climbed the northwest face of an unnamed and previously virgin ca. 6,000m peak on the long west ridge of Farol. The 1,000m route had ice up to 60° and a little mixed terrain close to the summit. However, only Barmasse

Cristian Brenna on pitch five (7b) of Up and Down during the first free ascent. The pitch above, which involved a 7c roof, provided the crux of the free ascent. *Hervé Barmasse/ Luca Maspes collection*

The left side of the south face of Raven's Peak (ca. 5,300m), Beusten Glacier, showing the line of Up and Down (800m of climbing, 6c/6c+ A1; Barmasse-Brenna-Chenal-Maspes, 2005). The route was later free climbed in a day by Brenna at 7c to give one of the hardest free routes in the Karakoram. The crux roof is marked. *Giovanni Pagnoncelli/Luca Maspes collection*

Hervé Barmasse following a difficult mixed section of Fast and Furious on the north face of Peak 5,500m. *Fabio Salini/ Luca Maspes collection*

reached the highest point. [This peak lies east along the ridge from Pk. 5,500m mentioned above and appears to be in a similar location to a summit marked Fiona Peak on Jerzy Wala's 2005 1:100,000 sketch map of the K6 and Chogolisa groups—Ed.]

Before leaving base camp on the Chogolisa, Brenna and I climbed many boulder problems up to Font 7b, and after four days working a particularly difficult problem, Brenna created Master of Survivor, at Font 7c/7c+, no mean feat for the altitude.

During the last week of our expedition Barmasse, Brenna, and I moved to the Charakusa Glacier to attempt a new route on Iqbal's Wall, a formation I climbed in 1998 with Natale Villa and Galen Rowell. On July 19 we climbed six pitches, up to 6b/6b+, using traditional protection but were

Farol Central Peak (ca. 6,350m) with the line of the south pillar, climbed by Cedric Haehlen and Hans Mitterer, facing the camera. The route gave over 1,300m of ascent from the glacier, the pair reaching the crest via the snow ramp indicated. They bivouacked once at the end of the long rocky section, below the final snowfields leading up to the summit tower. They rappeled the snow face to the left, between seracs and the pillar. *Hans Mitterer.*

stopped by bad rock on the final 100m. Two days later we repeated the first four pitches of Tasty Talking (300m, 11 pitches, III 5.10+, House-Prezelj-Swenson, 2004) on the southeast ridge of 5,200m Nayser Brakk, then rappelled into the gully on the right and continued to the summit via the classic British Route up the north ridge (300m, British VS plus aid; climbed free at 5.10-, Burnage-Hamilton, 1988).

LUCA MASPES, *UP project, Italy*

Central Farol Peak, probable first ascent. At the start of July our German-Swiss Expedition (Cedric Haehlen, Urs Stoecker, Rainer Treppte, and I) left for the Charakusa Valley. Like other expeditions in 2005, we were refused permits for K7 or K6 for security/safety reasons. However, we decided to go anyway and look at 5,000m-6,000m peaks, as we all felt there must be plenty of worthy objectives giving good climbing.

After acclimatizing with an ascent of Sulo Peak (5,950m), Cedric and I climbed the middle summit of the three Farol Peaks, via the striking south pillar. We camped on the glacier at 5,000m, close to the foot of the pillar, and started our ascent at midnight on July 26. We first climbed a big snow ramp leading to the start of the rock ridge at 5,650m. Arriving there at dawn, we were confronted with a demanding pitch of near-featureless vertical granite. The terrain above provided several pitches of challenging climbing, crossing loose flakes, followed by steep ice and mixed climbing through beautiful sound granite. Every tower and gendarme proved unavoidable, and between them was much deep soft snow, through which we had to wade, often up to our waists. Several vertical snow walls consumed much time and energy. Finally, we reached the end of the ridge at 8:00 p.m. and bivouacked under a cornice that formed the start of the summit snowfield.

Next morning we had a hard fight negotiating waist-deep snow, before reaching the summit tower. This final section began with a wonderful mixed pitch, but the last few rope lengths,

Negotiating one of the gendarmes on the middle section of the south ridge of Farol Central Peak. *Hans Mitterer.*

on steep smooth slabs covered with a thin layer of snow, demanded a lot more concentration. The last 30m of steep, waist-deep snow slope nearly exhausted us. We found no evidence of previous passage on the route and assume we made a first ascent. Jan Mersch and a German party attempted the route a few days before us and also found no trace of previous attempts. As to grades, we climbed several rock pitches between V and VI, a few meters of A1 on the last big gendarme of the rock ridge, two pitches of M6 or M7 on the first part of the pillar, and a pitch of M6 on the summit tower. Our altimeter read 6,350m on top, confirming our view that the West (Main) Summit (6,370m) was only slightly higher than us. The East Summit was around the same height and the Far East somewhat lower. Cedric and I descended by rappelling to the big snowfield, then on down between glacier and pillar. Although exciting, due to horrifying seracs, it was quick, and we reached base camp late in the afternoon.

During the next three weeks the weather was generally bad with only a few isolated fine days. We used these to repeat the popular British Route (north ridge) on the fantastic pyramid of Naysar Brakk (5,200m), the South West Couloir of Beatrice (ca. 5,800m), and a rock route (Asteroid Valley) on Iqbal wall (ca. 5,400m).

HANS MITTERER, *Germany*

Editor's note: In 2004 a guided CAF expedition of primarily young French climbers reported attempting Farol Central by the 1,400m south spur (TD+) and a summit they refer to as the Fourth Point of Farol (6,200m) via a line of icefalls, followed by big wall climbing (ED). It has not been possible to confirm their lines; they may have attempted the south spur of the West Summit.

Hassin Peak and the East Peak of Farol, attempts. On August 12 Steve Swenson and I, joined by Hans Mitterer from Germany, hiked up to the base of the west buttress of unclimbed Hassin Peak (ca. 6,300m) at the head of the Charakusa Glacier. Hassin is the local name for the mountain and means "beautiful peak." The following day we climbed 60° icefields, topped by a couple of rope lengths of near-vertical ice, to reach the crest of the buttress. We wound our way up, linking snow couloirs, dry chimneys, and strips of perfect styrofoam ice, as well as insubstantial slush tucked into the backs of corners. Just as the sun was leaving the mountain, we popped back out on the crest, where a ropelength or two of snow climbing yielded a promising spot for the bivouac tent. The summit was only 800m above; the next day we would leave the camping gear and make a dash for it.

Leaving the bivouac in the morning we climbed a moderate 60-70° snow and ice face, but as the day wore on, it warmed up considerably. By the time we were negotiating the final

Looking at the eastern rim of the Charakusa Glacier and the unclimbed Hassin Peak (ca. 6,300m). The route on the west buttress attempted by Mitterer, Slawinski and Swenson, and their bivouac site, is marked. Their highpoint was ca. 6,000m. The skyline ridge on the right leads up to K6 (7,282m). Peaks to the left of Hassin are also unclimbed. *Raphael Slawinski*

mixed ground at 6,000m, the sun was on us, rapidly turning the steep summit snow slopes to the consistency of cotton candy. The heat and the altitude were also taking a toll on us, slowing us to a breathless crawl. Though the summit lay less than 300m above, we were unlikely to reach it before dark. Finding safe belay and rappel anchors by headlamp would not be easy, and we were unwilling to commit to spending a night out with nothing but the clothes on our backs. Sadly, we drilled the first of many V-threads in a rare patch of ice and slid down the ropes. We regained the tent just as the sun sank below the horizon. The following morning, still under cloudless skies, we continued our descent, reaching the glacier in the early afternoon, after making a total of 30 rappels, each of 70m.

Steve and I made another attempt on Hassin Peak, but bad weather turned us back before we'd crossed the bergschrund. There was not enough time for a third attempt, so on August 22 we turned our attention to a striking ice line on the right-hand Farol Peak (ca. 6,200m). It looked like it might go in one push.

The evening before found us camped on moraines below the triple-summited Farol. By the time the sun rose, we were already cramponing up the lower slopes of our chosen couloir. We had made the approach in predawn darkness, crossing a wasteland of ice avalanche debris. But we were safe now, with nothing but rock walls rearing above, breached by a discontinuous white line. We roped up at the base of a steep curtain of chandeliers that made me feel like I was back at home in the Canadian Rockies. A couple of pitches of steep ice, followed by a short icefield, brought us to the base of what would prove to be the crux. The pitch went slowly, and by the time we were reunited at the belay, it was clear we would be hard-pressed to top out

The south face of the Farol Peaks. The left-hand or West Summit is the highest at 6,370m. The middle summit, Farol Central (ca. 6,350m), was climbed in 2005 by Haehlen and Mitterer via the south pillar facing the camera. The East Summit to the right is probably around the same height as the Central, while the Far East or Fourth Farol Peak is ca. 6,200m. The line attempted on Far East by Slawinski and Swenson is marked. French are also believed to have tried a route in this vicinity during 2004. *Raphael Slawinski*

before dark. Another pitch of steep, decaying ice awaited, and who cared if it led anywhere or not? It was climbing. From the snowfield at its top we finally got a close view of the blank, overhanging headwall blocking the couloir. As we began the rappels, at least we had the satisfaction of having climbed until we were stopped.

RAPHAEL SLAWINSKI, *Canada*

NANGMA VALLEY

"Barasa" or "Changi Peak," first ascent. Tomasz Polok and I established base camp on September 8 at 4,100m on the south side of the Nangma Valley, at the foot of Roungkangchan III. The north face of this peak is a prominent 500-600m rock wall, which we attempted twice in a somewhat heavyweight style. However, the granite was rotten, and the cracks were choked with earth, making the whole climb much less attractive than it had appeared from a distance. After our second attempt, our local guide, Alika from Khande, told us that a French party had climbed this wall by a route that was probably quite close to our planned line. We therefore turned our attention to the opposite side of the valley and the truncated ridges and buttresses of the better-known Changi Tower (a.k.a. Changui Tower, ca. 5,820m on Jerzy Wala's 2004 1:50,000 map), planning to do a climb in lightweight style on better rock.

Our new route climbs the southwest pillar of the final (lowest) tower on the southwest

Barasa or Changi Peak, a ca. 5,000m rock formation on the south-west ridge of Changi Tower's East Summit, showing Moonlight Pillar. In the background are peaks on the eastern side of the Nangma Glacier. *Jan Kuczera*

ridge of Changi Tower's East Summit. We called this ca. 5,000m formation "Barasa" or "Changi Peak." The route is 500-550m high and 900m long, with difficulties up to VII. Initially, there was 200m of straightforward, less-steep rock up to IV, which we climbed without belays. Above lay 14 harder pitches to the summit (we used 50m ropes). The difficulties generally increased the higher we climbed. After two pitches of IV+ were pitches of V and VI, with a final pitch of VII. The 13th seemed the hardest: grade VI smearing with no protection. The 11th pitch featured a sort of rock tunnel 20m long. Most of climbing was very delicate, with small edges and questionable protection in less than sound granite. Much of it, particularly on the compact slabs, was more or less unprotected and rather risky, due to slightly brittle granite. We protected ourselves mainly with Friends, seldom with pitons. We placed one bolt, on the last stance, as there was no possibility for anything else. Overall, the pillar is not very steep, but high up there are almost-vertical sections.

We completed the route in 11 hours on September 17, naming it "Moonlight Pillar." We took minimal gear and no warm clothes. We descended by rappelling 300m northwest into the gully between our peak and Changui Tower, then carried on down to the southwest. On pitches four and five we came upon rappel slings, which we think might have been left in 2005 by a team unknown to us.

The names for our peak come from our guide Alika, who had previously served other Polish parties. However, we are not sure whether the name "Barasa" refers to our small summit or a bigger part of the Changi Tower massif. Alika also had some sort of illustrated climbing guide to the valley, but in it was no information about climbing on our pillar.

JAN KUCZERA, *Klub Wysokogórski Katowice, Poland*

India

HIMALAYA

Overview. Forty-six foreign and 47 Indian expeditions climbed in the Indian Himalaya during 2005. These numbers were lower than normal. Among the foreign expeditions, more that half climbed on such standard objectives as Nun, Kun, and Kedar Dome. Many expeditions faced bad weather in mid-September, and some had to give up because of poor snow and ice conditions in early October. Expeditions also complained of problems in Uttaranchal State, where the government has imposed a stiff new fee structure. Apart from additional fees, there is confusion regarding approach routes (only designated approach routes are allowed), various permits (from the forest department, government of Uttaranchal, and the Indian Mountaineering Foundation) and permit procedures involving various authorities at Dehra Dun, Delhi, and locally). All this confusion dampened the enthusiasm of many parties.

There were two successful ascents of Kamet. The American team of Sue Nott and John Varco made an excellent alpine-style ascent in quick time. In his report Varco writes, "For some time only Indian teams were allowed to climb on this mountain, and there is much evidence of the high impact of large Indian expeditions, which travel with way too much gear and leave tons of trash in camps and on trails. This aspect needs to be looked into. It is a sad statement of outdated style. However, this year's Army expedition did a good job of removing the trash and was very friendly and helpful." Nott and Varco are of the opinion that only small-sized expeditions should attempt this popular high mountain.

An Indo-American expedition, jointly led by Divyesh Muni and Donald Goodman, enjoyed themselves climbing several unnamed peaks in the East Karakoram. It was a successful expedition, which climbed many virgin peaks and demonstrated how a mixed team can climb fine, safe routes and come back happy.

There was plenty of activity, but it was marred by tragedies and the fact that most attempts were directed toward easier peaks rather than challenging ones. Of the 47 Indian expeditions, many were to routine peaks. There were ascents of peaks in Spiti and Lahaul, like Khangla Tarbo II, Yunam , and Sanakdank, and also ascents of more difficult peaks, like Papsura in the Kullu. However, several notable Indian mountaineers died on different peaks. Dr. P. M. Das, with Inder Kumar, Nari Dhami, and two Sherpas, all experienced mountaineers, lost their lives on Chomoyummo in an avalanche. Inder Kumar and Nari Dhami had climbed Everest. Five army men, from the Air Defence Regiment of the Indian Army, died in an avalanche on Chaukhamba I. A ladies expedition, organized by the IMF and comprising various climbers from all over India, climbed Papsura (6,451m) at head of the Tos Nala. Seven women reached the summit but after a long day's climbing, Malabi Das from Kolkata became very tired. She barely managed to reach the highest camp and finally died of exhaustion—an example of human loss due to summit ambitions. She was an experienced and enthusiastic mountaineer, having climbed Sudarshan Parvat and Chhamaser Kangri—peaks higher then Papsura. Two porters died on the Gangotri glacier, bringing the number of Indian deaths in the Indian Himalaya to 13, a disproportionately high number for one year.

In a seminar toward the end of the year, suggestions were made to instigate organized rescue facilities and accident insurance. There was also talk of allowing satellite phones and GPS devices and revamping the fee structure. No one, though, knows when this will be done.

The I.M.F. elected a new President, H. P. S. Ahluwalia, in November. Major Ahluwalia, who climbed Everest in 1965, is an experienced mountaineer and organizer, and he leads a newly elected Governing Council.

HARISH KAPADIA, *Honorary Editor, The Himalayan Journal*

EAST KARAKORAM

Siachen region, Laxmi, attempt by northwest face. A 10-member team from the Indian Navy attempted Laxmi (Lakshmi; 6,850m), a virgin peak on the Teram Shehr Glacier. Lt. Cdr. Amit Pande, who was deputy leader of the Navy's Everest expedition in 2004, led the team, which reached Siachen Base Camp on April 23 via the Nubra Valley and Thoise Partapur. The weather was bad, with unusually heavy snowfall in April and May. The team took five days to reach the confluence of the Teram Shehr and Siachen glaciers.

They established base camp on the Teram Shehr Glacier at an altitude of 5,250m. From there they attempted Laxmi (6,850m) by the northwest face. They placed their only camp next to a narrow ridge at 6,000m, prior to getting established on the face and opening the route to 6,380m.

Good weather continued to play truant, and the team was confined to base camp for several days. The Indian Meteorological Department forecast a long spell of bad weather, with blizzards, so the expedition withdrew to a lower camp. During their stay at this lower camp they attempted Junction Peak, but on May 25 a minor avalanche hit a party, and three members suffered injuries. The team subsequently abandoned the expedition. Fanny Bullock Workman, with Italian guides, first climbed Junction Peak, in 1912. She named the adjoining peak Laxmi, after the Goddess of Wealth.

HARISH KAPADIA, *Honorary Editor, The Himalayan Journal*

Arganglas Range, "Thongsa Ri" (5,899m), first ascent, east ridge, southeast face; "Karpo Kangri" central summit (ca. 6,525m), first ascent, south face icefall; "Gjungma Kangri" (6,287m), first ascent, west ridge, north face to west ridge, north face direct; Pk. 6,082m, first ascent, southwest ridge; "Snow Dome" (6,289m), first ascent, northwest face. The 2005 Maitri (Hindi for *Friendship*) Karakoram Expedition was a joint venture of Indian and American climbers. The Indians were Ameya Chandawarkar, Surendra Anant Chavan, Rajesh Gudgil, leader Divyesh Muni, Vineeta Muni, Shripad Sapkal, and Cyrus Shroff. The Americans were Sally Annis, Don Beavon, Dave Creeden, Marlin Geist, leader Don Goodman, Natala Goodman, and Dan Sjolseth. Our liaison officer was Maj, Samsher Sing, and we had four high-altitude Sherpas from Darjeeling. The expedition left Leh on August 3 and returned on September 1.

Our primary aim was Pk. 6,540m, tentatively named "Karpo Kangri" [by the Indo-British expedition jointly led by Chris Bonington and Harish Kapadia, which visited the Arganglas region in 2001; Muni and Shroff were part of this team and saw its impressive northern flanks rising above the Phunangma Glacier—Ed.]. From Satti in the Nubra Valley [where the road over the Khardung La from Leh meets the Shyok River—Ed.] we approached via the Satti Lungpa valley, which led to the Spang Chenmo Glacier, south of the area visited by the 2001 expedition. Although there are no records of climbing from this valley, we presume an abandoned campsite and garbage stash found just above our base camp to be evidence that it was visited in 1964 by an Army survey party. We established base camp on August 9 at 5,140m on the Spang Chenmo moraine and advanced base on the 14th at 5,480m. Two days later we placed a high camp at ca. 5,900m on the Lung Tung Glacier, which flows below the southern flanks of Karpo Kangri.

Climbing on Karpo Kangri (6,540m) during the Maitri Indo-American Karakoram expedition. *Harish Kapadia collection*

During this time we reconnoitered various peaks, and on the 14th Beavon, Vineeta Muni, and Ang Tashi made the first ascent of Pk. 5,899m, later named "Thongsa Ri," by the east ridge. Next day Beavon and Geist repeated the route, while Shroff climbed the southeast face. By the 19th Annis, Chendawardar, Gadgil, both Goodmans, and Sjolseth had also climbed the mountain.

We made our first attempt to climb "Karpo Kangri" on August 17, using fixed rope. On the 19th Beavon and Geist climbed to the central summit (ca. 6,525m) via the south glacier icefall. They rose at 2:30 a.m. and reached the summit in 11 hours. They planned to continue to the east or west summit, depending on which appeared the highest. However, due to the lateness of the day, fatigue, snow conditions, and the prospect of an unplanned bivouac, they did not and reversed the route. Near the bottom they used the fixed ropes for descent. An early start and late

The unclimbed Satti Kangri rises opposite advanced base (5,480m) above the Spang Chenmo Glacier. *Harish Kapadia collection* return (they arrived in camp at 7:30 p.m.) meant they avoided most of the serious rockfall that made this route dangerous in the heat of the day. A subsequent attempt by Schroff and the Sherpas, employing fixed rope to climb to the east summit via the southern headwall of the east ridge, failed at 6,400m after a tremendous effort.

"Gjungma Kangri" (6,287m), which rises like a large nunatak out of the ice, was climbed on the 20th by the west ridge by Chandawarkar, Sapkal, and Ang Tashi. Using a variant approach, via the north face, Annis, Creeden, and Don Goodman also summited on the 20th by the west ridge. The following day Beavon, Natala Goodman, and Sjolseth repeated this latter route, while Gadjil, the Munis, and Samsher Sing climbed the west ridge. The first ascent of the north face direct was made on the 22nd by Beavon and Geist. They climbed the steep lower section unroped but belayed on the problematic upper headwall: a mixture of ice-covered rock, deep snow, and hard ice, including a few dry-tooling moves. On the 23rd Shroff and Ming Pemba Sherpa also summited the mountain, giving it the distinction of having been climbed by every member of the climbing team, as well as our L.O. and two Sherpa staff. Perhaps we should have named this peak "Maitri" after the friendships we established.

While the last ascent of "Gjungma Kangri" took place, Chandawardar, Gadgil, the Munis, and Sapkal traveled down the glacier and made the first ascent of Pk. 6,082m, via the south face to the southwest ridge. In the meantime Creeden and Sjolseth put in a long day scouting the glacier system south of "Snow Dome." They reached a high pass and reported that it appeared to give access to the Rongdu Valley. Crossing this pass would enable the team to make a nice three-day trek and circuit of the area upon departure.

On the 24th Annis, Beavon, Geist, and the Goodmans climbed "Snow Dome" (6,289m) by the northwest face and long west ridge, with Don Goodman piecing together an excellent route, as he had done on "Gjungma Kangri." They roped up for the steep glacier-covered northwest face, occasionally putting in protection.

We dismantled the high camps and descended to base camp on August 25. Forgoing further climbing attempts, all seven Indians and seven Americans, together with two Sherpas, crossed the unnamed glacier south of "Snow Dome" and crossed the pass explored by Creeden and Sjolseth to the Koyak Glacier. We found a reasonable descent to the Koyak Lungpa and on down to the Rongdu Lungpa, reaching the village of Rongdu on the 31st. During the last few days we saw jaw-dropping walls and cliffs that could keep a Yosemite climber busy for several lifetimes.

The expedition summited five peaks, explored numerous areas in the greater Lung Tung Valley, and completed a loop traverse connecting the Satti and Rongdu river drainages. It was a wonderful joint effort, with all 15 team members thoroughly enjoying themselves.

DON BEAVON AND MARLIN GEIST

Editor's note: Harish Kapadia mentions that "Snow Dome" was later called "Bukbuk" and Pk. 6,082 named "Rdung Ring."

ZANSKAR

"Peak Giorgio," first ascent, Amico Gio. Our expedition comprised Giuseppe Bonfante, Antonio Valerio Carrota, Silvano Colombo, Andrea Corti, Angelo Gnecchi, Giovanni Mazzoleni, Nerino Panzeri, Simone Ripamonte, Giampaolo Schiavo, Dario Valsecchi, and I as leader. Most

of us come from Lecco and are members of the Gamma Group. In August we visited the Shafat Valley in Kashmir at N 34° 05' W 76° 12' [a side valley of the Suru northeast of Nun Kun leading to the Kun Glacier—Ed.]. Here we made the first ascent of "Peak Giorgio," a 5,135m rock aiguille, by the northwest face. This peak lies south of Ringdom Gompa, and we established an advanced base below the wall at nearly 4,300m. The route. Amico Gio, had a vertical height of 900m but 1,100m of climbing. On our final push Carrota, Corti, Mazzoleni, Panzeri, Ripamonte, Valsecchi,

The Shafat Valley, Kashmir. Seen from the west (A) is the splendid unclimbed peak that was the original objective of the Italian expedition. The west-facing slabs of smooth granite are over 1,000m high. (B) is Peak Giorgio (5,135m), which the Italians climbed via the northwest face in 27 pitches at VII A1. *Giovanni Pomi*

and I climbed to the summit in 36 hours, with one camp on the face, reaching the top on August 15. We left five bolts and 30 pegs in the route. The 27 pitches were relatively sustained, from UIAA V to VII, with the 22nd pitch being A1. Prospective second ascensionists will still need to carry blades and angles. The large peak immediately to the north, which was our original objective, has huge granite walls.

GIOVANNI POMI, *Groupo Gamma, Italy*

Chhomotang Valley: Chhomotang I, Chhomotang III and Thorchok II, first ascents; Thorchok I, second ascent; Chhomotang II (No Name Peak), ascent. In summer 2004 we explored climbing possibilities in the Chhomotang valley, 85km west of Leh in the Zanskar Range of Ladakh. For some years trekking agencies have used this valley, because it offers an easy 6,000m summit on the way from Lamayuru to Kangi. The peak is referred to as "No Name Peak," and its first ascent seems not to have been reported.

During the 2004 exploration we identified five principal peaks in the same range as "No Name Peak," and the idea of a 2005 Chhomotang Valley expedition was born.

We approached using a 4X4 from Leh, via Lamayuru and the Fotu La (4,094m), until near Hiniskut, where a wide road leads into a gorge and gradually deteriorates into a footpath leading towards Kangi. We used donkeys in this section, though even they were unable to reach the village, and we had to send for reinforcements from Kangi. From the village we walked southeast up the Chhomotang River to our base camp at 4,900m

After an initial attempt on July 20 by Jordi Bosch (Barraca), Carles Figueras, and I, Figueras and I climbed the elegant north spur of Chhomotang I (5,865m) on the 24th.

After crossing the glacier northward, we reached the bottom of the spur at 5,415m and spent eight hours climbing the 450m of compact snow, ice, and mixed pitches that form an almost continuous 45-60° slope. There was a horizontal section at 5,640m that we called the "Plaça de l'esmorzar" (*Breakfast Place*). We graded the route TD, due to its committing nature

Chhomotang I (ca. 5,865m) and Chhomotang II (ca. 5,885m) in the Zanskar Range of Ladakh. Marked are the north spur of Chhomotang I (450m, TD, Bosch-Caros-Figueras) and the continuation along the east ridge of Chhomotang II. Although previously unreported, ascents of the latter have been made before via the northwest face (AD+). *Josep M. Sola i Caros*

Chhomotang III (5,740m) showing the route of the first ascent on the northeast face (Caros-Figueras-Garrijo, D 80°). *Josep M. Sola i Caros*

and difficulty of the mixed climbing. The summit, which had had no recorded ascent, comprised two enormous gneiss blocks.

We continued along the ridge westward to "No Name Peak" (5,885m). This 1km crest had all the qualities of an alpine classic and was more or less above 5,800m throughout. The first half consisted of blocks of compact gneiss, with several sections of F4+. We made three rappels. Beyond a col, the second half of the ridge had an unexpected ice step (100m at 70°) and a long horizontal crest. This summit is climbed by trekking parties via the northwest face (AD+, our descent route). The altitude of 5,885m recorded by our altimeters contrasts with the 6,045m published in most trekking guides.

We decided to change "No Name Peak" to "Chhomotang II" after discussions with locals in Kangi. They have been referring to the valley and its principal peaks as "Chhomotang" for a long time. We encourage trekking agencies to consider this proposal and remember that, in general, alpinists should make an effort to ascertain local mountain names and not simply to invent their own. Dialog with locals is the only way of respecting their inheritance.

On the 22nd Figueras, Inaki Garrijo, and I made the first ascent of Chhomotang III (5,740m), by the northeast face (D). There were significant crevasses on the glacier approach (50° maximum), and the final slope had a section of 80°.

On the 26th Bosch, Kim Bover and Figueras made the first ascent of Thorchok II (5,590m), by the northwest face. From the summit Bosch continued north along the ridge to make the second ascent of Thorchok I (5,740m). The route, which we graded PD, would make a nice acclimatization ascent. Thorchok I was first climbed on July 9, 2004, during the reconnaissance expedition, by Bosch and Figueras. In consultation with their local staff, they bestowed the name Thorchok (*Crown*) on the peaks because of their appearance. Thorchuk I lies west of Chhomotang III, and Thorchuk II is immediately south of its big brother. In 2004 Bosch and Figueras climbed the northeast face (800m, TD), which began with a 45° slope and continued with a 60m pitch of bad rock. Above, an ice face of 65-70° led to the summit, which was a 40m rock formation. They descended via the north face.

We recommend *Ladakh Zanskar* (1:350,000) from Nelles Verlag as a good general map of the region. However, Olizane (Switzerland) has produced a more detailed topographic map of the Kangi region, under the title *Ladakh-Zanskar – Centre* (1:150, 000).

JOSEP M. SOLA I CAROS, *Switzerland*

HIMACHAL PRADESH

MIYAR VALLEY

Castle Peak, north-northwest wall, 7 d'espases. Last year Eloi Callado and I went to India to climb the Neverseen Tower. We put up a new route on the west face called Mai Blau (*AAJ 2005*, pp. 367-8). This year I went back for a couple of months, not only to climb, but also to travel around the country. I like India; I like the people, how they live and also their mountains. So wild, so hard. Such an incredible country.

Back again in the Miyar Valley during September and October, I was lucky to climb a new route, "7 d'espases" (480m, V+ A3+/A4), in a remote area. I wanted to try it alone. That was my goal, something personal. The

The north-northwest wall of Castle Peak, Miyar Valley, showing the line of 7 d'espases (480m, V+ A3+/A4, Vidal). The vague arête just to the right of this line is the 2002 Slovak route, Sharp Knife of Tolerance (VIII+ A3, Koller-Kopold-Linek-Stefansky). Silvia Vidal

opportunity arose when a Spanish Young Alpinist Federation team also planned to go to the same area. Not wanting to travel alone, I contacted them to see if I could share transport and the approach march with them. It is one thing to be alone on a wall, but it is harder to go from Delhi to the mountains, and do all the organization in a country like India, on one's own. They agreed and were the best travel companions I could have wished for. Thanks guys!

They set up camp at Phalphu (3,900m) in the main (Miyar) valley. From there to my base camp at 4,400m was a one-and-a-half-hour walk up a subsidiary valley toward the Tawa Glacier. I decided to climb the north-northwest wall of Castle Peak, because it is steep and therefore easier for haul bags. I used a different system for hauling my two bags, because I weigh only 46kg and each bag weighed at least 50kg. I used a mobile pulley on the haulbag, which meant I needed double the amount of rope, and the system weighed more, but it preferable to not being able to haul at all, simply because I was not big enough.

I fixed the first 70m on September 17 and established my first portaledge camp at the top of pitch two. Next day I started a capsule ascent and spent 12 days (11 bivouacs) on the wall, finishing the route the 29th. I used only two camps on the wall, with the second at the top of pitch five.

There is an overhanging section, like a diving board, that takes you to the top of the face at 5,000m. I finished with the last 15m of the 2002 Slovak route Sharp Knife of Tolerance. From there it is possible to follow a ramp to a ridge. This ridge, which would be technical, could be followed for over 1,000m to the top of Castle Peak. Like the Slovaks, I didn't climb it and the next day rapped my route.

In terms of weather I had some good days and some bad days, but even on good days there was only one hour of sunshine on the wall. It was really cold, and ice on some of the compact walls made climbing difficult.

Climbing solo is different. You can share neither problems nor happiness. The feelings you experience are entirely your own. It is very intense, the best and the worst. But I had lot of fun up there.

SILVIA VIDAL, *Spain*

Paolo's Peak, first ascent, Via Pallaresa; Paolo's Peak, No Spice!; Pt 5,930m, first ascent, Antiparques; Iris Peak, Tinc Por; and "Brouillard Pillar," Tocati di Bola, Ocells a Vent. Last summer marked the end of the 2004-2005 course for members of the Young Alpinist group of the Spanish Mountaineering Federation (FEDME). The reward was a trip in September to the Indian Himalaya and unclimbed peaks of the Miyar Valley. We traveled with Silvia Vidal. Silvia knew the area, having been there in 2004. Thanks to her, the organization and logistics of reaching base camp was much simpler than if we'd had been on our own. Using her agent in Manali, we arrived at Phalphu (3,900m) in the main valley and set up base camp.

During the first week the weather was bad, but this allowed us to acclimatize at base camp. We then began to look for interesting lines. Oscar Cacho and I first went up the Tawa Glacier and made the first ascent of Paolo's Peak (5,460m), which is the third rock peak left (northwest) of Neverseen Tower. We climbed the narrow gully between the peak and Pt 5,700m to the right (M5 80°), then near the top slanted left up the rock of the southwest face to the summit (6a+). Via Pallaresa was 680m and TD.

Matias Cuesta and Jonathan Larrañaga made a second ascent of Paolo's Peak, by con-

From left to right on the Tawa Glacier, Miyar Valley: Paolo's Peak (5,460m), Pt 5,700m, Grandfather Ezio (5,750m). (1) Via Pallaresa (680m, TD, Baro-Cacho). (2) No Spice! (680m, TD, Cuesta-Larrañaga). (3) Denni-Marcheggiani (600m, 6c 70°, 1996). (4) West face attempt (700m, ED 6b A1 M5, Baro-Cacho). *Oriol Baro*

The final pitch (V) of Via Pallaresa on Paolo's Peak. *Oriol Baro*

Approaching the crux section (M6) of Antiparques on Pt 5,930m, Miyar Valley. *Oriol Baro*

tinuing up the last section of the gully to the col at the top and climbing the southeast ridge. No Spice! (5+ M5 80°).

Cacho and I then attempted the west face of Pt 5,750m, immediately left of Neverseen Tower. We climbed a diagonal mixed line (50° and M4) left, into the base of a huge left-facing corner. We retreated about half-way up this corner and around 700m up the face. This was certainly the best climbing I did throughout the trip; to our high point the grade was ED 6b A1 M5. [This is the same peak the Italians (see below) dubbed "Grandfather Ezio"—Ed.]

After another spell of bad weather, we had a look into the valley opposite. This neces-

The north faces of Pt 5,800m (left) and Pt 5,930m, Miyar Valley. Marked are the attempt to climb Pt 5,800m by Cuesta and Martinez, and the new route, Antiparques (950m, TD, Baro-Cacho). *Oriol Baro*

The west face of Paolo's Peak (5,460m) showing the line of Pallaresa. *Oriol Baro*

sitated crossing the river, which proved complicated. We set up a Tyrolean. We discovered a fine snowy peak of 5,930m without any known name and climbed it by the north face, which was cold. Our route, Antiparques (950m TD), required 19 hours of activity. We descended in 18 rappels.

Other members of the group made the following attempts and ascents: On a steep buttress on the flanks of Iris Peak, Victor Sans and Ferran Rodriguez climbed Tinc Por on September 18 (980m 6b). They reached the top of the buttress but did not continue towards the summit of Iris Peak. On a rock formation dubbed the "Brouillard Pillar" (5,240m) Cacho and Sans climbed Tocati di Bola (400m 6b A2). Both climbers returned with Larrañaga and Rodriguez to add Ocells a Vent (340m 6c A2). [Both routes lie on the steep wall left of the 2004 Urtasun-Viscarret route, Shakti (5+ A1).] On the north face of Pt 5,800m, the summit immediately left of Pt 5,930m, Cuesta and Martinez retreated at around three-quarters height after climbing a broad snow couloir and, halfway up, a right-slanting mixed ramp.

ORIOL BARO, *Spain* (WITH ADDITIONAL MATERIAL FROM XAVIER LLONGUERAS)

Editor's note: A Spanish couple from Navarra, Alberto Urtasun and Patricia Viscarret, also made a return visit in 2005 and climbed a new route on Iris Peak (ca. 5,300m), right of the existing lines put up by Italians and French in 2004. Ananda gave 800m of climbing at 6a+ and A2, apparently finishing on broad terraces some distance below the summit.

Buttress 5,650m, first ascent, via west face (Million Indian Stars); Pt 5,750m ("Grandfather Enzo Peak"), south face-southeast ridge. In August an Italian expedition led by Massimo Marcheggiani, and which included Nadia Benedettini, Mariano Fabrizi, Massimo Natalini, and I headed back to the Miyar Nala. After expeditions in 1992 and 1996, when he climbed four virgin peaks, including the now well-known Neverseen Tower (*AAJ 1997* pp. 274-6), Marcheggiani's goal was the unclimbed east pillar of Three Peaks Mountain. [This is Marcheggiani's name for the unclimbed 6,000+m peak at the head of the so-called Spaghetti Glacier, also known as Thunder Glacier, and locally called Dali Glacier. The west-facing rock wall overlooking the glacier has been attempted several times, and in 2003 Slovaks Dodo Kopold and Ivan Stefanski climbed to a 5,845m foresummit that they christened

The unclimbed Three Peaks Mountain near the head of the Dali Glacier (a.k.a Spaghetti or Thunder Glacier). The highest summit is around 6,000m. Spot the line on the east pillar facing the camera. *Francesco Camilucci*

Mahindra. The east side, overlooking the Tawa Glacier, has not been attempted—Ed.].

We established base camp at the usual place, just below the moraine of the Tawa Glacier at N 33° 01' 53.5" E 76° 48' 40.9" (GPS measurement). Our team was unable to attempt Three Peaks Mountain, but on August 31 and September 1 Marcheggiani and Natalini made the first ascent of a subsidiary buttress on the west face of the second peak to the right of Neverseen Tower. From Camp 1, at 4,950m on the glacier, their route followed an obvious Z-shaped feature: a sinuous couloir and mixed terrain followed by a complex and dangerous rock face. After a bivouac without a tent, the two climbers reached the top of the buttress at 5,650m, having finished via a beautiful crack system on the left. They named the route Million Indian Stars. It finished some distance below the summit of the mountain and was graded M6+ A1 and 5c.

After four days rest at Camp 1, Marcheggiani and Natalini made the second ascent of Pt 5,750m, climbed in 1992 by Marcheggiani, Di Vincenzo, and Miele by a 600m line up the south face and upper southeast ridge (ice couloir approach then 5c). This time the pair climbed the approach couloir all the way to the col between 5,750m and Neverseen Tower, then climbed the southeast ridge directly to join the original route. This gave pleasant climbing at 4c over rough granite slabs. They named the col "Tiziano Cantalamessa Col" and have proposed that the summit be called "Grandfather Enzo Peak."

Ice conditions in this area have deteriorated markedly since my visit in 1996. During last year's expedition stonefall seemed continuous, and it appears to be increasingly dangerous to climb on these beautiful peaks. Also, the Tawa Glacier has retreated significantly in the last 10 years.

FRANCESCO CAMILUCCI, *Italy*

"*Lotos Peak,*" *first ascent.* Michal Krol, a young mountaineer from southern Poland, and I set off in late August for a climbing trip to the Miyar Valley. Relatively few expeditions have climbed in this region, one of the first being an Italian team led by Paolo Vitali, which in the early 1990s attempted to make the first ascent of Neverseen Tower. Since then, exploration of the outstanding rock walls in the valley and its tributaries has mainly been carried out by Italian and Slovak parties.

Peaks on the east side of the Tawa Glacier. To date the altitudes of peaks in this region have never been properly measured and the various guesstimates by climbers often show inconsistencies from peak to peak. From left to right: Grandfather Enzo (5,750m but probably lower) with (1) west face attempt (700m, ED 6b A1 M5, Baro-Cacho), (2) Original Route (600m, 5c, Di Vincenzo-Marcheggiani-Miele, 1992) and (3) southeast ridge from Tiziano Cantalamessa Col (600m, 4c, Marcheggiani-Natalini, 2005); Neverseen Tower (ca. 5,750m) with (4) Horn Please (ca. 600m, VII, Di Vincenzo-Marcheggiani-Miele, 1992), (5) Mai Blau (ca. 650m, A3+ 6b 70°, Callado-Vidal, 2004) and (6) attempt on south ridge (five pitches in couloir then one pitch of 6b and A2; Casablancas-Llongueras I Orriols- Nadal, 1999). (7) southwest face (750m of climbing, VII- M6 80°; Kaszlikowski-Krol, 2005); (8) Million Indian Stars to the top of "Pt 5,650m" (but probably much lower), during an attempt on the peak southeast of Lotos (M6 5c A1, Marcheggiani-Natalini). *David Kaszlikowski*

Many summits remain unclimbed; most don't even have names. Large walls, similar in shape to but a bit smaller than Trango Tower in the Karakoram, shoot up from the glacier to almost 6,000m. The most interesting ones are located just above the Tawa and Spaghetti glaciers (the 2004 British expedition proposed ethnic names for these glaciers based on local research: Chhudong and Dali, respectively. See *AAJ 2005* p. 367). Neighboring glaciers have rarely been visited.

The Miyar Valley is about 100km long. We hired horses to carry our equipment, about 250kg (including 60kg of food that had to last for a month). The three-day trek into the valley completely surprised us. We passed flowery meadows, wild horses, and yaks, as well as many streams and small rivers. Mountains rose smoothly above us to 5,000m.

Larger walls started to appear just before base camp, which was at 4,000m. Before reaching it we met a small Italian team, which included Massimo Marcheggianni, the first ascensionist of Neverseen Tower, and the Spanish couple Alberto Urtasun and Patricia Viscarret. We climbed separately, but the atmosphere between us was very friendly, and we had an excellent farewell dinner party.

It took four days to transport our equipment up the difficult and unstable Tawa Glacier to an advanced base at 5,000m. From here we attempted the unclimbed peak to the right of Neverseen Tower. We had come prepared for every eventuality, including big-wall climbing (we had haul bags and a portaledge) but attempted this route in a lighter style. As the lower section of the wall remained invisible, we made an initial reconnaissance, putting up 200m of fixed rope.

After a rest day, we awoke at 3 a.m. and began climbing by headlamp. The first section, a steep ice slope, took two hours, while the line above was generally mixed. For comfort we decided that I should climb the rock sections in light rock shoes, and Michal would lead the ice. Michal ran up his sections placing hardly any protection. Rock pitches mainly followed cracks. Sometimes these were chocked with ice, and I regretted not taking an axe and leaving my crampons at base camp. At other times the rock was perfect for free climbing.

By afternoon the sun had melted the snow from the summit dome, and a waterfall was coming down the overhang above us. We had to go under the waterfall and in no time were soaked, particularly Michal, who had to belay me while standing under a curtain of water. I was hit on the forearm by falling rocks, which caused me to lose feeling and worry that the arm was broken.

It was late when we reached the final section leading to the summit. Although we had expected to find only snow on this last section, there was a surprising crack pitch. Finally, at 9:45 p.m. on September 5, we stood on the summit.

After leaving a short "message in a bottle" by one of the boulders, we started our difficult rappel descent, which continued throughout the night. Next morning at 8 a.m. we finally stood on flat, safe ice. A second after sitting on rocks, we were both out cold. The walk to camp, which should have taken half an hour, was prolonged by our falling asleep every few steps. We returned to advanced base after an ascent and descent of 28 hours.

The following morning, after 10 days at or above 5,000m, we decided to retreat to the lower valley. The weather broke and we knew the porters and horses would not wait more than a day at base camp. We had no choice. We gathered our equipment and with 50kg rucksacks began our slow, self-destructive walk to base camp.

We named our mountain "Lotos Peak," which according to my altimeter was 5,630m, not much lower than Neverseen Tower. Our route up the southwest face was 750m long, with difficulties of UIAA VII- M6, and ice to 80°.

This expedition was possible thanks to grants from the Polish Mountain Association, Alvika, and Tendon.

DAVID KASZLIKOWSKI, *Poland*

LAHAUL

Tela 2, attempt. A Polish expedition led by 70-year-old Andrez Zoinski and comprising 10 members attempted unclimbed Tela 2 (6,035m) on the Tela Glacier. After traveling by road over the Rohtang Pass and across Lahaul to Darcha, they trekked northeast to the Tela Glacier. This glacier has 10 peaks almost in a ring, and they are numbered from one to 10. The Poles attempted the north face of T-2 during August. However, they were hampered by bad weather and were only able to reach a height of 5,500m.

HARISH KAPADIA, *Honorary Editor, The Himalayan Journal*

Sanakdank, probable first ascent. This peak is situated near Gushal village on the Manali-to-Leh Highway, 7km before Keylong. From Gushal a seven-member team from the Climbers Circle, Kolkata, trekked southwest for two days to establish base camp on August 9 at an altitude of just under 4,600m. The team needed two more camps to get to the foot of the mountain. On the 15th Aun Kanti Das, Dibyendu Halder, and Tapan Kumar Mukherjee, with two high-altitude porters reached the 6,044m summit.

HARISH KAPADIA, *Honorary Editor, The Himalayan Journal*

Koa Rong II, rare ascent, west ridge. A 12-member team from West Bengal led by Govinda Mondal and employing high-altitude Sherpa support established base camp, on August 21, at 5,100m on the banks of Panchi Nala. After placing two high camps, Sanjay Bhowmik, Bikramjit Debnath, Sonam Lama, and Amiya Sarkar reached the 6,187m summit of Koa Rong II on the 28th from Camp 2 (5,895m). The climbers followed the west ridge. [This peak was first climbed by a Polish expedition in 1984 by the southeast ridge. It has received very few subsequent ascents, and it is not clear if any of these has been by the west ridge—Ed.]. The Koa Rong is a range of peaks that are the centerpiece of Lahaul. They can be approached from Pachi Nala.

HARISH KAPADIA, *Honorary Editor, The Himalayan Journal*

Koa Rong V, rare ascent, southeast ridge. A 10-member expedition from West Bengal led by Biplab Sengupta made a relatively rare ascent of Koa Rong V (6,258m), situated near the Suraj Tal and east of the Baralacha Pass. They placed base camp at 4,780m and established two more camps, the highest at 5,900m. On September 3 Raju Kumar, Subrata Mujumdar, Tsar Paul, Alamchand Thakur, Khemraj Thakur, and Nanakchand Thakur reached the summit by the southeast ridge, probably following the 1998 Japanese Route.

HARISH KAPADIA, *Honorary Editor, The Himalayan Journal*

KULLU

Kullu Eiger, second ascent, new route, west face to south face. In the autumn Oscar Pérez and I went to the Kullu Eiger, because our agent in India showed us a picture of the north face and an article written by the Scottish expedition that reached the top in 1996. This was our only information on what appeared to be a beautiful and spectacular peak. [The first ascent of Kullu Eiger was made on September 21, 1996,

Kullu Eiger from the south showing the line of the new route on the west face to south face, Baral Karasta, and (B) marking the top bivouac site. *Pepín Valdivia*

by Graham Little, Jim Lowther, and Scott Muir, after three bivouacs on the north-northeast face. Their route avoided the steep upper part of the Eiger's face by traversing out left to the northeast face. However, the route still presented difficulties of British E1 5b A1 and Scottish V. This team made a base camp below the wall at 3,740m and measured a summit altitude of 5,646m, making the face 1,900m high—Ed.]

After a few days trek up the alpine Parvati Valley, we established base camp at 3,820m, where the Glacier II valley joins the main Parvati Valley, directly below the Eiger's north face. This was in the same flat meadow as the Scottish base camp but on the opposite side of the Glacier II river.

The weather throughout the expedition was not good. It was always windy and cold at base camp, and each day there was snowfall by noon. We finally decided to avoid the terrible rockfall on the north face by attempting the west face in alpine style.

Climbing on the south face of Kullu Eiger during day three of the first ascent of Baral Karasta. *Pepín Valdivia*

The top section of the north face of Kullu Eiger. On the first ascent of this face in 1996 the three-man British team climbed first left and then straight up mixed ground toward the base of the prominent pillar (top left). They avoided the pillar on the left, climbing mixed ground between it and the left skyline to reach the summit slopes, which were followed back right to the highest point. A direct line on this face remains to be climbed. *Pepín Valdivia*

Big wall potential in the Indian Himalaya. The vertical granite headwall of "the prow" presents one of several enticing rock objectives in the Parvati Valley region. *Pepín Valdivia*

On September 29 we left base camp. We wanted to climb the first section of the wall in the afternoon, because it was in the sun, but we arrived too late and it started to snow, so we spent our first night at the base of the wall (4,300m).

Next morning we left early. It was cold, and the rock was icy. There was both grass and verglas in the cracks, so progress was slow and difficult. We front-pointed some sections of frozen grass with axes and crampons.

In the afternoon we reached the start of the west spur. Above, the way appeared to be blocked by a large tower. We decided to outflank this obstacle, only later realizing it was a shoulder on the ridge and not a tower. Our deviation was long and took us onto the south face. By nightfall we had reached 4,950m and by the time we got the tent up, it was again snowing.

On October 1 we started climbing late because it was so cold in the morning, but the day was perfect, sunny and windless. We climbed in rock shoes and made fast progress. The rock was perfect and the route a wonderful natural line. We reached the top of the wall at 2 p.m., and from there to the summit was only 15 minutes. Although we had decided that the north face was not 1,900m high (we think it more like 1,500m), it was still a bit of a surprise when we recorded 5,330m for the summit altitude. We can't be certain that our readings are accurate, but we are sure that both the heights of the north face and the mountain are ca. 300m less than those quoted by the Scottish team.

From the summit we rappeled to our top bivouac, where we spent another night before descending to base camp the following day. Our descent is fully equipped with pitons and bolts for rappels, though subsequent parties may find it less than straightforward to follow the route. We named our 1,000m line Baral Karasta, and belayed 18 pitches (generally sustained at 4 and 5), up to 6a+ and A0.

Pepín Valdivia, *Spain*

Editor's note: Two other members of the expedition, Cecilia Buil and Juan Gollanes, attempted the Throne (5,840m), a prominent feature in the South Parvati Valley. They appear to be under the impression that the mountain was unclimbed, whereas it received its first ascent on September 12, 1997, by the north ridge (Scottish II/III), by Kevin Kelly, Gordon Lennox, Scott Muir, and David Proudfoot.

The Spanish pair reached 5,300m on their second day but were then faced with a big avalanche-prone snow slope above a glacier that would lead to a point 200m below the summit. They retreated to wait for better conditions, but these did not materialize.

SPITI

Upper Pare Chu Valley, Pks. 6,206 and 6,080m, first ascents; Dhhun, second ascent. Our expedition from the Tokai section of the Japanese Alpine Club left Kaza (3,600m) in the Spiti River Valley on July 23. We trekked north up the Parilungbi Valley and over the Parung La (5,580m), dropped down the far side to the snout of the Parung Glacier (at the head of the Pare Chu Valley) and established base camp at 5,200m. [This approach followed the first section of the old trade route from Spiti to the large Tso Morari (lake) in Ladakh and onwards to Leh—Ed.] In 1999, inspired by the reports of Harish Kapadia, I visited this region, and our expedition made the first ascents of Umdung Kangri (6,643m), northwest of Gya, and Dhhun (6,200m), immediately south of Parilungbi (6,166m, climbed in 1987 by Kapadia's Indian expedition) at the head of the Pakshi Lamur Glacier. On the latter we thought the peak we were climbing was Lhakhang (6,250m), our main target. We reached the summit in poor visibility and on returning home discovered that Lhakhang lay 1½km farther south of Dhhun. It remained unclimbed and seemed the perfect target for 2005.

Our expeditions characteristically include older mountaineers, who still maintain an interest in exploration despite limited physical capabilities. When we asked for applications for this trip, we received many from elderly climbers with limited experience, so we included easier unclimbed peaks around Parang La as additional targets. There are many untouched peaks in this little-known mountain area, where it is still possible to satisfy one's curiosity for exploration, though it is not the place for super-technical alpine challenges.

The team split into two parties. The first, Midori Masada (50), Kunihiko Noro (64), and I (70), attempted two peaks northwest of the Parung La. We first ascended the easy Parung Glacier and placed a camp at 5,800m. On August 2 we left at 6 a.m. and followed a snow-filled gully to the top of Pk. 6,206m (height from the Russian map). It was technically easy, and we reached the summit, with our liaison officer and a porter, in two hours. The next day Masada and Noro bagged the unclimbed 6,080m peak immediately to the southwest, by the north face. Both these peaks were previously unclimbed.

The second party, Kiyoko Kanada (50), Takako Miura (62), Kazuhiro Mizuno (58), Tatsumi Mizuno (54), and Tokutaro Yanagihara (58), left base camp on July 28 and ascended the Pakshi Lamur valley to a camp at 5,100m. On the 31st they reached the glacier snout and set up a second base camp at 5,200m. On August 1 a reconnaissance to 5,600m showed the proposed route on Lhakhang to be too avalanche-prone, so on the 3rd they set out to make the second ascent of Dhhun. They established a high camp at 5,600m and at 4:00 the following morning started up the névé-covered north face. The five Japanese climbers, the liaison officer, and four porters reached the summit at 11 a.m. Unwilling to reverse the route, because of soft snow prevailing in the afternoon, they climbed down the rocky west face, though this turned out to be harder than anticipated.

TSUNEO SUZUKI, *Japanese Alpine Club*

A review of the mountains near the head of the Pare Chu. The Pare Chu lies northeast of the Spiti River, not far from the Indo-Tibet border. Since 1995 it has been easy for foreign mountaineers to gain access to the areas west of the Spiti River, but the regions north and east are restricted, so it is necessary to get reluctant Indian authorities to accept applications from other than local people or trekkers. There are five main venues that I would like to discuss:

(1) Peaks south of Umdung (4,880m) on the Pare Chu (river). In addition to the previously climbed peaks of Umdung Kangri (6,643m, climbed in 1999 by JAC Tokai) and Gyadung (6,160m, climbed in 1987 by Kapadia's Indian expedition) there are several unclimbed peaks, among which Pt 6,367m and Pt 6,321m are quite fascinating.

(2) Peaks north Dutung on the Pare Chu. Mountains in this area north of the Talking Valley have not been attempted. Notable peaks are 6,231m, 6,210m, 6,204m, and 6,122m.

(3) Peaks southwest of Kharsa Gongma, which is situated at the confluence of the Pare Chu and Pakshi Lamur rivers. There are two big unclimbed peaks opposite Kharsa Gongma: Pt 6,307m (6,401m on the Russian map) and Pt 6,320m a little farther east. The west and south flanks are nearly 1,000m high but composed of loose rock. The north sides look more promising, with small glaciers rising to both peaks.

(4) Peaks at the head of Pakshi Lamur. The glacier at the head of this valley is rather large compared to those in neighboring areas. It is surrounded by five peaks: Parilungbi (6,166m, climbed in 1987 by Indians), Dhhun (6,200m, climbed in 1999 and 2005 by JAC Tokai) and three unclimbed peaks, Lhakhang (6,205m), Pt 6,228m, and Pt 6,247m.

(5) Peaks surrounding the head of a side glacier west of the main Pakshi Lamur Glacier. There are four peaks here, two of which, Pts 6,240m and 6,100m, were climbed by an Indian (Bengal) party in 2004. The other two are beautiful, unclimbed, snow-covered mountains of 6,181m and 6,160m.

TSUNEO SUZUKI, *Japanese Alpine Club*

KINNAUR

Pts 6,132m and 6,154m, first ascents. These previously unclimbed mountains are situated at the head of the Armasong Nala, which drains into the Baspa River. A 13-member team from West Bengal led by N. Prasad Rao traveled via Sangla, Chhitkul, and Dunthi in the Baspa Valley to a base camp at Nithal Thach (4,380m) on the banks of the Armasong Nala. They established two further camps at 4,880m and 5,560m. From the highest camp both peaks were climbed on the same day, August 19, by the leader with Subrata Banerjee, Bimal Krishna Biswas, Sanjoy Ghosh, Somnath Hazara, Ajoy Mondal, Molay Mukherjee, and Dilip Tirky with four high-altitude porters: Kolbahadhur, Lalbadhur, Balwant Singh and Himmat Singh.

There are few 6,000m peaks in the Baspa. The Indo-Tibet Border Police have been active in the area for many years, and some of their officers have written authentically about the valley. However, there does not appear to be any written record of their reported ascents of the three high peaks north of Dunthi.

HARISH KAPADIA, *Honorary Editor, The Himalayan Journal*

GANGOTRI

Meru Central (Shark's Fin), east face, attempt. The Korea Meru Peak Expedition comprised Kim Sae-jung and Cho U-ryeong from the Extreme Leader Alpine Club, Lee Sang-woo and Jang

Seon-tae from the Bong-ahm Alpine Club, and Park Young-sik from the Gyeong-hee University Alpine Club. The team arrived at Tapovan base camp on August 8 to open a new route on the east face of Meru Central (6,320m), commonly referred to as the Shark's Fin. On August 11 they established advanced base at 4,300m and then took roughly five days to fix 500m of rope to Camp 1 at 5,400m. They continued fixing rope and after 15-days reached a high point of 5,800m, at the base of the rock wall forming the Fin. Rockfall during the day forced them to climb and ferry gear at night, until the small hours of the morning. Just preparing to start climbing on the Fin took 30 days.

On September 9 they began climbing the main rock wall, but the weather deteriorated. Over the next three days, despite consistently poor weather and high difficulties, they reached 6,000m but shortly after decided to abandon the route. They began a perilous descent in atrocious conditions. As their sole concern was self-preservation, they abandoned the majority of the gear and fixed line. Their equipment remains fixed on Meru Peak, as trials of the Shark's Fin does on their minds.

LEE YOUNG-JUN, *Korea (translated by Peter Jensen-Choi)*

Shivling (6,543m), north face and northwest ridge. Well-acclimatized after their second ascent of Muztagh Ata's southeast ridge, reported elsewhere in this *Journal*, Kazuya Hiraide (26) and Kei Taniguchi (33) arrived in Delhi on September 19 and by the 28th had established base camp at Tapovan. By then Polish and Czech parties attempting Shivling and a Korean team on Meru had given up, because of bad weather, and headed home.

The weather started to improve, and the Japanese pair spent from September 29 to October 7 reconnoitring their descent on the west ridge, looking at both the north and south sides of Shivling, and climbing the north side of Baby Shivling (5,500m) to complete their acclimatization. Their main objective was the unclimbed

Shivling North Face Route

▲ TOP(6513m)
ice&snow 60
▲ C3(6200m)
rock IV+~V
▲ C2(6070m)
hard snow 50~70°
60~70°
▲ C1(5650m)
rock IV~IV+
snow&ice 40~50°
▲ ABC(4745m)

A foreshortened view of the north face of Shivling (6,543m) showing the new Japanese line on the north face to northwest ridge (Hiraide-Taniguchi). The ridge bounding the left side of this face is the north ridge, first climbed by Japanese in 1980 but more directly in 1993 by Italians and with an impressive direct finish in 2000 by Huber and Wolf. The lower section of the Japanese route corresponds to the 1987 Czechoslovak Route, which continues more directly to the top section of the northwest ridge. The latter is still unclimbed in its entirety. *Kazuya Hiraide*

northwest ridge, which they planned to reach via the lower section of the north face.

On October 8 they left base camp with climbing gear, a tent, light bivouac bags, and food for five days. On a flat rock at the foot of the north face they made their first camp, at 4,750m. The following day they crossed a crevassed zone and front-pointed the initial snow and ice slope. They quickly reached the first rock barrier, which was to prove one of the key parts of the route. They were unable to dry-tool and had to resort to conventional rock climbing, cleaning snow from the rock as they went. They camped at 5,650m, in the lower section of the large funnel-shaped snowfield.

On the 10th the angle of the snow slope became steeper than anticipated, generally 50–70° but in some parts even steeper. The snow was hard and compact, and though they had feared this section might be avalanche-prone, there was actually very little danger. Small powder-snow avalanches sometimes occurred, but were harmless. Toward the top of the funnel-shaped snowfield the climbers stopped for the night, at 6,070m, and made a hanging bivouac.

On the 11th they tackled the second rock wall, which was another crux and led to the junction with the northwest ridge. Though the last part was difficult, they were able to exit above the big serac barrier. The ridge ahead was not so easy, and they had to remain roped. They set up their third camp at 6,200m.

On the 12th they ascended the upper part of the northwest ridge and, after surmounting a section of 60°snow/ice, reached the summit of Shivling at midday. Half an hour later they began the descent, stopping again at their top camp, so they could descend through the serac barrier in well-frozen conditions the following morning. From there they reached the Normal Route (west ridge), arriving at base camp the same day.

TAMOTSU NAKAMURA FROM INFORMATION PROVIDED BY KAZUYA HIRAIDE, *Japanese Alpine Club*

Editor's note: The northwest ridge integral is unclimbed, and the Japanese reached the crest via the lower section of the 1987 Czechoslovakian Route on the north face.

CENTRAL GARHWAL

Kamet, Normal Route, ascent. In the autumn Sue Nott and I spent seven weeks on an expedition to Kamet. We were plagued by horrible weather. On the approach from base camp to advanced base we got trapped between camps for five days while more than 3½m of snow fell. We had been in India for 25 days and only seen our objective, the unclimbed east face, for 10 minutes. And we still hadn't made it to advanced base, which is only a three-day hike from base camp in normal conditions.

Kamet (7,756m) is situated close to the Indo-Tibet border, and a peak permit for foreigners requires permission from both India and China. Receiving this permit would have likely been impossible without the help of Ibex Expeditions, our great outfitter. One condition of the permit was a strict six-week time limit. Our original plan was to acclimatize on the Normal Route (the northeast face, first climbed by Lewa, Holdsworth, Smythe, and Shipton way back in 1931), and, after resting, go for it on the east face. When nearly out of time, we had to compromise and go for the summit by the Normal Route. Two of the three teams with plans for this route had already pulled the plug. These large teams had many high-altitude porters and twelve climbing Sherpas. The mountain was covered with deep snow, and the avalanche hazard was high. On September 30 we left our one-tent advanced base at 5,500m and started up with light packs, five days food, and fuel. We found spectacular yet technically easy terrain on this historic route, but the upper snow slopes scared the crap out of us. Here, we broke trail in deep snow, finding sections of highly tensioned wind slab. These slabs would kindly remind us of our insignificance by giving off a more than subtle "whoop."

After five days of hard work we reached the summit at 1:30 p.m. on October 4, in strong afternoon winds. Upon returning to Delhi we heard news of a tragic season: eight climbers killed on other expeditions. Though we didn't get to attempt the east face, we had a great adventure and made many new friends.

JOHN VARCO

The ca. 1,800m-high unclimbed southeast face of Kamet (7,756m). With the obvious central line predominantly snow (though interrupted by more tricky rock barriers) and the relatively easy slopes of the Normal Route behind the right skyline, this face could succumb to an alpine-style ascent by a well-acclimatized party. *Satya Dam*

Pk. 6,123m, first ascent, east ridge; Bidhan Parvat, ascent, southeast face. A 10-member expedition from Kolkata, led by Amitava Roy, planned to ascend of Devban (6,855m). The team reached base camp at Thaur Udiar (4,095m) in the Amritganga Valley on June 26 and established three camps up the Devban Glacier. From Camp 3 Susanta Basak, Arupam Das, and Roy made the first ascent of an unnamed peak of 6,123m by the east ridge. On the following day, from the same camp, Das and Sherpas Gyalgen, and Tashi climbed the southeast face of Bidhan Parvat (6,520m). They did not attempt Devban due to avalanche danger. [Bidhan Parvat was first climbed in 1937 by Frank Smythe on his famous Valley of the Flowers expedition. The second ascent came in 1968, when the mountain was unofficially named by a team from Bengal, in memory of Sir Bidhan Chandra Roy, former Chief Minister of Bengal. Although unendorsed, the name seems to have stuck—Ed.]

HARISH KAPADIA, *Honorary Editor, The Himalayan Journal*

EASTERN GARHWAL

Changabang (6,864m), north face attempt. The Korean Changabang North Face Expedition was led by Chung Seong-kwon and had as members Ha Ho-sung, Kim Ji-sung, Lee Keun-tak, and Lee Min-sook. They arrived at base camp (4,600m) on May 3, established advanced base (5,200m) below the face, and on the 7th began fixing 250m of line up a moderate ice face that lay roughly 350m above the bergschrund and to the right of the 1998 Russian-American Lightning Route. Deteriorating weather made progress difficult, and the Koreans didn't reach the site of Camp 1 (5,700m) until the 16th. On the 18th, despite depressing snow conditions, they fixed more rope and hauled food and gear to Camp 1. They then made little progress until the weather finally cleared on the 24th. During the intervening time they ferried more gear to Camp 1. They reached Camp 2 (5,850m) on the 25th.

Although provisions were sufficient, the climbers realized that their remaining time was running short, and faster progress would be needed to reach the summit. They established a portaledge at Camp 2 on the 26th. The following day the weather remained clear enough for two members to work the route toward Camp 3, while three others rappelled to retrieve more rations from base camp and advanced base. The weather deteriorated again halfway through the ninth pitch, and the two lead climbers rappelled to the portaledge hoping for a positive forecast for the next day.

After a night of subzero temperatures, they were up at 4 a.m. in promising weather. However, the next two pitches (70m) proved a struggle. There were plenty of hook placements, but the thought of running it out for great distances was overbearing, and they opted to bolt every 8m until they reached more ice. From there, they climbed two more 50m pitches, at the top of which they placed two more bolts where the ice had thinned enough for granite to show through. Eventually, however, snowy weather again prevailed, and they rappeled into the night.

They spent the following days sitting out bad weather and trying to haul the portaledge to the next camp, but to no avail. On June 2 the weather cleared, allowing Kim Ji-sung and Lee Keun-tak to jug through pitch 14 and Ji-seong to lead another 50m aid pitch, before worsening weather forced him down. Soon after he returned to the portaledge, the snow showers ceased. The following day Ha Ho-sung aided pitch 16 using a plethora of exquisitely solid skyhook and talon edges. Although the proposed site for Camp 3 was still some distance away, it seemed attainable.

However, once again that cruel joke called snowfall returned. The expedition leader, Chung Seong-kwon, sat there feeling the toll of attrition, staring over at his partner, watching the snow fall even harder at their high point of 6,100m, and guessing how cold Ho-sung must be. Despite sufficient provisions, hope of good weather, time, and the will to stay on the wall had all gradually withered away with the falling of the snow. He knew they must go down.

The Korean Changabang attempt was graded VII WI5 A2. The team wishes to thank The North Face Korea and Korean Trango for their sponsorship.

LEE YOUNG-JUN, MOUNTAIN MAGAZINE, *Korea (translated by Peter Jensen-choi)*

Changabang, west face, Boardman-Tasker Route, attempt. The boulders basked in the sun, 9½km of them, wave after wave of rock misery. Waiting. The chance of breaking an ankle, breaking a leg, or being trapped by two closing together like the doors of an aircraft hangar, was ever-present. I hated it.

A new route on Changabang's west face sounded good a few thousand kilometers away, an age away with a team of four to spread the load. The intended team of four turned into a pair, Stu McAleese and I. A late arrival made it three. Olly Sanders was going to be in India, so it made sense to drag him along.

When we decided to climb the west face, we had the impression that the Nanda Devi Sanctuary had re-opened since its closure in 1982. This was not the case, and to climb on the west face we would have to approach from the north, via the Bagini Glacier. This caused several difficulties: we couldn't see the west face; the approach was now 9km over possibly the worse moraine I have encountered; and to reach the Bagini Ridge we were faced with a 450m climb resembling the North Face of the Tour Ronde in the French Alps.

The type of climb and the overall cost dictated we had more gear than I was accustomed to. A capsule-style expedition is not one I would normally consider, but the $6,500 that the IMF and local government charged, the $6,000 the agent charged, the flights, the freight, and insurance charges, all made for a total bill of $15,000. I am not proud to say the cost had a direct effect on style.

We spent seven days carrying and establishing advanced base and three more ferrying and wading, carrying, climbing, fixing, and hauling, until the rope hung 100m short of the ridge.

The snow started as normal mid-afternoon. Seventy-two hours later, after 1½m had fallen, it stopped. I had developed a tooth abscess, and our tent was buried. The decision to go to base camp was easy.

Nine hours of snow-covered boulders and dreaming of base camp comfort passed. Camp was not the haven we had hoped. The tents were flattened and covered in snow. Our kit had been left inside and had become a soaked-sodden mess. Rivers ran under, around, and through the tents. The ground looked like a rugby pitch at the end of a game.

Sanders left with Dutch who had been attempting the north face of Changabang. After four days of high pressure had melted the snow and turned the meadow into a barren, dust-driven desert, the hill called. McAleese and I answered.

When we reached advanced base after five hours, a huge concern was alleviated. The tent was intact, although two broken poles called for improvisation. However, the food stash was beyond improvisation. Animals had raided it, and we were now on a time line imposed by starvation.

It took four days in freezing, bone-numbing temperatures to reach the Bagini Ridge and another three to establish a camp. The angle of the slope leading onto the ridge from the Nanda Devi Sanctuary was a lot less than from the north. Pete Boardman and Joe Tasker had repeatedly soloed this ground with loads, escaping to the comfort of base camp. This was a luxury not available to us on the steep and technical north side. The gendarme between the col and our present position, the same spot as Boardman and Tasker's Camp 1 at 5,480m, looked difficult to pass, and I marveled at their tenacity.

The new route was not going to happen. Seven days of food remained if we followed a controlled diet. We decided to attempt the Boardman-Tasker line up the northwest ridge, knowing there was no chance to summit, but hoping for a miracle.

Miracles didn't happen. The weather became unsettled once more, the temperature plummeted, my tooth abscess returned, and after three days on the ridge we had only climbed 200m. However, following in Pete's and Joe's footsteps had been liberating. Respect for their achievement grew with every step. Some of the climbing we completed was mixed Scottish IV, with the meat of the route looming above: 800m of technical rock, hanging arêtes, overhangs, and blank walls with no obvious way. Boardman and Tasker stuck at it until they found a way and reached the summit, an awesome achievement that still waits a repeat. But the approach from the north does add logistical and physical difficulties.

On day five we decided this sort of existence wasn't fun and stripped the climb from our high point of 6,200m. On day six we descended, dragging all our kit to advanced base. On October 6 we left base camp.

Eight years have passed between the two expeditions on which I played at capsule-style. I find alpine-style gives more enjoyment and satisfaction, without the drudgery and monotony. You stick your neck out a little maybe, but there is much more in the way of reward—and it's cheaper. We thank the Mount Everest Foundation, British Mountaineering Council, and the committee of the Nick Estcourt Award for their generous financial support.

Nick Bullock, *U.K.*

Changabang, north face, attempt. Andreas Amons, Cas van de Gevel, Melvin Redeker, and I tried to climb 6,864m Changabang by its north face in the autumn. Arriving at base camp on August 25, we spent the first 12 days acclimatizing and load carrying to advanced base. The walk over the Bagini Glacier proved to be long and tiring, full of loose blocks. Although we were supposed to be in the monsoon, throughout this time the weather was perfect. On September 9 and 10 we fixed 300m of rope on the 1996 couloir, because we wanted to climb capsule-style with portaledges. [This line was tried in June 1996 by a British party, who retreated at 6,200m—Ed.]. The climbing was perfect, with superb, steep, solid ice.

The monsoon finally arrived, with seven days of rain, snow, and mist, or as our British neighbors, attempting the west face, put it, "fucking ming." When the weather finally cleared, we were unable to find our gear left under the face, even though we had tied it in and dug holes seven meters deep. About 10m of new snow must have accumulated below the face. With half our gear gone, we decided to climb in a lighter style. Again bad weather arrived, and with avalanches falling we retreated to base camp, which we left on September 29.

The weather seemed to be a bit off last autumn, with clear skies in August and rain in the middle of September. The north faces of Kalanka and Changabang looked absolutely great, but they are not places to be when snow starts falling.

MIKE VAN BERKEL, *The Netherlands*

KUMAUN

Nanda Devi East, east face, attempt. Marco Dalla Longa led a 12-member Italian expedition to attempt the first ascent of the east face of Nanda Devi East (7,434m). The team approached via Munsiary and the Milam Valley, establishing base camp on August 31. By September 7 they had placed three camps, the highest at 5,400m, on the central pillar of the east face. The team, which was primarily from the Bergamo region, split into three working groups, fixed ropes on the route and reached the top of the first tower on the pillar. From the 9th to the 18th a long spell of bad weather pinned them down at the higher camps. As the route was now out of the question, the climbers descended and turned their attention to nearby Nanda Lapak (5,782m). On the 23rd Ferruccio, Ferruccio, Perongelo, and Yuri reached the summit via the south ridge.

Toward the end of the expedition tragedy struck. Dalla Longa suddenly went into a coma and subsequently died of a stroke. The team's doctor suspected cerebral edema. Dalla Longa was relatively young and fit, and reportedly had no health problems during the expedition. The expedition had a satellite phone (carrying a sat phone is supposedly illegal for foreign expeditions), which could have saved his life as it was immediately used to arrange helicopter rescue. However, due to bad weather it took four days for the helicopter to arrive. The entire expedition was evacuated by air to Munsiary on the 27th and to Delhi on the following day.

HARISH KAPADIA, *Honorary Editor, The Himalayan Journal*

Nanda Kot, east ridge, attempt: Nanda Devi East, south ridge, attempt. Our approach to the Nanda Devi region began on August 30. After a three-day bus ride, six days walking up an ancient Indo-Tibetan trade route brought us to a base camp below Nanda Kot. Trails carved into the rocky gorge led from dense jungle, where we were sucked by leaches, up to high tundra. Sometimes they just ended in crumbling space, where landslides had laid waste. There were village names like Bogdwar and Lilam, and these, together with the local people, who ate dense bread while pulling on their water pipes, reminded us of Tolkien's landscapes.

By the third week our Nepali cook, Depender, was saying that he had never, throughout his 15 years working in these mountains, witnessed a worse spell of bad weather. Nearly two meters of snow had fallen; many tent poles had broken; slopes were loaded; we were chowing through our precious supply of books and rum; and even bouldering was out of the question.

Finally we got a break in the weather, and Chuck Bird, Sarah Thompson, Pete Takeda, and I started up the east ridge of Nanda Kot (6,861m), retracing the steps of a 1966 CIA-sponsored expedition, which placed a nuclear-powered surveillance device at 6,700m to spy on the Chinese. Toward the end of day two we were hit by a big storm at around 6,000m and took shelter in a crevasse. Pete Takeda takes up the story:

"We had two tents and set them up on narrow snow ledges that we chopped into the bottom of the crevasse. We must have angered the Goddess, for at half-past midnight, an avalanche poured into our cavern. It was as if someone had backed a colossal cement mixer up to the mouth of the cave and dumped hundreds of tons of cement. The snow sealed the entire entrance, save for a hole 1½ meters square. I'd felt the roar of the avalanche and somehow pulled myself from the tent in an adrenalin-crazed frenzy of thrashing and swimming. I was the only one of us to escape burial and was able to pull out Chuck before the debris could solidify around his head. Dragged from what had almost been an icy grave, he coughed up a handful of snow that had been wedged within his trachea.

We stood in the pitch black wearing only our underwear, all our gear now buried under tons of snow. The other two, Jonny and Sarah, had been tumbled to the bottom of our cave by force of the avalanche. They came to a halt near the edge of the bottomless crevasse. A meter farther and they would have either died from a vast fall or been hopelessly wedged under tons of crushing snow. As it was, I wrote them off as either dead or dying, and Chuck and I desperately dug with our bare hands in the dark for headlamps, boots, and gloves. At one point Chuck said, "You saved my life." Noting that we were nearly naked, in peril of losing fingers and toes, still facing more avalanches and the strong possibility that the cave might collapse, I responded, "No, I didn't."

Jonny and Sarah were buried but still alive. In a superhuman effort Jonny snapped a tempered aluminum tent pole, which had ended up near his face, to create an air pocket. With that primitive tool he ripped the snow-engulfed tent that was squeezing Sarah and him to death. Then, after extricating himself (naked except for a T-shirt), Jonny pulled Sarah from the remains of their tent.

After considerable effort the four of us located all our critical life-support gear. But the ordeal wasn't over yet. Around 6:30 a.m. another avalanche roared in, sealing us in what was fast becoming a tomb. I dug a wormhole through the debris, while Jonny cleared the snow from behind, ready to grab my feet and pull me out, if and when the ceiling collapsed. The tunnel was nearly five meters long before I finally broke through to the surface. Topside was a maelstrom of wind-whipped snow and constant avalanche, but at least we now had an air hole. A few hours later yet another avalanche passed over this hard-won hole, momentarily turning day into night, before finally sliding clear.

We spent four days in the cave and, when the weather finally cleared, ran for our lives.

We had little food, and our fuel supply was down to a half a gaz canister. During the harrowing descent, we were nearly wiped out by yet another avalanche as we crouched at the top of a 70m ice cliff. But we managed to pick our way down the treacherous slopes."

Across the valley an 11-member Italian expedition was attempting a new route on the east face of Nanda Devi East (the line Pete and I had planned to attempt). On their approach to the mountain a Hindu Holy Man asked the climbers to stop and make a puja ceremony for the mountain. They didn't stop. The Hindu said one of them would die on this trip. The day we were hit by the avalanche, the Italian team abandoned their route and 600m of fixed rope. Next day, just before leaving the valley, the 41-year-old leader, Marco Dalla Longa, an accomplished mountaineer, rose at sunrise to see Nanda Devi East in full glow. That morning, in full view of the mountain he'd grown to love, Dalla Longa fell unconscious and collapsed. During the subsequent night he died of what was afterwards diagnosed as a stroke.

A week later Pete and I were 200m below the summit of Nanda Devi East (7,434m), after having climbed for four days up the south ridge. I was at a hanging belay when the wind picked up, the snow started falling and the temperature quickly dropped. We had one 7mm rope, one cam, one picket, some stoppers and screws, and half a can of fuel. We had talked about "signs" the mountain might give us if she didn't want us "standing on top of her head" (as the head priest at the Nanda Devi temple had said). This seemed to be it. When fully committed to the descent, it was a bummer to see the weather improve behind us. Dwindling food, fuel, and energy precluded making another summit attempt.

After a visit to the Rishi Ganga and the taking of some water samples, we made it back to Delhi in time for terrorists to detonate three bombs. Two of them were in street markets around which we had wandered the day before. We watched the chaos from TVs in the airport, waiting to fly home.

JONNY COPP

SIKKIM

Western Sikkim, Lama Lamani North, first ascent, northwest flank and west ridge; Tinchen Kang, third ascent. In a 20-day round trip from Gangtok, between March 15 and April 3, we made three excursions on peaks in the Thangsing Valley of western Sikkim. Climbing with us were Kunzang Bhutia and Sagar Rai. The trip was an outcome of a trek to the popular Goecha La in the autumn of 2004, when we met Bhutia of the Sikkim Amateur Mountaineering Association. Both Bhutia and Rai are experienced young mountaineers who are active

Lama Lamani North (ca. 5,650m), western Sikkim, showing the route of the first ascent, up the northwest face to west ridge (AD+, Bhutia-Clyma-Payne-Rai). *Roger Payne*

in providing training for local guides and teaching rock climbing to young people in Sikkim.

After the standard trek from Yuksum to Thangsing, we reconnoitered and acclimatized on Tinchen Kang (6,010m). We followed what we believed to be the original route of ascent, climbed in 1998 by an Indo-British military expedition with fixed ropes and camps. Deep fresh snow made progress on the rocky wall below the northwest ridge slow and precarious. Having reached 5,100m on March 21, we decided to return to our valley base the following day.

An unclimbed peak due east of Lama Lamani. *Roger Payne*

After a rest and delay due to bad weather, we set off on the 25th to make a reconnaissance of the unclimbed Lama Lamani group. On the 26th we traversed from the northwest side of the group to the south ridge to look for a possible line of ascent. There were strong winds on the ridges and fresh snow underfoot. On the 27th we moved up to a position under the northwest flank of the mountain, which seemed to offer the best route of ascent. Next day we made a pre-dawn start and by 10 a.m. had made the first ascent of the north summit of Lama Lamani (ca. 5,650m). The climbing on the northwest flank and west ridge had been around AD+, mostly over snow, with rock steps and a good icy ridge. It was windy and cold on the crest, but the views were exceptional. We descended by the same route, doing some rappeling, and reached base that evening.

Tinchen Kang (6,010m) in the Thangsing Valley of western Sikkim. All three ascents of this peak have used the northwest ridge (left skyline). The first ascensionists, an Indo-British military expedition in 1998, approached the crest via the south flank facing the camera. The succeeding two parties gained the crest from the far side (north flank). On the third ascent, which was the first in alpine-style, the two-person party rated the route Alpine D. *Roger Payne*

After a day's rest just the two of us set off for an attempt on Tinchen Kang. Due to cloudy conditions we had not gotten a good view of the glacier on the northwest side of the mountain, yet despite previous glimpses of apparently threatening serac barriers, we decided to try this approach. We understood the northwest face had been climbed the previous autumn by a group sponsored by the Himalayan Club, Kolkata (*AAJ 2005*, p. 379). Strong winds limited progress on the first day, and we stopped to camp at 4,850m, near the start of the glacier slopes. Next day, in cold and windy conditions and deep snow, we reached the crest of the northwest ridge (junction with the 1998 route) and camped just below it at 5,400m. Despite appearances, the glacier route had not been threatened by seracs.

Next day, April 1, we made a pre-dawn start. Again we had to face deep snow and cold temperatures, but no wind. Getting onto the bottom of the rock wall was delicate (around UIAA IV- but probably easier when snow-free). Two fixed ropes were in place on the wall and led toward, then through, a short chimney with loose rock. Above, we reached the crest at the top of the wall. We now faced an ice wall and couloir. (On a previous trip Bhutia and Rai had reached this point but turned back because they lacked good ice-climbing equipment.) We followed the couloir, which was in good condition, for 150m and then exited onto the upper snowfields. Straightforward snow slopes led to the final summit pyramid, which we climbed on the west side to avoid a wide bergschrund. We reached the summit just before 2 p.m. Alas, warm air and clouds blew in from the southwest and obscured the view. On the summit were two snow stakes and the top of a fixed line that was otherwise buried. We removed one of the snow stakes as a souvenir for our friends at base camp.

The weather improved during the descent and allowed excellent views. We downclimbed and made three rappels to descend the rock wall. We reached our previous night's camp by 6 p.m. but, because the walkout was due to start the next morning, continued on down to reach base camp at 11 p.m. These two climbs, each made in three-day roundtrips from a base at Thangsing, demonstrate the potential for alpine-style climbs in West Sikkim.

We thank the Government of Sikkim and the Sikkim Amateur Mountaineering Association for making this trip possible, and the Mount Everest Foundation, British Mountaineering Council, and UK Sport for their support.

JULIE-ANN CLYMA AND ROGER PAYNE, *Switzerland*

Northern Sikkim, Chomoyummo, attempt and accident. In September the Indian Mountaineering Foundation (IMF) organized a high-profile expedition to Chomoyummo (6,829m) on the Tibet border. The nine-member team was led by the hugely experienced Dr. P.M. Das, Vice President of the IMF, and included two Everest summiteers and four experienced Sherpas.

While attempting the summit, seven members were caught in an avalanche. As they were swept down the slope they became entangled by the rope to which they were all tied. Five died, while two survived with serious injuries. The climbers who perished were Das, Inder Kumar and Nari Dhami (both of whom had summited Everest), Dawa Sherpa and Dawa Wangchuk from the Sonam Gyasto Mountaineering School at Gangtok. Details are sketchy, as the leading members died on the mountain.

Dr. Das was the Honorary Local Secretary of the Himalayan Club for Punjab. Hailing from Guwahati, Assam, he was a brilliant police officer who had won medals for bravery during the days of Punjab militancy. He had participated in 33 mountaineering expeditions, among

The southwest face of Chomoyummo (a.k.a Chomiomo, 6,829m) on the Sikkim-Tibet border. Dr Alexander Kellas made the historic first ascent of this peak in 1910 via relatively easy snow slopes on the Tibetan flank of the northeast (frontier) ridge. This route was repeated again in 1945 and again in 1986 by the Indian Army. It is believed that the side of the mountain shown in this photograph has never been attempted. *Lindsay Griffin*

which were Everest (reaching Camp 5 at 7,700 m), Mana and Mukut peaks (both 7,000ers), and Gorichen East (6,222m). With his death the Indian mountaineering world has lost a senior climber and able administrator.

HARISH KAPADIA, *Honorary Editor, The Himalayan Journal*

Northern Sikkim, Kangchengyao (6,889m), ascent from north. It is reported that a 14-member team from the Black Cat Division of the Indian Army made a rare ascent of this high peak in northern Sikkim. While the south side of this mountain is very formidable, the north presents relatively straightforward snow slopes, but being close to the Tibetan border and in an area of strategic importance, is only accessible to the Indian military. The team reached the summit on October 11. The first undisputed ascent of Kangchengyao was made in 1982 by an Indian Army expedition under Vijay Singh. However, the noted British explorer Alexander Kellas nearly climbed it in 1912, when he reached the lower east summit from the north.

LINDSAY GRIFFIN, *Mountain INFO, CLIMB Magazine*

ARUNACHAL PRADESH

Search for old pilgrimage route to Takpa Siri. In remote and rarely visited Arunachal Pradesh, much remains to be explored. One unexplored place had been the Subansiri River valley, in the central part of the area. In November and December a team from Mumbai explored this unique area. Prateek Deo, Wing Commander P. K. Sashindran, Sangeetha Sashindran, and I followed the ancient pilgrimage route towards Takpa Siri. Also known as the "Crystal Mountain," Takpa Siri (6,655m) is a peak just north of the border, near the Tibetan village of Migyitun, and is holy to the Tibetans, Monpas, and Tagins of Arunachal Pradesh. Traditionally a pilgrimage was undertaken every 12 years, starting from Chosam in Tibet. It followed the Tsari Chu valley to its junction with the Subansiri River and went up the Subansiri River valley to Taksing. The route then turned north along the Yume Chu. The pilgrimage would end at the holy Yume Gompa (monastery). This longer version of the pilgrimage, called *Ringkor*, was undertaken over a three-month period, and several thousand pilgrims passed along the route, staying in caves and bamboo shelters, called *Tsukang*.

Early explorers such as Bailey and Morshead visited this area from Tibet. Ludlow and later Kingdon-Ward also undertook the pilgrimage. In 1956 Tony Huber studied the pilgrimage in detail and wrote a thesis for his doctorate called "The Cult of the Pure Crystal Mountain." He recorded details of the route and various legends associated with it. However, the pilgrimage has stopped and a fine tradition been lost, because the McMahon Line or Line of Actual Control (LAC) separates Takpa Siri from the valleys of Arunachal Pradesh.

Our team followed the Ringkor route on both sides of the border, keeping as much as possible to Indian territory. From Guwahati, four days and 850km of road led via Tezpur, Itanagar, Kimin, Ziro, and Daporijo to Limiking and the starting point of our trek. The initial section involved a steep 600m climb and eventually led to Tame Chung Chung (*place of snakes*). From there we explored the Tsari Chu valley as far as Bidak, a little short of Maja, as farther on it became Tibetan territory. Later we explored the Subansiri valley and trekked to Taksing, the last village on the India side. From there you can look towards the LAC and the junction of the Chayal Chu and Yume Chu. The point where these two rivers merge is the start of the Subansiri, which flows down to meet the Brahmaputra on the Assam plains.

HARISH KAPADIA, *Honorary Editor, The Himalayan Journal*

The remote and rarely seen 6,655m peak of Takpa Siri, the holy "Crystal Mountain," which rises just north of the Arunachal Pradesh border with Tibet. The mountain remains unattempted, although in 1999 a small team, jointly led by Balwant Sandhu and Doug Scott. gained permission to approach the peak via the heavily forested Khurung Valley. Unfortunately, by the time the team had completed the long and arduous approach to base camp, nearly every member was either sick or injured, and the expedition was abandoned. *Harish Kapadia*

Nepal

ANNAPURNA HIMAL

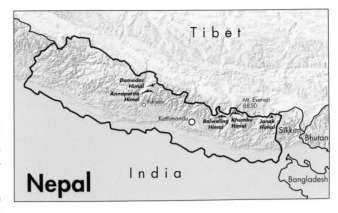

Annapurna, 14th for Viesturs, accident. The well-known American mountaineer Ed Viesturs went to Cho Oyu to acclimatize and then quickly to his last 8,000er, Annapurna I. The north face of this 8,091m mountain, the 10th highest in the world, is notorious for fatal avalanches. Viesturs went in the spring of 2000 and witnessed constant avalanching all across the face. He returned from having climbed no higher than 5,900m and declared he would never go there again. His next attempt, in 2002, was via the long east ridge, which he decided was not for him. So he was back on the north face after all.

This time he and his frequent partner, Viekka Gustafsson of Finland, already well-acclimatized, moved quickly up the face, pitched their high camp at just 6,900m, waited three days for the wind to drop, and were on the summit on May 12, less than two weeks after arriving at base camp. Viesturs was amazed by how free the face was from avalanching.

On the summit he felt it was "a dream come true. I had my doubts that I'd ever get there, because of our conservatism and its dangerous avalanching." He thinks he is the seventh or eighth person to scale all 8,000ers without using bottled oxygen [in fact, he appears to be only the fifth to complete all 14 without using oxygen on either ascent or descent—Ed.]. What next? "Now that I've gotten the 8,000ers out of the way, maybe some 7,000ers in Nepal; maybe Antarctica." He had no definite plans yet.

Viesturs and Gustafsson left the mountain on May 14 without having experienced avalanche problems. On the 18th four men from an Italian team led by Abele Blanc reached 6,300m in the same gully climbed by the American and Finn, when suddenly huge blocks of ice, some 3m square, came crashing down. Christian Kuntner, for whom Annapurna was the last 8,000er he had left to scale, received fatal internal injuries. Blanc, who was in the lead, was struck on the side of his head so hard that he was unconscious for 18 hours and has no memory of the incident. Two of his ribs were broken. (Annapurna was his final unclimbed 8,000er also.) The last two men going up the shallow couloir, Stephan Andres and Marco Barmasse, were not so seriously hurt.

ELIZABETH HAWLEY, *AAC Honorary Member, Nepal*

KUTANG HIMAL

Swelokan, south face and northwest ridge attempts. A small Japanese team became the first climbers to attempt the remote 6,180m Swelokan, which lies on the Tibet border north-north-east of Manaslu, in what is sometimes referred to as the Kutang Himal. Base camp was established at just over 4,400m in the upper Buru Gandaki, from where Sadmasu Kitagawa and

Hiroh Shogo had originally planned to attempt the south face. However, before reaching this point Shogo had been forced to retire by altitude sickness, so Kitagawa made his first attempt with Dorchi Sherpa. On April 27 these two reached only 5,200m, where a rock barrier blocked the glacier up which they were traveling. They moved base camp to the northwest and on May 2 camped at 5,400m on the southwest face. Next day they reached 5,800m on the northwest ridge, only to find the crest above was sharp, with loose rock and fresh snow. They gave up, though they noted that the south face would provide a good route for technical climbers.

TOM NAKAMURA *and the* JAPANESE ALPINE NEWS

DAMODAR HIMAL

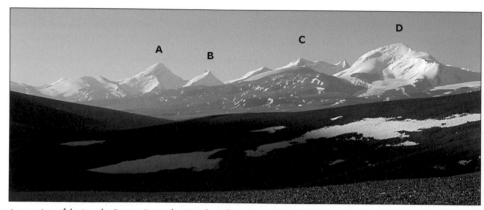

A rare view of the Lugula Group, Damodar Himal, and mountains of the Peri Himal from the northwest. Identifying little known peaks can be an inexact science but it is thought that (A) is Ratna Chuli (7,035m, first climbed in October 1996 by a large joint Nepalese-Japanese expedition along the west ridge over the 6,604m West Summit, climbed three times since), (B) is Pt 6,687m, and (C) is Pt 6,572m on the long east ridge of Lugula. Peaks behind C form part of the Peri Himal. (D) Is definitely the unclimbed Lugula (6,899m). *Peter Ackroyd*

Pt 6,417m, first ascent; corrections to some previous reports on Gaugiri.

In May 2002 Americans Peter Ackroyd and Jim Frush made the first ascent of Gaugiri, an often snowless but isolated 6,110m rock pyramid on the Tibet border. The Nepalese Ministry of Tourism places Gaugiri at 84° 11' 16" E, 29° 02' 45" N. This agrees exactly with its position as marked on the new HGM Finn map (Sheet 2984-13: the HGM Finn maps are generally considered the official cartographic reference to the Nepal Himalaya) and also with its reference in Classification of the Himalaya, a scholarly work published in the *AAJ 1985* by Adams Carter. However, the Finnish map marks the Damodar Kunda Lakes, a notable pilgrimage site, immediately below (and north west of) Gaugiri, where there are in fact a few small ponds at 5,420m. The true lakes lie some nine kilometers south (considerably further when walking this terrain) close to where sheet 2884-01 shows some very small lakes just north of the Namta Khola. This confusion led to the American pair separating from their porters and spending a night out without equipment before the team eventually re-united—see *AAJ 2003* pp. 385-386 for a full report. The American route up the southwest ridge was repeated by Austrians in 2004 for what is now believed to be the second ascent of the mountain.

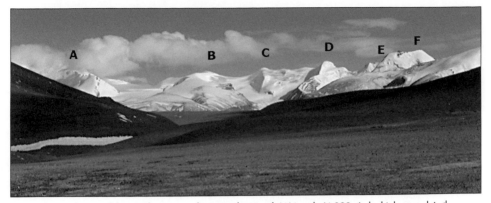

A rare view south toward the Lugula group in the Damodar Himal. (A) Lugula (6,899m), the highest peak in the group and located on the Nepal-Tibet border. (B) Bhrikuti Sail (6,361m, first climbed in 1982 by a Japanese expedition). (C) Pt 6,337m (also climbed in 1982). (D) Pt 6,358m (also climbed in 1982). (E) Kumlung (6,355m). (F) Pt 6,328m. The Damodar Khunda (ca. 5,000m) is hidden behind the foreground ridge in front of Pt 6,358m. *Peter Ackroyd*

In 2003 two parties were reported to have climbed Gaugiri (see *AAJ 2004* p. 393). Australian Anna Brooks and her naturalized Australian partner, Ken McConnell (from Scotland) trekked with their Nepalese team to the true Damodar Kunda, hoping to climb Gaugiri. They did not have a copy of the Finnish map and were not carrying an altimeter but during the trek met four climbers, three Spanish and one Andorran, who were on their way out of the area, believing they had just made an ascent of Gaugiri via the north face to north east ridge. Pep Aced and one of his partners both carried altimeters and confirmed readings of 6,270m on the summit. Unfortunately, it appears that in a report submitted in Kathmandu, the altitude was mistakenly transcribed as 6,720m. This led to a later assumption that as the Spanish peak must lie south of the true Damodar Lakes, it was possibly Khamjungar, the only mountain of that height in the region.

Talking with local goat herders based around the lakes, Ongdi Sherpa, the Australian's Sirdar, was told that the Spanish climbed a nice snowy pyramidal summit that was clearly visible south of the lakes (and which incidentally they were told was Gaugiri), but that the herders in fact referred to another peak a little further east in the range as Gaugiri (the name simply means "yak horn" and it is most likely that herders refer to several peaks by that title). The Australians decided to climb the same peak as the Spanish (via the same route) and after crossing the main Namta Khola and climbing a scree gully to an advanced camp, reached the summit by mid morning the following day (Alpine PD). The relatively short ascent and high snow line confirmed that the peak was nowhere near 6,700m.

Later, it became obvious to both Australian and Spanish groups that they had not climbed the Gaugiri of Ackroyd and Frush. Brooks re-examined her photographs, specifically relating panoramas with the topography of the Finnish map. Ackroyd provided further assistance. Brooks, and subsequently Ackroyd, concluded that while the Finnish Map marks a summit of 6,270m in the arc of peaks to the southwest of Damodar Khunda, it seems much more likely that both Spanish and Australians climbed Pk 6,417m, a little further to the southeast. This would actually agree with Aced's altimeter reading: although he measured 6,270m on the summit, his reading for the Damodar Khunda Lakes was c4,800m, which is actually around 200m too low. If there was no significant change in the weather during their ascent, the Spanish could well have climbed to over 6,400m.

Looking north from the summit of Pokharkan in the Damodar Himal. (A) Pt 6,358m, (B) Pt 6,337m, (C) Bhrikuti Sail (6,361m), (D) Pt 6,285m, (E) Lugula (6,899m), (F) Pt 6,760m, (G) Pt 6,260m and (H) Chako (6,704m). The big peaks to the right are officially unclimbed and lie on the Tibetan frontier. It seems likely that A and B, and possibly D were climbed by the 1982 Japanese Bhrikuti expedition. *Martin Scott*

Pk 6,417m: first ascent (October 8, 2003) by Josep Aced (leader), Serge Philippe Benet, Adria Font and Francesc Zapater; second ascent (October 21, 2003) by Anna Brooks, Ken McConnell (leader), Dendi Sherpa and Ongdi Sherpa.

LINDSAY GRIFFIN, FROM INFORMATION PROVIDED BY PETER ACKROYD *and* ANNA BROOKS.

PERI HIMAL

Kang Guru, avalanche tragedy to French expedition. The worst disaster ever to befall an expedition in the Nepalese Himalaya struck a seven-member French team trying to climb 6,981m Kang Guru. The only previous death on the mountain was that of a West German named Bernd Arenz, who died in a fall on October 24, 1985. On October 20, 2005, all the French and 11 of their Nepalese employees, who were inside their base camp tents after the members' late-afternoon tea, were swept by a giant avalanche into a deep gorge below. All 18 perished. These included 60-year old leader Daniel Stolzenberg, his wife, three high-altitude climbers, base camp cook and kitchen boys, and low-altitude load-carrying porters. Several other porters were outside their tents at the time and managed to survive. They trekked to the nearest village, Meta, where they met a French-Israeli expedition planning to climb another mountain in the area, Ratna Chuli. This team immediately informed the French embassy in Kathmandu of the disaster. (Because of snow conditions, the Ratna Chuli team made no attempt to continue to their peak).

During early attempts to retrieve the bodies, only one, that of Bruno Chardin, a ski resort manager, was found before the search was suspended due to more avalanches. In the meantime specialists in avalanche searches arrived from France with special equipment and two sniffer dogs. By mid-November, when they called off their work until early the next year, they had discovered only the bodies of another French member, Jean-Francois Jube, an advisor to the French Ministry of Youth and Sports, and a low-altitude porter, Manilal Gurung.

The previous record death toll by avalanche to a single expedition in Nepal occurred in April 1972 and involved a Korean team on Manaslu. Ten Nepalese, four Koreans, and one Japanese cameraman were killed when an avalanche struck their tents at 3:15 a.m. But most of the Koreans were inexperienced in the Nepalese Himalaya, whereas at least two of the Frenchmen had been to Nepalese or Pakistani 8,000m mountains, and all of them lived in mountainous parts of France. Stolzenberg, for example, came from Chamonix, was a professional guide and a professor at the prestigious ENSA (National School of Skiing and Alpinism), where he had worked for over 30 years. The leader of the Nepalese staff was an experienced Sirdar, Iman Gurung, who had summited Everest twice, most recently in May this year, as well as Cho Oyu twice.

It is easy to be wise after the event, and some people questioned the wisdom of the base camp's location, as it was surrounded by 35-40° slopes. One porter reportedly suggested that the camp be moved to what he considered a safer location downhill, but his proposal was not acted upon.

A noted French climbing instructor, Jean Coudray, who came to Kathmandu after he had discussed this subject with previous Kang Guru leaders, noted that the team had placed its base camp at the normal site. "In this area there is no place for base camp that is completely safe; there is no safer site than the one everyone has used." Furthermore, he pointed out, there had been continuous heavy snowfall for many hours. The result was a powder-snow avalanche, which is the worst kind, because it can travel at 200+ km/hour down a slope of 30° or more, and its target is impossible to predict: it can often shift direction.

Kang Guru is situated in the Manang region northeast of Annapurna. It lies east of Pisang Peak, which is favored by climbers preferring a lower mountain and less bureaucratic red tape for a permit. In recent years Kang Guru has been a favorite of some French commercial expedition organizers. The approach route goes through colorful mountain villages. It apparently was considered safe; as mentioned above, only one climber had died on the 27 previous expeditions, and that occurred two decades ago.

ELIZABETH HAWLEY, *AAC Honorary Member, Nepal.*

Editor's Note: this disaster is second only in terms of single-avalanche death toll to the 1990 accident on Pik Lenin, where 43 climbers were engulfed in a camp. The heavy storm responsible for this accident also trapped many nearby Annapurna Circuit trekkers, some of whom were eventually evacuated by helicopter.

Gyajikang, second ascent and first complete ascent of west ridge. A primarily French commercial expedition led by Paulo Grobel to 7,047m Gyajikang made the second recorded ascent of the mountain, via a partial new route, the West Ridge Integral. The first ascent of the peak was made in October 1994 by a large Japanese-Nepalese expedition (joint leaders Taichi Fujimatsu and Gupta Bahadur Rana), which put no less than 17 people on the summit. The team fixed 1,500m of rope on the northwest spur, which they climbed to reach the west ridge at 6,600m. The summit area was so vast that, according to one Japanese member, it would have been possible to play football.

Grobel's expedition approached from the south and established base camp at 5,200m, then set up Camp 1 at 5,700m, close to the foot of the west ridge. After passing an initial section of crumbly rock, they established two more camps before reaching the broad but crevassed summit plateau. They crossed the plateau to the highest point, gained on May 2 by Grobel with Maxime Blanc, Yves Exbrayat, Michel Gayton, and Jerome Jarry (all French), and Nicolas Hougardy (Belgian). They fixed the steepest section, 35-40° slopes above Camp 2, with 350m of rope. They estimated the overall grade of this potential Himalayan classic to be IV/PD+

Information provided by PAOLO GROBEL *from his website*

Editor's note: On September 26 seven Japanese led by 70-year old Shigeyoshi Kido, with three other members over 60, and seven Nepalese reached the summit via the northwest ridge, for the third ascent. It is believed they followed the 1994 original route.

MANASLU HIMAL

P2, second ascent, via partial new route. On October 13 Ukrainians Sergei Bublyk, Sergei Kovalev, Aleksander Lavrynenko, and Orest Verbytsky, from a five-member expedition led by Kovalev, made the second ascent of P2 (a.k.a. Simnang Himal; 6,251m) via the east ridge, which they approached from the Lidanda Glacier to the south. The first ascent of this peak, which lies on the long east ridge of Peak 29 southeast of Manaslu, was made in May 2001, the year in which it was opened, by Mistislav Gorbenko, Vadim Leontiev, Sergei Pugachov, and Mikhaylo Zagimyak. Those four Ukrainians reached the col on the east ridge from the Pungen Glacier to the north and were part of a large expedition that eventually climbed a new route on Manaslu (*AAJ 2002*, p.405).

ELIZABETH HAWLEY, *AAC Honorary Member, Nepal.*

JUGAL HIMAL

Gyalzen, attempt and map identity. Our four-person, primarily American party planned to attempt Gyalzen (6,151m) on the Tibetan border. We were not successful, partially due to bad weather but more because of confusion as to identity of the peak. Gyalzen stands close to Leonpo Gang (Big White Peak) and can only be seen clearly from farther away (30km from where it is possible to view the entire Jugal). The Gyalzen marked on the HGM Finn Map is not the correct peak. The peak climbed by the 1955 women's expedition and named Gyalzen is called Gumba Chuli on the map. This was confirmed by Evelyn McNicol, who accompanied our team and was part of the 1955 expedition. After figuring all this out there was no time left to explore Gyalzen, other than climb onto a ridge coming down from Phurba Chyachu.

BECKY HARRISON

Editor's note: The first ascent of Gyalzen Peak was made on May 11, 1955, by the south face and southwest ridge by British women Monica Jackson and Elizabeth Stark, with Sherpas Mingma Gyalzen and Ang Temba. It was named after Mingma. Evelyn Camrass, her name then, was the third U.K. member of this team from the Ladies Scottish Climbing Club but did not attempt the mountain. This is generally regarded as the first all-woman Himalayan expedition and is recorded in Jackson and Stark's book, Tent in the Clouds *(1956). The peak has only received two more recorded ascents, by Japanese teams in 1960 and 1961. There are several instances of peaks being misnamed on the HMG map, generally the result of HGM giving misinformation to map makers.*

ROLWALING HIMAL

Drangang Ri, second ascent, by a new route; Ripimo Shar, possible new route; Chekigo, first authorized ascent. The goals of the Academic Alpine Club Zurich expedition to the Rolwaling were Drangnag Ri (6,757m) and Chekigo (6,257m). The team members were I (Scottish, leader), Oliver von Rotz (Swiss, deputy), Monika Hronska (Swiss, medic), Paul Hartmann (U.S.), Beatriz Vidondo (Spanish), and Marco Scarsi (Italian). We were joined by the incomparable Dhan Kumar as sirdar/cook and the equally hard-working Phule as assistant. The final "member," our liaison officer, accompanied the expedition as far as the roadhead at Dolakha, doing a good job only as a living example of the corrupt and clueless Nepalese ruling classes. He had never been out of Kathmandu and was dumbfounded by the sight of our porters gearing up: "Are they really going to carry that?"

Drangnag Ri (6,757m) seen across the Ripimo Shar Glacier from Pt 5,965m on the Nepal-Tibet border. The new route via the west face and southwest ridge is marked. The peaks on the ridge running south (right skyline) are unnamed, the first being Pt 6,508m and the far right Pt 6,662m. Bruce Normand

Our first breakfast on the trail was disturbed by local Maoist rebels, one carrying a concealed revolver, who asked for 3,000Rs per foreigner to enter an area they controlled; we paid 2,000Rs ($28) each in exchange for a stamped chit authorizing our presence. The rebels also made good stereotypes of their role: Nepalese society's bottom-feeders who have found an easier living in threats than in work. The trek took us from the rushing blue waters of the Bhote Kosi under the ramparts of Gaurishankar and into the Sherpa region of the upper Rolwaling. At the natural dam of the Tsho Rolpa we turned north along the lateral moraine of the Ripimo Shar Glacier, and on April 24 found an acceptable site for base camp at Drangnak Kharka (4,900m). Directly above base lie Pk. 5,946m and Kang Nachugo, while across the glacier are the commanding bulk of Chobutse, the fluted peak of Dragkar Go, Pk. 6,665m, and other 6,000m points leading north to Drangnag Ri.

Looking southwest at Chobutse (6,686m, on the left), Chukyma Go (6,259m, rising above the cloud in the middle and situated on the south side of the main Rolwaling Valley), and Pt 5,981m (on the near right, above the Ripimo Shar Glacier). Chobutse (a.k.a. Chobuje) has been climbed at least three times, the first in 1972 by Germans, Gustav and Nikolaus Harder, Peter Vogler, and Wolfgang Weinzierl, via the northwest ridge facing the camera (between light and shade). The right skyline (southwest ridge) was climbed by New Zealanders in 1985 and repeated in 2002 by a Frenchman, solo. Bruce Normand

The unnamed Pt 6,662m rising above the east bank of the Ripimo Shar Glacier. There is no record of this mountain having been climbed. *Bruce Normand*

Unstable weather plagued our acclimatization, and a vanguard needed showshoes to reconnoiter up-glacier. Oliver and I, then Oliver and Paul, carried loads to a dump at 5,300m, before Paul and I established an advanced base, on April 30, at 5,500m on the Ripimo Shar Glacier, below the west face of Drangnag Ri. On May 1 we crossed the upper glacier to the snow dome of Pk. 5,965m, scoring the expedition's first summit but seeing nothing in the clouds.

The other four climbers later reached advanced base and enjoyed a beautiful day on Pk. 5,965m, with impressive views of Drangnag Ri, Pk. 6,705m, Menlungtse, and Kang Nachugo. Paul and I tried the west ridge of Pk. 6,705m, also referred to as Ripimo Shar, turning back in a whiteout at 6,500m. At base camp we planned strategy. The southwest ridge of Drangnag Ri was in much worse condition than in pictures we'd seen, and the north side was simi-

The west face of Chekigo (6,257m), showing the route followed by Normand and von Rotz. The bergschrund at the base of the final snow/ice face is at ca. 5,950m. *Bruce Normand*

larly impassable. Paul and I were the only takers for the technical difficulties of its west face.

Oliver and I started the summit campaign on May 7, with the west ridge of Ripimo Shar, enjoying spectacular sunrise views of Menlungtse and Cho Oyu. The "climbing" was mostly deep trail-breaking. Rising cumulus beat us to the summit, but there was no afternoon snow. The next day was cloudless, as Paul and I readied ourselves in advanced base.

The triangular west face of Drangnag Ri has a central buttress of pink granitic rock. The left side is heavily serac-hung, and the right is fluted and cornice-hung. The safest route skirts the rock on its right. By sun up we had crossed the snowfield below the buttress and were tackling four mixed pitches, the last a full ropelength of high-quality 80° ice. Beyond were more ice gullies and a soft-snow traverse, leading into a dripping but refreezing exit couloir, where night fell. At the top the ice turned to impassable meringue, and I fell 20m, landing back beside Paul, fortunately without injuring either of us. We found a crawl-through crevasse in a neighboring fluting and settled inside for a bivouac.

The weather next morning was perfect, but Paul had severe leg cramps and decided he wasn't going anywhere. However, we couldn't descend before dark, so I picked my way cautiously to, and then along, the convoluted ridge, across a snowfield, and onto the summit crest. Clouds blew in from the west but cleared partially as I reached the top, at 4 p.m. on May 10. I had excellent views of the Rolwaling and Khumbu. I retraced my steps, avoided the ridge by climbing down 60° ice on its east side, and was back at the cave by nightfall. Leaving at midnight, we made 15 rappels down our route to the lower snowfield and were back in base by evening.

Unstable weather returned as we moved to our final project, a lightweight attempt on Chekigo. Now well acclimatized, Monika, Oliver, and I hiked to a new base camp at 5,000m, arriving in a snowstorm. The next day we climbed the glacier, to be engulfed in a blizzard near the Manlung La (5,600m). The morning brought clear skies on a north wind, and we headed for the direct west face. Monika lacked the confidence to solo the exposed approach ridge, turning back to wait at high camp. Oliver and I wallowed into the snow bowl below the face, then climbed eight pitches of straightforward 55° ice/névé. We completed the first recorded ascent at 2:30 p.m. on May 15, behind returning cumulus. Our rappel descent was efficient and the walk-out quick, trading the narrow

Early morning on May 15, as Bruce Normand heads along the ridge toward the snow basin below the west face of Chekigo (6,257m). The main top is on the left. Normand and Oliver von Rotz made the first authorized ascent of this peak via the ice face directly below the summit. *Oliver von Rotz*

ridge for a sprint down a serac-threatened slope to reach high camp by dark.

The trek out was uneventful, although the bus journey back to Kathmandu may have been the most dangerous event of the expedition. For the team it was a successful venture and a rich experience, but also one clouded by the current state of Nepal. The Maoist rebellion is finally a countrywide scourge, met only with political and military incompetence and paralysis. The vanishing tourist dollar is being replaced by insecurity, poverty, and fear, reflected in more begging, more praying, less civility, and fewer smiles on once-bright faces. Can this sort of damage be repaired?

The Rolwaling expedition would like to thank the Academic Alpine Club Zurich for its generous financial support. We are indebted to Chris Bonington, Eva Hronska, and especially Takanobu Sakagaki for their help.

BRUCE NORMAND, *Switzerland*

Tengi Ragi Tau East, first ascent of peak via south pillar. In autumn 2004 a team of young French alpinists attempted to climb a new route on the northeast face of Tengkangpoche. They were unable to achieve this, due to high objective and avalanche dangers, and settled for a new route on Phamlahaka [a.k.a. Tangi Ragi Tau Southeast; 6,187m; first known ascent in 2002 via the south ridge; *AAJ 2003*, p. 382—Ed.], which they climbed via the striking southwest ridge (Le Sourire de Migma; *AAJ 2005*, p.389).

The team's main players returned in October 2005 for an attempt on the neighbouring, higher, Tengi Ragi Tau East and found much drier conditions than they had the year before. Maxime Belleville, Sébastien Corret, Louis Laurent, Julien Herry, and Xavier Vimal, all aspirant high mountain guides from Chamonix, spent time acclimatizing, with an ascent of nearby Par-

The south faces of the Tengi Ragi Tau group, Rolwaling Himal: (A) Tengi Ragi Tau (6,938m), (B) Tengi Ragi Tau East (6,650m), and (C) Phamlahaka (6,187m). (1) Southeast Face (Koichi Ezaki-Ruchia Takahashi-Pasang Tamang-Tul Bahadur Tamang, 2002; first official ascent). (2) Le Pilier du Grand Darbon (south pillar) (1,300m, ED 6b WI4; Maxime Belleville-Julien Herry, 2005). (3) Le Sourire de Migma (southwest ridge) (Maxime Belleville-Philippe Cou-dray-Julian Herry-Nicolas Potard-Xavier Vimal, 2004). *Maxime Belleville*

At the top of the first tower (ca. 6,000m) during the initial attempt on the south pillar of Tengi Ragi Tau East (6,650m). *Julian Herry collection*

chamo (6,279m), before returning to base camp to prepare for the main objective, the south pillar of Tengi Ragi Tau East (6,650m; the virgin summit between 6,938m Tengi Ragi Tau and Phamlahaka). The team spent several days ferrying loads and climbing rock pitches of grade F5 and 6. That the climbing went free, with some excellent pitches, came as a pleasant surprise; they had expected it to require aid. At 6,200m they were finally repulsed by fatigue and wind, so they descended to base camp, removing all their fixed rope and gear.

With 10 days remaining, Corret, Laurent, and Vimal left camp in search of projects for future visits. Belleville and Herry stayed, motivated by their objective, which now seemed possible, given a recent stable weather forecast. They went lightweight, whittling their sacks down to 15kg, plus a 20kg haul bag. The early rock pitches went easily and, leaving gear at 6,000m on the first bivouac ledge, they set off for the second day's climbing. After mixed terrain leading to the second tower, they passed their previous high point and were on unknown terrain. A "traverse of the gods" enabled them to avoid an overhanging gendarme and reach delicate mixed ground. Above lay a sharp arête, which had posed a question from the start. Two pitches of fine crack climbing (F6a, 6b) provided the key to this passage and, farther on, they discovered a good ledge for their second bivouac. The height was 6,400m.

Belleville and Herry started climbing again at 2:30 a.m. and reached the snowy summit arête at daybreak. Max led the way to the top, climbing steep snow slopes to a final two-pitch ice gully of 55°-80°. The two reached the flat summit at 11 a.m. on November 20. They named their route Le Pilier du Grand Darbon (1,300m, ED 6b WI4) in memory of Daniel Stolzenberg who, with a group of French climbers, was lost in an avalanche on the slopes of Kang Guru the month previous [see above]. The descent took two days and required 30 rappels.

Maxime Belleville on the summit of Tengi Ragi Tau East after the first ascent via the south pillar. The Khumbu Himal is well seen in the distance, with the familiar shapes of Everest, Lhotse, and Makalu to the left, and Chamlang, Kangtega etc. just to his right. *Julien Herry*

HILARY SHARP, *Vallorcine, France*

Tengkangpoche, attempts on north side. As of the close of 2005 Tengkangpoche (6,487m), west of Namche Bazar, had been attempted by eight expeditions since it was brought onto the permitted list in 2002. All but one of these tried to climb the impressive north side. [Although lines on the northeast face and northwest face have been climbed to the east and west ridges, respectively, they terminated a long way from the summit. The peak has received at least one unauthorized ascent, by Trevor Pilling and Andy Zimet in 1984, via the east ridge—Ed.] In spring 2005 it was the turn of the Japanese, Minoru Nagoshi and Hiroshi Matsushima, who tried to climb the left side of the northeast face in poor conditions. They gave up at only 5,100m when Nagoshi was hit by an avalanche.

In the autumn Canadians Will Gadd and Scott Semple attempted two lines on the north face. On October 29 they reached 5,200m on one line, and the following day the same height on another. Instead of finding the expected ice, they found unconsolidated snow, and the pair gave up due to the threat of avalanche.

ELIZABETH HAWLEY, *AAC Honorary Member, Nepal*

MAHALANGUR HIMAL - KHUMBU SECTION

Pasang Lhamu Chuli, south ridge attempt. The three-man Italian team of Alois Brugger, Hans Kammerlander, and Karl Unterkircher attempted the south ridge of 7,350m Pasang Lhamu Chuli (formerly Jasamba). [They were seemingly unaware at the time that it had been climbed in autumn 2004 by Slovenians, Rok Blagus, Samo Kremelj, and Uros Samec (1,550m, ED M5), as reported in *AAJ 2005*, pp. 391-2—Ed.]

In late April the three Italians established base camp at 5,200m and by May 5 had placed a camp at 6,300m on the ridge. However, they were plagued by changeable weather, plenty of snow fall, and almost constant high wind, which prevented them setting up a higher camp or making much progress on the mountain. Finally, on the 17th, all three set out at 4 a.m. in strong winds and poor snow conditions for a summit attempt. Brugger turned back, but the remaining two pressed on until they reached a point estimated to be 600m below the summit. Here they judged the avalanche danger to be extreme. They retreated and gave up any further attempt. To date the mountain, renamed to commemorate the first Nepalese women to climb Everest, has only four recorded ascents.

Adapted from the web site of HANS KAMMERLANDER

Gyachung Kang, fourth ascent from Nepal, via variants to southwest spur. On October 17 Hiroshi Hanada, Eisuke Shigekawa, and Tamting Sherpa from a seven-member Japanese expedition (Fukuoka University) led by Mitsuo Uematsu, reached the summit of Gyachung Kang (7,952m) for the sixth overall ascent and fourth from Nepal. In 1988 an expedition that included Hanada and Uematsu attempted the southwest couloir, joining the 1986 French Route on the southwest spur at a height of 7,200m. Three members pushed this line to 7,800m but while descending to Camp 4 at 7,300m, one of the climbers fell to his death, and the expedition was abandoned. Last year the Japanese followed a similar route but, when close to the top, traversed right for several pitches over new ground before reaching the summit. It would appear the 1986 French Route has not been repeated in its entirety. The Korean expedition making the third ascent of the mountain in 1988 mostly climbed the southwest face between the French Route and the original 1964 Japanese Route on the northwest ridge.

LINDSAY GRIFFIN, *Mountain INFO, CLIMB Magazine*

Kyajo Ri, first recorded ascent of southeast ridge. On October 24 Seth Hobby and I established base camp at 4,600m below the east face of Kyajo Ri (6,186m). Our plan was to climb the mountain from the northeast. Photos provided by our friend and trekking agent, Ang Karma, seemed to show a series of runnels and smears up the northeast buttress that led to the upper north ridge. Whether those runnels ever existed, or perhaps this was just a dry year, is not clear, but closer inspection proved there were no obvious lines.

The best option appeared to be the southeast ridge, which we knew to have been climbed to 5,600m in autumn 2002 by the team that eventually made the first official ascent of the mountain. [Kyajo Ri was first brought onto the permitted list in 2002, and in that year was ascended via the southwest ridge; *AAJ 2003*, pp. 394-396. The mountain is believed to have received unauthorized ascents before that—Ed.] On the 29th we left our camp around 6:00 a.m. and traversed under the east face to reach the glacier leading to the col at the foot of the ridge. Gaining the glacier turned out to be one of the cruxes of the climb, with a 40m section of 85° snowy, mixed terrain. Seth then led up through another delicate mixed band to the start of the ridge, where we found a cairn left by the 2002 party. Here we dumped the stove, second rope, and our second tools, in order to move as fast as possible on the technical rock above.

The first several hundred meters were mostly easy climbing on generally good rock, with difficulties never more than 5.7-5.8. Wild towers on the first half of the ridge forced us onto the east flank, and in bypassing the second tower we had to climb into a slabby gully that led to several hundred meters of absolute choss. We regained the crest via a pitch of 5.8 X and arrived below the final rock tower. There was no easy way to avoid this tower, so I downclimbed a little, then traversed to a series of good-looking holds that led round a corner. The holds were positive but the moves a few degrees beyond vertical; the sack and big boots, combined with the altitude of 5,900m, made it all feel serious. From a stance, a short pendulum got me to a ledge and easier climbing. From here we simul-climbed over easy rock and mixed terrain all the way to the summit ridge, which proved to be one of the most aesthetic mountain features either of us had climbed.

Kyajo Ri (6,187m) from a base camp at 4,600m to the east. The route followed by Americans Hobby and Kear, to make the first recorded ascent of the southeast ridge, is marked. *John Kear*

We didn't linger on the summit, approaching darkness and a cold wind prompting a hasty descent. We rappelled the southwest ridge and continued all the way down to the Kyajo Ri Glacier, below the south face. The only problem was that our camp was on the other side of the mountain. Tired, hungry, and out of water, we reached it by quality alpine suffering, with the biggest hurdle being climbing 600m of frozen kitty litter to regain the col at the foot of the southeast ridge. A few rappels and a glacier slog led us to our camp, 21 hours after leaving. We graded our route V 5.9 AI3.

JOHN KEAR, *AAC*

Cholatse, first winter ascent of north face, by new variants to French Route. Koreans Park Jung-hun and Choi Kang-sik reached the summit of 6,440m Cholatse at midday on January 16, having made the first winter ascent of the north face. The two arrived at base camp (4,200m) on January 2 and climbed East Lobuje to acclimatize. Due to the onset of poor

The 1,400m north face of Cholatse (6,440m) in winter. (1) Slovenian variant to 1984 American Route (northeast face to southeast ridge) (M6 6a 90°, Humar-Kozelj-Opresnik, 2005). (2) 2003 Korean attempt to 6,000m (110° mixed and aid sections, high point reached on October 30 by Kim Chae-ho and Hwang Young-soon). (3) Swiss direct finish (F5 M6 90°, Steck, 2005). (4) French Route (90°, Badaroux-Batoux-Challamel-Mora-Robach, 1995). (5) Korean first winter ascent (90° mixed and some aid, Park Jung-hun-Choi Kang-sik, 2005). (6) 2002 Korean attempt to 5,200m. *Peter Jensen-Choi*

weather on the 9th, the two men were unable to begin their alpine-style ascent until the 13th. They traveled as lightly as possible, packing for only one night out and two days climbing. They took a 55-liter rucksack, two 55m ropes (a 7mm and a 5mm Kevlar), 15 pitons, 10 slings, two quickdraws, four screws, a fish hook, three RURPs, two snow stakes, a bivouac sack each, one gas canister, one stove, two Sierra cups, power bars, power gel, coffee, cocoa, and only two biscuits between the two.

Cholatse (6,440m) from the west, showing the line of the Standard Route on the southwest ridge. This was the line descended by Koreans Park Jung-hun and Choi Kang-sik after their successful winter ascent of the north face. The accident took place just as the pair was close to the end of the glacier at the bottom of the picture. To the left of the Standard Route, the prominent West Rib (Collins-Selters-Walter, 1988) rises to join it above half-height. Left again is the difficult Northwest Ridge (Selters-Walter, 1988), and in profile to its left is the north face. The big peak on the right is Tawoche (6,495m). *Lee Young-jun collection*

Before sunrise the two men trudged through crusty snow to the main wall. They began the lower section with three pitches on a moderate 60° spur. After the fifth pitch they followed a seven-meter-wide, 80° couloir, where each pitch of blue ice took from 40 minutes to one-and-a-half hours. At around 1 p.m. the climbers reached a difficult section of black ice at 5,600m. One pitch above, at 5,650m, they made their first bivouac.

By 8:00 the following morning Park had worked through an overhanging section using RURPs and a hook. The pair then made a short traverse left and climbed four pitches of 75° mixed climbing to reach a fork in the couloir at 5,900m. Here, they made their second bivouac.

Park Jung-hun (left) with Choi Kang-sik at Cholatse base camp prior to their successful winter ascent of the north face. *Lee Young-jun collection*

The next morning they followed the right branch, a 65° couloir, and made their third bivouac on the northwest ridge, just five pitches shy of the summit. They began their trudge to the top by 8:00 the next morning, summited around noon, shot three rolls of film, then began their descent of the southwest ridge. To speed their descent, they left pitons and ice-screws and by 4 p.m. had made it down to walkable terrain. There they shortened the length of rope between them.

Low on the glacier Choi suddenly fell 25m into a bergschrund 1m wide and 50m deep. He broke a leg, and Park fractured ribs in his fall. By the time Choi had been brought to the surface, freezing darkness had descended. Despite being only four hours from the nearest habitation, Na La, their injuries, lack of provisions, and exhaustion forced them to bivouac for a fourth night. The two men reached Na La the next day and asked an elderly man to summon a rescue helicopter. Both climbers were successfully evacuated, but Park eventually lost eight fingers, while Choi lost nine fingers and all of his toes. All the camera film was lost in the bergschrund, and while Park returned the following spring to see if he could find the camera and film, he was unsuccessful. This ascent is the most dramatic and, despite the injuries, most acclaimed effort of all winter alpine-style first ascents made by Koreans.

LEE YOUNG-JUN, *Corean Alpine Club (translated by Peter Jensen-Choi)*

Cholatse, northeast face, second ascent with variant. At first believing they were opening a new route, Slovenians Tomaz Humar, Ales Kozelj, and Janko Opresnik climbed the steep and icy 1,300m northeast face of 6,440m Cholatse, more or less following the 1984 American Route to the upper part of the face (the Slovenians climbed an excellent 60m icefall right of the original line to gain the central gully system), before making a long traverse left to reach, then climb, the 1982 Swiss Route up the southeast ridge. The original and only route to ascend the entire face—a seven-day alpine-style push in November 1984 by Todd Bibler, Catherine Freer, Renny Jackson, and Sandy Stewart—remains unrepeated. The Swiss Route was climbed on the second ascent of the mountain by Nikolas Alpiger, Heidi Ludi, and Kancha Tamang, and 11 days later by Alpiger (again) and Werner Zaher.

The three Slovenians acclimatized by first climbing 6,083m Cholu Peak, then began their ascent of Cholatse on April 19. They were hit by bad weather on the second day, forcing an early bivouac in a snow cave. On the 21st they decided that, under the prevailing difficult and dangerous conditions, it would be best to escape to the crest of the southeast ridge as soon as possible. The three made a long leftward traverse below the upper funnel, reached the ridge, and a little higher bivouacked under a snow mushroom. Next afternoon they reached the summit. The technical difficulties of the Slovenian route were rated M6 6a+ and 90°.

They descended the 23rd by the southeast ridge. When 300m from the bottom, Opresnik, who had been suffering from altitude, fell whilst climbing down a short section unroped, but the two others managed to grab him. If he had been only slightly out of reach, he would have gone the full length of the wall below.

LINDSAY GRIFFIN, *Mountain INFO, CLIMB Magazine*

Cholatse, northeast face, third ascent, with variation finish. After our ascent of Kyajo Ri described above, we trekked to the foot of Cholatse (6,440m), arriving below the northeast face on November 2. This was Seth's second visit to the mountain. His proposed route followed a mostly continuous ribbon of ice up the face. Closer inspection convinced us that we could access the ribbon despite a blank section near the bottom. [At the time the pair was unaware that this face had previously been climbed—Ed.]

Seth Hobby at grips with the main ice flow in the middle of the northeast face of Cholatse during the third ascent. *John Kear*

The 1,300m northeast face of Cholatse (6,440m) showing (1) Swiss Route (southeast ridge) (Alpiger-Ludi-Tamang, 1982), (2) Slovenian variant (M6 6a+ 90°, Humar-Kozelj-Opresnik, 2005), (3) Hobby-Kear variant (VI WI5+ M6, 2005, starts via (2)) and (4) original American Route (VI AI5 5.9 A2, Bibler-Freer-Jackson-Stewart, 1984). The rectangular snow ramp leading to the crest of the ridge right of the number 4 is the top section of the French Route on the north face. *John Kear*

On Nov 7 we began climbing around 7 a.m. The first pitch was an amazing 60m flow of WI4+. A couple of traversing pitches and easy rock led to a buttress of unique turf climbing. The first pitch on this buttress we called "Turf Wars" (M4), not knowing that it was only a warm up for the climb's mental crux. The next pitch, dubbed "Tuff Reliance," was a bit of a third eye opener at M6 R/X. These pitches were the key to the climb and led us into the icy meat of the route. We continued for another 400m of excellent terrain, which included a couple of very cool and often thin pitches up to WI5+ M5, then after some 780m of climbing, at an altitude of 5,300m, we found a decent bivouac site.

Next morning, after an easy scramble up to a cave, the Hobbit (Seth) led a slightly overhanging cool whip, thinly plastered in a granite corner. Dubious protection insured that the Hobbit would send. A few hundred meters of easy ice and crunchy névé led to the heart of the route: a silvery blue ice flow 360m long. In the middle of the flow the "Dragon" bared its teeth. The first shot was a rock to Seth's right hand, which we first thought was broken. I set off on the next lead, only to be stopped by a second barrage of stone fall. Again, one of the rocks found the Hobbit's belay and smacked him on the head. We needed shelter fast, whether it was up or down. We chose up. Pitch after pitch of sustained grade 4 and 5 ice, combined with the rockfall, took everything we had. As darkness fell, we luckily found a safe, reasonably comfortable bivouac site, where we were able to pitch the tent, albeit in a precarious position.

On the following morning, leaving our high camp in place, we began simul climbing several pitches of 60° and 70° alpine ice. Then the route steepened, as we hit the headwall. The Hobbit headed right up into the maw and found himself in the middle of one of the highest-quality mixed pitches either of us had ever climbed. Steep black rock led through a series of bulges into a wickedly steep corner (M6), all with positive holds and great dry-tooling. I got the consolation prize above, a steep smear of 85° to 95° ice snaking up to the summit ridge. Six full pitches of AI4 led up the crest to the summit mushrooms; we arrived at the top in the dark a little after 6 p.m. It was cold, and there was no time to hang around. Sixteen rappels got us back to our high camp and our warm down bags, and the following day we rappelled the rest of the route, which we graded VI WI5+ M6.

JOHN KEAR, *AAC*

Editor's note: Hobby and Kear more or less climbed the same line as the Slovenians (reported above) to the base of the upper funnel. Here, they climbed up to the crest of the southeast ridge via a line approximately midway between that followed by the Slovenians in the spring and the more direct finish climbed by the Americans in 1984.

Cholatse, southwest ridge, winter attempt. Ross Lynn and I spent three days on Cholatse (6,440m) from January 30 to February 1, 2006. On the first day we climbed from base camp to the ca. 5,550m col at the foot of the southwest ridge, at one point having to cross beneath seracs to avoid a technical crevassed section on the glacier. A final 180m slope of 70° ice led to the col, which we reached by 2:00 p.m. We spent one night camped on this col, preparing for a one-day summit mission on the 31st. We left the col at 6 a.m. Some 300m of mostly rock climbing up the first buttress put us at a more level section of ridge, above which we simul-climbed. We reached the point where the sun-cooked southwest ridge joins the south ridge at around 3 p.m. Here we stashed unnecessary gear and charged for the summit. Two hours into it we realized that we were not going to make it before dark. Close but no cigar! We estimated our elevation to be 6,400m. At 5 p.m., with a building cold wind, we started heading down.

Due to an unusually warm, dry winter, the upper ridge gave us more technical difficulty than anticipated. There were many open crevasses and short steps that ate up our daylight. From our high point we had to make two rappels before reaching our stash of gear. We continued rappelling into the night and finally regained our tent around midnight. We estimated the temperatures we experienced on the mountain as somewhere between -12 and -20°C. During the descent I wore all my layers, including a down jacket, and my feet were cold. In hindsight we realized that an earlier start would have considerably increased our chances of reaching the top.

On February 1 we woke feeling tired and descended to our base camp. A few technical mistakes cost us the summit, but we now have more tricks in the bag for next time.

WHIT MAGRO

Tawoche, east-southeast face; Cholatse, direct finish to French Route; Ama Dablam, northwest face, attempt. While hundreds of climbers were in the early stages of their wanderings up and down Everest, one Swiss, Ueli Steck, was totally alone on the east- southeast face of Tawoche. He went to the base of the northeast pillar of this 6,495m peak, but saw there was too much loose rock falling down the couloir of his intended approach, so he went around to the east-southeast face. At 11:30 p.m. on April 24 he started for the face from his base at 5,200m, reached the summit in 4½ hours, and was back at base camp by 8:00 a.m. An hour after his return to camp, snow avalanches started coming down the face. "I didn't pick the perfect route," he commented. "It was dark." He had stayed on the face throughout his climb, but he thinks the best route is probably one leading to the southeast summit and from there traversing to the left along the summit ridge to the highest point.

ELIZABETH HAWLEY, *AAC Honorary Member, Nepal*

Editor's note: Steck's route on Tawoche climbed a left-slanting couloir/ramp on the far left side of the east-northeast face (sections of M5) to reach the big snow slopes that form the right side of the southeast face. These mainly consisted of 50-60° snow/ice, though in the upper section there were a few vertical ice steps through serac formations. He climbed the 1,200m line unroped.

His new line on the north face of 6,440m Cholatse is a direct finish to the 1995 French Route, finishing up the final section of the northeast face. He spent 37 hours on the climb, made one bivouac at 6,000m and compared the terrain to the north face of the Eiger, with rock to F5, ice to 90°, and M6 terrain.

On Ama Dablam he attempted to solo the third ascent of the Slovenian Route on the northwest face (Stane Belak-Srauf Memorial Route; ca. 1,600m, 5.7, AI 5, A2; Vanja Furlan-Tomaz Humar, 1996). He reached 5,900m, before retreating due to avalanche danger. Steck's account of his Khumbu adventures appears earlier in the Journal.

Lobuje West, southwest face, Korean Direct. A six-man Korean team comprising Kang Sung-woo (leader), Ahn Chi-young, Gwon Jung-hyo, Lee Tae-gyun, Eddy Park-Jun, and I made the first ascent of 6,145m West Lobuje's southwest face on April 16. The weather was good throughout, except for one day's snowfall. We fixed rope to 5,790m, from which point we climbed continuously to the summit, leading on a 100m 8mm rope. We left various pieces of gear and 600m of rope on the middle section of the route.

The ca. 900m southwest face of Lobuje West (6,145m), showing the line of the new Korean Route (27 pitches, 5.8 WI4). (1), (2) and (3) mark the bivouac or camp sites. The only known previous ascents have been from the opposite (east) side. *Peter Jensen-Choi*

Our route, Korean Direct, comprises three main sections. The first, led in rock-climbing shoes and not affected by serious rockfall, climbed the right edge of a triangular rock buttress that terminated at 5,430m. We rated it no more than 5.8. The second, a 300m ridge scramble with moves up to 5.7, involved exposed climbing over precariously loose, car-sized boulders that offered sparse protection. The final section, above the point where rock ended and snow began, started at 5,640m and had crux pitches of WI4. Rumors of a Japanese attempt in 1995 are dubious, as to our knowledge there are no journal entries, and there was no trace of any climbing being done near base camp or on the wall itself.

We established base camp on March 31 at 5,080m and spent the next five days scouting, organizing gear, and fixing line from 5,100m to 5,474m. On April 10 Ahn, Park, and I fixed line to 5,540m and the following day extended this to 5,700m. On the day after that we refixed rope, and, hauling more rope, gear, and food from base camp, continued our preparation for a summit push.

On the 13th Ahn, Gwon, Park, and I bivouacked at 5,430m, but the next day Gwon was forced to retreat, due to typical miseries of AMS. Ahn and Park fixed the remaining designated rope up to 5,790m. Thirty meters below this high point we cut platforms before darkness quickly enveloped us. Despite the waist-width ledges, this was a good bivouac, with clear skies, no wind ,and the distant glimmer of a Swiss soloist bivouacking high on the north face of Cholatse [Ueli Steck; see above—Ed.].

Our third day was equally slow, due to a relaxed start. The weather remained clear, and climbing commenced with me jugging up our fixed line and improving a mediocre anchor on an ice ridge. From there (5,790m) we climbed without fixed rope. Ahn pulled out a monster 90m lead along the right side of the ice ridge, and I finished with a 70m pitch up to the right of a large exposed granite slab, where we had originally anticipated finding a tent platform. There was none, and we spent the rest of the afternoon cutting a ledge at 5,900m, fixing safety lines, and cramming into the tiny two-man tent before night closed in.

On April 16 we were off by 6:15 a.m. with a few meager packets of dehydrated soup, nuts, and chocolate bars. This was our only chance of reaching the summit without starving the next day. I began by traversing left for 50m, then Ahn led directly up a steep ice gully to the top of an enormous snow terrace, just below and to the left of a building-sized cornice (WI4). Eddy led the second crux pitch (WI4), which led left of this large terrace and up the right side of a 50m+ steep granite headwall. I then traversed right and gained a gully of hard snow, rock, and ice, up which I climbed for more than 70m, placing mostly chocks and slinging horns. Ahn jugged the rope and led through, then finally Eddy reached the summit 50m above us. The time was 3:18 p.m. and we had climbed 27 pitches. [Base camp to summit was 1,000m, though the amount of climbing was estimated to be 1,300-1,400m—Ed.] Ahn and I followed and were able to straddle the saddle-like summit with our right legs on West Lobuje's northeast face and left legs down the southwest face. After taking pictures for 20 minutes, I led down, and we arrived back at our tent just as dusk blackened into night, our minds and hearts filled with the summit light.

PETER JENSEN-CHOI, *Corean Alpine Club*

The 700m Losar icefall, nestled into the north-facing hillside directly opposite Namche Bazar in the Khumbu. The first known ascent, in 1994, took three days but the route was soloed in just under six hours early in 2006. *Whit Magro*

Brady Robinson on low-angle terrain, approaching the 120m headwall of Losar icefall. The crux WI5 pillar is at the top of the climb. *Whit Magro*

Losar, ascent and possible future permit requirement. On January 10, 2006 Whit Magro and I climbed the stupendous frozen waterfall, Losar, which lies directly opposite Namche Bazaar. After 1½-hour approach, we took nine hours to reach the top, simul-climbing all but the last two crux pitches of the 700m route. The climbing was surprisingly moderate (WI3-4), with a little WI5 pillar at the top. We kept a steady, rather than frantic, pace and thoroughly enjoyed ourselves. It must be one of the greatest ice routes in the world. Over a dozen V-thread rappels got us back down in time for dinner in Namche.

We were in the region as volunteers for the Khumbu Climbing School, a program organized by the Alex Lowe Charitable Foundation (www.alexlowe.org), that strives to increase the safety of Nepali climbers and high-altitude workers through ice climbing, first aid, and English instruction. It seems that the only reason we got permission to climb the route was our affiliation with the ALCF. Jenni Lowe, President of ALCF, accompanied us to the park headquarters in Namche. After several hours of discussion and drafted letters, we received authorization. We learned that, shortly before our arrival, two Canadian climbers had been denied a go-ahead to climb the route, because they lacked a permit. Future parties should research the situation, as it may be that they will need a permit arranged and paid for prior to leaving Kathmandu.

On the 22nd Kris Erickson, Seth Hobby, and Renan Ozturk also climbed Losar. All three were affiliated with the ALCF and only received permission after protracted negotiations with park authorities.

BRADY ROBINSON

Editor's note: this icefall, which cuts through the north-facing pastures below Nupla (5,885m), had its first known ascent over three days in early 1994 by Catherine Destivelle and Erik Decamp, with photographer Beth Wald. They fixed ropes on the initial, thinly iced pitches.

Losar, solo ascent. Sometime after the ascent reported above and after I returned from an attempt on Cholatse's southwest ridge, I found myself back in Namche with a few days to spare. Losar allowed me to ascend and descend in just under six hours, by means of a leashless free solo.

WHIT MAGRO

Ama Dablam, Lagunak Ridge, attempt. Between October 1 and November 2, Tina Di Batista and I were members of a Slovenian Jubilee expedition to Ama Dablam. The expedition was organized to honor the 30th anniversary of the first Slovenian ascent of an 8,000m peak. In 1975 a Slovenian team (though in those days we were still Yugoslavia) climbed a new route on the south face of Makalu. Four of the seven Makalu summiters were on the 2005 Ama Dablam expedition, and all reached the top via the southwest ridge; Janko Azman, Janez Dovzan, Viki Groselj (expedition leader) and Marjan Manfreda. These four climbers were accompanied by Croatian Stipe Bozic, who was making a film.

Tina and I made an attempt on the Lagunak Ridge, which was climbed for the first time in 1985 by a Spanish–American trio, who completed the route using fixed ropes (this is the south ridge of Ama Dablam, which joins the Standard Route up the southwest ridge at ca. 6,500m—Ed.). We tried it in alpine-style. We started early in the morning of October 19. In the lower section we found fixed ropes along a rocky part of the ridge. We bivied below a small cornice at 6,070 m. Next day we continued over tricky mixed terain but by afternoon it had begun to snow. We waited for an hour at 6,250m but the situation was exposed and when avalanches started to fall around us, we began to rappel. We arrived at a safe spot below an overhanging rock wall after dark and bivouacked here at ca. 5,800m. Next day we continued rappeling and in the aftenoon reached the foot of the route. Shortly after, we were resting in the expedition Camp 1 on the southwest ridge. Next day weather was better, so instead of descending to Pangboche as originally planned, we decided to try the southwest ridge. We reached the summit on the 23rd.

TOMAZ JAKOFCIC, *Slovenia*

Everest, summary of events during the pre-monsoon season. Once upon a time—a decade ago— everyone knew that the period of good weather for summiting Everest was between May 5 and 15. Commercial expedition leaders set from the 6th to the 10th as their target. Later in the 1990s the weather pattern seemed to push the favorable period to later in the month, from the 18th to 25th, but never as late as June. That is, until 2004, when two Russians made the first June ascent, on the first day of the month. In 2005 a number of teams summited in June, after weeks of waiting for suitable weather, and didn't leave their base camps until the second week of the month.

Commercial expeditions were back in strength, and many were receiving daily forecasts via satellite from well-known meteorological centers, such as Bracknell in England. They wanted to know about impending snowstorms but were particularly looking for predictions about wind velocity on Everest, in order to know when there would be three or four continuous days of gentle breezes. They could then plan to send members and Sherpas up to the highest camp for summit bids. But not only commercial teams were closely following the forecasts; the small two-member parties did their best to learn what predictions the others were receiving.

The problem was that the forecasters were constantly getting it wrong. On the basis of inaccurate predictions, especially for the southern side of the mountain, climbers were going up and down like yo-yos and even trekking below base camp, tiring themselves out and becoming increasingly frustrated. Some independent climbers ignored the received wisdom, made their attempts to reach the summit, failed, and went home. "If it wasn't snowing, the wind was blowing," said one, who gave up waiting for a break in the weather. Other climbers, both independents and members of larger groups, stubbornly stayed till late May and early June. Many of these were finally rewarded with success.

On the north side a few teams summited on May 21 and 22, but then there was a gap until the 27th, after which parties continued to succeed until June 5. On the south side no one reached the top until May 30. This and the following day were those on which almost all successes were achieved; the others went to the summit on June 2 and 5.

This does not include the claim by a French helicopter pilot, Didier Delsalle, to have taken off from Lukla airfield, landed his Ecureuil on the 8,850m top of the world on May 14, stepped out of the cockpit, and stayed there for over two minutes, before flying safely back to Lukla. The Nepalese authorities denied his claim and invited him to leave the country for breaking rules.

A large number of unhappy climbers aimed to reach the top in the normal way, on their own two feet. They belonged to an unprecedented number of 101 teams on the mountain: 49 on the Tibet side, 42 on the Nepal side. They ranged in size from one foreigner without Sherpa support to an expedition on the northern side with 27 members and 36 supporting Sherpas and Tibetans.

In spring 2004, 64 teams went to Everest and only 10 (16%) failed. In spring 2005, out of the 101 groups an astonishing 48 (48%) failed to put anyone on top. There were 326 summiters in spring 2004, but in 2005 only 306 men and women claimed success.

An Australian climber figured how to beat the weather on the south side: go around to the north. Piers Buck originally planned to make a traverse from south to north and had permits to do so. He had gotten to only 7,500m on May 16, when the weather became unsettled for many days. However, on the north side people started getting to the top on the 21st. So he left the team he was with on the southern side, flew by helicopter to Kathmandu on the 23rd, and went by road to the north side's base camp. He summited on June 5 as a member of the expedition with which he had been given permission to descend.

Another late arrival at base camp on the north side climbed without any Sherpa support or bottled oxygen. Marcin Miotk was on an unsuccessful Polish expedition to the south face of Annapurna I and returned to Kathmandu in mid-May. But instead of going home he went to Everest, was at base camp on May 18, and made two summit bids. On the first he climbed with two Austrians but turned back at 7,900m, on June 1, because of strong wind. His second try was a success. Climbing alone from advance base camp, he was on top at 2:30 p.m. on June 5, the last person to summit during the season.

Back on the south side it was a miracle that massive fatalities didn't occur on May 4, when a huge avalanche of rock and ice crashed down from the west shoulder. It hit tents pitched at Camp 1 just above the top of the Icefall, but few people were occupying this camp at the time. Those in camp or nearby received relatively light cuts and bruises, except for a Sherpa whose back was injured. Numerous tents and the gear inside were lost.

ELIZABETH HAWLEY, *AAC Honorary Member, Nepal*

Kyashar, southwest face, attempt. From October 11 to 15 Jan Doudlebsky and Marek Holecek attempted the first ascent of the southwest face of Kyashar (a.k.a. Peak 43; 6,770m). This peak had its only official ascent in October 2003, by a multinational, Swiss-based team, via the west ridge and west face. The two Czechs began in the center of the southwest face and slanted up left to join the west ridge at 6,500m. It was cold, snow conditions on the ridge were bad, and both climbers were concerned about frostbitten toes. They estimated that to reach the summit would require a further one or two days of climbing, so they opted to

Kyashar (6,770m) from the Hinku Valley below Tangnag, with (1) being the first official ascent of the mountain. Steep snow slopes below the southwest face led to the 5,800m col at the foot of the west ridge. The crest above was followed to ca. 6,400 before moving left into a couloir on the west face (Broderick-Frank-Normand, 2003). (2) Is the Czech attempt on the southwest face, which reached the 2003 route on the west ridge before descending (M6+ WI6, Doudlebsky-Holecek, 2005) *Andreas Frank*

descend the west ridge. Although their route did not reach the summit, it joined an existing line, and the climbers have called it Ramro Chaina. Difficulties were about M6+ and WI6.

JAN KREISINGER, *Czech Republic*

Although the following event took place in the winter of 2006, it was such a notable tragedy that we include it in this Journal.

MAHALANGUR HIMAL - MAKALU SECTION

Makalu, winter solo attempt and tragedy. The well-known French mountaineer, Jean-Christophe Lafaille, 40 years old, vanished on January 27, 2006, while attempting to make an entirely solo ascent of Makalu (8,485m), the world's fifth highest mountain. The highest he is known to have reached is 7,600m, where he pitched his small red tent on the 26th [after almost six weeks on the mountain—Ed.] and from which he set out alone for the top early in the morning of the 27th. He reported his departure by satellite phone to his wife Katya in France. This was expected to be the first of several reports to her that day, but he never made contact with her or his base camp staff again. [Lafaille had remarked that he felt really up to it, despite the fact he hadn't been able to sleep, due to altitude and cold (down to -30°C). The forecast predicted slightly changeable conditions, with summit wind speeds possibly reaching 40-50km/hour—Ed.]

A helicopter search of the mountainside took place on February 4. Searchers included his wife, her brother, and Veikka Gustafsson, a Finnish mountaineer who had climbed with Lafaille and knew from his own ascent of Makalu the route Lafaille was following. They saw the tent but no other trace of him. The search team left a tent with sleeping bag, stove, food, fuel, and a few other necessities at base camp, in case he did manage to return alive. But Gustafsson knew there was no hope for Lafaille's survival, and thought he understood exactly what had happened to the Frenchman.

Ten years previously Gustafsson had climbed the same (Normal) route that Lafaille was. He had two climbing partners, Ed Viesturs and Rob Hall, but led most of the final part to the summit. He found numerous treacherous crevasses and fell into three of them. He was always belayed and emerged unscathed. Gustafsson is convinced the Frenchman fell into one and became fatally trapped.

Gustafsson considers Lafaille to have been "one of the world's greatest climbers." If he had succeeded, Lafaille would have been the first person to climb Makalu in winter. He had already attempted the mountain unsuccessfully in spring 2004, in an earlier solo bid by a different route, approaching the mountain from Tibet over Makalu II. Makalu was one of only three 8,000m peaks he had not yet summited.

ELIZABETH HAWLEY, *AAC Honorary Member, Nepal.*

Editor's note: beginning with Renato Casarotto's Italian expedition in January 1981, there have been 11 winter attempts on Makalu, which remains the only Nepalese 8,000m peak not to be climbed in winter, despite serious attempts by the great Polish winter specialists. While nearly all teams encountered good snow/ice conditions, higher up the mountain they found progress impossible in fierce winds.

Umbak Himal

Pabuk Kang, first known attempt. Two Japanese, led by the explorer-mountaineer Tamotsu Ohnishi, who specializes in visiting remote areas along Nepal's border with Tibet, planned to try the south side of Pabuk Kang [6,244m; just east of the Pabuk La at the head of the Yangma valley in the Ohmi Kangri Group, first brought onto the permitted list in 2003—Ed.].

On October 20 they pitched their advanced base camp at 5,550m just east of the Yanmakang Pass (a.k.a. Pabuk La, Dhangla Bhanjyang) and south-southwest of the peak. For the next three days it snowed, depositing 130 cm, and the two climbers abandoned their plans. On the approach to the mountain they met five parties of Maoists but paid only two of them, paying 2,000Rs or about $27 per member to each party.

Elizabeth Hawley, *AAC Honorary Member, Nepal.*

Janak Himal

Lashar I, first ascent of peak via south face; Janak, south face, attempt. I first saw the south face of Janak (7,041m) in autumn 2000, when leading an expedition to Jongsang, Pathibara, and Kiratchuli. From the upper Broken Glacier the southwest pillar looked like an excellent objective for a small expedition. The time for fulfilling this dream arrived in autumn 2005. The Slovenian Janak 2005 expedition comprised only the young climber Miha Habjan and I, though we were joined in Kathmandu by Padam Tamang, the expedition Sirdar and cook, Guirme Sherpa as his assistant, and our liaison officer, Gopi Lal Nepal.

After using local buses for the three-day drive to eastern Nepal, travel not only uncomfortable but also risky, we arrived in Taplejung. Surrounded by barbed wire and with a strong military presence, this village now seems like a fortress and was the last place on our journey toward the mountains that had any government power. After a seven-day approach we reached Lhonak, where we established base camp on September 29. In Chirwa, on the second day of our trek, we encountered Maoists. They didn't make any real trouble for us; we just paid them 2,000 Nepali Rupees per person.

On October 6, after short acclimatization trips around base camp, we went to our advanced base camp at the end of the lateral moraine on the upper Broken Glacier. After more than 9km of walking from base camp, we camped at 5,710m and the next day climbed the 6,096m [6,095m HGM Finn map] mountain above camp. [This was probably the third ascent of the peak, which was first climbed by a Anglo-Nepalese party in 1998—Ed.] We later continued to the south Tsisima peaks and after climbing Tsisima III, descended to base camp because of bad weather.

On October 10 we went for the next stage in our acclimatization program. Our goal was the nice pyramid of Lashar I, which is visible from Lhonak. [There is some confusion surrounding the names of Tibetan border peaks west of Janak. The old Swiss map, which appears to be relatively accurate in depicting the topography of this region and has been generally used as a benchmark for subsequent Japanese maps and the Kangchenjunga trekking map by Nepa Publications, places three border peaks at the head of the northerly branch of the Tsisima Glacier: from west to east, Dzanye (6,710m), Lashar I (6,930m), and Lashar II (6,860m). The new HGM Finn map, Janak Himal, does not name any of these peaks but gives them altitudes of, again from west to east, 6,581m, 6,842m, and 6,803m. On the Ministry of Tourism list of permitted peaks 6,842m and 6,803m are Lashar I and II, but Dzanye is quoted as 6,719m. This elevation is clearly marked on the Finn map as a border peak immediately northeast of Lashar II. Dzanye, as climbed by the Swiss Dittert, Lohner, Partgaetzi-Almer, Sutter, and Wyss-Dunant in 1949, via the northwest ridge, is definitely the peak marked 6,581m on the new map. Confused? So were the Slovenians, who for a long time after their ascent thought they had climbed Dzanye but now realize they climbed Lashar I—Ed.] After walking 11km in eight hours from base camp, we put our first camp at 5,610m (GPS) close to the start of the Tsisima North Glacier (Chijima on the HGM Finn map). The next day we climbed the glacier almost to its head and made a second camp at 6,200m, near the col on our expected descent route, the northwest ridge.

On our summit day, October 12, we descended to below the prominent snow couloir on the south face. The first part of the couloir is blocked by a big serac barrier, which we avoided on the left by ice slopes and a long traverse over loose rock. At daybreak we started to climb the main gully. Conditions were good and the angle from 50-60°, so we climbed unroped to the northwest ridge, not far below the summit. We reached the top after a climb of nine hours. The panorama was fantastic, but a strong and bitterly cold wind prevented us from enjoying it for long. We descended the northwest ridge until it became steep, then started to cut down the south face. We made five rappels to reach the glacier and were quickly at our tent. The same day we descended to the site of our first camp and made the long walk back to base on the 13th.

Since starting out from Taplejung, Miha had not felt well. Problems with his throat wouldn't disappear, so before attempting Janak we took five days rest. It didn't help but our

The south face of Lashar I (6,842m) in the Janak Himal, showing the line of the first ascent by Slovenians Miha Habjan and Andrej Stremfelj. *Andrej Stremfelj*

The south face of Janak (7,041m), seen across the upper Broken Glacier in eastern Nepal. (1) The route of the first ascent, in May 2006, by Andrej Stremfelj and Rok Zalokar via the ca. 1,150m southwest pillar. This will be reported in the 2007 AAJ. (2) The attempt on the south face to a high point at 6,650m, the plateau that forms a shoulder on the east ridge (Habjan-Stremfelj, 2005). *Andrej Stremfelj*

time was short, so on October 18 we regained our advanced base on the Broken Glacier. We rested most of the next day, making only a short reconnaissance of the approach to the southwest pillar. Late that evening we made a decision: with Miha still not well and the weather looking more dubious, we abandoned the pillar and attempted a shorter and somewhat easier route towards the right side of the south face, left of the obvious big serac. This was the line we had initially planned to use for descent.

The night was cloudy, forcing us to postpone our departure. Finally, at 4 a.m., we left the tent and two hours later were at the foot of the face. We climbed the lower section unroped, but began to belay ca. 50m below the serac. Seven pitches later we were on the plateau that forms a 6,650m shoulder on the east ridge. There had been two difficult sections: hard water ice around the left flank of the serac and mixed ground above. As we approached the ridge the wind became steadily fiercer, so strong that it broke ice from the rock walls to our left and bombarded the slope below.

We arrived on the plateau at nightfall. Crawling on all fours due to the wind, we were tired after climbing all day. The weather was cloudy, and with no moonlight we were unable to find the route to the summit. Without tents and sleeping bags, we had to find shelter immediately. Working hard for three hours, we dug a hole that gave us semi-protection from the wind. We sat and froze until 1 a.m. To keep warm we worked at enlarging the hole for the next three hours.

Next morning the weather deteriorated fast. A brief ray of sun was like a reminder from God that we needed to hurry. The wind on the edge of the plateau was even stronger than during the night, and we couldn't hear each other. We started to rappel, and soon it began to snow. In five minutes the whole face was being swept by avalanches. It was like a river. Often the rope would be pinned by avalanches, and we couldn't rappel. At 2 p.m, after 15 rappels, we reached the glacier, now covered with 40cm of fresh snow. The mist was so dense that we couldn't locate our ski sticks and had a difficult job finding our advanced base.

Guirme was waiting for us, and in the evening we all started our descent towards base camp. It was snowing so hard that route finding would have been more or less impossible without a GPS. We arrived in base at 7 a.m. and the same day packed our gear and walked out to Ghunsa. Two further days were needed to reach Taplejung, and on October 27 we flew to Kathmandu via Biratnagar.

ANDREJ STREMFELJ, *Slovenia*

Editor's note: Stremfelj returned in the spring of 2006 and climbed the southwest pillar of Janak.

Maoist activity in the spring. Maoists continued to extort funds from climbers. They charged Norbert Joos's Kangchenjunga six-member group 5,000Rs (roughly $70) per member. Another team, a Georgian and a Russian, on their way to Manaslu, were forced to pay a total of 52,500Rs ($745). This charge was calculated by the rebels at 100Rs per member per day. The climbing permit from the tourism ministry stated that there were seven members on this expedition, and it was valid for 75 days. The fact that there were only two members was of no interest to the Maoists. The Georgian leader, Gia Tortladze, later complained, "There are two governments in Nepal: one in Kathmandu and one run by the Maoists."

Mountaineers in the Everest region are not bothered by Maoist rebels, but one expedition traveling by road from Kathmandu to the Tibetan side of the range had a bad experience. Rebels had declared highways closed for five days in the area through which the Friendship Highway passes. The trekking agency for a large Russian-led expedition and several other teams arranged for the Royal Nepal Army to escort their convoys of vehicles on April 7, 8, and 9 to the border village, Kodari. They reached there without incident. However the Russian leader, Alexander Abramov, and one of his members, Sergei Kaymachnikov, were delayed leaving Kathmandu on the 9th, so they took a taxi to catch up with the team. Only 25km out of Kathmandu a small bomb was tossed through the open window in the back of the taxi where Kaymachnikov was sitting. Its explosion ripped off his heel, while some of its fragments penetrated the back of the front seat and slightly wounded Abramov. An army helicopter quickly flew the casualties to the military hospital in Kathmandu, where Kaymachnikov was treated until he left for Moscow on the 15th. Abramov drove to the border on the 16th, rejoined his team and climbed to their highest camp, at 8,300m.

To enforce their will, the Maoists also planted land mines at either end of a small bridge a few kilometers south of Kodari. Here an Everest expedition of Australians and a Dutchman, led by Tashi Tenzing, a grandson of Tenzing Norgay Sherpa, had to stop on the 13th and wait for three hours until an army bomb disposal squad detonated the mines.

ELIZABETH HAWLEY, *AAC Honorary Member, Nepal*

China

TIEN SHAN

Western Kokshaal-Too, first ascent of "Tombstone Tower." Fermented horse milk is a delicacy not to be missed. Especially if accompanied by freshly beheaded, blood-boiled lamb, goat yogurt, and yak butter on homemade fry-bread. The boiled goat head and intestine stir-fry topped off the gourmet meal. We devoured the food with sloppy slurps and grunts of delight. Our gracious hosts were two Kyrgyz families, living at 3,300m at the foot of the Tien Shan/Western Kokshaal-Too Mountains in northwestern China, in Xinjiang Province near the Kyrghyzstan border.

In 2000 I had received permission to enter one of China's most restricted regions of the Tien Shan Mountains. On that amazing journey, while on an untouched nearly 5,700m peak [Grand Poobah, a.k.a. Pik Byeliy; see *AAJ 2001*, pp. 400-401—Ed.], I got a glimpse of a huge valley of granite over the next ridge to the west.

We returned last July and August. We flew via Beijing to Urumqi, where our team of six Chinese officers loaded our 15 haul bags into two 4x4s and then had us heading west for three days over dusty, sandy roads. We skirted the Taklamakan Desert and slept in the Uygur-Muslim towns of Kurla, Aksu, and finally Ahqi. There, our liaison officer presented our permission papers and passports to the local military. After three hours he came out with good news; access was granted. However, we acquired a new team member, a local military officer who was armed and in full camouflage dress. We then all drove toward the snow-capped witch hats in the distance, toward the virgin valley of granite I'd discovered through secret channels.

"One of my goals was to stand on the summit with my brother, completely naked wearing only a Year of the Cock mask. Well, considering the temperatures, maybe one sock each." The Libecki brothers on top of Tombstone Tower, West Kokshaal-Too.

Above base camp we carried hefty loads for five days, 18km a day. We then took a day to scope routes, stretch, and eat. The wall we decided to climb reminded me of Sentinel in Yosemite, except that it was bigger, steeper, and completely virgin. All I could think about were sweet splitter cracks, snuggling on portaledges in storms, and standing on a tiny ca. 4,700m summit in China looking into Kyrgyzstan.

My younger brother Andy is an amazing musician, whose ability to rip up the banjo is astounding. When we first talked about this expedition, we made a deal: I would show him the experience of a big-wall first ascent, and he would show me how to play the banjo. This would be only his second climb ever: his first was a first ascent in Greenland.

I also had two goals regarding the tombstone-shaped tower we were about to climb: to come down alive, not necessarily without pain or injury but alive; to stand on the summit with my brother, completely naked wearing only a Year of the Cock mask. Well, considering the temperatures, maybe one sock each.

The first pitches were super-fun free climbing and, for a first ascent, surprisingly clean with little loose rock. But the smile-inducing 5.10 cracks turned into A3 seams and rotten A3/A4 pitches of kitty litter. Finally, after some tedious birdbeaks, I fixed to a high point about 300m off the deck.

Climbing capsule style gave my brother a chance to practice jugging, digest the exposure, and go through rescue scenarios. Climbing in an out of snow showers we fixed lines for a week and then committed to the wall. I needed to show my brother some additional techniques: how to go Number 2 on the wall; how to jug in space and horizontally. I taught him double hauls, Munter-mule knots, 'biner rappels, and hundreds of other variables in the big-wall equation.

From our highpoint, I was able to fix several more pitches. I decided that the extensive work involved in fixing all of our ropes as high as possible, and then do a push to the summit, would be safer and give us a higher possibility of success than doing another big haul. The upper part of the wall was treacherously loose. Flakes the size of pool tables looked like they could go. I spent an extra day rigging the fixed lines away from sharp edges and loose rocks.

We had now been climbing the wall for just over a week and had endured snow showers daily. Fast moving, time-lapse clouds threatened another storm at any time. I climbed a frightening pitch through a maze of giant leaning flakes and fractures, all relying on each other for stability. Once we were past this nightmare, an easy, unroped, 4th class scramble led us to the breakfast-nook-table-sized summit.

Thunder brought worry. I have no problem sitting out a storm, even if it lasts days. Storms offer time for rum, hot chocolate, and fantasy novels. But thunder changes everything. If lightning strikes home, everything will melt and our last few seconds of life would abruptly end with the sudden arrival of the ground. Even rum and hot chocolate won't ease minds if thunder roars. This is not the first electrical storm I have experienced here, and most likely not the last.

At base camp our sweet new Deering banjos waited. The goals of this expedition were soon fulfilled. My brother got the big-wall first-ascent experience, with thunderstorms, vertical toilets, plenty of hanging in space hundreds of meters off the ground, and summiting a virgin peak. Complete and utter satisfaction. By the time we got back home, I could play all of "Dueling Banjos." Squeal like a pig boy!

We named our route Libeckistan (500m, 5.10d A3+).

MIKE LIBECKI, *AAC*

Tomurty, far eastern Tien Shan, first ascent. The National Defense Academy Alpine Club of Japan organized an expedition to the Tien Shan to commemorate its 50th anniversary. The objectives were to climb Tomurty (4,886m), the highest virgin peak in the Karlik (Harlik) Shan and to explore the neighboring mountains of the far eastern Tien Shan, a range some 2,400km long.

Tomurty is located about 70km northeast of Hami in Xinjiang Province [a.k.a. Tomort and situated well east of the Bogda Shan at 43.1 N., 94.3 E—Ed.]. Although its height does not exceed 5,000m, it is well glaciated, and despite easy access, the little-known Karlik massif remains almost unexplored. The summit of Tomurty is a table-top ice-snow plateau, with glaciers several kilometers long descending on all sides.

Takashi Kawakami of our alpine club first reached the area near the mountain in the summer of 1996. and a Chinese party made a reconnaissance in late 1996 and early 1997. A Japanese party from Niigata Prefecture made an attempt in 2000, but they made a mistake on the approach and ended up in a valley from which they were not able to reach any of Tomurty's glaciers.

In the summer of 2004 one of our club members, Koichiro Takahashi, reconnoitered a possible climbing route, finding a way into the Kazantapute valley and a suitable line onto the glacier flowing southwest from the main summit.

Our 2005 expedition comprised I, Isao Fukura (57) as leader, Hiroyuki Katsuki, (25) and Koichiro Takahashi (43), plus a liaison officer, interpreter, and cook from the China Xinjiang Mountaineering Association. We arrived in Urumqi, the capital of Xinjiang, on August 7 and the following day reached the village of Badashi (1,800m) by road.

We reached base camp at 3,800m on the 9th, with the help of camels and mules. Over the next few days we ferried loads up the glacier and established Camp 1 (4,200m) on the 12th. On the 15th, after a reconnaissance the previous day, Katsuki and Takahashi left this camp at 7 a.m. in fine weather with a light wind and a temperature of -9°C. A crevassed glacier led to a 50° snow/ice face and eventually the summit, which they reached at 3:40 p.m. A GPS reading indicated an altitude of 4,892m. They returned safely to base camp the following day

ISAO FUKURA, *National Defense Academy AC, Japan*

KUN LUN

Muztagh Ata (7,546m), south ridge. On August 24 Valery Shamalo and I from St. Petersburg reached the main summit of Muztagh Ata via the south ridge. As we were well acclimatized after our ascent of Koskulak and had previous experience on the Kalaxong Glacier, we were able to reach the 6,100m col between Koskulak and Kalaxong in one day from the standard Muztagh Ata base camp. We made our first camp on this col at the head of the Kalaxong Glacier. The next day we climbed the ridge above to ca. 6,800m for our second night and by the following night had reached 7,200m, just below the saddle between Kalaxong and the main summit. The route had involved snow climbing almost throughout, though at two points we climbed rocky sections, as it appeared easier to progress on rock than break trail through difficult snow. Next day we reached the summit of Muztagh Ata, our biggest problem being cold temperatures and a strong wind, giving the feeling that autumn

The south ridge of Muztagh Ata (B; 7,546m), seen from the summit plateau of Koskuluk at c7,000m. The route of the first ascent by the St. Petersburg team is marked. On the second ascent, less than two weeks later, a Russian party also climbed Kalaxong (A; 7,277m). *Alexey Gorbatenkov*

was upon us. From the summit we descended the old Classic (1956) Route. Visibility was far from perfect, but the trail was well marked with red flags and easy to follow.

We passed below Kalaxong (7,277m; sometimes referred to as Muztagh Ata South), but on September 4 three members of another expedition, Dmitry Chijik, Vladimir Kagan, and Petr Yudin from a large Russian expedition led by Andrey Lebedev, repeated our route and also climbed Kalaxong.

ALEXEY GORBATENKOV, *Mountainguides.ru, Russia*

Editor's Note: The Lebedev expedition made the first ascent of Kalaxong via the South Ridge. The summit can be reached by an easy detour from the Original Route up Muztagh Ata, a route that is rarely followed today (climbed by the Sino-Russian expedition of 1956 but nearly completed in 1947 by Shipton and Tilman). In the early 1980s the Chinese moved Muztagh Ata base camp some distance further north and opened a new and more direct line to the summit, which has since become the established Normal Route. Who made the first ascent of Kalaxong is unclear, though it may well have been Shipton and Tilman. In more recent times there are unconfirmed reports of a Chinese ascent in 2000, when the team became badly lost on the descent.

Muztagh Ata, second ascent of southeast ridge, alpine style. In order to be well-acclimatized for their alpine-style attempt on Shivling during the autumn, 26-year-old Kazuya Hiraide and 33-year-old Kei Taniguchi climbed Muztagh Ata (7,546m), making the second ascent of the southeast ridge. This elegant line above the so-called Potterfield Glacier was first climbed in July 2000 by Americans Walter Keller, Dan Mazur, and Jon Otto in an eight-day alpine-style push, after they had first climbed the Normal Route. Hiraide and Tanaguchi initially acclimatized on the Normal Route (west flank) and then reached base camp at 3,900m on August 29. They established an advanced base camp at 4,500m on the 31st and then four high camps on the ridge as the two made their alpine-style push: Camp 1 at 5,400m on September 1, Camp 2 at 5,850m,

Camp 3 at 6,450m, and Camp 4 at 7,200m. On September 5 the pair reached the summit at 3:30 p.m. They descended the Normal Route, on the far side of the mountain, as far as 6,800m (usual site of Camp 3). On the 6th they reached the standard west-side base camp. Hiraide had carried skis up the southeast ridge and was able to use them to descend the west flank.

The two then crossed the Kunjerab Pass into Pakistan and made their way to the Indian border at Wagah, eventually reaching Delhi on September 19 and starting the second phase of their expedition.

KAZUYA HIRAIDE, *Japan*

The northern part of the Muztagh Ata Massif rising above the Kuksay Glacier. (A) Kalaxong (7,277m), (B) Muztagh Ata (7,546m), (C) Kuksay (Mustagh Ata North Peak; 7,184m). The line and camps of the Japanese alpine-style second ascent of the southeast ridge are marked: C1 (5,400m), C2 (5,850m), C3 (6,450m), C4 (7,200m). *Kazuya Hiraide collection*

The lower section of the north face of Koskulak (7,028m) seen from the lower Kalaxong Glacier. The first section of the new route climbed by the St. Petersburg team is marked. *Alexey Gorbatenkov*

The upper north face of Koskulak (7,028m), seen from the south ridge of Muztagh Ata: (1) The upper section of the northeast ridge (Moscow Aviation Institute expedition, August 2005), (2) north face (St. Petersburg team, August 2005), (3) west ridge (Moscow expedition, August 2005). *Alexey Gorbatenkov*

Koskulak (7,028m), first and second ascents by the west ridge and third ascent by the north face. Koskulak is situated in the Muztagh Ata Range and can be reached by the same route and logistics as Muztagh Ata itself. Until 2005 it remained unclimbed, neglected as other lower-altitude neighbors of Muztagh Ata and Kongur have been. The easiest route to the summit is quite obvious and does not require technical skills.

During the summer several expeditions attempted the mountain. The first to summit were Russians Leonid Fishkis, Dmitry Komarov and Alexandr Novik, who reached the top on August 10 via the west ridge. Two days later their route was repeated by seven members of another Russian expedition, from the Moscow Aviation Institute (they climb mountains as well as make airplanes).

At the same time two Russian climbers, Valery Shamalo and I from St. Petersburg, were attempting a more difficult route on the north face, from the Kalaxong glacier. This route had three distinct sections: an initial glacier and snow slopes; a rock barrier; steep snow slopes, followed by a large cornice and summit plateau. It was obvious that the main technical difficulties would be found on the rock barrier, but it was not clear from below how or even if the capping cornice could be climbed.

Above base camp and the Kalaxong Glacier was a long, steep slope of deep snow. Progress was strenuous and slow, requiring physical exertion rather than technical skills. We spent two nights out on this section, sheltering in crevasses. Above this slope lay the rock barrier, with an angle varying from 60-90°.

The main difficulties on the barrier were caused by thin ice or snow over rock, which made the climbing insecure and finding good belays difficult. We did not find any good bivouac sites in this section and had to make three consecutive sitting bivouacs. This section could be climbed faster, but we were not properly acclimatized and also had to haul the leader's rucksack. The barrier finished with steep snow slopes and scattered rock outcrops; here we established our last camp before the summit push. It was also our first comfortable night.

On our summit day, August 17, we had more strenuous deep snow before reaching the cornice, ascending only 100m per hour. The cornice was the last challenge. It was not possible to climb it with normal ice equipment, as the snow couldn't hold the weight of a climber, so we resorted to aid-climbing it using two snow anchors with ice gear. The cornice took two hours to complete, but from its top the summit was just 300m across a large snow plateau, which we crossed in an hour.

Although there may be other possible routes on the north face, we felt ours was the most logical and direct. We were also lucky with the weather. The nights were not very cold, which allowed us to be relatively comfortable during our sitting bivouacs.

ALEXEY GORBATENKOV, *Mountainguides.ru, Russia*

Yume Muztagh, first ascent. At 11:05 a.m. on August 1 all four members of our expedition succeeded in making the first ascent of an unnamed 6,345m peak in the Kun Lun Mountains. Although our average age was 61, all participated in every aspect of the climb, including load carrying, reconnaissance, and route selection. We did not employ local porters, horses, donkeys, or camels. Moreover, we received no outside financial and material support; the expedition, including a reconnaissance trip in 2004, was financed solely by its members. The party comprised a group of friends who have climbed together for decades and are well aware of each other's abilities and limitations.

The Xinjiang-Tibet Highway runs southeast from Kashgar along the southwestern edge of the Taklimakan Desert. At Yecheng the road splits, with the Highway running south, then southeast into the Lingzi Thang Plains, while a left branch continues east along the edge of the desert. We drove along the Highway for ca. 530m and made our base camp at one of the truck stops at Dahongliutan. Our proposed virgin peak was located 16km northeast of this point at N 35° 41'; E 79° 41' [These mountains are often referred to as the Aksai Chin—Ed.]. Our peak, the highest among a group of 6,000m mountains, lay at the end of a broad valley that curves towards the southeast. It is not visible from the road.

Because of the rich history and romance associated with the Silk Road, we were interested in the Kun Lun Mountains, rather than the better known Himalaya or Karakoram. A reconnaissance team in 2004 chose the mountain for its easy approach and, out of consideration for our ages, lack of great technical difficulty. So it was that on July 21, 2005, I (66) as leader, Hiromitsu Izutani (61), Toshikazu Kurimoto (56), and Eizo Maeda (61) arrived at Dahongliutan (4,265m). Although basic and without toilet facilities, the truck stop provided us with spacious and luxurious living quarters (compared to a tent), hot water, and a warm environment for recovery.

Conditions were such that we were able to drive eight kilometers across the desert and establish our advance base camp at 5,440m. The next day we placed Camp 1 on the shoulder of a scree-covered ridge at 5,800m. Above, a mixture of snow and rock led over a small top at 6,100m to a col on the far side at 6,010m, where we placed our second camp. We left here on August 1 and followed the snow-covered ridge crest, with a large cornice to one side, until a steep snow slope led to a junction with the north ridge. A gentle plateau extended toward the summit, which was a broad snow dome. We reached this easily and returned to Camp 1 the same day. We christened our mountain Yume Muztagh, a name that was later approved by the Kashgar Mountaineering Association. *Yume* means "dreams" in Japanese, while *Muztagh* is a snow- or ice-covered mountain in the local language of Uighur. All four of us are alumni of Kyoto University Alpine Club (KUAC) and members of the Academic Alpine Club of Kyoto University (AACK).

TOSHIO ITOH, *Japan*

Looking northwest into a high cirque close to the head of the Western Yurung Glacier, Kun Lun. The Russian expedition that attempted Pt 6,903m (a.k.a. Chongce Peak) thought all the visible peaks, which rise a relatively short distance above the glacier, were unclimbed. However, it appears that Pt 6,903m was climbed by two Japanese in August 1988, approaching up the East Chongce Glacier. *Otto Chkhetiani*

Unsupported crossing of the Western Kun Lun and attempt on Pt. 6,903m. In September a Russian team jointly led by Boris Malakhov and me, with Michael Bertov, Paul Demeshchik, and Sergey Zajko, made a northeast-to-southwest crossing of the Western Kun Lun. In this report we use the names that appear on old Russian maps from the end of 19th century. We have been on expeditions to Xinjiang since 1998, and our experience is that these names are much closer to local nomenclature than names on other maps. When it comes to glaciers, we have used names given by Chinese glaciologists.

We first traveled along the southern Taklamakan road to Keria (Yutian on Chinese maps) and then went south 75km to the village of Polu, which has been known to the outside world since the visits of Grabczewski and Przhewalsky. We hired donkeys and on September 9 left for a two-day journey to reach the Kar Yagde tributary. For the next month we did not meet a single person. The continuation through the Kurab-Darja Gorge involves approximately 50 river crossings and is described by Mark Newcomb in his article "Ultima Thule" (*AAJ 1997* p. 129).

This was our second expedition to this remote area. In autumn 2003 Andrey Lebedev, Malakhov, Alexander Zazhigin, and I left Goubauluk and travelled southwest over the Kudzhik-Bulak Pass, then on down alongside the Zejlik-Darja River to Yurung Kash. At this point we could neither travel along its banks nor ford the river. We retreated north, crossing a 5,880m

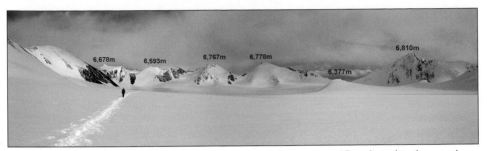

Looking southeast across the head of the Western Yurung Glacier, Kun Lun. All peaks in this photograph are thought to be unclimbed (and unattempted). Pt 6,778m is marked on the Chinese map as Yurung Peak. The 6,360m col, giving access to the East Chongce Glacier and crossed by the Russians, is situated directly behind Pt 6,377m. *Otto Chkhetiani*

The enigmatic Aksai Chin (7,167m), rarely seen from such close proximity and even more rarely visited by mountaineers. In this view from the southwest, the south ridge descends from the main summit toward the camera and the slightly lower north summit, Doufeng (6,957m), is visible behind. Both summits were climbed in 1986 via the south face to southeast ridge, which connected with the upper section of the south ridge. The main summit was reached again in 1997 by Japanese, and the north summit climbed from the southeast by French in 2006. *Otto Chkhetiani*

snow-covered pass and passing through two canyons before we regained civilization. We had to descend waterfalls, climb cliffs, and negotiate huge boulders. Steep walls towered 150-200m above us. We finally reached the large settlement Nur (southwest of Yutian).

Our 2005 way led much farther south than our 2003 explorations. After reaching a 5,140m pass, we headed south for 1.5km to visit an old volcano some 5,280m high. Below us lay the gravel floor of the Goubailyk Valley with its salty lakes, Achik Kel, Segiz Kel, and Ulug Kel, surrounded by a ring of 6,000m peaks and smaller volcanic cones. Later we climbed the 4,904m volcano, Achik Shan, which erupted in May 1951: we saw fields of volcanic ash and some freaky stone figures on the western banks of the Ulug Kel lake. Beyond, our route went down the left bank of the Yurung Kash (White Jade River), where we were lucky to find beautiful pieces of this fine stone on sandy terraces. This area is a paradise for animal lovers: we saw numerous herds of mountain sheep, goats, and yaks, while packs of wolves passed close to us.

We had planned to ascend the Middle Yurung Glacier, but it was obviously in surge. The badly fractured tongue had advanced 1.5-2km, cutting off the river valley. As far as we could see, travel up this glacier did not look feasible. Instead, we moved to the adjacent Western Yurung. This was also badly broken in its lower reaches, but we managed to ascend between the right edge and the moraine. Above 5,460m we continued on the glacier, where farther up we found fresh snow. This allowed us to use plastic sledges, but as we were often breaking trail through 60cm of snow, progress was still slow.

Finally, we reached the northern flanks of Pt. 6,903m and managed to climb to a height of 6,500m on this snowy mountain. Above was 300m of ca. 40° ice, accessed via a short snow slope. Unfortunately, fresh snow, the onset of stormy weather, and a resulting high avalanche danger forced us to retreat. [Pt. 6,903m is situated some distance west of Qong Muztagh, climbed by Japanese in 2000. The Russians believed Pt. 6,903m to be virgin, but it was climbed by Japanese in 1988; see *AAJ 1989*, p. 289 and *AAJ 2001*, p. 406—Ed.]

We continued through a 6,360m col between Peaks 6,775m and 6,840m and began our descent (toward the Lingzu Thang Plains) via the East Chongce Glacier. This was a fantastic journey with snowy peaks to the south and the impressive mountains of the Aksai Chin to the north. Close to the waters of the Gozho Tso were herds of Orongo antelope, yaks, and small groups of kiang. On October 7, having traveled unsupported for 28 days over a distance of ca. 400km, we reached the Xinjiang-Tibet Highway

OTTO CHKHETIANI, *Moscow, Russia*

SICHUAN

SHALULI SHAN

Xiashe (5,833m), first ascent. On October 13 Patricia Deavoll of New Zealand and I made the first ascent of Xiashe, via the south face and southwest ridge. We arrived in the region on October 1 accompanied by an interpreter, Zhengling Cheng (Lenny), and staff. Access to the area involved a three-day drive from Chengdu over very rough, uneven roads that crossed several 4,000m passes.

Our initial plan was to climb the north face of Xiashe. However, we discovered the north face to be

Xiashe (5,833m) seen after fresh snowfall during the approach from the Zhopu Valley to the north. The long unclimbed northeast ridge, rocky in its lower section, falls left from the summit toward the valley. The route of the first ascent follows the hidden valley to the right, in front of the north face, and crosses a col on the southwest (right skyline) ridge to reach the south face. This face was climbed to the upper section of the southwest ridge some distance right of the summit. The small peak in the left background is probably Pt 5,328m and unclimbed. *Karen McNeill*

"dry" and apparently out of condition. While acclimatizing we changed our goal to the longer, more aesthetic, rock-and-snow east ridge. These plans too became thwarted with the arrival of a weather system that brought frequent thunderstorms, which deposited up to 60cm of fresh snow. We maintained hope that the snow would melt, leaving the rock on the east ridge dry.

On October 8 a three-person British team arrived at base camp with the same climbing objective. [The British team reached the summit on October 17 via the north face, see below—Ed.] The arrival of a new team and the deep snow were just the incentive for us to try the peak via another route. We left base camp on October 10, collecting equipment from caches and making carries farther up the valley. It took two further days, wading through deep, unconsolidated snow, to get established at a 5,300m col on the southwest ridge, from which we felt we could make a summit bid.

We left high camp at 1 a.m. on October 13, descending ca. 300m to a glacier on the south face. We spent several hours in the dark ascending the snowy face. Fortunately, we'd brought snowshoes. We gained the southwest ridge around 5 a.m. and once on the crest we followed it directly to the summit. Daylight arrived at 7 a.m., and we reached the summit at 8:45 a.m. The fine weather afforded spectacular views of the Daxue Shan to the east and many other mountains in every direction. We descended the same route and arrived back at high camp by 2 p.m.

After returning to base camp, we spent the next four days resting and deciding on another objective. On October 19 a staff member drove us across the Zhopu pasture, getting as close as possible to the base of Jarjinjabo, a striking 5,812m peak ca. 15km northwest of Xiashe. After four days we established a high camp, but a storm arrived and lasted for over 50 hours. Unable to wait any longer, we abandoned our plans and on the 25th returned to the Zhopu Monastery, where the staff was waiting. The team was back in Chengdu on October 30.

The expedition was awarded a 2005 Shipton/Tilman grant by W.L. Gore.

KAREN MCNEILL, *Canada*

Xiashe, north face; Peak 5,690m, northeast ridge, attempt. It was Tamotsu Nakamura's telephoto of Xiashe's north face appearing in the *AAJ* that persuaded us to visit. We were looking for an objective that would require little acclimatization, was accessible, and not too difficult. The north face seemed to fit these criteria. However, we had also heard rumors of a previous unauthorized expedition, and these were later confirmed: a Korean team had indeed been to Xiashe in the late 1990s but was unsuccessful.

The north face of Xiashe (5,833m), seen from the northeast ridge of Pt 5,690m. The solid line shows the Douglas-Tunstall route and bivouac sites, while the dashed line shows their descent (southwest ridge to south face then back over to the north flank), which simply reversed the route followed by Deavoll and McNeill earlier the same month for the first ascent of the mountain. *Tom Prentice*

After three days' acclimatization and two days of driving at altitude to reach the Zhopu Valley, Duncan Tunstall and I left base camp on October 13 with three gas canisters and food for three evening meals. At 5 p.m. we reached a flat area at ca. 4,500m on a moraine ridge below the north face. Alarm clock issues meant we didn't start until 8 a.m. on the 14th. An easy snow slope followed by 10m of Scottish 3 and a long, rightwards-leading ramp led into the gully that runs the entire length of the face. Reaching this point, at an altitude of ca. 5,200m, took most of the day and involved punching up a mixture of consolidated and unconsolidated snow over loose rock. Stopping at 4:30 p.m., we dug a ledge for the tent and after a surprisingly bad night, made worse by spindrift avalanches, started again at 8 a.m., trailing the rope. The angle of the face steepened from 45°-50° to something more like 70°, and the climbing consequently became harder. We climbed a lot of Grade 3/4, but as we ascended, the covering of snow became less consolidated. Eventually, we broke out of the gully, to reach the crest of the spur that forms its left edge. This gave steep mixed climbing on rotten rock with sections of

Scottish 4 and 5. In fact, overall the route was quite serious with weird, fractured blocky rock and poor belays. On several occasions cracks split when torqued. Even when the climbing was not hard, there was no room for falling. With the summit ridge 150m above, it began to get dark. We eventually stopped at the right edge of a serac barrier extending from the summit and dug out half a ledge. The night passed very slowly.

Next morning was cloudy, and a little snow had fallen. After a brew, Duncan led a steep pitch of 4/5 on good ice and névé. I led a pitch on less solid but easier ground, belaying a few feet below the cornice. Duncan cut through this on solid ice, reaching the crest of the west ridge and the steps of the New Zealand and Canadian women who had made the first ascent of Xiashe several days previously. Less than five minutes later we reached the 5,833m summit and after a quick inspection of the east ridge, chose to follow the steps of the two women down to the west. By 4 p.m. we had reached the base of the ridge and pitched our tent. Next morning we made the long climb back up to and over the west col and slogged down through new snow to base camp.

Tom Prentice, our third team member, opted not to go on the north face and instead made a determined solo effort on the neighboring Peak 5,690m via its long northeast ridge. This peak, which is well seen from the silver mine on the road to Zhopu Monastery, faces Xiashe and, with it, encloses the west valley in a horseshoe. On the 14th Prentice set up camp at 4,600m in the hanging corrie clearly marked on Nakamura's map; the corrie forms the west side of the west valley. The following day Prentice ascended deep snow over boulders and scree to gain the northeast ridge. He followed the snow-covered crest around various towers until stopped by a prominent gendarme, where a western spur marked on Nakamura's map meets the main ridge at ca. 5,300m. Loose, unstable ground covered with unconsolidated snow, the lack of a rope, and diminishing daylight combined to force a retreat. Above, a long snow ridge appeared to lead all the way to the summit, and the route, which gives an excellent view of Xiashe's north face, should prove relatively straightforward for a pair of climbers.

The weather had been snowy prior to our arrival, and on our first night it snowed heavily, threatening our bargain basement Chinese tents with abject failure. However, this snow cleared quickly during the day, and although temperatures were never high, life was pleasantly warm in the sunshine. Good weather prevailed throughout our climb, ending during the night of October 16-17 with a big storm and a dump of fresh snow.

This region is as interesting for the strong Tibetan nomadic culture as it is for the climbing. Undermining this culture in the future will be a new village planned for the grassland. In addition, the presence of a silver mine and plans to upgrade the service road will also damage both the way of life and the area's considerable natural appeal.

Ed Douglas, *United Kingdom*

West Sichuan Highland, an exploratory visit and first ascent of Peak 5,160m. On the advice of Tamotsu Nakamura, a party from the Yamanashi Mountaineering Federation visited the unknown mountains of South Kham, Sichuan, from October 1 to 16. The area is located at the west end of the Litang High Plateau at approximately N 30° 10', E 99° 30'. It lies south of the Sichuan-Tibet Highway, north of the Genyen Massif (6,204m) in the Shahluli Shan and east of the Upper Yangtze (Jinshajiang or River of Golden Sand). To the best of our knowledge and that of Mr. Nakamura, there was no record of foreigners visiting the area since Brigadier George Pereira's tragic journey in 1923. However, Pereira didn't go to the mountains that we planned to explore.

The party consisted of me, Shigeru Aoki, as leader and six other members, including four from a university alpine club. We focused on exploring the region around a hidden glacier lake, Tsonahou Tso, in particular a group of unknown 5,700-5,800m peaks southwest of the lake. The highest, which is nameless, has an elevation of 5,870m. The second highest is called Xiangqiuqieke (5,863m), and there are two 5,700m peaks. The lake, which lies in Batang County, is comb shaped, 3.5km long, 600-700m wide, and 8km in circumference.

On October 5, after a four-day drive from Chengdu, we left the Sichuan Highway at road maintenance office 283 (4,392m) on the Litang Plateau and began our caravan towards the southwest. Four horses, 11 yaks, and 3 Tibetan muleteers dealt with our loads. We crossed a 4,950m pass and walked 20km the first day. This took us to a good camping location near the lake. We set up a base camp on a grassy spot at 4,600m, looking down on the lake. Beyond and to the southwest, 5,000m peaks were visible, as were snow-clad 6,000m peaks farther west. We stopped here for four days, during which the weather was bad, with snow every afternoon.

On the second day we explored Tsonahou Tso. It is a glacier lake damming a U-shaped valley at a height of 4,300m. The water was a beautiful emerald green. Player flags of local Tibetan Buddhists were fluttering on the bank and in the valley. On the third day all members ascended a nameless 5,160m peak from the north and studied neighboring high peaks, with Himalayan fluted ice, for as long as time allowed. The enigmatic 5,800m Xiangqiuqieke and other outstanding peaks were revealed to us. On the fifth day we started our return journey.

Shigeru Aoki, *translated by Tom Nakamura of the Japanese Alpine News*

Gongkala Shan

Gongkala Shan, foiled attempt to gain the mountain; Haizi Shan, attempt. In September and October Toto Gronlund, Peter Rowat, Dave Wynne Jones, and I attempted the peaks of Kawarani I and II (5,992m and 5,928m) in the small Gongkala Range of Western Sichuan. In two days by road from Chengdu we reached the town of Garze and spent three days reconnoitering the north and south sides of the Gongkala peaks. There were possible routes from the north, but they did not appear easy, and we decided the south side offered better prospects.

A good grazing trail led from the village of Khur Chong into the gorge of the Yalung Jiang River and around the hillside to a hanging valley directly below the southern glaciers of Kawarani I and II. From there it appeared possible to reach the ca. 5,500m col between Kawarani I and II. From the col there seemed to be routes to both summits.

Below the village were two or three apparently inactive monasteries. We stopped at the principal one but found no one to talk to. We continued to the village, where we found the people friendly and cooperative. We explained our plans and learned they were happy to assist us, making horses available to carry to base camp. On the afternoon of our first visit there was a thunderstorm with lots of large hail; this was not unusual, as it appeared the monsoon was not yet over.

Two days later we returned with our gear and had an uneventful journey to a base camp at 4,200m. The monastery showed its good will by providing a monk leading a large white yak at the head of the column. We were told he had been sent to bless our climb. There was no evidence that any climbers had been in this area before, so we could hardly have gotten off to a more auspicious start.

Four days later we had just completed carrying to a second camp at 4,800m when a delegation of around 40 monks came up the hillside and insisted we leave at once. They were from the same monastery that had assisted and blessed us earlier. They simply said that they had changed their minds as a result of two thunderstorms, which they believed we caused. They had no respect for our permit from the Sichuan Mountaineering Association and were thoroughly confrontational and unpleasant to deal with. We were clearly outnumbered, and after a long and unproductive discussion, during which distinctly non-pacifist attitudes were repeatedly displayed, we decided we had no alternative but to go down.

We spent part of the following day retrieving our gear from the depths of the monastery. Nothing went missing, but money had to change hands to get it all back. A protest to the civil administrator of the Garze Tibetan Ethnic Group Autonomous Prefecture, which governs this area from Kangding, drew only the comment that these monasteries can be difficult to deal with. (This gentleman himself is a reincarnate Lama.)

We are not the only party to have encountered difficulties of this kind in Western China. See, for instance, *AAJs* 2001, p. 408, and 2003, p. 410. Part of the problem may be the relative independence of the Garze Tibetan Prefecture from central control. The monastery's stated reasons for their actions have little credibility, as thunderstorms and hail were regular events in the area. Possibly the simple fact that we were the first outsiders to go into these mountains was enough to spook them, but it seems more likely that we got into the middle of a feud between monastery and village, which we could hardly have foreseen. (There was some fragmentary evidence for this.)

We were able to get our permit switched to Haizi Shan (5,833m) and spent our last 10 days attempting to complete the route which Geoff Cohen and I had tried on the north flank in spring 2004 (*AAJ 2005*, p. 415). Unfortunately, the weather was poor, and on October 10 we retreated in a foot of new snow from the bottom of the northern glaciers at 4,800m. The peak, we believe, is still unclimbed despite several attempts.

DICK ISHERWOOD, *Alpine Club*

DAXUE SHAN

Yala, west-southwest ridge, attempt. From October 20 to November 1 the GORE-AAIC First Ascents team attempted a new route on the west-southwest ridge of Yala (a.k.a. Yala Xeushan, Zhara, Ja-ra, or Haizi Shan, the King of Mountains, 5,833m). Our expedition started in Chengdu, as do all expeditions climbing in Sichuan Province. On the 20th we drove all day to a small town named Bamei, stopping briefly in Kangding to have the Ganzi Prefecture Mountaineering Association stamp the official red seal on our permit.

Bamei is a small, grubby place at the junction of three roads. Small, shabby auto repair shops, stores, and other hole-in-a-wall businesses necessary to the trucking industry have developed at this junction. Among this sprawl the old town still maintains some of its charm, and there is even a lovely Tibetan home, bequeathed with a courtyard flower garden. We stayed there that evening.

On the 21st we drove the short distance to the Taizhan Valley and from the roadhead employed horses to carry equipment to the natural hot springs. After a four-hour walk, we made base camp at 4,050m on grassy fields near the hot springs.

We then had almost 30cm of snowfall, but on the 24th it stopped and the sky cleared. I became restless and walked up to Camp 1. The route followed small, skinny couloirs. I placed camp in a large boulder field on the north side of the west-southwest ridge. The following day the entire team made the trip to Camp 1.

On the 26th Chen Cheng, Su Rongqin, Ma Yihua, and I, all guides working with the Arête Alpine Instruction Center in Chengdu, climbed to Camp 2 at 5,010m. The route followed the north face of the west ridge. When we reached the crest, the wind was howling, blowing directly from the south. We made camp on the leeward side, and Su Rongqin descended to base camp that evening.

A two-day storm had deposited a thick layer of unconsolidated snow on the primarily rocky ridge above, where initially the solid-granite crest was stepped, a horizontal section generally being followed by a steep rock face. Wind and blowing snow plagued our entire ascent, and the route proved very time-consuming. Two sections involved sack-hauling, while a few others required the leader to climb without a pack, then rappel and jumar back up with his sack.

We spent the night of the 27th in a half-erected tent on a small ledge at 5,250m. The next day we only managed to climb 147 vertical meters. The following morning we avoided the crest by a snow slope on the right, but when forced back to the ridge, were surprised to find it changed in character: narrower, steeper, and composed of large unstable blocks. Progress on less-steep sections often involved gingerly crawling along the crest, while the vertical parts involved climbing difficult rock in boots and crampons. One small section required easy aid.

We sited the last camp at a little over 5,500m, but by the afternoon of the following day, with obviously looser rock above, we realized we were not going to make the summit by the ridge. At 6 p.m., a little more than 200 vertical meters below the summit, we decided to rappel into the gully on the left. The gully would not only provide a campsite for the night, but hopefully we could downclimb it to a point where it met other couloirs, one of which we might be able to follow directly to the summit ridge.

We did not make a conscious decision to abandon our route that evening, but once we'd started rappelling, we kept going down. We descended for 15 hours through the night, enduring a storm with erratic, bitter cold winds and whipping spindrift, and finally reaching base camp at 9 a.m. on the 31st. Concentration during the descent was so great that at 10:47 p.m. an earthquake measuring 4.2 on the Richter Scale, with an epicenter just 20km away, occurred unnoticed. We rated the climb to our high point Alpine TD 5.10 A0. Despite a number of attempts to date, Yala remains unclimbed.

JON OTTO, *AAC and Arête Alpine Instruction Center, Chengdu, China*

QONGLAI SHAN

SIGUNIANG NATIONAL PARK

Jiang Jun Feng, Bipeng Valley, first ascent. Chris Chitty, Pat Goodman, Ari Menitove and I were to travel to the Qionglai Range to explore and make first ascents in the Shuangqiao Valley. However, during planning before we left for China, we heard about an adjacent valley called the Bipeng, which had only become easily accessible two years ago, because of a new road. This valley lies north of the Shuangqiao and just across a ridge from our primary objectives, but is approached from the other side of the range. This area was written up in *AAJ 2005* by Jon Otto, who gave us what information we had. When we got to China in mid-September, we met Jon and saw more photos of this valley. With the prospect of at least 10 unclimbed 5000+m rock peaks, we deemed it worthy and went there first.

We arrived at the trailhead in one day from Chengdu and stayed at a local hostel/guest-house. The weather was good the next day, and we were impressed with the valley and its offer-ings. We located a decent camp along the trail going up and over into the Changping Valley, right below one of the more striking peaks (Jiang Jun Feng, 5,202m) and a promising-looking wall of granite spires. The weather was good for two or three days, allowing us to acclimatize and make a reconnaissance. The northeast face of 5,202m was the obvious big objective for us, but as we prepared to begin a route, bad weather set in. For the next five or six days, rain, snow, and fog kept us in our tents or under the boulder we used as a cooking shelter.

When the weather began to clear on September 28, Pat and I made a quick unroped ascent of 5,202m, via the ca. 900m northwest buttress, a low-angle fin of rock just left of a giant talus field. We carried a rope and some gear but never even put on our climbing shoes. Most of the terrain was scrambling, but a few steps required climbing up to about 5.7. We climbed to the west summit, which we believe to be the tallest point on the massif. As it turned out, this was also the best day's weather of the trip.

Ari and Chris began a route on the northeast face. They came across a fair bit of loose rock and incipient features, interspersed with sections of good 5.10-5.11. They were climbing with no bolt kit and only a few pins. Ultimately they would have needed more of an aid rack to continue. As the weather window was again starting to close, they came down after five pitches. That same day Pat and I explored the wall of granite above camp and adjacent to Jiang Jun Feng. To our amazement this wall was made up of beautiful compact granite, covered with splitter cracks. Unfortunately, the cracks were completely filled with dirt and grass. Cleaning even one pitch would have taken hours. We did find a few clean cracks on a detached pillar at the base of the wall and installed anchors above three very good lines. Pat climbed the first splitter offwidth to place anchors, and we intended to return the next day to finish the other two, but we had neither time nor weather for cleaning the walls above. Bad weather set in, and we spent the rest of the trip toiling in the squalor of our tents or the cooking cave. This expedi-tion was supported by the AAC Lyman Spitzer Grant and Cascade Designs. Thanks to both for their generous assistance.

TOMMY CHANDLER

Editor's note: Tom Nakamura was probably the first foreigner to travel and photograph the Bipeng Val-ley. In 1998 he crossed from the Bipeng to the Changping via the 4,644m pass one kilometer west of Jiang Jun Feng. In AAJ 2005, p. 423, we reported an ascent of both Camel Peaks by Tom Chamberlain et al (first climbed by Charlie Fowler in 1994) as Pts. 5,202m and 5,484m. In fact 5,484m is a double sum-mited peak (the Camel Peaks) with both tops roughly the same height. On the 1:50,000 Chinese People's Liberation Army Map, Pt. 5,484m is West Camel Peak.

"The Angry Wife," first ascent, via north ridge (Raindog Arête); Daogou, first ascent, via south face (Salvage Op). In early September Jay Janousek, Joe Puryear, Stoney Richards, Paul Saddler, and I left Seattle for the Qionglai Mountains, with our main objective a new route on Siguniang (6,250m). After establishing ourselves in the Changping valley we climbed the west summit

of Camel Peak (a.k.a. Luotou, 5,484m), then set our sights on the northwest face of Siguniang, a 900m rock wall rising straight out of the glacier just right of the 2002 Fowler-Ramsden ice couloir. This magnificent wall tops out at nearly 6,000m; above, the summit of the mountain is guarded by seracs. Due to the height of the route and the fickle weather, we planned to adopt capsule-style, big-wall tactics.

Puryear, Richards, and I ferried loads up 1,500m to an advanced camp across from the base of the route at 5,100m. During a brief two-day weather window, Joe and I led the first four pitches up a corner system, which appeared to offer the least objective hazard. A series of troughs then blew into the Siguniang region. Joe, Stoney, and I took shelter in a portaledge at the base of the route for the next nine days, until it became obvious there was no chance of reaching the summit via this route. Having spent nearly four weeks working and waiting, with only a week

The Angry Wife (5,005m) in the Chiwen Gorge, Siguniang National Park. The line of Raindog Arête (550m, 5.10c) on the north ridge is marked. Joe Puryear

left in our trip, we decided to retrieve our gear. While double carrying loads back to base camp, we met a Russian team making a reconnaissance. The Russians were interested in a winter ascent of the northwest wall.

Back at base Stoney, Joe, and I decided to hike up the Chiwen Gorge for the remaining six days. As we passed west of Celestial Peak (a.k.a. Pomiu, 5,413m) the weather began to improve, and we set our sights on an attractive north-facing rock ridge higher up the valley. Dropping our packs under a large boulder, we began rock climbing in earnest at 4,500m. I led the first block of four pitches, the last of which was 5.10. Stoney led the next four pitches, following the line on the ridge between sun and shade. On his fourth pitch Stoney solved the 5.10c crux, which involved climbing thin, weaving, moss-filled cracks. Joe led the last two pitches to gain the summit at dusk. There was no evidence of a previous ascent, and we named the peak The Angry Wife (5,005m). Nine rappels down the east face led to the base of the route, which we named Raindog Arête (550m, 5.10c). We left only single pitons and stoppers on the descent.

The following day we hiked to the top of the Chiwen Gorge and reached a pass leading down to the Shuangqiao Valley. Knowing little about the valley into which we were descending, we were fortunate to discover a goat trail across the base of Chibu (5,450m) that shortened our descent considerably. As we rounded the base of Chibu, large rock towers emerged at the head of the valley. Of the three stunning rock summits, the main peak of Daogou, which had been attempted previously by Americans from the north, looked a particularly formidable challenge.

The south face of the main peak of Daogou (5,466m), east of the Shuangqiao Valley, Siguniang National Park. The line followed on the first ascent, Salvage Op (650m, 5.10d), is marked. *Joe Puryear*

On the cloudy morning of October 13 we hiked to the base, keeping right of a south-facing buttress. At ca. 4,700m we reached the head of a small, talus-filled cirque and began to climb a prominent drainage, where we found a direct line up the south face. The route began with a deep 5cm-8cm hand crack, but then the terrain eased, and we soloed low-to-mid-fifth class rock for the next few hundred meters, until the headwall steepened. The granite was excellent and on the headwall gave sustained 5.10 climbing above 5,000m. The crux was the summit block.

Joe describes the final pitch: "Unsure of which block was the actual summit, I led a difficult pitch on the east side, only to find that I had gone the wrong way. I rappelled back to a ramp and climbed around to the other side, where I found a horrifying series of ice-filled off-widths and chimneys. A 5.10d off-width over a bomb-bay chimney led to another chimney, with an overhanging chockstone. The mental crux came at the final block, where I had to chimney up a one-meter-wide gap, nearly 20m out from my last piece, and mantel onto the sloping summit edge." This lead was testament to the climbing skill Joe has developed in the Alaska Range.

We stood on the 5,466m summit before dusk, concerned that Joe had frost-nipped his toes. Stoney set the anchors as we rappelled 17 pitches to the base of the route, which we named Salvage Op (650m, 5.10d). We left only single pitons and stoppers on the descent.

CHAD KELLOGG, *AAC*

Changping Valley, first ascents of Chiwen, "The Little Prince," and Chibu. On September 11 Katy Holm, Aidan Oloman, and I left Vancouver for Rilong, a growing mountain town and access point for the Siguniang Shan National Reserve. From there we made reconnaissance hikes in the Changping and Shuangquao valleys. In the latter the walls are steep, with interesting architecture: fluted ridges and featured faces. However, it rained throughout our trip, and the granite looked slick, mossy, and unappealing. In contrast, our walk through the Changping was bright and sunny. We found an easily accessible

Aidan Oloman bouldering in the valley below Chibu (5,466m), Siguniang National Park. *Katherine Fraser*

hanging valley ringed by unclimbed granite peaks. It was an easy decision.

Back in Rilong we located Mr. Mah. He is a local horse packer, who has served multiple climbing teams; his trophies are fleeces and hats from past expeditions. Mr. Mah is a bargaining tactician who uses the language barrier to his advantage. He upsized us to four horses, yet he was fair, reliable, and entertaining. He dropped our gear by the river below our valley (two drainages north of Celestial Peak and the last main side valley to the west of the Changping before it starts its big bend to the west), and we carried loads up to a high camp.

The east face of Chibu (5,466m), showing the line of the first ascent by Canadians Katherine Fraser, Katy Holm, and Aidan Oloman. The climb gave 14 pitches on good granite to 5.10+. *Katherine Fraser*

We waited through four rainy days before attempting Chiwen (5,250m) on the south side of the valley. We climbed 10 long pitches in poor weather to the summit; some were 4th class (400m, 5.9). We attempted a 5,006m peak northwest of Chiwen, on the ridge towards Chibu. We first called the peak The Little Guy, but after he thwarted us three times we upgraded him to The Little Prince. We then bivouacked below Chibu (5,466m), the aesthetic prize of the valley. In a long day we climbed 14 pitches of sustained 5.9-5.10+, linking the steep gendarmes up the left side of the east face. The granite was good, and cracks were continuous. We descended our route in the dark. After waiting out a snow storm we finally summited The Little Prince (300m, 5.10+). We left the valley in slashing rain. In the 16 days we spent there we did not see anyone else.

The weather was poor to fair. It rained almost every second night, but when the sun does come out it dries the rock quickly. From local reports it seems that October is colder but has more consistent high pressure.

There is not a lot of unclimbed technical alpine rock left in the Changping, which is the more popular of the two parallel valleys for Chinese hikers and trekkers. However, a more thorough investigation of the Shuangqiao is warranted, a valley that has the advantage of being accessible by bus.

We acknowledge the support of the John Lauchlan Award and the Jen Higgins Fund.

KATHERINE FRASER, *Canada*

Editor's note: Aidan Oloman was killed by an avalanche in interior British Columbia in January 2006.

Putala Shan (5,428m), north face, solo. The north face of Putala Shan is an impressive big wall, which I have tried twice. I have not attempted the same mountain twice since 1990, when I made my last winter solo attempt on Fitz Roy in Patagonia. My first attempt on Putala did not go well. I hoped success would be the sign of my comeback, and I wanted to prove to myself that I was not finished as a climber.

I first saw Putala Shan in the autumn of 2003. I was trekking as part of my rehabilitation a year after my accident in Gyachung Kang. [In 2002 Yamanoi lost a total of five fingers on both hands and all of the toes on his right foot as a result of bad weather during an alpine-style

Seen from the northwest across the Shuangqiao Valley: the unclimbed Pt 5,592m (a.k.a. Barbarian Peak; left) and Putala Shan (5,428m). (1) Jiayou (north face) (850m, 18 pitches, 5.8 A3+, Yamanoi, 2005, not to summit). (2) Dalai Lama (west face) (800m, 22 pitches, VIII-, Grmovsek-Grmovsek, 2003). *Andrej Grmovsek*

ascent and descent of the north face of Gyachung Kang—Ed.]. Even compared to the big walls of places like Yosemite, the face on Putala seemed most attractive. In fact, I noticed many beautiful crack lines extending up to the crest. Although I made my final attempt after carefully evaluating my physical condition and cold weather equipment, the climb was as difficult as expected.

On June 25 we established base camp in a beautiful meadow at an altitude of 3,700m. My wife Taeko Yamanoi supported me as base camp manager, with a cook and an interpreter. On the 27th I carried equipment and provisions to the bottom of the wall, at approximately 4,500m, then spent a week fixing rope on the first 300m, in weather as bad as on my last attempt. Progress was difficult due to continuous rain and snow. As I chose a route following a large corner, ice fell on me frequently.

On July 13 I began in earnest my capsule-style attempt with a portaledge. The rock, especially on the lower part of the route, is solid granite, but as I climbed higher expanding flakes slowed my progress to about one pitch a day. Ice coating the rock prevented free climbing, so I was forced to use aid. Shortly after beginning, I got slight frostbite on my hands and feet, which are now my Achilles heel after my accident in 2002. Both my down jacket and sleeping bag were soaked, so my extremities were unable to recover, and as I was unable to sleep, I also began to suffer from exhaustion. To make matters worse, the sun never reached the face, and the snow and ice sticking to the upper part of the wall made the climb very stressful. However, on the 19th, the seventh day of my climb, I topped out on the crest at an altitude of 5,350m. I needed two more days to rappel the route and return to base camp.

Summary: first ascent of Putala Shan north face (not to summit) via Jiayou (Chinese for "come on" or "do your best"); 850m, 18 pitches, 5.8 A3+.

YASUSHI YAMANOI, *Japan*

Eagle Rock Peak, first ascent. A man wearing a leather jacket with a bloody knife in his hands stands by the roadside, digging inside the body of a slaughtered yak. We realized we were in China.

Christof Looser, Martin Ruggli, and I started out for the now-famous Quonglai mountains, 280km east of Chengdu, on September 25. Our goal was to establish a new route on one of the rock peaks north of Siguniang. Our information came from Tamotsu Nakamura.

After reconnaissance we set up base camp in the Shuangqiao Valley (Double Bridge Valley) at an altitude of ca. 3,500m. Recently a (horrible) road has been built into this valley to bring hundreds of Chinese tourists from one scenic spot to the next. The tourists stick pretty much to the road, leaving the rest of the valley quiet.

After a few days we discovered the beautiful, interesting, south face of Eagle Rock Peak (ca. 5,300m) south of Putala Shan. The summit looks like an eagle's beak and can be seen from the valley floor, but the south face is hidden.

Sichuan does not seem to be a place for those who like stable weather, and we had to deal with a mix of snow, rain, and clouds, with only a few spells of sunshine. During changable weather we set up high camp at 4,500m and ferried everything we needed. We had five 60m ropes: two twins and three singles. Due to continuing poor weather we fixed the first 240m (eight pitches). After 12 days (five days ferrying loads, three days fixing, and four days of bad weather) we set off for the big push. On the first day we jugged our ropes and climbed to the top of pitch 13, where we could fit a small tent. The next day we fixed three 60m ropes on the headwall. On the day after, October 14, we reached the previously virgin summit in evening light and returned to the tent, before starting our descent the

The south face of Eagle Rock (the ca. 5,300m South Summit of Putala Shan), showing the first ascent route, I Hate Camping (700m, 7a A3; Dürr-Looser-Ruggli, 2005). *Lukas Dürr*

following morning. In all, we spent seven days on the wall. Our route, which we named I Hate Camping, is about 700m long, 21 pitches, with difficulties up to 7a and A3. We placed a total of 13 bolts. The east side of Shuangqiao Valley sports many rocky peaks with big granite walls. There is great potential for future climbs, but many faces are slabby and lacking in features. As far as we are aware we were the only climbers in the valley during our time there in October.

LUKAS DÜRR, *Switzerland*

Editor's note: Eagle Rock Peak is the south summit of Putala Shan. The latter has three summits. The highest (5,428m) is the most northerly and was climbed in 2003 by Andrej and Tanja Grmovsek (see AAJ 2004, pp. 420-2).

Shuangqiao Gou, first ascents of "Pakla Shan," "Shuangqiao Peak," and the northwest face of Tan Shan. The Croatian Mountaineering Federation, to celebrate its 130th anniversary, organized a small expedition to Siguniang National Park. There were four of us: Darko Berljak as leader, Dubravko Markovic as doctor, and two climbers, Ivica Matković from Split and I, Boris Čujić, from Zagreb. Our trip lasted from September 13 to October 15. After reaching Rilong by bus, we took a ride into the Shuangqiao Gou (Two Bridges Valley), where we set up base camp. We then chose to climb in a smaller valley, a three-hour walk away. It was the valley where Slovenians

The northwest face of Tan Shan (4,943m) to the east of the Shuangqiao Valley. Marked is the new Croatian Route (450m, 6a+). This peak was first climbed in 2003 by Slovenians Andrej and Tanja Grmovsek via the south face (Don't Fly Away, 450m, VIII/VIII+). *Boris Cujic collection*

The south face of Shuangqiao Peak (5,100m) showing Kingdom of Heaven (780m of climbing, 6c+, Cujic-Matkovic, 2005). *Boris Cujic*

Andrej and Tanja Grmovsek had climbed in 2003 (see *AAJ 2004* pp. 420-422).

On the day after our arrival at base camp, Ivica and I set off for the first of our objectives: the northwest face of Tan Shan (4,943m), a peak first climbed by the Grmovseks via a hard route on the south face (Don't Fly Away, 450m, VIII/VIII+ obl). We climbed a new 450m route up a big dihedral system, with difficulties up to ca. 6a+. We rappelled the line, using only two bolts for anchors. A long period of bad weather then confined us to camp, even forcing us down to Rilong for a beer.

After 10 days we returned to our advanced base, but the following morning it started raining, and we couldn't even see the wall. At 11 a.m. it began to clear, and we started up a new route on a small wall 100m from camp, facing the route we had previously climbed on Tan Shan. The rock was wet, but after four hours we reached a 4,600m previously unclimbed summit. We christened the peak Pakla Shan (in honor of our own famous crag, Paklenica) and the route up the southeast face For Sanja and Adela (after our wives, who always support us). The length of the route was 450m and the difficulty 6b.

The next day, at last, was beautiful, and we started up our main goal, unclimbed Shuangqiao Peak (5,100m). We chose a fairly direct line up the south face. The rock was bad in the lower part but very good in the upper part. However, with a drill it would have been possible to make a nice route in the lower section. Our new route, named Kingdom of Heaven (the old Chinese name for Sichuan) was 780m long, with difficulties of 6c+. We rappelled the line of ascent.

The potential for long, hard big wall routes is this area is huge, even extremely hard climbs. Everything is cheap, and access is good, with approachs of from two to six hours from the vehicle. The best months are September and October, but rain or snow is normal. In winter there are nice waterfalls for climbing.

BORIS ČUJIĆ, *Croatia*

Editor's note: very recent information suggests that the south face of Shuangqiao may have been climbed in 2000 by Italians Gianluca Belin and Diego Stefani (850m: 6c and A1). They refer to the summit as Wong Shan.

CHENGDU REGION

Daxuetang (5,364m), first ascent. Daxuetang lies almost due south of Siguniang and is the highest peak within the boundaries of Chengdu city. It borders Wolong Giant Panda Nature Preserve, and we approached and climbed the mountain from that side. From Chengdu the Sichuan-Tibetan Highway leads through Wolong (the Giant Panda Research Center) toward Xiaojin and Siguniang. The trailhead is at Dengsheng (2,730m), right before the road starts switchbacking up toward the Balang Pass.

Boris Cujic high on Kingdom of Heaven, south face of Shuangqiao Peak (5,100m). Below and to the right, with the obvious smooth slabby wall, is Pakla Shan (4,600m), also climbed by Croatians Cujic and Matkovic. The new road up the Shuangqiao Valley is clearly visible far below. *Boris Cujic collection*

Daxuetang has several peaks, and the topography is confusing. Two are fairly close in height. In Spring 2002 Liu Jian, a newspaper reporter from Chengdu, claimed to have made the first ascent. However, it turned out that he summited Daxuetang's northernmost peak (Pk. 2), which is about 10m lower than the main peak, immediately to the south. In October 2003 a joint Japanese-Chinese team climbed the mountain, also thinking they were making the first ascent. However, they reached the same summit as Liu Jian.

The Goretex-Arête Alpine Instruction Center First Ascents team comprising Chen Cheng (Chengdu), Ma Yihua (Chengdu, leader), Su Rongqin (Fujian), Tselantou (Heishui County), and Zhang Jian (Chongqing) left Chengdu on May 21. From Dengsheng they walked up the Yeliu Valley and camped below the Baishuitai waterfall at 3,600m. On the 23rd they established base camp at 4,700m. Their route then followed the "Bowling Alley" on the northeast face of Daxuetang to Camp 1 at 5,250m. On the 27th Ma Yihua summited Pk. 2. But then two large rocks hit the tent at Camp 1, and the team retreated to Chengdu for a replacement.

On June 1 they again left Chengdu, to attempt the main summit. They followed the same route to Camp 1 but then traversed around the left side of a small pinnacle to reach a knife-edge ridge connecting Pk. 2 with the main summit. All five Chinese climbers followed the ridgeline southeast for 200m and reached the summit dome late in the afternoon. Due to the late hour they bivouacked on top before descending the following day.

JON OTTO

Tibet

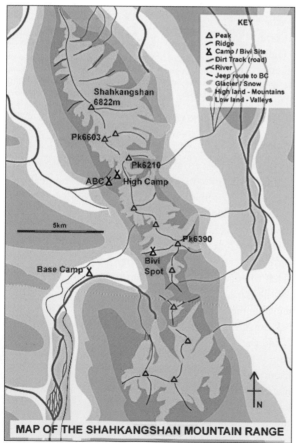

Central Tibet

Shahkangshan Range, Pt. 6,603m, southeast ridge, west summit; Pt. 6,210m, southwest ridge; Pt. 6,390m, west ridge; all first official ascents. Our team from Imperial College London approached the Shahkangshan Range from the south, via Saga. The name Shahkang-shan is that listed on the Alpine Club's Himalayan Index. However, other visitors have used the name Shar Kangsum.

During our first night spent in tents, water rushed through camp in the early hours of the morning, dramatically forcing us to evacuate the site. Quick thinking by our drivers and base camp staff minimized damage to and loss of equipment.

A landslide blocked the road that runs east of the Shahkangshan Range, forcing us to drive as far as we could up the western flank. We established base camp at the head of the valley (ca. 5,050m), midway along the western side of the range. From there a four-person team consisting of Naomi Bessey, Ben Gready, Joe Johnstone, and I headed north on foot to explore the higher peaks in the range.

Low cloud and poor visibility hampered our reconnaissance, but we finally established an ABC at ca. 5,500m. In a brief clear spell we set up a high camp at the foot of a hanging glacier (ca. 5,800m), from where Joe and Ben continued up to a snowy bowl, bivouacking at 5,950m in preparation for an attempt on Pt. 6,603m.

That night a storm rolled in, and all climbers were forced to sit it out for two nights while the bad weather deposited enough hail and snow to create a high avalanche risk. On August 3, with the weather starting to ease and supplies running low, Ben and Joe made a last ditch attempt. A snowy ramp led to the southeast ridge. Continuing through

MAP OF THE SHAHKANGSHAN MOUNTAIN RANGE

lightly falling snow, they followed the snow-topped, sharp crest, to a more rounded and steeply inclined snowy ridge with occasional cornices on the eastern side. Having waded through knee-deep snow in whiteout conditions all morning, the pair made the western summit, recording its height as 6,603m (Alpine grade PD+). Exhausted, they descended by the same route, arriving safely back at the high camp by mid-afternoon.

Daniel Carrivick on the col southwest of Pt 6,210m in the Shahkang-shan Massif. Ahead of him is the ridge leading south to the unclimbed Pt 6,500m (in cloud). *Daniel Carrivick collection*

After restocking ABC with food, the same pair headed farther north up the valley to attempt the highest peak, Shahkangshan (6,822m), via the southwest flank and southeast ridge. However, a few days later, as they were commencing their summit bid, three avalanches higher up roared down their intended line of ascent, forcing them to abandon their attempt.

Meanwhile, on August 8 Naomi and I reached the snowy bowl and headed up to the col southwest of Pt. 6,210m. Having set out along a mixed ridge toward the peak to the south (ca. 6,500m), it soon became apparent that the way ahead was longer and more technical than first envisaged. In building cloud we turned around, returned to the col, and headed northeast up a short snow slope with patches of scree to the summit of Pt. 6,210m (Alpine grade F+).

Taking advantage of the now settled conditions, we launched a lightweight assault on Pt. 6,390m. Leaving base camp at midday, we ascended a series of nightmare scree slopes to gain the west ridge. The ridge was no better, with similar terrain punctuated by areas of extremely loose, in situ bedrock. That evening we arrived at the snow line and bivouacked under clear skies. On the 10th we continued up the ridge on hard snow, past rocky bluffs, to gain a snowy plateau. From there we headed east up snow slopes and over a false top to link up with the heavily corniced east ridge, along which we gained the top (Alpine grade PD-). We returned to base camp the same day and started our return home that evening.

DANIEL CARRIVICK, *Imperial College, London*

Editor's note: the Shahkangshan Range lies west of, but nearly alongside, the Tsochen road and the highest summit, 6,822m, has received at least one unauthorized ascent.

HABUQUNG SHAN

Dobzebo, first ascent, via southwest ridge. When our team of four, comprising Alpine Club members Derek Buckle, Alasdair Scott, Martin Scott, and Bill Thurston, were searching for new climbing opportunities, we looked no farther than Tibet. Requiring a relatively unexplored region with interesting unclimbed 6,000m peaks, we eventually chose the Habuqung Shan range, which rises to the northwest of Lhasa and has reasonable access. One mountain in particular, Dobzebo, which possesses an impressive north face and rises in splendid isolation to over 6,400m south of the lake of Zuru Tso, attracted our attention and became our main focus.

Leaving London on September 25, our party flew to Lhasa via Beijing, before traveling by Land Cruiser to the village of Tsha-tse near the foot of Dobzebo. From here we established a base camp at 5,120m to the southwest of the mountain. Subsequently we established two further camps, at

Dobzebo (6,429m) from the village of Tsha-tse, showing the line of the first ascent to the south (and highest) summit. The north summit (6,412m) was also climbed by a different route during the same expedition. *Derek Buckle*

5,690m and 6,100m. We climbed the 30-40° glaciated south face above our high camp on October 8 and reached the 6,412m (GPS reading) north summit (Alpine PD). The view reinforced earlier conjectures that the southwest summit was indeed somewhat higher, but the double-corniced ridge leading to it was an unattractive option. We descended, in order to relocate our base camp farther to the north. From this second base camp, at 5,005m, we placed a third high camp at 5,503m, beside a large lake lying beneath the foot of the long southwest ridge.

After an early start on the 14th we climbed over steep broken ground to the crest of the initially broad southwest ridge. This narrowed considerably before reaching the summit ice field at ca. 6,100m. Straightforward climbing (Alpine F+) up the corniced ridge brought us to the 6,429m (GPS reading) southwest summit. A broad panorama stretched from the Himalaya in the south to the Lungmari group and beyond in the north. Loinbo Kangri (7,095m) was visible a little south of west.

We made a brief reconnaissance of the Lungmari massif before returning home. We are grateful to the Mount Everest Foundation and the British Mountaineering Council for their financial support for this expedition.

DEREK BUCKLE, *Alpine Club, United Kingdom*

NYANCHEN TANGLHA

Qungmo Kangri, first solo and first alpine style ascent, via south ridge. After a month of mountaineering in the central part of the Nyanchen Tanglha, Gerhard Gindl and I went to the far southwestern end of the range to make a reconnaissance of Qungmo Kangri (a.k.a. Jomo Kangri; Tibetan name Neiji Kangsang: 7,069m; N 29° 54.162', E 90° 01.521') and surrounding mountains. The only information we had was that the mountain had been climbed only once before, in 1996 by a Chinese-Korean expedition via the east ridge. However, I later found the mountain had received three previous ascents: on October 7, 1996, by the Chinese-Korean expedition via the south ridge; on May 17, 1997, by a Japanese expedition via the south ridge; and on August 15, 1999, by another Japanese expedition again via the south ridge.

We established base camp on October 6 at 5,450m after spending a day looking for the best site. This proved to be on the shores of a moraine lake, on the far side of which huge columns of ice stood in fragile equilibrium on the underlying bedrock. As we spent the following days exploring a possible route on Qungmo Kangri, it became obvious that the logical way was from the south, over a subsidiary south summit and on up the south ridge.

We went into the next valley west of base camp for a couple of days and climbed to the west-southwest summit of Qungmo Kangri (6,116m; N 29° 53.506', E 89° 58.694').

Qungmo Kangri (7,069m) from the Jumu Valley to the southwest. The line of the route up the south ridge climbed by Christian Haas is marked. This was the fourth known ascent of the mountain but the first one-day, alpine-style, and solo. The first ascensionists reached the crest of the ridge from the opposite (east) side. *Christian Haas*

We had fantastic views of the surrounding mountains, among others Qungmo Kangri West Peak. Apart from two days of snow, the weather was sunny with few clouds, but temperatures were starting to get very low.

On the last day before we had to leave, everything seemed to be right for a serious attempt on the main summit: the night was cold, the sky was clear, and the following night the moon would be full. However, Gerhard thought the route would be too difficult for him, so I let him sleep as I left the tent at 6.30 a.m. carrying minimal equipment.

As dawn was breaking on October 16, I had left the moraine and was heading east up a narrow ca. 45° couloir. At the top I found a snow anchor driven into the rock. At the time I thought it came from a previous attempt but later realized it must have been left by one of the successful expeditions. A slope of 45-50° led to the foresummit, from which I had to descend 50m on the far side to reach a ca. 6,000m saddle at the base of the south ridge. I took a short break to warm my toes and fingers in the sun. As the temperature was around -15°C, I wore my down jacket the whole day.

The saddle had a crevassed area, but this was well covered by debris from a huge snow and ice avalanche. The remaining 1,000m up the south ridge were exhausting and steeper than expected (average angle of 40-45°, with the steepest section at 50-55°). The lower 600m culminated in a hard shield of 55° snow, while in the upper part I had to bypass a rocky ridge on the left and then slant up left crossing large snow-filled crevasses. Close to the top the ridge became a moderately angled slope, before it reached a junction with the east ridge. After crossing a flat plateau I reached the highest point at 6 p.m.

The view was terrific, as this mountain overlooks all the surrounding peaks, which have a maximum height of about 6,600m. On the east-northeast horizon, perhaps 75km distant, I could see the great ice face that rises to all three 7,000m summits of Nyanchen Tanglha. To the northeast the deep blue of Nam Tso (lake) dominated the view. After hoisting prayer flags and taking pictures, I started my descent. I regained the saddle around 8 p.m., by which time the sun had gone down, and the moon was rising in the east. I used my head torch in the couloir, and when I reached the first cairn I'd constructed as a marker on the moraine, I knew I was going to make it back to base camp safely.

After 16 hours with hardly a break, I reached base camp at 10:30 p.m. Gerhard had prepared delicious noodle soup, which I ate and went straight to bed. No time to admire the bright starry sky and smooth moonlight outside the tent.

CHRISTIAN HAAS, *Austria*

Editor's note: The original ascensionists (and, despite the abandoned snow anchor found by Haas, maybe all three successful expeditions) approached the crest of the ridge from the east. Haas approached from the valley to the west.

Pajan Zhari (GPS 6,232m) from the east. Marked is the route followed on the northeast face and north ridge to make the first known ascent of this mountain southwest of Nyanchen Tanglha. *Christian Haas*

Pajan Zhari and "Gompa Garpo Ri," first known ascents. In September and October I returned to the Nyanchen Tanglha Range, situated about 80km north of Lhasa. In 2000 I had been in the same area with two friends, and we succeeded on three 6,000m peaks that had never been climbed before (*AAJ 2004*, pp. 427-428). In 2005 I was accompanied by Erich Gatt, who was also a member of the 2000 expedition, and Gerhard Gindl. This time we went to the valley immediately southwest of the main Nyanchen Tanglha massif, a huge ice-armored wall with three summits above 7,000m.

We first acclimatized around Lhasa, before visiting the Nyanchen Tanglha for one week only. In that period we went to the 5,816m pass at the head of the valley, enjoyed a terrific view over Nam Tso, the second largest salt water lake in Tibet, and climbed Gompa Garpo Ri (6,232m; GPS N 30° 20.440', E 90° 31.896'), a previously unnamed and unclimbed mountain directly northwest of Pajan Zhari. Gompa Garpo Ri means "White Monastery Mountain," and so named because of its broad white appearance when seen from the Nyanchen Tanglha Valley. I climbed directly up the northeast face, while the others followed the north ridge. We then returned to Lhasa and after two days of recuperation went back to our 5,332m base camp, which we regained on September 25.

Over the next five days we tried a new route on one of the 7,000m Nyanchen Tanglha summits. However, we were unsuccessful. On the last attempt Erich bivouacked without adequate equipment in a crevasse at 6,700m and was really cold when he returned to base camp the following evening.

Next day, October 1 and the last day of our stay, we left camp at 8.30 a.m. for an attempt on Pajan Zhari (6,221m on the Chinese Map). We had looked at the summit from adjacent mountains and decided to try the north ridge first. However, we had not been able to get a full view of the approach and on setting off were unsure how to reach the start of the ridge.

After an exhausting walk across pathless blocky terrain, we reached the glacier that provided access to the north ridge from the east. As the snow was still well-frozen, it was easy to cross a major zone of crevasses beneath the impressive ice-covered north face. At the end of the horseshoe-shaped valley Gerhard and I decided to reach a snow-covered ramp, from where we could get onto the north ridge without difficulty. To gain the ramp we had to climb a steep wall of black hard ice for about 30m. While we were doing this, Erich went up a steep snow-and-rock couloir on the opposite side of the valley to photograph our progress.

After reaching the crest at 1.30 pm, Gerhard and I continued upward in good snow along the 40-50° ridge. At the top we had to carry out a little reconnaissance to find the best way to avoid large cornices. At 3.00 p.m. we reached the highest point of Pajan Zhari (6,232m; GPS N 30° 19.724, E 90° 33.215).

Meanwhile Erich had taken a different route. After climbing the steep snow-and-rock couloir, mentioned above, to reach the crest of the northwest ridge, he turned away from the summit and followed the crest to a small rock peak. After he'd finished taking photos, he returned along the ridge and climbed to the point where Gerhard and I had reached the crest. This section before the junction gave some delicate climbing, at UIAA IV, around several towers of poor rock. Erich then followed our steps and joined us on the summit an hour after our arrival.

Together we enjoyed breathtaking views of the surrounding mountain scenery and the Nam Tso Lake, which presented a range of blue colors. The headman of Nyanchen Tanglha Village had given us prayer flags to present to the gods, and we threw them into the wind. After spending one-and-a-half hours on the summit, we began our descent. At the end of the north ridge a steep snow-covered couloir led straight down to the glacier below. We thought this would be easy, but the middle part turned out to be 45-50° hard ice covered by a thin layer of snow.

Before we finally reached base camp, we had to deal with one last challenge: the river we crossed in the morning had risen during the day. However, we negotiated it without getting totally wet. Next day we left for further adventures, in the southwestern section of the Nyanchen Tanglha Range, as reported above.

CHRISTIAN HAAS, *Austria*

NYANCHEN TANGLHA EAST

An introduction to the geography of the Eastern Nyanchen Tanglha (Nyainqentanglha) and a journey from the waters of the Yi'ong Tso to the primarily Bomi village of Bake along the lower Yi'ong Tsangpo. The "Alps of Tibet" east of the Himalaya spread from the Qinghai-Tibetan Plateau to the western rim of the Sichuan basin. The upper streams of Asia's five great rivers flow north to south, forming deep valleys. At one point these five rivers are squeezed into a span of just 150km before continuing their journey farther south. The Yangtze enters the Pacific near Shanghai, the Mekong enters the South China Sea, the Salween and Irrawaddy flow into the Andaman Sea and Rohit, and finally the principal river, the Tsangpo-Brahmaputra, flows into the Bay of Bengal (Indian Ocean).

The Nyanchen Tanglha East is located on the southeastern rim of the Qinghai-Tibetan Plateau and forms the watershed between the Yarlung Tsangpo and Salween River (Nu Jiang). To the north this is the Upper Salween, while to the south lie the two tributaries of the Yarlung Tsangpo: Yi'ong Tsangpo and Parlung Tsangpo. Numerous peaks have never been seen, let alone visited. The rivers erode the plateau into deeply carved valleys, and the topography is complicated. The highest peak in the main range is Sepu Kangri (6,956m), climbed by an American party in 2002.

The Po Tsangpo, a tributary of the Yarlung Tsangpo north of the Tsangpo Gorge, separates into the Yi'ong Tsangpo and Parlung Tsangpo at the confluence near Tongmai. The Yi'ong Tsangpo flows from west-northwest almost due east, then turns gradually southwards in the middle of Lake Yi'ong. The distance from the source to confluence is about 230km as the crow flies but the total river length is 286km, as it zigzags through deep gorges. We tentatively define the section (125km as the crow flies) from the source to Niwu (Nye) as the upper part, which belongs to Lhari County, and the section (105km) from Niwu to the confluence with the Po Tsangpo as the lower part, which belongs to Bomi County.

To the north and northeast of the lower Yi'ong Tsangpo lie the largest glaciers in East Tibet, such as Qiaqing (35km) and Jiangpu (21km), with stunning unclimbed 6,000m peaks soaring at their heads. Although there are no large glaciers to the south of the river, there are still challenging peaks of 5,600-6,300m.

A vehicle road has been constructed from Lhari to Niwu along the upper Yi'ong Tsangpo, but it is dangerous and vulnerable to landslides, which sometimes block traffic. The lower part, which flows through deep gorges, has no vehicle road, only a mule track along the right bank. However, it is not possible to follow even the mule road in its entirety with animals. Horses are unable to negotiate a section near Niwu, where to avoid a terrifically deep gorge, the route becomes a narrow trail clinging to precipitous slopes. The humid climate brings much snowfall, which feeds glaciers, forms impressive snow peaks, and grows beautiful conifer forests. Both sides of the Yi'ong Tsangpo resemble dense subtropical rainforest.

Bailey and Morshead reached Lake Yi'ong in 1913 and discovered it had only been formed 12 years earlier (see Bailey's *No Passport to Tibet*). In 1935 Kingdon-Ward traveled up the Yi'ong Tsangpo and was the first foreigner to complete the entire track from Lake Yi'ong to Niwu (Kingdon-Ward, *Assam Adventure*). In November 2005 Tsuyoshi Nagai (73) and I (70) became the first foreigners to repeat this journey, on my fourth attempt since 2001. I found Tangmai to be a hive of new construction, compared with my first visit in 1999, when it was a deserted village with a couple of shabby houses. We reached the Yi'ong Tso (lake) by Land Cruiser and then trekked northwest towards the Daoge Glacier, but were unable to see it due to poor weather. We returned and trekked up the lower Yi'ong Tsangpo to the village of Bake, where we were told we were the first foreigners ever to visit. A more detailed account appears in the 2006 Japanese Alpine News, Vol. 7

TAMOTSU NAKAMURA, *Japan*

Menamcho, attempt by northwest ridge; Kajaqiao, first ascent, via west face and northwest ridge. October 2005. Mick Fowler, Adam Thomas, Chris Watts, and I are stretched out on the dusty Tibetan tundra at the village of Tatse, not quite believing we are here. Across the valley Kajaqiao looms overhead, praying hands reaching to the sky and a plume of cloud cloaking the north face. It's taken 18 months of planning, two days driving, and nine permits to get here, and now we're less than half a day from base camp. [Original plans to attempt Kajaqiao in 2004 had been thwarted at the last minute by permit problems. See Mick Fowler's article earlier in this *Journal*—Ed.]

A week later base camp is 400m below us. Mick and Chris are setting off up the west face of Kajaqiao, and Adam and I are heading south across the glacier to reconnoiter a route to the foot of our goal, the south face. But it's hard work; the snow is never less than knee deep and frequently up to our thighs. The view changes every half hour, and Menamcho, the perfect replica of the Matterhorn if ever there was one, reveals more of itself with each step. We make the end of the main glacier by late afternoon and can see Mick and Chris bivouacking on the west face. As we settle down for a brew, an alternative plan begins to form. In this snow, the south face of Kajaqiao is still two days away and doesn't look as good as we'd hoped. But Menamcho is only one day away and the northwest ridge looks superb. Our spirits begin to lift and then soar above the exhaustion, as we realize Menamcho is our objective.

Looking south at the unclimbed Menamcho (6,240m), Eastern Nyanchen Tanglha, a little after dawn. On last year's attempt Phil Amos and Adam Thomas climbed directly from the glacier to the horizontal shoulder near the bottom of the right-hand (northwest) ridge, but retreated from this high point (5,880m) in bad weather. *Phil Amos*

Next day we head southeast up a steep convex slope and onto the glacier between Kajaqiao and Menamcho. Finally we reach the northwest ridge. We are only four kilometers from and 700m above base camp, yet it has taken three days of snow ploughing to get here.

We reach the shoulder that forms the start of the northwest

The spectacular peaks of Menamcho (6,240m) and Kajaqiao (6,447m), seen from the southeast in 2003 during an unsuccessful expedition attempting the first ascent of 6,359m Chukporisum (reported in AAJ 2004). Menamcho, the double summited peak on the left, is actually slightly nearer the camera than Kajaqiao. The large, triangular, snowy southwest face of the latter is clearly visible. The peak to the right is unnamed and unclimbed. *Adam Thomas*

ridge via four pitches, at Scottish IV/V, up the north flank. This is snow-covered ice and mixed ground: steep broken slabs and frozen rubble. We construct a ledge on the crest, erect the tent, and stretch out in relative comfort. The weather has been great for the last two days, and tomorrow night we'll be on the ridge with no hope of getting the tent up.

But tomorrow is a different story. By morning the weather has deteriorated, with strong winds blowing across the ridge, and temperatures of -20 to -25°C. In the 20 minutes it takes to pack up, I lose feeling in my fingers three times. "What's your gut feeling?" yells Adam. I point. "What's yours?" He nods. We hug. I can't believe it's happening, not again: our third trip in five years with the same outcome, turning back a stone's throw from the top. I begin to cry but stop when my tears start freezing. A GPS reading of our high point gives 5,880m, and at the time we thought the summit of Menamcho was around 6,400m, still a long way off. Finding out later that it was only 6,240m hurt. We descend the north side of the ridge, reaching the glacier with three 60m rappels. We have to remake our tracks down the glacier and arrive back at base camp the following day—the day that Mick and Chris summit. The A team had made it, whilst the B team were going home with their tails between their legs.

PHIL AMOS, *Alpine Club, United Kingdom*

Editor's Note: The photo in AAJ 2003, p. 134, which also appeared on the front cover of the Japanese Alpine News Vol. 2 (2002) is Menamcho (a.k.a. Chakucho), not Kajaqiao as captioned.

The first ascent of Kajaqiao (6,447m) by Mick Fowler and Chris Watts via the west face to upper northwest ridge (ca. 1,100m and Alpine TD) is reported earlier in this Journal.

An aerial view of Birutaso (ca. 6,650m) from the southeast. The route of the first ascent above Camp 4 is marked. The fluted pyramid in the right foreground is the slightly higher, unclimbed, Qang Dhen (6,691m), while the Lawa Valley is visible at the top of the picture. *Sean Waters*

Birutaso (ca. 6,550m), first ascent. After the last-minute permit fiascos that stymied an attempt to reach the Lawa Valley in 2004, Jo Kippax and I were apprehensive about how our 2005 attempt would work out. However, the permit process and access to the valley proved to be easier than expected, although we still didn't get permit confirmation until four days before leaving.

The Lawa Valley is a stunningly beautiful place, but access from the valley to the peaks turned out to be a tricky business. The Nyanchen Tanghla East did its best to wear us down with bad weather and snow conditions, but in the end we got lucky and on November 5 summited Birutaso, via the east ridge, which we accessed from the southern flank. We reached the top at 10 p.m. in very cold and windy darkness. After a long discussion we decided to avoid an error-prone descent by making an unplanned and chilly bivouac buried in impossibly loose snow at ca. 6,530m, just 20m below the summit. We groveled to the top again next morning in order to get a few better-illuminated photos.

It was the end of a long effort. We arrived in the Lawa Valley on October 6, made our base camp at 4,000m on the grounds of a local monastery, and spent the first 10 days trying to avoid bears and work out the best access route. At this stage it became apparent that we were trying to reach the wrong peak. The 6,691m mountain named Birutaso on Tamotsu Nakamura's sketch map is in fact a peak called Qang Dhen and lies on the south side of a large cirque, not visible from Punkar village. Birutaso is on the northern side of the cirque, visible from just above the village, and seems to be around 6,550m. It became apparent that the best means to access the mountain was over a high pass (dubbed Choirboy Col) below the peak Ura Drajhmo (6,060m). A much, much shorter and easier route above Kangpo Tso (lake) was thwarted by 600m of impenetrable rhododendrons. We reached Choirboy Col directly from the Lawa Valley not far above Punkar Village.

Conditions were a little trying; on only two days during the expedition did it not snow.

This reduced us to double and triple carries through knee- and thigh-deep (sometimes deeper) snow on our single push above advanced base. At steep sections through the icefalls we resorted to shoveling our way forward at a pitiful pace. We were avalanched in Camp 1 and then realized we had to drop 500m to round an icefall before beginning the traverse towards Birutaso. It took 12 days to reach Camp 4 in the cirque (about four km from base camp, as the crow flies). From here we made an attempt on the upper part of the route.

The summit was about 900m above Camp 4 and our route reached the upper east ridge via a couple of large couloirs that got progressively steeper and consisted of 10cm of rotten snow over bullet hard, dinner-plating, green ice. Once on the ridge less steep ground held deep avalanching snow on a series of large steps that led up to the summit cone. We climbed the first part of this final section in an evening alpenglow but ended with desperate wallowing in steep, bottomless snow. The last pitch to the summit consisted of just-in-balance, technical shoveling, creating an unconsolidated trench more than head-high up 65° snow: the only way to make upward progress. We felt the overall route was probably Alaskan Grade 5.

The Nyanchen Tanghla East is gob-smackingly beautiful, with thousands of incredible unclimbed peaks, unexplored glaciers, and unknown valleys, all covered in deep snow. Access from the valleys to the névés is not particularly easy, and it seems that high precipitation and deep snow is not uncommon.

The expedition received grants from The New Zealand Alpine Club, Mount Everest Foundation and the NZDF. More information can be gained from www.summitfootprints.com.

SEAN WATERS, *New Zealand*

HIMALAYA

Pts. 6,473m ("Free Tibet") and 6,063m ("Bochánek"), possible first ascents. Zdeněk Červenka, Čestmír Lukeš, and Irene Oehninger from the Czech Republic climbed two peaks close to the end of the long chain of mountains that runs northwest from Xixabangma over Kangboqen (a.k.a. Gang Benchen). The two summits lie at more or less the same location as a peak marked Tsalung (6,640m and south of the Tsalung La) on some maps. They are approximately equidistant from the Kyirong (a.k.a. Gyirong) to Saga road and the normal Nyalam to Saga road used to access Xixabangma north side base camp. They are clearly visible from the latter road where

There are still many easy virgin peaks in Tibet awaiting the explorer. On the left is the line followed by the Czech team to make the probable first ascent of Free Tibet (6,473m) in the Baka Kangri. The peak to the left is almost certainly unclimbed. The line marked on the right leads to the summit of Bochánek (6,063m), climbed by the same party. *Cestmir Lukes*

it runs south of the large lake of Pelku Cho and were thought to be previously unclimbed (there does not appear to be a record of their ascents). The three climbers approached by walking seven to eight hours south across the plateau and up the valley leading to the peaks. They then climbed the more easterly and higher peak, Pt. 6,473m (N 28° 41' 50.6", E 85° 25' 20.3"), on September 12, via the northeast slope, and named it Free Tibet. They climbed the more westerly peak, 6,063m (N 28° 43' 07.9", E 85° 25' 10.5"), on the 14th, also from the north, and named it Bochánek. Panoramic views from both peaks are superb.

THOMAS RUCKSTUHL, *Switzerland*

Risum, ascent of east ridge. On September 20 Isomi Okanda (61) of Japan and a porter made an ascent of the east ridge of 7,050m Risum (Fuqu in Chinese). Okanda followed the route of the first ascent, which was made on May 10, 1997, by Kazuyoshi Kondo and two friends. The expedition approached via the large glacial plateau northwest of Xixabangma.

TAMOTSU NAKAMURA *and the* JAPANESE ALPINE NEWS

Tsha Tung, first ascent. During my 2003 winter attempt on Xixabangma I noticed a small peak on the south side of the Phu Chu Valley just east of Eiger Peak (6,912m), as it was called by Doug Scott's 1982 Xixabangma expedition. Later study showed it to be a northerly outlier of Gyaltsen (6,151m). My Tibetan yak herder and camp assistant, Kesang Tsering, told me it was called Tsha Tung and was, as far as anyone locally knew, unclimbed. It looked like a perfect objective for a short, semi-commercial trip (I believe the correct phrase is "not-for-profit").

Later that winter I was guiding in Chamonix, when my client said he would be interested in a trying something new but not too difficult in the Himalaya. The seed of the

Looking more or less south from the slopes of Xixabangma down the snow-covered Phola Valley to peaks on or close to the Tibet-Nepal border: (A) Tsha Tung (5,995m), (B) Gyalzen Peak (6,151m), (C) Bhairab Takura (a.k.a. Madiya Peak, 6,799m), (D) Eiger Peak (quoted as 6,912m but according to contours on the Chinese Mi Desheng map likely to be less than 6,800m), (E) Lengpo Gang (a.k.a. Big White Peak, 6,979m), (F) Gur Karpo Ri (6,889m), (G) Ice Tooth (6,200m). *Lindsay Griffin*

A pile of partially burnt foam, plastic and other material adorns the base camp site used to climb the southwest face of Xixabangma. This, and other abandoned rubbish, is believed to be attributable to recent winter expeditions. *Victor Saunders*

idea was formed. The final team and camp staff were Jo Cleere, Vernon Gayle, Philip Jeffery, Victor Saunders, and John Tunney (all British), plus Kasang Tsering and Penpa Tsering (Tibetan Chinese), with Yie Xie and Huang Zhi Qiang (Chinese). Jo takes up the story:

"June 2005. Our plan had been to trek from the Xixabangma north-side base camp to the south-side base camp. The average altitude of our trek would have been around 5,000m giving us sufficient acclimatization for an attempt on Tsha Tung (5,995m). In the event we were unable to hire yaks at the last village before the north-side base camp. Lack of rain in the spring had been hard for the yaks and their herders didn't want to exhaust the animals on another expedition. The plateau in this part of Tibet is a barren and desolate place, and the villagers rely on their yaks for food and transport. In addition, the yaks are an important source of income during the main climbing season on Xixabangma, when they are used to carry loads. So, we were back in the 4x4 for another exciting drive to Nyalam (3,700m). The morning after our arrival we used yaks to carry loads up the first eight kilometers of the Phu Chu Valley to our base camp at Drak Po Che (a.k.a. Smaug's Lair, 4,070m).

"The most logical route on our peak was the wide, snowy east ridge. We used a couple of donkeys to carry loads up to Camp 1 (4,600m), located in a beautiful hanging valley fed by a couple of streams. The following day we scrambled up loose boulders and rock for about 400m

Part of the Langtang-Jugal Himal, viewed from the northeast above the Phu Chu Valley in Tibet. (A) The top section of this small, broad-topped summit a little southeast of Tsha Tung and just rising above the ridge is most probably Gyaltzen (6,151m). (B) Tsha Tung (5,995m). (C) Eiger Peak (quoted as 6,912m but according to contours on the Chinese Mi Desheng map likely to be less than 6,800m). The route taken on the first ascent of Tsha Tung via the east ridge is marked. A high camp at 5,135m was positioned close to the left edge of the picture. *Victor Saunders*

and then followed a rocky shelf, establishing Camp 2 (5,135m) at the snout of the glacier. June 19 was our summit day and initially involved moving westward on a broad glacial shelf and climbing a 100m 40° ice wall to the ridge. Seven hundred meters of snow led to the fine summit pyramid. As the clouds drifted in and out, we had an occasional glimpse of the fearsome-looking north face of Phurbi Chachu and a set of pinnacles at its eastern end, which we dubbed The Coolin Towers. The grade of our route equated to Alpine PD, and descent, following our route of ascent, was straightforward, with even some judicious glissading to ease tired legs.

"On June 21 we cleaned the area around base camp and bagged our tins to be carried down by yak, taking care to leave the camp as we found it. Then we finished our expedition with a trek up to the base camp under Xixabangma's southwest face. Here we found huge amounts of garbage left by recent winter expeditions. The piles of rubbish and debris were quite recent (winter 2004) and even included car batteries, which had been dumped next to the lake in the middle of the camp. They had been discarded together with large piles of plastic, unwanted gear, and gas canisters. It is unacceptable to leave camps in such a state."

Jo is right. It is quite unacceptable. Over the years there has been much informal discussion as to who is to blame for this type of execrable behavior. American and Nordic expeditions are often contrasted, favorably, with those of other nationalities. Sometimes the blame is laid at the door of the growing commercial expedition industry, but the more I visit the Himalaya, the more I come to the opposite conclusion: amateur expeditions often leave much more rubbish than commercial trips, possibly because commercial ventures have a vested interest in keeping their sites clean for future clients. At this camp site the most recent offenders had left a calling card; a bleached yak skull signed by members of the Italian-Polish winter expedition. The marker pen had been left alongside.

VICTOR SAUNDERS, *Chamonix, France*

Gaurishankar, northeast ridge attempt. The noted American mountaineer, John Roskelley, and his son Jess aimed to make the first ascent of Gaurishankar (7,134m) from its Tibetan side. The mountain defeated them as it had at least three earlier attempts from the north. [Although Don Whillans 1964 British expedition approached the Tibetan side of the mountain from Nepal and attempted the north face to northwest ridge, the northeast ridge was not attempted until 1997, when Japanese, Yasushi Yamanoi and his wife Takeo Nagao, climbed the ridge to 6,300m, at which point the way ahead looked steep, narrow and highly corniced. They retreated. The following year another Japanese team with the same objective failed to reach the base of the mountain—Ed.]

On a clear day the mountain is visible from Kathmandu on the northeastern horizon and was thought to be the world's highest mountain until the British Survey of India made more careful measurements. The first ascent was made from Nepal by John Roskelley himself in May 1979 via the southwest face, the feature seen from Kathmandu. However, the main summit (Shankar) of Gaurishankar has only been summited twice since Roskelley's success.

The Roskelleys were unable to get very far in their efforts on one of its northeast ridges, of which there are several. Their ridge comprised unstable rocks, "like a house of cards" and some of these had huge icicles hanging from them. John and Jess gave up at only 5,450m due to the dangerous terrain and the difficulty of the climb, which appeared to get worse the more they ascended.

ELIZABETH HAWLEY, *AAC Honorary Member, Nepal*

Menlungtse, north face attempt. In October 1999 I was the leader of a four-man U.S.-Canadian party that made the first attempt on the north face of Menlungtse. Our goal was a route at the eastern end of the north face, which we hoped would lead directly to the summit.

Though the route was predominantly on snow and ice, a serac high on the mountain's northeast face poses a serious obstacle to the final meters of the climb. We reached a buttress at about 5,600m, at which point a heavy snowstorm brought our attempt to a stand still. Discouraged by the prospect of avalanche-laden slopes high on the peak, we looked elsewhere and climbed a 6,262m peak (later named Milarepa) a short distance to the north.

In 2005 the team comprised two Russians—Yuri Koshelenko from Rostov-on-Dom and Nikolay Totmyanin from St. Petersburg—and I. We traveled the distance from Cho Oyu base camp by yak caravan, changing teams above the Rongshar village of Tadzan (3,915m) in order to spread out employment opportunities among the different villages.

We left Tsamboche (3,350m) on April 25 for a two-day trek with yaks past the ruins of Chuar Monastery (3,180m), then back up the Menlung Valley, and finally around the north side of Menlungtse to the gorgeous turquoise lake below the enormous north face. Base camp, at 4,800m, was at the same site as in 1999, a mere 20 minutes from glacial moraine at the foot of the north face.

In the six years since my last visit, the serac high on Menlungtse's northeast face had grown menacing, and that line now seemed unjustifiably dangerous. However, on the lower, west end of the two-kilometer-wide north face a rib separates the threatened central section of the wall from a steep rampart of rock and ice to the right.

The unclimbed north face of Menlungtse. (A) The Main (East) Summit (7,181m) and (B) West Summit (7,010m). (1) Route attempted by Brash, Buhler, and Price in 1999, with (H) their high point at 5,600m, and the dotted line for their proposed route above. (2) Route attempted by Buhler, Koshelenko, and Totmyanin in 2005, and their high point on the northwest ridge. (W) Is the initial icefall and (R) the ramp. *Carlos Buhler*

Nikolay Totmyanin on the first pitch of the ca. 200m icefall that formed the initial section the route attempted by the American-Russian team on the north face of Menlungtse. *Carlos Buhler*

To gain access to this rampart we would have to climb an initial 200m vertical rock band. Fortunately, we spotted a line of water ice cutting through the barrier. This frozen runnel gave access to 500m of ice fields and mixed climbing that led to the base of an imposing triangular black wall, which we could not avoid. Looking through binoculars, Yuri spotted a crucial iced-up ramp cutting through it from right to left. Above the ramp a 400m couloir continued back right to reach a small glacial shelf at ca. 6,300m on the northwest ridge. From here, a fluted snow/ice ridge led up for ca. 400m to the 45° summit ice fields, which in turn rose a similar distance to the west shoulder and junction with the 1988 British Route [to the West Summit—Ed.]. A long traverse east across the mountain's saddle-shaped glacier would lead to the main summit at 7,181m.

On May 14 we set off up the 1,600m face with about 10 days food and fuel. By the day's end we'd reached the top of the initial rock band and set up our tent. The second day we climbed for eight hours up predominantly 50° snow and ice fields, overcoming a short section of delicate granite slabs and an 80° water-ice pitch 20m high. We bivouacked below the triangular rock buttress and next day traversed right, then climbed up to a good tent site below an obvious rock overhang we had spied from base camp.

On our fourth day we climbed the ramp leftward through the triangular rock barrier but ran out of time before reaching easy ice. We were forced to rappel 40m to a 55° ice shelf and hack out a very small ledge, on which we sat out the night. It was thoroughly miserable, as almost continuous spindrift pummeled out backs and prevented sleep. By morning we were exhausted from the effort of surviving the undignified night.

We climbed on, and our prayers were answered late in the fifth day when we finally emerged onto the huge snow shelf at the top of the face (ca. 6,300m). We quickly found a nonmenacing, overhanging serac (if one can say that about any overhanging serac you're about to sleep under) and flattened a tent site. Now our spirits were high. Above, we could see the remaining ground to the shoulder, from where the traverse to the main summit did not appear complicated.

Next morning Yuri awoke with the uncomfortable sensation that his left arm was becoming numb. A previous spinal injury from a fall on the Dru was probably the cause, no doubt exacerbated by the miserable night of continual spindrift and possibly irritated by a subsequent uncomfortable sleeping position in our tent. He elected to rest while Nikolay and I fixed our three ropes on relatively easy terrain above the serac. When we returned, Yuri was still not feeling well. We therefore used some precious minutes on our satellite phone to talk with a doctor in the U.S. The diagnosis was puzzling, yet Yuri's condition did not suggest altitude sickness, so we elected to wait out the night. After packing up camp the following morning, Nikolay jumared the first rope. Yuri followed, but at the anchor he felt too weak to continue safely upwards. We made a tough but necessary decision. We all felt it was prudent to descend while Yuri felt strong enough to do so under his own power. We began to rappel at around 10:00 a.m.

Our descent of 35 pitches of steep terrain, close to the route of ascent, was time-consuming and tedious but not overly complicated. With a mixture of relief and disappointment, we slogged into base camp around midnight the same evening.

CARLOS BUHLER, *AAC*

Mount Everest, first free ascent of the Second Step, previously unreported. In *AAJ 2000,* pp. 378-9, Conrad Anker reported on his unsuccessful attempt to free climb the Second Step on Everest's Northeast Ridge. He rated the pitch 5.10 A0, concluding, "My inability to make the moves reinforces my belief that Mallory and Irvine were not able to surmount this formidable obstacle." On May 22, 2001, Austrian Theo Fritsche succeeded in free-climbing the pitch, but did not publicize his achievement. In recent conversations with me he supplied the following details: "From the beginning I was certain I wanted to climb Mount Everest without supplementary oxygen and without technical aids. … Below the cliff [the Second Step] I formed a clear impression of how to climb it without aid. I put my ice axe in my pack, cached one of my ski poles, pulled down the hood of my anorak to get a wider field of view and took off the cumbersome overmittens. … I saw to the left of the ladder a crack that offered the possibility of laybacking. At the end of the crack is a steep rise. I went directly over the steep rise, bridging out left. I then mantled to get my right foot on top of the block and to stand up, though it was very strenuous. … As for the rating, I would say IV+ to V- (5.6-5.7), the top part somewhat technical."

Fritsche did the climb free-solo, i.e., without protection, and completed the whole ascent without supplementary oxygen (Fritsche's fourth 8,000m peak, all without supplementary oxygen). Fritsche said he doesn't have a problem with Anker's rating of the pitch as 5.10 or VI+, as the chockstone/overhang at the top of the crack "might as well be in the V+/VI- (5.8) range." However, because of the shortness of this section, only two moves or so, he would give the headwall a lower overall rating.

We leave it to the reader to decide if this has any bearing on the Mallory mystery.

JOCHEN HEMMLEB, *German Alpine Club (DAV)*

Chomo Lonzo, North and Central Summits, first ascents. An eight-man French team of Stéphane Benoist, Yann Bonneville, Aymeric Clouet, Yannick Graziani, Patrice Glairon-Rappaz, Christophe Moulin (leader), Christian Trommsdorff, and Patrick Wagnon planned to attempt the huge northeast spur of Chomo Lonzo's unclimbed Central Summit. However, after arriving at base camp in April and inspecting the route as far as 6,100m, they decided there was far too much snow and transferred base camp to the west side of the massif. During acclimatization Benoist and Glairon-Rappaz climbed Chago (6,893m), the border peak northwest of Makalu II. They climbed the north face to reach the foot of the northwest ridge, then climbed the Nepalese flank of the latter to the summit. They descended the route, mainly by rappel. This appears to be the first time Chago has been climbed from Tibet.

On May 4 and 5 Bonneville, Clouet, and Moulin attempted the west face of Chomo Lonzo North (7,199m), retreating from 6,600m. In the meantime Graziani, Trommsdorff, and Wagnon made the first ascent of this summit, by the northwest ridge. They later returned, repeated their route to the North Summit, and continued with a committing and difficult traverse to the 7,540m Central Summit, though Wagnon stopped 40m below the top. The ascent alone took six days. Early in the climb they met Benoist and Glairon-Rappaz, who had completed a new route on the west face of Chomo Lonzo North. Named Unforgiven, this 1,100m line sported difficult mixed climbing and vertical ice. The pair descended the northwest ridge. The stories of these impressive ascents on Chomo Lonzo North and Central appear earlier in the *Journal*.

Kaluxung, first ascent. To celebrate the 90th anniversary of the Alpine Club of Keio University, Teietu Yakuwa led an expedition to unclimbed Kaluxung [6,647m; 6,671m on the Mi Deshing map—Ed.], south of Nojin Kangsang, approximately 150km southwest of Lhasa. A reconnaissance expedition in 2004 by a mature party of Japanese climbers confirmed suitability of the climb for older mountaineers. However, younger members of the club were strongly encouraged to participate. Unfortunately, none were able to take enough vacation to come, so the final team comprised Eiichiro Kasai (64), Tooru Mita (64), Tadao Shintani (61), Hisashi Tanabe (74), Shaw Watanabe (64), Teietu Yakuwa (69) and Yoochi Yamakawa (67). Because of our ages we had physical checks in a low-pressure chamber at the training facilities of the Self-Defense Air Force, Tachikawa Base.

Our arrival in Lhasa coincided with the end of celebrations for the 40th anniversary of the foundation of the Tibet Autonomous District. Lhasa had been transformed into a totally clean city with flags streaming everywhere, and the southern road to Shigatse tarmacked as far as Nakartse. In 2004, when we made our reconnaissance, it took two full days to reach Nakartse from Lhasa by way of Shigatse. Now the road via the Kamba La was very pleasant, and we were in Nakartse after a drive of only a half-day from Lhasa. The following day, September 13, we set up base camp close to the road on the north side of the mountain. Although we had a distant view of Kaluxung from there, we couldn't see the top.

Good weather prevailed, our acclimatization was almost perfect, and no one complained of bad headaches. We established three camps on the mountain, the highest at 6,150m. Although we were ready for a summit bid on the 21st, bad weather intervened and we returned to base camp. However, as the weather improved on the 27th, we all climbed back up to Camp 3. With our time in the area nearly up, unless we got a spell of fine weather in the next 24 hours, we would have to abandon the climb.

At 5:00 a.m. the next morning the sky was clear and starry. Kasai and Shintani left at 7:30 and after climbing a gentle slope, they jumared four fixed ropes on a steeper section and continued to the summit, arriving at 11.30 a.m. There they enjoyed a fine panoramic view of the vast Tibetan highland and the large Himalayan peaks that straddle the Bhutan and Nepal borders.

The ascent went very smoothly, considering the average age of the expedition members, 66. No one became sick, mainly due to our thorough acclimatization program and a stock of good food and equipment. We made it a rule to take all our garbage from every campsite and collected other trash around the base camp area.

With the opening of the railway to Lhasa and the development of infrastructure, such as roads, tunnels, and bridges, Tibet will become a major tourist destination. It is therefore important that we all embrace the concept of clean climbing, so the natural environment of Tibet can be preserved.

EIICHIRO KASAI, *Keio University AC, Japan*

Editor's note: Kaluxung, a broad plateau-like massif with a steep western flank, lies 11km east-southeast of the more popular Nojin Kangsang. A picture appears in the CMA's photographic reference, Immortal Mountains in the Snow Region.

Kula Kangri and Jiexiang, attempts. During April and May our small team attempted Kula Kangri (7,554m). Stephen Chaplin from the U.K., Laila Ojefelt and Lars Svens from Sweden, and I from Australia were the only people on the mountain, which has only had three previous ascents [all by the west ridge: 1986 Japanese, 1994 Austrian, and 1997 Spanish—Ed.].

We left Kathmandu on April 13 and on the 19th reached the village of Monda north of the mountain (ca. 4,200m) and the official Chinese Mountaineering Association (CMA) base

Kula Kangri (7,538m) from advanced base camp to the north of the mountain at 4,800m: (1a) is the original 1986 Japanese route up the west ridge, which short-cuts the initial section, (1b) is the route attempted by parties in the last few years. It rises directly from the Jiexiang-Kula Kangri Col (ca. 5,800m), where Camp 1 is normally sited. The positions of Camps 2 (6,300m) and 3 (6,900m) are marked. *Damien Gildea*

camp. On the 22nd we left the western end of the village (a separate place that we believe is named Pesa Tsun), as have other expeditions, and walked for five hours to advanced base camp at 4,800m. Typically, until then the weather had been good but on our arrival it began to snow lightly, which proved an omen for the next month. By May 3 we had established Camp 1 on the north slope of the Kula Kangri-Jiexiang col (ca. 5,800m), a site obviously used by previous expeditions. The route to this point had been fairly straightforward, with almost no crevasses on the glacier but plenty of calf-deep snow and nice views north to Nojin Kangsang (7,191m) and the Tibetan plateau.

After waiting out more cold and snowy weather, we started the west ridge on May 9, fixing some rope to 6,200m. We decided to fix because of the length of the ridge and a perceived need to carry quite a bit of food and gear, though none of us had climbed in this style before.

Though we later went beyond that high point, attempts to go farther up on the ridge were rebuffed by a surprisingly cold wind and generally poor weather. We often had a few hours of good weather early in the morning, but by 11:00 a.m. or so it turned bad again. Nights were cold, often with light snow until just before dawn.

On May 12 Chaplin and I attempted unclimbed Jiexiang (6,676m). We ascended to the col, moved a little south, then turned back west into a bowl beneath the east ridge, and climbed severely crevassed slopes with deep snow to gain the crest of the ridge around 6,000m. After moving up the ridge in poor visibility, we camped at 6,220m on easy snow slopes. The weather cleared but gave a cold night, −22°C inside the Bibler. An early morning start on the 13th got us up easy ground to 6,330m on the ridge, in close sight of the serac band not far below the summit. However, while we were taking a brief rest and re-sorting gear, clouds poured over from the southwest, the wind picked up, and the weather went from fine to bad in less than 10 minutes.

An unnamed and unclimbed 6,211m peak south of the Jiexiang-Kula Kangri col and ca. 15km inside the Chinese border. *Damien Gildea*

Negotiating the traverse around the upper seracs did not appeal to us in such weather, so we retreated in white-out conditions, avoiding our crevassed route up by going directly off the end of the broad ridge, coming out a few hundred meters north of Camp 1. [The only known previous attempt on Jiexiang took place in October 2004, when Ludovic Challeat's commercially organized French expedition attempted the east ridge on skis to a little over 6,000m—Ed.]

On the 14th we all ascended to our high point on Kula Kangri but were faced with more high winds, so we retrieved our gear and ropes and descended in defeat. On the 18th I attempted a small peak above the true right bank of the glacier on the long northwest ridge of Kula Kangri. A long approach over loose boulders and scree, followed by deep snow and strengthening winds high on the west ridge, forced me to turn back in the afternoon at ca. 6,100m, still some distance from the summit. We returned to Kathmandu on the evening of May 23rd.

Having not seen other climbers or expeditions since entering Tibet a month earlier, we were shamefully overjoyed to discover the dismal failure of so many other teams on big Tibetan peaks. It seems only those desperate enough to hang in at Everest could outlast the poor weather, which cleared in the first few days of June.

DAMIEN GILDEA, *Australia, AAC*

New Zealand

AUTUMN 2005-AUTUMN 2006

The Darran Mountains, summary. Despite their isolation and high rainfall, Fiordland's Darran Mountains are New Zealand's current forcing ground for rock climbing—both alpine and crag. The rock quality and virtually unlimited quantity of future lines provides an ample venue for those looking to push their own and New Zealand's standards. A driven few made last season a productive one, and now there are even more quality routes to tempt the motivated.

One area of notable activity has been the rock massif of Mt. Moir (2,072m) and its outlier peaks, the Mate's Little Brother and Moir's Mate. Already the site of the number of high-quality lines, the Mate's Little Brother saw some outstanding ascents over the summer. Jonathon Clearwater and Derek Thatcher returned to a project started the previous summer and, between bursts of rain, established another pitch on a project that cuts straight through the prominent overlaps of an existing line, Second Coming. Still unnamed, the new route has a pitch of 28 (freed by Thatcher), and is so far the hardest free pitch "up high" in the Darrans. Farther right on the same wall Kester Brown and Craig Jefferies added the five-pitch New Jersey Drifter (24, 21, 21, 21, 17). The line was rap-bolted, requires some natural pro, and is apparently of the highest quality. Brown also climbed new pitches leading to the prominent roofs on the right side of the north face of Mt. Moir. Richard Thomson, Richard Turner, and Dave Vass climbed a new rock route on the superb red wall that runs between Te Wera and Karetai. Statue Bro? is six pitches long with the crux at 19; it finishes just south of Karetai Col.

Also in late March, Tom Riley and Mark Watson fired up their petrol drill and initiated development of the northeast face of Barrier Knob (1,829m), which lies around the corner from the Labyrinth Wall. They spent six days establishing single- and multi-pitch routes, most notably: Quiet Earth (100m, 21), Sleeping Dogs (50m, 22), Goodbye Pork Pie (50m, 23), and with Allan Uren, the six-pitch route The Navigator (18).

Winter was typically quiet, but a keen few ventured out. Matt Quirke and Allan Uren made the fifth ascent, in thin conditions, of White as a Sheet (300m) in Cirque Creek.

British climber James Edwards teamed up with Gary Kinsey and Andrew Young to climb a new line on the southeast face of Mt. Talbot (Psychopath Wall). Actions Speak Loudest (400m; 4+) tackles a mix of turf, rock, and snow.

MARK WATSON, *New Zealand Alpine Club*

Queenstown region, summary. Queenstown's Wye Creek became New Zealand's focal point for sport-mixed climbing over the past winter. A number of climbers based themselves in the Wye valley cirque and developed mixed climbs up to grade M11. First to fall was an already bolted project, Greypower (M8), by Kester Brown. More bolting provided three more routes: The Rebirth of Cool (M7) by Brown, Pippi's Polish Circus (M8) by Johnny Davison, and the area test-piece, Northern Exposure (M11), again by Brown. These routes point towards a shift in attitude and the opening of horizons in New Zealand mixed climbing. Hopefully the development will continue.

Reminding us that the mixed climbing scene isn't all about bolts, Kester Brown and

Kester Brown on the first ascent of Northern Exposure (M11), Wye Creek. *Kester Brown collection*

Jono Clarke ticked off an old two-pitch project with shaky protection on the Telecom Tower (Remarkables), naming it The Fastest Indian (rock crux 20). Also on the Telecom Tower Rupert Gardiner and Andrew Mills climbed a new five-pitch line at a grade of about 3+.

In the summer Dave Bolger, Rupert Gardiner, and Cris Prudden ventured into the Stoneburn, climbing a five-pitch rock route on an outlier to Stoney Peak: The Sentinel (17).

MARK WATSON, *New Zealand Alpine Club*

Barron Saddle-Mt. Brewster Region, summary. It's tempting to call the North Buttress of Mt. Hopkins (2,678m) a "last great problem" of the Barron Saddle-Mt. Brewster Region. However, that would be misleading, as it's more the buttress being isolated and long, rather than technically hard, that has kept climbers off its heights for so long. However you look at it, the buttress is an obvious and compelling rock ridge, and it was great to see it finally climbed, in January. Kynan Bazley and Paul Hersey took the honors. They helicoptered to the base of Watkins, took 10 hours to reach the summit from the valley floor and then spent another two days to walk all the way out. Due to the remote and rugged terrain, they commented that in many ways the walk-out was as challenging as the climb. They graded the route 5+, with a rock crux of 17.

The twist to this story is that a month later Steven Fortune and Guy McKinnon also climbed the route and returned to Christchurch believing they had made the first ascent. Disappointment came when McKinnon opened the latest issue of The Climber a week after their return.

Winter saw a couple of prominent new lines established. On Mt. Huxley (2,505m) Sam Barron and James Edwards climbed an 800m route on the west face, spending the night in a hole near the summit. Edwards also teamed up with Steven Fortune and Paul Warnock for an 1,100m route on the southeast face of Mt. McKerrow (2,650m): Fortune Favours the Bold. In July Paul Hersey and Mat Woods climbed a grade 3 gully on the south face of Peak 2,200m.

MARK WATSON, *New Zealand Alpine Club*

Aoraki Mount Cook and Westland, summary. The west side of the Divide was relatively quiet this past year, with only two new routes reported. In the summer Craig Cardie and Allan Uren climbed an obvious and reportedly good-quality route to the right of Moonshine Buttress on Conway Peak (2,899m). Sunshine Buttress follows a direct line up a rock buttress, with a crux of 16.

In March 2006, Andrew Rennie and Graham Zimmerman climbed a new route on the southwest face of Mt. Matenga (2,665m) in the Franz Josef Névé. Mixed Blood is a four-pitch mixed route at 4 M5 WI3. The route is apparently "short and sweet" and provided "some very good, hard, and interesting climbing."

The other side of the Divide has seen little more new route activity. In March 2005 Michael Madden and Tshering Pande Bhote (Nepal) climbed a direct and obvious new line on the south face of Aoraki Mt. Cook (3,754m). Sherpa-Kiwi is graded 5. In late October Marty Beare and Johnny Davison climbed the prominent right-hand ice fang on 3,070m Mt. Haidinger's east face headwall, high above the Tasman Valley. Stealing White Boys is graded 5. A parallel left-hand line was climbed during winter 2004.

Just down the road from Mt. Cook, Nina Conradi, Thomas Evans, Mal Haskins, and Jason Tweedie climbed three new ice routes up the Bush Stream Valley. January 2006 saw Nico Hudak and Mark Watson head into the Reay Valley, east of Tasman Valley, in search of quality red rock. The pair climbed a prominent stepped buttress dubbed Max Johnson (seven pitches, 17) on a 2,235m outlier of Mt. Johnson. Later the same day the pair climbed a classic, sharp arête, Tim Fin (15, pitched and simul-climbed).

MARK WATSON, *New Zealand Alpine Club*

Canterbury region, summary. Showing that there are still plenty of new things to do in the Southern Alps, if you are motivated, Guy McKinnon ventured alone onto the northwest face of Malcolm Peak (2,512m) to make the first ascent of this 500m greywacke face, at 14. Malcolm Peak is on the Main Divide between the Lyell Glacier and the Heim Plateau.

MARK WATSON, *New Zealand Alpine Club*

Rock climbing, brief summary. Working from south to north, this report mentions only sample highlights of New Zealand crag climbing. Starting with the Darrans, where a lot of activity focused on Babylon and Chasm Crag, Derek Thatcher made the first ascent of Hammurabi (32) at Babylon, while Mayan Smith-Gobat made the first ascent Akathesia (28), a line previously bolted by Paul Rogers at Chasm Crag.

The Queenstown area has seen a lot of activity, both up high on the Remarkables and at Wye Creek, with the most notable event being Derek Thatcher's ascent of a long-time project named Homage (32) at Wye Creek.

In Wanaka, Guy Cotter and Ed Nepia finished a long-time project, to produce Taniwha (220m, 9 pitches, 24/25), a great-looking route that has already seen one onsight repeat, by Bruce Dowrick and Jon Sedon. There has been lots of other local cragging activity in Wanaka, as well as the release of a new, larger edition of the local guidebook

In Christchurch, Derek Thatcher ticked off a project linking terrain between Hung Like Elvis (26) and Bogus Machismo (29). This currently unnamed line weighs in at around 32. Kaz Pucia made the prestigious second ascent of Ivan Vostinar's testpiece, Centrifuge (32), while Mayan Smith-Gobat has been impressing everyone with some staunch sends, most notably Trogolodyte (30), the hardest grade yet climbed by a Kiwi woman.

MARK WATSON, *New Zealand Alpine Club*

AMERICAN ALPINE CLUB CLIMBING GRANTS

Fall 2004 and Spring 2005

The American Alpine Club grants program provides resources for climbers and explorers to attempt new challenges, conduct scientific research, and push the envelope of human accomplishment in mountain and polar environments.

For more information on all the grant programs, please visit www.AmericanAlpineClub.org

Expeditions labeled with an asterisk (*) are reported in the Climbs and Expeditions section of this *Journal*.

LYMAN SPITZER CLIMBING GRANTS

Tommy Chandler, Salt Lake City, Utah*
Putala Shan, Tan Shan, and other formations in the Siguniang region of China
$4,000

Samuel Johnson, Anchorage, Alaska*
Northeast buttress of Uli Biaho, Pakistan
$3,500

James Stover, Grand Junction, Colorado*
Southeast face of Kizil Asker, Western Kokshaal Too, Kyrgyzstan
$4,500

MOUNTAINEERING FELLOWSHIP FUND AWARDS (FALL 2004)

Jed Brown, Fairbanks, Alaska
West face of Mt. Hayes, Alaska
$800 (REI Challenge Fund)

Gabriel Coler, Shelburne Falls, Massachusetts
East face of University Peak, St. Elias Range
$800 (REI Challenge Fund)

Pete Dronkers, Reno, Nevada*
Stewart Valley, Baffin Island
$700 (John Hudson Fund)

Ryan Nelson, Durango, Colorado*
Southeast face of Mt. Dickey/South face of Moose's Tooth
$700 (Boyd Everett Jr. Fund)

Kevin Wright, Anchorage, Alaska
West Face of Mt. Hayes, Alaska
$400 (Boyd Everett Jr. Fund)

MOUNTAINEERING FELLOWSHIP FUND AWARDS (SPRING 2005)

Janet Bergman, North Conway, New Hampshire
Fitz Roy Group, Patagonia
$600 (REI Challenge Fund)

Colin Haley, Mercer Island, Washington
Alpine-style attempt on Nanga Parbat, Pakistan
$800 (REI Challenge Fund)

William Hinckley, Durham, North Carolina
Via Costa Brava on Mt. Probiscis and Club International on Bustle Tower
$350 (Mountain Fellowship Fund)

Nick Martino, Roeland Park, Kansas
Alpine-style attempt on Nameless Tower, Pakistan
$400 (Mountain Fellowship Fund)

Renan Ozturk, Barrington, Rhode Island
Alpine-style attempt on Nameless Tower, Pakistan
$600 (Mountain Fellowship Fund)

Chris Thomas, Columbia, Maryland*
Unnamed sub-peak of Mt. Huntington, Alaska
$600 (Rick Mosher Fund)

Andy Wellman, Centennial, Colorado*
New route on south face of Caraz II, Cordillera Blanca, Peru/Second ascent of west ridge of Huandoy Oeste
$350 (Mountain Fellowship Fund)

Book Reviews

Edited by David Stevenson

On the Ridge Between Life and Death: A Climbing Life Reexamined.
David Roberts. New York: Simon & Schuster, 2005. 415 pages.
Hardcover. $26.00.

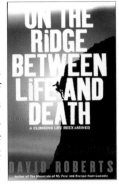

My introduction to the writing of David Roberts was by way of his
novella, "Like Water and Like Wind," published in the 1980 edition of
the celebrated mountaineering journal *Ascent*. At the time, Roberts was
best known for his groundbreaking climbs in Alaska, adventures that
dangled like fat hams to those of us who hungered for more than the
endless baloney of adolescence. As an aspiring alpinist, I rejoiced that
this piece of fiction, based loosely on the Maestri-Cerro Torre controversy, seemed to have been created to indulge my personal fascinations.
Sex, death, and lots and lots of climbing, these were the themes that Roberts distilled from his
experiences and imagination—although it seemed as though he'd been rooting around inside my
head as well. Reading and rereading his story, I remember feeling both exhilarated and vaguely
unnerved that Roberts seemed to be speaking directly to me (the fact that he set his tale in Min-
neapolis—my home turf—only deepened this conviction).

In the decades since, Roberts has pretty much abandoned fiction; instead, he's built an
enviable literary reputation and an oeuvre based primarily on adventure journalism that includes
a proclivity for risk-and-reward introspection. Meanwhile, having survived my own youthful and
rollicking indifference to the dangers of icy peaks, I have now reached the cusp of middle age,
where—like a salmon who has successfully completed her run and is a bit bewildered as to how
she should feel about that and what to do next—I find that Roberts is still talking to me.

On the Ridge Between Life and Death is Roberts' latest and perhaps final jab at a windmill
he first charged over 25 years ago in a landmark essay titled "Moments of Doubt." I say "latest
jab" because readers of this book who are familiar with Roberts' earlier work will find familiar material here. Once again, he recounts his significant mountain triumphs and tragedies
(indeed, some of this material represents at least the third or fourth go around for true Roberts
devotees), and again he lays it all out as pretext for reflecting upon the 800-pound gorilla lurking in the complex psyche of the mountaineer: "Is climbing worth the risks?" I say "final jab"
because of the exhaustive nature (over 400 pages!) of this new effort and the sixty-plus years of
perspective that ultimately lead Roberts to a new and compelling result. And I apply the metaphor of tilting at windmills, not because Roberts is undertaking a futile or misguided quest,
but because this is ultimately a deeply personal question that Roberts can really only hope to
answer for himself. For the rest of us, however, he certainly knows how to get the ball rolling.

Roberts' themes still include sex, death, and lots and lots of climbing. This time however,
he isn't making anything up. Although the jacket copy emphasizes philosophy over memoir, this
is misleading. In *On the Ridge Between Life and Death*, Roberts lays open his life—warts and

all—from teenage sexual fumblings to adult insecurities, in remarkable, even excruciating detail. Compared to reading the classic Homeric accounts served up by Terray, Buhl, and Bonington, reading Roberts feels decidedly voyeuristic. In less skilled hands, such candor and minutia might feel overwrought—like a cathartic exercise rather than content germane to the premise—but Roberts binds it all together with enough continuity and gripping adventure narrative to produce what is arguably the first truly honest climbing autobiography.

It's the means to an end. Roberts' full and eventful life is context for the friends and partners whose terms were cut tragically short pursuing the very activity that has given the author his identity. The difference, it seems, between the romantic notions espoused in "Moments of Doubt" and this new take on the measures of risk versus reward, is the realization that life is a cumulative and evolving experience—and that transcendence (or whatever it is we seek battling a mountain) comes via the more frightening, more difficult, and truly courageous act of meeting life's myriad challenges, day after day, year after year. The other profundity pushing Roberts to his conclusions is a newfound appreciation for the seemingly boundless depths of grief. Through interviews and correspondence with the close friends and families of his long lost climbing companions, he discovers that ripples in a pond of heartbreak never fade, but bounce endlessly from shore to shore, eroding the edges with as much force and definition as in the first moments after the falling pebble shocked them into being. Whether or not readers agree with Roberts' conclusions, these passages are certain to give climbers pause each time they tie to the rope.

So then, must we play it safe, just to avoid gravely wounding our parents and siblings? I don't think that's what Roberts is advocating at all. What he's telling me—writing with that uncanny ability to communicate as though he's addressing my personal insecurities about how to gracefully transition from one stage of life (and climbing) to the next—is that climbing can be a vehicle for growth, challenge, spirituality, etc., but it will not provide *the* answer. Lasting peace, satisfaction, transcendence—whatever we choose to call it—must be sought in more selfless pursuits. Roberts has clearly wrestled long and hard with the bugaboo of selfishness. Even here, in a volume dedicated to "reexamining a climbing life," it dogs him. A primary focus of Roberts' adolescence is the relationship with a girl he calls "Lisa." The fact that he paints himself as utterly self-serving throughout the affair is not out of step with the nature of young love (at least, not from a boy's perspective). And yet, by the time the relationship is over, the price Lisa has paid is considerable, with at least the potential to haunt her as completely as the death of a loved one. Surely, in the end, as Roberts gingerly explores the enduring traumas of long-ago climbing tragedies and paints them in a broader context, he must at least acknowledge the obvious parallel. Instead, Lisa's experience is marginalized—in truth, ignored—and she is reduced to a metaphor for failure. It seems a conspicuous and chauvinistic omission that will likely anger some readers.

Honest writing, however, demands no pretense or false modesty. What matters is not that readers like the author, but whether they believe him. I now recognize that in my very first encounter with Roberts' prose, it was his candid and unflinching voice that made my skin crawl. *On the Ridge Between Life and Death* feels even more personal and relevant. Here, climbers are likely to grin and cringe in sympathy with experiences and feelings that deserve conversation, but few are ever brave enough to voice. At the same time, non-climbers will find the best exposition ever crafted about why someone would risk life and limb to top a mountain.

DAVE PAGEL

I'll Call You in Kathmandu: The Elizabeth Hawley Story.
BERNADETTE MCDONALD. FOREWORD BY SIR EDMUND HILLARY.
SEATTLE: THE MOUNTAINEERS BOOKS, 2005. 24 PAGES OF BLACK &
WHITE PHOTOGRAPHS, 2 MAPS. 256 PAGES. HARDCOVER. $24.95.

For nearly five decades Elizabeth Hawley has played a stern, albeit
meticulous, Boswell to the Himalayan mountaineering community's
Samuel Johnson. Given the prominence of her name among alpinists,
it may come as a surprise to learn she has never climbed a peak or
even expressed any interest in doing so. "I am too lazy to walk the
mountains," she once joked in an interview. "Besides, I value good
food and a warm bed too much. I like to look at the mountains." Lucky
for mountaineering aficionados, she also likes to interrogate—some might say catechize—those
who do climb the peaks. Since the early sixties her practice has been to debrief all Himalayan
climbers as they pass through Kathmandu, both coming and going, and to record the details
pertaining to their ascents. Then she cross-references and authenticates the information in order
to render a judgment on the veracity and significance of the claims. Her diligent efforts resulted in an extensive expedition archive that serves as the basis for the American Alpine Club's
Himalayan Database. Although she is the world's most knowledgeable person about Himalayan
climbing, little in the way of biographical information has been available until now. Bernadette
McDonald's biography fills a significant gap in the cultural history of mountaineering.

In a flat but surprisingly effective prose style, McDonald presents her readers with Hawley's
life and personality. The figure that emerges is as striking—and as formidable—as the mountains themselves. Elizabeth Hawley was born into a reasonably well-to-do family in Chicago
in 1923. She attended the University of Michigan. After graduation she obtained work in New
York as a researcher for *Fortune* magazine. At age thirty-four, after eleven years on the job,
she found herself "a little bored," so she quit Fortune and embarked on wandering around the
globe, making her living as a journalist. Along the way she visited Kathmandu and liked what
she saw. In 1960 she returned to stay. At first she supported herself as a stringer for Time, Inc.
and by providing reports on the political scene in Nepal to the Knickerbocker Foundation,
an organization suspected as being a cover for the CIA. In 1963 Hawley made a major scoop,
thanks to her connections at the U.S. embassy, by breaking the news that the first American
expedition on Everest had not only summitted but made the first ascent of the west ridge as
well as the first traverse of the peak.

At this point—just shy of her fortieth birthday—she became the amanuensis of Himalayan
mountaineering. According to McDonald, "Elizabeth was always careful to ask detailed and
pointed questions of climbers when they returned to Kathmandu, and she was vigilant about
recording and reporting the truth." Kurt Diemberger refers to her "the living archive." And
Reinhold Messner recalls with affection: "When I came with crazy ideas to Kathmandu, she
was listening—she never said it was impossible."

The second half of McDonald's biography reads like a dance card of climbing celebri-
ties—Hillary, Bonington, Tabei, Babanov, just to name a few—and we encounter them *off* the
mountains, not so much "behind the scenes" but in the very foreground where history is written if not made. And yes, as with any story involving Himalayan climbing, it isn't long before
death makes its appearance. In the latter part of the book, every turn of the page seems to bring

another report of a mountain fatality. You get the impression that the Grim Reaper is the most successful of all Himalayan climbers. But rest assured, when he comes down from the mountains even he will have to make his report to Elizabeth Hawley.

Despite its abundance of information, McDonald's book does have limitations: to view the history of Himalayan mountaineering singularly through the lens of Elizabeth Hawley's life does entail significant vignetting—a falling off of light around the edges of the picture. One comes away from *I'll Call You In Kathmandu* with the nagging sense that a great many interesting and important stories—some involving Hawley herself—remain hidden in the shadows. In the final analysis, however, Hawley's life story serves as an admirable counterpoise to the bravado and bluster too often encountered in mountaineering literature and history. While she is notoriously shrewd at ferreting out the truth in climbers' claims, she can also provide the occasional psychological insight, as when she describes a certain climber infamous for his falsehoods as "a complicated man, as so many climbers are, and I have the feeling that he really believes his claims. I really think he is a Walter Mitty type. He lives in a world of fantasy and he believes he was successful." Yet on a certain level isn't this true of anybody who sets out to climb a dangerous peak? All climbing accounts are the stuff of dreams and heroic imaginings. In the rarefied air of the world's highest peaks, a human being might sometimes, forgivably, be inclined to continue the ascent beyond the actual summit into the realm of fantasy. Fortunately, Elizabeth Hawley has been around to bring us all—climbers and readers alike—back down to earth.

JOHN P. O'GRADY

The Villain: A Portrait of Don Whillans. JAMES PERRIN. SEATTLE: THE MOUNTAINEERS BOOKS, 2005. 360 PAGES, B&W PHOTOS. SOFTCOVER. $16.95.

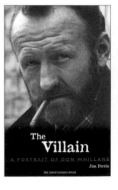

Here's a Whillans story I've been dining off for the last five years, told to me by a Brit climber who was 20 when Whillans died in his sleep at 53 in 1985.

A public schoolboy type enters the pub, his hands bloodied from a day of crack climbing. "Look at these," he says to his mates," I've been jamming all day. See how much skin I've lost. They're like raw hamburger!" Whereupon Whillans, at a nearby table, steely-eyed under the brim of his trademark cloth cap, thrusts out lily-white hands, knuckles up, and says "Them's jammer's hands, lad."

The incident, if it ever happened, may have taken place years after Whillans gave up gritstone jamming. In *The Villain* Jim Perrin tells us that gritstone cracks, in which Whillans excelled, were climbed without tape and ate up plenty of skin. But it's certainly true that good jammers lose much less of it than average: so the joke is that the upper class twit in the pub makes a show of his incompetence. Many of the Whillans' stories (true and false) celebrate proletarian emancipation just at the historical moment of decline in the class system's control of British climbing. Without Whillans' iconic status as a working-class hero, neither his climbing achievements, his wit, or prodigious talent as a brawler would have earned the fame that undergirds this book.

With enormous exactitude and sensibility, and painstaking fairness to everyone, Perrin gives a rounded picture of this man. And he does so without a word of psychological interpretation. His restraint in this regard is in perfect accord with his subject. Whillans' anti-social traits, as much as his achievements, seem to have emerged out of a non-dysfunctional childhood.

But although Whillans is the focus, what makes this a magnificent book is the social history of a great era of British climbing, sketched with loving detail by one of the participants. The controversies of the period are deftly handled, and Bonington, Haston, Scott, and lesser luminaries like John Streetly, Paul Ross, Al Harris, and others make cameo appearances.

The pity is that many who played a role in these times, as well as scores of potential readers, are no longer with us. Perrin demurred from publishing the manuscript until after the death of Audrey, Whillans' "good natured, long suffering" wife. Although she wanted a "warts and all" picture, Perrin decided that a full account of Whillans' parasitism, misogyny, bloody-mindedness, alcoholism, and numerous marital infidelities were more warts than Audrey needed in her closing years. Twenty years is a long time to sit on a book this good and give up maximum sales potential. Yet Perrin's attention to Audrey's feelings helps to balance the moral ledger that Whillans so infrequently consulted.

In the mountains Whillans now and again did demonstrate human virtue, when his alpine smarts and concern for others averted many a life-threatening crisis. But these qualities were more than balanced by an obdurate self-entitlement that alienated many: notably in his refusal to make a meal or brew a cup. And lo, what a surprise that after hitting the summit of Annapurna via the south face in 1970, he was marginalized and outmaneuvered for a place in British expeditions. Even the decade previous to that triumph had not been exactly covered with glory. As Perrin sees it, Whillans' fire burnt out quickly. "Before he is even out of his twenties, the Alps are beginning to fade from focus and his rock climbing pioneering is over." Later, Perrin says Whillans had the air of one "unloved by the gods who bestow good fortune"—in stark contrast to the favor shown his old climbing mate, Joe Brown, who continued to climb and pioneer new routes into his seventies, and is rich, celebrated, and happily married besides.

The final treat in *The Villain* is Perrin's descriptions of cragging—notably in a long digression about gritstone. Years of experience come pouring out in prose of amazing power. These few excerpts should give a taste of it. "The keynote to gritstone climbing is aggression… characteristically they [these climbs] deal with inordinately large quantities of pain and fear." He also makes fine distinctions between a typical Whillans route and a Brown route. Whillans' rock climbs were bold and in your face—an "affront" Perrin says at one point. (Such was once the power of his reputation that any truly daunting local crack was dubbed a Whillans route, often ones he'd never tried.) Brown's climbs, however, were seldom obvious, and required "lateral thinking, adjustment, balance." "On gritstone the difficulty of Joe's climbs is something to do with keeping enough of that flooding aggression back (into oneself) to channel into guile and technical inventiveness…. With Don's routes you always knew that if you wound yourself up to a particular pitch of focused aggression, you'd get up them without having to think too hard about it."

In the end *The Villain* left me with a dull ache as I considered my library shelves and the biographical material on dozens of climbers far greater than Whillans (Terray, Cassin, Robbins, Bonatti). If only they'd been delivered up from the past by a talent like Perrin's, how much richer the annals of mountaineering would be!

JOHN THACKRAY

Editor's note: The Villain received the best book award for Mountaineering History at the Banff Mountain Book Festival, 2005 and was co-winner of the Boardman-Tasker Award, 2005.

Possessed by Shadows. DONIGAN MERRITT. NEW YORK: OTHER
PRESS, 2005. 239 PAGES. HARDCOVER. $22.00.

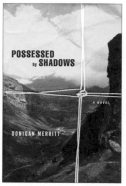

Some alpine climbs are so visionary that regardless of their success
or failure, by expressing a concept worthy of realization or by posing
a problem for future generations to solve, they deserve both attention
and praise. Within the medium of words and narrative, *Possessed
by Shadows*, a novel by Donigan Merritt, makes such a venture.
Although ultimately flawed, the book's effort to bridge the genres of
climbing and literary fiction represents a worthwhile and ambitious
project that this reader hopes may inspire future attempts.

A graduate of the Iowa Writers Workshop, Merritt comes from
a writing school that applies its own minimalist, light-is-right style to language; the late Frank
Conroy, Workshop director from 1987–2005, used to admonish his students that writing was
like climbing a mountain: you couldn't carry any extra baggage. Merritt's spare and carefully constructed novel, about a woman dying of cancer who travels from California to the mountains of
Slovakia to climb with her husband and to relive her past, reflects well on this tradition.

Taking as its central metaphor the Greek myth of Eurydice—the young bride hovering
on the threshold between life and death (as the Rainer Maria Rilke epigraph describes, "already
possessed by shadows"), who fades in the instant her husband turns to embrace her—the novel
uses climbing to explore a multitude of liminal spaces: between life and death, action and philosophy, the personal and the political.

Likewise, it finds itself between audiences. At times it seems too basic for anyone who
has ever tied into a rope, with its textbook-style explanations of Münter hitches and of common
crag behavior—as the dying woman, Molly, has written in her diary about the first time she met
her husband, "I assumed he was trying to pick me up, which is the principal reason men talk to
women in climbing areas." Other times, the novel's matter-of-fact and often technical descriptions of climbing scenes risk boring a nonclimbing audience. Passages such as the following,
"I liked the pitch. It has great holds, good pockets for the toes. It was slightly off vertical, a bit
less than 90 degrees in most places. Near the top, the wall fell away to a featureless slab, but at
an angle that made friction climbing possible," read like informational, but unimaginative trip
reports. Of course as a literary climbing novel, the text may be aiming for an impossible objective, or at least a "futuristic" one, to borrow a familiar term from climbing magazines, and its
achievement may await both new literary techniques and an expanded public of people who
read good books—and who climb—two activities that are still less than mainstream.

Yet if the book's laudable failure to close the gap between genres leaves the reader with a
sense of void, it's within that emptiness that lies a more profound, underlying problem: how to
compose a compelling, meaningful aesthetic in a postmodern world that denies its inhabitants
both mystery and hope, offering in exchange only images and shadows. The cipher-like characters chase *ersatz* objects of desire—climber x sleeps with climber y because y slept with z, and
because x is in love with a, who is unattainable. Behind this incestuous dance, the unmitigated
agony of thirty-three-old Molly, whose descent into illness will become a death without rebirth,
loss without redemption, asks repeatedly the question of how she and how any of her fellow
characters can assert their own existence and achieve their real desires.

Perhaps in complement, the flat, pseudo-Hemingway tone creates a limbo in which even the words themselves seem deliberately to avoid any form of soaring beauty, fulfillment or catharsis—"I ordered a beer and the waitress who brought it to me smiled at my accent. A prostitute asked in Slovak if she could join me and I let her. She asked if I spoke German. I used a candle on the table to light a cigarette for her. In Slovak, she asked if I liked her and I said no. She crushed out the cigarette as if it were my hand and left the restaurant."

With such an emulative style, the language takes few risks; it remains as constrained by structure and rationality as the characters themselves, who, even in their sexual abandon lack convincing passion, and whose affairs, revealed one by one, fit into a far-too-elegant, almost mathematical design to be natural—just as their climbing is too perfectly heroic (particularly in the opening rescue scene) to be believable. (And here the reader makes a natural comparison to David Roberts' *Like Water and Like Wind*, an alpine-climbing novella whose author is brave enough to portray the messiness of real human emotions, the inscrutability of desires, and the failure of heroism.)

And yet near the beginning of the story, Merritt has written two extraordinary sentences, which in themselves contain the entire novel—and beyond it, a whole universe, whose every gesture and word have been hollowed out, and whose hope of presence and transcendence becomes the most inconsolably haunting and beautiful shadow of all: "Molly stood near the rock and touched it with her hands. It looked like she was praying, but actually she only warmed her hands and recalled the corn kernel texture of the rough granite."

Climbing, the novel seems to tell us, may be an illusory form of redemption and solace, and yet it is all that many of us ever find.

KATIE IVES

Mountain Rescue—Chamonix Mt. Blanc: A Season with the World's Busiest Mountain Rescue Service. ANNE SAUVY. TRANSLATED BY SUE HARPER. LONDON: BÂTON WICKS, 2005. 300 PAGES. SOFTCOVER. £14.99. $34.95.

Anyone who has climbed very much in Chamonix recognizes the sound—the ominous thwock, thwock, thwock of a rescue helicopter. Knowing that, on average, one person dies every week in the mountains above Chamonix, you get a hollow feeling in your stomach. "Ask not for whom the helicopter thwocks...." Then you try to put it out of your mind. Focus on the route, the view, the summit, the cold beer at the bottom of the *téléphérique*, anything but what that helicopter is up to. Screw your karma down tight and keep going.

Mountain Rescue—Chamonix Mt. Blanc is the diary of a climber who took the opposite approach, spending an entire summer with the Chamonix rescue service—the Peloton de Gendarmerie de Haute Montagne, or "PGHM." The author, Anne Sauvy, is a scholar who has been climbing since she was in school. She became known in France as the author of *Nadir*, a novel (published only in French) that involves a mountain rescue. In the course of writing *Nadir* she did a lot of research on the PGHM and got interested in its operations. Ultimately, she spent the entire summer of 1997 with the PGHM, keeping the diary that became this book, translated into English in 2005.

Ms. Sauvy's life that summer consisted principally of hanging out at the PGHM's headquarters adjacent to the helipad from which the rescues—often as many as a dozen a day—are launched. Over the summer, she got to know the pilots, rescuers, doctors, and mechanics who ran the PGHM, as well as some of the rescued. Most rescues do not involve heroically snatching injured climbers off the face of the Dru or the Grandes Jorasses. The typical fare is retrieving climbers who have become exhausted on the standard route up Mt. Blanc, are stranded in bad weather, or have sprained an ankle jumping a crevasse, or hikers who have gotten lost or simply have fallen off a footpath. Virtually no one dies while being rescued. Thanks to the helicopters, rescues that would have taken a week back in the 50s (two classics of which are recounted) are now effected in an hour.

July was fun. Many were rescued, no one died, and the author helped out a few of the injured. August was not fun. As if the mountain gods had awoken from their slumber to claim their yearly tribute, the summer's body count climbed inexorably back into line with the annual average. Some days the PGHM operated more as undertaker than a rescue service. One of the rescuers himself died in a climbing accident not related to any rescue. A Russian climber was stranded on a ledge on the Dru for several days in a storm with the body of his fiancé, who had been killed by rockfall while standing next to him. While these tragedies were unfolding, tabloid photographers circled the helipad like jackals, on the lookout for cover shots. The author thought of dropping the project, but was persuaded to continue.

In addition to an interesting account of the PGHM's activities that summer and a description of some of its techniques, the book offers an insider's perspective on life in Chamonix that most climbers never glimpse. Climbers tend to pass through Chamonix on their way to a *téléphérique* and a route, the only points of contact being shops, restaurants, and bars. Extended or multiple trips simply multiply that experience. Almost all of the books on Chamonix are written from that same perspective. This book offers a different angle—Chamonix as a place where people live, work, attend funerals, and discuss not only the latest first ascent or accident, but the attendant media coverage and even some of the occasionally ensuing litigation.

Another interesting result of the difference in perspective is a look at the climbers from the vantage point of the rescue service. The rescued run the gamut from climbers with severe injuries who apologize for inconveniencing the PGHM or Eastern Europeans who offer to walk down on broken limbs because they are afraid they will be charged and can't afford to pay, to those who demand to be rescued because they are tired and then berate the rescuers for making them wait while they were inconveniently off saving some other climber's life.

In the end, the book is a tribute to the PGHM. They can't change the fact that mountain climbing is dangerous, but they emerge as a dedicated group who are pleased to shift the odds in your favor when you are in their mountains.

JOHN MCINERNEY

Into the Unknown: The Remarkable Life of Hans Kraus. SUSAN E.B. SCHWARTZ. LINCOLN (NE): IUNIVERSE: 2005. 306 PAGES. SOFTCOVER. $21.95.

Hans Kraus lived the life most of us dream of. Few manage to balance, let alone excel at, both a professional and recreational career the way Kraus did. He was a visionary and bold climber on the weekends and a brilliant back doctor during the week. In both areas, Kraus relied on good sense and experience over high-tech equipment. Moreover, Kraus was a man of principles, humility, and loyalty who never let his fame within the climbing, medical, or political circles get to his head. His rich life makes for a gripping and inspirational story.

The book is well-researched and passionately written. Schwartz relies on short and focused chapters of around four to five pages. This clear structure comes at the expense of long, flowing narratives, but this is not necessarily a bad thing. Schwartz's writing is refined and concise. In each chapter she manages to express the essence of the theme without unnecessary literary decoration. Climbers beware, however! A reader who expects the typical mountaineering adventure book may find the climbing sections too short. There are indeed some gripping portrayals of Kraus's most memorable adventures in the Alps and at the Shawangunks, but the book spares all details of Kraus's trips to the Bugaboos and the Tetons. This is a strength and not a weakness of the book, however. Kraus was much more than a climber and hence a book about him cannot relegate his other accomplishments to the sidelines. If you are willing to learn a thing or two about modern European history, back pain, the intrigues of the Washington political scene and, more importantly, about a truly remarkable man, then this is definitely a book to read.

Part One examines the life of Kraus and his family in Europe. Born to a successful Austrian businessman, Kraus experienced the all-too-familiar struggle between doing what he loves and what he is expected to do. One of the strengths of this section is how well Kraus and his family's experiences are tied in with larger history. The first half of the 20th century was of course a turbulent period in Europe. In between chapters on Kraus's climbing adventures and his time in medical school are chapters on the ever-changing political and social landscape of Austria. Readers who are particularly history-savvy may disagree with some of Schwartz's historical interpretations. Overall her scholarship is solid, however.

After the Nazis came to power in Austria the Kraus family immigrated to New York. The next four parts of the book cover Kraus's climbing and medical career in the U.S. Kraus became what Schwartz calls a "founding father" of the Shawangunks. Schwartz seamlessly narrates the daring, if not reckless, undertaking that was establishing first ascents in the 1940s and 50s. Besides climbing over 60 first ascents in the Gunks, Kraus served as the area's unofficial proprietor, ensuring access and checking the qualifications of new climbers. Even though the book is written for flatlanders as well as climbers, I appreciated that Schwartz does not waste much space explaining climbing techniques and terms in the main text. For the most part this is taken care of in footnotes.

As a doctor Kraus was equally bold and respected. His ability to cure any and all back pain through "unconventional" means peaked with his invitation to work as President John F. Kennedy's back doctor. Kraus dedicated numerous hours to this difficult case without ever asking for compensation or political favors. It is also notable, Schwartz points out, that Kraus did not capitalize on his relationship with JFK by publishing memoirs immediately upon his death, as so many other White House regulars did. Similarly, Kraus treated all who came to his clinic and charged them according to what they could afford.

Kraus pioneered the theory that exercise, in and of itself, is healthy. Although this is taken for granted today, some of Kraus's teachings on back pain was news to me but certainly rang true. Schwartz's efforts in sifting through medical jargon and explaining the medical concepts in a clear fashion are remarkable.

The final part explains how Schwartz came to write the book. As so many patients before her, Schwartz came to Kraus as a skeptical yet desperate back pain sufferer. The story of Schwartz's relationship with Kraus is, in and of itself, touching. It also reaches beyond this last section of the book. Schwartz weaves images of her interviews with Kraus into the narratives of his earlier life. This duality of stories throughout the book is quite powerful.

My only genuine complaint about the book is the title. As far as I'm concerned, "Into the…" has been overused on the cover of mountaineering books. But one should never judge a book by its cover anyway. Schwarz's achievement is nearly as remarkable as the life of Hans Kraus. His was a story that had to be told, and Susan E.B. Schwartz has done so in a most graceful way.

MARTIN GUTMANN

On Thin Ice: Alpine Climbs in the Americas, Asia and the Himalaya. MICK FOWLER. FOREWORD BY CHRIS BONINGTON. LONDON: BÂTON WICKS, 2005. HARDCOVER. 24 PAGES OF COLOR PHOTOGRAPHS; 18 MAPS/DIAGRAMS. 224 PAGES. £18.99. $45.00.

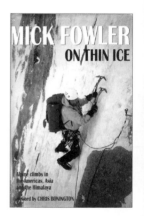

This, Fowler's second book of climbing memoirs, picks up more or less in 1995 where his first book, *Vertical Pleasures: The Secret Life of a Tax Man*, leaves off. The subtitle of the first book speaks to one of Fowler's great charms: he's a working person like most of the rest of us, with limited vacation time and two children. Both books are essentially a series of trip reports; thus the greatest strength here is that these are reports of amazing climbs done in pure alpine style on spectacular peaks such as Taweche, Changabang, Arwa Tower, and Siguniang.

At the book's center is his 1997 climb on Changabang's north face. The expedition was made up of three pairs of climbers with Roger Payne and Julie-Ann Clyma on one line and, as it turned out, Andy Cave and Brendan Murphy sharing a line with Steve Sustad and Fowler. Far less than half of the 35 pages of this account are devoted to the actual climbing. Fowler is particularly good with the preliminaries–dealing with bureaucracy and acclimatizing, but toward the end of his description of the climbing I was surprised to realize they had been on the line for 13 days. The sense of duration is lost in his relatively compressed accounting. The hardest thing for writers to describe about climbing seems always to be the actual climbing.

Fowler sets a very high standard for the purity of his climbing style: "the sense of exploratory, adventurous climbing was seriously compromised by us following Andy and Brendan up the face." This despite seeing no other Westerners since very early on the approach. Fowler's description of the climbing is generally casual until the end, when events turn undeniably grim. Yet, the continuous difficulty of the climbing comes through in subtle moments such as: "Steve eased the belay strain by tying his rucksack into ice screws and sitting on it with his legs dangling free"–which made me realize I'd never placed a screw so solidly in my life.

If his self-deprecating writing style may sometimes prevent us from understanding just how difficult the climbing is, the photographs are consistent reminders. The photo "Day 4 pitch 1 [Changabang]" is captioned "Glassy icefields became both taxing and boring after a time." The "taxing" aspect is obvious, but "boring"? It would keep my attention. The 24 pages of photographs are consistently excellent both in their composition and reproduction, yet miniaturized to fit as many as six frames on a page—this is not a coffee-table book, but one wishes it were.

Fowler writes in an understated, self-deprecating style that has been a staple of British climbing writers going back to its inception. He invokes the old bad boy image on the book's first page by recounting the anecdote about Al Rouse "reputedly drinking vomit from Noel Odell's Everest boot." But Fowler's close to 50 years old and not much of a bad boy himself. I have always enjoyed this stance as a way of having ones' cake and eating it too. They're doing these very imaginative, very strenuous climbs and pretending it's nothing, all a lark, but still worthy of cranking out a couple books describing them. Fowler bemoans (humorously!) his lack of physical conditioning throughout, yet when climbing seems capable of summoning the strength and endurance of superheroes. Wish I knew how—reminds me of an old cartoon showing a math problem which includes as a variable the words "and then a miracle occurs" in order to produce the correct result.

Finally, the Changabang climb turns desperate with Fowler and Sustad falling after summiting and Murphy swept away in an avalanche on the descent. Very little is said about Murphy's death. In the account's closing moments Fowler asks "was it worth it?" and gives us a nine-line answer that we've heard before, perhaps even in our own heads. It's not the most introspective of answers and yet has the great advantage of being, at least, true.

Another strength of the book is the diagrams and the footnotes. The diagram "The Torture Tube, Bivouac no. four" on Taweche has to be one of the most horrifying climbing drawings I know, ranking up there with the diagram from an old edition of Wilkerson's *Medicine for Mountaineering* depicting a technique for removing an impacted stool.

The book opens with a description of receiving the "Mountaineer's Mountaineer" award in 1989 and closes with him winning both the Golden Piton Award from *Climbing* and the Piolet D'Or for his and Paul Ramsden's remarkable climb of Siguniang, at 6,250 meters, the highest peak in the Qionglai Range, China. Fowler describes their route, The Great White Dyke, as "a long vertical basalt dyke stuffed with ice which at several points looked very steep." The diagram notes, more precisely, 5 meters of 95 degrees around bivouac number four! (*Alpinist* #1 features a photo spread of the route which does it justice.) If there was any doubt, this book confirms that all these awards were very well deserved.

On Thin Ice, which received the best-book award for Mountain Literature at the Banff Mountain Book Festival in 2005, is inspiring at every turn. Fowler's humility is a nice touch and while I believe it's genuine, this is no ordinary bloke, this is a truly extraordinary climber.

DAVID STEVENSON

The Forgotten Adventure: Mount Everest, The Reconnaissance, 1935. TONY ASTILL. FOREWORD BY LORD HUNT. INTRODUCTION BY SIR EDMUND HILLARY. SOUTHHAMPTON: LES ALPES LIVRE, 2005. 359 PAGES, NUMEROUS BLACK & WHITE PHOTOGRAPHS, AND 2 FOLDING MAPS PLUS A UNIQUE DOUBLE DUST-JACKET OF A 1935 COLOR TOPOGRAPHIC CONTOUR MAP OF MT. EVEREST'S NORTH FACE IN TIBET BY MICHAEL SPENDER. £30.

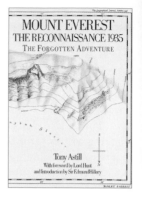

It was, claimed Eric Shipton famously, "a veritable orgy of mountain climbing." In May 1935, Britain's best mountaineers, including Shipton, longtime climbing partner Bill Tilman, plus 15 Sherpas, among them a 19-year-old novice, Tenzing Norgay, embarked from Darjeeling on the fourth-ever Mt. Everest expedition. In large part because no expedition book was later penned by Shipton, their 27-year-old leader, the 1935 Everest Reconnaissance Expedition has remained largely unknown and unlauded. No more! Seven decades later, *The Forgotten Adventure* reveals the never-before-told climbing adventures of three of the twentieth-century mountaineering's most revered icons reveling in the Himalayan glory of their youth. By any yardstick its successes were stunning. Everest's summit was not reached, yet in various combinations, Shipton, Tilman, Edwin Kempson, Dr. Charles Warren, Edmund Wigram, and New Zealander Dan Bryant ascended a staggering total of 26 peaks in the Everest region—all over 20,000 feet and all but two first ascents.

British mountaineering historian Tony Astill has finally published his heroic recounting of the 1935 Everest Expedition. Utilizing long-lost diaries, letters home, plus journal and book extracts, Astill has recreated in absorbing and fascinating detail the journey to and from the mountain and the climb-by-climb successes of Shipton's team. *Forgotten Adventure* is an intimately told, romantic, seat-of-your-pants tale of 1930s exploratory mountaineering. The team accomplished the first ascent of virtually every major peak on Mt. Everest's northern Tibetan side, then also made the grim discovery of the body of Maurice Wilson, the demented English non-climber who had perished the previous year while attempting Everest alone via the North Col.

Yet this team's triumphs, planned "in half an hour on the back of an envelope," traveling "lightly equipped and shorn of superfluous baggage," cost a mere tenth of Britain's previous military-style Everest expeditions. As Tilman rightly quipped: "An expedition is a party with too many people in it." While the deep monsoon snows thwarted their efforts on Changtse—Everest's north peak—no other Himalayan expedition in history has ever bagged so many virgin summits. Tilman and Wigram climbed an astounding 17 peaks each! Shipton and Bryant also obtained the first-ever photographs and views of the Khumbu Icefall, making Shipton think it would "go."

And although Tilman and Bryant had difficulty acclimatizing, this 1935 expedition unknowingly set the stage for Everest's first ascent eighteen years later. It was the first of Tenzing's eventual seven Everest expeditions, and Shipton so enjoyed Bryant's company that in 1951 he invited another Kiwi mountaineer, Edmund Hillary, to join his recon of the Khumbu Icefall in Nepal. Thanks to Astill's monumental efforts, mountaineers can experience this "final chapter" in Everest's history through the climbers' own words and beautiful, never-published black and white photographs—and the rest IS history. As this is a self-published book, please order directly from the author, at his email address: alpes@supanet.com.

ED WEBSTER

Let My People Go Surfing: The Education of a Reluctant Businessman. YVON CHOUINARD. NEW YORK: PENGUIN PRESS, 2005. 261 PAGES. HARDCOVER. $26.95.

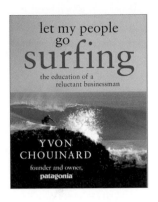

This review assignment made me nervous. I have to pass judgment on a book by climbing legend and environmental hero Yvon Chouinard—which is scary—and the damn book sounds like one of those business yawners—*Who Moved my Seventh Habit,* or whatever? About as appealing as an offwidth under a cornice, right?

Here's the good news. My mental skies brightened as soon as I flipped the pages. *Let My People Go Surfing* turns out to be a new kind of business book; readers experience Patagonia's company history as an unlikely adventure narrative from backyard shop to billion-dollar operation, with frequent tales of expedition and excitement from the peaks and the waves.

Let My People Go Surfing gives us an autobiography of Yvon Chouinard in the context of his company and his awakening environmental conscience. Indeed, this latter conscience is the story behind the story of *Let My People Go Surfing.* You see, environmentalism is barely a concern for the young Chouinard, but seeps into his ideas in the late sixties, and by the 70s is shaping product decisions, until the 90s when environmentalism is not only a factor in production choices, it's the reason for the company's existence. Let me confirm that last part: Chouinard is adamant that Patagonia exists to make money for environmental causes.

Chouinard's book fascinates with examples of Patagonia's bold and uncompromising environmental choices. For instance, in 1970 Chouinard Equipment was the country's biggest climbing hardware supplier, and most of that hardware was pitons. A climb on the Nose that summer showed Chouinard the steady degradation of the granite cracks due to years of nailing. As a result, he and Tom Frost decided to get out of the piton business. What's interesting here is the way environmental choices are not business hara-kiri; instead, they position the company to innovate and anticipate novel developments. In the case of the pitons, the innovation was stoppers and hexes, and soon they were selling these chocks faster than they could make them.

Let's look at some other environmental cruxes in Patagonia's history. (If this were a climbing biography, we'd be talking about the key ascents that define the legend.) What does it mean when a clothing company takes its primary fabric—cotton—and insists it be organically grown? It means that Patagonia's cost for materials nearly doubles. But, in 1994 the company's board voted to be organic by 1996, and the result was a trip all the way down the production chain—through cotton brokers, to suppliers, to the farmers themselves. Patagonia has stimulated demand for organic cotton, and influenced other apparel industry leaders to, finally, encourage organic cotton farming. Again, this principled decision has led Patagonia to a bigger market share. Chouinard concludes: "Every time we've elected to do the right thing, even when it costs twice as much to do it that way, it's turned out to be more profitable." So here's the real Patagonia mission and the mission of this text—showing the corporate world that green business not only works, but is a profitable best choice for company practices.

Maybe there are deep and shameful secrets about Patagonia somewhere, but I don't know them, and *Let My People Go Surfing* just made me feel glad to have a closet full of their stuff. The book describes Patagonia's other progressive innovations that distinguish it from the suit and tie business world—like a tradition of on-site childcare, a corporate headquarters without executive suites, a recycling initiative for their own old products, and a commitment to the flextime policy that gives this book its title. So, in Chouinard's story, Patagonia employees are not only allowed but urged to get out and surf or climb or demonstrate, and thereby replenish the cup of vigor that brought them first through the door.

Now I'm not a business guy, and there were a few dull spots in the text for me. Breaking the company practices into eight discrete philosophies—e.g. "Product Design Philosophy," "Distribution Philosophy," "Image Philosophy"—seems like the bland self-referentiality of Human Resources drones I've resented in the past (you know who you are). But, *Let My People Go Surfing* prusiks out of this particular crevasse with its radical message: Business can be the Green Revolution.

Patagonia is about action, and not about profit: "Our main reason for being in business is to work on changing the way governments and corporations ignore our environmental crisis." This action extends from supporting activist groups and a self-imposed Earth Tax of 1% to the power of example. "If Patagonia can continue to be successful ..., then we perhaps can convince other companies that green business is good business, and they can gain the confidence to take a few steps in the right direction." So, Chouinard's story is the story of a company finding its purpose in environmentally aware business practice. This is much more than preaching to the Birkenstock choir about recycling; it's an address to the shiny-shoe-set positioned to reshape industry. The striking thing is that Chouinard's quest for responsibility and for relevance makes surprisingly good reading.

To sum up: behind the jokey title, there's an edge to this book that slices the soft and comforting illusions from the American lifestyle. Here's a capitalist telling us the perils of growth, a manufacturer talking about industrial toxins, a garment maker angry about the consequences of dyes and pesticides. Chouinard's title is rooted in a revolutionary anger from the Old Testament, where the Lord tells Moses to tell Pharoah "Let my people go." So, though we associate the line with Moses, it's actually God who says "Let my people go," and this isn't the New Testament God of love and forgiveness here, this is the tooth for a tooth, blood on the ground, Lord God of the Hebrews we're talking about—as Pharoah found out down the road. My point is that *Let My People Go Surfing* is its own Exodus. It's a call to revolution from a Beatnik prophet for whom climbing was an alternative to the strait-laced expectation of the 1950s. Today, Patagonia is setting a counter-example to a Pharoah's culture of suburban sprawl, faceless mutual funds, and insidious consumption that entangles us all.

I think this is a book for most anyone. If you happen to run a major corporation, have one of your interns retrieve it ASAP. If, like the rest of us, you're starting to think about reducing your ecological footprint, *Let My People Go Surfing* is an entertaining inspiration.

Jeff McCarthy

Breaking Trail: A Climbing Life. Arlene Blum. New York: Scribner, 2005. Black and white photos. 313 pages. Hardcover. $27.50.

If ever there has been an iconic figure in the canon of women's mountaineering literature Arlene Blum is she. Blum can be considered a pioneer in women's mountaineering in line with other great women mountaineers such as Fanny Bullock Workman, Annie Peck Smith, and Isabella Bird. Alongside the earlier female accounts of adventure, in *Breaking Trail* Blum combines the genres of memoir and adventure writing beautifully. *Breaking Trail* is a unique and insightful glimpse into the heart, mind, and soul of Arlene Blum, one of the world's most accomplished female mountaineers.

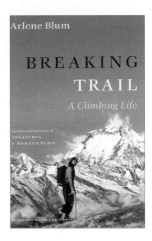

Arlene Blum was born in the heart of the Midwest to German and Russian Jewish parents. For most of her life she was encouraged to find a nice Jewish husband and settle down into the comfortable and rewarding life of a wife and mother. Through recollections of her past, written as forewords in each of the chapters, her story unfolds. These flashes of childhood memories, that have remained locked up in a heart-shaped secret diary until now, parallel the many adventures, failures, and triumphs alike, that Blum encountered as a woman in education, adventure, and with love.

As an academic, with a PhD in biophysical chemistry, Blum has accomplished many professional firsts. Blum attended Reed College and eventually went on to UC Berkeley to complete her PhD. Throughout her course work Blum tirelessly worked for the betterment of the global community. Through her efforts as a scientist she is one, among several others, responsible for research that exposed the use and implementation of toxic flame retardant chemicals in children's pajamas. Blum and colleagues demanded the recall of millions of pajamas in the United States and developed a flame retardant to be used that is safe and nontoxic. Academically, Blum was "breaking trail" through her dedication and tireless research.

Throughout her young life and her later adult life as a mountaineer and explorer, she also began "breaking a trail" that had for so many years remained "unbreakable." Blum was responsible for the first all-women's expedition to Denali, which was a success despite negative pressure from the male climbing community and the media. Several years later, after having participated in the tragic Pamirs expedition of 1974, which claimed the lives of eight members of the Russian women's team, Blum was invited to participate in the 1976 Bicentennial American Everest Expedition. Then in 1978 she organized the first all-women's expedition to Annapurna, the world's tenth-highest mountain. The Annapurna expedition was significant for many reasons. With a successful summit Blum's American team members would be the first Americans to climb Annapurna, and even more significant was the fact that this expedition would produce the first women to climb Annapurna. In an effort to raise the needed $80,000 the women participating produced and sold T-shirts that coined the infamous phrase "A Woman's Place is on Top." Two expedition members successfully reached the summit while two others died during their attempt. The expedition was both a success and a tragedy, something that Blum internalizes and writes of in this compelling narrative. In the final chapter of *Annapurna: A Woman's Place* she writes: "On Annapurna our entire team took the risk, made the commitment. Only time will reveal its full consequences. As Maurice Herzog declares at the end of his book: 'There are other Annapurnas in the lives of men.' And in the lives of women as well." While it is unfortunate that tragedy overshadowed this momentous event (likely more so because it was an all- female team), it can not be argued that Blum was not "breaking new and unexplored trail."

Blum "breaks trail" further not only through writing of her adventures and successes, but in dealing honestly with her failures as well as her life's journey, both personally and emotionally. Blum honestly, openly, and effectively confronts the psychological problems she suffered as a result of her troubled childhood. Blum's mother gave birth to her in the 1940s when the idea of postpartum depression was not understood or verbalized. Her mother underwent shock therapy to help "heal" her disease. Blum's parents separated before her birth, which left her to be raised by her grandparents. Throughout Blum's adult life she suffered emotionally and mentally because of the separation that she encountered as a baby and her childhood. This suffering manifested itself often, leaving Blum in uncontrollable states of depression and fear of abandonment. Blum parallels these mental and physical "Annapurnas" throughout her memoir, not only successfully but masterfully.

Breaking Trail is a must read for anyone interested in mountaineering, gender studies, psychology, and memoir, for Blum traverses all these areas as effectively as she has the high places of the world.

SARAH VAUSE SNOW

Learning to Breathe. ANDY CAVE. LONDON: HUTCHINSON, 2005. 276 PAGES. £18.99. $44.95.

This remarkable debut memoir, co-winner of the 2005 Boardman-Tasker Award and winner of the best-book prize for Adventure Travel in the 2005 Banff Mountain Book Festival, recounts an equally remarkable trajectory in the life of one of Britain's finest mountaineers. Andy Cave grew up working class in Yorkshire, the son and grandson of coal miners. At the age of 16, he took up work himself in the Grimethorpe pit, performing some of the most dangerous and brutal labor in the "civilized" world for menial wages. Cave might well have spent the rest of his life underground (the Grimethorpe pit is 3,000 feet deep) but for Margaret Thatcher's meddling with the industry, which led to a prolonged miners' strike, which in turn allowed the lad to scratch the restless itch that drove him from local crags to the Alps and ultimately to the Himalaya.

In 1986 Cave turned his back on the family profession to devote himself to climbing—without, at first, any hope of making a living from his passion. Instead, he dedicated himself to school, eventually earning a PhD in socio-linguistics. His dissertation? A study of the dialects of the miners with whom he had grown up.

Some of the most vivid passages in *Learning to Breathe* evoke life in the coalmines. Not only does Cave capture the claustrophobic terrors of the deep, dark shafts and tunnels, but his ear is pitch-perfect for the dialogue of his grimy cronies. The gallows humor of these "hard men," exposed daily to the hazard of crippling accidents and even death, makes Don Whillans sound cheery. Overlying the whole way of life is the relentless bleakness of the lifelong poverty from which Cave makes his daring escape.

Thus the climbing passages, which at first alternate with the episodes in the mines, sing with the lyric joy of that escape. As Cave discovers that he's better than merely good as a climber, his ambitions escalate wildly. Reading about the young man's dream of limitless ascent in the far-flung ranges, every mountaineer will be reminded of his or her own youthful urge for transcendence on rock and ice.

If there is a single missed opportunity in this memoir, it may be that Cave does not quite exploit the perspective of his grad-school learning and his mountain craft to reflect more deeply on the self-transformation he has wrought. There is much to be said (as, for instance, Sebastian Junger does in *The Perfect Storm*) about the irony of seeking risk in a dangerous pastime versus enduring risk in a daily job. Is mountaineering, after all, a luxury for those of us who will never have to work in a coal mine?

But this is a mere quibble. *Learning to Breathe* is a wonderful, unique book. And its climactic chapters, about a drawn-out, ultimately tragic epic on Changabang, unfold in climbing narrative as gripping as anything written in the last several decades.

David Roberts

Broad Peak. Richard Sale. Translations from German text by Michaela Gigerl and John Hirst. Ross on Wye (UK): Carreg Ltd. 2004. 208 pages. £22.50. $45.00.

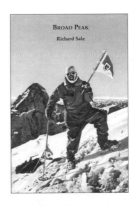

Broad Peak was short-listed for the Banff Prize for Mountain Literature in 2005; one can only surmise that this was based not on the book itself, but on its admirable premise. In 1957 four Austrians, Marcus Schmuck, Fritz Winterstellar, Herman Buhl, and Kurt Diemberger made the first ascent of Broad Peak, an 8,000-meter summit, the twelfth highest in the world. Further, they did so in groundbreaking style: unsupported by high-altitude porters, without bottled oxygen, lightweight, and fast-moving. The climb may not have been recognized as it ought to have been because after Broad Peak the climbers went off in ropes of two: Schmuck and Winterstellar to climb Skil Brum, and Buhl and Diemberger to climb Chogolisa. On the descent Buhl walked over a cornice in a whiteout, and the only man to accomplish first ascents of two 8,000-meter peaks was lost. Buhl's death took some of the well-deserved publicity from the Broad Peak ascent, and a chapter in Diemberger's *Summits and Secrets* became the best-known version of events. This beautifully written impressionistic account never sets out to tell the full story of the expedition, but tells a very personal story by a young climber, focusing mostly on the tale of Buhl and himself.

Sale claims that he wishes to tell the full story here and to give Schmuck and Winterstellar their long overdue credit. Fine, who would wish to deny them credit? Diemberger would, if you believe Sale. I don't.

I recommend Diemberger's original essay to you. Diemberger never says anything negative about Schmuck and Winterstellar. And even though Sale clearly has an axe to grind, he never really disputes anything of substance in Diemberger account, either. Instead Sale fills his book with petty speculation, much of it seemingly intended to demonize Diemberger. By "petty" I mean, for example, notes from Diemberger's diaries accusing others of not doing their share of camp chores. By "speculation" I mean statements that assume the language of speculation but in fact are judgments, for example: "Perhaps Buhl was already distancing himself from someone he considered a rival who had won the first exchange." There are dozens of such instances herein.

In the end, I felt that while Sale may have set out to be objective, somehow in the process the opposite happened: he lost sight of his goal of praising Schmuck and Winterstellar and became intent on critiquing Buhl and Diemberger. The result is that he puts forth a single point of view, one that assumes that Diemberger and Buhl were essentially dishonest, lazy, and/or unfit. I simply didn't believe it; Sale's account seemed to deconstruct itself.

It is indeed regrettable that Buhl's death diverted the spotlight from Schmuck and Wintersteller's achievements, but not so regrettable as the fact of his death. Honor those achievements by remembering what Sale says in his introduction: "It must never be forgotten that the Austrian climb was one of the landmarks of mountaineering history and that, whatever friction there was between the four men during the climb and after it, the ascent of Broad Peak stands as a monumental achievement." That line appears in the last paragraph of the introduction; avoid the muck that follows it.

DAVID STEVENSON

IN BRIEF: NOTES FROM THE BANFF MOUNTAIN BOOK FESTIVAL, 2005

The 2005 Banff Mountain Book Festival competition received more than 150 entries from eight countries. Although this was narrowed down to 39 finalists, it was one of the most impressive years in the 12-year history of the festival for quality writing in the mountain literature genre. To submit an entry into the competition, contact banffmountainbooks@banffcentre.ca.

A brief selection of the more noteworthy Banff books not reviewed in this *AAJ*:

Mountain Ranges of Colorado, John Fiedler (Westcliffe Publishers, $75.00) winner of the Best Book for Mountain Image. This coffee table book chronicles the 28 distinct ranges of Colorado's southern Rockies. One jury member described it as "A wonderful testament to the observation that luck favors the prepared and persistent . . . A great eye coupled with wonderful technique and then married to a beautifully produced book."

The Rage: Reflections on Risk, Steve De Maio (Rocky Mountain Publishing, $16.95) is a collection of essays and poetry that describe what De Maio calls "the rage"—a combination of strength, experience, focus, and rational analysis that saw him through first ascents in the Canadian Rockies in the late 1980s. One jury member described it as "Honest, personal, bold, and well-expressed reflections on the inner workings of one climber's mind."

The Longest Climb: Back from the Abyss, Paul Pritchard (Constable and Robinson Ltd. 7.99) Picking up where *The Totem Pole* leaves off, this book describes Pritchard's emotional and physical recovery after near death by rockfall and subsequent paralysis. The jury found it "continuously excellent and interesting."

Bradford Washburn: An Extraordinary Life: The Autobiography of a Mountaineering Icon. Bradford Washburn and Lewis Freedman (Westwinds Press, 27.95). This accounting of "an extraordinary life and a life worth telling" is anecdotal in nature and foregrounds Washburn's professional life, focusing more on early accomplishments. The jury found it "intrinsically interesting."

Losing the Garden: the Story of a Marriage, Laura Waterman (Shoemaker & Hoard, $24.00) Laura Waterman's view of life with her husband Guy who killed himself on Mt. Lafayette in midwinter. "A terribly compelling book" that describes "how this family lived in them [the mountains] and with them." Described by a jury member as "Sad and hopeful at the same time."

BERNADETTE MCDONALD, *Director, Banff Mountain Festivals*

In Memoriam

Morgan Harris 1916-2005

The last of the great Yosemite climbing pioneers of the 1930s has died. Morgan Harris, during his 88 years, lived an astonishingly rich life, serious climbing being only a small part of it. This obituary will necessarily emphasize his climbs over a short career—some eight years. But I must unfortunately (for this is a journal of exploits done in the mountains) gloss over his greater triumphs: his professional life as a scientist, his excellent family, his fabulous birding career. Climbing is not everything. Morgan was truly a Renaissance man.

Morgan Harris

Born in Idaho, he soon ended up in the San Francisco Bay area, a good move, for he fell in with the Sierra Club Rock Climbing Section, a group of Young Turks formed in the early 1930s to climb in untouched Yosemite Valley. A week after his 19th birthday, in 1935, he teamed up with Dick Leonard and Jack Riegelhuth to make the first ascent of the towering Washington Column. This was a pretty bold achievement, in my opinion, for even today there is no obvious route up this 1,300-foot, seemingly vertical wall. (Their route, called the Piton Traverse, remains to this day a mystery. Where did they actually go? A later route, more direct and popular, meant that the 1935 climb was soon destined to fade from memory.)

A climb that a vast number of AAC members have done, or at least heard about, is the Royal Arches. Here again is a Yosemite route without an obvious line. Harris, by 1936 a junior at the University of California at Berkeley, had studied the cliff with binoculars. He knew the giant curving arches couldn't be climbed, but off to the left lay non-overhanging terrain, studded with trees and blessed with cracks. One attempt, in torrid weather, failed, and he spent a week in the hospital recovering from sunstroke. After yet another attempt, Harris and two others succeeded in October 1936. The climbing on the route was not too tough, but the routefinding and rope techniques proved daunting. One new procedure, called by Harris a "swinging rope traverse," overcame a blank section. This was likely the first "pendulum" done in California.

Later the trio reached what Harris later described as "an old tree-trunk," a feature soon to become famous as the Rotten Log. This 25-foot-long, foot-thick dead log bridged a chasm, affording a unique method of reaching the other side. Harris had spotted this golden trunk from the Valley floor and hoped it would be strong enough to hold his weight. It was, though it vibrated crazily as he led across it. Many thousands of climbers shuffled along this shaky pole in the decades to come; it finally parted company with the rock in the spring of 1984.

Harris was on a roll. On the following day he and two others tried to reach the top of Sentinel Rock from the north, but failed. The next day, beginning a long and fruitful climbing partnership, he teamed up with David Brower to make the first ascent of Cathedral Chimney, the huge gash separating the Higher and Middle Cathedral rocks. The following day the pair were first up Panorama Cliff, the somber wall rising above Vernal Fall. Thus, in the space of four days, Harris made first ascents of three major Valley features and attempted one more.

Harris and Brower utterly dominated Yosemite climbing in the mid- and late 1930s, establishing nine more routes together, including long and involved climbs such as Yosemite

Point Couloir and the Circular Staircase on Sentinel Rock. Harris ended up with 14 Valley first ascents.

Of one ascent together, Brower wrote about Harris climbing upward in "wet tennis shoes." He went on to say, "I couldn't discover how he led the pitch and still don't know. While I prefer to think it was because we were hurried and I was carrying the pack, I nevertheless had to use that forbidden handhold—the rope."

After World War II Harris remained an active backpacker and wilderness skier. On New Year's Day 1955 he was cross-country skiing near Lake Tahoe when he came upon a fresh avalanche track with three trapped skiers yelling for help. One man, they yelled, is over there and completely under. Harris quickly dug out Allen Steck, blue and near death.

Of his non-climbing life, the challenges and kudos were just beginning. By 1945 he was teaching in the zoology department at UC Berkeley, remaining there for more than 40 years, and as chair for 11. He specialized in cell biology, making significant contributions to the biological mechanisms of drug resistance.

I once wanted to ask him a question about the old days and so called his home. His wife, Lola, replied, "He's at work; try him there." He was 77 that year, working at the Berkeley campus, still fascinated with his research. We shall miss his dedication, his gentleness, his humanity. If our last years were as calm and as productive as Morgan's, we should count ourselves blessed.

STEVE ROPER, *AAC*

ROBERT F. KAMPS 1931-2005

Bob Kamps *Carrie Sundra*

Having lived this long, I've found the most important measure of our climbing days is not what grades or climbs we achieve, but what we get from it all down deep, especially our times with others. On these counts, my friend and longtime climbing partner Bob Kamps got full measure. He loved moving well and precisely on rock. His footwork, finesse, intensity, devotion to good style, and winning smile told you joy was his. As well, he made scores of lasting friends across three generations, influencing both their climbing and their lives. Twenty-four spoke from the heart at his memorial at Stoney Point in L.A. and numerous others did the same at www.BobKamps.com. Listen to a few of those he met along the way (quotes edited to fit space):

"The climbing/bouldering ethos we had was primarily due to Mr. Kamps. Over the years I've by now seen various big names climb—at Camp 4, Stoney, Smith, but of all, two people stand out in terms of the control and precision of their climbing and presence on the rock: Bob Kamps and ...."—John Reed

"In the course of 25 years of doing outdoor sports, I have only met a handful of beings that have had Bob's blend of humility, core, and accomplishments. He set the high bar." —Brett Valle

"His true legacy is his effect on other people and his ability to help them grow through his gentle encouragement and acceptance ... that is his true legacy."—Chris Wegener

"I found Bob did most of his talking about climbing through the act of climbing.

He was a master of teaching by example. I don't think he did it intentionally. It was what made Bob."—Kevin Wright

"I knew how great Bob was not just for his climbing ability but for who he was as a person. People he had never met would see all this in just a few moments. Bob was many things to me, a climbing mentor, and most importantly, a true friend."—Jim Wilson

Bob began climbing before how-to books or gyms. Captivated by the mountains while visiting Yellowstone National Park in 1955, he recruited anyone who could walk as a climbing partner and invented techniques on the fly. For example, he cut a U-shaped trough in a dirt hummock to rappel off Pilot Peak after a successful ascent. Later, he learned the basics through the UCLA Bruin Mountaineers and the Sierra Club.

The highly publicized first ascent of the Diamond of Longs Peak with Dave Rearick in 1960 was perhaps his best-known climb. He preferred challenging, shorter crags to big walls, with lots of sun and friends nearby. His personal favorite first ascent was Lucky Streaks in Tuolumne Meadows, a wispy, sweeping series of steep cracks on Fairview Dome.

Bob always climbed in good style. He never rested on the rope when he fell, but instead lowered to the last stance and started again. He placed bolts sparingly, by hand, often from difficult positions, and was one of the first to write about bolt ethics, in a 1966 article for *Summit* magazine.

As Bob got older, it was natural for climbers everywhere to stop to watch him: usually leading, craggy legs sticking from cutoffs, strong, sinewy arms poking from a frayed T-shirt; gray hair, leathery skin, gold-rim glasses, maybe fiddling with impossible protection. No wonder a post at Bob's website says, "I think now … climbing … has less to do with age than … desire, preparation, experience, and vision"—J.W.

Bob's passion for climbing is reflected in the sheer number of his ascents: more than 3,000 routes over 50 years; 162 first ascents (2/3 were 5.10 or higher); 25 first free ascents. He appeared regularly and recognizably at Yosemite, Tuolumne Meadows, Joshua Tree, Tahquitz, southern deserts, southern states, Midwest, East Coast—just about every climbing area in the U.S. He climbed at his top standard to the end (age 73) when his heart stopped as he reached for a hold at the local climbing gym. A life to envy.

Both Bob and loving wife Bonnie of 46 years were elementary school teachers, enabling them to enjoy summers in the mountains. He left teaching to deal in antiques and collectibles, calling himself "Entrecrapeur." He did well in his chosen pursuit, allowing him to help out many a young climber in a pinch.

I can't say goodbye to Bob Kamps. He and I climbed together since the early '60s. He gave me my climbing technique and mentality. He was father to me when my parents died early in my life. He fought well with me over politics and religion. He ranted with me in the days when climbing styles made big changes. He maddened me in his stubborn way of carrying too little hardware. He gave me things out of the blue. He saved my life at least once, as I did his. For me, Bob lives on, climbing a remembered pitch, sharing a summit and later the tale, smiling, punning, loving the days.

My thanks to Bonnie Kamps, Steve Roper, Jim Fulmis, and Kevin Wright for assistance in preparing this obituary and to all quoted here. For a database of Bob's climbs, pictures, and tributes from friends, visit www.BobKamps.com. For other obituaries, see *Climbing* July 2005 and *Rock and Ice* June 2005.

TOM HIGGINS, AAC

Vera Komarkova 1942-2005

Vera Komarkova, a strong and courageous mountaineer, talented and respected plant ecologist and teacher, fiercely dedicated mother of two sons, and a loyal and caring friend, died of complications of breast cancer treatment on May 25. She could be outrageously blunt; she had a wicked sense of humor, a fatalistic streak, and a high standard of honesty. Vera set ambitious goals and worked hard to achieve them. She was full of fun and serious at the same time, and never boring.

Vera was born on Christmas Day, 1942, in the small town of Pisek in the former Czechoslovakia. Her father was the eminent botanist Jiri Ruzicka, a specialist in Desmidiales, a large order of

Vera Kormarkova in Leysin.
Robert Hutchison

mostly fresh-water algae. Vera entered Charles University in Prague in 1959 when she was nearly 17, graduating in 1964 with an MSc in biology. She was married in 1963 to Jiri Komarek, a fellow botanist and alpinist 11 years her senior. She spoke five languages: English, German, French, Czech, and Russian. After graduation her first job was in the Krkonose National Park near the border with Poland, where she wrote a small guide to the park flora.

Vera started climbing while at university and during the next 10 years put together an impressive resume of summer and winter climbs in the High Tatras and other areas of the Carpathian Mountains, as well as in the Western Alps.

During the political thaw leading up to Prague Spring, Vera and three women climbing friends had the crazy idea to walk to the 1968 Summer Olympics in Mexico City. They called themselves Slapoty, which means "Footprints" in Czech. They crossed Austria and Switzerland, then walked through France and England and took passage on a ship from Liverpool to Canada. After walking nearly 5,000 miles, the team arrived in Mexico City in time for the games. While in Mexico they climbed Ixtaccihuatl and other peaks and Vera was briefly married for the second time to Esquinoza Aquillar. The women of Slapoty would remain lifelong friends.

The Russians invaded Czechoslovakia in August of 1968. The border was closed in October of 1969, but somehow Vera managed to emigrate to the United States in 1970, followed by her third husband, Vladimir Farkas. She arrived already a fully trained plant ecologist and enrolled in graduate studies in botany at the University of Colorado, receiving her Ph.D. in 1976. Her thesis, "Alpine Vegetation of Indian Peaks Area, Front Range, Colorado Rocky Mountains," was published as a two-volume monograph in 1979 and remains the best example of Braun-Blanquet methods in North America. Adold Ceska, a fellow Czech botanist who emigrated at the same time, said, "...she was the greatest phytosociologist the U.S. has ever known."

I first met Vera when she came to my home in Palo Alto seeking an American woman to propose her for membership in the AAC. Highly qualified, she became a member in 1973. AAC membership was an important recognition to Vera; she would go on to write accurate and interesting articles for the AAJ about four of her major climbs and speak about one of them, Cho Oyu, at the 1984 annual dinner.

Vera combined field trips to the North Slope of Alaska with climbing opportunities, including the third ascent of Doonerak in the Brooks Range in 1975, in which I participated. The following year Vera would climb the South Buttress of McKinley with a six-woman team led by Kate Persons. In 1977, with the Czech climber Tomas Gross, she would complete a very difficult extended new route on the southeast face of Mt. Dickey, above the Ruth Glacier in the

Alaska Range. After fixing the first five pitches, they spent 23 days on the ascent. The climb totaled 47 pitches and they nearly ran out of food. Vera said she felt like a bird on a wall.

When Arlene Blum decided to try for Annapurna in 1978, I immediately suggested Vera, by then a naturalized American citizen, as a member. We shared a tent on the walk in, and Vera collected plants along the way. As they accumulated, we had a joke: press release: climber killed by falling plant presses. We enjoyed the camaraderie of the Sherpa fire in the evenings, and we were climbing partners during the first and last parts of the expedition. On the summit day I felt fortunate to be climbing with Vera again. We agreed that the Sherpas, Chewang and Mingma, were part of the team, and if they wanted to summit they deserved a chance. That day we were a team of four roped together, more symbolically than because of technical difficulty. It was very strenuous going because of the breakable crust with cotton candy underneath. Vera was significantly stronger on the summit day than I was. At one point I asked if we could take a break, and Vera said she didn't think so! Chewang added, "Slowly going, summit," which turned out to be true. Fortunately Vera had enough energy to take a summit photo.

With the deaths of Vera Watson and Alison Chadwick-Onyszkiewicz two days later on the second summit attempt, the aftermath of the expedition was difficult for everyone, and I had no contact with Vera for several years. She almost single-handedly organized and led the American Women's Expedition to Dhaulagiri I in 1980. They attempted the difficult Pear Route on the north side. Heavy winds led to avalanche conditions, and after the death of a member of the support team they mutually abandoned the attempt after reaching 23,300 feet. While on a business trip the next summer I visited Vera in Boulder. We both broke out laughing when I saw she was quite pregnant. Her first son, Mipam Moudry, was born a month later. In keeping with Vera's Buddhist beliefs, his name was chosen from the book title, "Mipam: the Lama of the Five Wisdoms," Moudry meaning "wise" in Czech.

In the next few years Vera continued her work as a research assistant at INSTAAR, the Institute for Alpine and Arctic Research, at the University of Colorado. She made several botanical trips to the Antarctic Peninsula and also visited China and Tibet. In 1984, still ambitious for high summits, she climbed Cho Oyu with the small team of Dina Sterbova and the two Nepalese climbers Ang Rita Sherpa and Nuru Sherpa. They were the first women and Vera was the first American to summit; at 8,201 meters, or 26,900 feet, it was Vera's personal altitude record.

Vera's second son, Dorje, was born in 1985. Because her European training in plant ecology was not appreciated here at the time, Vera did not find a permanent academic position in the U.S. With two young sons to raise, she gave up expeditionary climbing. Moving back to Europe in 1986, closer to her parents, she took a teaching position at the American College in Switzerland in Leysin. She taught a variety of science subjects and became Professor of Science and Information Technology. The computer lab at the college was very much her project. In addition, she taught classes at another school, and in her spare time continued to write papers, articles, and book chapters. I visited Vera twice, in 1994 and 1996; the second time I walked in unannounced and found Vera, her mother, and an 11-year-old Dorje all working on illustrations for her father's third, still unfinished book. The bedroom was piled high with boxes of unfinished botanical projects, just like the tent on the Annapurna approach.

As a single mother of two, Vera did not choose an easy path, but she was proud and self-reliant and worked extremely hard to provide for her family. She endured much pain in recent years, undergoing and recovering from two hip replacement surgeries. Rereading her annual Christmas letters over the last 10 years, one finds dedication to her family, unending projects, humor, trenchant comments about the political scene, much concern for the recipient, but no self-pity. Typically, she told no one but her immediate family about her illness. She leaves behind her mother, Tatiana Ruzickova, of Pisek in the Czech Republic, and her sons Mipam and Dorje Moudry, in Switzerland, Mipam in Bossonnens and Dorje still in Leysin. She had hoped to retire to the Czech Republic in a few years, and her ashes were interred there in Pisek in a family tomb.

IRENE BEARDSLEY, *AAC*

HEATHER L. PAUL 1970-2005

Heather Paul

The most touching part of Heather Paul's memorial service occurred near the end. A nurse and several physicians she had worked with came to the podium and paid tribute to an aspect of her life that we mountain comrades had wondered about.

Over 300 friends gathered on a perfect Jackson Hole summer day, at a ranch at the foot of the Tetons. Heather had died few days earlier from a fall while descending Cloudveil Dome. Family and friends reminded us that Heather moved to Jackson Hole after graduating from ASU in 1992 because of the beauty, the people, and because, she discovered while working a summer job, it felt like home. She arrived with energy, enthusiasm, and athletic talent, credentials as a bicycle racer, and an urge to become proficient as a climber, but timid about venturing into the mountains. She never expected to climb the Grand Teton.

Subsequent speakers filled us in on Heather's achievements during her Jackson Hole years—three new routes in the Tetons, four in the Wind Rivers; old classics like Blackfin, Serendipity Arête, Italian Cracks; ski descents of Wister, Apocalypse Couloir, Pinocchio Couloir; the 2003 North American Randonée Series woman's champion; car-to-car marathons to and from the Wind Rivers' Fremont Peak in eight hours, Downs' Mountain in 14. Her first 11 climbs of the Grand were by 10 different routes.

Everyone had stories of meeting her hurrying along a trail—on foot, on skis, on a bike. One friend related how she checked caller ID before answering early-morning phone calls because it might be Heather, whose infectious enthusiasm would have them out in the hills whether she was up for it or not. Another painted an image of Heather far more evocative than a list of her accomplishments—skinny bare legs, huge pack, blond hair, bouncing along the trail. Paul Horton, her longtime partner, summarized Heather: whatever the activity, she was thrilled just to participate, just to be there. Heather's close friend Nancy Johnstone simply remembered her as epitomizing the meaning of friend.

Among the tributes to her energy, I heard an untruth. Someone related how on the Sunday before she had climbed the Grand, then gone directly to work. Not so. She had descended from the Grand and, with a few hours to spare, had stopped by a cookout I was having at my cabin, then worked all night.

When it seemed that Heather's mountain life had been fully memorialized, a nurse came to the podium and spoke, then a doctor, then others. A year before Heather had completed her nurse's training and gone to work at St. John's Living Center. We mountain comrades had wondered how someone with her energy coped with geriatrics. We needn't have worried. Jackson doctors tend to travel—one was a Physician Without Borders—but they couldn't escape Heather. Each described her concern for her patients, the passion she put into caring for them, the urgent e-mails and calls to their pagers that found them half way around the world. It turned out that they knew Heather as well as we did. Her most fundamental attributes—the impulse to do the right thing the right way, the ability to connect with others, and the generosity of spirit—touched everyone.

JOE KELSEY

P. JIM RATZ 1952-2005

Jim Ratz reached an extraordinary number of people with his wisdom and deep friendship. In the weeks after his death in a climbing accident in Sinks Canyon, Wyoming, it became clear that the depth and frequency of communication I shared with Jim was not unique. Over 500 people from as far away as Tokyo, Taiwan, and Kenya gathered to remember him at a memorial service in Lander. He was a trusted advisor on any issue—personal or business—to a great number of people. To all who confided in him, he was our "go-to guy." He was 52 when he died on May 4.

Jim Ratz *Phil Powers*

I first came to know Jim during his years with the National Outdoor Leadership School (1973-1995), which culminated with him serving 11 years as executive director. Under Jim's leadership, NOLS grew in both size and scope: he opened the Patagonia, Southwest, and Canada programs, and published *Soft Paths*, the authoritative book on minimum-impact backcountry travel. Jim was also instrumental in starting NOLS's research and public policy programs, as well as Leave No Trace.

In 1999 Jim and I joined Rob and Kathryn Hess to purchase Jackson Hole Mountain Guides. With Jim as president and guide, we grew substantially and opened operations in Cody, Wyoming, and Moab, Utah, which added to the existing offices in Jackson and Las Vegas. Guides and clients were extremely fond of Jim as an employer, guide, and friend.

Jim was very active in civic leadership and involved in many organizations. Beginning in 2000 he served as a director of the American Mountain Guides Association, serving as the board's vice president since 2002. He devoted himself to the Lander Valley High School swim team, was director of the Lander Swim Club Board, an official of USA Swimming, and on the Board of Review for Wyoming Swimming Inc. Other organizations he was involved with included: cChairman of Leave No Trace, Inc; Advisory Board of the World Wilderness Congress; Rotary International; American Alpine Club; Natural Resources Defense Council; Association for Experiential Education; National Speleological Society; Advisory Board of the Rawlins District Bureau of Land Management; recipient of the first National Partnership Award from the U.S. Forest Service and Bureau of Land Management; member of the Wilderness Working Group of the Society of American Foresters; Founder, NOLS 1994 Wilderness Risk Management Committee and Conference; Founder, NOLS Wilderness Medicine Symposium

1986; Founder NOLS Wilderness Education and Leadership Symposium 1985; and cofounder NOLS Wilderness Research Colloquium. He was also an Eagle Scout.

Jim's work and love for the mountains frequently took him into the Tetons and the Wind Rivers, and occasionally to more distant peaks including Denali, Aconcagua, and Kilimanjaro. He also loved sunny afternoon climbing with his friends in Sinks Canyon, where he made numerous first ascents.

While Jim dedicated his life to outdoor education and the preservation of wilderness, he was passionate about preserving as much time as possible with his wife, Lantien, and their children, Mei (16) and Willy (12), to whom he was devoted. Friends of the family have organized a memorial fund for college or any other need of Mei and Willy. Donations may be sent to The Jim Ratz Memorial Fund at the Wyoming Employees Federal Credit Union, 873 W. Main St., Lander, WY 82520; (307) 332-3120.

PHIL POWERS, *AAC*

Brief obituaries of other AAC members may be found in the quarterly American Alpine News.

NECROLOGY

James K. Angell, Jr.
John William Augenstein
Mads Aulum
Patrick Clark
Henry E. Everding, III
Hubert J. Favero
Benjamin B. Franklin
Charles M. Hampton

Bob Hardy
Morgan Harris
Scott David Hyslop
Robert F. Kamps
Vera Komarkova
David R. Mahre
Robert W. Milne
Heather L. Paul

P. Jim Ratz
Kenneth L. Rinehart
Christine Seashore
Philip E. Sharpe
Johnny Soderstrom
Fred C. Tuttle

CLUB ACTIVITIES

EDITED BY FREDERICK O. JOHNSON

CASCADE SECTION. On February 3 Section members were invited to see a slideshow, *The Chola Shan Expedition and Mountaineering in China*, at the Mountaineers Clubhouse. Two AAC Cascade members, Tina Nef and Bruce Frank were a part of this six-person expedition, and Tina became the first American woman to climb the peak, a rarely climbed mountain in the remote Shaluli Mountain Range of Western China. A two-day van ride along the ancient "tea-horse" road took the team from the metropolitan city of Chengdu to a Tibetan town, Manigange. The team joined forces with a team of Chinese and Tibetan climbers for the final push to the 20,360-foot summit.

On November 30 Andy Selters presented a multi-media show on the history mountaineering in North America. The show stems from his 2004 book, *Ways to the Sky*, which won top honors at the Banff Mountain Book Festival and the National Outdoor Book Awards. With images of historical climbs from every decade and from peaks from all over the continent, Selters' hour-long presentation charted the progression of mountaineering and its basis in our culture. His previous books include The *Mt. Shasta Book and Glacier Travel and Crevasse Rescue*. The event, which was well attended by Northwest climbing luminaries, was sponsored jointly by the AAC, the Climbing Club of the University of Washington and Pro Mountain Sports.

On December 16 a special event was held to start a drive for support of a relief effort for victims of the Pakistan earthquake. AAC member Steve Swenson and Arc'teryx representative Marshall Balick initiated the process and REI provided the space and planning support. We heard some entertaining and sometimes harrowing stories from Jim Wickwire, Dee Molenaar, Jim Whittaker, and Steve Swenson about their experiences climbing in Pakistan. The one unifying theme was just how wonderful the local people were that they met on their travels and how much they helped these climbers in times of need. Mark Fisher, who had just returned from doing relief work in Pakistan, showed us some of the conditions that people are living in, including sleeping under tarps in the extremely cold, snowy weather. Many items were donated for an auction and over $11,000 was raised at the event. During the following two weeks there was an incredible outpouring of support and in addition to being able to ship 460 boxes of gear (tents, sleeping bags, blankets and jackets), over $45,000 was donated to the AAC Pakistan relief fund.

PETER ACKROYD, *Chair*

OREGON SECTION. The Oregon section has had a very busy year. Richard Bence Oregon section web master has kept the section in touch and working with Jeff Alzner and others to organize functions. Richard Bence hosts the Oregon section web site (http://ors.alpineclub.org) and as well as the Madrone Wall web site, (www.savemadrone.org).

We had big ice year in the Columbia River Gorge during mid December and mid February with two incredible ice formations, a rare occurrence. See Climbs & Expeditions for more information. Wayne Wallace along with Mike Layton gave a good talk about their escapades in the North Cascades for the Oregon Section and Access Fund. This took place at the Old Market Pub as a benefit for the Madrone Wall. Keith Daellenbach has published important newspaper articles in the local publications to help save the Madrone Wall. Kellie Rice of the Access Fund continues to be an important figure in the fight to save Madrone. I coordinated with the Ice Age Flood Institute and Mark Buser of the Columbia River Chapter to help create an ice age flood corridor, which includes the Madrone wall. There has also been renewed interest by Congress because of the nearby impact site of the Willamette meteorite. Richard Bence and I of the Oregon section, Kelly Rice of the Access Fund, and the Lewis and Clark College Outdoor Program, together completed the installation of a rescue cache at Broughton's Bluff. The AAC Oregon section donated the rescue litter.

Neale Creamer, Jim Onstott, and Friends of Silcox Hut, along with Timberline, continue to perform difficult maintenance tasks on Silcox Hut, an excellent base camp for emergency south side rescue operations. Oregon section member Jeff Sheets, of the Friends of Silcox Hut, is also on the safety committee for *Accidents in North American Mountaineering*.

Ruth Henneburger, a Ph.D. student, searches for extremophiles (www.astrobiology.com/extreme.html). Ruth wanted to sample at specific depths from the 40-meter cliff of the Hot Rocks Fumerole on Mt. Hood. Because of the strong sulfur gases, Ruth and I carried two 3,000 psi aluminum cylinders of nitrox, along with diving gear to the Devil's Kitchen for a one-hour descent into the "Devil's Hole." Dr. Steve Boyer belayed off two pickets. The steep rock-hard sulfur mud slope was slippery and at the limit of free climbing without crampons. Although we had on glacier glasses, the hydrogen sulfide stream badly burned our eyes and exposed areas of skin. Ruth published a paper, *Hunting Extremophiles in the Devils Kitchen*, producing the phylogenetic trees from the DNA analyses and cultures of her previous 2004 samples.

Oregon section member, Bob Speik hosted Royal Robbins at the Tower Theater in Bend. Robert is the president of the Traditional Mountaineering and raised funds with the Robbins lecture for a central Oregon land trust (www.traditionalmountaineering.org). Oregon Section members were active in many other ways as well. Doug Hutchinson, Tom Bowman, and pilot Pete Pupator climbed in Alaska during March, completing first ski descents in the Talkeetna range. Jeff Alzner's trip to the North Cascades and Canada yielded lots of climbing; Jeff is presently working on a Mike Bearzi biographical movie in Colorado. John Harlin climbed the north face of the Eiger and worked on an upcoming Imax movie that centers around the climb and his father's life called *Alps: Giants of Nature*. It is scheduled for release in March 2007, when his book, *An Eiger Obsession: In the Shadow of Dad's Mountain*, should also appear. And I spent two months in Namibia and South Africa running the Sossusvlei desert observatory and making a number of ascents on the Mesas in the Sossusvlei desert region. Bob Lockerby, Klindt Vielbig, Tom Bennett, and I are volunteering with the construction of the new Mazamas headquarters in an old church.

The Oregon section also raised money, tents, and clothing that was shipped to Pakistan by the AAC. In total the section has now raised $7,500 for the Alpine Club of Pakistan for earthquake victims. Among the fundraising tools were The Cascade Mountain Film Festival, a local effort organized by Jeff Alzner and Richard Bence, and the traveling version of the Banff Film Festival. For these events we had over a dozen volunteers from the AAC and the Mazamas.

BOB McGOWN, *Chair*

SOUTHWEST SECTION. After an extended period of dormancy, the Southwest Section was revitalized in 2005. It began with a formal complaint letter sent to the Club's headquarters, filled with threats of canceled membership dues, and was replied to with an opportunity for David Rosenstein to assume the reins as Chair. With the help of Ellen Lapham, Sierra Section Chair, the first-in-a-long-while Section event was held in Joshua Tree. It was a film night, with beer and popcorn, and all proceeds were donated to "Friends of Joshua Tree," a local nonprofit that raises money for JSAR (Joshua Tree Search and Rescue). All seats were full, with people standing in the aisles and in the open windows of this quaint JT venue.

After time spent analyzing the Section and its shaky viability in its preexisting state, attempts were made to reach out to a more diverse audience that may more accurately represent the face of the current climbing community. The result was likely the first-ever AAC sponsored event that focused primarily on bouldering and the young climbers who tackle those incredibly challenging problems. At Galen Rowell's Mountain Light Gallery in Bishop, we had a full house of young boulderers (and a select group of local alpinists such as John Fischer) who came to drink beer and watch multimedia presentations from Natasha Barnes (top female boulderer), Damon Corso (top bouldering photographer), and a sneak peak at the new bouldering video, Soul Cal, directed by Paul Dusatko.

One of the most exciting developments for the Section and the Club as a whole was the introduction to the Board for a proposed Joshua Tree Climbers Ranch, a walk-in campground situated outside the park boundaries close to the town itself. At the Flagstaff Board meeting $5,000 was committed from the 2005 Budget to help pay for utilities at the Ranch as well as some picnic tables. An extensive due diligence process followed, spearheaded by AAC Past President Jim McCarthy, which involved legal matters as well as a tour of the property in person. At the Annual Meeting in North Conway, New Hampshire, the Board agreed to sign a Letter of Intent to develop and lease the property from the land owner (a local JT climber and Club member, who expects no profit from the arrangement). Furthermore, the Board committed to raise an additional $50,000 as seed money for the project, to be modeled in spirit after the Teton Climbers Ranch. A warm thanks to Ellen and Jim for their efforts to make this possible.

The Section would like to express its relief that R.J. Secor (author of The High Sierra) survived a 1,000-foot fall on the slopes of Mt. Baldy, arguably one of the longest falls possible in Southern California. We hope you continue to heal well, RJ.

Looking ahead, much work remains to be done regarding both Section activities and the Climbers Ranch. It is the hope that these efforts will serve to invigorate the Section and its members as well as the greater regional climbing community, which is truly one of the most extensive bodies of climbers anywhere. Those of you interested in being involved at any level should feel free to contact me at bagtrango@yahoo.com.

DAVID ROSENSTEIN, *Chair*

NORTHERN ROCKIES SECTION. In September, Doug Colwell, after close to 10 years as Section chair, passed the baton to Brian Cabe. Much thanks to Doug for his past and continued service to the Club.

Zone II of Castle Rocks State Park opened to new route development on October 29, with orientation at the Castle Rocks Ranch House. Several members attended and completed new routes. Castle Rocks State Park is located in Idaho, adjacent to the City of Rocks National

Reserve. In conjunction with the Access Fund, members of the American Alpine Club were instrumental in developing the climbing management plan for Castle Rock State Park, which opened for the first time to the public in May 2003. For additional information on the area, see: http://www.idahoparks.org/parks/castlerocks.aspx; http://www.accessfund.com/regions/state/id.

Section members worked with Jason Keith of the Access Fund to develop a climbing-oriented response for the scoping phase of the new Zion National Park Backcountry Management Plan. The Access Fund sent a letter to the Park Service in October.

Brian Cabe worked with the Zion Canyoneering Coalition to craft input and solicit support for comments for the scoping phase of the ZNP Backcountry Management Plan. Brainstorming at meetings with the ZCC board resulted in a letter generator, which produced over 100 comment letters. According to ZNP, the Draft Backcountry Management Plan/EA should be available for public review and comment in the fall 2006.

Several section members supported and provided input at a planning meeting hosted by the Access Fund concerning the BLM's Indian Creek Corridor Recreation Management Plan in conjunction with the Outdoor Retailer Winter Market 2005. Indian Creek, located 50 miles south of Moab, Utah, is one of the world's premier crack climbing destinations. See also Friends of Indian Creek: http://www.moabdesertadventures.com/foic.htm.

Local Organizations/Web sites of interest to climbers in our territory: http://www.boise-climbers.org, http://www.saltlakeclimbers.org, http://montanaclimbers.org, http://www.serac-club.org, http://wasatchmountainclub.org.

BRIAN CABE, *Chair*

CENTRAL ROCKIES SECTION. For the third consecutive year, the Section sponsored and helped fund the Waterfall Ice Roundup in Cody, Wyoming, on February 18-20. Some 50-60 climbers from five states traveled to Cody to attend this event, which is also known as "the friendliest little ice festival in the Northern Rockies," to sample 99 local ice routes, demo equipment, and enjoy the catered food and evening slide programs. For the first time, an AAC staff member, Membership Services Coordinator Jason Manke, attended. Section Chair Greg Sievers has written a letter to the editor of *Climbing* magazine regarding the possible over-use of V-threads for ice climbing anchors and rappel stations. Numerous V-threads, slings and rap rings have been found in the drainages below Cody's waterfalls. This littering has prompted concern from the U.S. Forest Service in Cody. We hope to enlighten climbers to reuse or replace existing rappel station material before authorities become more involved in the matter.

In March we co-sponsored a dZi Foundation fundraiser in Estes Park at the Trail Ridge Outfitters store. Local legend, armchair mountaineer, historian, and walking encyclopedia on the Himalaya, Dale Vrabec provided an enlightening view of trekking in Nepal in the 1970s. Images and stories of the Makalu and Everest regions were enjoyed by all. The evening event raised $1,000 for the dZi Foundation, which implements, supports, and funds projects to improve the basic quality of the lives of people primarily in Ladakh, Nepal, and Sikkim.

The Section advertised for proposals and offered to assist a Section member to attend the Bulgarian Alpine Club festival in Vratsa, Bulgaria, during September 21-25. Kevin Frederick was the lucky recipient. The Federation of the Bulgarian Alpine Clubs (with support from the Mayor and the Municipality of Vratsa and Vrachanski Balkan Nature Park) hosted the event. Despite rainy weather, the festival hosted 150 climbers from many countries near and far. During his three days at the festival, Kevin gave a presentation highlighting inspiring places to climb in Colorado and Wyoming. The festival was a great experience, and everybody even managed to sneak in some climbing between the rain and the beer.

This was the fifth year that the AAC hosted the Lumpy Trails Day at Lumpy Ridge in Rocky Mountain National Park, This fine crack climbing destination in Estes Park offers high quality granite with 1- to 6-pitch long routes. This year on October 23 the 63 volunteers— Front Range climbers, Club members, and Park Services employees—collaborated to improve the climber access trails to The Twin Owls, one of the most popular and photogenic rock features at Lumpy Ridge. The result was a complete "face lift" of over 500 vertical feet of extremely rugged mountainous trail. Over 133 wood and rock steps and seven drains were installed to help check storm runoff, control erosion, and act as stairs.

Finally, the year's activities ended as they began with a fundraiser. In October Heidi Wirtz provided a video image program of climbing travel to Siberia and Nepal. Liz Scully was instrumental in organizing the grassroots event, which raised $1,000 to assist several young Nepalese children to attend school in Kathmandu. The evening was co hosted by the CRS, which provided locally made, custom embroidered AAC shirts and jackets for the raffle.

GREG SIEVERS, *Chair*

NORTH CENTRAL SECTION. The North Central Section of the AAC continues to make progress toward having more communication, camaraderie, and interaction within the Club. Major projects for 2005 included further work developing a Section web site, clean-up days at two areas, and further communication with the Minnesota Department of Natural Resources regarding closed areas at the most popular climbing destination in the Minneapolis/St. Paul area. A small social was held at an indoor climbing gym and restaurant in Stillwater, Minnesota, in October.

As background, Inter-State State Park lies along the St Croix River bordering Minnesota and Wisconsin. Because of the river valley, the geological formations are spectacular. The routed climbs vary from 5.3 to 5.12 and are about 50 feet long. In July 2001 there was a large rockfall that necessitated closing 40 percent of the Minnesota side. The North Central Section continues to work with the DNR to point out the closed areas as well as plan for the possible re-opening of part of the area. In addition we had a garbage pick-up day at the park in June. With five members in attendance, the day included some climbing and a barbeque, along with a meeting with the State Park staff. The Section was also represented at a clean-up day in July at Blue Mounds State Park in Luverne, Minnesota, on the border with South Dakota. This area has had a big increase in the number of climber visits over the past five years. It is small and there was a little garbage, but a fun day was had by eight of our members.

SCOTT CHRISTENSEN, *Chair*

NEW ENGLAND SECTION. The year began on a celebratory note when Bill Atkinson was honored at the home of Rich and Andrea Leonard on his 80th birthday January 13. The 90 guests, including representatives of both the Appalachian Mountain Club and the AAC, gathered to salute Bill, who is known to many as "the hub of the Boston climbing community." Under his chairmanship since 1997, the New England Section has been one of the most active in the Club.

Seventy intrepid mountaineers braved the winter's blast—seven inches of treacherous snow—to attend the Ninth Annual New England Section Dinner on March 12 at Northeastern University's Henderson House in Weston. Our special guest was Kurt Diemberger of K2 renown. Kurt delivered a cultured and sympathetic presentation of his mountaineering life, his philosophical outlook, and especially his K2 experiences. In addition , AAC President Mark Richey gave a lively description of the successful annual meeting in March at Ouray, Colorado. Mark was accompanied by his wife Teresa, the second Peruvian woman to summit Huascaran Sur (6,746m), and daughter Natalia, who assisted with the door prizes.

We were especially graced by the presence of Brad and Barbara Washburn, who helped us get the annual dinner started 10 years ago by offering Brad's stunning photographs for exhibit at the first dinner

Paul Dale, our accomplished auctioneer, succeeded in his fund raising efforts to benefit the Section by selling a day in the hills with President Mark Richey, another with guide Marc Chauvin, and a beautiful mountain photograph by our own reception area exhibitor Chris Dame.

Once again we met in June at Nancy Savickas's alpine refuge in Albany, New Hampshire, to enjoy the camaraderie of fellow climbers and to sample the grill, snarf down Nancy's excellent hors d'oeuvres, bite into some corn-on-the-cob, and share a glass of wine or a few beers. At least 30 guests attended from far and wide, including old timers Henry Barber, Ted Church, and Malcolm Moore.

Our Halloween gathering attracted more ghosts than expected owing to the threat of rain. However, the rain held off and several parties came in from climbs on the Cathedral Ledges and elsewhere on the cliffs of New Hampshire. In the evening more than 20 Halloween revelers showed up at Nancy's place for her hors d'oeuvres, grilled food and refreshments, followed by Rick Merritt's showing of summer slides of Africa and his ascent of Kilimanjaro.

Many of our members were active during the year climbing on five continents. Unfortunately, space limitations prevent a more detailed account of their accomplishments.

BILL ATKINSON, *Chair*, AND NANCY SAVICKAS, *Vice Chair*

NEW YORK SECTION. The New York Section hosts a variety of outdoor and indoor social events throughout the year. Among the perennials is a Winter Outing held each year in the Adirondacks, as well as a June get-together at the Ausable Club there. However, it is perhaps best known for its Fall black tie dinner, now in its 26th year and held this year on October 29 at Manhattan's Union Club. Looking for a change from the usual expedition slide show, we asked Eric Simonson, head of International Mountain Guides in Ashford, Washington, to share with us some personal insights on climbing from the guide's unique perspective. His talk, *Confessions of a Mountain Guide*, especially resonated with an audience who regularly rely on mountain guides to lead their major adventures. Eric spoke about the importance of experience, instinct, and also plain old-fashioned luck, even for a professional like him, in determining happy outcomes. In one expedition to Nun, one of his Dutch clients experienced problems with a broken crampon. The ensuing delay resulted in his team not being on the slope when it suddenly avalanched, killing all in its path.

Simonson praised the growing skill and professionalism of Nepalese and Tibetan guides. The day is not far off, in Eric's opinion, when guiding on Everest will be outsourced in large part to these, similar to much of U.S. manufacturing, and Americans and Europeans will function primarily as expedition organizers and marketers. Globalization, it seems, is spreading everywhere.

In addition to Eric's main talk, one of our local members, Susan Schwartz, presented a short retrospective on the late Dr. Hans Kraus, pioneer Shawangunk climber, close friend and partner of Fritz Wiessner, and equally famous as JFK's back doctor and as an early advocate of physical fitness. Susan had just written and published Kraus' biography, *Into the Unknown*, which was a finalist at the Banff Mountain Book Festival and is reviewed in this Journal.

As usual we welcomed and introduced each of our new members as well as those attending with 25 or more years of Club membership. New members received their AAC membership pins while the quarter-century group received certificates of appreciation and a pewter membership badge.

Dinner profits were divided between the *American Alpine Journal* and the AAC Library.

At the Dinner we were happy to welcome Phil Powers, the Club's new Executive Director, on his first official trip to New York. At the Dinner Phil announced the Club's Pakistan Earthquake Relief Initiative, a drive to collect and ship gear to stricken mountain villagers in that country. Almost immediately a team of Section volunteers went into action and assembled tons of gear, including tents and clothing, all donated by local members. These were collected, sorted, and transported to JFK Airport for shipment overseas. Special thanks go to Holly Edelson and Richard Ryan for their hands-on efforts in collecting and cataloguing the material, and to Todd Fairbairn as well for transforming his apartment into a temporary warehouse. This is no insignificant sacrifice given the small size of New York City dwellings.

From time to time, we get requests from foreign visitors to experience the famed overhangs of the Gunks. This was the case last June when Ed February, a professor of botany from South Africa lecturing at Princeton, let it be known that he would like to try his hand on High Exposure and other Gunks classics he had heard so much about. It turns out that Ed is not only a noted scholar, but perhaps South Africa's most famous black climber, a pioneer responsible for opening up the sport to black South Africans. Our own Bob Hall and Steve Miller immediately responded, and the trio had a superb day on the cliffs. This was the subject of a write-up and photos in the *American Alpine News* and Section web site.

In July a group of New York Section members, including Roland Puton, Garrett Bowden, Julie Floyd, and Mark Kassner, joined Frederick Selby in an expedition he organized to Mongolia. One of the highlights was a visit, on foot and horseback, to the far western border with Kazakhstan where there are numerous unclimbed 4,000m peaks. While the group was weathered off Khuiten Uul, they succeeded on Naran.

A fitting end to our fiscal year was a delightful September Sunday in the country hosted by Olaf and Gitta Soot. Between swimming, volleyball, and climbing in the Soot backyard (yes, the Soot's Greenwich property contains a 50-foot high outcrop with a variety of technical routes) as well as excellent food and drink, "Olaf's Outing" will result in fond memories for the 40 or so members who attended.

Stay in touch with AAC events in New York, including our outings and social events, by logging on to: http://nysalpineclub.org. This is the colorful and informative handiwork of Vic Benes, a retired Bell Labs scientist, who created and maintains the Section web site.

PHILIP ERARD, *Chair*

INDEX

COMPILED BY RALPH FERRARA AND EVE TALLMAN

Mountains are listed by their official names. Ranges and geographic locations are also indexed. Unnamed peaks (eg. Peak 2,340) are listed under P. Abbreviations are used for some states and countries and for the following: Article: art.; Cordillera: C.; Mountains: Mts.; National Park: Nat'l Park; Obituary: obit. Most personnel are listed for major articles. Expedition leaders and persons supplying information in Climbs and Expeditions are also cited here. Indexed photographs are listed in bold type. Reviewed books are listed alphabetically under Book Reviews.

SUBMISSIONS GUIDELINES

The *American Alpine Journal* records the significant climbing accomplishments of the world in an annual volume. We encourage climbers to submit brief (250-500 words) factual accounts of their climbs and expeditions. Accounts should be submitted by e-mail whenever possible. Alternatively, submit accounts by regular post on CD, zip, or floppy disk. Please provide complete contact information, including e-mail address, postal address, fax, and phone. The deadline is December 31, through earlier submissions will be looked on very kindly! For photo guidelines and other information, please see the complete Submissions Guidelines document at the American Alpine Journal section of www.AmericanAlpineClub.org.

Please address all correspondences to:
The American Alpine Journal, 710 Tenth Street, Suite 140, Golden, CO 80401 USA; tel.: (303) 384 0110; fax: (303) 384 0111; aaj@americanalpineclub.org; www.AmericanAlpineClub.org

INTERNATIONAL GRADE COMPARISON CHART

To download the complete "American Alpine Journal International Grade Comparison Chart," including alpine and ice grades, go to: www.AmericanAlpineClub.org/AAJ

This chart is designed to be used with the *American Alpine Journal* to help decipher the difficulty ratings given to climbs.

Seriousness Rating:

These often modify the technical grades when protection is difficult.

R: Poor protection with potential for a long fall and some injury.

X: A fall would likely result in serious injury or death.

YDS	UIAA	FR	AUS	SAX	CIS	SCA	BRA	UK	
5.2	II	1	10	II	III	3			D
5.3	III	2	11	III	III+	3+			D
5.4	IV- / IV	3	12		IV-	4			VD
5.5	IV+		13		IV	4+			VD
5.6	V-	4	14		IV+	5-		4a	S / HS
5.7	V / V+		15	VIIa		5	4	4b	HS / VS
5.8	VI-	5a	16	VIIb	V-	5+	4+	4b	VS
5.9	VI	5b	17	VIIc		6-	5 / 5+	4c / 5a	HVS / E1
5.10a	VI+	5c	18	VIIIa	V	6	6a	5a	E1
5.10b	VI+	6a	18	VIIIa	V	6	6a	5b	E2
5.10c	VII-	6a+	19	VIIIb		6+	6b	5b	E2
5.10d	VII	6b	20	VIIIc	V+	7-	6c		E3
5.11a	VII+	6b+	20	IXa		7-	7a	5c	
5.11b	VII+	6c	21	IXb		7	7b	5c	E4
5.11c	VIII-	6c+	22	IXc	VI-	7+		5c	E4
5.11d	VIII	7a	23			7+	7c	6a	
5.12a	VIII+	7a+	24	Xa	VI	8-	8a	6a	E5
5.12b	VIII+	7b	25	Xa	VI	8	8b	6a	E5
5.12c	IX-	7b+	26	Xb		8	8c	6a	
5.12d	IX	7c	27	Xb		8+	9a	6b	E6
5.13a	IX+	7c+	28	Xc		9-	9b	6b	E6
5.13b	IX+	8a	29			9-	9c	6b	
5.13c	X-	8a+	30	XIa	VI+	9	10a	6c	E7
5.13d	X	8b	31	XIa	VI+	9	10b	6c	E7
5.14a	X+	8b+	32	XIb		9	10c	7a	E8
5.14b	X+	8c	33	XIb		9+		7a	E8
5.14c	XI-	8c+		XIc		9+		7b	E9
5.14d	XI	9a				9+		7b	E9

YDS=Yosemite Decimal System; UIAA=Union Internationale des Associations D'Alpinisme; Fr=France/Sport; Aus=Australia; Sax=Saxony; CIS=Commonwealth of Independent States/Russia; Sca=Scandinavia; Bra=Brazil.